DAVID KATZ is widely acknowledged
life and music of Lee Perry. As a journ
features on reggae to a range of publications around
including *Uncut* (UK), *Grand Royal* (USA) and *Reggae Magazine*
(Japan), and recently he compiled and co-annotated *Arkology*, a triple
CD box set of retrospective Perry material issued by Island Records.

People Funny Boy

David Katz

PAYBACK PRESS

First published in 2000 by Payback Press, an imprint of
Canongate Books Ltd, 14 High Street, Edinburgh, EHI ITE

Copyright © 2000, David Katz
The moral rights of the author have been asserted

10 9 8 7 6 5 4 3 2 1

British Library Cataloguing-in-Publication Data
A catalogue record for this book is available upon request from the British Library

ISBN 0 86241 854 2

Typeset by Antony Gray
Printed and bound in Great Britain by Creative Print and Design, (Wales)

CONTENTS

Foreword by Rainford Hugh Lee 'Scratch' Perry   VII

Introduction by David Katz   IX

INTRODUCING MYSELF: *From Kendal to Kingston*   1

CHICKEN SCRATCH: *The Studio One Years*   15

GIVE ME JUSTICE: *The Upsetter Emerges*   40

THE RETURN OF DJANGO: *International Success*   69

SOUL REBELS: *The Upsetter and the Wailers*   102

BEAT DOWN BABYLON: *Building the Ark*   137

HURT SO GOOD: *Early Fruits of the Black Ark*   180

ENTER THE DRAGON: *Black Ark Album Abstractions*   217

POLICE AND THIEVES: *The Golden Years of the Black Ark*   245

CITY TOO HOT: *The Excessive Apex and Sudden Fall of the Ark*   296

THE RETURN OF PIPECOCK JACKXON: *The Partial Rebirth and Ultimate Destruction of the Ark*   327

I AM A MADMAN: *Years in England*   369

THE SECRET LABORATORY: *A Base in Switzerland*   415

Notes to the Text   463

Selected Albums Discography

     Lee Perry Productions, plus Perry vocal and club albums   467

     Vocal guest appearances   489

     Albums co-produced or engineered by Lee Perry   491

Selected Bibliography

     Books   495

     Booklets, pamphlets and liner notes   498

     Newspaper and magazine articles   498

Selected Videography   503

Selected Radio Broadcasts   503

Index   505

Acknowledgments   534

FOREWORD

by Rainford Hugh Lee 'Scratch' Perry

Thank you David Katz
You have my blessings on this special book.
The future facts of life reality knock.
God bless you
Good luck
Success
From President £ee £eo $cratch Perry ABC Love.
Mr Ghost writer
The buyer will be very pleased with this book of
    Rainford King Hugh Perry rain all over the Globe.
Park to parks
Streets to streets
Lane to lane
Black Ark rain.
I rain facts of life
$un of £ord Thunder
Black Ark God Zadkiel
X29, 1999.
Kids God
Kids King
Kids Lord,
Lord Jesus Christ God
INRI.
One Love
X INRI
Jah Love
Enjoy this.

INTRODUCTION

I first met Lee 'Scratch' Perry, face to face, in January 1987 at Dingwall's nightclub, a few weeks after I left the relative tranquillity of San Francisco to complete my studies in the grey chaos of London. I had been captivated by his music since my teenage years, exposed to it through the many reggae radio programmes broadcast on Bay Area community stations, and already had a first article about Scratch published in the underground magazine *Wiring Department* before leaving the US. I hoped to interview the maestro at Dingwall's, but Scratch had little inclination to speak to me then; instead, he spent most of the evening performing rituals, blowing herb smoke through a wooden recorder placed in alternate nostrils, and grabbing electric lights with his bare hands while blowing a whistle. He did, however, take home the article I had written about him, and summoned me a few days later to a South-east London studio, where I found him filming himself with a tripod-mounted video camera while voicing a new version of 'Exodus'. Scratch requested I bring him 13 stones from the banks of the Thames, which he placed inside the video monitor; when the engineer later told him the track length was 13 minutes and five seconds, he found 'the other five' stones evidently missing from his video set.

Before the day was done, he presented me with a silver ring adorned with a winged death's head, which I was to wear on a finger of the hand I wrote with: Lee Perry thus appointed me his 'Ghost Writer', bestowing the highest of honours and heaviest of burdens on a journalist who was decidedly green. Scratch had apparently been seeking a writer to help create a book on his life, and was taken with my comments on his autobiographical song 'Introducing Myself', in which he directly challenged Reagan, Thatcher, the Queen of Great Britain, and the Pope; though other journalists were bemoaning him as a lost cause at the low end of his career, Perry understood that his message was still reaching me, and took my arrival as a sign. Despite my ongoing protests that others might be better suited to the task, Scratch insisted that his choice had been made.

I then held – and continue to hold – Lee Perry's music paramount as the most striking, inspirational and meaningful sounds I have ever encountered, and it was long clear that his unique artistic vision has made him one of the major creative figures of the twentieth century, but it took many months for me even to consider attempting the daunting and clearly Herculean task of penning a document on the life and work of Scratch; meanwhile, through regular contact with the man, I found myself being drawn into what can only be described as another world – a whimsical and pre-ordained universe laden with spiritual significance and the symbolic truths of nature, where retribution awaits the unsuspecting and unseen forces are constantly at work, where there is no such thing as an accident and everything happens for a reason.

I spent the majority of the next two years in Perry's company, spending time with him nearly every day. London then ceased to be his home base, though it has continued to be mine; we have since inevitably spent less time together, but have continued to meet and converse by telephone at key intervals.

Once Scratch and I no longer lived in the same nation, I began an early draft of this book, but after completing the first 50 pages, it was clear there were major gaps in my knowledge. I thus began to concentrate on interviewing other significant individuals in his life, ceaselessly gathering data and eventually constructing other drafts over the years; in completing what you now hold in your hands, I conducted interviews with around 200 people, in addition to holding countless discussions with the man himself – yet I cannot help thinking that another 12 years of research would still have me barely scraping the surface of Perry's life.

In many ways, this book is not the entity that either Lee Perry or I originally conceived. Scratch once informed me that he wanted this text to take the form of a comic book; another time he seemed more concerned with the number of pages it would have as opposed to its actual content. But most perturbing has been the fact that Perry seemed to think the book would write itself, presenting me with an endless series of riddles or blank replies to questions brought by his repeated challenge of 'anything you want to know, just ask me'. Perhaps the only thing truly predictable about Scratch is his very unpredictability, and his perpetual moodiness has meant that direct questioning has often been out of the question. The Scratch I came to know weaves a constant, conflated stream of parables and riddles, speaking often in rapid, abstract sequences that are not easily translated, the verbal conflagration of a mind on fire. Some life events have proved traumatic for Lee Perry and his family, and to confront such demonic memories has sometimes proved impossible; consider, for example, the following typical exchange: 'What about this book you're writing,' Perry would often glare at me. 'But Scratch,' I once protested, 'there are still many things I need to know to make a proper start.' 'Anything you want to know, just ask me,' he insisted. 'OK, tell me about your parents,' I suggested, not knowing that he had been denounced by his mother and had not spoken to her for several years, 'were they farming people, or . . . ' 'Blood claat David, you no see it? Me dead already, me is a ghost,' was all he had to say about the subject. Other times, different happenings from diverse eras have become blurred in a mind that has perpetually worked overtime, making a muddled and often misrepresented history all the more confused; for example, he once spoke of the destruction of some of his studio equipment in the early 1980s as being partially motivated by King Tubby's murder – an event that did not take place until 1989. These combined elements and various others have made a standard biography ultimately untenable.

On the other hand, Scratch has always been perfectly frank when ready to describe a situation to me, or when he had something specific to relate; other times, he has dictated specific passages for verbatim inclusion. The shifting nature of our relationship over the years has inevitably resulted in the texture of this book, which now centres on a mixture of the testimony of others along with Perry's own. His connection to everyone of significance in Jamaican music and other major figures outside it has also given rise to the need for the inclusion of other voices in this book.

Those familiar with the vengeful punning of Lee Perry's proclamations may already be prepared for baffling and contradictory statements from Scratch himself, but the unfortunate truth is that statements from many of his associates may add to the confusion rather than alleviate it. I was often presented with differing accounts of significant events, particularly regarding recording sessions (for instance, three people claimed to have played bass on 'Judge Dread'), but also about more general and personal happenings. I am aware of moments when misleading information was deliberately stated for various reasons (such as justifying a bootleg release or dubious song-writing claim, or furthering a long-standing grudge); more often, those interviewed simply had difficulty remembering the circumstances of sessions or events from 20 or 30 years ago. Memory is a peculiar thing, and statements given in good faith are themselves not necessarily accurate; additionally, it is worth noting that the regular use of ganja has been noted by many to result in short- and long-term memory loss. Furthermore, those who have delved into the murky, uncharted waters of Jamaican vinyl releases will already know just how little data were recorded until recently; a lack of precise dates has meant the chronology of this book may not seem entirely logical throughout.

As with other texts on Jamaican music, this book is bound to have errors and omissions that will later be brought to light, and I apologise for them in advance (though I would like to point out that certain lesser creations have purposefully been neglected due to space and time constraints; much as I would like to have dissected every song Scratch ever recorded, such an action would see publication indefinitely delayed).

Having stated such concerns, I will note that every effort was made to minimise errors through re-checking any contradictory elements that arose with those concerned. Ultimately, the greatest source of help in this aspect came from Lee Perry himself, whose stringent checking of a draft of this book in May 1999 resulted in a number of significant alterations, particularly to Chapter 11; Scratch has my ultimate gratitude for his willingness to listen to and comment on the entire text, which I read to him over the course of a few days in Düsseldorf.

In seeking to chart the particular life journey of Lee 'Scratch' Perry, this book attempts to illuminate the endless creativity that has marked his incredibly complex body of work; it also seeks to explore the mass of contradictions that lurk behind the ethos of his legend. Scratch has been so far ahead of his time for so long that a broader recognition has come late, and this book is partly concerned with making clear precisely why so many have attested to his genius – a word that is grossly overused in popular music, but entirely justified in this instance.

Lee Perry has been concretely involved with every significant phase of Jamaican music, and his creative innovations have found a broader resonance in a range of other genres, from American rap and hip hop to British punk, jungle, ambient and trip hop, from Japanese electronica to European avant-garde and techno. Though Scratch is now a hip name to be dropped from the mouths of pop stars, his individuality and unpredictability have seen him reap fewer rewards than some of his students – most notably Bob Marley, Jamaica's most famous son, whose career was largely shaped by creative interaction with Perry. It is through the exploration of such links that this book attempts to show the importance of Perry's vision, and trace its lasting impact on a number of music styles.

At the same time, I have tried to make sense of the complicated alternative space created for Perry's unique spiritual vision while simultaneously detailing the particulars of an invariably unique lifestyle. If the mysteries of Rastafari seem confounding to outsiders, then Perry's particular brand of cosmology is doubly so; though often baffling and far from simple, I have done my best to explain its significance in his life and work.

To be relatively objective, I have consciously left a number of key points open to the interpretation of the reader. Scratch remains an enigmatic figure, partly of his own design; many of his actions, as with his work, are simply open to interpretation. Though many describe him as a genius in this book, others degrade him as a madman, accuse him of being a *ginal* (con man) or dismiss him as a charlatan; the readers must ultimately form their own impression. Similarly, I do not claim that my descriptions of Perry's music are gospel truths. Though I have tried to be as accurate as possible in my contextual explanations of the material, readers will have to draw their own conclusions about the worthiness of the records mentioned.

Accounts of Jamaican music have often tended towards the mythical, with depictions of Marley as a saint or deity being particularly troubling. Though mysticism has played an important role in Perry's life (as it has to some degree with the majority of the island's musical figures), I have consciously avoided an overdramatised or eulogised portrait. Lee Perry may be one of the most original and inspired men to ever walk the face of this earth, but it is perhaps important to remember that he is only a man – despite a creative vision that has rendered him somewhat beyond the constraints of ordinary mortals. Similarly, Scratch has been likened to other popular figures, such as free-form jazz pioneer Sun Ra, wacky funk star George Clinton, and eccentric artist Salvador Dali, but such comparisons are ultimately futile in the face of Perry's singular trajectory.

I am also aware of the limitations I have brought to this text through my situation as a young outsider. I have spent far less time on the blessed island of Jamaica than I would have liked, and a portion of the music described in this book was recorded before I was born. Lee Perry has noted that he came 'before his time', and it is worth pointing out that he certainly came before *my* time. This has partly influenced my decision to frame this book around testimony of those who were present at the events described in its pages, aided by minimal contextual commentary. I personally feel that the best historical portions of this book lie in the words of the true experts on Jamaican music who are quoted throughout it: the musicians, singers, producers, and engineers who have themselves created it. Scratch's own words, of course, speak for themselves.

As with other writers, I have found that the printed word does not do justice to the essence of Jamaica's spoken patois, but point out that I have not attempted to Jamaicanise nor Anglicise quotations. Instead, I have tried to reproduce spoken statements as accurately as possible, in keeping with each individual's particular use of language.

This book is also the culmination of my own long and difficult journey in an adopted land, and it has seen me travel to several world destinations in search of accurate information. My ultimate motivation in following through with what has seemed a pointless, and indeed torturous, endeavour at times is simply to help Scratch achieve the greater glory he is due while he is still alive to benefit from it. Lee Perry is one of the few who truly deserves the title of living legend; the foolhardy speculations on his sanity detract from the creativity that has resulted in some of the most inspiring and visionary sounds yet to grace the ears of the human race. Above all, I hope this biography has helped to clarify the importance of his creations.

DAVID KATZ
London
August 1999

INTRODUCING MYSELF:

From Kendal to Kingston

'I'm an artist, a musician, a magician, a writer, a singer; I'm everything. My name is Lee from the African jungle, originally from West Africa. I'm a man from somewhere else, but my origin is from Africa, straight to Jamaica through reincarnation; reborn in Jamaica. Superman comes to earth 'cause him sick and tired; I'm not sick and tired because I'm learning what goes on, so when we get frustrated, that is when the music come down by rain drops to support all here with a broken heart and don't know what to do. I have been programmed; many people who born again must come back to learn a lesson . . . have you heard of ET? I am ET, savvy? Savvy?'

Lee Perry has spoken of his origins in many contradictory ways. He has claimed to come from Jupiter, once said he was born in the sky, and has often named Africa as his true birthplace; Perry has additionally suggested that his empty body was taken over by space aliens after an undocumented death. According to family members, however, his arrival came in the height of the Depression era in the rural town of Kendal, the third of four children born to Ina Davis and Henry Perry. Like many peasants the world over, his family grew in an environment marked by centuries of exploitation and neglect, and the remoteness of the region he was raised in has contributed to the absence of accurate or consistent information about certain particulars of his early life.

Even his very given name and date of birth remain points of contention, perhaps somewhat appropriate for a man who has kept elements of his life shrouded in mystery. His given first name was Rainford – sometimes spelled Reinford – his middle name Hugh, but he was soon given the pet name Lee by his mother, and it was this pet name that the world would come to know him by.

As with many other poor country folk, there is still confusion about his exact date of birth, with conflicting information and a lack of official records contributing to the uncertainty. A variety of dates and places have been put forward at various times by numerous sources, and Perry's habit of adding a year to his age when speaking of it publicly has added to the confusion. The most consistent information indicates Lee Perry was born in Kendal on Friday, March 20, 1936; he entered the world on a payday under the star sign of Pisces.

Regardless of the particulars of the day he arrived on the planet, Lee Perry is certainly of humble origins. He was born to a poor family in an underdeveloped part of Jamaica where few amenities or provisions had been established; the island was then a British colony that was being stripped of its very goodness through intensive plantation farming.

Hanover Parish lies at the Northwestern tip of Jamaica, about the farthest point on the island from Kingston, and the town of Kendal is buried deep in its interior. In a terrain marked by parched and largely inhospitable land, interspersed with the stifling humidity of the untamed bush, farmers found some success with staple foods like yam and cassava, but the crop on which the entire region's commerce relied was sugar cane, made the focal point of the Parish during slavery days; bananas had been established as a second plantation crop, but by the time Lee Perry was born, many of the bananas growing in Hanover had succumbed to a detrimental disease.

Ina Davis never knew her grandparents, but when they were born, many locals could still remember when Busha Aide was the overseer of this area. A sadistic brute who took a perverse pleasure in publicly punishing and denigrating his workforce, Busha Aide and his wife Mary ruled over Kendal and the surrounding districts of Grange, Prospect and Cauldwell with an iron hand. The slaves he controlled were mostly assigned the task of harvesting sugar cane, which was exported from the nearby port of Lucea to keep well-oiled the wheels of capitalism upon which the British Empire relied, and Ina's family was descended from the slaves he exploited.

Born in Kendal on Sunday, April 12, 1915, Ina Davis was the result of a liaison between Jane Anne Horton and Jonathan Davis; her parents never married, and both had several children of their own from previous relationships. Her father passed away when she was young, and Ina was raised in the harshness of poverty by her mother, growing up with her mother's other children Philippe, Mary, Celeste, Sammy, and Gussie. She also came to know some of her father's other children, including Elsie, Sue, Amy, Man-Man, and a boy called Ira who died when he was young. Her mother farmed on a nearby ridge, struggling to grow enough to feed the family, and when Ina came of age, she took up sewing to support herself and contribute to the family welfare. In her later years, she would be referred to universally as Miss Ina.

At age 16, she began a relationship with Henry Perry (sometimes referred to as Cornel Perry), an 18-year-old who had grown up in the same village. 'I did know him from school days when me is a small girl,' Miss Ina recalled. 'He come from the same place, Kendal.' Perry was a contractor who did roadwork, and the young couple soon began a family. Their first child, Beryl, was born on September 29, 1932 and given the pet name Dulcie. Lesbert was born on December 29, 1934, and, as the first-born son, he became known as Sonny. After Lee's birth in late March 1936, a final child, Icelyn was born on February 28, 1938 and given the nickname Sitta.

Growing up in Kendal, Lee Perry was just another barefoot country boy who would walk with his siblings up the hill to school with empty pockets and a hungry belly. Lee's mother remembered him as 'a lively little boy' who was well liked by his peers, though prone to mischief making when older. In his younger days, he felt a natural affinity with his older brother Sonny; the two not only resembled each other physically, but Sonny was his only male sibling and the one closest to him in age.

'In growing up days we was very poor but we never bow, nor trouble no one, we are very honest,' Sonny noted. 'When we were growing up, we used to love each other and never war. In the early days, all 'bout, anywhere is me and him. Me never left him, me always be like a bodyguard for me smaller brother.'

Apart from attending Kendal School, sometimes the children were recruited to help their mother plant and harvest crops. 'When we no go to school we were around in the bush with me mother,' Lee's sister Sitta noted, 'and he would romp and all them things.'

'We mother did poor and we daddy did poor so we just take it easy and work and help out,' added Sonny.

At this time, the family attended Rock Spring Church, an Anglican congregation in Kendal, though most of the family have indicated that the church was not central to their lives then. More meaningful to Miss Ina was the Ettu dancing her mother passed down to her; this ritualistic form of African dance centres on representations of natural phenomena, and is retained for special occasions such as Nine Night, the culmination of funeral celebrations held when a member of the community passes away. Though Jamaica's colonial slave masters were intent on wiping out all cultural practices the Africans had brought from their homeland, a proliferation of underground activities saw certain customs retained and adapted, and those the slavers did not see as threatening were occasionally tolerated. Ettu thrived in remote bush communities, and its survival allowed Miss Ina to retain a link with the ways of her ancestors, preserving traditions that dated from before the forced migration of her foreparents to the bleak reality of captivity In a hostile foreign land. Another surviving African custom that had a more pervasive influence on the lives of the villagers in Kendal was a universal belief in the spirit world, with the existence of benign and malevolent spirits and their corresponding powers to assist or harm viewed with absolute gravity. Such beliefs continue to be the norm throughout most rural areas of Jamaica, despite a majority adherence to Christianity.

Though Henry Perry's work could be relatively lucrative, there were also periods when he was without work or was poorly paid for his efforts, and there was often a scarcity of food in the Perry household. Two meals a day was the norm, and sometimes the children would have to make do with one and whatever scraps they could find to share with friends during the day.

'When we go to school, sometimes a penny a day we get to carry to school,' Sonny remembered. 'One penny a piece, so we have to take it easy, buy cool drink and patty and bread . . . all eat the one, we show love from that because we all share.'

By the time Lee Perry was ten, his father left the family home for good. He had become involved with another woman in Green Island, a larger town nestled on a nearby murky bay, and after they married he eventually emigrated to England. Miss Ina and the children were left to struggle on their own, and the next few years were very difficult for the abandoned woman and her four hungry children.

With the passing of time, Ina Davis eventually came to be courted by Granville Blythe, a kind gentleman who retained the position of 'Head Man' on the Paradise Saxham sugar-cane estate located some miles away from Kendal in an area called Prospect. Once the heart of Busha Aide's domain, the concern was then run by Alan Blair, a wealthy landowner of part-Indian extraction. After marrying Granville Blythe, Ina brought her children to his house in the small settlement of Grange, a few miles from Kendal in the general direction of Prospect. The children got on well with their stepfather, and Mr Blythe made it clear that he was equally fond of them. 'He did like them, he took them as him own,' Miss Ina noted. 'They get on all right, no problem.'

Once settled in Grange, Ina and Granville began to have children of their own, beginning with Veta Aneta, born August 29, 1949, and given the pet name Girlie. The family began attending the Church of God in Green Island, one of the African-influenced churches where hats were worn and the Lord was praised through song, accompanied by rhythmic clapping and the banging of tambourines; though the services were more exciting than those of the Anglican Church, the religion still played a relatively peripheral role in their lives. Sonny, Lee, and Sitta were then attending Green Island School, a good three-mile walk away, while their older sister Dulcie had gone to Negril in search of work.

Though other family members have refuted this, Lee Perry has said he found school a perpetual burden, a pointless exercise in which the archaic methods of instruction tried to force conformity to a highly alien European model; the very language of his lessons was incomprehensible to him, and much of the experience was marked by cruelty. His small size and quick mouth made him an easy target for the teacher's cane, which his brother Sonny remembered as being in constant use: 'The teacher rough, and the teacher beat, but the teacher teach you good. I know me take the licking and me better off now.'

Lee's size also made him an easy target for the bullying of older students. He was particularly troubled by a larger girl named Pernel Davis, a cousin from his mother's side who used to torment Lee and one of his closest friends, until the wily youngster struck back with a razor blade in the school yard one afternoon. 'We did have a good friend named Manzie,' Sonny related, 'but one girl, big and coarse, she did fight the guy and the guy afraid. One day when the gal start to fight Manzie, Lee come up and give around three slashes . . . and it's under Saxham Bridge he go hide. When him come out, him get flogged still, the old lady beat him. Anything we do when we little, them flog we for it.'

After the incident with his cousin, Lee began to carry a knife with him everywhere he went, which he would sharpen with a piece of stone he carried in his pocket. The school bullies didn't trouble him any longer, but the generally oppressive and alien nature of school continued to be anathema to him. He dropped out at age 15 at the start of the 1950s, having only managed to reach the fourth grade. 'I learned nothing at all,' Lee later said of his schooling, 'everything I have learned has come from nature.' [1]

One of nature's lessons came when he was up in the hills, tending the family goat. 'He used to tend the goat and one Sunday morning he go and buck him big toe and have to go to the hospital in Lucea,' grinned Sonny. 'He never wear shoes in those days. The nurses them love him, doctor and everybody.' Not long after Lee's broken toe had healed, Miss Ina gave birth to another boy: Desmond was born October 29, 1952, and given the pet name Lloyd.

As Lee began to come of age, he was feeling increasingly constrained by his environment. There was little to keep him in Grange, and his only solace came through music. His greatest motivation came from dancing to music that inspired him, and many remember him as being an impressive dancer at an early age. 'The crossroads is where the dancehall used to be and he couldn't pass it!' his brother Sonny remembered. 'He have a crowd around him, crowd of gal and boy and every one of them are friends, he never have no enemy.' But rousing his peers at the dancehall was not enough to keep him in the region, and as soon as an opportunity arose, he was gone.

Lee Perry spent much of his teen years and early twenties ambling around the west and south of Jamaica, motivated by an unseen spiritual force. 'Everything that's going on, he later explained, there's some big spirit behind me who send me to do the thing that I must do.'[2] The youth he spent in Kendal and Grange was defined by the impoverished conditions of the district, and the toiling endured by his family in the cane fields was a downgrading experience of perpetual oppression.

Slavery had been banished from the island for over a century, but the values of the slave system ran deep, and those of African descent continued to bear the brunt of the divisive practices of colonialism. As the young Rainford Hugh watched his parents' ceaseless toil, he tried to picture if this too was to be his lowly destiny. He had seen his mother, stepfather, elder brother and sister, and most of his peers endure hours of back breaking labour, cutting cane in the fields for a mere pittance, but Perry's nature would never allow him to be beaten down and endure such work.

'I wasn't one of the working type. I loved to play games like dominoes. I never like to work, because I don't wish no one to be a slave. I want to be worked by my mind, not work by my body. I don't wish my body to be harmed. I really know this is the only body I've got and I've got to protect it, so I don't wish my body any hard work, I wish my body only the best work, the best things that entertain me; I wish not to be bored. Whenever I have a job, I would be very bored.' [3]

After dropping out of school, Perry stayed for a while in the vicinity of Grange, 'mostly playing domino. I was loving domino; I was a domino champion, cannot lose, always win. I become a professional domino game winner, go tournament and all them things.' [4] As a domino champion, Perry learned more skills than just slapping the dominoes on the table: he would study the faces of the other players while keeping his own face expressionless, trying to use his unseen senses to determine what move to make next. 'Through dominoes I practised my mind and learned to read the mind of others,' he later revealed, adding, 'This has proved eternally useful to me.' [5]

During the post-war economic boom of the early 1950s, Perry travelled to the Parish of Clarendon in search of work:

'We see a lot of guys go to Clarendon, they come back with bicycles and nice clothes. I say, "Wow, things looking good," because when they come back from Clarendon they're wearing different clothes, because they go and work for it. There was a lot of us who didn't have enough work, so we say, "This guy looking so nice, let's go Clarendon, and see what's happened to Clarendon." Me and my friend go Clarendon too, and I start to work for more than a year, get myself some nice different clothes and buy myself a bicycle and come home.' [6]

Lee made the journey to Clarendon with his brother Sonny and a friend named Douggie whom everyone called Bogus. 'Him carry we down and we no have no money,' Sonny noted. 'He take care of we until we start work, but me know me work and Lee, him no work yet. More time when me work, what me get, me share it between me and him.'

Although Perry was superficially drawn to Clarendon for practical reasons, he later explained that his motivation behind this relocation was really a love of music: 'Because I used to go to dance, I want to go to all the dances, and then I have a bicycle to take me to the dance quicker.' [7]

'He start to think he is a dancer, go to dances and always win,' remembered Ina Blythe.

Back in Grange, he used his bicycle to take him to dance competitions held in Jamaica's western parishes during the sugar-cane crop season.

'Me and my friend keep going to the dance, Westmoreland and everywhere, so I become the dance champion, win all the dance, the best dance. The "Neat Little Thing" they call me, the "Neat Little Man". From there I start to go into the music, and start to have the love for the dance music that can make me do funny things, some Yankin' and some crazy thing before rock and roll. Those days things was really nice, boogie woogie and blues, and jazz and all them things, but we would like the wild type of dancing, roots music . . . Me think about it, and find meself from the dancing, I want to get into the music now.'[8]

A regular attendant at such dances was Lee's cousin Stainton 'Archie' Moore; born April 17, 1938, he is the son of Miss Ina's older sister Mary. Archie noted Perry's growing fame as a dancer in this period: 'When him come all a Grange Hill (in Westmoreland) and have dance 'round a Mint Road and all them place, crowd come gather waiting to see him and Manhill and a guy named Manzie. He used to dance with Amy, the daughter of a musician named Smith who used to have an orchestra band in Grange Hill. When them dance, everybody just hold on and watch them.'

It was partly Lee's mastery of a step called the Yank that made him a repeated dance champion. According to Winston Blake, operator of the Merritone sound system and label, the drastic movements that characterised the Yank resulted in many injuries, and a dancer who could Yank well was treated with much respect. 'The music in the '50s that was really dominant started out with a slow type of thing which is like the New Orleans type of music, Shirley and Lee. They had a thing them called the Yank, that was a big dance in Jamaica, so big that a lot of people dislocate their hips doing it. They had a big (announcement) in the paper, "No bed at the hospital for Yankers", because people Yank themselves out of control.'

While Lee was Yanking his way towards glory, his mother gave birth to another boy on October 29, 1956; named Milton, he was given the nickname Poppa Son by his older sister Girlie.

In the mid-'50s, the Jamaican government designated a new tourist development in Negril on the westernmost tip of the island, and Perry got a job there driving bulldozers and shifting boulders in the early stages of the region's development. 'He even drive a tractor in Negril, dynamite all rock with electric dynamite,' recalled his brother Sonny. 'He like those things, but it dangerous!'

Besides concentrating on the task at hand, Perry tuned into the sounds associated with construction, focusing on the energies of the machines as they came into conflict with nature. 'I liked the power,' Perry later remarked. 'That BRRRRRRR from nine 'til six, BRRRRRRR from the engine up the gearstick into your arm. It builds up lots of power.'[9] He worked for some months in Negril, before moving on to a couple of other jobs in Westmoreland where he drove a yellow Caterpillar bulldozer. He later explained that mysterious events, 'miracle gifts' and 'blessings from God',[10] occurred during this construction work, resulting in his eventual migration to Kingston towards the start of the 1960s.

Perry later stated that while shifting boulders in Negril,

'I get an overload from throwing stones down there for maybe two weeks. I started making positive connection with stones, by throwing stones to stones I start to hear sounds. When the stones clash I hear the thunder clash, and I hear lightning flash, and I hear words, and I don't know where the words them coming from. These words send me to King-stone: to Kingston. Kingston means King's stone, the son of the King; that's where the music's coming from, so I go up to King's stone, because the stone that I was throwing in Negril send me to Kingstone for my graduation.' [11]

What Perry has seldom mentioned about his time in the Negril area is that he met and married a woman who lived near there in the town of Little London as the 1950s were drawing to a close. On the road between Negril and Savannah La Mar, Little London was then largely inhabited by the descendants of Indians who had emigrated to Jamaica as indentured servants in the 1800s, and the family Ruby Williams came from was no exception to the rule. Affectionately known as Tootsie, the attractive young woman lived with Lee Perry in Little London for about a year and a half before their wedding, which was instigated largely by the pastor in the local Church of God – a church Perry was baptised into during their courtship. The wedding was a quiet affair, with none of Perry's family present, and the marriage itself would not last long. 'We get married when I was about 25 and she was about 18,' Perry recalled.

Perry spoke with fondness of their time together, and noted his disappointment when the relationship broke down within a matter of months. 'We lived together for about eighteen months. Then we wanted a change and the pastor suggested we get married, but after the marriage we only lived together for six months. When you just met somebody, the vibration you get off a new love is nice; it take for a time until we find we weren't living cooperatively, because after a while you get to find the true facts of the woman that you deal with. She never show what she is like at the very beginning, that she only love siler and gold and money; she could do sewing but never wanted to work by it, so she go the Montego Bay to try to live off others. Then I went to Kingston.'

Though Lee Perry had been born into poverty and did not take well to institutionalised education, his independent spirit and impulsive nature ensured he would never remain stagnant for long. He was already aware of creative urges springing up within him in his teens, and the life of wandering he began then was largely a search for the means to express himself creatively; indeed, the majority of his life would be spent undertaking exploratory journeys to better interpret and express his ideas about the world through song. By the time Perry was working in Negril, he had a strong desire to make it as a singer, and he knew that the only opportunity for him to realise his dreams lay in the nation's capital. He thus heeded the wisdom of his guiding spirit and made the journey to Kingston at the start of the 1960s.

In the years following World War II, while Perry was enduring the last of his school days, there were several important advancements being made in Jamaican popular music. A number of different styles were being experimented with by local players, and the method of dissemination of recorded music also contributed to concrete changes.

On the live scene, Jamaican big-band jazz groups began to perform at clubs and hotels on the island. They mostly played the music of the American groups who had created the genre, but also featured other Caribbean styles like merengue and calypso, additionally forming Jamaican variations of jazz through their own complex compositions. Among the most popular to tour the country was a band led by saxophonist Val Bennett, while a group called The Arawaks, led by pianist Luther Williams, also commanded a large following. Eric Deans' Orchestra was immensely popular in the capital, enjoying a long residence at the Bournemouth Club in East Kingston, playing six nights a week at the height of their popularity. Another hot band was led by Redvert Cook at the upmarket Glass Bucket club, where the clientele was largely composed of upper class Jamaicans who were white or of mixed race but with light complexions; down at the Blue Mirror on Neal Street, American GIs would cavort with the resident prostitutes while a band provided musical atmosphere. At the Coney Island gambling arena on East Queen Street, a house band with a shifting lineup was also blowing hot jazz six nights a week.

Down in the Dungle, in the heart of West Kingston's most notorious ghetto on the edge of the municipal garbage dump, there were other musical rumblings that were to have a strong impact on Jamaican popular music. This is where the ghetto was harshest, where only the most resilient could thrive, and daily survival came as something of a miracle. Since the 1930s, the Dungle had become the haunt of the Burru men, a lowly community of criminal outcasts who had migrated from rural Clarendon. At the very bottom of Jamaican society, the Burru men had retained the drumming traditions of the Asante tribe from whom they had descended, and had a long history of rebellion and criminality that stretched back to slavery days.

Burru music revolves around a trio of hand drums: the large bass drum (pounded with a stick) and the *funde* hold the rhythm, while the smaller *kette*, or repeater drum, takes the melodic lead. Historically, the Burru have been among the most defiant of Jamaica's people, and they have used their music to express this defiance. Derived from a fertility ceremony that accompanied a masquerade dance, Burru music was later associated with a variety of social functions, including the greeting of prisoners returning home or morale boosting for incarcerated prisoners that were soon to be released. Although the Burru warriors played an important role in fermenting insurrection during slavery, their propagation of African traditions meant that they were seen as backward in the Eurocentric aftermath of post-emancipation Jamaica. But the

Burru held immense appeal for another group of outcasts visible in the ghetto from the early 1930s: the Rastafari.

Rastafarianism has been written about at length elsewhere, and the varying accounts of the religion have resulted in perplexing and contradictory portraits, especially in several texts by white academics whose lives are far removed from those of the faith. Without wishing to further this process, I shall briefly recount below certain salient points of particular relevance.

The Rastafari began to emerge in Kingston and various rural areas after the crowning of Prince Tafari Makonen in 1930 as Haile Selassie, Emperor of Ethiopia. Various street preachers interpreted a statement attributed to Marcus Garvey to mark the event as the fulfilment of biblical prophecy, and it is partly the great reverence held for Garvey among the Jamaican poor that gave the Rastafarian movement its initial impetus.

Born in the parish of St Ann in 1887, Garvey was a radical revolutionary who fought tirelessly for black self-determination through the Universal Negro Improvement Association. A champion of Jamaica's poor black masses, Garvey sought to establish voluntary repatriation to Africa through the Black Star shipping line. Although Garvey was hounded out of Jamaica by the authorities in 1916, was imprisoned in America for fraud when the Black Star line collapsed in the 1920s, and later died in England in poverty with few of his goals realised, his revolutionary ideals had a profound and wide-ranging affect, and his influence can be seen in diverse places such as the American civil rights movement and Kwame Nkrumah's revolution in Ghana.

Throughout his lifetime, Marcus Garvey gave a series of eloquent and fiery speeches, several of which are said to have contained cryptic prophecies. Echoing the Bible's description of the African continent, Garvey made frequent reference to Ethiopia, referring to it as the 'land of our fathers' and expressing a belief in 'the God of Ethiopia'. In one such speech, said to have been delivered in 1927, Garvey is supposed to have proclaimed, 'Look to Africa, for the crowning of a black king, he shall be the redeemer.' In 1930, when Ras Tafari Makonen was crowned Haile Selassie I, Emperor of Ethiopia, taking the title of Negusa Negast, the Elect of God, King of Kings, Lord of Lords, Conquering Lion of the Tribe of Judah, the downtrodden of Jamaica took note.

Whether or not Garvey actually uttered the prophetic words, his Jamaican followers took the crowing of Selassie as a sure sign of divinity, boosted by passages from the bible such as 'Princes shall come out of Egypt, Ethiopia shall soon stretch out her hands unto God' in Psalm 68 and 'Weep not! Behold, the Lion of the Tribe of Judah, the Root of David has triumphed. He is able to open the scroll and its seven seals' in Revelation 5. As new religious leaders like Leonard P. Howell, Joseph Nathaniel Hibbert, Claudius Henry, Robert Hinds, and Prince Emmanuel Edwards began to galvanise support for the faith by proclaiming that God was black and that the rightful place for black Jamaicans was Africa, various sectors of the black peasantry responded enthusiastically, and myriad forms of the Rastafarian movement took root in the early 1930s.

The different strands of the faith continued to grow, notably among the inhabitants of the sprawling ghettos of Western Kingston, and a fertile intermingling eventually took place among the Rastafari and the Burru. It is said that the Rastas were searching for a music that would reflect their veneration of African culture, so they borrowed the music of the Burru, in turn providing them with a religious and spiritual doctrine. In the '40s and '50s, many jazz musicians began to accept the faith, and late night jam sessions would echo into the night from various Rasta encampments.

Although live jazz music tended to be more popular with the wealthier sectors of the population, it was the emergence of another musical entity that really captivated the majority of the island's music lovers: the sound system. Sound systems became a fixture of Jamaica's post-war economic boom, the first having appeared after Jamaicans returned from periods of work abroad, cutting sugar cane in Florida or picking crops elsewhere in the American South. Custom-built in Jamaica or brought back from the USA, the huge portable systems used hefty amplifiers and public-address systems to blast music through rows of massive speaker boxes; a lasting impression was inevitably made on the listener through the sheer power and volume of the sound. Set up at dances, many of which were held in the open air, the sound system's selector would spin the hottest American rhythm-and-blues records to catapult Jamaican dance fans into enthusiastic action, egged on by over-the-top microphone commentary from deejays that revelled in comic exhortations of verbal wit, outrageously exaggerated hep-cat imitations of black American radio disc jockeys. With an entry price of about two shillings and the ability to penetrate the country towns that did not have proper music venues, sound system dances had a wider appeal to the general Jamaican public, and did not carry the same restrictions or elite connotations as much of the live jazz scene.

Sound system competition was fierce, with operators relying on exclusive records brought back from America that they alone could play to keep their supporters loyal. Fats Domino, Shirley and Lee, and Louis Jordan were immensely popular with dance fans, but the sound system operators found that they needed to get their hands on particular records by lesser-known artists. Only outstanding tunes that were out of the ordinary would retain the dancers' interest and stop them from seeking more exciting sounds at an opponent's set. Open confrontations began in the form of the 'sound clash' where two systems would battle each other in clubs like the Forester's Hall on North Street, the Pioneer Club in Jones Town, and outdoor venues like Chocomo on Wellington Street and the King's Lawn on North Street.

The first sound to really take off was Tom the Great Sebastian, run by a certain Tom Wong, whose skilled selector was a man called Duke Vin. Based at premises on Pink Lane, off Orange Street, the outfit was in operation in the late 1940s, and Vin, born in 1928, continued to rule the dancehall at the start of the '50s, keeping an edge on the competition through the steady stream of records sent to him by a friend named Juan in America. Sounds like Sir Nick the Champ on Charles Street, Count Smith the Blues Blaster in Greenwich Town and Count P. the Whip all emerged as challengers to Vin's popularity, but his more varied selection (which included a repertoire of merengue and Spanish music, as well as rhythm and blues) held sway until the appearance of a more concrete challenge provided by two men who used force to ensure their popularity: Duke Reid and King Edwards.

The Duke, born Arthur Reid, was a flamboyant and intimidating figure who bludgeoned his way to the top of Kingston's popular music scene. His ten years in the police force had left him with a fondness for firearms, a close association with the Jamaican criminal underclass, and strong links with certain factions of American organised crime; one of Duke Vin's childhood memories is of Sergeant Reid behind the wheel of a Black Maria, passing Vin while he was on his way to school.

Duke Reid's wife Lucile (a.k.a. the Duchess) had won the National Lottery, allowing the Reids to establish the Treasure Isle Liquor Store on Bond Street, which also became the headquarters of Duke's musical operation; they also ran a restaurant and dry cleaners on the same corner.

Well-versed in the skills of intimidation, his Duke Reid the Trojan sound system (named after his Bedford Trojan truck and featuring the selector Leroy 'Cuttings' Cole and a disc jockey called Clifford) became the largest and most successful sound in Jamaica, largely through the strong-arm tactics of the Duke and his henchmen. Vincent Edwards, a friend of the Duke who operated a set called King Edwards the Giant from premises on the border of Waltham Park and Spanish Town, was another man who used violence to establish the success of his system.

Duke Reid was a man who often walked with a rifle. He kept a loaded .45 magnum clearly visible in the holster at his waist, and retained a .22-calibre pistol inside his waistcoat for good measure. Reid was a large man who liked to throw his weight around, and had a legion of rough ghetto-dwellers and off-duty policemen who were always willing to lend a heavy hand after getting tanked up on Duke Reid's rum – men like the greatly feared Whoppi King, a notorious criminal commonly known as Public Enemy Number One for his ruthlessness. Adding to Reid's fearsome reputation were heavy rings worn on every finger, many of which were imported from the occult De Lawrence organisation in America; though De Lawrence material could not legally be imported to Jamaica, Reid is said to have bribed post office staff and customs officials to ensure their safe delivery.

King Edwards also built up a crowd of roughnecks who did not hesitate to sabotage the competition, and both men became the new rulers of sound in the early 1950s as the more popular sets found their equipment being smashed up and shot at with increasing regularity.

Many a sound couldn't take the pressure and were flattened in Reid's and Edwards' wake. Tom the Great Sebastian, the reigning champ, stuck his tail between his legs and moved to the Silver Slipper club out at Cross Roads, where things were safer, but after Duke Vin quit Jamaica for good in 1954 to became the first sound system operator in England, Tom's days of glory were over. He phased out the sound some time thereafter, and is said to have committed suicide in the early '60s.

The successful challenger that eventually emerged was Sir Coxsone's Downbeat, a set run by an enterprising businessman named Clement Seymour Dodd; Coxsone was the name of a Yorkshire cricket batsman, and Dodd picked up the nickname while batting in his youth at All Saints School.

Born in Kingston on January 26, 1932, Dodd's father was a successful contractor mason who helped build the massive Carib Theatre located at the Cross Roads section of Kingston; he also built several other theatres in rural parishes. From the early 1950s, Dodd's mother ran Nanny's Corner, a restaurant located at the corner of Laws Street and Ladd Lane that she later converted into a liquor store; equipped with a Morphy Richards radio, the restaurant's customers could enjoy the latest by Billy Eckstein, Sarah Vaughan, Lionel Hampton, and Louis Jordan. In his teenage years, Clement found work as a cabinetmaker, and later trained at the Ford garage on Church Street after completing a course in automobile mechanics before seeking more profitable employment as a crop picker in the American South. In the early 1950s, after working on American farms, Dodd saw black Americans earning good money spinning rhythm and blues at outdoor dances and city block parties, and thus began to contemplate entering the music business.

According to the late George Peckings, a long-time associate of Coxsone, Dodd came into the business almost accidentally, after he met a man on a farm in America who had been buying rhythm-and-blues records to bring back to Jamaica. When the man disappeared, Dodd decided to bring back the records himself, and promptly delivered them to Duke Reid, who was an old friend of the family. It was, in fact, Dodd's mother who had furnished Duke with his original signature tune: the instrumental 'My Mother's Eyes' by Tab Smith. Coxsone began to make guest appearances on Duke Reid's sound system with his growing stack of vinyl, and after seeing the effect his new discs had on the ecstatic Jamaican dancing public, Dodd became determined to give Duke a run for his money by starting his own sound system.

Dodd has stated that he began visiting Rainbow Records in the heart of Harlem on 130th Street in 1954, bringing back a stack of boogie-woogie and jazz discs. He sought out the most impressive hi-fi equipment available in the USA, and established a base in Kingston with the help of his mother at a newer branch of the family liquor store on the corner of Beeston Street and

Love Lane; Coxsone also began selling imported American 45s from the premises.

From the late 1950s, Coxsone Dodd and Duke Reid maintained a heated rivalry, and it was straight into the middle of their pitched battles that Lee Perry would step when he first arrived in Kingston. Though neither took him seriously at first, they would both come to recognise and appreciate his talents after seeing the creativity he was capable of harnessing – a peculiar creativity that could be entirely beneficial to musical entrepreneurs. He may have been nothing more than a little man fresh from the country with some very peculiar ideas, but the big sound men would soon learn that Lee Perry's ears heard things that they could not, and his very strangeness would see him become a key player in the creation of a distinctly Jamaican music.

CHICKEN SCRATCH:

The studio one years

Having already spent a fair amount of time in sizeable towns in the Parishes of Clarendon and Westmoreland, Lee Perry was not as green as some of the other youths who arrived in Kingston straight from the heart of the country, but life in the sprawling overcrowded capital was still quite unsettling at first.

Perry's closest relative in town was his cousin, Archie Moore, who was then working as a shoemaker; having lived in Kingston since 1950, Archie knew his way around and proved to be a generally useful ally. Esmee Davis, a childless maternal aunt, was also working in Kingston as a hat maker, and Perry occasionally slept at her place during his early days in Kingston. Extremely short of money, he began spending nights at a shop operated by a tailor from Hanover named Lawrence at 45 Spanish Town Road in an area of Kingston known as Dog Park; after closing time, Perry would fight with other fresh arrivals from Hanover to retain a bit of floor space to sleep on.

Lee Perry was nurturing a dream of making music, but without any form of employment, Kingston life was proving to be tough. Archie Moore recalled the harsh nature of Perry's early days within the city: 'It reach a stage where him have one suit 'pon him back and him go and buy himself a T-shirt so that him could change him shirt. When him go out and come back them thief the shirt, and him have to put on back the same shirt that he did have on before.'

Back at the family home in Hanover, Miss Ina had given birth to a final daughter on January 29, 1960; named Lorna, she would later be known as Miss Nelle.

Perry's arrival in Kingston coincided with another important musical change: local talent was beginning to be regularly sought by sound system owners for recording. After relying on purely imported music for several years, the sound men began to record local singers and musicians for one-off 'specials' – songs cut only on acetate for exclusive use on their sound. Duke Reid is said to have begun the process, with Coxsone soon following, and part of the impetus for this practice stemmed from the belated success of recorded mento.

Mento music had long been a feature of Jamaican country life. It evolved from Junkunu, a West African harvest ritual that survived the purges of slavery. To the basic African structure was added European melodies, Cuban rumba beats, and other Latin American influences to form a vibrant music that was distinctly Jamaican in character, though it shared some common ground with the inter-island calypso style through lyrics that were often satirical.

Although mento's popularity began to wane in the 1930s with the increased emigration of rural peasants to the Kingston conurbation, it is the style that was featured on the first discs to be recorded and pressed in Jamaica. In the late 1940s and early '50s, a Jewish Jamaican businessman named Stanley Beresford Motta released a series of notable mento and calypso 78s. Born October 5, 1915, the enterprising Motta began his working life as an apprentice at his uncle's garage, but quit to open his first radio-parts shop at 10C East Street at the age of 16. In 1934, he became a pioneer in his field by introducing the popular Sylvania lighting systems to the island, and subsequently established a successful appliance rental outlet at 109 Harbour Street. His early music sorties included debuts by artists such as Lord Flea, Count Lasher, Monty Reynolds' Calypso Clippers and an immigrant from Trinidad known as Lord Tanamo, backed on later recordings by a band that included a young pianist from Darling Street named Theophilus Beckford and a guitarist based in Jones Town named Ernest Ranglin. A self-taught musician born in Manchester, Ranglin also recorded Hawaiian guitar music on wax cylinders for another entrepreneur before the Motta 78s.

Motta's chief source of competition was provided by Ken Khouri, who began producing records on his Pioneer label in 1954; in September of that year, he opened a monophonic recording facility and pressing plant called Federal that was to become a focal point for the subsequent rise of Jamaican recording artists. Before the opening of Khouri's studio, the only stable recording premises on the island was another one-track facility at Radio Jamaica Rediffusion, a station that had sprung from the ashes of the government wartime station Radio ZQI in 1950.

The Mento records produced by Motta and Khouri were aimed at the overseas 'ethnic' market that was then infatuated with calypso, but the records were met with little interest abroad. However, airplay on RJR partly influenced the sound men into taking risks on the singers and players that were directly in their midst, although the songs they began recording were based on American boogie-woogie and R & B instead of mento.

In September 1959, the Jamaica Broadcasting Corporation was set up as an alternative to the airwave monopoly enjoyed by RJR. As the sound system bosses began to increase their number of official releases, both stations began a gradual aggrandisement of the Jamaican content of their playlists. Another important part of this process was played by the talent shows held in various Kingston theatres, several of which were regularly held by a man named Vere Johns Jr; the Lanneman's Programme was a similar contest presenting budding talent. Many aspiring young singers emerged from the spotlight at contests held at the Ambassador, Ward, Carib, Palace and other theatres to get the push needed to bring them to the attention of the few record producers that were active in Jamaica.

Just as the 1960s were coming into view, the radio charts were being ruled for the first time by local Jamaican talent, with the first number one coming in Laurel Aitken's 'Boogie Rock', released in September 1959 by Stanley Motta's Caribbean Recording Company. Born Lorenzo Aitken in Cuba in 1927 to a Cuban mother and a Jamaican father, Aitken lived in Jamaica since the age of eight. As a teenager, he was hired by the Jamaican Tourist Board to sing calypsos to tourists in Kingston Harbour. Aitken continued to rule the boogie era with songs like 'Boogie In My Bones' and 'Little Sheila', recorded soon after the Motta hit for a young white entrepreneur named Chris Blackwell.

Blackwell would eventually become one of the most successful promoters of Jamaican music and remains a controversial figure in many ways. Born in England on June 22, 1937, Blackwell spent his formative years in Jamaica and was later educated at an elite English public school. His mother was Blanche Lindo, a Jamaican of Jewish descent who was at the paramount of Jamaican society when Chris Blackwell was born.

In 1492, the same year that Columbus 'discovered' America on behalf of the Spanish regent, all Jews were banished from Spain. In 1580, Spain overtook neighbouring Portugal and furthered its concerted persecution of Jews. The majority of the Sephardic Jews who inhabited southern Europe were thus hounded out of the continent by the purges of the Spanish Inquisition, and some eventually arrived in Jamaica by a circuitous route, Blanche Lindo's foreparents among them.

Originally, Jews occupied a fairly low social status in Jamaica. A complex social hierarchy based on skin tone had been established on the island early in the English colonial period, and elements of this hierarchy profoundly influence attitudes towards race among Jamaicans today. The system placed white English rulers at the top, with their Scottish and Irish lackeys just below. Next were the illegitimate mixed-race children of whites and slaves, known as 'mulattos' or 'coloureds'. At about the same level or just beneath were Jews and freed slaves, but the Jews later occupied a higher status after becoming allied with the plantation owners during slave insurrections.

Rising slowly in Jamaica's shifting social structure, the Lindos made their fortunes from rum and sugar towards the end of the days of slavery, and emerged as one of the 21 families said to have taken control of Jamaica in the 20th century, given esteem by the ruling class but viewed with fear and loathing by much of the general population.

Joe Blackwell was an Irishman who had become an officer in the Irish Guards, and he met Blanche Lindo on one of her trips to England in the 1930s. Like the Lindos, the Blackwell family had also reaped substantial benefits from the colonial situation through the Crosse and Blackwell Foods

Company, though Joe Blackwell himself was on the periphery of such imperial fortunes. Upon moving to Jamaica, he became a major in the Jamaica Regiment.

As the wayward son of two wealthy and powerful families, Chris Blackwell relied on his parents' connections for some of his early occupations. He was sent to England to become an accountant at the powerful Price Waterhouse company, but it provided too little challenge for him, so Blackwell abandoned his apprenticeship to try and make it as a professional gambler. Returning to Jamaica in 1958, he served briefly as aide-de-camp to Sir Hugh Foot, the Governor General of Jamaica. In 1959, Blackwell left the island again, this time heading for America with his father. He spent several months in New York, becoming friendly with prominent jazz musicians and generally being inspired by the music scene. Within six months, he returned to Jamaica and established two labels to promote local talent – Island and R & B – thus beginning a long and complex involvement with the Jamaican music industry. Besides his success with Laurel Aitken, Blackwell also had early hits by singers Wilfred 'Jackie' Edwards and Owen Gray.

Another notable and ambiguous figure entering music production at this time was Edward Seaga, an American-born Jamaican of Syrian and English parentage. The son of a wealthy businessman who made his fortune from a travel agency, Seaga studied anthropology at Harvard, where some say he was recruited by the CIA. Like Blackwell, Seaga's involvement with Jamaican music would be long and complicated, and his later incarnation as a Jamaican politician is clearly linked to his early involvement in the music industry. Seaga had supervised the earliest-known recording of African-inspired religious folk music in Jamaica in 1955 for an album that appeared on the Smithsonian Folkways label; in 1959, he began releasing popular Jamaican 45s through the West Indies Records Limited or WIRL label, scoring a big hit with 'Manny Oh' by the Trench Town duo of Joe Higgs and Roy Wilson. Another early success came through an instrumental called 'Dumplings' by the Dragonaires, led by a young bassist named Byron Lee, who would himself emerge as one of the most influential figures in the Jamaican music industry.

Born in Manchester June 27, 1935, Byron Lee was the eldest of two sons born to a Chinese immigrant father and black Jamaican mother. Lee's father came to Jamaica from Kowloon, Hong Kong, to teach English to the children of Chinese migrants who had settled in Jamaica after working on the Panama Canal; his mother came from a family of Junkunu dancers and mento musicians in the rural Balaclava area. After learning to play the piano in boarding school, Lee became a professional football player for the Jamaican national team before pursuing a career as a bass player and bandleader. As a light-skinned member of Jamaica's middle class, Lee would gain a success and credibility among the wealthier sectors of the population that ghetto musicians were unable to achieve – despite the fact that the Dragonaires would later base their music on the appropriation of ghetto styles. After Edward Seaga left the running of WIRL to associates of his father while embarking on a political career in the early 1960s, Byron Lee became the bandleader for the rival Federal Studio, but would later become more concretely involved in WIRL's operations through his continued friendship with Seaga.

Although Duke Reid is said to have recorded local artists for sound system specials earlier than Coxsone, the popularity of his material was gradually superseded by Coxsone's product. Coxsone was keen to point out that although he and Duke were rivals, the rivalry was based on mutual respect, and that they retained a working friendship despite their ongoing competition. 'The rivalry was clean, it was more of a musical challenge. I respected Duke because he was my senior by a couple of years, but what kept me there was that I was more musically knowledgeable than Duke in terms of what rhythms could be danceable or acceptable. When we started recording locally, I had the stronger set of records but Duke was always there trying and whatever it costs, Duke would find the money and get it done. It kept me on the ball trying to produce better stuff, but in the early days we had exchanged songs, like I give him "Green Island" to release on his label and he gave me "Eastern Standard Time" and some other songs.'

Among Reid's most successful early releases were blues-tinged instrumentals like 'Duke's Cookies', 'The Joker', and 'What Makes Honey', all issued on his Treasure Isle label between 1959 and 1961; he was also working with artists like the Jiving Juniors (a trio featuring Derrick Harriott, Maurice Wynter, and Eugene Dwyer), but Coxsone was to achieve far more success with the group. Dodd, meanwhile, was grasping the nettle and finding success with material on his All Stars and World Disc labels. A recording session in 1959 yielded a number of hits, including 'Time To Pray' by Basil Gabbidon and the Mellow Larks, 'Marjie' by the Dewdroppers, featuring pianist Aubrey Adams, and 'Muriel' by singing duo Alton Ellis and Eddy Perkins, but the song that caused the biggest sensation by far was 'Easy Snappin' '. This innovative record, sung and played by pianist Theophilus Beckford (accompanied by the Blues Blasters band, led by bassist Cluet Johnson) prefaced changes that would soon be brought to the prevalent beat, as Beckford himself has noted.

'When I started, there was no Jamaican music much around, it was pure foreign tune. Somewhere down in the end part of 1956 I start my music, a whole lot of people used to gather 'round and want to know what kind of music that I playing.' [1]

The Jamaican boogie style was gradually giving way to the new rhythm of an emerging hybrid coming up from the nightclubs and back streets, and 'Easy Snappin' ' was the first nod towards this new direction.

Another notable Coxsone production from this period was 'Freedom' by

Clancy Eccles. Born December 19, 1940, near Highgate in the Parish of St Mary, Eccles moved often as a child as his father was a builder and tailor who uprooted the family as needed to satisfy work commitments. In his teen years, Eccles settled on the North Coast, where he tried to make it as a singer, becoming friendly with artists like Higgs and Wilson, the Blues Busters and Busty Brown. He began promoting shows at the White River Club, presenting himself and a fire dancer to a small audience, but the performances did not gain him much exposure. In November 1959, Eccles participated in a talent contest Coxsone Dodd held at the Ward Theatre in Kingston and, though Tony Gregory was the triumphant winner of the event, Eccles was the first of the contestants Coxsone chose to record. Backed by Clue J's band, Eccles cut 'Freedom' and 'I Live And I Love' for Dodd at Federal shortly after the talent show, but the songs were not released for several years – despite their massive popularity on the Downbeat set, built up on acetate by selector Count Machuki.

When 'Freedom' was finally released, its original message was virtually overlooked in favour of a new meaning, with conservative Jamaica Labour Party politicians using the song to protest against Jamaica's membership in the Federation of the West Indies, pushing for full and immediate independence from Britain apart from neighbouring colonies. In 1958, Jamaica had joined the other 12 English-speaking Caribbean islands as part of what was meant to be a new nation, with independence from Britain planned for all in 1963. But by 1961, trade-union leader Alexander Bustamante – who had formed the JLP after failing to take control of the People's National Party, headed by his cousin, Norman Washington Manley – began a vociferous campaign with Edward Seaga against the Federation, using Eccles' 'Freedom' as part of their platform of Jamaican nationalism, despite the song's original statement of the desired repatriation to Africa of Jamaica's black populace. As Eccles explained, 'We were talking about repatriation, a back-to-Africa thing, but the politicians used it as a slogan to mash Federation and give them an independent look from Britain. They used it as their tool, but going for political independence wasn't our thing. We were thinking about an African movement where we could go to this big motherland and become somebody there.'

Eccles provided further hits for Coxsone like 'River Jordan' and 'More Proof', both recorded in July 1960. He also tailored suits for many of Dodd's artists, including Tony Gregory, the Blues Busters, and several of the backing musicians who would eventually be known as the Skatalites. He also began promoting shows with Dodd, but ceased working with him in 1962 after discovering that Dodd was taking a greater portion of the profits. Not wanting to infringe on the exclusive contract he had signed with Dodd, Eccles avoided singing for a period and returned to promoting shows, finding success with artists like the Clarendonians from 1963. Before his final rupture with Dodd, Clancy Eccles enountered Lee Perry at Coxsone's shop on Beeston Street.

They established a friendship there that would prove to be long and fruitful, far outlasting their initial connection as agents manipulated by the same boss.

It was while Duke Reid and Coxsone Dodd were battling to control the local talent that Lee Perry first arrived in Kingston in the early 1960s. As a dance champion, Perry was instinctively drawn to where Kingston's hottest musical action was to be found, so Treasure Isle Liquors was, naturally, his first port of call. He had heard that the Duke had started to record local artists and offered his songs and other services to Reid, but the Duke's initial response was not positive.

'I go to Kingston and I try Duke Reid,' Perry recalled, 'and him never ready for me, because he didn't ready for my type of thing.' [2] Reid let Perry hang around for a couple of weeks, but refused to record him and did not pay him much attention. Duke is said to have been troubled by the small man's presence; there was something unnatural in Perry's eye and, when his gaze fixed on you, it was as though he was seeing through you, or looking at something else that was far and distant. Perhaps Duke had occasionally seen such a look before in his days as a policeman, in the eyes of those who scraped a precarious existence amongst the poorest slum dwellers who were saying that God was an African.

Although Reid thought Perry was not ready to make it as a singer, he was aware of the country youth's songwriting ability, and it was Duke's unwarranted use of Perry's lyrics for a better established singer that would see Perry leave Reid's stable for the rival camp of Coxsone Dodd. According to both Perry and Dodd, the parting incident took place at Federal studio, where Reid and Dodd were conducting recording sessions on the same day. Reid had heard Perry singing a song whose lyrics he found impressive, but thinking that Perry's singing voice was not properly developed, he gave the lyrics to popular hitmaker Stranger Cole – without seeking Perry's permission first.

When Wilburn Theodore Cole was born, he resembled no family member and was thus given the nickname Stranger. He was first brought to Duke Reid's attention by his older brother Leroy, the selector of Reid's sound system; at his audition, Reid was impressed by an original composition, 'In And Out The Window', which he recorded with the more established Eric 'Monty' Morris. When Morris' recording quickly reached a number one chart position, Reid asked Cole to prepare for his recording debut, which yielded two further hits: 'When You Call My Name', a duet with Millicent 'Patsy' Todd, and 'Rough And Tough', a taunting solo effort. Both songs reached number one chart positions in 1962 and retained their popularity well into the following year.

Joe Higgs was present when Duke Reid quarrelled with Lee Perry, and named 'Rough And Tough' as the song using Perry's lyrics; he has said that when Perry protested about the situation, Duke flattened him with a hefty punch. Both Perry and Coxsone Dodd had difficulty remembering exactly which song caused the incident, and Stranger Cole insists he wrote the song after being challenged by a romantic rival: 'I never really tell many stories about 'Rough And Tough', but I really made it from a girlfriend I had. We were very young then, and I had a disagreement with her with another guy, talking about who was slick, in pretty clothes and all that. We had a little fallout, so I went away and made the song; it's all coming out of a little love affair.' Whether it was 'Rough and Tough' or some other number, this unwarranted use of lyrics led to Perry leaving Reid's area for the less established camp of Coxsone Dodd.

As Coxsone recalled, 'Scratch came from country and he was hearing all these local musics. He wanted to get into the business, so he used to hang out by Duke's session or my session. How we really get together that first time, Perry come by Federal and he and Duke in the focus. He vexed and I asked him what happened and he explained to me that the song that going to record in there is a song that steal from him. There was a song that cause him and Duke to get into a fracas, he did sing it and rehearse fe him and Duke go record it over. So seeing he and Duke and some of the guys clash, I came in and pacify it, and realising he was outnumbered at the studio I took him away from the crowd and whatever was happening. At that time, I had to advise him, I said "In future, you don't sing your song around to let people hear it, 'cause sometimes they will have a better voice and they'll sing the song." We had a good talk, then he went back to the country and when he came back, he stop visiting Duke and then started by me and in no time I created a little job for him.'

Perry noted that he felt generally compelled to leave Duke Reid because of Duke's arrogance and negative attitude, the unsolicited use of his lyrics appearing as one liberty too many. 'It was really true that it was a song that I write and Stranger Cole was singing it, and I said to Mr. Dodd "That is my song" but there was many more Duke didn't want me to sing. We join forces to drop a bigger guy who said he was the biggest guy in town, and we small guys, the likkle got big and make him feel it. The pressure with Duke, you couldn't take it because Duke never have no sense about humanity, him just figure that him is a bully. You would be afraid of his gun – though he's not going shoot you, he have gun like a whip, and he can skin you. He thinks he's the boss, but him have no feelings that you could go with him and enjoy yourself; like Mr Dodd, he's always like a kid. You can go to the people and you can share their thoughts and you enjoy saying words and laugh, make your own entertainment. With Duke, you cannot have people like that around make their own entertainment, 'cause he's a boss.'

A quiet youth with a country air about him, Perry soon won the confidence of Coxsone, who took 'Little Lee' in as part of his growing entourage. 'I used to love dancing. I see dancing as a physical exercise for energy for sustaining of your body. I always trail music for exercising, so we met in the dancehall,' Perry said of his first link with Coxsone. 'I want to sing, those days I just want to try because I have ideas, but Coxsone was the only one that give me the first try.' [3]

By this point, Perry had found digs in the crowded West Kingston slum of Vineyard Town. Although he began as a mere errand boy for Dodd, Coxsone was able to see Perry's potential usefulness in ways that Reid could not. Because the Downbeat sound system was a smaller set, Perry found that Dodd had an openness that Duke Reid lacked; he also chose to stick with Downbeat because the set then had the reputation of an underdog.

'I see Coxsone as a struggler, he was struggling under Duke Reid's pressure. Duke Reid was well heavy, with bigger boys. If you have the most bad boys amongst you, then you're stronger. It started from there, then me have to be, compulsory, be on Coxsone's side now.' [4]

Dodd described the initial position he created for Perry as that of a 'handyman', though Perry himself was to speak of his role in terms of a 'gopher', or apprentice. Once he had permanently settled in Kingston, Perry remained around Coxsone and was gradually accepted as one of the crew. The wild dance steps that the short youth employed made an impression on Dodd, as did the fact that he had briefly worked for the mightier opposition, and Perry was soon a regular fixture at Downbeat's dances. Dodd initially employed him to run errands, including the delivery and collection of recorded material pressed at Federal's pressing plant, but his contributions were quickly to become more concrete. Though many particulars of this period remain hazy and unclear, both Perry and Dodd agreed that Coxsone first recorded him a few months after Perry became part of Dodd's team.

Over the years, Perry has given widely varying statements about his time of first contact with Coxsone. In an early interview for *Black Music*, Perry implied that he was already working with Coxsone when Dodd first began recording in the 1950s, though he would later claim that this was not the case. Dodd himself has adamantly insisted that Perry did not begin working with him until 1961 or '62, and Perry has recently agreed that his link with Coxsone dates from about that time.

Dodd himself recalled his first recording session as being in 1955, yielding songs like 'My Baby' by Jackie Estick, 'I Love You' by Bunny and Skitter, and 'Shufflin' Jug' by Clue J and the Blues Blasters. After giving the tunes ample sound system airplay, he eventually released them on the first of many labels he controlled.

Dodd spent much of the mid-to-late '50s building up the importance of the Downbeat sound, and one of the variety of tasks Perry performed was to further this aim in the early 1960s; his chief involvement with Coxsone's set was to deliver hot vinyl fresh off the press and to observe which new tunes proved popular. It has been reported elsewhere that Perry was selector and operator of Downbeat's sound system in this period, but both Perry and Dodd have indicated this was not so; selector and operator were never among his duties, nor was he involved in transporting or setting up the sound. 'I might go at certain times to see what was happening or bring new songs to give to the selector to play,' Perry clarified. 'I would check the direction of the people: if it's this cut we want or that cut we want, or if you like this one, maybe we should make another cut of it.'

One of the friendships he formed through working on Coxsone's sound system was with a teenager from Milk Lane named George Phillips who was initially employed by Dodd as a box loader; he would drag the heavy speaker boxes onto trucks to transport them to a sound system dance, helping to set them up and ensure the smooth running of the gear upon reaching their destination. Born in downtown Kingston circa 1942, Phillips left Jamaica to join his father in England at the start of the 1960s; upon his return to Jamaica in 1965, he would begin recording and producing under the alias Phil Pratt, and his friendship with Perry would prove to last for many decades

It was within weeks after Perry shifted his allegiance from Duke Reid to Coxsone that he first auditioned at the shop and rehearsal studio Coxsone ran near the Ward Theatre. One of those present at Perry's audition was Bibi Seaton, a singer that had recently caused a stir on the Downbeat sound with a song called 'Only You', recorded at the same session as Ken Boothe's hit 'Prevention'.

Born Harris Lloyd Seaton on September 3, 1944, he was originally known as Bibi due to his eternally youthful baby face (though later credits often list him as BB). Seaton had been an informal member of the Rhythm Aces and had performed at talent contests as part of the duos Bibi and Babs with Barbara Bloomfield and the Diamond Twins with Winston Delano Stewart, and would later form one of Jamaica's most successful groups, the Gaylads, with Stewart and Maurice Roberts. Seaton was to become one of Coxsone's most trusted pair of ears as an A & R man and auditions supervisor, but when Perry first appeared for an audition, Seaton only had a few recordings under his belt and had not yet risen in the hierarchy. Seaton recalled the scene as amusing: 'He came and he auditioned with a song called "Chicken Scratch" and that's how he got the name. They didn't take him because Coxsone said he wasn't any good, and we were all laughing because we didn't think he could sing. We started calling him "Chicken Scratch" until it come down to "Scratch", but he stayed with Coxsone and started to be like a handyman and do all these things around the place.'

Along with the Mashed Potato, the Chicken Scratch was one of the most popular dance steps in Jamaica at the time, and Perry's song was a celebration of the crazed jerkiness that dancers would display to accompany the shuffling sway of their favourite R & B hit.

Although the audition was initially unsuccessful, Coxsone decided to test Perry's ability in the studio shortly after, and cut 'Chicken Scratch' at a Federal session using the core musicians who would later become the Skatalites.

Though the song was not released on vinyl, it gradually proved to be enormously popular in the dancehalls where Coxsone retained it as an exclusive sound system acetate. Coxsone then decided to present Perry with his standard recording contract for vocalists, and in late 1961 Perry signed a five-year agreement to record exclusively for Mr Dodd.

It was around this time that Lee Perry moved to 4 ¼ Water Street where he rented a room on the same block where his boss Clement Dodd was living; his estranged wife Tootsie then came down from Montego Bay to join her husband in Kingston. Though Lee Perry had been hoping that she would return to him since she first left their home in Little London, their time apart and personal differences meant the relationship could not be rekindled; she thus left Kingston shortly after and returned to Montego Bay. As Perry recalled, 'I was expecting her to come back. I did love her, definitely, and I say "OK, I going to wait and see if she want to come back," but when she come back, it could not work. We were waiting to get the truth, then we don't have to wait any more because we find out it can't work.'

By the time 'Chicken Scratch' became popular, Perry was firmly in the ranks of Coxsone's sound defenders, men who were employed not only to protect the sound from rival sabotage, but also to ensure that Downbeat stayed at the forefront of the musical arena and retained an edge over Duke Reid. Other key members of the crew previously included George 'Peckings' Price and Prince Buster.

Born Cecil Campbell in Kingston in 1938, Buster was raised on Orange Street in the heart of the downtown area by strict Christian parents; his mother worked at a match factory and his father was a railway employee who was a staunch supporter of Alexander Bustamante. Buster was approached by Coxsone in late 1957 after Dodd and Count Machuki saw him chasing a notorious bad man called Mean Stick down Luke Lane with his knife drawn; Buster was in pursuit because Mean Stick's gang had robbed him during a dice game the week before. Originally a follower of Tom the Great Sebastian, Buster held vengeful feelings against Duke Reid after Reid's thugs chased Tom out of town; though Buster initially had reservations about being in a rival camp to the rough neighbours he had grown with, the chance to get back at Reid proved too hard to resist, and Buster shifted his base from the corner of Luke Lane and Charles Street to Coxsone's junction at Love Lane and Beeston Street.

Buster was useful to Coxsone in a variety of ways. Trained as a professional boxer, he was often used to provide the muscle that would ensure the sound was not vulnerable to sabotage. Buster was also adept at spying, and while employed by Dodd, he would venture into a rival's territory to note the exclusives retained by the competition, something Perry himself would also become quite adept at. As Buster explained, 'Coxsone and Duke Reid used to bring records in from America and when Duke Reid had a record that he didn't have, people put that record on a pedestal. When Coxsone and Duke would go away and bring back a copy, that became their own master recording, and they would bootleg the thing on blank labels, so I am the one who used to go to the dances when Duke Reid play and listen to records, go and tell Coxsone who the artists are, try to discover the name through the lyrics.'

Perry added the following particulars of the art: 'You go to the dance where other people playing and listen to the songs, what the people like more and you know exactly what goes down or what you're supposed to throw. Like you had (King) Edwards, big sound system, and then you pass by and listen to what he's playing that you don't have, and if me know a song that the people like me just tell Coxsone, "They like this one" so we can version it somehow.'

It has been implied elsewhere that Prince Buster was still working for Coxsone Dodd when Lee Perry joined the team, but all three insist Perry joined shortly after Buster left – though an oft-recounted incident reveals the Prince was still close by and willing to still step in when needed. One night a Downbeat dance at the Forrester's Hall had been infiltrated by Duke Reid's heavies. A fight was started that soon turned ugly, and Coxsone fled the premises while Perry was given a knock-out punch. Buster then appeared just in time to fend off the attackers, dragging the unconscious youth to safety after a considerable battle. 'Even now them call me "Friend of the Underdog",' laughed Buster. 'It was their dance but I wasn't with Coxsone any more. I really helped him (Perry) out there, and I guess that must have brought me and him closer. People in Jamaica will tell you that most of the fights or problems I get into wasn't from me – I'm always defending somebody.'

Though Coxsone was expecting a concrete fight from Duke Reid, the true challenge to his popularity in the early 1960s came from Prince Buster, the mutinous former member of his crew who had unexpectedly emerged as a main source of competition. At the start of the decade, Buster felt experienced and inspired enough to stand up on his own two feet. Tired of taking repeated blows and knife wounds for a man who kept himself far from danger and was not known for his equal distribution of accumulated wealth, Buster planned his own record-buying trip to America in 1959, but was removed from a team of crop pickers on the morning he was supposed to depart, his hands having taken 'too much blows' to pass a final physical inspection. He worked briefly for the competition, producing hits like 'Let George Do It' and Eric Morris' 'Humpty Dumpty' for Duke Reid, and eventually brought Rico Rodriguez, Drumbago and Jah Jerry to JBC studio for his first production, 'Little Honey'. His first record shop was located at 47 Charles Street near Luke Lane, just round the corner from Dodd's Orange Street shop, shared with a woman named Claudette who did dressmaking and hairstyling on the premises; he then moved to a larger shop across the road at 36 Charles Street. This second shop was owned by a certain Miss Blake, an aunt of sound system operator Winston Blake; it had previously been the site of a bakery and base of noted sound system Son the Junior Sebastian (a.k.a. Son's Junior). It was here that

Buster based his Voice of the People sound system, issuing records on the Wild Bells, Olive Blossom, and Voice of the People labels.

The first hit Buster issued as an independent producer was the Folkes Brothers' 'Oh Carolina', a truly monumental recording. Although the lyrics were of a fairly straightforward love ballad and the music generally in the boogie-woogie mode, it was the inclusion of Burru drumming by the renowned Rastafarian drummer Count Ossie (Oswald Williams) that really set the song apart. Though Buster was never a Rastafarian himself, later opting for the Muslim faith, he, like Perry, was instinctively drawn to the power of their music, a music that carried forgotten echoes of an African past in the drumming triumvirate of bass, *funde*, and repeater.

Count Ossie had endured so much police harassment by the end of the '50s that he had fled to the Wareika Hills overlooking Eastern Kingston, and when Buster first approached him for a recording session, Ossie is said to have thought Buster was trying to ridicule him, so deep was society's prejudice against the Rastafarians – or anyone seeking to present an awareness of an African identity in Jamaica. But Buster persisted, and despite efforts by Duke Reid to sabotage the recording session by double-booking JBC's one-track studio, the results were truly phenomenal. Through exposure at sound system dances, popular demand for the song grew so intense that both RJR and JBC radio stations had to overturn their ban on the single, and both eventually gave it ample airplay.

'Oh Carolina' launched Buster as a formidable competition that Coxsone would not be able to shrug off. Soon Buster's popularity was so great that Count Machuki fled Downbeat's set to deejay for Voice of the People, forcing Coxsone to deejay on his own set temporarily, before locating suitable replacements King Stitt (Winston Sparkes), King Sporty, and a youth called Opie. When Buster announced he was leaving, Coxsone had laughed, but Buster quickly got his own back by providing competition Coxsone was not prepared for.

Prince Buster's departure had direct consequences for Coxsone, and Perry's arrival at Coxsone's camp would see him filling some of the void created by Buster's absence. Perry thus found himself rapidly rising in the ranks of Coxsone's crew: though conflicting dates have again been put forward over time, Perry definitely found himself being rapidly promoted by Dodd.

'From since '59 coming up '60 me start audition singers in Coxsone's little shop down Orange Street. Any artist me feel good enough me say Downbeat "select this one fe session, record him." And him listen 'cause he spot me as a man with talent and he loved to work with people with talent. Him always believe in the people I choose and always give me a free hand.' [5]

In this new role as auditions supervisor, Perry changed the face of the music that Dodd was recording, and through his selective backing of upcoming talent, played an important role in the shaping of Jamaican pop.

'At first, when I was working with him, I was just going around with him. Those days him have some people amongst him who want to go with him that him feel good with, people he could talk with, and me was one of them. It happened that sometime when lots of singers come to sing, and want him to hear, sometimes he's so busy, he asked me to do the audition, to listen to them. So sometimes me did listen until it advance.' [6]

The years preceding independence in the early 1960s were marked by a series of struggles, as Alexander Bustamante and Norman Manley battled to gain control of what was clearly soon to be an independent nation. As the island struggled to shrug off its colonial yoke and break free from Britain, so were Jamaican musicians struggling to shake off the American hold on their music; they sought to create a sound they could truly call their own. As Perry later noted,

'Jamaica had roots thing from long time but being so close to America we slumber. Then something come and wake we up and we take these things and make them more powerful, take control, start get more powerful than American in soul and song.' [7]

The wake-up call came in ska, an infectious new beat that was harder, faster, and generally more Jamaican than the shuffle beats of boogie-woogie or R & B. Punctuated by a staccato rhythm guitar that placed emphasis on the second and fourth beats, ska began to emerge in the late '50s and early '60s, becoming the music of the day by the time Jamaica gained its full independence from Britain on August 5, 1962. Although early ska vocals retained echoes of rhythm and blues beneath the quirky beat, ska gradually became more up-tempo, characterised by wild drumming and full horn sections adapted from jazz ensembles.

Building up the ska sound for Kingston's small circle of producers were a number of key musicians: the drummers included Arkland Parks, known as Drumbago, and a youth from Portland named Lloyd Knibb. On upright bass, Cluette Johnson began to be superseded by Lloyd Brevett, a tall young Kingstonian taught to play by his father who was a bassist for a big jazz band; as Brevett couldn't read music, he would sometimes be replaced by Lloyd Mason, bassist in a military band. Ernest Ranglin was contracted to Federal records as musical arranger and lead guitarist in 1959; an important creator on the ska scene, he would also play rhythm for other producers and even played bass for Prince Buster. Another notable axe man was Jerome Hines, a.k.a. Jah Jerry, a versatile player equally adept at rhythm and lead. Keyboard duties continued to be handled by Theophilus Beckford, Aubrey Adams, and Cecil

Lloyd, with Richard Ace filling in when Lloyd didn't turn up; newcomers like Gladstone Anderson were also gradually making an impact in ska. Another important keyboard player was Jackie Mittoo, a teenager from St Ann who was brought to Coxsone by Bibi Seaton after playing with the Sheiks and the Rivals, ultimately becoming a key member of Coxsone's team in the ska years. On mouth organ (or harmonica) was Charles Cameron, an expressive player known on the scene as Charlie Organaire. The leading saxophone players included Roland Alphonso, an immigrant from Cuba of mixed parentage who had played in Eric Deans' Orchestra and Redvert Cook's group; Tommy McCook, another member of Eric Deans' band; Carl Bryan, known as Cannonball after Cannonball Adderley; and younger players such as Headley Bennett and Lester Sterling. On trombone, an eccentric and talented songwriter named Don Drummond was a major creative force; his Cuban immigrant friend, Emmanuel 'Rico' Rodriguez, also built a strong reputation playing in the Rastafarian community in the ghetto. The hottest trumpet players were Oswald 'Baba' Brooks and Johnny Moore, known as Dizzy after Dizzy Gillespie.

Many of the horn players had learned their craft at the Alpha School For Boys, a strict reform institution for destitute youth located in the heart of the ghetto; others, like Roland Alphonso, got a start at similar institutions such as St Aloysius and Stony Hill Schools. These musicians recorded for all the leading producers in different combinations, emerging variously as the Baba Brooks Band, the King Edwards All Stars, Drumbago's Band and so on. The group that would emerge to define the genre was the Skatalites, said to have been officially founded in June 1964, though together as a unit from an earlier time. Centred on the nucleus of Lloyd Knibb, Lloyd Brevett, Jah Jerry, Jackie Mittoo, Tommy McCook, Roland Alphonso, and Don Drummond, other members drifted in and out of the group, and these players had been working together in various capacities for several years before their official formation, most regularly in the Coney Island house band.

By the dawning of Jamaican independence, Lee Perry had already brought Coxsone considerable success by insisting that he record the Maytals, a vocal trio consisting of Frederick 'Toots' Hibbert, Nathaniel 'Jerry' Matthias and Ralphus 'Raleigh' Gordon. Matthias, who hails from Clarendon, had recorded solo material such as 'Crazy Girl' for Duke Reid in 1958, but his career did not take off until the Maytals formed in Trench Town some time later, after he and Gordon heard Hibbert singing while working in a local barber shop. What distinguished the Maytals from other vocal trios was the emotional religiosity of Toots Hibbert's lead; as both his father and mother were preachers in a Seventh Day Adventist church in May Pen Town, his singing always contained the emotive qualities brought forth by a religious experience. When the group turned up for an audition at Coxsone's shop on Orange Street one Sunday in 1962, Perry told Dodd to record them right

away. Although they had been turned down by several other producers, there
was something in their sound that spoke to Perry, and he insisted that Dodd
take them on.

After signing an exclusive contract with Coxsone, the group began belting
out the hits. Their first record, 'Hallelujah', went straight to number one, as did
their second release, 'Fever'. In 1963, the group enjoyed their biggest hit of all,
a thrilling spiritual number called 'Six And Seven Books Of Moses'. Though
Dodd was providing their management, it was Perry and Jackie Mittoo who
were often present in the recording sessions, 'vibesing' with the musicians and
helping to arrange material. As Perry himself later said, 'I the man force
Downbeat take on Toots fe work. We go to the studio and he give "Six And
Seven Books Of Moses" and rip it up!'[8] The song would be the last hit they
provided for Dodd; like Count Machuki, they left Dodd's stable to work for
Prince Buster, choosing not to renew their contract in 1964. Though Toots
himself insisted that Perry's contribution to their Studio One material was
minimal, he did acknowledge Scratch's role in their acceptance by Coxsone:
'Scratch always work for these people. He tell them, "Go listen what Toots
have, go listen what the other guy have." That's what he have to do with it.'

Although the Maytals gave Dodd the edge over his old rival Duke Reid
and emerging competition provided by Chinese Jamaican producer Leslie
Kong (for whom the Maytals would later record much successful material),
Prince Buster proved to be the hardest opposition going in 1961 and '62.
'Carolina' was still causing shock waves some years after its initial release, and
when Buster attacked Dodd in the enormously popular 'Bad Minded
People', it was Perry who came to the rescue with lyrics aimed to counter
Buster's attack.

Lee Perry had plenty of material of his own by this time, some of which
he had been playing around with since before his arrival in Kingston. He
would adapt folk melodies and traditional tunes with his own original lyrics,
but Coxsone was still hesitant to record him freely; he feared Perry's voice was
too untrained and amateurish for sophisticated city audiences. 'He was kind of
folkie and full of ideas,' Coxsone once stated, 'but his songs needed
construction.'[9] Coxsone wasn't yet willing to issue songs featuring Perry as a
vocalist, but he had seen Little Lee's accuracy in predicting hits, and was
impressed by his lyrical jabs. In late 1962, Dodd thus began using Perry's lyrics
for some of his other upcoming artists, including Delroy Wilson and Chenley
Duffus, and Perry also began 'banging percussion' on some of Downbeat's
material.

Born in Kingston in 1948, Wilson was Jamaica's first child star,
recording for Dodd in the high-pitched voice of adolescence when he was only
13 years old. Among the material Wilson voiced for Coxsone was three songs
co-written by Perry. 'Joe Lieges' was a direct reply to Buster's 'Bad Minded
People'; as Buster was trying to steal Coxsone's 'lieges' (glory) from him, Perry

came up with the lyrics, which he later said were about 'people who just want to take and don't want to give.' 'I Shall Not Remove', based on a spiritual standard, was also aimed at Buster, while 'Spit In The Sky' (which Bibi Seaton said he and Scratch wrote at the corner of Orange Street and Charles Street in front of a chemist that sold tasty patties) was a song using proverbs to express a similar message.

'Buster come out the strongest, him held the scene for about a year or two straight,' Perry once remarked. 'We young guys would go along and write songs to counteract Buster's sounds – songs like me write for Delroy Wilson, "I Shall Never Remove" and "Spit In The Sky". And we killing off Buster backwards!' [10] Perry also noted the following particulars about songs he and Coxsone aimed at the Prince: 'Buster was trying a little thing. At that time he was looking like a personal fight, so Mr Dodd have to use Delroy Wilson to trace him back. It was a little joke fight, because Mr Dodd have Delroy Wilson and we write a piece for Delroy about "I shall not remove". When it comes to battling, Mr Dodd always have a thing to do with words, he sees words as funny and I see words funny as well. We always want to add another word to it to make it match and rhyme, and we become a battleaxe. That is the way him is, when he say one I say two and we build up on it and make it connect to an explosion in a laugh and he knows it is a hit; they call it common sense and an invisible force.'

Another singer Perry wrote lyrics for in this period was Chenley Duffus, an accomplished tenor with a broad and readily adaptable vocal range. Born in the town of Roland Field on February 10, 1938, Duffus was raised between Kingston and Spanish Town while his father worked for the United Fruit Company. After touring Jamaica with Vere Johns from the age of 12, he was eventaully brought to Federal studio in 1958 for the recording of three songs for High Lite Haberdashery, a company run by a man named Smith – a.k.a. 'Little Wonder' – from premises at the corner of Spanish Town Road and Duff Street. Heavily influenced by American blues singers like Joe Turner, Louis Jordan and Ben E. King, Duffus' debut 'Million Dollar Baby' was sung in such a convincing American style that it was a hit in the States as well as in Jamaica. When Coxsone took Duffus away from Smith in the early '60s, he and Perry immediately began collaborating, beginning a long friendship and musical association.

Duffus' first tune for Coxsone was 'What A Disaster', a song Duffus said sought to end the vinyl feud then being propagated by Prince Buster and Derrick Morgan. 'When they do "Black Head Chiney" and "Blazing Fire", the three of us were good friends, so I get right in the middle and write "What A Disaster". Lee Perry was a banton writer for Coxsone, he was my good pal, so everything that I'm going to write at the shop, I rope him in. Even "What A Disaster", me and him was having lunch when a madman give me the idea, just a guy passing come to the traffic lights and say "What a disaster!", so I say

"Perry, this is it man! Let's go!" We go right over to the shop, and in ten minutes we finish "What A Disaster".'

An even bigger hit was 'Fret Man Fret', another banton song that Perry co-wrote with Duffus, this time attempting to 'throw words' at Prince Buster. 'Perry's always busy,' Duffus noted. 'Like I say, he's one of the best banton writers in Jamaica. He give you all kinds of ideas: rhythmic, lyric. When Perry's around, you can look for hit songs. Believe me, he's full of ideas.' Perry also wrote a song called 'Leticia' in this period that Dodd refused to let him record; instead, he changed the title to 'Lolita' and gave it to Duffus to sing.

Noting the success of the songs he had co-written, Dodd finally gave Perry the go-ahead to record steadily by late 1962, and his first tunes continued to attack Coxsone's competitors. Perry's vinyl debut, 'Bad Minded People', was the first of several records aimed at Prince Buster; further attacks came with 'Mad Head', a parody of Buster's smash hit 'Madness', 'Prince and Duke' (a.k.a. 'Royalty', 'The Prince, The Duke and the Sir', or 'Me Sir'), which also took a swipe at Duke Reid, 'Prince in the Back' and 'Don't Copy'. 'Old For New', which related warnings in proverbial terms, would prove to be Perry's first issue abroad when it surfaced in London on the R & B label in 1963.

Other material recorded in 1963 included the spirited 'Never Get Weary', which imparted the qualities of a hymnal in ska, while 'Cannot Wrong and Get Right' (a.k.a. 'Can't Be Wrong') was a moralistic number introduced by a horn line lifted from the 'London Bridge' nursery rhyme. The more personally revealing 'Man And Wife' was somewhat more disturbing, relating the tale of a man whose wife sleeps with his brother.

Musically speaking, these sorties all had commonalities. Marked by the slow shuffle of ska as it gradually formed to distinguish itself from boogie, each song contained prominent mouth-organ licks and loping acoustic bass lines. On some tunes, Coxsone's initial wariness seemed justified, as some felt Perry had a tendency to sing off key, but his lyrical wit typically made up for the occasional lapse in a vocal delivery in tense recording sessions where everything was recorded live by one microphone. Dodd also felt that many of the tunes were strong enough to license for pressing abroad on the R & B and Ska Beat labels run by Rita Issels and Benny King in London's East End. Perry's earliest recording, 'Chicken Scratch,' also continued to enjoy popularity in the dancehall many months after its initial appearance.

As 1963 drew to a close, other concrete changes were brought to Downbeat's operation, most significantly in the establishment of his Jamaica Recording Studio. Located at 13 Brentford Road in the Cross Roads area, the studio was housed in the premises of a former nightclub called The End. Construction work was supervised by Headley Jones, with Coxsone's father providing assistance, while Coxsone's cousin Sid Bucknor installed the electrical equipment, including the original one-track recording machine previously installed at Federal (who had recently purchased two-track equipment). By this point, Coxsone controlled several record labels including D. Darling (named for his mother, whose maiden name was Doris Darlington), Rolando and Powie (named in reference to Roland Alphonso), Coxsone and Muzik City. The latest label to carry Coxsone's product was named Studio One, and this moniker quickly became the name that the studio itself was known by. The musicians that would make up the Skatalites quickly became the house band at Studio One, and the leading singers of the period all flocked to record at the premises.

Not long after the studio opened its doors, a rough and undisciplined group called the Wailers presented themselves for recording, brought to a Sunday audition by Alvin 'Seeco' Patterson, a percussionist who had previously worked with calypso singer Lord Flea. Formerly known in the neighbourhood as The Teenagers and schooled in the art of singing by the revered Joe Higgs of Higgs and Wilson, the Wailers were then an unruly five-piece based in Trench Town, composed of Robert Nesta Marley, Peter McIntosh, Neville Livingstone, Junior Braithwaite, and Beverley Kelso. Marley had previously recorded 'Judge Not' and 'One Cup of Coffee' for Leslie Kong, but the rest of the group had not yet succeeded in making a recording debut. Quickly sensing the potential beneath their anxious and amateurish appearance, Coxsone arranged to record the group after signing them to an exclusive five-year contract. As always, Perry and Jackie Mittoo were present when the Wailers first arrived at Studio One, and both came to know the group in this professional situation. Their debut single, 'It Hurts To Be Alone', was pressed in limited quantity on blank labels, and Lee Perry was given the task to initially promote the disc and group through sound system airplay.

The Wailers thus joined the growing roster of Studio One success stories, making a quick impact on the Kingston music scene under Dodd's tutelage. Coxsone Dodd is said to have acted as something of a surrogate father to Bob Marley, arranging for him to live in a small room adjoining the studio; he also made sure that Bob was presented as the leader of the group. Behind the scenes, Lee Perry also had his role to play in the presentation of the Wailers as stars from the start of their time with Dodd. Along with the auditions he was supervising, the records he was distributing for Dodd, the songs he was voicing himself and the percussion he was providing on many sessions, Perry's latest responsibility was to see that the Wailers became the most successful group on the island.

1964 and '65 were years of refinement for both Perry and the Wailers at Studio One. The Wailers were strengthening their output, becoming more competent as songwriters, and clarifying their direction after releasing a number of hit singles – though Coxsone's insistence that they record a high proportion of American cover tunes saw them partially neglecting their stronger original material. Early members Junior Braithwaite and Beverley Kelso left the group, as did occasional member Cherry Green, leaving the robust core of Bob Marley, Peter Tosh, and Bunny Livingstone (later known as Bunny Wailer) intact.

Meanwhile, as the ska pace picked up, Perry's music was changing and becoming more complex. His version of Ernie Doe's humorous 'Mother In Law' was one of the first songs Perry tried to the faster beat, and had Perry howling and yelping in a frenzy as he implored his mother-in-law to stay out of his romantic endeavours. He had moved away from attacking Coxsone's rivals to wage more general warfare on social injustice on songs like 'Help The Weak', 'Bad Minded People', and 'Wishes Of The Wicked', while 'Trial And Crosses', 'John Tom', and 'Gumma' (a.k.a. 'Gruma') all made use of proverbs and folk sayings, backed by female choruses. Some of this material was being issued in the name of King Scratch, partly in the boastful manner of the sound rulers like Duke Reid and King Edwards, but partly also as Perry began to ponder on his cultural identity as a misplaced African descendant in a foreign land.

He was often paired with two female backing singers who were dubbed the Dynamites at Studio One – though the duo was not recording on their own according to both Coxsone and Scratch. 'We just label them the Dynamites,' Coxsone explained, 'they was no active group that was singing by themselves, they were just a backing group. It's two girls who only do harmonising; they didn't do any recording of themselves.' Perry has suggested that one of the Dynamites was Marlene 'Precious' Gifford, who was also a member of the popular Soulettes trio, but others have contested this idea; what is clear, however, is that Perry himself went on to cut a few tunes using the Soulettes for harmony – though precisely which is also a source of contention.

The original Soulettes were Alpharita Anderson, her cousin Constantine 'Vision' Walker (also known as 'Dream'), and 'Precious' Gifford. Anderson was born in Cuba to a Jamaican father and Cuban mother, and returned with her parents to Jamaica as a baby, where she was raised by her Aunt Viola; she made her stage debut at a talent show at the huge Carib Theatre. Walker was the son of Vesta Anderson, a politically active sister of Viola who followed Marcus Garvey; Precious Gifford came to know the pair through her high-school friendship with Anderson.

When the Soulettes arrived at Studio One, Coxsone placed them under the guidance of Bob Marley, who was already proving to be something of a driven perfectionist despite his youth and relatively short experience in the music business; according to Rita, they first backed up Scratch on 'Roast Duck', one of a glut of rude songs Perry recorded from late 1964 as his hungry libido began noisily to pronounce itself on record.

'The only one I can recall we did is a song called "Roast Duck". You might find one or two more, but it wasn't something that we did often because we weren't back-up singers, we were a group – the number-one female group in Jamaica. Scratch wasn't really a singer at that time, he was just a right hand for Coxsone when he had auditions, and one day he said he had a song to do and we listened to it and everybody was amused by it, so we sing the background on it.'

Rita noted that although the song was popular on release, a live Kingston performance drew a distinctly negative result. 'We did a concert with him at the Ward Theatre singing "Roast Duck", but we were stoned off stage because nobody knew Lee Perry as a singer; it was his first appearance, and everyone said "Get off the stage!" '

'The audience never like it,' Perry confirmed, 'because Jamaican people never like my music until foreign people start to like it. From long time me make music for Jamaicans and them never like it, so I don't expect anything from a Jamaican audience. I don't expect anything from Jamaican people; I know these people wasn't ready for me, but I still have to test them.'

The Soulettes are also credited as backing vocalists on some of Lee Perry's subsequent releases, two of which exhibit a harmonic depth not present on his previous material. 'Please Don't Go,' a minor hit in 1965, has Perry stating happily that he will ignore the pleas of his former partner who is begging him to stay, while 'By Saint Peter' was another song that related folk sayings to a snapping ska beat; both were licensed to Chris Blackwell for pressing abroad on the UK branch of his Island label.

Similarly suggestive songs recorded in the same period as 'Roast Duck' include 'Hold Down', the first of many to use food as a metaphor for sex – in this case, he sang of a woman who had eaten too much 'honey' – and 'Open Up (Cook Book)', which explored a similar vein, though perhaps not as subtly as the former. By the time Perry recorded the despicable 'Jane Ann And The Pumpkin' (a.k.a. 'Rape Bait'), he was steadily gaining a reputation as one of the slackest singers on the island.

Thankfully, Perry was never one to be stuck in the same groove too long, and not all the material he created in this period was slack. His version of Dee Clarke's R & B hit 'Just Keep It Up', for example, was a mournful tirade by a heartbroken lover; 'Deacon Johnson', among the last material he recorded with the Dynamites, was another adaptation of a folk tale or country tune, notable also for its flipside, 'Rinky Dink', on which Roland Alphonso blew a fresh melody over the rhythm of 'Hold Down'. Discs like these reveal the ceaseless creativity of Jamaican producers and artists, who would re-use original rhythm tracks as an opportunity for a new instrumental, an alternative vocal, or deejay interpretation. Perry and Coxsone were already creating such alternative 'versions' by the end of the ska era. Re-using previously issued rhythm tracks as the basis for further recordings, they were thus able to generate something exciting and new without needed to start from square one.

Perhaps the most important song he recorded in this period was 'Hand To Hand, Man To Man', on which he was joined by the Wailers on backing vocals. A spiritual song that again spoke in proverbs and religious metaphor, 'Hand To Hand' was infused with hidden meanings, and the dramatic potential of a musical connection between Perry and the group is hinted at on this first combined release.

It was around this time that Peter Tosh brough Leonard Dillon to Studio One for an audition co-supervised by Scratch. Born in Portland on December 9, 1942, Dillon learned to sing in the Seventh Day Adventist Church that was the centre of his community; after impressing the crowd at a local stage show through his vocal talent, he was given the nickname 'Sparrow'. Moving to Trench Town at age eighteen, he began working as a stonemason and hanging out with the Wailers. Dillon recalled the circumstances of the audition: 'It was Coxsone present, Peter (Tosh) because he had to play the guitar, Lee Perry, and Jackie Mittoo. It was a little joke too because when I sang the four songs, everyone started to laugh. I was so upset and ashamed, not knowing what they were laughing about. They said the way that I'm singing the song was as if I'm going to eat up everything! That was the first time I met Scratch and also Jackie Mittoo, they was around listening while you sing.'

His audition successful, Dillon cut four tunes for Dodd under the name Jack Sparrow before returning to building work; later he would form the Ethiopians with Stephen Taylor and Aston Morrison.

It was in 1965 that Perry began a relationship with Pauline Morrison, someone who would prove to be a central figure in his personal and business life for many years. An alluring and secretive young woman from Trench Town, Pauline was born on February 6, 1951; her family came from a village on the Portland side of the Blue Mountains, where her grandmother, Miss Hilda, was a domestic worker for wealthy white landowners. Perry first met her at the door of the Gold Coast, where she would often appear on Sunday nights without money; one week, he allowed her to enter without paying, thus initiating their relationship at a time when he was literally twice her age. 'She was not anything big, so they lock the door all the while and she begging to come in,' he later explained. 'How many times she beg to come in, and one time I let her in at the dance, and when you let them in to the dance, you know say you go to bed with them, because them time we go with a whole heap of girls.' Shortly after, she moved into Perry's rented room at 4 1/4 Water Street.

Pauline was a ragamuffin girl from the ghetto, already hardened by the harshness of Kingston life. Some say she was a go-go dancer at this time, though if this was the case, Lee Perry was not aware of it. Her high cheekbones gave her a coarse beauty enhanced by her mysterious air, and Scratch would later learn that she had previously been the girlfriend of singers Toots Hibbert and Lord Tanamo.

When Pauline Morrison first met Lee Perry, she was already pregnant with her second child; in 1962 she had given birth to a son named Derrick Lord, but the relationship with his father did not last, and the boy was primarily cared for by Pauline's older sister. When Pauline gave birth to a daughter named Michelle at Jubilee Public Hospital on January 17, 1966, Lee

Perry raised her as though she was truly his own first-born, despite not knowing who her biological father was. 'I don't know if the child is for Toots or Lord Tanamo or for who. I didn't even know that Pauline was Toots' girlfriend 'til after Toots wasn't on top any more and was working for me, then I discover that they were talking nice and knew each other long time. Later on I find out that she was Toots' girlfriend in Trench Town. Lord Tanamo was Pauline's boyfriend too, me never even know that either, but when he start to sing, girls love singers so all ugly Tanamo have pretty girls like Pauline, understand?'

Around the time of Michelle's birth, Perry sent for his younger half-sister Veta to come from Hanover and help care for the newborn; she stayed at Water Street for about three months and then returned to the country.

From the very start, Lee and Pauline's relationship was as volatile as it was passionate, and though they quickly grew close to one another in the startlingly fiery confines of their love, they would also endure stormy periods of problematic unrest.

Other vinyl efforts surfaced in late 1965 and early 1966, including a forgotten dance number called 'Do The Push Push', heavily laden with sensual imagery that lingered on every beat; 'Feel it Up' (a.k.a. 'Sugar Bag') alluded to the hidden sweetness of a woman. The more politically relevant 'Run Rudies Run' was also issued on Coxsone's Supreme label in this period, featuring the Gaylads on harmony vocals behind Perry's wistful lead. In the mid-1960s, it was clear that Kingston had a serious 'rude boy' problem on its hands, and 'Run Rudies Run' was the first record on which Perry voiced his views on the phenomenon.

In the late 1950s, 'rudies' had begun to creep forth from the most disenfranchised portions of disaffected communities in the harshest parts of the ghetto to form fearsome gangs that began to terrorise Kingston. Excited by the hyper-real displays of cinematic violence regularly screened at downtown theatres like the Rialto, the rude boys sought to emulate their foreign movie heroes by bashing, slashing, and shooting their way to the glory of a short-lived retribution, in which they would take what society had denied them by the most direct and brutal means. Some of these rudies had been recruited by sound system proprietors as 'dance crashers'; they would smash up a rival sound system, destroy its equipment and beat, knife or rape those attending a rival's dance. Others began to commit random crimes just for the hell of it.

By the mid-1960s, larger gangs with an evident hierarchy had formed along territorial lines in the ghettos of West and East Kingston, where other battles were being avidly fought by the two main political parties who were clamouring to control a Jamaica that had only been independent some few years. Edward Seaga, the man who had established the WIRL recording studio and label, was steadily rising in the ranks of the ruling JLP. As he moved deeper into politics and farther from the music industry, he sought to profit from the existence of the rude boys. In exchange for money, arms, housing and protection from police, Seaga recruited members of the fearsome Tivoli Gang to be 'enforcers', i.e. henchmen who would keep his West Kingston constituency loyal to the right-wing JLP.

Soon the opposition PNP, led by socialist Michael Manley, sought to redress the balance through the recruitment of their own rudies – most notably using the Spanglers gang, originally a group of dance crashers from the Back O' Wall district who were loyal to Duke Reid's sound. The result was a steady escalation of violence, culminating in the declaration of a month-long state of emergency in 1966.

In the ska and early rock steady years, many singers sought to address the problem of rude-boy violence. The Clarendonians' 'Rudie Bam Bam' and 'Rude Boy Gone A Jail' were two of the biggest anti-rude-boy hits for Studio One, as was the Wailers' early 'Simmer Down'. Other songs, like Derrick Morgan's 'Tougher Than Tough', Peter Tosh's 'I Am The Toughest', and the Wailers' 'Let Him Go' (a.k.a. 'Rude Boy Get Bail') and 'Jailhouse' were more ambiguous or openly pro-rudie. Perry's 'Run Rudies Run' was a light-hearted warning to the rudies, appealing to them to change their evil ways lest they reap a similar fate to the bad deeds they were sowing, and reminding them further of the biblical commandment 'Thou shalt not steal'.

It was around the time of 'Run Rudies Run' that Lee Perry made some of the first concrete works with the Wailers, strengthening a bond which would bear greater fruits in years to come. Perry, the Wailers, and the Soulettes were working in extreme closeness at Studio One in this period, and it was by a process of natural progression that they enhanced each other's performances on disc. On February 10, 1966, the connection between the Wailers and the Soulettes was solidified when Bob Marley married Rita Anderson, and the repercussions of this link were immediately evident in the music that was born from such connections. The symbolic importance of such early intermingling is most evident on songs like 'Rub and Squeeze', a slightly rude number with lead vocal by Perry and harmonies by the Soulettes over the same rhythm used by the Wailers for their hit 'Put It On' (featuring backing by the Sharks, with harsh lead guitar lines provided by a young guitarist named Dwight Pinkney), a song said to have been repeatedly spun at Bob and Rita's wedding. A further such link can be seen in 'Pussy Galore', a massive hit in 1966 in which Perry sang of the dubious virtues of the alluring female character from the James Bond film *Goldfinger*. Not only did the Wailers provide harmony vocals that were deep and broad, but the rhythm track made use of an alternative take of 'Rude Boy Ska', an earlier Wailers' tune. One of the most interesting songs the Wailers recorded during their time at Studio One, 'Rude Boy Ska' was another of the songs that Perry helped arrange, its peculiar structure placing an adapted line from the Impressions' 'I've Got To Keep On Moving' in the middle of a string of Jamaican proverbs.

When contemplating the early links between Perry, the Wailers, and the Soulettes, it is important to remember the closeness of all parties. Each artist had been living in the Trench Town vicinity, and was sharing the same streets, cinemas, and places of worship as well as working together for the same boss. In short, they were all part of a close-knit social and musical community. These early links would later gain a stronger resonance when Perry re-encountered both groups away from the constraints of Studio One.

1966 would be a year of momentous occurrences for Scratch; several events were to result in substantial personal changes that would ultimately herald a new direction. Since his arrival in Kingston, Perry's status had slowly risen, but when he stopped to think about the reward he was getting for his efforts, a dark cloud of depression and anger seized him. He began to harbour resentment when he took stock of the glory his boss was reaping by the sweat of Perry's brow; he thus took some time out to look into himself and, knew the situation could not continue. A breeze of change was blowing in his direction, and as he pondered on that breeze, he realised he had no choice but to move out on his own.

GIVE ME JUSTICE:

The Upsetter Emerges

By the end of 1966, Lee Perry was feeling increasingly frustrated by the runnings at Studio One. In the years he toiled for Clement Dodd, Studio One's status had risen from that of an underrated challenger to the virtual ruler of Kingston's musical roost, and Perry had been instrumental in implementing the change. Of the myriad tasks that Perry performed for Dodd, his supervision of audition sessions and distribution of new discs proved to be essential factors in the success of Studio One, and his influence on the playlist of the Sir Coxsone's Downbeat sound system greatly enhanced the popularity of the set.

Once Dodd began recording local artists in earnest, it was Perry's ear for talent that often brought him his biggest selling acts, and although it was Dodd who re-fashioned groups like the Maytals and the Wailers, their growing popularity owed much to Perry's largely unseen promotional efforts and musical arrangements.

Perry provided Dodd with one of the biggest hits of 1966, the risqué 'Pussy Galore', and his similarly lewd 'Rub and Squeeze' and 'Doctor Dick' (about an 'injection specialist' and his female patient) were also big sellers that year. Perry voiced over 30 tunes for Dodd, 22 of which were licensed for pressing in the UK and several were substantial hits. Some songs, such as the enormously popular 'Chicken Scratch' and 'Joker In The Ring' (a ska re-casting of the children's play song 'Brown Girl In The Ring') were never officially released, being reserved instead on acetate for exclusive airing on the Downbeat sound system; others Dodd felt were not up to par and thus were never cut.

Despite the enormous popularity of 'Chicken Scratch', 'Pussy Galore', and other King Perry material, Dodd continued to be unimpressed by Perry's singing voice. He thought nothing of using Scratch's lyrics for his younger singers, and made it perfectly clear that he did not rate Perry as a vocalist. 'He took my songs and gave them to people like Delroy Wilson,' Perry once angrily recounted. 'I got no credit, certainly no money. I was being screwed.' [1] It was bad enough that he received no payment for his lyrics, but what also bothered him was that Dodd refused to credit him as writer of the songs, instead substituting his own name in the credits (although the Jamaican issue of 'Fret

Man Fret' was an exception to this rule). Thus, the lack of proper financial reward for his efforts greatly irked him, and the largely absent Dodd taking credit for all and sundry made things worse.

Another bone of contention was Dodd's enduring disapproval of music expressing Rastafarian sentiment. Although most of the Studio One musicians and a growing number of singers were Rastas, Coxsone would not allow them to record songs openly expressing their beliefs, though Delroy Wilson's 'Lion of Judah' – another of the songs Perry had written – was innocuous enough to escape his censure in 1963.

After the visit of Haile Selassie to Jamaica on April 21, 1966 the Rastafarian community was ecstatic. Perry was among the tens of thousands present when the imperial plane landed at Kingston's Palisadoes airport, and he was deeply moved by the spectacle.

'I saw him when he came to Kingston in 1966. 12,000 Rastas were waiting for him at the airport. The prophecy said that one morning a single white dove would fly over the assembled Rastas followed by a short shower of benediction. His plane came from the East, coming out of the dawn and it rained when the plane landed. The chalices were being passed around and people were smoking herb with our flags, our rockets, our spliffs and our music, and above all the Abeng horn that was the rallying instrument of the Maroons in the bush two centuries ago.' [2]

Although Perry had not yet fully embraced the faith, this visit of the Emperor made a deep impact on him, and he began to listen to the Rastafarians' reasoning with greater interest. He had long felt an affinity with the Rastas who made up much of his community, and was also greatly appreciative of their inspirational music, heavy sounds underlined by the African spirit that would inspire his wild dances.

Coxsone was not as anti-Rasta as Duke Reid, who retained a blanket policy against Rastafarian music for the whole of his career, a move that would eventually cost him dearly. As pioneering toaster Dennis Alcapone once remarked,

'Duke Reid was more or less the man that Rasta lick up against . . . He told me point blank, him don't want no Rasta lyrics. That was the main reason for the downfall of the Treasure Isle studio in the later years. The Rasta lyrics were revolutionary and that was the lyrics that was selling.' [3]

Coxsone did allow the recording of occasional Rasta instrumentals featuring Burru drums, especially after repeated insistence from keyboardist and arranger Jackie Mittoo, and would later change his policy towards the music when Rastafarian tunes became the rage at the end of the decade. But Dodd's reluctance to record adventurous or rebellious music styles in 1966 filled Perry with ever-greater amounts of frustration. Perry was angry that the musicians had to stifle themselves in their music, and Dodd's sustained timidity in the musical realm was becoming increasingly bothersome.

Part of the problem may have stemmed from his boss's auspicious success. The bigger producers like Coxsone and Duke Reid were earning sufficient money to place some distance between themselves and the ghetto; even Prince Buster had moved to the lower-middle-class suburb of Washington Gardens after his success with 'Oh Carolina' and other hits that were popular abroad like 'Wash Wash' and 'Madness'. Although their business premises were in the urban centre of downtown Kingston, this residential distance meant that the producers were not always in tune with the exciting musical innovations emanating from Trench Town and the surrounding ghetto areas, and the bosses' stifling of the musicians' creative processes fostered much general resentment.

Already over 30 years of age, Perry felt a worsening constraint with Dodd as his distant but continual overseer. When he thought of the many responsibilities he had taken on, Perry felt bitter at his lack of recognition and repayment from the Studio One controller, a bitterness that grew more troubling with the passing of each day. Thinking back over his meandering teen years when he was more of his own man, in the constant limelight as a domino king and 'Neat Little Man' dance champion who at least received the recognition he was due, Perry knew it was time to make another change. The unseen spirit that had guided him from construction work 'to King-stone for my graduation' was speaking to him again, gently urging him to step away from Coxsone Dodd.

> 'It's when me leave him, and things wasn't going nice and I think he could be treating me better. I wasn't working with him as he employ me to work, I was just giving him my service, and him give me a money sometimes. I was just giving him my free service, until I see like maybe him take advantage, and don't respect me after I give him service, so I decide to leave him. I tell him I'm going to my country for a month or so, and I didn't go nowhere. I was staying in town, I didn't go to my country; I go to the studio. It was what happening between me and him that I have to leave because I wasn't getting any justice. And the songs them that I want to sing, him think them wasn't ready, that I didn't have a good voice to sing. That is what he think, so I decided that I have something that him no have, so I tell him I'm going on a holiday. I didn't go to a holiday, I go to the studio behind him back.' [4]

In Perry's role as record distributor for Coxsone, he had built up a network of friends and friendly acquaintances that worked in every aspect of music production. He had come to know all the leading musicians, singers, and toasters, as well as pressing plant workers, sound system operators and record-shop owners, several of whom were beginning to try their hand at music production. 'The people know me because I started off with the cats in the ghetto,' Perry later said. 'I had a crowd out there so whatever I want to present to them they accept it.'[5] Such was Perry's reputation as a vocalist, popular record selector and predictor of sure-fire hits, that it wasn't hard for him to find someone outside Studio One willing to take a gamble on his singing talents.

The first songs Perry recorded away from Coxsone were for Carl Johnson, a.k.a. 'Sir JJ', a producer recently emerging on the scene from record-vending premises at 133 Orange Street. The first tune, 'Give Me Justice', was an impassioned plea for the justice he felt was being denied him at Studio One, and was the first of several songs aimed directly at Coxsone's head, doubly ironic, as the song was surreptitiously recorded in Dodd's studio on an occasion when Coxsone was absent. 'Why take advantage of the innocent ones?' Perry sang forcefully over the bouncing ska rhythm, 'Soon it will be a change of plan . . . Give me justice!' Issued as the single's A-side was 'Such a Good Woodman' (a.k.a. 'The Woodman'), an innuendo-laden tale about an unfaithful wife, notable for its use of a recurrent piano chord that is noticeably out of tune.

Like much of his work at Studio One, the disc was licensed to Rita Issels and Benny King in London, where it appeared on their Ska Beat label. Although his work with Sir JJ was limited to this outing, it is already indicative of a freedom that was being denied him under Coxsone's thumb, both in the musical experimentation of 'The Woodman' and in the frank admonishments of 'Give Me Justice'.

As 1966 gave way to 1967, important changes were being brought to Jamaican popular music, as the frantic pace of the ska era gave way to the slower, more spacious, rock steady period. The big-band jazz that ska was based on gave way to a sound created by smaller groups who formed themselves primarily as studio ensembles. Rock steady was thus marked by an increased use of guitar and keyboards with a decreased use of horns, allowing for a greater scope of musical and lyrical expression. Certain key musicians were to develop the greater musical potentials of rock steady, including Tommy McCook, saxophonist and musical arranger of the Supersonics at Treasure Isle since the break-up of the Skatalites in 1965, and Jackie Mittoo, organist and musical arranger of the Soul Brothers at Studio One. However, much of the old guard of ska was trying to make sense of the new sound, and a set of younger musicians was on the rise. The most impressive of these new acts belonged to two related groups: Lynn Taitt and the Jets and the All Stars. Lee Perry worked with both groups soon after his departure from Studio One, and it was partly the receptive dynamism and general adaptability of the All Stars that would allow him to expand his musical creativity.

Born during World War II in San Fernando, Trinidad, Nerlynn Taitt became a noted steel-pan player in his teens. In the late 1950s, he acquired a guitar from a Swedish sailor and briefly joined the Dutchey Brothers quintet as a rhythm player, forming the Nerlynn Taitt Orchestra in 1960. In August 1962, Byron Lee arranged for Taitt to back Lord Melody and other calypso singers at Jamaica's independence celebrations. Taitt remained in Jamaica and joined the Sheiks, a popular live band featuring bassist Lloyd Spence, saxophonist Felix 'Deadley Headley' Bennett, vocalist 'Honey Boy' Martin, and pianist Jackie Mittoo. Taitt and Spence later formed the Cavaliers with organist Winston Wright, trumpeter Johnny Moore, and drummer Lloyd Knibb, who brought Taitt to his first recording session in the mid-1960s to record the monumental 'Shenk I Sheck' with Baba Brooks, Roland Alphonso and Don Drummond. Duke Reid began to use Taitt regularly for rhythm on hits like Justin Hines' 'Carry Go Bring Come', and Taitt occasionally sat in with the Skatalites at Studio One. Taitt then formed the Comets with trombonist Ron Wilson and singer Honey Boy, backing up Prince Buster on a four-month tour of England in 1967, after which the Comets eventually evolved into the Jets. Along with Taitt on lead, the typical nucleus of the group included bassist Brian Atkinson, drummer Joe Isaac (a Studio One session man), sometimes replaced by a drummer called Ferguson, and keyboardists Gladstone 'Gladdy' Anderson and Winston 'Brubeck' Wright (whose nickname was sometimes corrupted to 'Bluebeck'). Contracted to Ken Khouri's Federal recording studio in 1967, they backed up Hopeton Lewis on 'Take It Easy', a huge hit that helped inaugurate the rock steady genre, and Taitt's intricate picking style soon became the preferred guitar sound in rock steady, just as Ernest Ranglin and 'Jah Jerry' Hines' styles had added flavour to many a ska hit. Taitt has said that this picking style evolved from the rhythms of the steel pan, which he would try to emulate on his guitar strings; the shimmering lines and ringing notes were meant to emulate the trembling solos of traditional steel drum playing.

Linked to the Jets was the All Stars, a conglomerate of rising musicians featuring lead guitarist Lynford 'Hux' Brown, bassist Clifton 'Jackie' Jackson, and keyboardists Winston Wright and Gladdy Anderson. Lorraine 'Ronnie Bop' Williams would typically be on rhythm guitar, though others would occasionally take his place, with Lynn Taitt sometimes making a guest appearance on lead. Winston Grennan and Hugh Malcolm were the most consistent drummers for the group, and Denzil 'Pops' Laing would often be on percussion. Perhaps the main structural difference between the two groups was that Taitt was the clear leader of the Jets, whereas the All Stars was a more democratic outfit, though Gladdy eventually emerged as its chief arranger.

With a wealth of musical experience between them, this group truly was composed of 'All Stars', and their composition of seasoned hands and young unknowns gave them the best of both worlds. Depending on whom they were recording for, the group was called by various names and used a shifting line-up, but certain key musicians remained constant throughout.

Winston Grennan had much performing and recording experience behind him. Born to a musical family in the town of Duckenfield, St Thomas on September 16, 1944, six of Grennan's uncles had formed the Scott Brothers big-band group, and his Uncle Christer played trumpet with saxophonist Val Bennett's band from the late '40s. Grennan made his way to Kingston in 1959, and later befriended Lee Perry while hanging around Coxsone's Muzik City premises. After boxing for a period in Mexico, Grennan recorded as a vocalist under the name Winston Richards, but success was elusive. Comedy duo Bim and Bam (Edward Lewis and Aston Wynter), old friends of one of his uncles, offered Grennan a place in an upcoming performance, and he was soon touring the country as a member of the cast and playing piano in the Caribbeats backing band, a group led by guitarist Bobby Aitken, brother of Laurel. Grennan then became the Caribbeats' regular drummer, opening for the Skatalites at the 300 Club in Waltham Park and at the Bournemouth Club at Bournemouth Beach.

After recording for various producers, the Caribbeats eventually dis-banded in the mid-1960s as Aitken became more committed to the church. Grennan then formed the Meditators with Roland Alphonso, recording at Studio One before moving on to work with the Supersonics at Duke Reid's Treasure Isle studio. Before joining the All Stars, Grennan's drumming helped provide rock steady with a beat that still carried tension despite its slower pace. Grennan himself noted that the beat was influenced by religious and folkloric music: 'In the country they used to have people who go out there and preach on the street side. I used to go with those people and play drums for them, and at Christmas time I would play masquerade drums for masquerade people, so I have all these little sneaky beats, but no one knows.'

Hugh Malcolm was another drummer with a very particular style. While Grennan's idiosyncrasy was to place his cymbals behind his drum kit, the definitive element of Hugh Malcolm's drumming was a reliance on furious drum rolls, giving a sense of urgency to many a tune. Malcolm was also a baritone vocalist who recorded a few gospel-tinged sides for Coxsone.

Jackie Jackson also came from a musical family. Born on March 27, 1947 in Kingston, Jackson's uncle was Luther Williams, the piano player who led a big jazz band called the Arawaks, popular in the post-war years. Jackson's aunt taught him to play piano, but a 1962 nightclub visit changed his musical direction when he saw Lloyd Brevett play bass. Jackson played in a small band called Ty and the Titans, and later joined Lester Sterling's Cavaliers. After that band broke up, Jackson received a surprise visit one day from Tommy McCook, who asked him to take his old mentor Lloyd Brevett's place as bassist in the Supersonics. The first record Jackson played on was 'Girl I've Got A Date', a number-one hit for Alton Ellis which signalled the approaching rock steady era. As the resident bassist at Treasure Isle, Jackson earned ten shillings a side, playing on all the hits by Duke Reid's most successful rock steady acts.

Lynford Brown was born on December 4, 1944, in Port Antonio. His school nickname Fordie changed to Fordux, later evolving to Hux. He started

singing in a school band called the Playboys, and taught himself to play guitar
after sending off for a music book advertised in the back of a comic. In 1962,
the Playboys performed at a birthday party in Port Antonio, attended by
members of the Vikings band. After the performance, Vikings Victor and
Sonny Wong approached Brown, and asked him to come to Kingston to
attend an audition, where he was selected to join the group.

Led by bassist Desmond Miles and featuring trumpeter Bobby 'Willow'
Ellis, saxophonist Headley Bennett and vocalist Derrick Harriott, the Vikings
was one of the hottest live acts on the Kingston ska scene, and Brown gladly
accepted their offer; he relocated to Kingston, renting a room on Lyndhurst
Road near the studios of RJR. The band played a variety of musical styles in
clubs on weekend nights, leaving the musicians free to attend recording
sessions during the week.

Around the time the Skatalites broke up, Bobby Ellis brought Brown to
Studio One, where he joined the nucleus of the Soul Brothers as a rhythm
guitarist. Brown played rhythm on hits for groups such as the Jamaicans and
took his first solos on the Clarendonians' 'Rude Boy Gone A Jail' and the
Heptones' immortal 'Fatty Fatty'. It was at Studio One that Brown first met
Lee Perry, who he noted 'used to give a lot of joke'. In 1967, Brown left
Coxsone's stable to play rhythm guitar on Lynn Taitt's sessions, backing a
score of artists for Leslie Kong, of which the most successful was the
Melodians. Brown picked up many pointers from Taitt, including how to 'ska'
with all six strings, and how the use of heavier strings would give his Hoffner
guitar a deeper tone for solos.

As a foreigner in Jamaica, Lynn Taitt had begun to feel the pressure of life
as an outsider despite the fame rock steady had awarded him. His gently lilting
Trinidadian accent made him stand out all the more, and though he was a
leading guitarist of the rock steady era, many directed envy at the outsider.
Thus, when he was offered a contract to be musical arranger of the house band
at the West Indian Federated Club in Toronto, Taitt jumped at the chance
and departed for Canada on August 8, 1968; he was never to return to Jamaica.
Once Taitt was off the island, Hux Brown would play in the All Stars full time.
According to Brown, the advent of the All Stars 'was more or less like a jumble
group came on the scene'.

Gladstone Anderson was another experienced member of the group.
Born June 18, 1934 in Jones Town, Gladdy was taught to play the piano at
home by his maternal uncle, the noted keyboardist and bandleader Aubrey
Adams. In the late '50s, Adams was playing organ for Duke Reid and
introduced Gladdy to Reid as a pianist. He remained a constant element of
Duke's productions from the boogie period onwards, and was also a crucial
contributor to the ska and rock steady recordings of Coxsone and Leslie Kong.
It was Gladdy who was typically in charge of musical arrangements with the
All Stars.

According to Jackie Jackson: 'When the singer comes to sing a song we would say "Go over to the piano, go over to Gladdy." Gladdy will run it down first, and the rest of the band will stand and have a listen to the progression, the melody, and Gladdy will tell us where to go. Nine times out of ten, Gladdy is always the first person to catch a song.' Gladdy himself remarked, 'If a one come with a song, I is the one who put it in chorus and verses and solo, and arrange the bass line and all like that. It's just the musical knowledge that I really born with.'

Like Jackie Jackson, Ronnie Bop began his professional career after Tommy McCook brought him into the Supersonics. He was born Lorraine Williams on November 8, 1942 in Spanish Town, but was soon called Ronnie (or Rannie), the nickname Bop eventually taking the place of his surname; the second of seven children, Williams was raised by his mother, who was treasurer and secretary of a local church. In the rock steady era, Tommy McCook saw Williams playing at the Maracas club in Ocho Rios, and was so impressed with his steady licks that he brought him to Kingston to join the Supersonics as a rhythm guitarist; his recording debut came on the Ethiopians' smash hit 'Expo '67'. The reputation he established as a Treasure Isle regular would see his talents made use of in several other bands, including the short-lived El Dorados and the more lasting Hippy Boys as well as the All Stars.

Winston Wright, born 1944, had also been recording for Treasure Isle before joining the Jets and the All Stars, while Headley Bennett had been part of the shifting early line-up of the Skatalites. This combination of relaxed experience and youthful guts and enthusiasm gave the All Stars a spontaneity and vitality that was lacking in some of the more established studio bands, and they soon became the most sought after session men on the island. When they eventually came under Lee Perry's direction, the combination would prove to be most invigorating.

With the rock steady beat creating a new buoyancy in the music, Perry was itching to get back into the studio, but he didn't have much ready cash, nor did he have an outlet for his product. He began scouting around for someone to enter into partnership with, and ended up making a series of one-off recordings throughout 1967 as he sought to find his feet away from the solidity of Coxsone's stable.

As he hung out with his musical peers, a number of recording opportunities presented themselves. Despite Perry's acute lack of cash, the reputation he had built up at Studio One, coupled with his ability to improvise, fulfilled his determination not to be excluded. One of his first appearances on disc after 'Give Me Justice' was a spoken guest spot on 'Get Ready, Do It Steady' by a female harmony group called the Alpines, backed up by Bobby Aitken and the Caribbeats; the disc may only have been issued in limited number on blank pre-release, and the particulars of the recording session remain obscure.

Scratch then began collaborating with Prince Buster, basing himself for a period at Buster's shop at 36 Charles Street. Buster brought Perry to Federal to voice two love songs, 'Give It To Me' and 'Call On Me', but the tunes were not very popular; it was the direct collaborations between Perry and the Prince that proved to be more substantially successful.

The songs Perry voiced for Coxsone Dodd often dealt with social injustice, and material he cut with Buster continued to question the failings of Jamaican society. The Prince had already scored a number of hits with politically relevant rude-boy themes, including 'Rude Boys Rule', 'Don't Throw Stones', and 'Shanty Town', but it was the disc he recorded at WIRL with Perry in 1967 that was to be the most far-reaching rude-boy epic ever: 'Judge Dread'.

Aside from being an instant success, 'Judge Dread' is a complex record with plenty of subtle references to the legacies of colonialism still largely conditioning Jamaican society. In his guise as Judge Dread, a saviour from Ethiopia, Buster castigated the rude boys by condemning them to 400 years' imprisonment for their acts of senseless violence against their fellow suffering black people. Over a brilliant rock steady rhythm provided by the All Stars, in which Jackie Jackson's bass line is built roughly on the melody of the 'Baa Baa Black Sheep' nursery rhyme, Buster reels off a list of crimes and punishments.

Perry and Buster's brother Fitzroy, appearing as the defendants Adolphous James, Emmanuel Zechariah Zacchepon, and George Grab-and-Flee, proffer a series of unconvincing denials, eventually collapsing in tears as the sentences are pronounced. Prince Buster revealed the weighty circumstances that led to the song's creation:

'That time the gun had just come to Jamaica, and the police were so afraid; they wouldn't arrest certain people and the court was too lenient on wrongdoers through fear of repercussions and it had gotten out of hand. I went to Scratch and said "I don't like this!" Scratch said "But you can't do this," him was a little bit nervy because if him name go 'pon it, he might even get killed out a street. All them who turn gun men, we all went to school together, so we not exactly friends but we know each other; but what cause "Judge Dread" fe make is when they shut down Denham Town School and rape kids inna the school and the teacher have to run with her panty, that was enough for me. The whole West of Kingston was under fire that time, because people no used to gun, and the gun just panic the whole society, and it wasn't functioning as it should, so I decide to put back some teeth inna the judicial system at the risk of my own life. If somebody was going to that studio and make that record, the first time it play, they would have to run and go hide somewhere, 'cause it was going against people who evil, gangster. I tell Scratch "Come" and just give him the part and we go inna it to put back teeth in the judicial system in Jamaica. Inspectors of police, about two judges and all decent respectful people come down a me shop and shake me hand because they hear that play on the radio; nobody dare to speak out, but I am entitled "Voice of the People" so I must.'

Technical engineer Sylvain Morris noted that the end result of 'Judge Dread' was shaped partly by Perry's keenly active creative process, after he came up with some of the dialogue on the spot at WIRL. 'Scratch was the one who instigated it, him make a suggestion and him and Buster just go about it. Scratch is an extraordinary individual. He's a creator, he creates things which is abnormal and unusual.'

Perry detailed the process by which he assumed his role on the recording, noting a hidden significance in the name Buster assigned his character: 'I was saying if him think it might be a war, me would be like the accused, so it just come out of his mouth that I am Emmanuel Zechariah Zacchepon. I don't think even now he know the meaning of Emmanuel, but it all come back because it was a revolution: Emmanuel means "God amongst his people"; he give me the name because he look into a book, see it there and just think it was a movie. If you are an artist you are open, and Prince Buster have open ears – he can hear words too.'

The immediate and broad success of this disc was such that it spawned many imitations and sequels, including some recorded by Jamaican immigrants in England. Buster himself re-used the original rhythm for 'The Appeal', in which one Barrister Dreadlock fails to set the rudies free, and 'Barrister Pardon', in which trombonist Rico Rodriguez inspires the Judge to allow the convicts to dance their way to freedom. Buster also used the rhythm for the thematically unrelated 'Musical College'. Such is the enduring popularity of the tune that updated versions of the rhythm and its scenario continue to be cut in the 1990s, the most recent being 'The People's Court' by dub poet Mutabaruka.

In 1967, Buster and Perry also worked together on 'Johnny Cool', a two-part saga in which Buster takes vengeance on the marauding rude boys. As the Prince explained, 'When you go out in the night time, you have a set of man in Jamaica who just rape. Because they were so bad, people used to get scared to say they raped them. They stop a girl by Trench Town late one night, and I go after them at a dance, so in the song I say "I'm a ice box man, Johnny Cool." If you listen to the tune, you will understand it: "Them mess with my girls, sometimes I become a icebox man." Sometimes you don't have to cuss a lot of bad word and all that, all you have to do is just cool.' The song also incorporated a medley of popular tunes, such as the Jamaicans' 'Ba Ba Boom' (a hit for Treasure Isle), and the Impressions' 'Minstrel and Queen'.

Perry provided further vocals on records for Buster such as the eerie 'Ghost Dance' in this period.

Unlike his experience with Coxsone, Perry felt that Buster treated him fairly. 'He and money was all right,' Perry said of Buster, but money wasn't the largest motivation for King Scratch when he linked up with the Prince: Perry saw his work with Buster as something pre-ordained; he had been sent to Buster to fulfil part of his destiny.

> 'I was just on a trail to do a job. That's how I get involved, not to be a bully like the rest of the guys. I didn't in it 'cause I want to make money but then I realise I need money. I was doing the job I was programmed to do; Prince Buster was in it.'[6]

Perry also emphasised that he and Buster had a mutual respect that neither retained for Coxsone, for both felt that Dodd had taken advantage of them.

> 'Prince Buster believe in excercise. He can defend himself, he's a fuckin' tough guy. I love him! If a guy tried to do me anything, Prince Buster would kill him instantly without even thinking. Coxsone might be a shame of a coward, but Prince Buster would go right to you and say "You move you bumba clot!" '[7]

After Buster spent some time abroad on tour, Perry returned to freelance operations. Falling back on useful industry connections, he made an arrangement with WIRL's manager, Clifford Rae, where he could record now and pay later; they would take care of the session and pressing fees, until money was raised through record sales, while Perry would supervise other sessions for them. He was also distributing records for WIRL on a little Honda 50, the smallest motorcycle then available. Perry thus sneaked back into the studio to take another swipe at Coxsone with the playfully scathing 'Run For Cover', in which King Scratch warned of the volley of musical blows he would send to Coxsone through the recording of superior product. With harmony provided by the Sensations (a group whose members have included Jimmy Riley, Cornel Campbell, Aaron 'Bobby' Davis [a.k.a. Dego], Buster Riley, Jackie Paris and Radcliffe 'Douggie' Bryan) and Lynn Taitt's supreme picking filling out the bridge, 'Run For Cover' was a formidable attack by Perry in the rock steady mode. The single's B-side, 'Something You Got,' was a soulful cover of an R & B hit by New Orleans vocalist Chris Kenner. Also recorded at the session were 'Wind Up Doll' and 'Whup Whup Man', songs that expressed Perry's attitude towards women: his love was eminently available, but he preferred to spread it around with no strings attached.

Seeking to squeeze the maximum mileage out of what seemed certain to be a hit, Perry voiced two further songs over the 'Run For Cover' rhythm: 'Set Them Free' and 'Don't Blame The Children'. Credited on release to the Defenders, 'Set Them Free' was Perry's answer to Prince Buster's 'Judge Dread', with Perry appearing this time as the Barrister Lord Defend to point out to the Judge that the rude boys were forced into their life of violent crime by a crooked system that upheld the racially divisive values of colonial Jamaica. In a relaxed rhyming testimony, Lord Defend sought to explain that a true understanding of the situation must overturn their convictions by right:

'They are from a poor generation,
Having no education, no qualification
So they are driven to desperation.
Can't get a job, they have been forced to rob.
I'm not suggesting that they should, but as you know,
A hungry man is an angry one . . .
Your Honour, as you already know, that robbery was
                                        from creation
For it was robbery that befall the black nation.
Our ancestors once ruled this world and all its gold
But now they are poor.
Who stole the gold?
Your Honour, could you answer me that question?
If you can't, then there must be silent thief as well
                                        as violent thief.'

'Don't Blame The Children' continued this defence of the rude boys, allotting the true blame for their predicament to a society that sought to denigrate their blackness through a meaningless education that glorified European injustices, indefinitely continuing their state of disempowerment that followed on from 400 years of colonial rule.

Although the sessions at WIRL weren't costing him anything upfront, the situation wasn't really earning him anything either, and he was eventually removed from his post as resident arranger and hit-spotter by a man with better-established industry contacts: Bunny Lee. Born on August 23, 1941, in Greenwich Farm, Edward Lee was the oldest of ten children born to a shoemaker and his wife. After leaving school, he did electrical work before joining United Motors in the parts department, later moving to its chief competitor, the Kingston Industrial Garage on Church Street. Friendly with singers such as Derrick Morgan, Laurel Aitken, Jackie Edwards and Owen Grey, Lee entered the music business as one of Duke Reid's hired hands in 1962; the heavy-set youth's task was to see that Reid's product was played on the radio 'by any means necessary'. He also performed a similar function to a lesser degree for Coxsone Dodd and Leslie Kong while still working in the auto-parts business. As his involvement in the music business increased, it was only natural that he begin recording. 'My boss hear say I was down the country promoting Desmond Dekker's festival song and me and the boss have argument – I leave and they pay me twenty pounds and I run my first session. Duke Reid give me the studio time free and Lynn Taitt just take the twenty pounds and get him band, has a drink and just plays four tunes for me. We did a tune with Lloyd and the Groovers with Derrick (Morgan) talking, "Do It To Me Baby" and "Music Field" with Roy Shirley.'

The roll of blank tape for this session was provided by Phil Pratt, another producer whose product Bunny Lee was promoting. Though Pratt lacked the economic muscle of the bigger fish, he was an insightful producer and talented singer who had been gradually making his mark on the music scene since his return to Jamaica in 1965. His debut recording, 'Safe Travel', was made for Coxsone Dodd, but when Coxsone declined to issue it he began to produce his own material. In 1966, he produced Horace Andy's debut 'Blackman's Country' and Ken Boothe's 'The One I Love', scoring his biggest hit with the vocal 'Reach Out', issued on the Caltone label. Caltone and Wiggle Spoon were labels run by a man named Mr Calneck whom everyone called Ken Lack, and Pratt was operating the John Tom label at this time from downtown premises shared with Lack at 15 Mark Lane.

Of the material recorded at Bunny Lee's debut recording session, 'Do It To Me Baby' was issued on Caltone, while 'Music Field' was released on WIRL after Lee replaced Perry as WIRL's arranger. Shortly after, Bunny Lee established the Lee's label as an independent producer.

Once ousted from his post at WIRL, Perry moved over to the Beeston Street premises of Joel Gibson, another record shop owner who was entering the production field. Born in Montego Bay in 1945, he worked on the American naval base in Cuba's Guantanamo Bay, like many other poor Jamaican males who came of age in the Cold War years. Returning to Kingston in the mid-1960s, he began selling records from a television-repair shop downtown. After forming the JoGib record label in 1966, he became known on the music scene as the producer Joe Gibbs.

Like Perry, Gibbs didn't have much money, but he knew that producing music would earn him much more than simply selling records from his shop. Gibbs entered the business by recording Roy Shirley, and the first disc they cut made a serious and lasting impact. Born in Kingston during World War II and raised in Trench Town by his mother (who is said to have the gift of healing), Roy Shirley grew up in a spiritual community centred on a Revivalist church. Given encouragement by rising star Jimmy Cliff, his first record was 'Shirley' for Leslie Kong in the ska years, for which he was paid ten pounds. After writing the lyrics of the song 'Hold Them', Shirley approached Coxsone Dodd, who told him to return in three years' time because he didn't feel the youth was ready to sing. Determined to get the song recorded, Shirley was brought to Joe Gibbs by a mutual friend called Jimmy who had been stationed with Gibbs in Guantanamo Bay.

Recorded in one take, 'Hold Them' was a massive success. Shirley's peculiar voice, thin and quivering one moment, deep and gravelly the next, led the way with a chilling effect as he tried to emulate the feeling the Salvation Army band had brought him. A related song called 'Be Good' was also recorded, containing more of an uplifting feel with similar lyrics over a faster rhythm based on the same two chords.

As the buzz went around about this new sound, Coxsone sought to cash in on it by having Ken Boothe, Studio One's 'Mr Rock Steady', record his own highly popular cover version. Although the success of Boothe's re-cut began to affect sales of the original, Gibbs' name had already been established on the scene as a producer of note.

The only other threat to the success of 'Hold Them' was posed by another popular Roy Shirley song that Lee Perry had arranged at WIRL just as 'Hold Them' was picking up steam. Shirley says that he first recorded 'The Winner' for Bunny Lee at WIRL, but that the stamper was deliberately ruined by former Treasure Isle engineer Byron Smith who was then cutting discs at WIRL. Shirley then re-cut the tune with Perry at the controls, and it began to challenge the success of 'Hold Them' through radio airplay – though 'Hold Them' ultimately held sway.

Shirley noted that Bunny Lee was initially helping Joe Gibbs, but moved over to work at WIRL after building up 'Hold Them', causing Perry to lose his position there: 'I took Bunny Lee to Joe Gibbs to help him, because Bunny Lee was known as one of Jamaica's greatest dancers, he could dance a thing named "Mash". Everywhere he go, a lot of people leave out of the dancehall and watch him dance; him mash up 'nuff dance and create road block, so me know he's an exciting guy. Some radio guy who used to work at RJR – Jeff Barnes and him brother – Bunny Lee had those man, so I bring him in to help Joe Gibbs to move the material, which he did. Bunny Lee came on the scene when "Hold Them" was established, and people know that he was the man who do that, so I go back to WIRL and show the boss who named Mr Rae, "This is Bunny Lee, the man who help get that tune in the charts." Scratch was just a guy who earmark some record, so them see Bunny Lee as a greater potential. When you have a tune to record, Scratch take that man in the studio and Scratch arrange out that thing, but he didn't have the crowd and he didn't have the contacts that Bunny Lee have, so the company would have seen it more beneficial to get rid of him and bring on Bunny Lee. When Scratch leave him job, he walk and tell people me and Bunny Lee come and get him out of him job from WIRL, which look like it was true, but we never say he couldn't produce.'

With Lee in Scratch's former seat at WIRL, Perry decided to join forces with Joe Gibbs, his recent adversary and former rival. While Gibbs began to stake his claim on the ghetto record industry, Perry became an increasingly important force in his operation. Scratch would work closely with the artists in the studio, developing a distinct musical style. 'He was like the producer,' Jackie Jackson said of Perry's work with Joe Gibbs. 'Scratch would come into the studio and say "Play this for me: doo doo, doo doo, doo doo, doo doo, ding ding" and we play it, or he might say "the drum, give me this beat". He's not a musician, but he can relate to you what he wants that kind of way.'

When Perry began working with Joe Gibbs, Errol Dunkley had already scored Gibbs a hit with his cover of Gloria Lynn's 'You're Gonna Need Me'.

Born in the West Kingston ghetto of Denham Town in the mid-'50s, Dunkley began singing and dancing along to jukebox records as a child in his mother's bar. When barely in his teens, he recorded a few songs for Prince Buster, and was eventually brought to Joe Gibbs' attention by Bunny Lee after Dunkley turned up at WIRL with a letter from his youth-club leader stating he was entitled to an audition. Dunkley was Jamaica's second child star, brought into the business as competition for the rapidly maturing Delroy Wilson. One of the first tunes Perry arranged for Gibbs was 'Please Stop Your Lying', an even bigger hit than its predecessor. As Dunkley recalled, 'Scratch was a freelance producer, he's got a good hearing for sound. Joe Gibbs at the time, he was just the guy who's spending the money. Lee Perry's the guy who could compare with the musicians. When (Gibbs) tried to tell them what to do, they just laughed, because him couldn't talk to them in the term of music. It's like he's just the guy who put up the money. Later on, him get an idea of things still.'

For the rest of the year, Perry worked closely with a variety of artists for Gibbs, including future percussionist Uziah 'Sticky' Thompson, then a popular deejay known as Cool Sticky. Born on August 1, 1936, in the rural district of Mannings Mountain, Thompson was the third of five children born to a poor contractor. The family's poverty meant that Thompson was unable to complete his education, and at age 15 he moved to Western Kingston in search of work. As the ska era approached, Thompson was one of the many box lifters assisting Coxsone Dodd with the running of his sound, and his friendship with Lee Perry dates back to this period. Gradually, King Stitt began passing the mike to Thompson at dances because of his ability to make certain sounds with his mouth, and when Coxsone heard these sounds, he recorded Thompson's vocal oddities on the Skatalites' hit 'Guns of Navarone'. The success of the song saw Duke Reid using Thompson for the exciting introduction of the Skatalites' 'Ball of Fire', and the lasting success of this rival hit saw Thompson toasting regularly on the Treasure Isle sound system. It was while toasting on Duke Reid's sound that his capacity to excite a packed audience led to his peculiar nickname: 'When I started to play Duke Reid's sound, it always stick up-stick up, so they just put the name on me, Sticky.' In the late rock steady period, Sticky provided Scratch and Joe Gibbs with a dynamic toasting style on songs such as 'Train To Soulsville', an outlandish take on the Ethiopians' 'Train To Skaville' given a James Brown workout.

A number of significant vocal groups were also finding success with Perry and Gibbs at this time, including the Overtakers, led by a young singer from Trelawney named Leo Graham, the Mellotones, led by a youth named Winston Francis (not to be confused with the Studio One singer of the same name), and the Versatiles, led by Junior Byles.

Keith Byles Junior (a.k.a. Chubby) was born in Kingston in 1948 and raised in the ghetto of Jones Town; his father ran a business downtown and his mother was a schoolteacher. Junior was his father's apprentice when he formed the Versatiles in 1967 with his friends Ben 'Louis' Davis and Dudley Earl, who was part-Indian of extraction. Though each member of the Versatiles could sing lead, and the group frequently sang their songs in unison, Byles would eventually emerge as the one most committed to music, and his strong and distinct baritone had an expressive edge not present in the voices of the other group members.

Lee Perry was working for Joe Gibbs when the Versatiles made their recording debut, cutting three songs with Lynn Taitt's band under Scratch's direction. Surfacing from the session was 'The Time Has Come', a 1967 Festival song competition entry that led to a series of performances by the group around the island. The group would later record for Perry away from Gibbs, and Byles was to become a significant ally in the following decade.

Perry also brought the duo of Stranger and Gladdy to Gibbs' attention, providing him with a couple of big hits that had been recorded independently. Cole's highly successful career as a lead and harmony vocalist had seen him recording heavily for Duke Reid and Coxsone Dodd in the ska and rock steady years. After later making hits with Ken Boothe on which Gladstone Anderson was the keyboard player, Stranger and Gladdy began working together as a singing duo, beginning with a couple of self-produced numbers called 'Just Like A River' and 'Seeing Is Knowing'.

Gladdy noted their initial difficulty in generating interest in the songs: 'We did them at Duke Reid's studio, and when we ask Duke Reid to distribute it for us, Duke Reid say "Oono gwan try it fe oono self." At that time we didn't have no funds, so when he disappointed that way, we go to Miss Pottinger.'

Stranger Cole noted Scratch's role in the problematic dissemination of the hits: 'The studio was given to me by Duke Reid and all the musicians played for free for me. I took them to Mrs Pottinger to distribute, but I wanted to get a little money upfront, and she didn't want to give me any money. I knew Lee Perry from his early days as a singer, he come for rehearsal at Duke Reid, so I know him from way back before he was at Coxsone or before he was with anybody . . . Lee Perry decided to take me to Joe Gibbs with the songs, Joe Gibbs like them and decide to release them for me and Gladdy. He gave us £200 upfront, and I've never received any more royalties up until this day.'

With Gibbs' popularity rising and his productions gaining a higher currency on the ghetto hit parade, Scratch was determined to send a more high-profile message to his former mentor, Coxsone Dodd, and did so in the form of his latest personality: 'The Upsetter'. Over a buoyant All Stars rhythm on which Lynn Taitt was doubled-tracked to play two different guitar lines, Perry queried Coxsone's 'gravelicious' and 'covetous' nature. He was 'greedy', 'red-eye', and could not be satisfied, Perry proclaimed, but the avenging Upsetter was on the musical rise, chasing Coxsone away with a vinyl upper cut.

'That tune has a meaning,' Perry later explained. 'After spending time with Coxsone and the amount of work that I did and the pay that I got . . . I was hurt about the whole deal.'[8]

In another interview, he stated that 'He treat me good as a friend but not cashically. He was a nice pal, but at the time there was only a few man with the money to back ideas so sometimes a man just take away your ideas and don't give you the right rewards.'[9]

Though Perry and Dodd would later have a series of further clashes and reconciliations, Scratch would ultimately voice his gratitude to Dodd for starting him off in the music business. 'I don't have a reason to hate Mr Dodd. What I do is upset him and teach him a lesson, and I did really even forgive him as well. Duke Reid didn't give me no chance, he take all me tune, but even if Coxsone only give me one pound a week, it doesn't matter; I was just giving Mr Dodd my service and he was giving me some food because me didn't have any at the time. Me get to that me not sleeping in the tailor shop any more; I could afford to rent a place, whatsoever likkle money he give me and what likkle me can achieve for my side, me can make it and me live. If I was waiting on Duke Reid I would still be in the tailor shop, so though it was one likkle money Mr Dodd was giving me, my word was going out on record.'

Lynn Taitt noted that the musicians structured the overall composition of 'The Upsetter' after Perry sang them the melody in the studio: 'He was going to have a recording session with Gladdy Anderson and Jackie Jackson, and I think it was Drumbago on drums. I arranged the song in the studio. He sing the song, we listened to it, and then Gladdy said "Taitt, you have any introduction?" and we work it up together. If Scratch don't like it, he say, "No no no, change that!" ' In contrast, the flip side of 'The Upsetter' was 'Thank You Baby,' a song that exposed a more loving side of the Upsetter's nature.

Perhaps the most successful material Perry arranged for Joe Gibbs was with the Pioneers. Sydney Roy Crooks (a.k.a. 'Luddy'), the founder of the group, was born in Westmoreland on February 24, 1945. The son of a cane farmer and his wife, Luddy grew in various rural locations before moving to Trench Town at age 17. Once in Kingston, he formed a loosely structured street-corner group variously called the Spectaculars or the Counts, with musicians such as Glen Adams, Earl 'Bagga' Walker, Maurice 'Blacka Morwell' Wellington and Lloyd 'Gitsy' Willis, but the group never found success. Luddy later formed the first version of the Pioneers with his brother, Derrick Crooks (a.k.a. Joe) and a lad called Winston Hewitt, but lack of interest from record producers meant that the group had to finance their own recording debut with money provided by Luddy's mother. 'Good Nanny' and 'I'll Never Come Running Back To You' were recorded at Treasure Isle with a group called Al and the Vibrators (led by bassist Linval Martin) as the backing musicians; both self-financed tunes surfaced on Ken Lack's Caltone label but achieved only limited success and the original group split after Hewitt migrated to Canada. Luddy said that a chance encounter with Joe Gibbs on

Beeston Street led to the creation of a new Pioneers duo for the number one hit 'Give Me Little Loving', recorded one night at WIRL with the All Stars. 'When I was about to voice the song I looked outside the studio and I saw a little boy sitting on a stone. I said "Hey, come here man, you can sing?" He sung the harmony for "Give Me Little Loving" and his name was Jackie Robinson. After that I said to him "You are one of the Pioneers from today" and he became the lead singer of the Pioneers.'

Though Perry was not present for this initial session, his involvement in later Pioneers material ensured that they continued to produce hits for Gibbs. 'Scratch used to move very good with Joe Gibbs and all of us,' Luddy readily consented.

Ever willing to make further use of a good rhythm, the Upsetter slipped into another cloak on the flip side of the Pioneers' 'Jackpot' on a version of Stranger and Gladdy's 'Seeing Is Knowing'. 'Kimble' was credited on release to the Creators, but was in fact Perry quietly proclaiming himself to be the one-armed villain of *The Fugitive* television series that was gripping Jamaican viewers at the time, with breaking bottles and cracking whips underlining his lyrical delivery. 'Kimble' is worthy of note not only for the range of sound effects that Perry placed over an otherwise unblemished rhythm, but also for its indication of Perry's tendency to *become* other characters, to drift so heavily into an alter ego that he actually lives that character's experience for a time. In this particular instance, he may only have been 'Kimble' for the duration of the record, but the Upsetter was a persona that would remain with him to infinity.

While Gibbs continued to pick up steam off Perry's concerted efforts, Scratch himself found that the recognition and financial independence he sought was far from evident. If he had been under any illusions about being in partnership with Gibbs, the assertion of the more ruthless side of Gibson's character soon made it readily apparent that this would never be the case.

Perry found himself to be in a situation that was all too familiar. He had broken away from Coxsone Dodd only to find himself treated no better by his new boss, Joe Gibbs. When he confronted Gibson one night, their quarrel turned ugly, and Perry struck out on his own after a heated and quarrelsome parting. His shoes were soon filled by his friend Niney, another young record salesman and freelance producer who gradually became the new creative force beneath Gibson's business acumen. 'That was just night-time work,' Niney noted, 'because I used to work for Bunny Lee during the days, and Scratch. Night time was like my hustling with Joe Gibbs, earn some extra money.'

Though many Jamaicans are known more by their pet names or stage personas than their given names, Niney had the added confusion of being given two different names by his parents: his father named him George Boswell, but he was raised by his mother as Winston Holness. When he lost a thumb in a work accident, he became better known as Nine Finger or Niney.

Born in Montego Bay on December 7, 1944, Niney first met Perry in the town
of Lucea in Hanover, where Niney was hanging around young musicians like
guitarist Eric Frater at Rusea High School. 'We hook up in the teens. He was
the greatest dancer, because Mashed Potato was the type of dance that time,
and he was the King of Mashed Potato. That's why they called him Chicken
Scratch, 'cause he could dance. From there we hooked up in town, we meet in
town again, and from there I beside Bunny Lee and Lee Perry.'

Financial considerations were certainly becoming more concretely im-
portant to Lee Perry by the time he left Joe Gibbs as his domestic
responsibilities were increasing. He had moved his family to a larger space on
Johnson Terrace in Rollington Town to make way for a new family member:
Pauline gave birth to Marvin Hugh, Scratch's first child, on April 11, 1967.
Initially referred to as Django after the hero of Sergio Corbucci's spaghetti-
western films, his mother later gave Marvin the pet name Sean in reference to
Sean Connery, star of the first series of James Bond films.

For much of the mid-1960s, Lee Perry was a regular fixture at WIRL. He
had long been friendly with Lynford Anderson, who was not only the engineer
at WIRL studio, but also oversaw much of the mastering process for records
pressed by WIRL. Known to his friends as Andy, Anderson was born in
Clarendon on July 8, 1941. Moving to Kingston in 1959, he worked briefly as
an accountant, but left soon after to work for RJR as a log keeper. In the early
'60s he was laid off, but was subsequently re-hired as a trainee engineer when
another staff member got fired. Exhibiting a natural flair for sound engineering, Anderson stayed at RJR for two more years, recording and mixing
material such as Prince Buster's '30 Pieces of Silver' on the studio's one-track
monophonic recorder. He was later approached by Ronnie Nasrallah, manager of the Dragonaires, who had bought into WIRL's operations with Byron
Lee after Edward Seaga took the band to America to perform at the World's
Fair in 1964. The studio's proprietors, Clifford Rae and George Benson, had
supervised the building of the West Indies recording studio at 13 Bell Road in
the early 1960s, originally installing a two-track recorder on the premises;
when Lee and Nasrallah joined the team, they upgraded the studio to four
tracks, and established a lucrative distribution deal with Ahmet Ertegun's
Atlantic Records.

Graeme Goodall, an Australian who then resided in Jamaica, had been
the studio's engineer since its inception, and he trained Anderson for a
significant period before emigrating to England, where he established the
Doctor Bird label in 1966. Soon Anderson was an integral part of WIRL's
operation, performing many vital functions for the company. 'I used to record
and master almost one hundred songs a day, for foreign and local. I used to
have to work right through the night, after working in the studio, then go
down and cut again until four in the morning. Byron Lee was paying him a
dollar for each one, so at night if you cut twenty you'd get twenty bucks.'

Perry made most of his valuable contacts and closest friendships while he was working for Studio One, and his connection with Anderson dated from his time with Dodd. 'He used to come down with records for Coxsone, cutting the masters. He was the runaround, the guy who take them over for Coxsone. We get to know each other, and after work we'd hang out.'

After his rupture with Joe Gibbs, Perry attempted to form an allegiance with Anderson and Barrington Lambert, then WIRL's trainee engineer, as Perry himself later noted.

'That's where I start my own self there, with a guy named Andy. He was the engineer at West Indies and he had a friend named Barry, so the three was working, walking together and talking together all the while. We live in one unity, so we happy, whether we in the studio or not we always talk.' [10]

Anderson had also been hoping to begin producing his own records, and he started off by persuading the session musicians to let him record them for free at the end of a day's work, beginning with a cover version of 'South Parkway Mambo' by the Bop-A-Loos. As Jackie Jackson remembered it, 'We were there recording, and we got to know him as a nice guy. He said to us, "Me have a likkle one, I beg you a song now." By this time we were there all day recording, it was one of those days when we had made about fifty pounds, so we were in a good mood. He said "I beg you a one song," we did it and forgot about it. There was no question of money, we did it for him.'

Hux Brown said this was a fairly common occurrence at that time: 'We guys was pretty close, and when we're recording, in them days it was no big thing. We didn't know this music was going to go nowhere. More or less, all of us guys had other jobs – we used to play in hotels and play in other bands too. I used to play at the Sheraton, but our day job was recording. We didn't really need that much money, so we could afford to do something for some of those guys.'

Though Anderson was initially unhappy with the song, he would later have Lloyd Charmers turn it into something else by overdubbing sprightly keyboards over the rhythm and voicing it himself as 'Pop A Top' after being inspired by a Canada Dry advertisement. 'Pop A Top' was a massive success, and Anderson re-used the rhythm countless times for a number of experimental versions.

In 1967, Anderson formed the Upset label in collaboration with Lee Perry; Anderson claims he coined the name after a billboard caught his attention. 'I was driving along one day and I just see a commercial, "Are you having upset stomach?" And I say, "Oh, that's a damn good name for a label!" I started the label, but at the time, Lee Perry didn't have a label. Then, afterward, he decided to branch out, said he was going to start his own one, Upsetter. He say he's going to upset one, so he's the Upsetter.'

Anderson's Upset label began with the Gaylets – a female harmony trio led by a popular dancer from St Andrew named Judy Mowatt. Born in the tiny riverside village of Industry in the foothills of the Blue Mountains, Mowatt learned to sing in the African-influenced Pocomania church her mother belonged to. As Judy's mother had her children while still a teenager, Judy and her two older sisters were raised by their grandmother, a woman who did domestic work for a rich family in nearby Gordon Town. At age seven she went to stay with her father's relatives in Hanover, living off the land in a rural community until the age of twelve; she then moved to Gold Street in the heart of downtown Kingston.

There was a radio in the tenement yard where she lived with several other families, and Mowatt was greatly inspired by singers like Ella Fitzgerald and Nancy Wilson, whose music was broadcast on The Voice of America. It was after hearing such music on the radio that Mowatt became determined to make it as a singer, though it was as a dancer that she would give her first stage performances.

By 1967, Mowatt was working as a salesperson for the Colgate Palmolive Company, and was also touring around the island with a creative dance troupe. The troupe rehearsed at the Baby Grand Club in Cross Roads, and it was there that she first met Beryl Lawson, who was one of her dancing peers. Lawson had previously formed the Gaylets with Merle Clemenson and Dawn Hanchard, but the group had fallen into a period of inactivity. After hearing Mowatt's singing voice, Lawson asked her if she wanted to join a group, and the Gaylets were thus re-formed with Judy Mowatt, Beryl Lawson, and Merle Clemenson.

Not long after their re-formation, the group came into contact with Lynford Anderson, who decided to use them for harmonies on recordings made around the time of his classic 'Pop A Top'. Merle began a brief romantic liaison with Anderson, and the group subsequently recorded a number of other tracks for him, including a cover of the soul hit 'Something About My Man'. As dancers and singers coming up on the Kingston music scene, the attractive Gaylets found themselves attending many parties around town, and it was at just such an event in one of Kingston's many hot spots that they first came to know Lee Perry.

Scratch was clearly happy to remain in their company, and requested that they join him on an overtly rude duet called 'How Come', recorded late one night at WIRL with Lynford Anderson towards the end of 1967. A late-rock steady number on which a squeaky bedroom door and sighing vocals underlined the record's sexual nature, 'How Come' was fairly light-hearted sleaze. It was with a certain amount of embarrassment that Judy Mowatt recounted the recording of the song, and the peculiar circumstances of a concert connected with its aftermath: 'That was one of the worst things I have ever done. My self esteem then was not as it is today. If somebody would have brought that to me years after, I would not have done it, but as a young girl in the business, you would like to hear yourself on radio. We really wanted popularity, and Scratch was kind of moulding us. We had so much respect for Scratch, sometimes you can respect a person and that person is disrespecting you and because of the respect that you have for the person you allow them to use you. Scratch asked us to do it one night, nobody much was in the studio, so we went in and we covered our shame with the darkness and the door of the studio and we did the song, hoping that he would not let anybody know that it is us. We never saw that maybe one day he would have wanted us to go on stage and perform it. Then one Christmas morning now, they had the stage show at Ward Theatre and this particular morning, Scratch was dressed like a magician and he asked us to come and perform the song with him. We were so afraid and ashamed, but we didn't want to tell him that we didn't want to do it because we didn't want to lose face. God was so good that riot broke out before Scratch went on and the show mashed up.'

Perry was also working at this time with Clancy Eccles, another important force now gaining currency on the music scene in Kingston. After his rupture with Coxsone in 1962, Eccles had been promoting shows around the island, notably with the Clarendonians in 1963 and the Wailers in subsequent years, but his earnings from the concerts were not steady enough to allow him to stop working as a tailor. He thus continued operating from his sewing premises adjacent to Prince Buster's record shop at 121 Orange Street, still far from abandoning his musical ambitions. As ska changed to rock steady in the mid-'60s, Clancy began recording sporadically for producers like Sonia Pottinger, operator of the Tip Top record shop a few doors down from Buster and first female record producer to emerge in Jamaica. In late 1966 or early 1967, he joined forces with Scratch and burst back onto the scene, recording a series of hits at WIRL that were to have a strong influence on the direction of Jamaican pop, starting with Eccles' own 'What Will Your Mama Say'. As Eccles remembered, 'Scratch was like my A & R man then. I knew Scratch from he came from the country, Coxsone was by Beeston Street then and I met Scratch and Niney. I was about leaving Coxsone and Scratch and I get on very well. I believe Scratch is a great songwriter and top A & R man. For the recording sessions, I would give Scratch my panel (mixing desk) to help on a session, because Scratch understand sounds very very well. He's a self-taught soundperson, but I believe he has a little more than the ordinary. When we start getting very close, he and Pauline was living in some place in Rollington Town in '67. He was working then with West Indies Records Limited, with Andy Capp. We did "What Will Your Mama Say," "Darling Don't Do That", and I did "Feel The Rhythm" in 1967.'

'Feel The Rhythm' was something else entirely – it used a driving beat that was entirely new. The rhythm was so intense that Eccles spent much of the song describing its effects: you either danced the rhythm, or 'upset' the rhythm. He also used the song to give remarks about many of the negative aspects of human nature. As Eccles explained, 'It was just a novelty as far as I'm concerned. People may take it serious but it was no seriousness to me, it's just that you feel the rhythm, you love the rhythm, so you dance the rhythm or upset this rhythm, you understand? Because if you're trying to reach the top, they want to see you drop, and if you don't try at all, the people stand by the wayside and say that you're a lazy boy, and if you win a lot of money, everybody will come along and eat it, and when it down and out, none of them going to help you out.'

Part of what made 'Feel The Rhythm' stand out was the guitar work and musical arrangement provided by Ernest Ranglin. Eccles had been using Lynn Taitt's band on his earlier material, but Taitt's demands for upfront payment led to Eccles seeking a different set of musicians. Although it did not have a definite name yet, Eccles and Perry were clearly fashioning a new sound. The new beat was most notable on 'Feel The Rhythm,' though the high register of Monty Morris provided the biggest hit at the time with 'Say What You're Saying'.

According to Eccles, Scratch brought Eric 'Monty' Morris to his attention after discovering him singing one night. 'Scratch Perry heard him doing some songs in Heathfield Road, right below Coxsone's studio. Scratch took me there and he played two songs on his guitar and I loved both of them and I took him to Treasure Isle studio, same time I did "Please Stay" with Larry Marshall and "Two Of A Kind" on that session.'

Eccles and Perry made further use of the 'Say What You're Saying' rhythm on 'CN Express' and 'You Were Meant For Me,' the first re-cast as a deejay cut with bottles being played as train whistles, the second a Perry vocal ballad. Eccles noted that 'CN Express' made reference to the masses of people who were leaving Jamaica for England, with additional vocal exhortations provided by Uziah 'Sticky' Thompson.

Scratch was also producing hits for Mrs Dorothy Barnett, a former secretary of Coxsone Dodd who established the Deltone label towards the end of the rock steady era. One of Scratch's first production hits for Deltone was 'Combination', the recording debut of a high-pitched tenor named Keeling Beckford, nephew of pianist Theophilus Beckford. Born on North Street in downtown Kingston on June 13, 1954, Beckford and his younger sister were sent in their infancy to farming grandparents in St Mary after their father emigrated to England; it was as a member of the Presbyterian Church Choir in St Mary that Beckford's vocal talent was first noted. At age nine, he was sent to live with a wealthy maternal aunt who lived on Lady Musgrave Road in New Kingston, and spent much of his teen years hanging out on Orange Street with other aspiring singers such as Jacob Miller, Dennis Brown, Roman Stewart, and Freddy McGregor. It was while accompanying his uncle to sessions at Studio One and Federal in the ska years that Keeling Beckford first met Lee

Perry; he later encountered him more closely through auditions at Clancy Eccles' shop. Beckford recalled the details of his debut recording, which was arranged by Mrs Barnett after Beckford passed his audition: 'The song was recorded at WIRL. When I arrived, there was a session going on at the time: Tennors was doing "Ride Me Donkey". After their time done our time start, and Lee Perry was in charge. The drummer was Hugh Malcolm, "Snapping" Theophilus Beckford on piano, guitar was Ronnie Bop and Lynn Taitt, bass was Jackie Jackson and the horn man was Val Bennett. I did one tune on that session, the engineer was Andy Capp.'

The success of the song prompted Barnett to record a further dozen songs with Beckford, but Scratch was not involved with those recordings. He did, however, produce a number of other hits for the label with the Versatiles, who had continued to record for Gibbs after Perry's departure, under the guiding hand of Niney. When the financial situation with Gibbs proved disappointing in 1968, the group began recording for Deltone, working with Perry on songs like 'Teardrops Falling', 'Someone To Love', and 'Action Line'. Although one such number, 'Children Get Ready', sold fairly well in Jamaica, the group received little financial reward, forcing Byles to join the Kingston Fire Department and pointing to an uncertain future for the group.

Through his many links on the music scene, Lee Perry eventually established a connection with Harry Palmer, one of three brothers who operated the Pama group of record labels in England, then the chief rival to the larger Trojan records. Harry Palmer had come to Jamaica in late 1967 to license product from Clancy Eccles and Alton Ellis, and later established strong links with Bunny Lee after Lee made a first trip to England in February 1968. Perry arranged for Palmer to buy the Gaylets tune he had recorded with Anderson for £100, but when the song was pressed in England on the Pama label, it ended up being credited to Lloyd Terrel, the given name of the singer, producer and keyboardist known as Lloyd Charmers.

According to Lynford Anderson and Archie Moore, the first song Perry then proposed to the Upset team was 'Honey Love', an innocuous cover version of the Drifters' tune by an unknown adenoidal crooner called Burt Walters – someone Perry found singing barefoot on the streets of Rockfort in East Kingston, a 'sufferer' who is said to have been emotionally unstable. 'Perry came to us and said, "I have some ideas to produce a song," cost about thirty pounds each. Barry and me put the money up because Perry didn't have any money.'

The song was recorded hurriedly in the middle of the night to keep costs to a minimum. Although the A-side of this record was entirely unnoteworthy, the B-side was a shocker: 'Evol Yenoh' was the same song with the entire vocal track played backwards; Walters' saccharine sentiment thus appeared as the fervent pleas of a tongue possessed, the sweet banality of pop turned on its head to produce something startling and alien. Such a radical representation of a singer's voice was unheard of in 1968; even the

Beatles had dared only to reverse a mere half a vocal line on their experimental song 'Rain'. In the Upsetter's hands, low on finance but high on creativity and wit, even the most unremarkable of songs could thus be transformed into something entirely other.

According to Archie Moore, when Anderson had 300 copies of the single pressed, Perry was only able to find the money to pay for half of them. He and Moore took the records on Scratch's Honda 50 to various record shops: KG at Cross Roads took some on consignment, Harry J paid cash for some upfront on Orange Street, and Patricia Chin at Randy's gave Scratch a hefty cheque for the remainder. The pair were thus able to go back to Lynford Anderson with payment for the other half that had been pressed, which they peddled to other Kingston record outlets.

Although 'Honey Love' did not make much of an impact on release in Jamaica, it allowed Walters to buy a new pair of shoes; after Lynford Anderson arranged for the song to be issued abroad by Trojan, the team recouped their initial investment. Anderson noted that Perry was ready to press on with more recordings, but his partners were reluctant to continue. 'We did the song in about an hour and it was not a big hit. We sold the song for £100, at that time it was a lot of money. He said he wanted to continue with the business, I said whatever he wanted to do was fine. Then Barry said he figured he should get more. Barry said "I'll take my money now," so I said "OK, I'll take mine too." Barry and I went straight to the racetrack with thirty-three pounds each, and we lost the money! Lee Perry, he's not working so he doesn't gamble.'

Despite the failure of the song to become a hit and the reluctance of his partners to continue backing him, Perry was determined to soldier on and make his mark. He began recording and pressing small quantities of material, which he would sell from a corner of Clancy Eccles' shop. Most early releases were issued on blank label discs, rubber-stamped 'Upsetter Records, Produced and Distributed by Lee Perry', but a few appeared on the Upset label, whose original illustration featured a machete that was dripping blood – symbols suggesting the magic arts of Obeah. Derived from African animist traditions, Obeah or 'Science' is widely believed throughout the Caribbean to be able to inflict damage on a foe or provide protection from enemies, and the early Upset label gave ambiguous hints of hidden powers.

Early Upsetter sessions yielded a version of Acker Bilk's 'Stranger On The Shore' by veteran saxophonist Val Bennett, and 'Nonesuch', another tale of racetrack losses by the Mellotones, who agreed to do some recording for Perry after moving away from Joe Gibbs. Perry had been hankering to show Gibbs the error of his ways, and although 'Nonesuch' had subtle thematic echoes of the Pioneers' 'Jackpot', Perry had been planning a more direct vinyl attack in that direction. Not only was he eager to burst Gibbs' bubble, he also knew he was capable of becoming as successful as his rapidly advancing peers: Sir JJ was striking big with the Ethiopians, Sonia Pottinger with the

Melodians, and Bunny Lee with the Uniques. Although Perry's independent material had not yielded any big hits, his creative urges forced him to move forward. His goal was to create a new and different type of music, and all he needed was some particular inspiration that would carry him in the right direction.

In the end, the inspiration came from a most unsuspected source in the spring of 1968. As Lynford Anderson recalled, 'One night he say "Let me buy you a drink," so we stopped at this bar close to my house and there was a church there. The church was doing Revival stuff when we were drinking. When we left, Scratch starting rocking. They had this real band with drum and bass and guitar and everything. The next day Lee Perry came and said "I've got the idea for a song."'

Perry himself recalled the inspiration as coming 'from touring the night':

'At them time, me used to go out town and stay late, drink one or two little beer, thing like that. And one night me walking past a Pocomania church and hear the people inside a wail. And me catch the vibration and say boy! Let's make a sound fe catch the vibration of them people! Them was in spirit and them tune me in spiritually. That's where the whole thing come from, 'cause them Poco people getting sweet.'[11]

Pukumina or 'Pocomania' church services retain some of the most powerful vestiges of African culture to survive the purges of colonialism in Jamaica. Through the dark centuries of slavery, in which Africans were stripped of their humanity to keep well-oiled the cogs of capitalism upon which the British Empire relied, African forms of cultural expression went underground. As in other parts of the Caribbean, slaves in Jamaica propagated African forms of religious worship through secret ceremonial societies. In the ceremonial rites of Pukumina, the faithful would be visited by ancestral spirits who would take possession of their bodies after a ritual involving music, singing, and dancing.

After slavery was abolished on the island in 1838, branches of the Baptist faith fused with Pukumina, resulting in the emergence of highly Africanised forms of Christianity after the Great Revival of 1860. Revival Zion churches began to practise forms of animal sacrifice, with ritualistic dancing, drumming, and singing becoming central tenets of their ceremonies. In these settings, Jamaican slave descendants were allowed to retain vital elements of their cultural identity in an oppressive social structure that had tried its best to erase all remnants of African culture.

Perry attended services at a variety of churches in his formative years, each with a strong African viewpoint, and his indoctrination at the Church of God in Little London had a particularly strong effect on him. 'As I was baptised by water,' Perry once remarked, 'I was staying close to the Church of God and the Holiness Church.'[12] Perry's experiences within these churches kept the practices of Africanised Christianity close to his heart, even if he had drifted away from the Church after settling in Kingston. He had been raised in an environment where spirit possession regularly occurred in Pentecostal or Revival Zion churches, and the midnight mass he stumbled upon with Lynford Anderson spoke to somewhere in the depths of his very soul. Perry stopped in his tracks and listened, taking in the message from the crescendo of emotive wailing emanating from the Pocomaniacs. He knew then that he had found the basis of the beat he had been searching for.

The following evening, Perry made his way down to WIRL a bit later than usual, hoping to find the musicians already warmed up and in a more receptive mood. He explained what he wanted to Gladdy, Jackie Jackson, Hux Brown and the rest of the crew, and then the tape was rolling. The vibe was right, the band was tight, and the session was getting well hot. Scratch was behind the mixing console while the rhythm was being laid, Clancy Eccles providing a guide vocal until the musicians got the music how Scratch wanted it. Once the rhythm track was down on tape, Perry went into the voicing booth and ripped through the vocal recording. In imitation of the Pukumina session he had witnessed the night before, he kept his voice gruff and unrestrained in the choruses.

The resultant sound was startling, the beat truly frenetic. It contained an unfettered urgency and frustrated clamour that went against the relaxed pace of the waning rock steady, but instead of hankering back to the American jazz influence of ska, this crazy, pounding beat went in another direction, with Scratch's re-interpretation of the midnight Pocomania revealing the transmogrified suffering of Africans transplanted to a hostile and alien environment.

Although the melody made a mockery of the Pioneers' 'Longshot' that Perry had helped craft for Gibbs, Gladdy's piano chords here had echoes of gospel, Hux's guitar spun in rapid bursts of aggressive energy, and Winston Wright's organ provided a peculiar melody line beneath Perry's angry snarl. Between the repeated refrains of 'Why, why, people funny bwoi', Perry's lyrics lashed out at Joe Gibbs, reminding him how Gibbs had turned his back on Perry after reaping rewards stemming from Perry's own creativity: now that Gibbs had his 'Jackpot' of hits from the Pioneers and other artists developed by Scratch, he was stuffing his belly full of rice and peas, the song proclaimed, while Perry and his family were starving. To further emphasise this point, Perry over-dubbed the famished bawling of his infant son through various portions of the song.

'The ideas about "People Funny" is one hundred percent of the human beings in this planet with flesh and blood are users. They only use people for their ideas and for their thoughts, for their gift and their talent and their blessing, so people are funny, extremely funny, extraordinary funny, wickedly funny.' [13]

For the disc's flip side, Perry used a version of Bob Dylan's 'Blowin' in the Wind' that he had previously recorded with Burt Walters, complete with mechanical wind-storm effects. 'That is a song anybody can love – a song that you must love,' said Perry of Dylan's original. 'From school days and dance days, I used to hear songs like those. Then the guy bring me the idea, he have a funny voice and want to make it, so we put it together.'

With these and other songs committed to tape, Anderson says that Perry was again hindered by a lack of funds. Anxious to get 'People Funny Boy' out on the street, Perry went to a distributor known as KG who would often advance money to small producers wishing to press potential hits: 'He didn't have any money to press or nothing, so he went to KG and told KG about it. Them print a thousand and put it out, the radio play it a couple of times, and they said "OK, print ten thousand." It became a big hit and them take it to England (where it appeared on Graeme Goodall's Doctor Bird label). KG press the record, and he sell it to KG at a price! It's a lot of money, they would make like twice the amount. It was pressed on blanks, there was no label. Ten thousand blanks! It was all illegal stuff they used to do those days. Nobody get paid, nobody registered nothing.' Perry later indicated that the song sold a staggering 60,000 copies on its initial release, allowing him to buy his first car: a model S Jaguar imported from England.

Gibbs attempted to counter the attack with 'People Grudgeful', mimicking the melody and reversing the lyrics of 'People Funny Boy', but the feeble mockery lacked originality and paled in comparison to Perry's creation. A further riposte came on 'Pan Ya Machete', in which Gibbs warned the Upsetter directly that 'Little sins can lead to big things', further berating Scratch with the sound of a whining puppy. Although Gibbs and Perry were publicly feuding, the animosity, as usual, would not prove to be permanent, and the bitter humour of such vinyl jousts ultimately emphasised that the Upsetter had indeed emerged as a force truly to be reckoned with.

In the history of Jamaican popular music, no sound had been created quite like that on 'People Funny Boy'. The Upsetter had truly arrived as an independent producer, and so had a new genre of Jamaican popular music.

Musicians and historians are still arguing over what was the first reggae record, and in some ways such ponderance is futile as different artists and producers seek to stake their claim as originators. For example, Alva Lewis claims it was his guitar sound that made a later hit called 'Bangarang' the first reggae record, while Gladdy Anderson says it was his organ shuffle on 'Everybody Bawling'. Bunny Lee agrees that 'Bangarang' was the first reggae song, but claims it was down to Glen Adams' organ riffs. According to Ernest Ranglin, Scratch and Clancy Eccles originated the style on an earlier collaborative session: 'We were the first people who did reggae music – Scratch and Clancy Eccles, they were the two producers and I was the arranger with a tune by Clancy named "Feel The Rhythm" and a next one by Monty Morris,

"Say What You're Saying".' Countless other songs have been suggested by an array of people involved in the music.

Whoever may have been first, Niney recounted an argument surrounding what the new music would be called after the recording of 'People Funny Boy' and 'Feel The Rhythm' in which Scratch expressed his direct opposition to the term reggae: 'Scratch was fighting us. He said "Hey man, I don't like the name reggae because reggae is thief and gun man," he fight it. Clancy Eccles is the only one who go with it. The first thing, they come with four names: Lynford Anderson come up with "chuck chuck," they come up with "peeling skin" and they come up with "streggae" because when they say "reggae" or "new beat", they wasn't going off of the good things, they were going off of the bad things. Just like some guys out there fire gun and you will say "Gun Hawk," well "chuck chuck" and "peeling skin", "reggae" and "streggae" is some careless girl that walk the streets. That was what they used to call the girl them before – like you see a girl out there and she acts a way, you say "Go away, you is peeling skin, you is chuck chuck," that means when you peel the food them, you're going to dash it away, like when you wash the rice, you're going to throw away the water. So it was nothing good, but in those days reggae wasn't in the dictionary.'

It is true that Larry Marshall's 'Nanny Goat' for Studio One had already signalled that rock steady was passé, but as with the beat of 'Feel The Rhythm,' the music of 'People Funny Boy' was far more extreme. This driving new beat that contained the pent-up energy of centuries of injustice and frustration may not yet have had a proper name, but already a dance step was springing up to the peculiar rhythm. In giving birth to 'People Funny Boy', the Upsetter had fully inaugurated a different beat, and from this beat would come the music that would eventually be known as reggae, regardless of the fact that Scratch himself would never be happy with the term.

THE RETURN OF DJANGO:
international success

After the tremendous success of 'People Funny Boy', Scratch had far more ready cash at his disposal, and finding appropriate housing for his family was top priority. They briefly occupied a rented space off the upper end of Molynes Road, edging away from the city towards the quieter suburban areas on the Northwest outskirts of Kingston; they then rented a home at 2 Canewood Crescent in the suburb of Washington Gardens, just off the main thoroughfare of Weymouth Drive.

Shortly after moving into the neighbourhood, Perry acquired a large property with a small yard around the corner at 5 Cardiff Crescent, a comfortable three bedroom house more suitable for his expanding family. While the area was hardly considered upmarket, it was certainly removed from the extreme harshness of the downtown residences, and allowed Perry and his family to retain a bit of breathing space; being a home owner also gave Scratch a new-found sense of security.

He began holding regular recording sessions at WIRL several days a week, recording many different songs at each session. Working late into the night, the perfectionist Perry would record repeated takes of each song, until the musicians played the music exactly as he pictured it. Despite his inability to read music, Scratch always knew exactly what he wanted, and retained a dictatorial demeanour when at work.

For the rest of 1968 and the early months of 1969, Perry's recorded output began to increase. He was still sharing many of his sessions with Clancy Eccles, whose own productions were steadily gaining the favour of Jamaica's music fans, and began sharing sessions with Striker Lee more regularly; Niney was also often present when he worked. Scratch was still typically utilising the talents of the loosely structured All Stars, who recorded for Perry as the Upsetters, occasionally being named the Upsetter All Stars on some discs. But Perry was not the first to name his band the Upsetters: the original group was a set of New Orleans session musicians active in the 1950s. The first Jamaican Upsetters was a live band led by Roland Alphonso, who gave a notable performance in the Papine district of East Kingston during the independence celebrations of 1962. Active shortly after was a vocal group called Ossie and the Upsetters who recorded songs like 'Turn Me On' and 'True Love' for Coxsone in 1964 and 'Si Senor,' 'Country Girl' and 'Strange Country' for Leslie Kong in 1965; the group has also been named on some releases as the Checkmates.

'I remember when that group was recording for Cocksone,' Perry clarified. 'I was there, but had no involvement with them.'

By the end of 1968 Scratch had designed a proper label for his Upsetter releases, most of which had previously been issued on blanks. Like the early Upset label, the original illustration had machetes, scorpions, and drops of blood flanking a red Upsetter logo – symbols that again suggested the magic arts of Obeah. As Perry once noted, it was his former employers and other propagators of social injustice that Scratch now sought to upset:

> 'That was the same vibration about the treatment of Coxsone and the rest of them that I did form this Upsetter label. I determined, say "If they take my good deed and good favour and handle it like that, what I have to do is form a shield to protect myself", so I call upon that shield Upsetter. I really decide was to upset him, and I really upset him, it was no joke.' [1]

Another time, he remarked that the label was designed specifically to upset wrongdoers:

> 'The Upsetter label don't come to upset the dance people, because the dance people are here to dance and to chant down Babylon. The Upsetter label really come to upset the heads of government, the council of churches, the politicians and the gun men, the gun boys and all the evil forces. Upsetter records come to upset the seven devils and all the demons of age, all evil corrupted soul and corrupted spirit. The Upsetter no come to fight against flesh and blood.' [2]

For the rest of 1968, Perry recorded original material with established artists and rising talent, experimenting with multiple uses of the same rhythm in the process. The Mellotones provided a few other strong songs for Perry late in the year, including the amusing 'Uncle Charley', in which the named uncle was accused of turning 'a wine head', emerging as the 'king of the bottle' through repeated bouts of drunkenness. The song employed a bold Upsetter arrangement, with Perry and the group making retching noises of alcoholic excess over a bouncing rhythm punctuated by a tin whistle. Perry used the same rhythm for another take by the group on 'Uncle Desmond', in which the accused refutes the insalubrious claims, again with much coughing and spluttering included in the mix. The Ethiopians, then a duo composed of Leonard Dillon and Stephen Taylor, recorded 'Cut Down (On Your Speed)' and 'Not Me' for Perry that year, creating two unrelated songs on the same chugging rhythm.

Between the spring and summer of 1968, Scratch began working with a teenage singer from Port Antonio named Derrick Burnett. Although their initial collaboration produced little material, Burnett would later become a close friend who performed a variety of functions for Perry. The eldest of nine children, Burnett learned to sing in the Baptist church his family attended in Port Antonio. One of his closest friends was Murvin Smith Jr, another young singer from the same area who would begin to record in the early '70s as Junior Soul; Smith gave Burnett the nickname Watty when he was eight years old due to the effect a prominent stutter had on his speech.

By 1968, Burnett had formed a duo with his friend Jimmy Nelson, alternately called Derrick and Jimmy and the Soul Twins. They began travelling to Kingston every Sunday to try to get recorded, but did not find much initial success. Although the other producers rejected them, Burnett said Scratch was willing to give the group a try on hearing a song they had written called 'Pound Get A Blow', a commentary on changes brought to Jamaica's currency: 'I went to Duke Reid and he said "You're too young, come back in five years." I was so scared of Duke because he's a man who have gun with him . . . Scratch came down there and I asked him if I could come for an audition so he gave me one. When Scratch first heard the idea, "Look here now, pound get a blow, Canada and America trying to capture Jamaica, they gave us dollars and cents to replace pound paper," Scratch say "Wow, it's a great idea," so we started from there.'

Burnett noted that the rhythm was laid at West Indies and voiced later at Treasure Isle. 'When I went to do the vocal I was so nervous that I couldn't do it. Toots from the Maytals come and said "Scratch, he is nervous, he will do it," came in the studio, and hugged me and I did the song.' Though the tune did not fare well when issued abroad (where it was miscredited to the Bleechers), 'Pound Get A Blow' was fairly successful in Jamaica, where it placed at the annual Festival Song Competition held to commemorate Jamaica's independence. 'We did it for the Festival thing and we came third in the island in Festival '68, that was the Festival that Desmond Dekker won.' Scratch later used the same rhythm for a saxophone cut by Roland Alphonso called 'Roll On'.

A trio of songs co-written and recorded by Perry in 1968 indicated the problems and uncertainties prevalent in his mind despite the success of 'People Funny Boy': 'What a Botheration' by the Mellotones spoke of hard times and no money, with the protagonist forced to play the lottery as a desperate last resort. On a different Perry vocal, also called 'What a Botheration,' he sang of greeting the approaching Christmas season with torn pants and empty pockets over a sprightly keyboard melody from Gladdy; his car battery was dead, so he could not try his luck at the races and the lottery was out of the question. The hauntingly beautiful 'What A Situation' (a.k.a. 'Give Me'), voiced by Slim Smith at a session arranged by Scratch and Bunny Lee, spoke of the terrible confusion brought on by the suffering of ghetto life and its resultant domestic and romantic failures.

Other resentful numbers followed, adapted from earlier concepts that continued to be of relevance in his life. For example, 'You Crummy' took another stab at a former partner that Perry momentarily held a grudge against – in this case, Clancy Eccles; the song was cut at another session co-arranged by

Bunny 'Striker' Lee. 'Look how we used to be very good pals,' Perry lamented wryly in the lyrics, 'we even share the same gal. When you were down and out, I help you out, but now that you reach the top, you push up your mouth. Boy you really crummy fe true . . . '

Eccles responded in kind with 'Don't Brag Don't Boast,' questioning Perry's rhythmic authority and turning his accusations against him. Another take on the same theme was 'People Funny Fi True', a Perry vocal expressing similar sentiments to those of 'You Crummy' and 'People Funny Boy'.

In a more experimental vein, Perry got saxophonist Val Bennett to sing two songs, a cover of the blues standard 'Baby Baby' and a jumpy tune called 'Barbara', the only known examples of Bennett as a vocalist. Scratch was also experimenting with deejays when it was not yet fashionable to record them, beginning with Sir Lord Comic on 'Django Shoots First' (a.k.a. 'Bronco'), a record notable on several levels. The title and theme of the song came from one of a series of *Django* films made by Sergio Corbucci, surreal and violent epic tales of underdogs in the days of the Wild West that Scratch and his peers were greatly inspired by. A complex and playful creation, the organ melody line of 'Django Shoots First' was based on 'Old Man River', the theme of a Broadway musical written by Jerome Kern in 1927, while the bass line seems adapted from 'One Step Beyond', a Jackie Mittoo instrumental for Studio One; Comic's slow drawl and voiced imitation of gunshots turned the rhythm into an emulation of Django's cinematic exploits. Sir Lord Comic was one of the first deejays to make it to vinyl with the recording of 'Ska-ing West' in 1967, and this follow-up for Perry indicates the forward-thinking approach Scratch applied to his music, taking risks that kept him ahead of his competitors through the exploration of daring new concepts in recorded sound.

Perry's most successful production after 'People Funny Boy' came from the Inspirations, a duo composed of Trevor Shaw and Ransford White. Shaw was born in Redwoods, St Catherine on November 30, 1949 and was re-united with his mother in Western Kingston at age 16. In later years, Shaw would achieve fame as Jimmy London. Ransford White was of part-Indian parentage, and his brother Doraney was in the Techniques; he would later be known as Billy Dyce. The Inspirations often hung out in the Techniques' rehearsal premises on King Street, and the duo became friendly with Roy Shirley, who helped them find their way in the music business. Their debut was 'I Need Money', recorded for Sir JJ at Linden Pottinger's small studio off Molynes Road. When the tune failed to make much impact, the group decided to work with Lee Perry, initially recording 'Tighten Up' at WIRL, but re-voicing it at Studio One. 'You Know What I Mean' was another song the group recorded for Perry at this time. Despite the success of 'Tighten Up', the group felt Perry was not giving them much attention, so they moved on to work with Joe Gibbs shortly after.

Another big hit came just after 'Tighten Up' in an emotional rendition of

Stevie Wonder's 'A Place In The Sun' by a young singer from Denham Town named David Isaacs. Born on June 9, 1946, Isaacs began his career singing at a talent contest held by Clancy Eccles at the Palace Theatre. In the mid-'60s he became a record salesman for Studio One and made his recording debut with the hit 'I'd Rather Be Lonely' for Ronnie Nasrallah. Greatly inspired by the Dells, Curtis Mayfield and Jackie Wilson, Isaacs became a singer in the Comets towards the end of the rock steady period which ultimately lead to the recording of 'A Place In The Sun'. As Isaacs recalled, 'I said to Lynn Taitt one time, "I would like to cover back this tune because it is a favourite of mine." He said that I would have to check a producer, so I came down Orange Street one evening and I went to Clancy Eccles with it. Clancy Eccles was doing tailoring that time, he said to me he liked the song but why don't I try and give Upsetter it? The two of them had a shop side by side, Upsetter on Charles Street and Luke Lane corner, and Clancy on Orange Street corner. I went to Upsetter with it and right away, he took me in Coxsone's studio. I can remember that the intro, it was this guy that used to play with Fabulous Five, a keyboardist that they use (Grub Cooper). Scratch used him on the session and right away, it was a hit. It did well in London and Harry Palmer came down and offered me a contract, but I couldn't go to London at that time. Because I was new in the business, I didn't really want to take the gamble. I wanted to be more mature so I stick with Upsetter and keep recording with him.'

Clancy Eccles noted that it was Scratch's relentless determination to get things right that resulted in the strength of 'A Place In The Sun'. 'I was running a session by West Indies Records, and Scratch was there with me and didn't have any hit record. At the end of the day Scratch said to me, "Boy, David Isaac's tune sound good," so I said, "Hear now what happen: you deal with that song." He took the song from me and he went to Coxsone and did the voice over, and it took him a very long time to get the voice the way he wanted. He turned it into a very good song, he actually got better than what I probably would have gotten out of that record, 'cause I probably wouldn't have put so much time. I believe it took around 16 hours to really do it, he went there around three days 'til he got it right.'

In 1968, reggae was getting hot in England, and after 'People Funny Boy' proved to be a big hit, the top reggae labels established regular licensing arrangements with the Upsetter. The two top groups of companies issuing Jamaican records in England at this time were Trojan and Pama, with Trojan being the more firmly established of the two. The Trojan label was originally founded in July 1967 by Chris Blackwell, who had steadily become the most important promoter of Jamaican music in Britain since moving his base of operations to London in 1962. A complement to the UK branch of the Treasure Isle label, Trojan was originally established to issue Duke Reid material in the UK. Lee Gopthal, a Jamaican of Indian descent, was an accountant who was also the landlord of Blackwell's business premises; he began playing an important role in the music business through the establishment of the Beat and Commercial distribution company, which handled Jamaican and American material. He and Blackwell formed a partnership in 1968, and Gopthal began to take charge of Trojan while Blackwell was out in the field, pursuing various licensing arrangements with American soul producers and British rock acts as well as Jamaican reggae producers and artists.

The Pama label was established by three black Jamaicans in 1967 as competition to Blackwell's group of labels. Like Gopthal, much of their financial backing was supported by the rental of property owned in Northwest London. Harry Palmer was initially the main man in charge of licensing material, with his brother Carl, an accountant, taking care of the books; another brother, Jeffrey, founded the London Apollo Club, a showcase venue for black talent in nearby Willesden. Unity, Crab, NuBeat, and Gas were all established as subsidiary labels in 1968, with Punch being added to the group in 1969.

When 'Tighten Up' was issued in the UK on Trojan (credited on release to the Untouchables), it proved to be just as successful as 'People Funny Boy', particularly with the white working-class skinheads who were emulating Jamaican popular culture through dance steps, bravado, and sharp dress. The hit spawned a series of cut-price *Tighten Up* compilation albums on Trojan, grab-bags of varying quality that were sold for around 15 shillings. The first volume of *Tighten Up*, released in 1968, contained three of Perry's most popular productions: the hit title track, David Isaacs' 'A Place In The Sun', and Val Bennett's 'Spanish Harlem', bringing the early Upsetter sound to the forefront of the reggae scene in England.

As Perry's fame grew, so did his immediate family. On December 30, 1968, Pauline gave birth to a second son whom the couple named Mark Anthony but who became known as Omar after the viewing of a film starring Omar Sharif. It was only after Omar's birth that Perry made the legal arrangements to file for divorce from Ruby Williams, who did not contest the action; though Scratch would subsequently be free to re-marry, a series of complicated circumstances would ultimately see him avoiding matrimony, and he and Pauline were thus never officially wed.

As with the birth of his older brother, Omar's arrival was heralded as a fortuitous event, and marked the start of what was to be a momentous year. Indeed, the positive changes experienced in 1968 would seem somewhat insignificant in comparison to the advances achieved by the Upsetter in 1969. It was to be the first of many prolific years for Perry, in which he would unleash a startling amount of new material, now that he had a greater capability to let out the many ideas that had been crowding up inside him for years.

In the early part of the year, Perry remained chiefly at WIRL, which had been re-named Dynamic Sound after its pressing plant had been destroyed by a mysterious fire in late 1968 – which some say was started deliberately. West Indies had been affiliated to WIRL Barbados, and the new name partly served to sever links between the two companies, but also to draw emphasis to the new eight track studio constructed at 15 Bell Road by Byron Lee.

Scratch also began using Randy's, a newer studio run by the Chin family at 17 North Parade, upstairs from their large record shop and distribution premises. Vincent Chin had entered the music industry as a jukebox distributor in the late 1950s and later opened the small Randy's record shop on East Street, stocked with discs from jukeboxes that had been taken out of action. By the time he and Patricia Chin moved Randy's to a larger shop on Parade in 1962, he was already a formidable record producer through product issued on his Randy's label. Once their studio was up and running, Vince arranged for his brother Victor to begin issuing their material on a New York branch of Randy's from his small electronics shop on Schenectady Avenue in Brooklyn, with other material issued on Keith's by Keith Chin, another brother who had emigrated to Brooklyn. Much of the product Perry recorded at Randy's would find its way to New York on their labels, the first of several tenuous links with record companies based in America.

The establishment of the Upsetter Record Shop at 36 Charles Street provided Perry with a previously lacking solidity for his business enterprises and a badly needed base for his musical endeavours; the premises had previously been occupied by Prince Buster and Derrick Morgan.

When Perry's cousin Archie injured his hand while working at a shoe-making factory, Perry informally hired him to assist with the running of the shop. Archie was eventually joined by Delroy Phillips, a downtown bad boy known as Jubie who had previously been in a gang run by a roughneck called Schoolboy. When Schoolboy moved his activities to Spanish Town, Jubie began to turn away from badness through seeking guidance from Scratch.

As the record shop became more successful, Perry opened an audition room in the back, and groups began to congregate there to display their talent and grab the ear of the wiry producer. The Green Door Saloon was later attached to the shop, where ranking ghetto toughs like Claudie Massop would while away the hours drinking beer; a herbman named Dizzy who sold weed and 'ital' meals from a shack that backed onto the shop made sure that food and spliff were always available for customers.

As the reputation of the Upsetter record shop grew more widespread, prominent industry personnel began to frequent it. Harry Palmer was to make his presence known there, and a number of sound system operators would often call in for hot material. The soundman who came most often was also one of the most prominent: Merritone's Winston Blake made frequent appearances, and played a direct role in establishing the Upsetter's popularity by giving his material exposure at the Copacabana club in East Kingston, and later at a venue Blake ran called Peyton Place in the posh Jack's Hill district.

The closeness of Perry's shop to 'Beat Street' meant that he was in constant contact with other producers, and such closeness led to some working relationships developing into lasting friendships. One such contact established in this time was with Rupie Edwards, an independent producer and vocalist who ran the Success record shop on Orange Street.

Born on July 4, 1945 in the town of Goshen, St Anne, Edwards was raised in Edward's Peace, St Catherine from the age of three months. An only child, his father worked on plantations as a driver, while his mother eventually landed a job as a government receptionist in Kingston. When Edwards reached age 13, he joined her in town and made his performing debut covering a Pat Boone song in a Vere Johns contest at the Majestic Theatre in East Kingston. After training as a mechanic, he began working with Bunny Lee at United Motors, but was also playing piano at the Kittymat Club, a night spot run by Horace Forbes on a rough section of Maxfield Avenue near Spanish Town Road. He started his recording career in 1961 with 'Guilty Convict' for the Hi-Light label, and sporadically recorded specials for Bells sound system. Edwards then formed the Ambassadors with Junior Menz, cutting 'Amen' and 'Mother's Choice' for Harry J, before venturing into self-production in 1966. It was through their mutual friend Bunny Lee that Edwards and Perry came to know each other better, and the friendship shared by Edwards' long-term girlfriend and Pauline Morrison would see Rupie and Scratch furthering their camaraderie.

The popularity of *Tighten Up* indicated that Lee Perry's productions would continue to be in demand, so Trojan arranged for him to make the first of many trips to London in 1969 to establish the UK branch of his Upsetter label. They began issuing a high volume of singles on Upsetter in March 1969 and scheduled a debut album called *The Upsetter* for a summer issue on Trojan, though circumstances would see its official release delayed until early November. Pama records also began issuing a large amount of Perry-produced singles at this time, though most of the hit-bound material was placed in Trojan's hands.

The cover of *The Upsetter* showed a dapper Perry, resplendent in a green velveteen jacket, flanked by two attractive young women in a forest. Of the twelve tracks compiled on the LP, nine were organ instrumentals, which was quickly becoming Perry's new passion. He was working with a variety of groups and solo artists in 1969, but he began to find a greater fulfilment in creating instrumental music, particularly songs where an organ would take the lead. Perry used the instrumental as a way of providing an aural accompaniment for the visions in his head – visions that were then influenced largely by spaghetti westerns, spy films and monster movies, as can be seen in the titles 'Man From MI5', 'Wolfman', and 'Thunderball'.

The vocal tracks on the album were all cover versions of American songs. Busty Brown provided two, while the third was credited to the Muskyteers. Brown, also known as BB James but born Clive Smith, was a baritone singer who began his career as a dancer on the North Coast with the Bow Tie Brothers. He joined the Crepe Souls as a singer in the early '60s, recorded for Llans Thewell and the Celestials by 1966 and Clancy Eccles in 1968. On *The*

Upsetter album, his version of the Bee Gees' 'To Love Somebody' infused the song with an honest urgency somewhat lacking on the original, while the slow blues of 'Crying About You' kept up the emotion contained on the American version. The Muskyteers – better known in Jamaica as the Silvertones – was a trio led by the husky baritone of Delroy Denton that had recorded extensively for Duke Reid and Coxsone Dodd earlier in the decade. On *The Upsetter*, their version of Brook Benton's 'Kiddy-O' retained shades of the original's country-and-western flavour.

Many of the instrumentals on the album were Upsetter mutations of American hits, most of which used rhythm tracks that had previously been voiced. Thus, 'Tidal Wave' used an organ to recreate the tear-jerking melody of 'He'll Have To Go', 'Soulful I' was Winston Wright's particularly skilful organ take of 'Since You Are Gone', and 'Heat Proof' was an unvoiced recreation of Otis Redding's 'Too Hot To Handle'.

Several other groups and solo singers recorded sparse material with Perry in the spring and summer of 1969. The established artists he recorded included Eric 'Monty' Morris with 'Can't Get No Peace'; Ernest Wilson of the Clarendonians with 'Another Chance' and 'Freedom Train' (issued in true stereo with vocals in the right channel and rhythm in the left), joined by his former partner Freddy McGregor for 'Just Once In My Life'; and the Termites, a duo based in Waterhouse composed of Lloyd Parks and Wentworth Vernal, with an odd number set in Paris called 'I'll Be Waiting'.

Perry was also working with less-established talent in this time, including the West Indians vocal trio. Composed of Eric Donaldson, Hector Brooks, and Leslie Burke, the West Indians had worked briefly for Sir JJ and Lloyd Daley, and it was the staggering falsetto of Eric Donaldson that made the group stand out. Despite the strength of songs like 'Oh Lord', 'Dirty Dozen', 'Never Get Away' (a.k.a. 'Caught You Red Handed') and the broken-hearted 'Strange Whispering', the material they recorded with Perry that year did not prove as successful as their work for Sir JJ and the group disbanded shortly after when a member migrated to Canada.

Scratch issued a couple of notable songs by the Righteous Flames in this period, though neither was a hit. Sometimes a duo, sometimes a trio, and sometimes just one man alone, the Righteous Flames was founded by Winston Jarrett, a singer who favoured spiritual material. Born in Lime Tree Gardens, St Anne, on September 14, 1940, Jarrett's father was a deacon in the Church of God. Jarrett moved to Jones Town in his childhood, and formed the Flames in the early '60s with Eggo 'Baby G' Gordon to back Alton Ellis after his singing partner Eddie Perkins emigrated to America, but when Ellis toured the UK with the Soul Brothers towards the end of the decade, Jarrett recorded solo for Coxsone and Buster before moving on to work with Scratch.

An early and somewhat uncharacteristic Righteous Flames number recorded for Perry was 'Mini Dress', which Jarrett voiced alone. He also recalled recording a song 'Water the Garden' around the same time, but it may not have been issued. Perhaps the most notable was 'Zion I Love You', a somewhat later track featuring the lead vocals of Jarrett's roommate, another young singer from Trench Town named Danny Clarke; the religious spirit of the tune was emphasised by a church organ line from Winston Wright. According to Jarrett, receiving payment from Scratch could sometimes be problematic, so he left Perry's stable to begin his own productions: 'When I did "Mini Dress" for Scratch, he didn't want to pay me no money. Thirty pounds in cheque, I have a hard time to get it changed . . . some time it bounce.'

The Bleechers was another rising trio that Perry helped build up in 1969. The group was led by Leo Graham, a young man with a distinctly high and thin voice, with harmony provided by Wesley Martin and his friend Sammy, the latter a former member of the Mellotones. Born in the district of Johut, Trelawny on December 15, 1941, Leo Graham was the second of ten children born to a family of farmers. At the age of 22, Graham moved to Kingston to stay with his aunt at 27 Upper Regent Street. In the rock steady era he was a member of the Overtakers, recording 'That's the Way You Like It', 'Girl You Ruff', and 'The Big Takeover' for Joe Gibbs.

The Bleechers took their name in reference to ravers who stay up all night seeking action – a practice in Jamaica known as 'bleeching'. Upon their formation in 1969, the group recorded a handful of songs for Lee Perry, the most entertaining of which was 'Check Him Out', which advertised the sweet music to be found at the Upsetter record shop. Leo Graham noted that he wrote the song unprompted after being inspired by Perry's productions: 'I just decide to advertise it, bring it to him and him like it.' Other numbers recorded for Perry include 'Farmer in the Den', 'Everything for Fun', and 'Ram You Hard', a rude number oddly credited abroad to John Lennon and the Bleechers; 'Ease Up' and 'You're Gonna Feel It' were recorded at Dynamics and credited as Byron Lee productions, but were in fact the work of Lee Perry.

Perry's other notable 1969 productions included work with Pat Satchmo, Jamaica's answer to Louis Armstrong; his versions of 'Hello Dolly' and 'Boss Society' re-cast the tunes in a particularly Jamaican mode. Another Jamaicanised cover version of an American pop standard came from David Isaacs with Jim Reeves' 'He'll Have To Go', while 'Since You Are Gone' was an original ballad. Pat Kelly provided more love songs with a cover of James Carr's soul smash 'Dark End Of The Street' and 'Give Love A Try' (which was an alternative take of 'Since You Are Gone' with different but related lyrics); another Pat Kelly number, 'How Long Will It Take', was a huge hit in Jamaica and the UK that was credited as a Bunny Lee production but which Scratch was keen to point out was recorded by him after Bunny Lee left the studio on another co-managed session.

The most moving Busty Brown composition of 1969 was 'King Of The Trombone', which lamented the terrible death of Don Drummond in a

Kingston psychiatric ward. Later in the year Perry did a one-off with the Gaylads, whose song 'If You Don't Mind' contained a serious message beneath its tight pop harmonies. 'In those days, people used to look down on the dreadlocks,' BiBi Seaton explained. 'I'm just trying to say to them "Don't watch the clothes and the hair". As long as you're clean and your heart is clean, everything is cool.'

On the instrumental front, Scratch began more serious experimentation, exploring diverse influences and styles with a variety of different musicians. In addition to Winston Grennan and Hugh Malcolm, he began using a young drummer from the rough downtown area near Oxford Street named Lloyd Adams – better known as 'Tin Legs'.

One of the many drummers who was tutored by Winston Grennan, Tin Legs' style was characterised by furiously fraught drum rolls that often arrived off-beat, adding a dynamism to what could be otherwise straightforward rhythms. According to Grennan, Tin Legs' first recording session was a disaster. 'I couldn't make the session so I send Tin Legs. I sat down Tin Legs and trained for about a week to go do the session, because I know who Duke Reid is and I know what he like. I said "Duke like this sound, this is what you have to do for him." When he get inside . . . he couldn't hold the beat so Duke get mad, bust two shots under his legs and the drum stool and scare him. The guy get nervous, piss up himself, and try to look for a way to run out of the studio. When Duke come back and asking where is the drummer, the engineer say he saw him running in the street like a mad shark.'

Despite this initial failure, Tin Legs soon became one of the most sought-after drummers on the island, and Perry would put his extreme expressions to good use on many a tune, the first of which was 'Drugs and Poison' in 1969.

The other young drummer Perry began working with from early 1969 was Paul Douglas. Born and raised in Ocho Rios, Douglas also came from a musical family. His uncle Clarence was a drummer and his cousins Trevor and Rigley performed cabaret as the Douglas Brothers. Paul's father Edwin was a percussionist who learned many different beats while stationed in Latin American locales in the army, and Paul began by learning various Latin and free-form jazz beats from him. As the Douglas family was active on the North Coast entertainment scene, his parents were close to Tommy McCook, who arranged for Paul to audition at Treasure Isle in early 1969. One of the earliest hits he played on was Phyllis Dillon's 'Moonlight Lover', but Douglas was only coming into town on weekends at this stage. By the time the All Stars were backing up the Wailers for sessions that would create Leslie Kong's *Best Of The Wailers* album, Douglas was one of their most regular drummers and was playing often for producers like Clancy Eccles, Lee Perry, and Byron Lee.

Perry also began to vary his choice of keyboardist. He had been relying mainly on the organ talents of Winston Wright of the All Stars, along with Gladdy or Theo Beckford on piano, but was soon working with younger, less established players. One of his most successful keyboard instrumentals was 'Night Doctor', a hit included on *The Upsetter* album, but Scratch himself was not responsible for the recording or creation of this song. The funky organ riffs of Ansel Collins are what made 'Night Doctor' special, and it was Collins who not only wrote and arranged the song, but organised and supervised its recording independently a full year before he licensed it to Scratch.

Born on April 16, 1948, Collins was the son of a barber who grew up around the notoriously harsh ghetto area of Maxfield Avenue in Kingston 11. The oldest of nine children, Collins was encouraged by his mother to become a performer, and made his debut in 1960 at Vere Johns' Opportunity Hour at the Carib Theatre, singing 'A Star Is Born' with Sonny Bradshaw's group. He then formed an unsuccessful duo with a girl named Patsy Clark, and later became a vocalist with Bobby Aitken's Caribbeats, voicing 'I Tried' with the group for Coxsone Dodd in the rock steady period. He was also the group's featured vocalist on a stage show called *Baldhead Rooster* with Bim and Bam.

Rehearsing at 26 Galoway Road with the Caribbeats, Collins was taught to play drums by Winston Grennan, eventually providing the beat on songs like Delroy Wilson's 'This Heart Of Mine'. Hanging around the yard during the day with little to occupy him, Collins was encouraged by Bobby Aitken to practise the piano, and began to play keyboards on Bunny Lee's recordings, beginning with the session that produced Slim Smith's 'The Beatitude'.

Towards the start of 1968, Collins became leader of the RHT Invincibles, a band formed by a Rastafarian bakery owner who had an uncanny resemblance to Selassie; known as Father Good'un, he ran the Rainbow Healing Temple on Spanish Town Road. Collins arranged for the band to record a session at Federal studio which produced four songs, of which the outstanding number proved to be the instrumental 'Night Doctor', with Collins making full use of the studio's Hammond Baldwin organ, complete with swirling Leslie effects unit. The other three songs were vocal tunes: one was voiced by Lloyd Parks, who was then occasionally guitarist for the group (along with another player called Scotty), another by Bertram 'Ranchie' MacLean, the group's rhythm guitarist, while a third song called 'Diplomat' was voiced by an aspiring young drummer named Lowell Charles Dunbar who had recently joined the group; then known as Charlie, he would later be more commonly known as Sly due to his love of the music of American funk band Sly and the Family Stone.

The youngest of three children born to a pair of airport employees, Dunbar was born in Kingston on May 10, 1952. He spent his infancy in the Windward Road area, moving to Waterhouse at the age of six. It was while attending Trench Town Comprehensive School that he became infatuated with music after seeing a school performance by Ken Boothe and the Gaylads; he then began carefully noting the techniques of session drummers, seeking advice from upcoming sticksmen such as Carly Barrett, Mikey 'Boo' Richards and 'a guy by the name of Duckie', as well as established veteran Winston Grennan.

By the age of 17 he had formed the Yardbrooms with some neighbour-hood friends, but only managed one performance with the group at the Teen and Twenties Club off Waltham Park Road before it faded away. Shortly after this debut gig, Dunbar attended a rehearsal of the RHT Invincibles, and sat in with the band after their regular drummer Lloyd 'Tin Legs' Adams went home early. Impressed by his playing, Ansel Collins brought him to Federal for the four-song session. Though Dunbar's vocal performance may have left some-thing to be desired, he could keep the beat like a metronome; his drumming gave 'Night Doctor' a solid backing, and Collins had him replace Tin Legs .

Hampered by a lack of available funds, Collins began to sell the vocal songs to other producers, including Coxsone Dodd. Collins noted that after hearing of the successes Scratch was having with instrumental tunes, he eventually brought a dub plate of 'Night Doctor' to the Upsetter Record Shop some time after committing it to tape. 'I know Scratch a long time, from Coxsone days. In those days, I could only record and wait for somebody else to do the releasing for me. It easy to find studio time, but to release songs, you have to have money. I do "Night Doctor" and I have it there for one year. I gave it to Scratch on dub plate and someone stole it away. Then he found it back and he checked me and said that he wanted the song. I give him the song and he release it and give me a money. I give him the tape, and it went in the British chart, sell like hot bread. After a while he give me some more money. He's the best one out of all of them for me (financially) . . . he remember me.'

Once Scratch had his hands on the master tape, he created an alternative saxophone take of the song called 'Thunderball', which was also included on *The Upsetter* LP. Collins was also featured on 'Man From MI5', another spooky organ instrumental that was fairly successful in the UK and Jamaica.

Perry followed up 'Night Doctor' with 'A Live Injection', a song that was to make a strong impact on the British charts towards the year's end . Using the rhythm of 'Babam Bam' by the Ravers, Winston Wright let loose on the organ, churning out furious scales and rapid chord bursts from the full length of the keyboard. The final instalment of the theme came in 'Medical Operation'. Based loosely on the Meters' 'Sophisticated Sissy', 'Medical Operation' was the first recording Perry made with the Hippy Boys, a group that would play an increasingly important role in Scratch's creations for the rest of 1969 and into the early '70s. Though he still considered the All Stars to be the Upsetters, the Hippy Boys would gradually fill their shoes on a more regular basis.

The Hippy Boys had a complicated history of which much has been written that is questionable. The group's lead vocalist was Max Romeo, who had known Lee Perry for a long time. 'I knew Scratch from when he was at Downbeat. He produced most of Studio One's stuff: all these old Wailers, Gaylads, Alton Ellis, Ken Boothe, Scratch was the producer actually, because most of the time these sessions (were) happening, Downbeat is on the road, taking care of business, so he was there vibesing and doing all these things.'

Born Maxie Smith on November 22, 1944, near Alexandria in St Ann, Max came to Kingston aged ten to live with his father after his mother emigrated to England. He said he 'became like a renegade child' when he found he couldn't get along with his stepmother, and was raised 'partly among strangers' after running away from home. After coming across Mr Denham – a wise elder who encouraged him to follow his heart and try to make it as a singer – Maxie was one of many talented but hungry youths who hung around Studio One trying unsuccessfully to be recorded. By 1966, Max was working for Ken Lack's Caltone label as a salesman and errand runner, and began recording for the label as leader of the Emotions, a group he had formed with two friends, Kenneth Knight and Lloyd Shakespeare. Their debut, 'Rainbow', reached number two on both Jamaican radio charts, but Max eventually left the group due to bickering about who was to lead it. He then began selecting records for a small sound system that used to play in Longstone Road in the ghetto known as Dunkirk in East Kingston, and stayed close to his friend Bunny Lee, who was rapidly rising as a popular producer active on the Kingston music circuit. According to Romeo, it was Lee who eventually gave Max his stage name. 'How that name came about, I was standing at this guy's gate, talking to his daughter one morning. I was there from about eight o'clock in the morning talking to her. I stand in a particular pose, and this guy push his bicycle up the road to work. Well, shortly after he left, I leave, but I came back, standing in the same spot with the same pose (in the evening); he came from work, about to go in, and he look and me, and say, "Wait! Same spot, same pose? You must be Romeo!" So all the guys start laughing, they just start calling me Romeo. Bunny Lee catch onto the name and say "Why not call yourself Max Romeo?" '

Max Romeo, Bibi Seaton and others believe the origins of the Hippy Boys can be traced back to one of the periodic break-ups of the Gaylads around 1967. As Seaton recalls: 'Mrs Pottinger split up the group. She wanted Delano to sing and to control him . . . Delano Stewart used to be in the Hippy Boys, and Maurice (Roberts) used to play with them sometimes too. Max Romeo used to hang out on our corner, every singer used to hang out on our corner, because we had a band, and people could rehearse and the band was good.'

Max Romeo added the following particulars: 'The Hippy Boys begins after the Gaylads band broke up. I had the bass player and the drummer with me, which was Maurice and Sean. This guy named Webbie, Web Stewart (former guitarist with Bibi Seaton and the Astronauts, who built his own guitars) was the lead guitar for the band then.' The group was active on the live scene and began to attract a large following, including two penniless brothers who were hoping to become professional musicians: Aston and Carlton Barrett.

Aston Francis Barrett and Carlton Lloyd Barrett grew up in the heart of downtown Kingston with their parents and older sister in conditions that were circumscribed by poverty. Born on November 22, 1946 at 26 Beeston Street, Aston grew in the same yard where saxophonist Val Bennett lived; members of the Skatalites often congregated there to rehearse. Aston became known as Family Man because of the several children he had spawned with different women by the end of his teen years; like Roland Alphonso, he went to St Aloysius School. He grew unruly in adolescence and was sent for a year and a half to the Cobbla camp in Manchester, run by the Jamaica Youth Corps; while at the camp, he tried his hand at the piano and sang in a five-part harmony group called the Jiving Crackerballs. 'My first approach was singing, but I have a voice like a frog!' laughed Fams at the memory. 'I sing bass, so I said maybe I should play it on the strings.' Upon returning to Kingston, he worked at Sampson's Metal Shop and Chin's Welding Works, where he was joined by his brother Carlton, who was two years his junior.

The Barrett brothers had long been inspired by music – the Wailers' 'Simmer Down' having had a particularly strong effect on Family Man – but the Barretts had no available money for instruments or tuition, so the pair facilitated their own learning by hanging around the studios and nightclubs near their downtown home. Carly fashioned some drums out of paint tins and disused pots, while Fams made a plywood bass in the woodwork shop at Chin's. 'My real first bass, I built it myself. It was a one string, I use a curtain rod. I put a board and string on the bottom to lift the string off the fret, and when I pick it, it goes 'ping ping ping ping' and when I rush it, it go 'tong tong tong tong'. I was playing it like a upright bass. It was ska time in Jamaica, we had my favourite band called the Skatalites, so I listen to all the favourite musicians them, and I imitate the sound. My favourite bass players was Lloyd Brevett, Jackie Jackson, and Lloyd Spence. I pattern their (lines), then improvise.'

Fams was not as tall as Brevett or Jackson, but his stocky frame and large, wide hands are perfectly suited for his chosen instrument, and his ability to play by ear meant he was soon excelling on his rudimentary one-string bass.

Jackie Jackson vividly recalled Family Man's eagerness to learn: 'I can remember in the olden days when I used to record at West Indies, Family Man used to come to the recording studio because he knew Rannie Bop. That time he wasn't playing bass yet. I can remember he came in one particular day and said, "Bassie, can I look at your bass?" I said "Yeah mon!" While we were in the console room listening to the playback, I hear this bass playing the same thing that we just recorded. When I went 'round, there was Family Man playing the bass line, and him say, "It sound right? This is right?" And I say, "Yeah, you are right! If you like it, and you want to do it, keep at it and one day you will become a bass player." He used to come to the recording studios so we got to know each other, and when I am doing a session he would come and listen, and when I record a song and put down the bass, he would pick it up and play the same line right away.'

Max Romeo recalls that Fams and Carly had their first lucky break after the original Hippy Boys rhythm section failed to show up for a live gig. 'Family Man and his brother Carlton, anywhere we play, they always go with us, that's before they even start playing music. Web Stewart was giving Family Man pointers and notes and things like that. When they started off, Carlton was playing tin pans, Family Man was playing a one-string banjo! They started off following the Hippy Boys. This particular night, the bass player and the drummer didn't show, and Family Man and Carlton said they would sit in. Well, after much reluctance, we decided "OK, let them play." The first song they did was "Puppet on a String". I was singing lead vocals on the band, they played a few rhythms and it sound good on the gig. From then on, we said "OK, you're the bass player and the drummer," and that's how they emerged. We started playing at another club named Baby Grand, and Lloyd Charmers came by one night to hear us, and take them into the studio. "Watch This Sound" by Slim Smith, that's the first record Family Man played on; Lloyd Charmers produced the session. That's where their career started right off, until they went over to the Upsetters.'

A slow and soulful rendition of Buffalo Springfield's anti-war hit 'For What It's Worth' featuring drums by Winston Grennan, guitar by Bobby Aitken and Ansel Collins on piano, 'Watch This Sound' by the Uniques (then a trio composed of Slim Smith, Jimmy Riley, and Lloyd Charmers) first appeared on the Tramp label, run by a Chinese Jamaican from Greenwich Town named Winston Lowe; the tune also became popular with expatriate communities in the UK and USA after being licensed for pressing abroad.

Around the same time that Fams and Carly joined the group, Web Stewart left the Hippy Boys to be replaced by the more competent Ronnie Bop on lead guitar; two other core members joined the group after playing with Fams and Carly on a significant recording session for Bunny Lee.

The group's organ duties were handled by Glen Adams, a tailor from Jones Town who had previously been popular as a singer. Some time after the war, Glen's mother was working in Curaçao where she became involved with a chemistry teacher from St Vincent; after becoming pregnant with Glen, she returned to Kingston to raise the child. In addition to working as a milliner, Glen's mother was a singer and dancer who began promoting stage shows, putting on a notable dance with the Jiving Juniors in 1957. Soon after that show, Glen formed a little singing group with some school friends for an appearance at one of Vere Johns' shows at the Palace Theatre. He appeared alone at a subsequent contest and was taken by an agent named Caledonia Robinson to appear on cabaret shows at the Havana, Bungalow, and Penguin clubs alongside the Blues Busters and the Indian Rubber Boy. Glen's older sister Yvonne was also a popular singer who recorded with Roy Panton ('Meekly Wait and Murmur Not') and Derrick Morgan ('Two Roads Before You'), and it was while rehearsing a love song called 'Wonder Thirst' that she had written that Glen caught the attention of Clement Dodd. Dodd took Glen into the studio, and though 'Wonder Thirst' never gained an official release, it was popular as a sound system dub plate. With Ken Boothe, he then formed the duo Ken and Glen, placing second with a song called 'I Remember' at the first Festival Song Competition, held at the Ward Theatre in 1966. They also backed up Stranger Cole on his number one single 'Uno Dos Tres'. Glen subsequently became a member of the original Heptones when they were a five-piece, but left the group briefly to join the Pioneers after Winston Hewitt migrated to Canada, appearing on their early releases 'Shake It Up' and 'Good Nanny'. Continuing to earn a living as a tailor, he eventually emerged as an informal musical director for Duke Reid.

At Treasure Isle, Adams brought singers like Joe White to Duke's attention, and arranged 'Woman A Come' for Margarita Mahfood, the dancer whom trombonist Don Drummond lived with and eventually murdered in 1965. 'I would deal with her day upon day,' Adams remembered fondly. 'Mr Reid send her to me to spend time. If I was a little bit older, probably she would be my girl.'

Working often at Treasure Isle in the mid-'60s, Adams began collaborating with Bunny Lee around 1967, arranging material and providing harmony vocals in exchange for studio time. Adams was unknown as a keyboardist, but a certain October '68 session for Bunny Lee at which Scratch was present was to result in his gravitation towards the organ and his assured membership of the Hippy Boys. 'Bunny Lee had a session I was supposed to sing on. That's when we went to the studio, and the musicians, Hux Brown and Jackie Jackson, none of them didn't turn up. The musicians said they weren't working, Bunny Lee didn't pay them for a session before. Lloyd Charmers was there and Family Man, Carly. Duke Reid is the one who say that they need a pianist, so give a try. I usually rehearse all the artists with my guitar, I didn't really play no piano.'

Adams said that the first song of the night was 'Bangarang', an adaptation of an American melody that alto saxophonist Lester Sterling was working on. 'I tried to play the piano but it didn't work out, so Lester Sterling asked us to switch, make Lloyd Charmers play the piano and let me play the organ. I'd never played the organ before.' It was the first of eight songs that Adams would play organ on that night, and he would stick to the instrument ever after. Another big hit from the session was Slim Smith's 'Everybody Needs Love', on which Glen was given some assistance from Lloyd Charmers. 'When I look back on it, we didn't even know what we were doing. I got some lead from Charmers, he tell me "play that". He didn't shy us, although you had some other professional musicians didn't want to play with us.'

Making his recording debut as a guitarist on the 'Bangarang' sessions was a young singer and axe man named Alva Lewis, popularly known as Reggie, who would become the Hippy Boys' rhythm player from then on. Reggie was born in Manchester on April 16, 1949, the youngest of ten children. At age sixteen he settled with his brother on West Avenue in the centre of the Greenwich Farm community. After being sent a Fender electric guitar and a semi-acoustic Gibson by an elder brother who had emigrated to the States,

Reggie learned the basics of music from neighbours like Derrick Morgan and the Melodians. His style was marked by a choppy aggressiveness, and was to influence other players as the predominant musical style began to change again. 'When me start play now, it's like me play a different sound, it sound different from every other sound out there. Bunny Lee and Slim Smith carry me down to Duke Reid, and from the first tune me lick now, "Everybody Needs Love" and "Bangarang", they all start to strum a different style.'

Another early song the Hippy Boys were featured on was Derrick Morgan's 'Hold You Jack', again produced by Striker Lee. According to Max Romeo, Lee wanted to re-use the rhythm for a slack number, but couldn't find a singer willing to voice it.

'If a rhythm was made, I would write songs and ride the rhythm. Bunny Lee came with the idea to me about doing a slack song, because they were heavy into Blowfly and all these type of artists who was doing rude songs, "Shitting on the Dock of the Bay" and all those things. They was really into Blowfly then, that's an American artist. I wrote the song, but I didn't want to sing it, and everybody he go to refuse to sing the song. Slim Smith don't want to sing it, Roy Shirley and John Holt and "No way", Derrick Morgan said "No, not me. It's my rhythm, I just did 'Hold You Jack' on the rhythm." So Bunny Lee came back to me and said "OK, if you don't do it, you're out of here. You can't stay around, you have to do it." So I said "OK." It was in Studio One, Coxsone himself was at the control board. I went 'round the mike and I start when the rhythm start, "Every night, me go to sleep, me have wet dream." Coxsone shot off the board and get up and say "Bunny, where you get that fool fool singer from?! I won't be a part of this foolishness! What kind of idiot business that you bring me into?" By this time now, Errol Thompson, "ET", he was an apprentice then at the studio. Bunny Lee say "We rent the studio, and we no really want a man to dictate to me how fe run my session. This man going fe do this tune and if you don't want fe do it, let the apprentice come." So ET come 'round the board, and ET did the session. He (Bunny Lee) went to England to do some business with Pama with a bunch of tune, then he threw mine in as a make up, and that was the birth of "Wet Dream".'

Despite a BBC radio ban of the song because of its rude lyrics, 'Wet Dream' was a number one hit in the UK in 1968, remaining in the charts for a staggering 26 weeks. It did much to establish Max Romeo's popularity abroad, though initially in the context of a novelty singer.

Just after the session that resulted in the voicing of 'Wet Dream', Lee Perry used the All Stars for a cover version of 'Sick and Tired', a late-'50s New Orleans boogie-woogie hit by Chris Kenner, whose style was similar to that of his more famous contemporary, Fats Domino. However, Perry was not happy with the vocal he tried to lay down at WIRL, and left the recording unreleased for a period of time. Unknown to him or the band, this initial recording would prove to be one of the most successful of their careers.

It was with a former member of the Hippy Boys that Lee Perry would record one of his most socially relevant tunes of 1969: 'No Bread and Butter', credited to Milton Morris but actually the debut solo issue by Milton Henry. Born in the central Kingston ghetto of Allman Town on January 19, 1950, Aston Milton Henry was one of seven children born to a carpenter and his wife. In the rock steady era, the tall and deep-voiced singer formed the Leaders with Keith Blake, a large-framed youth from Greenwich Farm who would later be known as Prince Allah; together with other neighbourhood singers such as Roy 'Soft' Palmer, the Leaders recorded a few songs for Joe Gibbs before going their separate ways. Henry then passed through a group called the Progressions with Rudy Mills, Patrick Hearty and Derrick Bucknor, all singers who had been recording at Studio One as the Jets; the group produced an album, *Reggae To UK With Love*, distributed abroad by Pama. Henry then took Max Romeo's place in the Emotions, and the group went on to record numerous songs for Sonia Pottinger, including 'You Can't Stop Me', the rhythm of which was used for the Hippy Boys' hit 'Dr No Go'. Henry also played guitar for the Hippy Boys in this period, but left the group after walking off stage during a marred performance at the Globe Theatre.

When Milton Henry attended his Charles Street audition, he presented Lee Perry with a song that his friend Tony Russell had written about the strife brought on by a hungry belly. Impressed with the deep tones of Henry's strong and expressive voice, Perry recorded 'No Bread and Butter' straight away, starting Henry on his lengthy, though somewhat sparse, solo career.

Lee Perry first began using the Hippy Boys for his backing band because he was searching for a sound that would be new and different. The All Stars were providing countless hits for all the leading producers in Kingston, and their previously original sound was becoming far too common, something Jackie Jackson readily recalled. 'In them days, everybody wanted to have a nice band. Mrs Pottinger, Tip Top label, Leslie Kong, Scratch, everybody wanted their own sound, and everybody approached us and said "Listen, we want you to record for us exclusively." We said "No, we can't do that! We don't want to, we can't do that." And Scratch went and found Family Man and his brother Carly, Reggie and Glen and that's the birth of the Upsetters, but the Upsetters was never a band of musicians. As a matter of fact, Upsetters is Scratch. Scratch and his label is the Upsetter, and whoever went in there and played, the end product is the Upsetters.'

Perry himself has noted that the naming of his group fitted in with his wider ideas about the function his music was serving, and that he sought to change the group when their sound became too predictable:

'Those days, any musicians me use, me used to call them the Upsetters. That was the image in me mind, the group that me want to have. Whether now or the other generation me must name them the Upsetters,

because whatever set of musicians, me want to upset – like upset
politicians, upset government, upset parson, upset Pope and people like
those, and me music me can use to upset them, so me have to have a set
of people working with me as musicians named the Upsetters . . . Any
musicians me use, they call them Upsetters. At them time me used to
have Jackie (Jackson) and Hux Brown, Hugh Malcolm, and then after a
while it become, play it fe everybody, everybody music sound the same
way. So then me want a different set of musician or a different set of
music, so Barrett them come. Them was young and they wanted to do
something, so me let them do something how me wanted to do it, and it
sound different from the set of musicians me used to use before and call
them the Upsetters, so me call the Barretts now the Upsetters 'cause them
was with me now.' [3]

The Hippy Boys first worked with Scratch through their mutual links
with Bunny Lee. Perry was still sharing the odd session with Clancy Eccles at
Dynamics, helping to arrange material like King Stitt's 'Vigorton 2' with the
All Stars (who recorded for Eccles as the Dynamites), but he was working more
frequently with Bunny Lee at Randy's, where Errol Thompson had become
the engineer after his apprenticeship at Studio One; Niney also began to sit in
on their sessions. When Perry initially linked with the Hippy Boys, they had
not been long in the business and did not have much material recorded, but
hits created with Scratch and Striker soon found them in greater demand.

In October 1968, Fams and Carly had provided producer Lloyd Daley
with his first big hit, a record called 'Uglyman', sung by a group called the
Scorchers; from his premises in Waltham Park Road, Daley sold over 50,000
copies of the tune. Lloyd Daley established the Matador sound system in the
late '50s, and recorded a few early shuffle numbers with members of the
Skatalites in 1958; in 1965 he married Deanna Deans, daughter of the great
jazz band leader Eric Deans. After his sound system was destroyed by police in
1966, Daley decided to return to record production, and achieved only minor
hits before the recording of 'Uglyman'.

The Hippy Boys were also instrumental in solidifying the popularity of
producer Harry Johnson, a former insurance salesman who found success in
record production with the Beltones' 'No More Heartaches' in 1968; an even
greater success was the instrumental 'Liquidator', a soulful number originated
in part by Fams and Carly and given its title by Scratch at Randy's studio after
it was mixed by engineer Sylvain Morris. Family Man proudly recalled the
group's early successes: 'The first promoter we worked with was Bunny Lee.
Bunny Lee and Lee Perry was close friends, so we keep working for Bunny Lee
and Lee Perry, and did one or two for the Matador Mrs Pottinger, and also
Harry J. We did a track as the Emotions and we did the instrumental called "Dr
No Go" for Mrs Pottinger. Then for Harry J, there was a track that we did for

a guy called Tony Scott, a song called "What Am I To Do", and then he sold the rhythm to Harry J, and I tone up the organ in Randy's studio for Winston Wright, he was known as "Brubeck", and he did this instrumental called "The Liquidator". We originate that rhythm, it was covered by the Staple Singers.'

The group were also backing artists for Joe Gibbs, but the bulk of their work continued to be cut in joint sessions controlled by Bunny Lee and Scratch. 'Lee "Scratch" Perry and Bunny Lee was the more kind of ghetto promoters, what you call down to earth. We like a little down to earth thing, so we play for anyone, but we're mostly with Lee "Scratch" Perry and Bunny Lee.'

By the time Harry Palmer appeared at the Upsetter Record shop in August 1969, Lee Perry had recorded plenty of material with the Hippy Boys and had many All Stars tracks in reserve. Palmer brought back two albums' worth of material to Britain, much of which had been recorded earlier in the year. He released the first collection in 1972 as *Clint Eastwood*, drawn largely from popular singles issued by Pama and aimed squarely at the Jamaican immigrant community. Nearly half of the tracks on *Clint Eastwood* were instrumentals, and numbers like 'Return Of The Ugly', 'For A Few Dollars More', 'Taste Of Killing', and the title track revealed the pervading influence of Westerns on the Upsetter sound. Retaining something of a harder edge, even the vocal tracks on *Clint Eastwood* contained a raw energy not present on *The Upsetter*.

Issued in October 1969, the 'Clint Eastwood' single was one of the most popular Western-inspired nuggets to come out of Jamaica in the late 1960s and early 1970s. According to Clancy Eccles, 'Clint Eastwood' was made partly in answer to 'Van Cleef', one of Eccles' biggest 'dollar' hits, cut in salutation to the toughness of actor Lee Van Cleef. 'When I did "Van Cleef" Scratch went out and did "Clint Eastwood". He go on my record changer and played "Clint Eastwood" and make me hear "Clint Eastwood tougher than Lee Van Cliff". It was just a joke.'

Perhaps the strongest answer of all came from Lloyd Charmers on the Hippy Boys' 'Vengeance', on which Charmers warns the Upsetter that he is coming to take his throne, chasing Scratch and Niney out of town, over a rough-and-ready rhythm. Although such vinyl rivalry was based on enjoyment, Clancy Eccles noted that the competition could sometimes become tense in reality. 'I remember Scratch come down to Chin's bar at the corner of Orange Street and Beeston Street with his suit and gun holster, it was around 1970, during the Django "dollar" series. That was where we come and drink because I had the record shop right beside the bar and Scratch is on the other street, quite near. He and Glen Adams and Reggie came down there, wanted me to be afraid, so I lift up Scratch in the air to drop Scratch 'pon him head, and Scratch whisper in me ears, "We just a do this fe make record sell you know," so I just put him down and walk out of the bar. Scratch understand the gimmicry of recordings and he always try to get them to sell, that's a very good thing. It was a joke thing, and after that stopped, record sales dropped.'

Aside from the Western-inspired material, the *Clint Eastwood* album had other current Upsetter vocal and deejay material. 'What Is This' (a.k.a. 'Ba Ba') and 'Selassie' were two hot tunes from the Reggae Boys, a singing duo made up of Glen Adams and Reggie. They had previously scored a big hit for Joe Gibbs with 'Mama Look Deh', which enjoyed number-one chart position for 13 weeks. "Mama Look Deh' give me my first car,' Reggie noted, 'one little Honda car me have that time what me buy from Jeff Barnes for £350.'

'What Is This' began life as 'Little Suzy', a love song Watty Burnett had tried unsuccessfully to voice. By this time, Burnett had settled in Allman Town with his brother Fitzy, and was trying to establish himself on the music scene as a singer and bass player. When Burnett failed to deliver a satisfactory vocal, Scratch had Glen Adams overdub a frenzied organ line which became the instrumental 'Cold Sweat' (also issued as 'Power Cut'). Then Glen Adams and Reggie added the vocal that transformed the song into 'What Is This'.

Though 'Selassie' sounded like a pop song, it was in fact a warning to the heathen about the powers of the true and living God of Rastafari. Family Man, Carly, Glen Adams, Reggie, and Max Romeo had all accepted the manifestation of Rastafari in their lives by this time, while Perry himself was grappling with its messages and meanings, which were both liberating and disturbing. Though outwardly the fashion-conscious Perry bore the trappings of a 'soul man' with a finely combed small Afro and manicured moustache, some have stated that Perry was already taking the rasta message seriously, and he clearly had been pondering on its import since Selassie's visit – though Max Romeo remembered him as being a rasta sympathiser, who respected the group but did not yet fully share their religious beliefs, a view supported by several family members. Perry himself has said that although he was 'soul man from ever since', he held rasta beliefs in his heart 'from ever since'; he suggested that regardless of his appearance, he may have inwardly accepted the faith without yet acknowledging it outwardly.

Reggie recalled that 'Selassie' was another semi-spontaneous creation, which perhaps partly accounts for its buoyant vibrancy. 'We just go inside the studio and say "What a gwan?" and man say "Come and go talk about Selassie" and we just go there.'

Perry was always keen to exploit the full potential of a solid rhythm whenever possible, and 'Selassie' was no exception: He stripped the recording to its core for a stunning alternative version underscored by religious orthodoxy. 'Rightful Ruler' featured the drumming talents of Count Ossie, wailing and guitar work from Peter Tosh, and the chanting of Psalm 1 by U Roy. Ossie had been absent from recording for much of the mid-1960s, retreating to the Rastafarian community of Wareika Hills after work for Prince Buster, Coxsone Dodd and a producer from Spanish Town named Harry Mudie earlier in the decade. The Wailers had been working with Leslie Kong, but had temporarily broken up, due to one of Bob Marley's hiatuses at his mother's home in

Wilmington, Delaware, so Peter Tosh was active as a freelance guitarist and organist. Tosh would often be clowning around at Randy's, spontaneously laying down an organ cut of whatever tape was rolling; so it was with 'Rightful Ruler', on which Tosh contributed guitar and emphatic shouts of religious fervour. Taking the lead was U Roy, the top toaster of the day and one who took his role as a messenger of Rastafari very seriously.

Born Ewart Beckford, the young U Roy was raised by his granny in the Jones Town area of Western Kingston, close to the emerging musical hotbed of Trench Town. His proximity to lively downtown areas meant that he was exposed to the excitement of the dancehall scene at an early age. According to U Roy, his own musical apprenticeship began when he started attending sound system dances at age 11. 'When I was to going to school I ask my grandmother if I can go during the weekend time and do that. That was like '65 or '64. I used to ask her to go to the dance and play, but sometimes she used to be saying I have to be studying my lesson, I have to do my homework. No matter how she flares up and go on, I still have to sneak away and reach, because that is my best fun! I only used to like to watch football game or cricket, but I don't play those games. Wherever sound system is playing, I'll be there, listening to every tune. At that time, every tune that play on the radio, I know it; every tune that a sound system play, I know them.'

He soon began chatting on sounds like Sir Dickies (also known as Dickies Dynamic) and later Sir George the Atomic, his stage name U Roy originating from a family nickname. 'The name was just given to me by my smaller cousin. My family, sometimes they call me the nickname, (when me) just a pickney, they call me Hugh. Then my cousin who's small, one day we're playing, and I hit him hard with a piece of stick. He said to me "Hey U Roy, you hit me hard, I'm going to tell my grandmother," and this name just stick.'

In 1967, U Roy became the toaster for King Tubby's Home Town Hi Fi. Tubby's given name was Osbourne Ruddock, but he was called Tubby from a corruption of his mother's maiden name, Tubman. Tubby was then the disc cutter at Treasure Isle studio, having taken over from Byron Smith who had gone to work at WIRL. Tubby and U Roy were both instrumental in establishing the practice of version and the subsequent popularity of the dub and deejay styles. Tubby was among the first to begin manipulating mixes on dub plates, dropping the vocal down to reveal the bare rhythm that pulsated beneath its surface, later to be cut back in, strikingly modified by echo or reverb. Ruddy Redwood, a light skinned man who operated a sound called Ruddy's Supreme in Spanish Town, is now also acknowledged as an earlier pioneer who obtained a steady supply of exclusive Studio One and Treasure Isle remixes for his sound.

U Roy on the mike at Home Town Hi Fi was quite a spectacle, and his dynamic and lively toasting won him much admiration and respect, as did his open espousal of Rastafarian beliefs. Around the start of 1970, U Roy was to change the face of Jamaican music through a fluid rapping style where he would interject his toasting continuously through rhythms, shifting the role of the deejay from incidental commentator and noise maker to that of a lyrical sage whose contribution was as valid and important as that of the singer. His work with Duke Reid would see him become a major sensation, resulting in a series of number-one hits. This would seriously upgrade the status of the deejay nearly a decade before rap music would begin to be made in the USA, and the popularity of U Roy's art came as a surprise even to him. 'I didn't think that something like this would ever happen and that it would still be going on until now. At the time it was like it was a joke! A deejay is just a person who comes to a dance, he talks over the mike and puts records on and read the invitation where the next dance is going to keep. Who could ever tell that this thing would ever reach like this, people having number one on the chart!'

When Lee Perry arranged for U Roy to voice 'Rightful Ruler' at Randy's in the summer of 1969, the toaster had already recorded a couple of other songs for Keith Hudson, a producer and occasional dental technician who had scored a hit on his Inbidimits label in 1967 with Ken Boothe's 'Old Fashioned Way'; his shop was near Randy's on Parade. Like Perry, Hudson understood that the deejay needed to be given proper space to express himself on a rhythm, and 'Dynamic Fashion Way' left plenty of room for U Roy's message. 'A whole heap of people bla bla bla about it but I was the first person put U Roy in the studio,' Hudson stated in the mid-'70s. 'When I took it to the radio station, it's like they was saying "we could never play this music, it's strange and it's funny."' [4]

Travelling to the USA shortly after recording U Roy, Hudson shelved the tunes temporarily, making 'Rightful Ruler' the toaster's vinyl debut despite its later recording date. 'My first tune I ever do was "Dynamic Fashion Way" with Keith Hudson,' U Roy stated in clarification, 'and then I do "Earth's Rightful Ruler" for Scratch. Those tunes didn't get very far, them sell a couple hundred.'

Despite its low sales, 'Rightful Ruler' is an important disc on several levels. It was first and foremost a direct expression of belief in Rastafari, entirely undisguised and issued without apology at a time when the mere hint of such a belief could result in a beating, imprisonment, or worse. It was also the most bass-heavy version yet produced, a thunderous and majestic sound that heightened the primordial intensity of the record. Even more peculiar was the song's beginning, which was grafted from the start of another Burru record, Ras Michael and the Sons of Negus' 'Ethiopian National Anthem' (issued earlier on the Zion Disc label and based on the anthem of the UNIA). 'Rightful Ruler' thus shows how Perry was reshaping his creations through the new application of cut-ups, restructuring the deejay in a central role and relegating the bass as his main instrument.

Other deejay cuts by Cool Sticky found their way onto the *Clint Eastwood* album, including 'Dry Acid', a boastful delivery based on the American radio mode, and 'I've Caught You', in which Sticky barks incomprehensible slogans over an organ cut of David Isaacs' version of Ben E. King's 'Can't Take It Anymore'. Also recorded around this time was 'OK Corral', perhaps the most surreal deejay record then issued, on which U Roy croaks the law of the urban jungle: 'An eye for an eye, a tooth for a tooth, if you want I, don't argue, just shoot.' Over another inordinately bass-heavy rhythm, augmented by breaking glass and rapid machine-gun fire, U Roy barks a fierce warning to those who dare insult the Rastafarians – be they rude boy, gunman, skanky producer or politician.

The album's title track sold well in Jamaica and enjoyed widespread success in Britain in the early months of 1970 (though Perry felt that Pama had not promoted the record to its full potential). One of several versions of The Coasters' 'Yakkety Yak', 'Clint Eastwood' was a quirky instrumental led by a throbbing cowbell and punctuated by an odd squeaking sound. 'He play a little Christmas hammer in it,' Bunny Lee recalled, 'a toy dolly hammer.' The original take was a fairly faithful cover version voiced by Perry himself, while the B-side, 'The Tackro', was far more extreme; unleashing a crazed abandon only hinted at on 'Kimble', Perry was now appearing as the only thing uglier than Lee Van Cleef in *The Good, The Bad, and The Ugly*, using echoing shoots, whistles and burps to emphasise the point. Another single marked by the extreme ends of Perry's imagination came in 'Mad House', a song where he tried to capture the feeling of a mental-asylum ward through crazed scat-vocal gibberish and startling sound effects. What Perry was doing as a matter of routine on records like these was far beyond the limits of other producers; in his ceaseless urge to express abstract ideas, Perry was pushing things far beyond their accepted limits.

Another big hit on the *Clint Eastwood* album was 'Prisoner of Love', a more conventional vocal credited on release to Dave Barker. Born David Crooks in the ghetto of Franklin Town in 1948, Dave was raised by his grandmother and three uncles when his mother emigrated to the UK in 1952; his father was a sailor who emigrated to America before Dave's birth. Dave endured so many beatings at the hands of his uncles and schoolteachers that he developed a noticeable stammer, yet when he opened his mouth to sing, people would always stop to listen. Tuning into American radio station WINZ as a teenager, Dave was greatly inspired by James Brown and Otis Redding, and he began trying to emulate the style of the 'Godfather of Soul'.

His first street-corner group was called the Two Tones, formed with a friend named Brenton Matthews and a guy they all knew as Fathead; their initial attempt at recording proved to be a failure. 'We got as far as into the recording studio, with Tommy McCook and the Supersonics. Duke Reid stood there with pistol in him waist and handcuff and all them things. The band came in with the intro, and when my turn come for me to come in, I froze! No voice! They kept trying for about three, four takes, and I just couldn't respond at all.'

While practising with a friend on Cable Street, Dave was approached by

Glenmore Brown, an older, taller singer who was becoming established as a vocalist through duets with Lloyd Robinson. 'Me and Glen start to practise, and it was coming up to independence time. We wrote an independence song and appeared on stage at the Carib Theatre with the Vikings. At that time, Bob Marley was also on the same bill, and I was surprised how the people responded. Bob came out with a song which also had something to do with the festive time. How the people responded to Bob was quite strange, because they sort of laughed at Bob on stage, which to me didn't feel right. You see how things work? Right now, the ones who laughed isn't laughing any more.'

Glen and Dave recorded material such as 'Lucky Boy' for Harry J, using the All Stars at Federal, and appeared regularly at noted nightclubs, including one at the Portland Manor Hotel. They also recorded material for Coxsone Dodd, including 'In This Whole World', a cover of a Sammy Davis Jr song, and 'Lady Lovelight'. Dave noted that he was also doing manual work for Studio One at this time: 'I used to work in the pressing plant for Coxsone Dodd, alongside we I-dren from Heptones, Earl (Morgan). Me and Heptones and everybody, we got on well.'

According to Dave, it was Glen Brown that first brought him to Scratch's attention, resulting in his launch as a solo artist. 'One night, we were walking past Randy's recording studio down by King Street. At that time Scratch had a green and black Jag, which he transported from here (UK) to there (JA). This car drop this short, slim guy, with fancy-dress business and a whole heap of guys behind him, and it was all excitement. Everybody was just "Scratch, Scratch, Scratch!" Randy's door open, and we find ourselves in with the crowd too. We go upstairs, Busty Brown was amongst the lot. Scratch put this tape on, and the rhythm was a rhythm (over) which Slim Smith did a song called 'Slip Away' (a highly successful Bunny Lee production). Scratch wanted Busty to sing something, to do something on that particular track. They tried and tried and tried, and the booze and the weed was flowing. I was in the corner, checking out everything, and getting stoned as well, and Busty tried and tried and tried, but him just couldn't contact with that track. Then Glen Brown go say to Scratch, "Scratch, you have I-dren out there named Dave, you know. Bwoi, you hear him man, try Dave, man, Dave would touch this track now," and Scratch say "Yes? Who named Dave? Dave! Dave! Come 'round the mike, man. You feel you can tackle this tune here?" We put on the headphone, and Scratch run the track, and from I hear, me just start sing, "Baby, baby, yeah, you made me a prisoner . . . " And me go right through, me sing non-stop.'

Dave said that Lee Perry was so taken by his spontaneous burst of lyrical creativity that he began jumping around the room with joy. 'From I did "Prisoner of Love", everybody in the studio, there was this excited buzz. Scratch could not control himself. Then him start to drink and smoke. Then him look 'pon me and him say, "Your name Dave. Now you want a stage name. Give me you full name." I say "David Crooks." Him say "No mon,

Crooks?! No mon, Dave Crooks can't work, mon. That no sound showbiz at all." Then the man just suddenly come out with "Barker. Barker! Dave Barker, man!" And the Dave Barker stick. Everybody come out of the studio buzzed! I felt so excited, because when they played the track back, I'm saying to myself, wait, this is me do that?! The next day, Scratch go to pressing plant and every place and the music just start to tear down the whole of Jamaica.'

The biggest hit Perry scored in the UK in 1969 came as something of a surprise, even to Perry himself. 'Return of Django' was an instrumental version of Chris Kenner's 1958 hit 'Sick and Tired', which Scratch had recorded with the All Stars at Studio One on the same night 'Wet Dream' had been voiced and the 'Yakkety Yak'/'Clint Eastwood' rhythm had been laid. He had tried unsuccessfully to voice the song at WIRL, but eventually chose to issue it as an instrumental. 'I'm not sure if it was Lee Perry (singing),' said Lynford Anderson, 'but the voice didn't come out, so he released the rhythm. It come out as "The Return of Django" with nothing on there. It's supposed to be "Oh Babe" ("Sick and Tired"), he call it "Return of Django". He went to England and they gave him a lot of money. More or less, that's how Lee Perry started. He got a lot of money and he went back and forth to England.'

'Return of Django' had been the second single issued on the UK Upsetter label. Though it sold fairly well among the Jamaican immigrant community, it initially made little impact on the general public until the autumn of 1969, when it made a belated appearance in the pop charts. Sustained mainstream popularity would eventually see its use in a radio and television advertising campaign for Cadbury's Fruit and Nut chocolate bar.

Once the song hit, Trojan re-released the single and a brief UK tour was quickly scheduled, but the tour was unfortunately delayed due to a serious domestic problem, possibly halting the record's rise in the UK pop charts. As Family Man recalled, 'When we were to come on tour to carry ("Return of Django") to number one, Scratch have an accident, like he get a stab in his arm from one of his ladies, so we have to wait two months. By the time we come here we could only reach it to number five.'

Lee Perry's sexual appetite has always been difficult to satiate, and fidelity was not a virtue that he often felt comfortable with. He had a long-standing reputation as a ladies' man, now heightened through his fame on the music scene and visible wealth. 'When Scratch in a woman house for the first time and him want to drink ice water and she no have no fridge, Scratch just get a phone and phone for a fridge,' Bunny Lee recalled. 'Him used to have a big, four-ply cheque book.'

Scratch had an air of excitement and wealth about him: Always immaculately dressed, with a large, gaudy gold ring shining on the pinkie of each hand and even his goatee and moustache groomed, Perry was irresistible to many women, and the feeling could often be mutual.

An early relationship was struck with a woman of Chinese extraction called Lou, who eventually left the island. 'Lou is a Chiney girl where me lend some money through Scratch and she went to America,' Bunny Lee noted, 'Put all £150 in the bank for her, never see her again. £150 them days you have to get bank statement!' A brief affair in 1969 with a woman called Junie produced a son, Delano Perry, but Scratch had little contact with either of them after the birth, and Junie herself would also eventually emigrate to the States. By the autumn of 1969, he had became strongly involved with a short, light-skinned woman named Melanie Jonas – a highly attractive young woman who Scratch came to know through Judy Mowatt. Jonas and Mowatt had been working together for Colgate-Palmolive, and it was while raving together at a nightclub that Jonas first came to know Scratch; like Mowatt, she also had ambitions to be a singer, but perhaps lacked the necessary talent to achieve this goal. Her relationship with Lee Perry quickly grew serious, and the pair were often spotted together.

When Pauline Morrison – who was again pregnant with another of Perry's children – inevitably discovered the affair, she attacked Perry with a knife, inflicting a deep wound in one arm that required several stitches. While Perry recovered from his injuries at the hospital, a panic-stricken Pauline fled with the children to Perry's mother's house in Hanover, where she said nothing of the incident, until a telegram from Scratch informed the family of the events. Although Pauline temporarily moved out of Cardiff Cresent, spending a period on her own in Rollington Town, such violence was not to mark the end of the affair, and Perry continued his clandestine liaison with Jonas until she eventually emigrated to the USA; he even took her to Hanover at one point to meet his mother.

It was also during the time of his affair with Melanie Jonas that Lee Perry was involved in a serious car accident near Kingston's chief cement works. Scratch himself had no driving licence, and normally had his stylish Jaguar chauffeur-driven by Val Bennett, until an argument ended the arrangement. On one particular evening, Scratch and Melanie Jonas had been drinking with a Bermudan who worked at JBC and two other work associates named Frankie and Justin; Frankie was a runaround man for Clancy Eccles, while Justin worked in a similar capacity for Scratch. Hearing of a function in Port Royal, the five sped off into the night: Scratch and Mel were in the Jaguar, with the Bermudan at the wheel, and Frankie was driving a motorbike with Justin riding pillion. In a show of machismo, the drivers began to race; someone lost control along the way and the car collided with the bike, killing Frankie and seriously injuring Justin. As Perry recalled, 'I didn't have no licence, that's how Val Bennett get into my life. Val was a saxophonist when we used to do those rhythm and blues like "Return of Django" and Val was in those things; me have a car and didn't have no licence so Val was driving me around. I don't know what happened with Val, there was some argument and me and Val wasn't driving the car no more. Then there was a guy who was working at JBC, come from one of them small islands, he was working on the radio station and used to come and get friendly with me. One night we want to go up to Port Royal, he say him have licence so we say "Let's go." Justin and Frankie who work with Clancy was riding on a bike, Justin was working with me too. The driver was drinking, and they was drinking so they was riding careless as well, riding to see who can ride faster and go in front of the car and get knocked off. Justin was riding the bike and him get crippled and the other guy dead. Me wasn't driving; me have the small islander driving and give the police statement.'

The Bermudan driver thus served a long jail sentence after being convicted of drunk driving. Malicious rumours would later surface that the bike was intentionally hit after Perry accused the men of stealing his records or because Pauline was said to be having an affair with one; certain foes even alleged that Scratch himself was at the wheel, driving drunk – but Perry has flatly denied such suggestions, citing his police statement as proof of his innocence. 'Anything what look very nasty, is me that,' Perry explained, 'but I'm not nasty enough to kill Frankie and scupper Justin.' The car was later purchased by Clancy Eccles, after Scratch left it in a garage during his British tour.

Perry had originally planned to bring the All Stars to tour as the Upsetters as they were the musicians that played on 'Return of Django', but the group is said either to have had other engagements or felt that the fee offered was too low. 'It just didn't happen,' Jackie Jackson remarked, 'it was one them things. We knew of it, we heard about it, and everyone was excited. We all said "Hey, all right!" and then it just petered out.'

'It was Jackie them that played the tune, but me wanted to do Family Man them a favour,' Scratch explained.

Lee Perry thus arrived at Heathrow Airport on November 22nd 1969 with Family Man, Carly, Reggie and Glen Adams, the nucleus of the Hippy Boys, who had become his second string of Upsetter musicians; Melanie Jonas also travelled to London, remaining in Britain with Scratch for a number of weeks. Val Bennett was originally meant to attend the tour, along with a second guitarist; the initial plan was the have Ronnie Bop on lead and Reggie on rhythm, later changed to Reggie on lead and Lloyd 'Gitsy' Willis on rhythm after Bennett and Bop were removed from the proposed line-up (Bop's commitments with the Supersonics caused his exclusion). Eventually, the small available budget and other personal circumstances resulted in such other musicians remaining behind in Jamaica.

Also present on the flight were George Dekker, Jackie Robinson, and Sydney Crooks, the members of the Pioneers vocal trio, who were scheduled to complete a separate tour backed by a mixed band called Sweet Blindness. Both groups were initially housed in the Arama and George Hotels in Praed Street, in the middle of the bustling and somewhat transient Paddington area.

'The first time the Pioneers came up to England, we come up on their billing in '69,' Family Man remembered, 'and Pioneers stay in England from that time. Both of us come up then, Pioneers and Upsetters, but we had our own band together and they got some other rhythm section.'

'The group I brought over wasn't really the Upsetters,' Perry later insisted. 'Most of my hits was made by Gladdy's band: Winston Wright, Hux Brown, Jackie Jackson, Hugh Malcolm, and Gladdy.'[5] Whether we consider them the Upsetters or the Hippy Boys, the band was brought to the UK for a six-week tour – an unprecedented action for a Jamaican band. They were also flown to Holland for a live appearance on a television show called *Shoo Be Do*, which was broadcast in the UK on *Top of the Pops*. 'I remember we fly over just to do the TV show,' Family Man said proudly, 'it was just one cut, one take, and we did it like we were professionals. We were all in different colours, it's a beautiful show.'

The Upsetters tour kicked off on Novemebr 28th at the Up The Junction club in Crewe, followed by an appearance the next day at Manchester's New Century Hall, where the audience was largely composed of skinheads. On December 1st they played the Chesterford Grange in Coventry, followed by the Tonbridge Six in One club December 3rd, Hook Youth Centre the 4th and Dunstable California Ballroom the 6th. Their London area debut came before an audience of mostly Caribbean migrants at the Kensal Rise ABC Cinema on a double bill with the Pioneers on the 7th, followed by the Purley Orchid and London Bag O'Nails the next day and the Southampton Adam and Eve club on the 10th. An appearance at Huddersfield New Theatre took place on the 12th, followed by a return to the London area for performances at the Ruislip Bourne School and London Golden Star club, the Kennington Oval Rooms and Streatham Silver Blades. They played the Bookham Youth Centre on the 17th, followed by the Bournemouth Locarno, Devizes Corn Exchange, Margate Dreamland club and Bournemouth Pavilion, and performed at the Torquay 400 Club on Christmas Eve. Boxing Day found them at the Basildon Locarno, followed by a gig at famed Caribbean landmark the Dalston Four Aces club and another at the Crystal Palace Hotel. In the new year, they hit the Sheffield Shades club on January 2nd, 1970, followed by performances at the Boston Gilderdome and Derby Clouds. They had a three night run at the Birmingham Rainbow Suite from January 8th, and finished the original tour commitments at the East Sheen Bull on January 11th.

Reggie also recalls being brought to Cardiff for a BBC2 interview. 'I think Tom Jones was there the same day,' he laughed, 'they were asking us what about this reggae? and them play the "Return Of Django". Family Man didn't come on that interview, he stay at the Edwards Hotel; it was me and Carly and Glen.'

They were brought to England by a booking agency called Commercial Entertainment, run by two white entrepeneurs who had previously been in a close harmony group called the Next Move: Bruce White and Tony Cousins. White was born in London on November 24, 1942; he became a singer with the band in the early 1960s after working at his father's printing company. Tony Cousins' real name was Anthony Bautista; born in the British protectorate of Gibraltar in 1944, he took the stage name Cousins after joining the group on drums. Though independent producer Mickie Most expressed interest in producing the band, they split up in 1965 without ever having made a record. Noting that agents seemed to earn more than musicians, White and Cousins then decided to set up a booking agency in Gerrard Street, where they initially booked small bands into youth clubs and American Air Force bases in Britain. By 1967, they had developed a close friendship with Graham Goodall, who was then operating the Doctor Bird and Pyramid labels in the UK. Through Goodall's connection, Commercial Entertainment made arrangements with Leslie Kong to bring Desmond Dekker to Britain just as 'Israelites' was entering the pop charts in 1969; Dekker ended up touring successfully throughout Britain and Europe after the company secured numerous bookings.

Seeking to expand Commercial Entertainment's roster of Jamaican artists, Cousins began travelling to Jamaica, where he solidified his link with Kong and initiated contact with other producers; subsequent live dates were scheduled in Britain for acts such as the Maytals and the Ethiopians.

The unofficial road manager for the Upsetters' British dates in 1969 was Clifton 'Larry' Lawrence, a Jamaican resident in London who would later become more concretely involved in record production. As Lawrence noted, 'Lee Perry came over here with the Hippy Boys. They work in Tropical Palace, that was in Kensal Rise. They did a live show there, and they did live shows in Birmingham, up and down the country, Bournemouth and all those places. The record ('Return Of Django') was in the chart at the time, they was on *Top Of The Pops* and everything. They came over to do a tour, they played Manchester and everywhere. I used to have to take them around, guide them around the place. Daytime, he would want to go shopping; in the evenings, we'd go to nightclubs and rave together.'

Commercial Entertainment had initially hoped to present an additional six week nationwide package tour featuring Desmond Dekker, Jimmy Cliff, Max Romeo, the Upsetters, the Pioneers and the Harry J All Stars to commence in late January with a gala event at the Royal Albert Hall. Unfortunately, the tour was scrapped after skinhead disturbances saw club owners cancel most of the scheduled dates. Further UK appearances were made by the Upsetters after Commercial Entertainment arranged other bookings: they played with Dekker, the Pioneers, Symarip and Noel and the Fireballs at the Purley Orchid on January 13th and at the Ilford Palais the 14th (without Symarip); they then appeared on their own at a club called Toffs in Folkestone on the 17th, the Bedford Hotel in Balham on the 18th, the Alladice Hotel in Brixton on the 23rd, the Gala Ballroom in Norwich on the 24th, the Tower Pier in Great Yarmouth on the 25th, and gave a final performance in Cirencester on January 30th.

Conditions on the tour were generally difficult and chaotic, with many arrangements made at the last minute, further complicated by Perry's own spontaneous agenda; as Bruce White noted, both band and agency were repeatedly subjected to Perry's unpredicatble whims. 'Scratch was running his own thing and really cherry-picked what he wanted to do. One night he decided he was going on stage, the next night he decided he wasn't; one time I can recall he decided he'll play a triangle, that was probably somewhere like Birmingham. He's a great talent but he's got a mind of his own. Whatever took his fancy you had to do.'

Despite such inconsistencies, the tour itself was generally perceived as a success, and led to 'Night Doctor', 'A Live Injection' and 'The Vampire' also achieving UK chart positions. By the middle of December, a *Return Of Django* album had been complied; billed as the Upsetters' debut LP, the collection of organ instrumentals duplicated some of the tracks from *The Upsetters*, and was officially released by Trojan on January 2nd 1970.Though Perry's first real taste of British life came in a consistently icy winter, he was fascinated by what he encountered in Britain and began to consider relocating to London.

As the tour ground to a halt, the Upsetters found themselves cast adrift in London. Doing business with both Trojan and Pama, Perry was journeying between Kingston and London for much of the winter of 1969–70, and left the band largely to fend for themselves. Scratch also had some important social events to attend, appearing in London as co-best man with Harry Palmer at Bunny Lee's wedding. Sometimes he stayed at the Northwest London home of the Owens family – Jamaican immigrants who often housed visiting artists as their mother was an old friend of Jeffrey Palmer. Tony Owens, who had left Jamaica to join his mother in London in 1967, had recently won a song competition at the London Apollo club as leader of the group Tony J and the Wild Ways; their successful entry 'Telephone Line' was co-written by Alton Ellis, another frequent guest at their home. Years later, Tony would emerge as an important ally with concrete involvement in Perry's work; during Scratch's early London visits, the Owens family link often provided him with a comfortable and friendly place of rest.

Having no such connection of their own, the Upsetters band was not so fortunate. Left largely to their own devices, they received only minimal assistance from Larry Lawrence. 'They finished the tour, and they wasn't actually signed to Scratch or nothing like that, so they were trying to do their own thing. At that time, I actually end up with the band, because Scratch had to go back and forth to Jamaica, so he's left them with me to take care of. They had to move out of the hotels and everywhere that they was living when the tour was finished, and they had to start finding digs for themselves and they had to live, so they had to work sessions for other people to keep their life going. I can't tell you what happened with the "Return Of Django", who get money out of it, that is not my department. I just know that they say that they wasn't actually getting money from that deal. In Jamaica at the time, most of this music was made by session players really, and when the bands are put together, they don't really have nothing to do with the deals, they just go to work for the money off the gigs.'

Meanwhile, Bruce White and Tony Cousins were beginning to enter into record production, having sold half the shares of their booking agency to Trojan, who re-named it Trojan Artists; Trojan would later take over the agency entirely. White and Cousins persuaded the Upsetters band to make the best use of their time in England by recording an album's worth of instrumental material in London, which Trojan would release as *The Good, The Bad And The Upsetters* in 1970 after a planned deal with President records fell through. White and Cousins then formed the Creole label as an EMI reggae subsidiary after meeting EMI's managing director Roy Featherstone at a convention.

Although it bore the Upsetter name, Perry stated he had no involvement with the project and was out of the country when most of it was recorded. Production credit was given to 'Bruce Anthony', a pseudonym used by White and Cousins on records that they financed. Somewhat lacklustre in comparison to their authentic Jamaican efforts, the frigid atmosphere that permeated the disc rendered it significantly less popular on release. Scratch would periodically express resentment about the album in subsequent years, and seems to have never gotten over what he felt was its improper titling. 'I didn't know anything about that,' he explained. 'That was after they want to play their own game, so I leave them on their own. I was not involved, and I've never heard that album yet.' Scratch later attempted to get his own back by having stickers printed with a different track listing to use the Trojan sleeves for an alternative Jamaican Upsetter album of his own largely instrumental productions, but the disc seems to have been issued in only the smallest of quantities and its exact circumstances remain obscure; highlights included a steel-pan version of the 'Bum Ball' rhythm and a deejay cut of the Inspirations' 'Same Thing All Over'.

1969 was in many ways a turning point for Lee Perry. He had moved away from the conventional vocal in favour of instrumental re-inventions of previously fashioned rhythms and general sonic experiments. He had a better home for his family on the outskirts of the city, and retained a mistress downtown. His record shop was becoming a focal point for the burgeoning talent of the area, his productions so sought after that he had to hire help with sales and distribution. His tour of the UK had caused more than just a flicker of interest from the British press, who were normally dismissive of the validity and worth of Jamaican music. 1969 had brought the Upsetter to the attention of large audiences outside Jamaica for the very first time, but 1970 would herald events that were to rock the very foundations of the music world.

SOUL REBELS:

The Upsetter and The Wailers

As a new decade was dawning, Lee Perry continued the experimentation that had seen him rise to the attention of the world outside Jamaica. He had been consumed by music for the entire 1960s, with all else in his life taking a second place, and had found fame and fortune after struggling to establish himself as an independent production force. Now that Perry had various avenues in Jamaica and abroad with which he could pursue his creativity, he sought to make the best use of such opportunities for self-expression by delving further into uncharted sonic territory. Always aware of the power exerted by his secret spirit guide, he was pondering what form the next exciting sound would take, how it would come to him, and what significance it would bring to his life. As he began to mature as a musical creator, he again sought to change the focus of Jamaican pop through sounds and ideas that were challenging and different.

1970 began with several new creations, the first of which was certainly the most important: on February 4, Pauline gave birth to Marsha Rachel Perry at St Andrew Public Hospital; she would soon grow to be her father's favourite child. In later years, Marsha's broad forehead would earn her the nickname Martha, after her resemblance to one of the daughters of Selassie. Shortly after Marsha's birth, another child would be brought into the Perry household after Scratch's sister Girlie gave birth to a son called Renal, who was adopted by Scratch and Pauline; in keeping with his habit of renaming everyone, Scratch gave the boy the nickname Enoch.

Lee Perry had already established his own Upsetter sound system by this time, operated by his record salesman/bodyguard and general assistant Jubie. Sticky was an occasional toaster on the set in its early days, later replaced by Jah Stitch; though the sound was small and operated sporadically, it retained popularity downtown for much of the decade. Another concrete boost to the popularity of the Upsetter label came through Scratch's sponsorship of a weekly radio show on JBC; for an hour every Thursday night, nothing but Upsetter music was broadcast.

Early 1970 also saw the release of two more Perry produced album collections: *Many Moods Of The Upsetters*, handled in the UK by Pama, and *Scratch The Upsetter Again*, released in the UK by Trojan. *Many Moods* had been assembled in August 1969, and its title aptly suggested the range of influences Perry incorporated into his productions. Like its predecessors *Clint Eastwood* and *The Upsetter*, the album was made up mostly of the instrumental version experiments that Perry had begun to master, with a few vocal cover tunes thrown in for good measure. The surreal album cover showed Perry in several different 'moods', ranging from the suave 'detective' to the unseen 'invisible', and again emphasised his status as a rampant swinger and charged sex symbol through shots of him with bikini-clad bathing beauties on the beach. Of the vocal content, David Isaacs' version of Ben E. King's 'Can't Take It Anymore' was another tear-jerking lament of failed romance, Pat Satchmo's 'Boss Society' was complemented by a serene re-working of the rude 'Goosy' calypso as though it too was a Louis Armstrong song, and the Temptations' 'Cloud Nine' was given a fairly faithful work-through by Carl Dawkins. The re-worked instrumentals included an organ cut of 'Selassie', re-titled 'Ex Ray Vision', a heavily over-dubbed cut of 'Check Him Out' called 'Soul Stew,' a sombre organ take of 'I'll Be Waiting' called 'Low Lights, and an organ version of 'Taste Of Killing' called 'Beware'. The truly manic piano and organ duet on the 'Uncle Charley' rhythm, called 'Prove It', was originally attempted with a saxophone, but was executed as a keyboard duet after a few takes, while 'Mean And Dangerous' (which had tentatively been titled 'Sign of the Times' during the recording session) was a cut of 'Stand By Me', also using overdubbed piano, organ, and sax, completed after nine abortive trial takes. A steel-drum version of Joe South's 'Games People Play' concluded the British pressing of the album, with another steel-drum track called 'Extra' being included on Jamaican pressings.

Issued in late February *Scratch The Upsetter Again* had nine instrumentals, including organ cuts of 'Return Of The Ugly' as 'Bad Tooth', and 'King Of The Trombone' as 'Outer Space', while 'Take One' was a cut of 'Medical Operation', on which the organ had been removed. The three vocal numbers were Dave Barker's version of the Shirelles' 'Will You Still Love Me', the heartfelt 'She Is Gone Again' by Alva Lewis, and former Vagabonds member Count Prince Miller's 'Mule Train', complete with zoological sound effects.

As Perry began to increase the amount of reverb on his overdubbed instruments, he also began a thematic shift with his titles: since Tip Top had spoiled his medical series, he moved over to the sounds of 'Bad Tooth' and 'The Dentist', and in reference to the fierce competition between Kingston's upcoming producers, Scratch proclaimed himself the winner instrumentally on 'The Result'.

Although the competition had often been ruthless, a fraternity existed amongst the struggling ghetto promoters, and Perry continued his tradition of helping to inaugurate the careers of other producers. When Alvin Ranglin started the GG's label, Perry gave him a helping hand in 1970 with what was to be one of his first hits: 'Man From Carolina', an organ re-working of the Folkes Brothers' 'Oh Carolina', introduced in an eerie fashion by Perry himself. Later in the year, Scratch would be instrumental in helping Niney to establish his Observer label after he too broke away from Joe Gibbs; Perry was even partly responsible for getting Niney to abandon his previous moniker of the Destroyer in favor of a more lasting title. As Niney later noted,

> 'I did name Destroyer before. When I decide to start out on my own, I remember Lee Perry come down and said to me "I am the Upsetter so you can't destroy me," fussing, fighting about "Who you going to destroy?" so one day I said, "That name there really sound a way." I don't know how it come, but gradually I go to the artwork guy and said I want to change my label, name it Observer.' [1]

Perry also licensed material from Martin Riley in this period, a singer from Jones Town who occasionally entered into self-production and would later be more famously known as Jimmy Riley. Born Martin James Norman Riley on May 22, 1954, he was the second of eight children whose father was a night watchman at the Myers rum plant and mother a seamstress in a clothing factory. At Kingston Senior School, Riley became friendly with Slim Smith who was already a member of the Techniques group with Winston Riley (no relation), Franklyn White, and Frederick 'Dadum' Waite. Unable to join the Techniques, Riley formed a rival group called the Sensations with Cornel Campbell, Aaron 'Bobby' Davis and Buster Riley, Winston Riley's brother. The Sensations became one of the leading harmony groups, and backed up Scratch on the sides he cut at WIRL, though Riley could not recall the material. Later, Riley left the Sensations to form the Uniques with Lloyd Charmers and Slim Smith after Smith fell out with Winston Riley over money; the Sensations were then briefly a trio until Jackie Paris joined, making the group a quartet again.

Riley said he originally met Perry through hanging out with Bunny Lee and Slim Smith on Orange Street. 'Because I used to hang with Bunny Lee, I was always on the street. At that time, Slim Smith used to live at the back of Muzik City at the apartment upstairs, and Scratch's record shop, Upsetter, was across the street on the lane. We used to smoke herb chalice a lot in the big yard besides Scratch, so going between the house and the shop we always saw Scratch, just run into each other like that.'

In addition to his work with the Uniques, Riley was also occasionally recording and producing his own solo material. One such issue was a rude number called 'Self Control', with vocals by Riley and Val Bennett's daughter Faye, a gutsy associate of Bunny Lee who was happy to provide lewd sounds on slack songs. After issuing the tune on his own Civic label, Riley later licensed the song to Scratch for pressing abroad on the Upsetter label, but the confusing circumstances of its foreign release eventually saw Archie Moore split away from Lee Perry and his crew. As Moore recalled, 'I was running the record shop and Jimmy Riley did a record named "Self Control". It didn't do well down here, so somebody pirate it and go to England with it and release it. Scratch knew about it but it wasn't Scratch's business, he wasn't the one who do it. Every time I call up there (England) I hear the record playing and I say if it playing like that it selling. Jimmy asking at the time and I tell him that the record doing well up there and him wouldn't believe me, so me asked Scratch to give me a chart when him coming down. When me get the chart me see that the music was (at number) thirteen, so me show it to him and me say "If it ram thirteen, then it must sell some money." I had a sister named Rosie who worked at an office, I told her to ask one of them lawyer man to write a letter and scare (the record company in England), and them send some money come give him. One day now it was like a meeting called between everybody, discussing who make Jimmy know, and him reveal say it's me tell him. Me tell him to keep him mouth (shut), 'cause he get a nice money out of it, fix up him car and all them things, and then he let me down. From one argument to the other, a fight started but them never really allow we to fight it out, because me fight with a guy that was working with Bunny Lee and Scratch run right between and him get a severe lick inna him ears and him couldn't hear. The guy break a bottle and cut me so me draw me ratchet and run him down, cut him right by Charles Street. They sew him up at KPH (Kingston Public Hospital), and them sew up my arm. Then basically me break ranks with them; anywhere you see trouble, you try and get out of it.'

Perry suggested that Archie was removed partly because of Pauline's claims that he was pocketing extra money from the till, though he noted his cousin may not have been aware of the malicious gossip. Once he left his post at the Upsetter record shop, Archie concentrated on building up his own sound system; operating since the late 1960s, the set was called Caveman because many said Archie's prominent forehead made him resemble a Neanderthal.

Caveman's departure meant Scratch needed someone else to run the record shop, as the Upsetter spent more time away from the premises. 'Me don't want to go to the shop because too much guys always want to beg,' Perry explained, 'so me just collect the money at weekends, or when they want record me go and give it to them.' Jubie, operator of the Upsetter sound system, took a more prominent role for a while, and Pauline remained regularly present until Perry hired Pat Francis to be his chief record salesman.

Born on August 29, 1947 in Point Hill, St Catherine, Patrick Lloyd Francis was one of ten children born to a farmer and his wife. When his father remarried after his mother's death, Francis was unable to get along with his stepmother and left home at age 12 to head to Kingston. He inevitably wound up in Trench Town, where he befriended Theophilus Beckford, Eric 'Monty' Morris and Toots Hibbert. Greatly inspired by Beckford's 'Easy Snappin', Francis formed a group called the Eagles with Carlton Brown, recording 'What An Agony' for Studio One in 1966. He later formed the Meditators with Paul Aston Jennings, recording 'Darling Here I Stand' for Studio One and 'Look Who A Bust Style' for producer Rupie Edwards in 1969; Francis was also selling records for Edwards and was instrumental in establishing the success of songs like Dobby Dobson's 'That Wonderful Sound', Joe Higgs' 'Burning Fire', and the Gaylads' 'My Jamaican Girl'.

After recording a few solo tunes, he approached Lee Perry with a Rastafarian song: 'I always know him at Studio One but never really get to do work with him until we meet at 36 Charles Street. Then we rehearse and I do a song named "King of Kings":"Let us give thanks to the King of Kings, he's the Lord and the Lord of all, the Conquering Lion of the Tribe of Judah, and the Elect of God and the Light of the World, His Imperial Majesty, the Emperor Selassie." I voice that song at West Indies, the band was man like Hux Brown, Jackie Jackson, Ronnie Bop, Easy Snapping on piano, and Winston Grennan on drums. When I do that song, he said I seem to be a lucky man; then after I would be a salesman too for Lee Perry. You'd have to go from shop to shop and try to put out the record to the people, make them know that it's a good record, try to get it off the ground. I was a salesman for about two years for Rupie Edwards, then another three years for Lee Perry.'

By late 1969, Scratch had begun to record fewer singers to concentrate more fully on instrumental productions. The initial exception was Dave Barker, who recorded fairly steadily for Perry as both singer and deejay from the summer of 1969 to the start of 1971. The next hit the pair created after 'Prisoner Of Love' was 'Shocks Of Mighty', voiced some weeks after their initial work together, using a cut of the Inspirations' 'Bhutto Girl' that Scratch had obatined from Bunny Lee; the rhythm had originally been created by Ronnie Bop at Dynamics. Present at the session was Martin Riley, who first met Barker when he was hanging around the Techniques group, trying to become a member.

'Martin used to move around with Scratch and Bunny Lee a lot. Most times he would either be with Bunny Lee or Scratch,' Barker noted, recalling Riley's assistance with the 'Shocks Of Mighty'session. 'That particular time, he came along to the same Randy's recording studio, it was closer to where Scratch's shop was, and Randy's studio sound was very clean and nice.'

Despite Riley's moral support and the strength of the rhythm, Barker said he had difficulty with his delivery on the first attempt at voicing 'Shocks Of Mighty'. 'Scratch played the track and I found it hard to respond to that track at that time. Scratch could not understand that it's not all the time a certain vibe comes to you. If the vibe isn't there, don't care how you force and force, it won't come. He got very upset and stormed out of the studio, which made me very upset too. Imagine the first time I go into the studio and gave him – baff! – one cut, "Prisoner of Love", and everything was nice and sweet. But this time we go in, and the vibe was not there, and the man go get upset. I started saying to myself, this man kind of lack understanding.'

Two weeks later, Perry and Barker had another go at the same rhythm, this time with Dave adapting lyrics from Slim Smith's 'Born To Love' for a vocal cut called 'Set Me Free'. 'We went back into the studio with the same track, and can you believe, from the man play the track – one cut again! As the track started playing, I started to sing, "It seems I was born, born to love you, babe, and sometimes I wonder why, why, I love you, babe." I go through that one cut, the man start him excitement, jumping up and down again! It's not to say I write out words, it's just vibes. From the man put the tape on, the words start to flow in my mind, and as them come in my mind, them come out. That cut there, straight right through, done, and Scratch up and down again, him can't contain himself. Then him say, "All right, bwoi, the flip side is a version. Wha'ppen, you feel you can do a talking?" "Yeah mon, I will try mon." Him play the rhythm, and me deh deh, "This is . . . Shocks of Mighty! This is a bad bad . . . " Him say "All right, you have 'Shocks of Mighty', suppose before you say 'Shocks of Mighty' you say 'This is . . . Upsetting!' " I go 'round the mike and me say "This is Upsetting! Shocks of Mighty! Hit me back!" Oh my gosh, right into it, and we just one cut again! And Scratch was just dancing all over again, come out of the studio, couldn't walk man, stoned!'

As with 'Prisoner of Love', both 'Set Me Free' and its version 'Shocks of Mighty' contained an anxious spontaneity that proved to be exciting to fans of Jamaica's music. Both in Jamaica and abroad, Barker's euphoric outbursts over the tightly wound rhythm of 'Shocks of Mighty' made a particular impact, and Scratch knew he had a hit when he first aired the tune at a prestigious nightclub uptown. 'Randy's had a cutting machine, cut slate, same place in the studio. The engineer at that time was Errol Thompson, he was brill. Scratch cut a disc there immediately, and we jump inna Scratch car and we go up to the clubs uptown by Half Way Tree. He used to cut the slates, go to the club, and check the people them response to the music. From Scratch put on the slate, and we start, "This is upsetting!", the people them shocked, because it's the first time they hear something like that. It's a club where everybody's in tables and chairs, sort of a groovy spot where everybody sit down, a few people might be dancing. From Scratch put on the slate and them hear this thing blast out, "This is upsetting! Shocks of mighty! Hit me back!", slowly the people them start to get up on dance floor, and everybody start move, and Scratch say "Yes! Yes!" Then him release it, and I hear say it come across and did well here (in the UK).'

Dave also noted that Scratch was responsible for 'Lockjaw', a song he voiced as a deejay for Duke Reid towards the end of 1969. Even though Duke Reid's men had beaten Perry up when he worked for Coxsone, Perry and Reid later enjoyed a friendship, as did Duke Reid and Prince Buster, another of Reid's former targets; Perry also retained a tempestuous friendship with Coxsone Dodd and Joe Gibbs throughout the years. Dave Barker recalled Perry's arrangement of the 'Lockjaw' session: 'Me and Scratch go by Duke Reid and go upstairs in the studio, say hello to Duke. Scratch and Duke were good friends, and me overheard Duke Reid saying to Scratch, "I have a music here, and I want a deejay, but the deejay I want is a deejay that can sound like an American. I don't want no ordinary deejay business 'pon it." Me hear him say to Duke, "Me have the man, mon, Dave will do it." Him call me, say "Dave, go and sing for Duke now. Duke have a music, me want you fe help out Duke." Duke say to me, "Perry say you is the Yankee man." Me say "Aye", nervously, because when him have him gun and all them thing there . . . Him say "Well, listen to this track here. Me want you do the Yankee thing, mon." Him play the track, and say "Me want you to talk something at the front, and inna the rhythm, me want you fe ride it." We exchange ideas, what to go on the front, and him say, "Well, me want it to sound like, bwoi, it a go everywhere, like it a spread all 'bout, all over, like coast-to-coast business, man." From him say "coast-to-coast", me say "Yes! 'Coast to coast, the sound of now!' He go to the engineer and he say "Take this – 'From coast-to-coast, the sound of now'." Him start to get excited.'

Dave's emphatic delivery over a choppy rhythm arranged by Tommy McCook propelled 'Lockjaw' to the top of the charts, seriously reviving Duke's flagging career as a producer. 'I got an inkling he probably was going flat businesswise, that tune there make him surface back,' Dave recalled, 'serious thing. Everywhere you go it's "Lock Jaw".'

As 1969 gave way to 1970, Perry continued working with Dave Barker, next enjoying a minor hit with a cover version of Blood Sweat and Tears' 'Spinning Wheel', which Perry recorded as a duet between Barker and Melanie Jonas. As with their previous hits, Barker noted that an element of spontaneity was often the key to success. 'One of the thing with Scratch is when he's going to the recording studio he's not someone who say, "Listen man, I'm going to the recording studio tomorrow or next week", to prepare certain songs or lyrics or anything like that, him just say, "Come, make we go studio." He springs these things on you. We went into the studio and we play the track, and him say he would like me and Mel to do that track. We run it down a couple of times and we did that particular track, which surprisingly didn't turn out too bad.'

After the success of the song, Perry established the Spinning Wheel label to provide further financial support for Melanie Jonas. Releases on Spinning Wheel included 'Haunted House', 'Double Wheel', and 'Land of Kinks', all instrumental cuts of 'Spinning Wheel', plus material from otherwise unknown singers O'Neil Hall and Chuck Berry Junior; issues on the label pressed in the UK brought Jonas considerable income. 'A big chance was there to give her some money because I did like her,' Perry recalled. 'She wasn't looking the type that rough, she was clean skin, looking nice. She was looking different and she give me a good vibration, so why shouldn't I give her a start?'

Meanwhile, Perry's own Upsetter label was thriving, both on the instrumental and on the vocal front. By now Scratch had built up a large catalogue of backing tracks, enabling him to select particular rhythms whenever a specific idea came to him. He continued to record cover tunes of foreign pop hits, but was not content with merely licking them over; most were thoroughly mutated, especially on the version side. 'I did have a collection of pop songs that did mean something to me,' said Perry in reference to his source material. 'Most of them we used to (make cover versions), put the (instrumental) tracks down until me see somebody who might look like them can do it, then run the track and give them the words.'

Thus, Dave Barker's version of King Floyd's popular American blues number 'Groove Me' was cut in two different formats, one a fairly faithful fast soul version, the other a slow and sensuous reggae cut. 'Melting Pot' was the song that brought one-hit wonders Blue Mink to the top of the British charts in November 1969, and Perry was significantly taken by the song's message of the power of love to transcend racial barriers to record a version with Melanie Jonas, credited on release to the Heaters. Perry's rendition was led by a throbbing bass and conga drum, lending the song a nuance of African elements that emphasised the song's thrust of ethnic melding. The version side, 'Kinky Mood', was a playful experiment in mixing, with the already prominent bass brought ever closer, the piano and organ beneath being rhythmically boosted and withdrawn without warning. Similarly, Steam's 'Na Na Hey Hey (Kiss Him Goodbye)' was subjected to Upsetter kinks with the melody played by what seems to be an organ fed through a wah-wah pedal. And as he and Melanie Jonas explored the depths of carnal activity before her emigration ended their affair, he proclaimed himself 'the kinkiest' on a similarly structured instrumental called 'Land Of Kinks'.

As Perry was putting together such odd innovations in instrumental sound, the Wailers were on the verge of joining forces again after a period of inactivity. Bob Marley's months in America with his family had seen their temporary withdrawal from the scene, and he was eager to begin recording new material he had been working on in Delaware. Late in 1969, Marley had been sent registration papers for the American military draft; refusing to fight in the Vietnam War, he immediately returned to Jamaica. Peter Tosh and Bunny Wailer had been largely dormant in his absence, and Bob is said to have initially been reluctant to join back with them, owing to friction generated by his departure, but eventually the group was reunited.

The Wailers left Studio One not long after Perry split with Dodd. They had also been frustrated by Coxsone's business practices, and decided to try to make it on their own. But the few releases they had put together for their own Wail'n Soul'm label had not sold sufficiently to keep the label going, and the recordings they made with the All Stars for Leslie Kong were also not sellers. Although they were finding survival difficult without backing, they were determined not to return to either Kong or Dodd, and held dreams of forming their own self-sufficient company in the future.

Some relief had come in 1968, through the signing of a somewhat questionable contract with JAD. The company had been formed by the

American singer Johnny Nash, his manager, Danny Sims, and producer Arthur Jenkins. Sims and Nash had initially been attracted to Jamaica because of the low cost of recording, and were significantly impressed by the Wailers in general and Bob Marley in particular to begin recording demos of the group in the hopes of breaking them into lucrative overseas markets.

Besides having solid connections with American and European music industries, Sims was also said to have had strong links with elements of American organised crime, and he would remain a controversial figure in the group's progression for several years to come. Despite dozens of tracks being recorded for JAD at Dynamics and Federal from late 1968, little had been released at the start of the 1970s, and promised exposure abroad was also elusive. The Wailers were thus looking for a different outlet to achieve their goals, and Bob Marley's open ears knew precisely where to find it.

The exact sequence of events has proved difficult to unearth accurately, with much contradictory information being supplied by various sources who were actively involved in the events, but the Wailers certainly sought out the Upsetters in the spring of 1970, and the combination was to prove unbeatable, with Perry directing their creations. According to Family Man, his initial meeting with the Wailers came when Bob Marley sought to use the Hippy Boys' rhythm section for a self-produced single called 'Black Progress'; they subsequently came together under the aegis of Lee Perry for some of their strongest work. Fams recounted his first meeting with Bob: 'We used to do backing for any artist. One time Bob was in Europe and the States amongst his mother, and he back to Jamaica now and decide to get back in the music. He'd been listening to all the sound what's hot in Jamaica, and out of the blue he heard this song "Watch This Sound". He liked that bass sound, so he was inquiring for the bass player who play that bass for his session. He check a friend of mine who is Alva Lewis, popularly known as Reggie, guitarist from the Hippy Boys/Upsetters. He gave me the message and he take me to where Bob hang out, and Bob was there rocking and smoking some chalice, so he says, "Stay here, I soon come back when I finished talking to him," and he went away for about 45 minutes to an hour. When he come back, Bob said to him, "What happened, Reggie, I asked you to do a favour for me. What happened to the man I asked you to get?" He say, "I bring the man come long time! See him over there?" Bob look 'pon me and say, "Oh, this youth there? A you named Family Man?" Me say "Yeah!" He laugh and say, "Is really you name so? So you is the right man then!" He didn't know it was a youth, he thought it was a more professional, elder person.'

Lee Perry has also named the Hippy Boys' rhythm section as one of the significant factors that led to Marley approaching the producer – an approach he felt unable to refuse when confronted with the immediate honesty of Marley's vision.

'That's why Bob came when he come into it, because I was creating that sound, and the young musicians, Family Man and Reggie, them hear the sound and they wanted to join it, so them come by me and decide say they want to play some music for me. They was ready to play that kinky, funny type of idea that I had. Bob was with Coxsone; after I left Coxsone, the thing wasn't strong with Coxsone anymore, and even Bob's thing was shaking. The Wailers' thing was shaking, everything shake. When me leave Coxsone, everything gone reggae, so Bob went away, maybe to America, and all 'bout, wherever him going him hear that funny sound that I had. He go to England and he hear it and he come back to Jamaica and say "Scratch, you have a sound, and honestly I really want to work with you" I say, "I don't really want to work with no singer at the moment," because I was just making instrumental, I was really burned and bitter after the Coxsone treatment, and I decide to upset. When I look 'pon Bob, it was like somebody sent him. From inside, I didn't want to do it, definitely, 'cause I didn't need no help from Bob or nobody. I did have a upsetting vibration and it was good enough for me, but Bob hear it and want to join it. I said, "OK then," but when I look I see that someone really sent him because he need help somewhere. I say, "Let me hear the songs that you have to sing," he sing this, "My cup is overflowing, I don't know what to do." I said to myself, as a producer listening to an artist's inspiration, this is a true confession, it's the truth! His cup run over and don't know what to do, so he need help. I didn't say that to him, but I think about it. I listen; I didn't want to take him on, because I didn't need no help and I didn't want to use any singers, 'cause them was behaving so stink and so rude that I didn't want to get involved, just wanted to do instrumentals. But then, I looked and I hear somebody's inside dark, and I want to hear what the person say, so I tell him to let me hear what song him have to sing and him say his cup overflowing and he don't know what to do.' [2]

Perry's home in Washington Gardens was fast becoming crowded with additional mouths to feed. In addition to Marsha and Enoch, the family also had an extra guest: Bob Marley was temporarily lodged in the front room so that he, Perry and the spirits could work more closely together.

'I give Bob a room there in my yard to live, Bob was living there. Bob was having my front room, and the room that Bob was staying in, that's where I have my genie. I have a real genie, I don't know if you believe in genie but I have a real genie. My genie's not in a bottle, (it's) the breeze, the bag of breeze. He was living in the genie room and absorbing the power of the genie to do the job because I didn't hear a singer, and he didn't have the personality and the looks and the complexion and the hair, even though it wasn't dread when he come. So after him gather the power and him get mighty strong I know it was real power, and he put on the dread and decided to take over. And he did it, he did really take over.' [3]

While Bob was a guest in the Perry household, he and Scratch worked on several songs together. Later, the pair would travel to the rural area where Perry had been raised to work on other songs together, staying briefly at the home of Perry's mother in Hanover, a place Perry would often bring his growing children over the years.

Perry also claimed that it was he who convinced Bob to reinstate Bunny and Peter for the songs they were working on together, creations that they saw not as reggae music but instead as revolutionary soul.

'I was working with Bob and Bob didn't want to go back with the Bunny and Peter thing. I say, "Well, I think you should do it with this soul revolution for special reason, because the three of your voice blend very good like an angel, to manifest your work on this soul revolution." That was a revolution – a spiritual revolution, fighting against government pressure and things like that, so he say, "I'll take your advice and call 'em back," otherwise there would be no more Peter and Wailer when the Coxsone thing break up. It was my idea to put them back together; he alone didn't want to do it. Bob wanted to sing with me alone without them, but I said, "No, you need them for special work like "Sun Is Shining", you need the harmony." ' [4]

And so it was that one of the greatest musical partnerships the world has ever known came to fruition: the incredible combination of Lee 'Scratch' Perry and the Wailers.

Working solidly together for the rest of 1970 and part of 1971, Scratch and the Wailers created music that would prove to be timeless. The Wailers were the hardest and most original vocal trio on the island, and the Upsetter musicians were creating the toughest rhythms under Perry's limitless artistic vision. Just as he had created something new with 'People Funny Boy', Perry was now in the process of changing the reggae beat, and the Wailers would be the ones with which the new sound was realised. 'When the people hear what I man do them hear a different beat,' said Perry in an often quoted passage from 1977, 'a slower beat, a waxy beat – like you stepping in glue. Them hear a different bass, a rebel bass, coming at you like sticking a gun.' [5]

Although Perry coaxed brilliant performances from each of the Wailers, it was his special relationship with Bob Marley that resulted in much of the strongest material. As his own father had abandoned him at birth, Marley sought out a series of surrogate father figures throughout his life, and Perry seemed to fulfil this role for a brief time, but in their relationship Perry generally was treated more like an elder brother or at times a demented uncle. Scratch's best strength was his ability to teach, and many have testified to the concrete changes his coaching brought to the Wailers' singing. As Clancy Eccles noted,

'Perry was always a fan of Bob Marley. He loved Bob, he feel like Bob is the best singer in the world. But Bob Marley never used to sing like how he sings now, then he used to sing a different way, but Perry used to sing that way how Bob Marley sound now.' [6]

Jimmy Riley backed up Eccles' testimony. 'He was the one who taught Bob Marley to sing really, that's the honest-to-god truth. The way Bob Marley sing is the way Scratch sing, for real. Bob Marley used to sing a different way before he start singing with Scratch; if you listen to Studio One Bob Marley and when he start working with Scratch, it's a different way. Scratch is not really a singer, but Scratch can express himself; he's slower in a different kind of way. That style is effective because you hear what he's saying more, so Bob Marley pick up that style and work with him.'

What Lee Perry did was to transform the Wailers' sound by paring it down and gearing it more towards Jamaican ears as opposed to simply aping the styles of their American vocal heroes. Perry spent weeks rehearsing with the group in the back of the Upsetter Record Shop, restoring their confidence in their own creative abilities and persuading them to reach higher heights through a presentation of music that was a more honest expression of their true selves than material they had recorded previously for others. From the recording of 'My Cup' in the summer of 1970, Scratch and the Wailers created a string of exceptional songs together that remain as outstanding works of both their respective careers. Recording in Randy's Studio, the group cut over two albums' worth of material with Perry by the end of the year, songs that helped change the direction of reggae, giving it a harder edge and a more natural, indigenous focus.

It was also the percussion of Sticky that would lend a certain ambience to these songs. Shortly before the recording of 'My Cup', Sticky found his true calling at one of Scratch's recording sessions, transforming himself from deejay to percussionist: 'I just found myself in the studio with a grater, start play grater and Scratch say "Yeah mon." Then after the grater I get two piece of stick, they call it grillo. Scratch know me have the vibes to do any likkle thing, he always call me and I try to put out, 'cause we did love Scratch. Me and Maxie (Romeo) stick 'mongst Scratch daily, so sometimes Scratch go into the studio and make all a rhythm with no guitar, and me have to use my percussion to play rhythm. Even on one of Bob's songs, it's just percussion a do the rhythm, because the man go down a the studio with him bag a tape and don't see no drummer.'

Sticky's percussion would lend a subtle African feel to the backdrop of the Wailers' rhythms, his unobtrusive licks and skilful timing quietly enhancing the works. The songs were generally infused with a more rebellious spirit, containing a sense of spontaneity and youthfulness, stemming largely from the solid Upsetter rhythm section and crisp engineering work from the young Errol Thompson.

But this intense fusion of the Wailers and Upsetters was not without friction; a smooth transition it certainly was not according to those present. It was typically money that would cause a rupture, and the first instance of Scratch seeking another band to back the Wailers stemmed largely from financial concerns. Scratch had learned that Striker Lee had hired an upcoming group of Greenwich Farm musicians called the Soul Syndicate to play a marathon recording session for a mere $200; he thus approached the band to record a quiet and introspective number Bob had written called 'Sun Is Shining'.

According to rhythm guitarist Tony Chin, the Soul Syndicate evolved from the Rhythm Raiders, a group formed by a shoemaker named Meggy in 1967. Born on September 28, 1948, Albert Valentine Chin was an only child whose father was a salesman and fisherman and mother a domestic worker. Chin's mixed parentage is a direct reflection of the different ethnic groups that compose Jamaican society: he is half black, one quarter Chinese and one quarter Indian. Chin grew between Greenwich Farm, Trench Town, Spanish Town and Waltham Park, and spent a couple of years in St Andrew and Negril with a family friend called Miss Williams. In his teen years, Chin's father bought an acoustic guitar from a local drunkard and Tony began to learn chords from a school friend named Morris Gregory. It was Gregory who knew the shoemaker and aspiring guitarist on Maxfield Avenue called Meggy who had two electric guitars and a drum set; Gregory told Chin that Meggy was was looking for a set of musicians to join him and a drummer called Elgin who had accompanied Meggy to town from a rural area. Through another connection made by Morris Gregory, Tony Chin had become friendly with another neighbourhood guitarist named George Fullwood, who Chin drafted into the group.

Born in Kingston on October 30, 1950, Fully was the second of three children born to a sheet metal worker and his wife. He lived in the Rae Town ghetto of East Kingston until age six, when the family moved across to the Western Kingston ghetto of Greenwich Farm. Fascinated by music at an early age, Fully made his first guitars out of sardine cans. When his father realised Fully was serious about music, he had a work colleague teach his son the basics of guitar, but the youth was soon more capable than his teacher.

When Tony Chin told Fully that he knew someone who was seeking a bass player, Fullwood had not yet played a bass guitar, but knew how to play the lower strings of a guitar as though it was a bass. Tony Chin thus brought Fully into the group as a bassist, and the early line-up of the Rhythm Raiders was complete.

In 1967 and '68, the Rhythm Raiders played at various Kingston nightclubs, and appeared on stage shows around the island backing artists like Roy Shirley and Stranger Cole. But Meggy and Elgin were far older than the other band members, and had difficulty keeping up with the group's musical progression. By 1969 there were some personnel changes: drummer Max Edwards briefly joined the group, and was quickly replaced by Leroy 'Horsemouth' Wallace, who had been practically adopted by Fully's parents after spending time at the Alpha School for Boys. Prone to causing fights and generally unreliable, Horsemouth was replaced by a tall young drummer from Greenwich Farm named Carlton 'Santa' Davis, who Fully had grown up with; Davis' mother, who worked at a local dry cleaner's, often left him in Fully's care.

Somewhat younger than the other group members, Santa got his nickname from a skating accident one Christmas that left his face red and swollen. He was an only child who was fascinated by the synchronised beats of marching bands from an early age: each day, on his way home from school, Santa used to pass a Catholic church on the corner of St Joseph's Road and Waltham Park Road, where he would hear the marching music that so captivated him. At age ten he auditioned to join the church's Junior group, but his playing was so proficient that they put him straight into the Senior group, where he remained for the next five years, learning to play bass, tenor, and snare drums. Bobby Aitken used to give guitar lessons to some of the church's band members, and he gave Davis some pointers on how to play the eight-bar rock steady beat. At age 14, Santa joined the Graduates, a live band formed by one Kofi Kali, a Jamaican who had spent time in New York and was heavily influenced by the jazz of John Coltrane. The Graduates featured Earl 'Wire' Lindo on keyboards, Richard Daley on guitar (later more famous as a bassist with Third World), and Earl 'Bagga' Walker on bass. Regularly performing at nightclubs such as the Blue Mist on Slipe Road, the Graduates played a mixture of musical styles including ska and calypso. Their manager, Mr Reece, got them a series of gigs in Ocho Rios backing up Ken Boothe, Alton Ellis, Hortense Ellis, and Joe Higgs, but the band broke up when they learned that Reece was taking advantage of them financially. It was in late 1969 that the Rhythm Raiders were in search of a drummer, and Santa found himself joining his friend Fully's group after a successful audition.

By the time Santa joined the band, the guitarist Meggy had been replaced by Cleon Douglas, who was a strong vocalist, as well as a competent lead guitarist. Douglas had grown up in the same yard as Tony Chin, and it was Chin who had first taught him to play guitar. George Fullwood's father had taken over management of the band by this time, buying some inexpensive instruments and basic amplifiers, and also building cymbal stands for their use.

Taking a suggestion from Fully's older brother Lucky, the group changed its name to Soul Syndicate after the personnel changes in 1969. Many additional members would subsequently drift in and out of the group. When

Santa completed the line-up, keyboard duties were being handled by someone called Scotty; other keyboardists to spend time with the group would include Earl 'Wire' Lindo, Tyrone Downey, Augustus Pablo, Glen Adams (who used to sew the band's uniforms), Tony Johnson, and Jah Macka, but it was Keith Sterling, younger brother of saxophonist Lester Sterling, who eventually joined the group full time. Alva 'Reggie' Lewis would briefly be a member, and after Cleon Douglas emigrated to America in early 1970, another young Greenwich Farm resident named Earl 'Chinna' Smith became their regular lead guitarist.

Born in Kingston on August 6, 1955, Smith was raised by family friends in Greenwich Farm, right next door to Bunny Lee. Both his father and godfather ran sound systems; his father, a roofing contractor, ran a sound called Smith's that Bunny Lee used to operate, while his godfather, a fudge seller, ran a sound called Down South the President. As a little boy, Earl tried to emulate his father and godfather on a toy sound system made out of broken records, which earned him the nickname Tuner after a type of hi-fi amplifier. Pronounced in strong patois, Tuner soon mutated to Chuner, which eventually was corrupted further to Chinna or Chinner.

It was as a young boy that Chinna first encountered Lee Perry, who often came to visit his neighbour, Bunny Lee. 'I remember this likkle man used to dress neat. He used to come down to Bunny Lee with his attaché case, used to walk come down East Avenue. That time him have some tight up pants, never out of him attaché case. Because Striker a godfather, all of the man them have to come check the don Striker Lee, every man used to come hang out at Striker Lee. Mrs Lee have this bar named Mother in Law, so everybody just come check when we draw weed. East Avenue was *the* Avenue then.'

Around the same time that he noted Scratch's dapper presence in the neighbourhood, Chinna began to be fascinated by the guitar, and was quickly fashioning replicas out of sardine cans and fishing line. In his early teens, Chinna formed a neighbourhood singing group with his friend Earl Johnson (later known as Earl Zero) and a youth known as Rush It, and the trio began sitting in on the rehearsals that Soul Syndicate held three nights a week at their base on Ninth Avenue. After borrowing a guitar from a cabinetmaker named Mr Eastman, Chinna asked Cleon Douglas to teach him the rudiments of tuning, thus paving the way for him to successfully emulate what Douglas played. As Chinna spent so much time at Soul Syndicate rehearsals, he soon found that he had mastered their full repertoire, and when Douglas was preparing to migrate to America, Fully thus made arrangements for Chinna to join the group. Chinna recalled playing his first gig with the band at the Spanish Town Theatre – a performance which went down well with the audience, but which only earned each band member the ludicrous sum of 25 cents.

Through their close personal friendships and highly developed musical skills, Soul Syndicate would grow to be a highly respected group through work with producers such as Niney and Keith Hudson, but when Lee Perry first used the group, they had only recently cut their studio teeth. In fact, they had not done much more than their lengthy session for Bunny Lee, at which they produced material by a group from Falmouth called the Twinkle Brothers (including a song called 'Miss World'), and a set of songs with Slim Smith and the Uniques; their following session for Phil Pratt resulted in John Holt's hit 'My Heart Is Gone'.

Though Chinna's school attendence meant he was not present at Scratch's session, he remembered Perry's motivation in seeking out Soul Syndicate. 'I used to be there at school, that's why I missed the session when Scratch come and call them to do "Sun Is Shining". Even though Scratch used to have the Upsetters, Scratch always want a different sound, so he tune into Soul Syndicate, come down and hear the band. We did do some sessions for Phil Pratt, some bad tune, and Bunny do some tune, pure hit rhythm. The word go out that Soul Syndicate wicked, so Scratch come in and draw them now fe do the "Sun is Shining".'

Santa Davis noted that Scratch was typically directive in shaping the overall feel of 'Sun Is Shining'. 'The first thing for Scratch was a song with Bob Marley called "Sun Is Shining". It was me, Fully, Cleon Douglas, and Tony. The first time I ever be in the studio with Scratch, it was an experience. This guy's head is full of ideas. People like Scratch and even Niney, they shaped sound in a new way, to make a music that had never been played in Jamaica in that time. They used to come up with ideas that other producers wouldn't have. They would actually arrange the music, they would show you things. Scratch wanted a particular type of mood in the song, he didn't want any eight-beat or anything going on, it would distract from the rhythm. I was playing and he took away the high hat, he said 'You play this song without the high hat.' I said in my mind, 'How am I going to do that?' but then, as a musician, you have a challenge so we play the song without the high hat, that's why it sound open. That's how that song was made, without the high hat. You hear no high hat on that song.'

Though the Upsetters remained Lee Perry's house band, the next time there was a quarrel about money, he decided to use the less financially demanding Soul Syndicate again, this time under more difficult circumstances and with less readily pleasing results. Recorded soon after 'Sun Is Shining', 'Duppy Conqueror' was one of the most original and classic songs the Wailers had yet recorded. A duppy is a chaotic spirit, forced to roam between the spirit land and our visible world if the body it inhabited in life was given an incomplete burial or lay in a grave that was desecrated; captured by a worker of Obeah, a duppy is believed able to cause serious harm to the living. One of the many songs that Marley and Perry put their heads together to create, 'Duppy Conqueror' ultimately spoke of the strength and prowess of Bob Marley, the

Tuff Gong who had returned to shake up Kingston and its music scene, and Perry's influence is evident in both the lyrics and arrangement of 'Duppy Conqueror'.

> 'One Saturday I was doing some recording at a little shop in Orange Street. I said well look here, Bob, I want you to write a tune with "yes, me friend, we on the street again" in it. He gave me the third line, I gave him the fourth line and so on. We started to work together and the ideas started to flow 'til finally we made the tune "Duppy Conqueror".' [7]

Reggie Lewis noted that he acted as something of a catalyst in the writing of the song, which he recalled as having been written in the back of the Upsetter record shop. 'Me there 'mongst Scratch and me say, "Scratch, you no see you get soft. Upsetters is soft." Scratch say, "Soft?! Call Bob for me," and me jump inna me likkle car, me go call Bob, me see Bob sit down 'pon him box right at his yard gates, and me say, "Scratch call you." Him say "What Scratch a call me for now? Just let me go inside and change me clothes." Me say "Come in the car same way, mon." Bob took up him guitar and put it in the car back and come barefoot same way and we go down to Charles Street and go 'round the back there . . . you have a man who have a little set-up named Dizzy, him sell herb, and after two chalice Bob say, "Wha'ppen? What you a call me for?" Scratch say, "Give him a little drink, man," because Scratch have a bar right there named Green Door Saloon, right there in Charles Street . . . That's how "Duppy Conqueror" write.'

The recording of 'Duppy Conqueror' proved to be most problematic – and the problem, as Family Man noted, was primarily financial as usual. 'There was a session Scratch was planning after they write the song "Duppy Conqueror", but at the time, I didn't have the cash to pay my rent, so I says "Scratch, I need some money!" He says "You a come to the session?" I says, "Well, I better go somewhere else to look some cash. If I don't make it, I'll feel better trying." '

When the band's demands for outstanding payment were met only by Perry's excuses, they left in a huff and refused to provide backing. Scratch thus turned again to their understudies, the Soul Syndicate.

For the original recording of 'Duppy Conqueror' at Randy's, Tony Chin played lead guitar and Cleon Douglas handled rhythm, along with Fully on bass, Santa on drums, and Glen Adams on Wurlitzer organ; Peter Tosh later overdubbed additional organ riffs on the tune. When the rhythm had been initially laid, Perry was not certain about the sound of the junior musicians, so he asked the opinion of Family Man and Reggie when they appeared at his shop on Charles Street. As Fams recalled, 'He bring in the Soul Syndicate and they do the rhythm for "Duppy Conqueror" and he cut a dub. When he see me he called me in the record shop and said, "You didn't come, listen to this." When I listen to it, he say, "What you think?" I say, "It's nice, it's good, but that not 'Conqueror' rhythm. You have to book a different time, that's not what we started out." That rhythm end up being "Mr Brown", and we went back and we do the proper rhythm for "Duppy Conqueror", that was special!'

Perry agreed with Family Man: the Soul Syndicate rhythm was good, but it was not fit to be the 'Duppy Conqueror' rhythm. He left the tape in the can momentarily and made arrangements to re-build 'Duppy Conqueror' with the usual Upsetters. Family Man, Carly, Glen Adams, and Reggie made their reparations with Scratch and went back with him, the Wailers and Sticky to Randy's to cut the rhythm again, and the resultant 'Duppy Conqueror' created a rage when it hit the street on a blank label release a few days after. 'Randy's himself operate the board,' Reggie noted, 'and a one cut.'

Its version flip side, 'Zig Zag', presented the raw rhythm with accentuated organ and guitar, a sparse cut that emphasised the song's jagged edges. Several subsequent pressings later appeared in Jamaica and abroad as the song increased in popularity, and Perry quickly re-used the rhythm for 'Upsetting Station' (a.k.a. 'Conqueror Version 3'), a far-out 'talking' cut in radio-jock mode by Dave Barker. Joe Gibbs sought to cash in on the record's success with an instrumental re-cut called 'Ghost Capturer', but Perry eventually got his own back by re-pressing Gibbs' version with added mechanical laughter effects as 'Bigger Joke'.

Shortly after the success of 'Duppy Conqueror', Perry and the Wailers had another hit with 'Soul Rebel', a song the group had given a half-hearted attempt with Danny Sims. Perry's version fully restored the song's raw power, which Sims had flattened out through a cheesy horn and doo-wop vocal arrangement; even the stammer that Bob had been cultivating over the years was stripped down to its minimal base on the Upsetter version to allow him to express better the pride and optimism Marley carried in his rebellious spirit. The slow proclamations of 'Soul Rebel' went beyond mere boasting and posturing; the song is instead a highly autobiographical number in which Bob dismisses the neighbourhood gossip to revel in the insurgent forces contained in his inner being. 'I arranged the music for that,' Perry stated categorically in 1975, 'He wrote the lyrics.' [8]

As with many subsequent sessions, the perfectionists Marley and Perry insisted that several takes were recorded with slight variations until they correctly captured the essence of the tune, and the Wailers themselves issued alternate versions of the song with entirely different lyrics as 'Run For Cover', which surfaced on the Power label around the same time and later on Tuff Gong. According to Scratch, it was he who suggested Marley use the name Tuff Gong for his label. 'I give Bob the name for Tuff Gong. He was looking for a name to call his record company, we were working together and I call it something like Soul, and it didn't work, so we was looking for a name and going down Orange Street. We almost reach Beeston Street and Orange Street corner, he say "Scratch, I'm looking for a name for my label." Me say "Call it Tuff Gong", that was on Orange Street and Beeston Street.'

'Soul Rebel' was followed up by 'Man to Man', another song Marley and
Perry had written together. Re-recorded years later as 'Who the Cap Fits' when
Marley had permanently become a solo artist, the song used proverbs to
explore the wickedness and treachery that our closest friends are capable of
inflicting; the version side, 'Necoteen', showed the sharp edges of the Upsetter
accompaniment that lay beneath the Wailers' ethereal harmonies. As Perry was
again hampered by constraints on his time and finances, the pressing of this
single was arranged by retail record mogul KG; shortly after, Perry arranged a
distribution deal with Sonia Pottinger to alleviate problems associated with the
pressing and distribution of new material.

Medley fever was shortly to grip the nation through singles by the
Gaylads, Errol Dunkley, the Heptones, and others, and Perry was among the
first to set the trend. He had the Wailers lay down a combination track called
'All in One', made up of several of their previous hits such as 'Bend Down
Low', 'Nice Time', 'One Love', 'Simmer Down', 'It Hurts To Be Alone', 'Love
And Affection', and 'Put It On'. The original Jamaican issue of this single split
the medley over two sides, and included the sound of a master tape being rewound in the mix, making explicit the editing process and harking back to the
'hits of yesteryear' at Studio One; on later UK pressings, the medley was
compressed onto one side of a single, with a few bars of 'Duppy Conqueror'
tacked onto the end.

While 'Duppy Conqueror' continued to make waves across Jamaica, the
island was also gripped by a strange and frightening phenomenon: A duppy
was said to be speeding through the land on a three-wheeled coffin, on top of
which three 'John Crows' (buzzards) were perched, one of which was asking
for a certain Mr Brown. It was said to have been originally sighted in
Mandeville, re-appeared in Sligoville, was driven through Spanish Town, and
arrived in downtown Kingston by the Old Harbour Road. When Glen Adams
appeared on Charles Street one morning, he found a sizeable crowd searching
for the coffin right in front of the Upsetter record shop, and quickly put
together some lyrics about the situation.

The origins of the tale remain obscure, and many conflicting statements
have pointed to diverse beginnings. Adams recalled it stemming from a
murder case in Mandeville, while the *Daily Gleaner* reported it being related to
a case of petty theft in the same town; Bunny Wailer has also said that it may
have been linked to a publicity drive by Brown's funeral parlour in Kingston.
Regardless of its origins, belief in the tale provided the perfect vehicle for a
song, and 'Mr Brown' became the most successful of several tunes that were
quickly recorded to comment on the situation.

As Lee Perry himself later stated,

'In Jamaica you have Obeah man that chant Obeah and all kind of ism
and schism, and send out ghost and send out duppies, terrorise the

people. Then we discover that people in Jamaica can tell a quick lie. Somebody in Jamaica work a quick lie, say there is some ghost going 'round in a coffin, looking for a man named Mr Brown. But it wasn't (true), somebody just want to say something to scare people, and people believe in it and people get frightened. So we go to the studio and make this song about this ghost-talk coffin saying, "Have you seen Mr Brown?"It was just like a publicity stuff, a joke.' [9]

After putting together some lyrics, Glen Adams went to voice the song that afternoon at Randy's over the original 'Duppy Conqueror' rhythm that the Soul Syndicate had recorded, but Perry suggested that the Wailers voice it instead. To emphasise the ghoulish nature of the song's subject, Bunny Wailer supplied the maniacal laughter worthy of a Hammer horror film that is featured throughout the song, while both Glen Adams and Peter Tosh laid down spooky organ riffs. In Jamaica, the song initially sold around 15,000 copies, enough to make an impact but not nearly as strong a seller as 'Duppy Conqueror'; later 'Mr Brown' would be one of the songs that brought the group to the attention of a wider audience in Britain through a Trojan re-release.

As summer turned to autumn, Lee Perry concentrated his efforts on perfecting the Wailers' sound. He rehearsed them rigorously in the back of the Upsetter record shop, preparing them for the recording of an album and gearing them up for live performances around the island. Even when Perry took time out to record the odd song with other artists, the Wailers were usually involved in some way. Dave Barker's 'What A Confusion' is a case in point. 'What A Confusion' began life as 'Screwdriver', another kinky instrumental led by the quavering organ trills of Winston Wright; beneath swinging horns and honking, oddball sound effects, echoes of the 'Duppy Conqueror' rhythm lay buried in the mix. According to Dave Barker, Perry later fashioned lyrics to fit the rhythm, and his chosen vocalists were again the Wailers. 'Bob, Bunny, and Peter were supposed to be the ones who should have done a song named "What A Confusion". I don't know what happened, but somehow Scratch asked me to do it. Can you believe that it is me and Bunny Wailer that did that song? Bunny harmonised with the fine voice on top of my voice. It was after a while I found out that it was the Wailers who were supposed to have done that song.' Similarly, it was the musical contributions of the Wailers that partly made Little Roy's 'All Africans' (a.k.a. 'Cross The Nation') such a great record.

Born in Whitfield Town on February 25, 1953, Little Roy's given name was Earl Lowe. A short, quiet youth with a prominent set of front teeth, he made his first record at Studio One towards the end of the rock steady era. Initially credited incorrectly to the Gaylads, 'I'm Going To Cool It' was a song his big brother Campbell had written while watering the family garden. 'I followed two of my school mates to Coxsone, Barrington Bailey and Errol Burgess. They went to do an audition for Jackie Mittoo, we were in the same class at school. After they finish singing, Jackie Mittoo says to me, "So what you're doing? Sing me a song." I sing that song that I heard my brother singing, and Jackie Mittoo recorded me the next day. After that I went to Prince Buster because me and him were living in the same neighbourhood, Washington Gardens. Some times in the morning before he wake up, I try to sing a song for him, so I ended up singing two songs for Prince Buster, "It's You I Love" and "Reggae Got Soul".'

It was Buster who gave Little Roy his stage name, but his first real hit came in 1969 with 'Bongo Nyah', recorded with a young singer called Donovan Carlos as The Little Roys for producer Lloyd the Matador. ' "Bongo Nyah" is the starting of me as a youth getting conscious towards Rastafari,' said Lowe of the song's inspiration. 'The lyrics was even dreader than that, but the producer decided to water down the material.'

'Bongo Nyah' achieved instant success, and enjoyed a number-one position in the Jamaican charts for several weeks. Lowe continued to record for the Matador, working with the Hippy Boys on further hits like 'Hard Fighter', but was displeased by what he felt was censure by the cautious producer who was reluctant to record lyrics that were too radical.

Hanging out in Washington Gardens, Lowe began to be drawn towards the Rastafarian faith, largely through a local dread called Vill who was also close to Lee Perry. 'In Washington Gardens, one of my brethren named Vill have a dreadlocks. Vill and Vincent, they came from Trench Town, from the Pen, the Ghetto. They moved into this area, I would say it's a middle-class area, Washington Gardens. Them youth give me enough inspiration towards Rastafari. Those Rasta brethren, they used to sit in and read the Bible every day, and smoke a lot of ganja, a lot of chalice. Them brethren show me the way to Rastafari to have to accept it.'

As Lowe's consciousness of his African heritage began to increase with his acceptance of the Rastafarian faith, he approached Perry with another song whose message he did not want diluted. Since the release of 'Rightful Ruler', Perry had become known and respected for his willingness to record Rastafarian music or songs with an otherwise radical slant, and Lowe was confident that Perry would not tamper with his challenging lyrics. In his own material, Perry had recently begun an oblique expression of identification with the challenge presented by the Rastafarian creed. The ominous single 'Sons of Thunder' was an attempt to capture the essence of God's power and proclaimed the invincibility of his Rastafarian servants. Although the song itself might not have seemed out of place in one of the surreal spaghetti westerns Perry and the Upsetters were so fond of, 'Sons Of Thunder' can be seen as similar to his 'OK Corral' release: it was a warning of the powers of Rastafari, and portrayed them as a group not to be trifled with. With such releases in mind, Lowe brought his material to Perry, and a session was quickly booked at Randy's. 'I link up with Lee Perry from those days after "Bongo Nyah". From I was going to school, Lee Perry lived about three houses from me in Washington Gardens. I lived on

Hampton Crescent and Lee Perry lived on Cardiff Crescent. Some evenings I go to his record shop and I usually just come home with him and Pauline, they were just three doors from me. I did ("All Africans") because I was reading a Marcus Garvey book. It's like he was saying "Don't cross the nation" and certain things he was explaining, like the word "Negro", we are not Negroes because it's a downgrading word. A lot of black people don't know that, that's why I had to sing a song like that. I recorded it at Randy's; Peter Tosh played guitar, Bunny Wailers played the *kette* on that song. Bob was there too, all Wailers was there 'cause that was Lee Perry's crew at the time.'

Although the song was later credited as a Bob Marley and the Wailers track when issued in the USA, Lowe insists that they did not sing on the session. 'It was me and Ewan Gardiner, he eventually became Ian in Little Ian Rock (a group Little Roy later formed with Gardiner and Anthony Ellis). If you notice, it's a song kind of building from "Bongo Nyah" actually, they are the only two songs I have that sound similar.'

Through his renewed link with Bob Marley, Scratch also issued a tune with the Soulettes, who Rita Marley had re-formed with new members Hortense Lewis and Cecile Campbell (the latter a sister of former Uniques member Cornel Campbell, then leader of the Eternals); Rita had come to know both singers at Studio One. Their fairly tame version of the Beatles' 'Let It Be' was issued on the UK Upsetter label while the Wailers were regularly recording for Scratch; the song was most notable for the group's invoking of Jah's name in the choruses.

Meanwhile the Wailers were building up a solid armoury of hit records and quality songs, some of which were issued on singles in the latter months of 1970. Despite the high volume of popular Wailers material, Perry had assembled, his Festival song competition entry for 1970 was 'Water More than Flour' by the lesser-known Al and the Vibrators; the song, which dealt with rising food prices and labour shortages, was not among the successful entries.

In contrast, the Wailers continued their onslaught of hits with 'Dreamland', another song that may have been first issued as a Winston Wright organ instrumental, though Bunny Wailer's stunning vocal version was recorded earlier. Bunny's strong tenor remained clear and expressive while stretching to the higher ends of the aural spectrum on what was perhaps his strongest and most complex composition to date. Like much of Bob Marley's material from this period, 'Dreamland' was ostensibly a love song, but its heady imagery was infused with a subtle spiritual content. 'Dreamland' conjured images of a distant land, far from the oppressive restrictions of Babylon, where a peaceful and idyllic life could be reclaimed by right. Complemented by a slow and spacious Upsetter rhythm provided by Fams, Carly, and Reggie, with a particularly expressive lead guitar provided by Soul Syndicate's Tony Chin, 'Dreamland' captured the just rewards the faithful knew they would receive in Zion.

Speaking of the song many years later, Perry said:

'Real, everything is real. It wasn't nothing was a joke, because the "Dreamland" represent where life come from. Life is a dream. Judgement is a dream. Creation is a dream. It's a real thing, it's not a joke. We call it real magic. I was planning to put him over Curtis Mayfield, but his behaving is not good enough . . . But the voice inside could do anything, super. The voice is good but if you are the personality behind the voice, if you are not good enough to handle the voice, the voice can't be anywhere, can't help you.' [10]

The above quote shows the tension that was building behind the music. While Scratch and the Wailers were perfecting their creations together, there was a growing resentment building on both sides. Many who were present have said that Scratch and Bunny never got on, and their distrust of one another later blossomed into full-blown animosity. The year in prison that Bunny had spent for possession of ganja had hardened him, and his reputation as something of a loose cannon meant that people tended to stay out of his way. A deeply religious person, Bunny had a tendency to retreat so deeply into his faith as to become uncommunicative, and even he and Bob were said to go for long periods without speaking in this era.

In 1975, Perry spoke of some of Bunny's strengths and foibles in a highly illuminating article by Carl Gayle in *Black Music*.

'Bunny is a good singer, I like Bunny's voice very much. The "message" that Bunny writes is not so easy to understand, like Bob and Peter would write. See Bunny is a man who believes in a thing (the doctrine of Rastafari) so much that he gives himself less time to think. He would do great if he give himself more time to think . . . See, he's a guy that don't like you to rough him. If you cool with Bunny, you can get anything out of Bunny.' [11]

While relations between Bunny and Perry continued to be strained, the close bonds Scratch had built up with Marley also heightened displeasure from Peter Tosh, who felt the dictatorial Perry was destroying what little democracy was left in the group. Bob was being touted not only as the star but enjoyed a position as Perry's confidant, and Peter Tosh and Bunny Wailer both felt slighted. Money matters were a regular cause of further tension, and Bunny found it particularly difficult to trust the wily producer. But, despite these slowly escalating problems, 'Dreamland' was a success that spawned many imitations. One of the high points of Bunny Wailer's long and varied career, 'Dreamland' has consistently remained in his performing repertoire ever since.

Not long after the recording of 'Dreamland', Perry was brooding over the power exerted by the three biggest recording studios in Jamaica: Ken Khouri's Federal, Coxsone Dodd's Studio One, and Byron Lee's Dynamic

Sounds. In many ways, Perry and other upcoming producers were at the mercy of these industry giants, particularly Federal and Dynamic, who controlled the manufacturing of local product as well as its recording; they were also known to be closely aligned with those who held the nation's political and economic power – particularly Byron Lee, who had been brought into the business by Edward Seaga, the rising star of the JLP. If an independent producer was getting too big for their britches, the giants would not hesitate to exercise their power and squash the challenger like a bug, and Perry was growing gradually more resentful of the control they exercised over the aspirations of ghetto promoters like himself. To address the problem musically, he began working on the song that would become the Wailers' 'Small Axe', recorded with Jackie Jackson, Hux Brown, and the rest of the All Stars at Dynamics.

One of the few songs the Wailers and Perry created together to feature a full horn section, 'Small Axe' pointed the way towards the slower and more complex beat that would become popular in the early 1970s. Vibrant hand drumming and a scalding wah-wah lead guitar gave an added edge to what was a thoroughly scathing admonishment.

> 'One Sunday morning I get up and sort of think over the whole thing and I got this idea. I said well "if they are the big three we are the small axe". And I started to write that song. Then I got stuck at a certain part so I bring it to Bob. Bob read it and started to sing a melody. Bob created the melody for that. We were stuck for about three quarters of an hour and I went for a Bible . . . we saw it there, "Why boasteth thyself, oh evil men," that come from the Bible. That was when the beat change again. After that we go straight into an album titled *Soul Rebels*.' [12]

Clancy Eccles stated that part of 'Small Axe' was written in the toilet of his shop – a spot he says Scratch often used to compose lyrics. 'Many of these songs was written at my place. Although Scratch was around the road, Scratch use my toilet at my record shop. Scratch would pass me with a roll of toilet paper and a piece of cement bag, and when him coming back it was a song written on the cement bag. Sometimes I don't even remember he was there, because him round there all two or three hours, sitting on the toilet and writing the songs. I remember "Small Axe", when him coming back him say "Why boasteth thyself, oh evil men, if a so a so . . . " '

By the winter of 1970, the Upsetter had a stockpile of Wailers material, much of which would surface as the album *Soul Rebels*.

The *Soul Rebels* album marked a departure for the Wailers in that the LP was not merely a collection of singles. A mixture of love songs with other understated agendas and pure, unadulterated rebel music, *Soul Rebels* was perhaps the most personal and revealing set of Wailers songs yet to appear on album. It opened with the aforementioned 'Soul Rebel', which was still popular some months after its release as a single. 'Try Me' was a fairly ordinary love song given that extra bit of edge through the adaptation of the biblical lines 'I am black and comely' towards the end of the song, while 'It's Alright' recounted Bob's late-night work in a Chrysler assembly plant in the USA. 'No Sympathy' was a trudging number from the tortured soul of Peter Tosh, on which he wailed out the alienated anguish brought to a Rastafarian whose awareness of his African heritage violently clashed with the society he lived in that placed no value on its worth. Delivered with much conviction, 'No Sympathy' was earmarked to be a single in the UK, with a bouncy Soulettes track called 'Boy Named Tom' on the other side, but the record never made it past the test pressing stage, just one of a dozen or so Upsetter singles that Trojan planned to include in their catalogue in the early '70s, but were never actually released. 'My Cup' was Marley's aforementioned confessional that started the whole ball rolling with the Upsetter, while 'Soul Almighty' was a quirky number inviting the listener to do a variety of popular dances to the new and heavy beat of the upsetting Wailers.

An alternative version of 'Soul Almighty' provisionally entitled 'Shocks of Mighty', or 'Shocks Almighty', was also recorded as a duet by Marley and Perry but not issued (until 1994), a soulful toast that again emphasised the closeness of the pair. Tapes of the session reveal that halfway through the voicing of the duet, something happened, and the rhythm was abruptly stopped. 'Somebody inside a mar the spirit,' Perry shouted angrily, attempting to chase away the bad vibes by feeding a good dose of echo around the control room.

On side two of *Soul Rebels*, 'Rebel's Hop' updated the 'Rude Boy Ska' medley the group recorded for Coxsone with a fuzzy wah-wah guitar and driving percussive licks from Sticky, including also portions of the Temptations' 'Cloud Nine', a favourite of both the Wailers and the Upsetter. 'Cornerstone' used passages from the Bible to lend a serious air to a cheeky plea for love, though the true religious potential of the rhythm would not be realised until a later re-cut as 'Jah Is Mighty'. '400 Years' was the most direct and revolutionary statement yet to come from Peter Tosh's critical pen, a truly anguished plea for his fellow black people to uplift themselves by refuting the injustices of slavery that had ruled their lives for centuries. Tosh's political stance had grown steadily more radical through the late 1960s, but it was only with the recording of '400 Years' that he began to express his political beliefs concretely in his music. 'No Water' was Bob's titillating request for a wet nurse to quench his sexual thirst, while 'Reaction' was a prophetic bit of grainy urban soul that spoke of the impact their music would have on the world, rocking and shocking unsuspecting listeners from their rough and tenuous existence in a Jamaican shanty town. Throughout the album, Perry and ET made certain that the Wailers' voices were given added prominence in the mix, and the dynamic vocal interplay of 'Reaction' showed just how tight their harmonies had become over the years. Closing out the album was a version of '400 Years', confusingly mistitled 'My Sympathy'.

It is worth noting that 'Soul Rebel' and '400 Years' do not feature Family Man; playing bass on those songs was Lloyd Parks, a vocalist and bassist who had strong links with Scratch dating back several years. Born on May 26, 1948, in Kingston, Parks had risen to fame as half of the Termites singing duo at Studio One, but was also a talented and expressive bassist. He had also played guitar in the RHT Invincibles with Sly Dunbar, Ansel Collins, and guitarist Ranchie McLean. When approached for the Wailers sessions, Parks was playing bass with Bobby Aitken, Ansel Collins, drummer Neville Grant, and guitarist Phil Grant in the Thoroughbreds, the house band at a club called the Stables on Red Hills Road.

Soul Rebels was one of a trio of Perry-produced albums issued by Trojan Records towards the end of 1970; after their stampers were cut in the UK, Perry also pressed copies of these discs in Jamaica for the local market. The first to surface, *Eastwood Rides Again,* followed the typical Trojan formula for Upsetter compilation LPs by mixing older singles like 'Dollar In The Teeth', Val Bennett's 'Baby Baby', and Sir Lord Comic's 'Django Shoots First' with newer instrumentals. Fresher material like 'Popcorn', 'Catch This', 'Power Pack' (based on the Temptations' 'Cloud Nine'), and an instrumental cover version of Eddie Floyd's 'Knock On Wood' were heavily slanted towards the funky sounds of American soul, while numbers like 'Red Hot' and the eerie 'Tight Spot' (whose rhythm would also be used for the Heptones' excellent 'Revolution') were pared down to quasi-dub form, pointing the way towards evolving sounds of the future.

Dave Barker's *Prisoner Of Love* album featured some of his biggest hits, including the title track, 'Shocks Of Mighty', 'Set Me Free', and 'Runaway Child', as well as his version of Bob Dylan's 'Blowin' In The Wind' and The Wailers' 'My Cup', but Dave has indicated he felt the album was compiled hastily, and contained some material that was not up to par. 'That is a next sore point again. I was sort of surprised with Scratch and annoyed with him for doing that because the tracks he put together for that album, some tracks were good and some tracks were bad. I said, "Why not let us concentrate on doing a proper album?" Songs that were done spontaneously and somehow didn't work out right, which he had also ditched, he brought them together for the album which displeased me immensely. At that time, (it) was also putting a blot on my ability as an artist. It's strange. As far as I'm concerned, that isn't an album.'

Although the album sold modestly, Barker was soon to be propelled to greater international stardom as part of the duo Dave and Ansel Collins with the huge hit 'Double Barrel', recorded for producer Winston Riley.

As 1970 gave way to 1971, the Wailers continued to go from strength to strength in the material they recorded with Lee Perry. Later sessions at Randy's yielded another crop of exceptional material, much of which was issued in Jamaica in 1971 as the album *Soul Revolution.* Even stronger than *Soul Rebels,* *Soul Revolution* marked a point of departure for the Wailers, in which their work was more serious and mature by definition. The hits they had created with Scratch helped the fermentation of a greater creativity, and their familiarity with and closeness to the Upsetter's rhythm team resulted in a sound that was all their own, characterised by a confident tightness and fearsome vocal deliveries. 'Keep On Moving' was a full re-working of the Impressions' 'I've Got To Keep On Moving' that the group had taken a stab at with Perry at Studio One, and featured Bunny's shrill imitation of Curtis Mayfield in the bridge. 'Don't Rock My Boat' was a re-working of an earlier song, turned by Scratch into a stunning proclamation of romantic concord in a slow and moving version voiced by Bob alone with a sparse musical backing. At Studio One, the message of the original 'Put It On' had been easy to miss in the frantic jump-up of a crowded ska arrangement; here Perry completely restructured the song to emphasise its spiritual and religious nature. Guiding the trio of vocalists in unison through a slow and balanced rhythm track, Perry procured a powerful delivery radiant with spiritual undercurrents through a gradually increasing rhythmic pace, culminating in the furious drum rolls and excited exclamations worthy of a Revivalist prayer session. 'Fussing And Fighting' was an urgent plea for ghetto unity, followed by the 'Duppy Conqueror' hit. 'Memphis' was a funky instrumental led by Peter Tosh on melodica, the toy keyboard's chords and melody line meandering curiously; traces of a guide vocal can be heard faintly in the background, indicating a probable previous attempt to voice the rhythm. On side two, Bunny Wailer took the lead on 'Riding High', singing of an elusive love over a choppy rhythm with an elaborate organ line, while 'Kaya' was a paean to marijuana, the wisdom weed so beloved by the Wailers, Scratch, and countless multitudes around the planet.

According to Scratch's younger brother Milton, 'Kaya' was written during one of Scratch and Bob's visits to Miss Ina's home in Hanover. 'My bigger brother Sonny, the Rasta one, he always keep a long locks. They was smoking herbs in the house, herb run out and they get some money to buy some herbs and the rain set up to fall at the same time, so they tell him he must ride a bicycle to go and buy the herb. The rain was falling and they said he must go and buy the herb before the rain fall and so the lyrics come up. They said they want Kaya before the rain is falling, and then now they start to rehearse it the same place, because Bob have him guitar. I would say it's between Scratch and Bob come up with the lyrics, but I can remember as a little youth, by saying the word to my bigger brother, he just came up with the idea, put it in lyrics, and they just start from right there.'

'Kaya' sold fairly well as a single in Jamaica and the UK in 1971, and is significantly the first 'herb' song recorded by either Perry or the Wailers. 'African Herbman' was a Ritchie Havens song re-worked to stunning effect through an exceptional vocal arrangement that makes the best use of Havens' excellent lyrics, while 'Stand Alone' was a tale of love's treachery given a fairly emotive work-through by Bob. 'Sun Is Shining' was another Marley solo vocal, nicely complemented by the pleasant strains of Peter Tosh's melodica echoing the cadence of his voice atop a smooth rhythm from Soul Syndicate and Glen Adams. The last song on the album was 'Brain Washing', a dash of righteous anger from Bunny Wailer that indicted the entire educational system through a peculiar refutation of nursery rhymes.

1971 began with a couple of notable journeys that would have definite consequences on the future of the Wailers/Upsetter combination. In November 1970, Johnny Nash had travelled to Sweden to begin working on the film *Want So Much To Believe*, in which he was to play a dance instructor who became involved in an ill-fated romance with a Swedish air stewardess. Nash was also asked to contribute to the film's soundtrack, and arranged for Bob Marley to join him in Stockholm in the early part of 1971 to work on material for the film with his backing band, Rabbit and the Jungles, led by a keyboardist from Texas named Johnny Bundrick.

With Bob again abroad, Perry continued working with Bunny Wailer and Peter Tosh, though never as closely as how he worked with Bob. Perry recorded a couple of strong Peter Tosh compositions in this time, the first of which was 'Downpressor', a version of the spiritual 'Sinner Man'. The Wailers had recorded an earlier version of the latter at Studio One, but as with 'Put It On', this version for Perry had greater strength, the pace of the rhythm allowing for a stronger expression of meaning. Informed by the I-words of Rastafari dialect, Tosh drew out the meaning of each word, augmented nicely by interjections and harmony from Bunny. Perry later recorded Tosh's dejected 'Brand New Secondhand', a sad statement from a jilted lover that showed off the range of Tosh's baritone. Scratch would later sing his praises to Carl Gayle:

'Peter is another good writer. He writes how he feels. Any time Peter writes a tune he writes it for a reason. He doesn't do it just because he wants to sing a song, he does it because it means something to him, because you done something to him or he's saying something about somebody or something. He doesn't do things for a quick price. He does it because he wants to send a message.' [13]

Perry was also employing Peter and Bunny's harmonies as backing for other artists, including Ras Carl Dawkins, a fiery young singer with an unrefined quality in his voice. The son of Joe Dawkins, a drummer who worked with Sonny Bradshaw and Baba Motta in the post-war years, Carl Dawkins was born in St Catherine on August 1, 1948. He grew in East Kingston, where Slim Smith and Jimmy Riley were his school mates at Kingston Senior School, but spent much of his youth hanging out with other singers and musicians in the ghettos of the West, becoming close friends with the Wailers by the time they linked up with Scratch. Dawkins was brought by Slim Smith to Sir JJ's shop on

Orange Street for an audition in the rock steady era, hitting immediately with 'Baby I Love You' and 'Hard Times', but was forced to take a break from music after being arrested for herb possession. After his release, he recorded a few other tunes for JJ and began promoting shows, eventually linking with Scratch and the Wailers for a version of Freddy McKay's 'Picture on the Wall' and an original called 'True Love'. 'True Love' was particularly embellished by the soaring harmonies of Bunny and Peter, their unrestrained voices adding a greater urgency to Dawkins' emotionally laden lead. 'We did have such a nice relationship,' Dawkins recalled fondly, 'and Perry was always there to help we along, inspirational and spiritual and heavy.'

It was around this time that Dawkins also began fronting a band called the Youth Professionals, which Family Man had formed to play at the Green Mist, a disreputable venue in Vineyard Town. 'A little before we move out of Upsetter time, I re-form a little band and call it Youth Professionals,' Fams remembered. 'It was Carl Dawkins who was the lead vocals at the time, and I was training our other keyboard player, Tyrone Downey, and also Touter.'

Tyrone Downie was then just a schoolboy, but Family Man could see he had talent. Downey said that Family Man originally wanted one of his school mates to play keyboards in the band: Horace Swaby, a light-skinned and somewhat frail accountant's son from the lower middle-class Havendale district who was just bringing the melodica to prominence through recordings with Herman Chin-Loy under the stage name Augustus Pablo. Horace Swaby and his brother Douglas had established the Rockers sound system in the late '60s, and often bought records from Herman's Aquarius record shop in Half Way Tree; when he turned up at the shop with a melodica he had borrowed from the daughter of a prominent lawyer, Herman took him straight to the studio to record him as Augustus Pablo. Swaby noted that Herman had come across the name Augustus Pablo in a Mexican magazine, and first assigned it to Glen Adams, who was then his standard session organist, but when Adams left the country the day after he played organ on 'East Of The River Nile' – Pablo's second recording and first big hit – the stage name passed permanently to Swaby. 'East Of The River Nile' owed much of its popularity to Lee Perry, who had created the rhythm and sold it to Herman Chin-Loy; in later years, Pablo and Perry would merge their unique talents on a number of highly successful collaborations.

As Tyrone Downey recalled, Pablo's demanding schedule as a session musician meant he was too busy to play in the Youth Professionals; instead, he suggested to Family Man that Tyrone be allowed to join. 'Augustus Pablo and I were in the same school, and Augustus Pablo tell Family Man say, "You have a youth named Tyrone Downey," 'cause Augustus Pablo was doing his own Augustus Pablo thing, he never really wanted to be in a band or nothing. Thanks to him, I was introduced to Fams, and started playing with Youth Professionals, which really was a band playing in a little striptease club at the weekends, but these musicians were the top session musicians at the time and I was blessed and lucky to have been there and to have played with them. Fams took me anywhere he went. Anything he did, I was there.' When Tyrone was unable to play, another teenager named Bernard Harvey (a.k.a. 'Touter') would sit in, while Tin Legs took care of the drum duties.

In 1971, Perry was also re-using the rhythms of his Wailers hits for new alternative versions with other artists. 'Small Axe' proved to be one of the first hits of the year, so Perry got Dave Barker to voice a deejay version as 'Shocks '71'. An alternative Wailers vocal version was released shortly after as 'More Axe', with its version side 'The Axe Man' being a Burru cut featuring Rasta percussionists Bongo Herman and Les. The 'What A Confusion' rhythm was used for U Roy's 'Earthquake', another startling piece of Scratch innovation, in which he double-tracked two different toasts from U Roy, which ran over the rhythm simultaneously, as though Roy was in conversation with himself. Perry also cut U Roy on a version of 'Dreamland' called 'Rhythm Land', which appeared in limited quantities on a blank-label pre-release after Perry journeyed to England with the Soul Revolution master tapes.

Unfortunately, Perry ultimately failed in much of his mission in England, and returned to Jamaica highly dissatisfied shortly after. Although stampers were cut on this brief journey, Trojan declined to issue the *Soul Revolution* album in the UK.

'We made *Soul Revolution* because *Soul Rebels* was so successful. I asked Trojan to push these guys. They said I'm wasting my time because they can't make it, because they can only sell to the West Indian market. And *Soul Rebels* did well here but through lack of promotion it didn't do what we expected. And then he (Lee Gopthal) wasn't interested in *Soul Revolution*. And then it was like he was trying to tell me to forget these guys because they'll never make it. I said, man, you're crazy.' [14]

With a UK release out of the picture in 1971, Perry eventually went one step further in Jamaica. Copies of *Soul Revolution* appeared first on Perry's Maroon label, the name of which paid tribute to the runaway slaves who formed fearsome independent communities where an African way of life was upheld in some of Jamaica's most inaccessible spots. The Maroon pressings quickly sold out, so Perry re-pressed the album on his Upsetter label, and then issued a limited number of *Soul Revolution II*, a proto-dub instrumental version of the LP.

Soul Revolution II was another first, presenting the entire album with all the vocals removed to lay bare the rhythmic foundations. Though dub albums would later become commonplace, presenting remixed songs on which the vocals would disappear and re-appear, bathed in delay or other effects with the equilibrium of the mix radically altered, *Soul Revolution II* presented the pure rhythms plain and simple. To date, no one else has issued an album quite like

Soul Revolution II, and it thus remains another of the Upsetter's unequalled innovations.

The sleeve of *Soul Revolution II* hinted at various elements of the Wailers and Upsetter connection: using photographs taken by Glen Adams in Perry's front yard in Washington Gardens, the three Wailers were shown brandishing pistols, rifles, and other automatic weaponry. In the central photo was the ringleader himself: Lee Perry, in the process of doling out the guns. With Bob and Peter dressed in overcoats and Bunny wearing a Mexican poncho, the group seem to be somewhere between the radical pride of the Black Panthers and the gratuitous violence of Al Capone or Django. But lest we take the scenes too seriously, one photo reveals the weapons to be the plastic toys of Perry's children, as harmless as his son's miniature dump truck.

Soul Revolution II cast the songs in a completely different light, the voiceless rhythms revealing hidden musical flourishes previously buried in the mix. 'Keep On Moving' featured a dynamic interplay between piano and organ and rhythm and lead guitar; the blues guitar line that led the tune became heightened, as did intricate tapping on the cymbals and high hat. 'Don't Rock My Boat' placed the bass in front, with subtle percussion revealing itself as integral to the force of the rhythm. 'Put It On' and 'Fussing And Fighting' became led by the plaintive saxophone line that was a mere flicker on the vocal versions, and the organ can be heard to mingle with the fancy trilling of a piano on both tracks. 'Duppy Conqueror Version 4' was driven by bursts of organ, a ghostly guitar and that subtle but vital percussion, while 'Memphis', *sans* melodica, was revealed to be a fast-paced slice of Upsetter blues. Piano and organ interplay was again exposed on 'Riding High', while the loose guitar strumming that drove 'Kaya' placed the tune somewhere between flamenco and merengue. The guitar and organ of 'African Herbman' ensured its mournful quality remained intact instrumentally, while 'Stand Alone' revealed the melancholy strains of a melodica deeply hidden in the mix. The skeletal form of 'Sun Is Shining', with the lead melodica removed, became a shuffling organ rhythm in stop-gap time, while the picking that lay beneath 'Brain Washing' reminded listeners how closely related some of this music was to rhythm and blues.

The Wailers were the best vocal trio on the island, but *Soul Revolution II* showed that the Upsetters were the hottest session musicians and that, with or without the vocals, *Soul Revolution* was music of an unbeatable standard.

After the Swedish film and its soundtrack were completed, Johnny Nash and Danny Sims took Bob Marley to London. His time in Sweden was confusing, often unpleasant, and ultimately counterproductive; the film was a critical failure, and would fold one week after its release the following September, while the soundtrack that Marley worked on would never be released. Much money had been wasted by Sims and his crew, notably in a high-stakes card game, and the promised wealth and fame remained far from Marley's grasp.

In London, Marley was joined by Peter Tosh and Bunny Wailer to record backing tracks for *I Can See Clearly Now*, the next Johnny Nash album; Marley was also counting on Sims to arrange a record deal between himself and CBS. Sims housed the Wailers in a rundown hotel in Bayswater, a transient district where prostitution openly flourished, and Peter and Bunny were dismayed by their working conditions. The trip proved not to be significantly rewarding, and they were all relieved to return to Jamaica towards the end of the spring.

At this point, the Wailers had become thoroughly disillusioned with all the Jamaican producers and promoters – and Peter Tosh and Bunny Wailer were particularly eager to break away from Scratch. Around this time, the group began operating from a place they called the Soul Shack, selling records, Peter's hand-carved combs and freshly cooked food from a shop formerly occupied by Roy Shirley; according to Shirley, the group surreptitiously took over the premises while he was touring abroad. 'When I come to England here, Bob Marley take away my shop. I had a big record shop where Joe Gibbs' record shop used to be there at North Parade, right beside Randy's. I had a shop there many years before that, and I come to England on tour with U Roy and Max Romeo . . . all I heard now was Bob Marley took over the shop, pay 'nuff money 'pon the rent. I was here, I wasn't paying any rent, so obviously a man come, kick off the door and Bob just go into there . . . Joe Gibbs take over that place when Bob left it.'

After their return to Kingston, the Wailers had been rehearsing a song called 'Lick Samba' at the shop, a complex number with a broad Caribbean lilt. When the song was ready to be recorded, the group opted to produce it themselves, but Marley felt that Perry's touch was still required, and retained him as engineer on the actual session. The vocal arrangement of 'Lick Samba' was dense, almost cluttered, and so much lay beneath Marley's wounded but playful vocal that it was difficult to take it all in. There is scattered baritone from Peter, odd interjections from Bunny, and a rousing female chorus by Rita Marley and friends. The chords of a melodica were blown lightly in one corner of the mix, and a wooden fish gave the song an additional percussive twist.

Glen Adams had begun to spend periods of time in New York, so Family Man brought Tyrone Downey in to take his place on the session. Although he had already played on Carl Dawkins' 'Walk A Little Prouder' for Bunny Lee, he was still such a youngster that Scratch and the group referred to him as 'Baby Tyrone'. 'I was like 13, 14 years old and I was a Wailers groupie, always hanging out at the record shop. It wasn't called Tuff Gong at the time, it was called Soul Shack. It's just when Bob was going to join up the Wailers and the Upsetters (rhythm section), that's when I met Scratch and I started playing some sessions with Fams.'

Tyrone remembered Perry as generous with herb and ideas, but not so generous with payment. 'Lee Perry gave me my first spliff, the first time I remember smoking herb was in his yard. Lee Perry for me, out of all the producers, he was the one who was more crazy, and crazy people are geniuses, so for me he was a genius. He knew how to feel the music, and he knew how to relate to the musicians. Lee Perry, Duke Reid, they have a way to make you say . . . they don't know music, they don't know shit about music. He'd say, "Give me zoing, man" and "Zoong zoong zoong zoong paff! Chikee-crash!" And Duke Reid even write it down, like long strokes, short strokes, hold, like hieroglyphics . . . Hearing from other musicians, they talk about Duke Reid, it seemed to me like between him and Lee Perry, they were like conductors. These guys, they never had the coat with the tails or the stick, but they knew what they wanted and they knew how to relate to the musicians. Scratch is a genius. He don't like to pay musicians, but you cannot knock his geniosity. He don't have a lot of generosity, but he sure have a lot of geniosity.'

Shortly after 'Lick Samba,' the Wailers severed their links with Scratch, and robbed him of his rhythm section in the process. The break came with 'Trench Town Rock', an exclamatory tour de force celebrating the power of their ghetto music, issued on their own Tuff Gong label. Released in the early summer of 1971, 'Trench Town Rock' was number one in Jamaica for five months straight; it instigated a self-determined success the group had never seen before. With the Barrett brothers now officially accepted members of the group, the Wailers would never again let themselves be at the mercy of the whims of Jamaican producers. As Family Man put it, 'The producers in Jamaica, upfront, them never too really overstand the business. We get to understand that as time goes by, so them make little mistakes for themselves too. And then the Wailers were as forceful, and we (the Barrett brothers) were as forceful too, so we decided to do something on our own. We said that we're going to let these promoters sing and play for themselves, and so we try to get it together.'

Perry later claimed it was partly Bunny's jealousy that drove the Wailers away from Scratch.

'When him see that the power has been given to Bob, and him feel it, him start to encourage Bob against me. Me cause nothing fe him . . . Bob meet some more bigger people, encourage away Bob and all them things. So what happened to Bob, it wasn't Bob's fault, because some people go funny, a lot of people funny.' [15]

In their time spent with the Upsetter, the Wailers had progressed dramatically. The close tutoring Marley had learned under Perry's wing had not only strengthened his resolve but had radically altered his approach to singing, and the intonation and phrasing he had learned from Scratch took the nation by storm; with time, it would move audiences the world over. Though Tosh and Livingstone were happy to distance themselves from Perry, Marley retained a respect for the troublesome craftsman, and would return to his side at crucial moments later in his career. Although a variety of problems had caused an untenable rift between the Wailers and Scratch, the deep bonds that existed between Bob Marley and Lee Perry were too strong to be totally severed simply because of cash or ambition.

There have been various conflicting reports of threatened or actual violence between the Wailers and Scratch that is said to have ultimately led to their parting. While these have proved difficult to substantiate, they certainly indicate the likelihood that things between them were often far from harmonious.

One of the most drastic examples has been recounted by Bunny Lee. The group are said to have given Perry a severe beating – particularly Peter Tosh – when 'Duppy Conqueror' was a hit due to the low amount of payment they received for the tune, their attack supposedly resulting in Perry's hospitalisation. However, it is hard to believe that the tale has not become exaggerated or embellished with the passing of time. Would Perry and the Wailers really have gone on to record two albums' worth of material together after the three singers put Perry in the hospital? Perry has flatly denied such questionable claims.

Bunny Wailer has also spoken of a tense meeting between Perry and the group in the back of the Upsetter record shop. The Wailers were trying to recover money they felt Scratch owed them, and were being met with a determined but nervous resistance. Eventually, they realised that the bottle in the middle of the table was full of acid, which Bunny said he suspected Scratch was planning to hurl at him. Again, Scratch has denied the claim. 'That was his suspicion,' he retorted, 'there was no acid there, that come out of his thoughts. They always think me have something to do them something, but it was only in their thoughts because they know I wasn't a chicken.'

We will probably never know the exact details of such rumoured occurrences or the precise circumstances of the Wailers' departure from Scratch, but what remains overwhelmingly clear is that the work Perry and the Wailers did together changed the face of Jamaican popular music, with the new vocal phrasing and Jamaicanised structure of their rebel material preparing the Wailers for the international stardom that they were soon to achieve upon signing to Island Records.

Lee Perry has since made a series of confusing and contradictory statements about the Wailers, and they continue to be subjects that elucidate extreme reactions from him when brought up in conversation or at interviews. But regardless of the odd statement to the contrary, Perry continues to uphold his love and respect for Bob Marley, an artist whose work he consistently valued for the whole of his career.

In 1975, Perry did not hesitate to make this perfectly clear in Carl Gayle's article in *Black Music*.

'As far as I'm concerned, every song that Bob Marley sing is good. That is the only artist in Jamaica that I really admire and nothing Bob can do can be wrong as far as I'm concerned. I just like the way he's professional. I think he's the best. I and him can ever quarrel 'cause there are certain things between me and Bob that no one understand. We work together, we have ideas and in Jamaica, professionally and musically we are blood brothers man so there's nothing he can do wrong for me. You see, I believe in originality and Bob is an original . . . Most of the time I have a pen writing while he's singing. And I write and he sings it. I don't tell no lie, Bob Marley great man!' [16]

He also acknowledged the contributions of the other group members, stating, 'They all play a great part in the Wailers. You see even the harmony section, there's no harmony in Jamaica can sound as good as Wailers' harmony.' [17]

Although the Wailers had moved away from Scratch by the end of 1971, Bob Marley would never keep himself too far for long. And if the Wailers thought they had other fish to fry at the time, so did the instructive producer they chose to leave behind. Lee Perry had no qualms about devoting more time to instrumentals, and there was a wealth of vocal talent still knocking on the door of the Upsetter record shop. But the work he and the Wailers created together as the 1970s began still remains some of the best music to be recorded on the island of Jamaica, and many consider it far superior to the group's subsequent international releases. Lee Perry echoed the sentiment of a legion of fans around the world when he later described the Wailers' Upsetter recordings as 'The best. Can't finish. The records will continue to live forever. Those recordings can't die.' [18]

BEAT DOWN BABYLON:

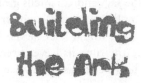

Building the Ark

As the Wailers began drifting away from Lee Perry's grasp in 1971, Scratch continued to scour the field for other outstanding talent, and a series of notable one-off recordings was created with other artists that year. A number of these songs contained a serious message, marking a gradual shift in Perry's material towards more weighty matters. This was perhaps partly influenced by his close contact with the militant Wailers, who had drawn out the most religiously and politically committed elements of Scratch's character, helping to re-define his work even as he was re-defining theirs.

The bulk of Perry's non-Wailers material from 1971 was by virtually unknown artists, some of whom were re-named or miscredited on release. For example, 'Mount Zion' was a repatriation tune credited on its UK issue to the Righteous Souls, with songwriting credit given to the Righteous Brothers. The flip side of this record, 'All Over,' was an attack on illiteracy credited to Eccle and Neville, but a Jamaican issue of the song (as 'Once A Man') named Milton Henry as the artist. 'Iniquity Worker', another weighty tune perhaps sung by the same duo featured on 'Mount Zion' was credited on issue to the Faithful Brothers. Exactly who these artists were has not been clarified, though Winston Jarrett suggested that they may have been previously unrecorded singers from the countryside hoping for a lucky break: 'Those guys come from the country, they was some little hills group. 'Nuff of them used to come up by Scratch and do one or two tunes and that's it.' To complicate matters further, when the 'Mount Zion'/'All Over' single was issued in the UK, production was credited mysteriously to Perry Marvin, a peculiar inversion of Scratch's oldest son's name, suggesting either a publishing arrangement to benefit his children or perhaps some obscure joke.

'You Can Run' warned the evildoers what the righteous would eventually do to them over an extremely tight Upsetter rhythm embellished by fiery brass. Credited on a UK release to the Hurricanes, lead vocals were handled by Danny Clarke, who had also written the lyrics. Born in Trench Town on August 7, 1953, Clarke was raised partly in Kingston by his father, who sold flowers at the racehorse park, and partly by his stepfather, who was a farmer in Clarendon, after his mother emigrated to the UK in 1960. Clarke made his recording debut for Coxsone Dodd with the tunes 'Free Angela Davis' and

'Working Time,' but the single appears not to have been released. He had a brief spell with Winston Jarrett in the Righteous Flames around 1970, and then began singing with Lloyd Forrester, another occasional Righteous Flames member who later joined the Jays and Chantells groups. On 'You Can Run', Clarke says he was joined by Forrester and 'a guy from Trench Town called Dennis' in a prototype of what would later be the Meditations. Clarke also indicated he was not aware the tune had ever been released in vocal form: 'Scratch told me he didn't like the vocals so he wasn't going to put it out. He did want us to re-voice it, but we didn't get the time to go back into the studio. I didn't know he even released it! I heard it as an instrumental, but I didn't know the vocal came out.'

The rhythm would later be re-used for several hard-hitting instrumentals, perhaps the most interesting of which was 'Rob Oil', a melodica version by drummer Leroy 'Horsemouth' Wallace issued on Syd Bucknor's Jamcan label in 1974. Born in Kingston in 1947, Wallace was taught to drum at Alpha School by Lennie Hibbert and played in the Mighty Vikings and Soul Syndicate bands in the late 1960s. He also voiced a deejay record for Coxsone, for whom he had worked as a printer, under the pseudonym Mad Roy. Horsemouth's approach to rhythm was underscored by the beats of pukkumina and Junkunu, and Perry began using him as a session drummer in the early '70s, partly due to Winston Grennan's imminent departure to America and partly through a perpetual quest for a different beat.

Another serious song that Perry had involvement with in 1971 was Max Romeo's 'Ginalship', recorded at another joint session run by Scratch and Striker Lee. A song about the political wickedness that was destroying Jamaica, 'Ginalship' was set to the melody of the folk song 'Old Fowl Dead In The Market'. As Max Romeo explained, 'In those days, when you're writing songs, you have to be close to a melody so it touch a chord in somebody and they can relate to it. You had to do it that way, because it was a new beat, so the rhythms and melodies can't all be new. You have to be as close to traditional as you can, in order for them to get that taste . . . "Ginalship", it's a political thing. In those times, the political pressure was brewing up, it wasn't there full-scale like now. The ginal is the politicians who are hiking prices every day, not doing anything for the people but they're reaping a lot. Ginalship is the act of being a crook, "Crookedness mash up the country", that's what I'm really saying in that song.'

Romeo later re-used the rhythm for 'Labor Wrong', a direct attack on the policies of the JLP, and 'Man In Your Life', a song that was a coded warning to Bunny Lee that his wife was being unfaithful. Issued on Romeo's The Truth label, both sides named the singer under the alias Johnny Stud.

One of the outstanding though somewhat overlooked Upsetter releases of 1971 came in 'Give Me Power', by a harmony group called the Stingers. Written by a certain L. Tibby, the song was infused with Rastafarian overtones, invoking a religious power and noting the liberating aspects of unity and righteousness; its version side, 'More Power', stripped the rhythm down to its core elements, elevating the bass and drum. A deejay cut by the otherwise unknown King Iwah – also called 'Give Me Power' – quickly followed, notable not only for its freshly overdubbed organ part, but also for the version's use of alternative Stingers vocal lines and odd vocal sound effects provided by Lee Perry. This version was a fairly successful seller among the Jamaican immigrant community in the UK when issued by Trojan in 1972; its 1971 Jamaican release was on a new label Perry controlled called Justice League.

Apparantly inspired by the Justice League of America comic book series, each Justice League single bore the legend that the disc was 'produced and directed by Upsetter – Wonder Man', emphasising not only the marked difference of each of Perry's personas, but also the filmic quality of so many of his releases. As producer and director of product on Justice League, Perry was putting the movies in his head into his listeners' ears by pressing up his visions on vinyl. Another label inaugurated in early 1972 was Wizzdom, a pun on the verbal wisdom and aural wizardry of Perry's creations, while the obscure Hermes-like symbol that graced the label emphasised the magical and scientific qualities of each disc.

Other less serious but still noteworthy Upsetter material released in 1971 included 'Run Up Your Mouth', a tale of love coming undone through gossip (credited to the Hurricanes on a Spinning Wheel single and to Rob Walker on a UK Upsetter release), and 'The Creeper,' a plodding rhythm with zany jive talk from deejay Charlie Ace (a.k.a. Valden Dixon), operator of the Swing-A-Ling mobile record shack. Mahalia Saunders provided a trio of fairly faithful cover tunes of blues and soul standards, 'Piece Of My Heart', 'Tip Of My Tongue', and Elvis Presley's 'Suspicious Minds', while David Isaacs performed vaguely convincing versions of 'Knock Three Times' and 'You'll Be Sorry' for Perry at Coxsone's studio; a more satisfactory effort was his version of Solomon Burke's 'Just Enough', made more emotive by Glen Adams' organ skills.

Glen Adams and Milton Henry put together a cover of the soul song 'Never Had A Dream' with Adams providing a free-form organ interpretation of the tune on the B-side, while Winston Wright gave a soulful organ workout on an instrumental called 'Example'. Perhaps the most noteworthy instrumental created that year was 'All Combine', a muzak medley that brought the Upsetters into the realm of elevator music through soft horns and a plonking piano and organ duet dubbed over peculiarly adapted versions of the 'Yakkety Yak'/'Clint Eastwood' rhythm, Andy Capp's 'Pop A Top', Max Romeo's 'Maccabee Version', Derrick Harriott's 'Solomon' (written by Junior 'Soul' Murvin), Glen Ricks' 'Holly Holy' (originally by Neil Diamond), and the Wailers' 'Mister Brown', 'Duppy Conqueror', and 'Sun Is Shining.' As medleys go, 'All Combine' was certainly one of the strangest; it marks another first for the Upsetter in his unabashed fusion of raw rhythm and instrumental schmaltz, a theme later explored in greater detail by producer Harry Mudie.

In the early 1970s, adding string arrangements to reggae records increased a song's likelihood of receiving radio airplay in the UK, and Perry was among the first to try this ploy on selected discs. One of his few successes in this format was a cover of the Monkees' 'I'm A Believer', which Perry voiced in London with the singer DD Dennis in 1971.

Denzil Lynward Dennis was born in Manchester on October 13, 1945; after his father emigrated to America and his mother to England, Dennis went to live with his uncle in Waltham Park and attended Saint Aloysious Catholic school. His elder cousin, Lloyd Daley, started a sound system in 1957 called Lloyd's Stereophonic Hi-Fi, which later became known as Lloyd the Matador; Dennis and Daley used to hide under Duke Reid and Coxsone's speaker boxes and record their specials on a Grundig machine for clandestine airings on Daley's set.

A closeness to the West Kingston musical fraternity and friendship with Derrick Morgan and Prince Buster led to Dennis' debut recordings for Duke Reid in 1962 as half of the duo Cosmo and Denzil with partner Frank Cosmo. Of the six songs they cut for Duke, 'Take Your Belongings' and 'Bed Of Roses' so impressed Melodisc Records' boss Emil Shalit that he arranged for the pair to travel to England to record further, but Cosmo's father was relying on him to assist at the Tower Isles Hotel where he worked, so Dennis ended up making the journey alone. In the UK he hit with 'Love Is For Fools,' produced by Laurel Aitken and featuring English jazz musicians Ronnie Scott and Red Price, but after a few more Blue Beat releases he began recording under the alias Alan Martin for the Rio label. Rio was formed in 1963 by Shalit's former partner William Record, an American whose new business partner was his wife Noreen, a woman who hailed from Trinidad; Dennis remained solidly with the label into the mid-1960s. After recording 15 songs for Rio, he teamed up with Dandy Livingston and Pat Rhoden as the Brother Dan All Stars for the newly formed Trojan label, scoring a big hit on his own with 'Hush Don't You Cry' in 1968. He began recording songs as DD Dennis around this time, replacing his middle initial L with the first letter of his first-born son Dave's name.

In 1970, when Perry was in London on one of his many business trips, Dennis had a big hit in the reggae charts with his strings-laden reggae version of Frank Sinatra's 'My Way', produced by Laurel Aitken for Pama. Perry was sufficiently impressed by the hit to build the 'I'm A Believer' rhythm in Jamaica, which he brought up for Dennis to voice in 1971 at Chalk Farm studio. Backing vocals were provided by the Carols, a trio of white English girls who often sang back-up on Pama discs, and Scratch later overdubbed strings at Tony King's studio in Hammersmith with Tony Hartley's assistance. Strings were also prominent on an instrumental version of the Temptations' 'My Girl' that was cut for Pama in this period and pressed in limited number on an Upsetter blank.

Laurel Aitken had produced another hit in 1970 with 'History Of Africa' by the Classics, a duo composed of Denzil Dennis and Milton Hamilton, and Scratch was sufficiently inspired by the tune to voice the Classics on a cut of 'Cherry Oh Baby' around the same time as 'I'm A Believer'. To confuse matters, not only was the song was re-titled 'Cheerio Baby', but it was backed with the somewhat stronger 'Civilization', credited also to the Classics but featuring a different group of Jamaican singers. While in the UK, Perry also cut a version of the throwaway pop tune 'Sex Education' with the Classics in this period, along with the stronger 'You Gonna Miss Me' by Owen Gray.

As Chalk Farm studio was then the preferred recording facility for reggae in London, Perry would make increasing use of the premises in the early 1970s. Located in a former dairy building on Belmont Street, close to Camden Market in North London, the studio was opened in late 1968 by engineer Vic Keary. Originally an eight track facility, Chalk Farm was upgraded to 16 tracks a few years later.

Born in London in 1938, Vic Keary began working as an engineer in the late 1950s in Dennis Preston's prestigious Lansdale studio, located in Holland Park. He was mostly working with traditional jazz artists like Acker Bilk at Lansdale, but began recording 'bluebeat' material for Emil Shalit's Melodisc label by 1961, and it was Shalit who would later provide much of the financial backing for Chalk Farm. In the mid-'60s, Keary took over the old Radio Atlanta studio at 47 Dean Street, in the heart of the West End, and began recording rock steady and reggae with artists such as Sugar and Dandy. He then established the three-track Maximum Sound studio on South London's Old Kent Road, which was quickly upgraded to four-track; the facility was often used by visiting Jamaican producers such as Prince Buster and Bunny Lee.

Keary's assistants at Chalk Farm were Mike Craig, Neil Richmond, and John Smythe, and part of what added to the studio's overall reputation was the custom-built mixing desk created by Keary and Craig; between 1969 and 1974, much of the reggae recorded in Britain was created at Chalk Farm, particularly material for the Trojan and Creole labels. Though Bunny Lee had more of a regular presence there, Lee Perry made a substantial number of recordings at the studio in the early 1970s, while some of his work for Pama records was recorded at Tony Pike's studio in Tooting.

Perry always had an ear for spotting deejay talent, and he continued to issue hot product with deejays in the early 1970s. Some of the best toasting records Perry created in this period were with Dennis Alcapone, who had already established himself as a leader in his field by the time of their first collaboration. The youngest of eleven children, Alcapone was born Dennis Smith on August 6, 1947, in the town of Crooked River, in the district of Culloden in Clarendon. While still an infant, Dennis was sent to Kingston to be raised by an older sister whose husband ran a downtown dry cleaner's; the sister later ran a bar and liquor store on Waltham Park Road. Trained as a welder, Dennis began attending sound system dances in his teens, initially following El Toro, whose deejay was King Cry Cry (a.k.a. Michael Williams, later known as Prince Far I), and Kentone, whose deejay was a man called Pompadoo, but the sound that clearly had the biggest and most lasting influence on him was King Tubby's Hometown Hi-Fi with U Roy on the mike. 'Tubby's was definitely the greatest sound ever to come out of Jamaica, in terms of the arrangements and the equipment and everything else. The technology and everything was just mind-boggling really. Them time, when you listen to King Tubby's sound, it look like it going to blow your mind. I listen to a lot of the sounds, like Duke Reid, Coxsone, and the whole of them, they was just normal sound, bringing out normal voices with normal bass and everything. Duke Reid and Coxsone, I think their tubes was 807, which is some big tubes, and their bass, it was heavy but it was not as round as the KT 88 that Tubby's came with. KT 88 was a smaller tube, and his bass was something else, it was just round like when you're kneading flour. With the 807, when the bass hit the box, you hear the box vibrate, but Tubby's now, the bass was just so solid. Then he brought in reverb, which wasn't introduced to the public before, reverb and echo. When U Roy would be announcing a dance and he would say, "This coming Friday night-night-night-night-night-night-night . . . " that was brand new to everybody in Jamaica. Everybody was so fascinated by this thing, "All roads lead-lead-lead-lead-lead-lead-lead to the place called the Gold Coast Beach," it was mind blowing, man, for that reason. Tubbys have some steel (speakers) they used to put up in the trees, and when you listen to that sound system, especially at night when the wind is blowing the sound all over the place, it was wicked!'

Just as rock steady began changing into reggae, Dennis started his own little neighbourhood sound system with two friends, named El Paso after Marty Robbins' country-and-western ballad. By this time he was working at the Jamaican Public Services on Orange Street, and he began building up the sound's selections through contact with all the record shops on 'Beat Street'.

After El Paso began to attract a wide following through Dennis' toasting abilities, he made his recording debut in 1970 for Keith Hudson under his given name, and went on to enjoy strong successes as Dennis Alcapone with Coxsone Dodd, Duke Reid, and Bunny Lee, for whom Dennis scored a hit in 1971 with 'Ripe Cherry', a version of Eric Donaldson's Festival-winning classic, 'Cherry Oh Baby'. It was this rhythm that would initiate collaborations between Lee Perry and Dennis Alcapone in late 1971, and the pair would continue their fruitful collaborations through 1972.

According to Alcapone, Perry first recorded him as a substitute for Lizzy, who had previously collaborated with Dennis on the first deejay combination records ever made. Lizzy was then the star deejay on Prince Jammy's sound system, a Waterhouse set established by King Tubby's childhood friend and future apprentice Lloyd James in 1962. Alcapone noted that he began working with Perry almost accidentally, though he had been aware of Scratch's importance on the music scene for many years: 'I used to see Scratch from he was at Coxsone. Coxsone had a grey Buick, and whenever you see Coxsone, you see Lee Perry, he was always sitting beside Coxsone in the front seat. In them days, when he did tunes like "Doctor Dick", Scratch was always with Downbeat. Before I get involved in recording, I used to go by Music City, Coxsone's store on Charles Street, to buy records, and Scratch was always there. He was Coxsone's right-hand man, anywhere you see one, you see the other. When him and Coxsone parted company, he took over Prince Buster's record shop that was on Charles Street, him and Pauline was always there, and him and Bunny Lee becomes good friends. Scratch see Bunny as a shoulder to lean on really, because him and Downbeat is not friends any more. You have to have somebody in your corner because Downbeat is a man who thump you down, you can't go against that man because he is heavy, so Scratch now was friends with Striker, and Striker's wife Marva and Pauline was friends. Them used to go in the studio and make rhythms, give each other rhythms and so forth. How I start get to work with Scratch, when I did "Ripe Cherry", Scratch made a version of it, and him wanted to put Lizzy on it. Bunny did give him a cut and he put on a trombone and made a trombone version. I remember I just went and buck up on the session that day, I went to Bunny Lee's shop to look for him, and Marva told me that he was down by Randy's, so I went down there, went upstairs inna the studio and I hear this rhythm and Lizzy was inside trying to do it, but Lizzy couldn't get the basic idea of what they wanted, so I was trying to direct Lizzy from behind the glass and tell him how to attack the rhythm. Bunny said, "Dennis, go in and tell him," so me actually go in and illustrate to Lizzy. Scratch said, "What you did on the rhythm, we'll have that," but I didn't want that. For a start, I just did "Ripe Cherry" on the same rhythm, I didn't want two songs on the same rhythm. I went in there to show Lizzy how to ride that rhythm, and Striker said "That's all right, mon," and Lee Perry said "Yes!" so that's how the tune "Well Dread" come about.'

Enhancing Dennis' ferocious but measured toasting was a trombone melody from Vin Gordon, a graduate of Alpha School who had built his reputation at Studio One; the rhythm was then made more Upsetterish by the stabbing chords of an overdubbed organ and fragmented rhythm guitar and bass. 'Well Dread' was not so much an adaptation of 'Cherry Oh Baby' as an Upsetter re-creation, in which the bedrock of the original rhythm was mutated into something that bore its likeness while also being apart from it. While other producers were typically issuing fairly standard version sides, Perry saw each version as an opportunity to test the limits of music production, and made use of the version format to satisfy his ever-growing experimental urges.

Further experimentation came through work with undiscovered deejays. From his early recordings of Sir Lord Comic and Cool Sticky, Lee Perry had always had an ear for a deejay's potential, and he was not afraid to take chances with toasters who had little or no recording experience. So it was with the young Winston Thompson, a deejay variously known as Prince Winston, Winston Prince, Prince Cool, Winston Cool, or Youth Winston, but who would later come to greater prominence as Doctor Alimantado.

In the early '70s, Tippertone sound system was on the rise, and Thompson was one of the set's star deejays. Thompson recalled that he had cut only a couple of sides for small independent producers before being approached by Lee Perry for recording after Perry saw him in action at a Tippertone dance: 'I did some recording with a couple of people before I record with Upsetters, but in Jamaica, you just know people by them first name; you don't know much about them, them just wander in your life and wander out again. You do a couple of records and that's it, but Upsetter was one of the up-and-coming producers at that time. He was very outstanding in his work, everybody knew that. I used to deejay in a sound that was the sound in Jamaica at that time, and the Upsetter came to one of the dances. The next day I was by a shop looking at some records and he said I should come and do some songs for him, but I didn't really take it up at the time. Then he used to have a sound named Upsetter too, and one of my friends, Jah Stitch, and a youth named Jubie used to play Upsetter sound, so when his sound was playing we used to go and listen to the sound. That's how it came about really.'

Thompson initially recorded a trio of toasts for the Upsetter: 'Maccabee The Third' over a cut of Max Romeo's 'Maccabee Version', 'Chapter Of My Heart' on the 'Piece Of My Heart' rhythm, and a toasting cut of 'Tip Of My Tongue'. None of these versions made a serious impact at the time, perhaps because Thompson was still largely unused to the recording environment, though he would subsequently prove his ability on further versions for the Upsetter and other producers.

The definitive rupture between the Wailers and Scratch had robbed Perry of more than just his most successful vocal trio. When the Barrett brothers followed the group overseas in 1972, it would prove to be a permanent defection; they were no longer part of the Upsetter camp, but bona-fide members of the Wailers' band from then onwards. Additionally, Glen Adams had basically emigrated to New York, though he did return to Jamaica on several occasions, while Ronnie Bop had moved to London in 1970, where he began producing records for Pama; after his own record shop in Roman Road proved unsuccessful, he became involved with Count Shelley's premises in Finsbury Park. Although these players had created a sound unlike any other on the island, Perry soon got over their departure by recruiting what he referred to as the 'Third Generation' of Upsetter musicians. On bass, he began using Lloyd Parks, Val Douglas of the Now Generation band and Ranchie McLean, who also played rhythm guitar, while drum duties were shared between Tin Legs, Leroy 'Horsemouth' Wallace, and Hugh Malcolm. With Glen Adams spending an increasing amount of time in Brooklyn, Perry began using organ players like Ossie Hibbert, while his horn section consisted of trombonist Ron Wilson, occasionally replaced by Vin 'Don D Junior' Gordon, and trumpeter Bobby Ellis; horn parts were later fully controlled by saxophonist Tommy McCook, who was arranging much of Perry's material at this time. But what Perry was clearly most affected by was the absence of Bob Marley in his daily life. Marley's departure from under Scratch's wing severed a deep friendship, leaving a kind of void not only in his professional life but also on a far more personal level. He and Marley had become very close through their work together – some have said perhaps a bit too close – and Scratch found himself searching for an artist not only of Bob's calibre, but one with a similar seriousness, determination, acerbic wit, and general vibes.

Perry was seeking an artist whose talents he could cultivate, but the artist also needed to be an inspired challenger with notions of his own. He sought a singer and songwriter who was adaptable enough to be able to handle the peculiar rhythms he was fashioning, and who had enough non-standard ideas of his own already partly developed. He was looking for someone who would be receptive to his guidance, but also one whose outlook and inspiration would be different enough to cause Perry himself to take note. By the end of 1971, when Perry recorded 'Beat Down Babylon' with Junior Byles, he realised that Byles was just the singer he had been looking for.

Junior began recording solo material with Perry in 1970, though he continued to be backed by the Versatiles on some recordings. His debut solo single was 'What The World Is Coming To' and 'Live As One', both songs that revealed the caring nature of Junior's troubled soul, exposing an emotional and sensitive interior that sought to embrace the greater goodness of his fellow man whilst shunning the many wrongs and injustices of an evil and unequal world. Credited to King Chubby on a UK release, the A-side of the single had a full string section and vocal chorus arranged by Tony Hartley at Tony King's studio in Hammersmith. Locating the song firmly within the more acceptable mode of pop-reggae, the strings were added in the hopes of boosting British radio airplay for the single, but ultimately did not achieve its desired effect – perhaps partly because they distracted attention from Byles' powerful delivery and strong lyrics.

Both songs ultimately showed something of Byles' great concern with humanity as a whole, and his tendency to take such matters extremely seriously would see his life plagued by mental illness and repeated arrests. Once Byles demonstrated a commitment to the Rastafarian faith, tension arose between him and his parents and he would remain somewhat estranged from his family for several years. Like Bob Marley, he perhaps saw in Scratch something of a sympathetic father figure, and their relationship would also prove to stretch beyond mere business deals and music production.

In 1970, Perry was far too busy with the Wailers to give Byles the attention he was due, but with the group far from his agenda in late 1971,

Perry had the time and inclination to respond to Junior's great potential. Though their Festival song competition entry 'Rub Up '71' flopped, the extraordinary power contained on 'Beat Down Babylon' showed that Junior was definitely deserving of Scratch's undivided attention.

Over a driving rhythm provided by the Now Generation band, augmented by the startling sounds of a cracking whip, Byles sang with an optimistic determination of how the Rastafarians would beat and whip the oppressive forces of Babylon into submission, aided by the Almighty Himself; the lyrics were based on a song written by one of Junior's long-time friends, Harold Meikle:

> 'Said me no like kinda Babylon
> Said me no dig them kinda wicked men
> For I'm a righteous Rastaman
> And I am a dread dread one-high man
> I and I going beat down Babylon
> I and I must whip them wicked men
> Oh what a wicked situation
> I and I starving
> This might cause a revolution
> And a dangerous pollution
> I and I going beat down Babylon
> I and I must beat down Babylon
> I and I going whip them wicked men
> I and I going beat down Babylon
> Whip them, whip them, Lord . . . '

'Beat Down Babylon' was one of the first studio recordings to feature the Now Generation, and their link with Lee Perry was made by Tin Legs, then a regular session drummer for Scratch and Bunny Lee. The Now Generation has a complicated history, and many musicians would pass through its ranks in their formative years. The group evolved from the Mighty Mystics, formed at a Kingston technical college by guitarist Mikey Chung, keyboardist Geoffrey Chung, and bassist Val Douglas in 1968. Douglas, who was born on July 22, 1950 in the village of Broad Leaf in Manchester, taught himself to play guitar and piano after being sent to a Kingston boarding school by his parents, who were both schoolteachers; when the Mystics formed, he was persuaded to switch to bass. After the band split into two rival groups, the Fabulous Falcons and the Mighty Virtues, Mikey Chung and Val Douglas formed the Now Generation in the summer of 1969 with Tin Legs on drums and Augustus Pablo on keyboards, who was shortly replaced by Glen Stair (who in turn was replaced by Joe Cooper, later keyboardist with the Vikings); other early members included Ernest Wilson and Keith Rowe on guitar. The group's long tenure at the Stables club, one of the hot spots lining the Red Hills Road, helped establish their reputation in Kingston, and they would ultimately emerge as one of the most reliable session bands on the island once their line-up had been stabilised.

On 'Beat Down Babylon', it is the loping bass of Val Douglas that gave the song its melodic pace and overall shape, complemented by understated guitar from Mikey Chung, with Earl 'Wire' Lindo's organ melody helping to mark the song as a spiritual oratory.

'Beat Down Babylon' was an instant success, and its continued popularity would see Perry usher in 1972 with a series of further cuts on the same rhythm. Though Junior's follow up to 'Beat Down Babylon' was a quieter, more introspective number, the song was equally powerful. Recorded at the same session as Bunny Wailer's 'Dreamland', 'Place Called Africa' was a moving portrait of a young Jamaican grappling with his African heritage, and remains an outstanding release for its skilful instrumental arrangements and insightful lyrics:

> 'There's a place called Africa far, far away
> There's a place called Africa many miles away
> Mom says that's where I'm from
> And I know she can't be wrong
> Take me back to Africa
> Mama how did I get here?
> She said "Once upon a time my son
> They stowed us on a ship
> We had to work and slave each day
> The boss he took our pay
> But a brighter sun has come today
> And they can't stop us come what may
> A time will come for you and I"
> She bowed her head and cried
> Mama please don't cry . . . '

Perry gave the song a finely balanced mix, presenting the percolating lead guitar of Tony Chin atop the smooth rhythm played by Family Man, Carly, and Reggie, helping to emphasise the deep feeling Byles sought to convey. The first deejay version of the song Perry cut was by Dennis Alcapone, a U-Roy-styled toast augmented by sound effects; issued on Justice League in scarce numbers, the song was backed by 'Jah Rastafari', a religious chant that rode the rhythm of Dave Barker's 'Prisoner of Love'.

It was shortly after this release that Perry assembled *Africa's Blood*, the latest in his series of mostly instrumental collections assembled for Trojan Records. *Africa's Blood* had only two straight vocal tracks: 'Isn't It Wrong', a heartbroken harmonic number by the Hurricanes, and 'Do Your Thing,' a soulful groover from Dave Barker that had all the energy of a James Brown

single. The disc's sole deejay record was a far more competent issue from
Winston Prince, 'Place Called Africa Version 3' over Junior Byles' hit rhythm.
The remaining twelve tracks mixed instrumental takes of classic Upsetter
rhythms with freshly created instrumentals, many of which were inspired by or
adapted from American soul hits. Songs using the more traditional Upsetter
rhythms included an organ cut of 'Dreamland' by Winston Wright, 'Long
Sentence', an organ cut of Junior Byles' 'Poor Chubby' by Glen Adams, and
'Well Dread Version 3', perhaps the most inspired update of all. A bongo cut
of 'Cherry Oh Baby' credited to the Addis Ababa Children, 'Well Dread
Version 3', transformed the rhythm of what was originally a trite love song
into the religious glory of a Rastafarian grounation ceremony. Of the
remaining derivative soul material, a harmonica cover version of Otis
Redding's 'My Girl' and 'Move Me' (a sped-up version of 'Groove Me') were
the most obvious, but other tracks like 'Saw Dust', 'Not Guilty', and 'Bad
Luck' (an instrumental cut of 'Run Up Your Mouth') also revealed that Perry
and the Upsetters were continuing to draw strongly on elements of African-
American soul – although such elements were always digested thoroughly and
playfully re-cast to better suit Jamaican palates.

If the musical content of *Africa's Blood* showed Perry moving closer to the
soul sounds that were inspiring him, further indication that he had picked up
some of its liberating messages came through the album's cover photo and
title. Unlike the velveteen chic of *Return of Django* or the casually stylish
polyester and wool worn on *Scratch the Upsetter Again*, Perry was now wearing
little more than his jewellery and his woman an African headdress, displaying
themselves for all the world to see as regal people proudly aware of their
African foreparents. Though largely an instrumental disc, *Africa's Blood*
proclaimed a belief in the uplifting elements of black pride through its very
name, echoing expressions of the black power movement in America.

> 'That LP is really based on being black . . . just a feeling, telling the
> people this is the blood of Africa. So once it's done, black and white have
> to appreciate everything in it 'cause I love black, I love white, I love
> everyone.' [1]

The continued success of 'Beat Down Babylon' saw Perry returning to
the rhythm for a number of inspired alternative cuts. The flipside of the
original single, 'Ital Version', was another aural experiment on which Perry
used reverb to alter sounds he made with his mouth, while an uncredited toast
filled out the background of the rhythm. Next came Dennis Alcapone's 'Alpha
and Omega', on which Alcapone chanted biblical proverbs between Byles'
disappearing verses; its version side, 'King Alpha', was basically the same as the
A-side but with the toasting removed to uncover a fairly straightforward dub.
'Ring of Fire' (subtitled 'Babylon Chapter Five') was an absurd instrumental
cut, featuring a phased trombone from Ron Wilson, which began by

incorporating the melody of Johnny Cash's 'Ring Of Fire' before collapsing into anarchic brass mayhem, while 'Bet You Don't Know' by Chenley Duffus and the Soul Avengers turned the burning rhythm into a somewhat tame love song by adapting a ballad he originally recorded for King Edwards in the boogie era.

Although Duffus' cut did not have much impact on its initial release, it would prove to be a hit in Egypt some 25 years later due to the inclusion of the line 'You're a good woman and a fine girl' sung in the Amharic language, which Duffus was teaching himself at the time.

Further cuts brought the song back to its original theme. 'Babylon's Burning', by Maxie, Niney, and Scratch had Max Romeo giving further evidence of what the Rastas would do to the wicked over a bass-heavy cut of the rhythm punctuated by thunder claps and a percussive shaker, with Niney, Earl Morgan, and Barry Llewellyn from the Heptones joining in for choral vocals, while upcoming toaster Jah T furthered the biblical attack from the Upsetter station on the ominous flipside, 'Lion Of Judah'. Junior Byles himself gave the song a more specific re-interpretation on 'Informer Men', railing against police informants in the community while Jah T reached from beyond the Seven Seas of Galilee to spur Junior on to a greater castigation of their foes over a version of the rhythm that made use of an eerie ringing telephone. 'Outformer Version' (a.k.a. 'Babylon Chapter 10'), the final cut Perry issued of the rhythm in 1972, kept snatches of Byles' new vocal drifting in and out of the mix in a rhythmic yet haphazard manner, in an ever-adventurous quest to test the limits of what could be an acceptable presentation on record.

We have already seen that Perry had helped establish the version phenomenon from his early days at Studio One, and he had remained consistently fascinated by version as a means of expressing himself. But now Perry was taking version one step further, with the creation of no less than ten cuts of the same rhythm, each startlingly different and unique while also being linked to the original.

The popularity of 'Beat Down Babylon' was so great that other producers also began fashioning their own re-cuts of the rhythm, though no outside version proved to challenge the popularity of the Upsetter originals; producers trying their hand at re-creating the rhythm included Keith Hudson and Maurice 'Blacka Morwell' Wellington, a freelance producer who would eventually form the Morwells group with Louis Davis and Eric 'Bingy Bunny' Lamont.

Meanwhile, Byles and Perry were going from strength to strength in the material they were creating together. Two of the more interesting and overtly political songs Junior Byles recorded with Lee Perry were 'King Of Babylon' and 'Pharaoh Hiding', both songs commenting on the 1972 election battle between Hugh Shearer and Michael Manley. Since independence in 1962, the conservative JLP had remained in power, and although much of the 1960s saw relative economic prosperity for the nation, the general world recession of the early 1970s had drastic consequences for Jamaican society. A quarter of the overall population was unemployed, imported goods had reached a premium outside the grasp of much of the population, and the gap between rich and poor was clearly worsening. The JLP had always run the country to serve a wealthy minority at the expense of the poor majority, and many saw the aging Shearer as being greatly out of touch with the needs of the Jamaican people. Michael Manley had taken control of the PNP from his father in 1969, and was appealing to the people in a populist campaign that saw him cast as Joshua. He toured the country with a musical bandwagon, supported by Clancy Eccles, Bob Marley, and others, sporting a 'Rod of Correction' said to have been given to him by Haile Selassie. This greatly increased his popularity amongst the poor and downtrodden, and his fiery socialist rhetoric held immense appeal, despite origins that placed him firmly inside the ruling elite he claimed to be challenging.

After a solid decade of JLP rule, the country was ripe for change, and in recording 'King of Babylon' and 'Pharaoh Hiding', Junior Byles was express-ing his support for Manley, likening Shearer to the evil Nebuchadnezzar in the former and the Egyptian Pharaoh, hiding from the vanquishing Joshua, in the latter adaptation of a spiritual hymn. But the expression of such support could have a high price, as Bunny Lee was to find during the run-up to the 1972 election. Max Romeo's scathing 'Let The Power Fall' caused much offence at JLP headquarters, and when Striker voiced the singer Bill Gentles on a related tune, he fell foul of Prime Minister Shearer and his henchman, Edward Seaga. 'Max Romeo make a tune named "Let The Power Fall On I", but at that time now, there's a good imitator out there named Bill Gentles, he do a tune that go "Take the Rod from off our backs Fari, can't get no rice and deliver people." Is the biggest tune ever make in Jamaica, the tune sell by thousands. Seaga keep a meeting under Bustamante's statue the Sunday night when the tune come out, and Shearer there 'pon the stage, him and Seaga and the whole crowd of Labour people, and them say Maxie sing the tune and no poor Maxie at all. Maxie no have nothing fe do with the tune, but the brother sound like Maxie 'pon it for true, "Can't get no rice or coconut oil" and all them things there. Things really tough in Jamaica them times, and Seaga and the man Shearer there 'pon the scene and they say, "A few days ago the people was bawling that the Rod was on their backs, can't get no rice or no flour, hear the song that the same man Maxie Romeo sing." Maxie Romeo is the man that sing "Let the Power Fall on I", now he is singing "Take the Rod off our backs . . . " and me and Maxie get hot. Maxie move to the States, so a man come fire some shot. Me hide in a pig pen, and the big man come and say, "Where the boy them?" and just run through there, so me just there inna the pig pen and them passed. Me go a hospital and them say me get shot inna me hand, but I can't say it's shot I get inna me hand, probably is something cut me, I never see the bullet.

Them dress the hand, so the people make one big thing out of it. Me all the night in the hospital, Shearer come and it big news. Them send me a whole heap of different police, man a start say me is a Labourite . . . But it's just a song me make, and them shoot me.'

It was around the same time that Striker was wounded that Lee Perry experienced some car trouble, crashing his Thunderbird into a Washington Gardens ditch due to a faulty front end; Scratch was also fortunate in avoiding any serious injury, though the car itself was significantly damaged.

In addition to their political content, Junior Byles' 'King of Babylon' and its instrumental version 'Nebuchadneezer,' are also musically interesting. Recorded at Randy's with the Impact All Stars, Lloyd Parks' original bass lines particularly stand out; in addition to having plenty of rest stops, the bass pattern was interspersed with frantic, high fingerings that slide down the neck of the bass, creating a sensation of spiralling pitch not then utilised by other bassists. In 1971, Perry had begun making use of Parks' abilities as a solo vocalist and bass player when he had not really established himself in either realm; Parks' version of B J Thomas' 'Mighty Clouds Of Joy' showed just how strong his abilities were, while his playing and singing on 'Professor Ironside', a hilarious homage to the wheelchair-bound private eye played by Raymond Burr, showed Parks' amiable sense of humour and general adaptability to Scratch's whims. With Scratch's guidance, Lloyd Parks managed to squeeze surprising sounds from his instrument, with furious patterns and odd timings taking the bass out of the realm of reggae and closer to free-form jazz. Parks was keen to point out that Scratch was very insightful about his musical capabilities early on: 'I did a song named "Mighty Clouds Of Joy" and I think that is the time he could identify my talent as a bass player. I used to do songs for Randy's, Impact label, in the studio band. Whenever anybody is recording, they call me, Ansel Collins, Sly, and so on, and I play on "Nebuchadneezer" by Junior Byles. When I play that song, I play that line and I play some things, and the man say, "Boy, what's making that sound? It's just something different." Scratch was one of the greatest producers that Jamaica has ever seen. He get things out of me that I didn't even know I had inside of me as a bass player. At that time you had bass players like George "Fully" Fullwood, Family Man; Robbie (Shakespeare) was coming too, and you have discussions, "Who is the best bass player?" Scratch would say "Lloyd Parks, I want you to hear this little guy!" He predicted what is happening now, like whenever a song is playing on the radio that I play on, the disc jockey says "Lloyd Parks, the greatest bass player in Jamaica!" '

Perry re-used the 'King of Babylon' rhythm for Dennis Alcapone's 'Master Key', on which Alcapone's edgy toast is offset by another Ron Wilson trombone line; the song was fairly popular in both Jamaica and the UK, where it appeared on a Trojan various-artists collection called *Version To Version*.

Another hugely successful Byles/Perry collaboration was 'Da Da', a largely nonsensical song that came third in the Festival Song Competition in 1972 (first place was 'Pomps and Pride' by Toots and the Maytals). The song featured a smooth horn section and backing vocals from the Jamaicans, a group that had won the 1967 Festival with 'Ba Ba Boom'. A more interesting but less successful version was 'Come Da Da', cut without backing vocals but with the horn section still in place. On 'Come Da Da', Chubby and Scratch sang largely incomprehensible gibberish in affected voices, including Scratch murmuring one of his favourite sayings: 'Matthew, Mark, Luke and John, drop the knife and spoon and nyam with your hand.' To those who were able to make out the lyric, this cryptic expression suggested an abandonment of European table etiquette in favour of African eating customs; according to Scratch, the saying was adapted 'from the Bible. It said before the fork and knife was here you had to eat; you're not going to not eat because you don't have any. These (hands) are your fork and knife, original(ly).'

The version side of 'Da Da' was called 'Festival Da Da', and while the Jamaican pressing of this song on Wizzdom featured a fairly standard dub, the UK pressing of the same song utilised not only a different mix but began with a livid proclamation from Scratch: 'In thee, oh Jah, I put my trust, deliver I from confusion.' 'Come Da Da' and its version also began with a revealing proclamation: 'I-lee plant in a righteous water, and the increase comes from Jah,' referring to the blessed weed they were growing and smoking. By now he had been significantly affected by the Rastafarian faith to proclaim a belief in it openly on record and to begin using the I-words of Rastafari dialect.

The use of I-words by Rastas was part of a concerted effort to convert 'word-sound' into power through an intense and selective re-shaping of Jamaican english. It involves the substitution of syllables that are deemed negative with the more uplifting 'I', the sound of which suggested all things 'high' and therefore closer to God. Thus the syllable 'ban' of the word 'banana' must be removed, for as a natural and life-giving fruit, the item cannot be 'banned'; the word 'I-yana' is seen instead as a preferable and elevating description. Marijuana was brought to Jamaica from India by indentured labourers, and the strong weed became known as 'collie' through a corruption of Kali, the most potent Hindu goddess who is responsible for the cyclical destruction and re-birth of the world. But as 'collie' can also be a lowly dog, perhaps one who might even dare to piss against the walls of Babylon, Perry names it as 'I-lee' in 'Come Da Da' as his belief in the Rasta way was slowly intensifying.

Though some had him down as a mere Rasta sympathiser due to his preference for a 'soul man' Afro and neatly trimmed facial hair, others recognised him as having already embraced the faith from within. And even if he retained the physical countenance of a 'baldhead', at least the unshaven beard he began to wear around this time was pointing him in the general direction of the Rasta dress code. These issues were dealt with by Scratch and

Junior Byles on 'Hail To Power,' the version side of 'Pharaoh Hiding', in which a disguised voice asks, 'Well sir, do you think it's right for a baldhead man to claim that he's a Rasta?' to which Junior – himself a Rasta with no locks – answers, 'It all depends on his heart.'

'Beat Down Babylon' and 'Da Da' had made Junior Byles a star, and he would continue to work with Scratch for a number of years. The pair worked solidly together for the rest of 1972, and by the start of October they had recorded over a dozen tracks, of which ten of the best were selected for Junior's debut LP; called *Beat Down Babylon* after his phenomenal hit, the album was issued in November by Trojan in the UK and Canada (through Montreal's Trans World Records) and by Dynamic in Jamaica.

Except for the Festival song, each track on the album showed the depth of feeling Junior was capable of imparting, and the majority of the disc dealt with themes affecting the wider society as a whole. 'Joshua's Desire' implored Jamaica's youth to heed Michael Manley's pleas for unity, while the autobiographical 'Poor Chubby' reminded us of the thin tightrope Junior was walking as a suffering young Rasta in Babylon. Even the love song 'Don't Know Why' opted for a quiet honesty as opposed to the falsity of clichés. With every song a winner, *Beat Down Babylon* remains as the finest album of Junior Byles' career, and is perhaps the strongest Upsetter-produced album of a solo singer.

The pair enjoyed a further hit in 1972 with Byles' rendition of the ballad 'Fever', an oft-covered number that was a huge hit in jazz for Peggy Lee. Byles' version was cut over another curious Upsetter rhythm that included a false start and plenty of movement in a heavily reverberating mix; the original cut of the rhythm was 'This World', voiced by Milton Henry and Junior Byles. As Henry explained, 'Devon Russell wrote that song "This World". "Fever" is on the "This World" rhythm, "This World" is the original song so everything else come after that. I did the original 'This World' first up at Randy's, with Lloyd Parks playing bass and Reggie; Junior Byles was doing backing vocals.' When 'This World' was released, it was credited to King Medious, an alias Henry noted was inspired by the Sixth and Seventh Books of Moses.

Though 'This World' was a moving plea for peace and love, it was not nearly as popular as Byles' 'Fever'. The widespread popularity of Junior's version would give rise to a number of further cuts on the rhythm, including Jah T's 'Lick The Pipe, Peter' and Augustus Pablo's ominous melodica cut, 'Hot And Cold'. Pablo recalled his contribution as involving a naturalistic form of experimentation brought about through the general 'vibe' of the session. 'That was like a experiment, I take my instrument and just play. It's no miracle thing or nothing like that, it's just natural vibes. Everybody look 'pon the past and wonder how we plan this out, but we don't really plan; it was just Jah vibes. Now that everybody get big off that, everybody acting like they're professional, but it was just natural vibes. Anybody tell you anything else is a lie they're telling.'

Milton Henry would later voice an alternative take of the rhythm as 'Follow Fashion' for Alphonso Bailey's Globe International label. Bailey had been involved in manufacturing records at Dynamics before opening a record shop on Hagley Park Road; after producing early work by Freddy McGregor, he bought cuts of a number of Perry's rhythms for his own productions.

Lee Perry spent much of 1972 and '73 recording at Dynamic Sound. Dynamic was then the leading studio on the island, and had top-of-the-range equipment that was outside the reach of most other Jamaican studios; in November 1972, it made a further quantum leap towards the future by installing the first sixteen track machine on the island. Such state-of-the-art facilities allowed for a broader, cleaner, and more complex arrangement of sound, and Scratch became very comfortable working in its well-equipped environment. He already had a rapport with Barrington Lambert, who had been the junior engineer under Lynford Anderson at WIRL, and he quickly established an understanding with Dynamic's new head engineer, Carlton Lee. Perry's talents had been noted by studio boss Byron Lee after the recording of 'Small Axe', and Lee had Scratch perform a variety of duties for Dynamic in this period, including taking charge of their A & R roster. Lee noted that he began to make use of Perry's services after observing Perry's ear for potential hits: 'Dynamic Sound was the studio that had 90% of things happening here. When Leslie Kong was alive and you had Bob Marley, Toots and the Maytals, the Maytones, the Gaylads, the Melodians, all those groups coming in. After that era you had Johnny Nash coming down to record and then Lee Perry was one of the producers we had. When Lee Perry first come, what attract us to him was that he had tremendous talent. He could recognise a hit, out of all the producers we had worked with, his ear for a hit before it was actually recorded – he had that gift in his head. A lot of producers have to hear the song first to say it could be a hit but he could generate the hit from day one. I remember once he came and he brought this guy called Junior Byles and he brought some things from "Small Axe" with Bob Marley. He was a tremendous producer that we were very happy to be associated with.'

Lee explained that Perry's work at Dynamic was based around informal bartering that suited his needs as well as the needs of the studio: 'We had four A & R people working as in-house production for us: Lee Perry, Bunny Lee, Tommy Cowan, who did Eric Donaldson's "Cherry Oh Baby" and Boris Gardiner. We had kind of a joint production deal where (Perry) would do stuff for us, we would release some of it under our label, some under his, and he would get production royalties or sometimes he would waive his production fees for facilities we have, like studio time, stamper-pressing or distribution. Then he never had the cash to finance his operations, so we would take his talent in the studio and in return, give him cash to counter the production costs. He would go and make another record with somebody else, and he would press them here, we call it third party licensing.'

Perry's UK various-artists album release of 1972 was *Battle Axe*, the latest in his series of hodge-podge collections for Trojan. As usual, the disc combined a majority of peculiar instrumentals with the occasional unaltered vocal, though *Battle Axe* showed Perry moving closer to what would later be commonplace practices in dub through mixing that playfully re-cast the material. For instance, Delroy Wilson's hits 'Cool Operator' and 'I'm Yours', cuts of which Scratch obtained from Bunny Lee, were not presented in the ordinary forms that ensured they were hits, but were mixed instead as quasi-dubs to include only a fraction of vocals, placing the recordings in an entirely different context; Little Roy's 'Don't Cross The Nation', here confusingly credited to Mark and Luke, underwent a similar transformation. Dave Barker's 'Groove Me' and a Clancy Eccles re-cut of Theophilus Beckford's 'Easy Snapping' were both stripped of their vocals entirely, while David Isaacs' vocals on 'Knock Three Times' were replaced by a swirling organ and phased horns, turning a most innocuous rendition of a cheesy love song into a psychedelic instrumental oddity. The 'Cherry Oh Baby' rhythm that Scratch had so artfully mutated into 'Well Dread' was here presented as the raw rhythm of 'Cheerio', while the rhythm of Andy Capp's 'Pop A Top' was faded jerkily in and out of the mix as 'Pop A Pop'. Only Junior Byles' 'Place Called Africa' and Carl Dawkins' 'Picture On The Wall' were left with their vocals intact, while 'Rough and Smooth' was yet another Rastafarian number by an uncredited vocal duo. The remaining three instrumental tracks were 'Battle Axe' (a.k.a. 'The Axe Man', featuring Bongo Herman and Les), 'Dark Moon' (a saxophone version of 'Blue Moon', recorded some years earlier), and 'Earthquake' (by Winston Wright).

Overall, *Battle Axe* continued the progression of experimentation shown on the previous Trojan Upsetter collections. While the reggae beat was gradually slowing down, Perry was also ensuring its sound became more complex. As his access to better studio equipment allowed him to better satisfy his greater propensity to alter the mix, the innovations Perry came up with were given greater credence on the Jamaican music scene. The Upsetter was then at the forefront of Jamaica's musical revolution, and many other producers would take inspiration from his innovations, seeking to emulate his obscure technique that was resulting not only in a series of hits but in a unique and startling sound.

Besides the album releases and his work with Junior Byles, Perry produced a number of other notable singles in 1972. Perhaps the biggest hit for another artist was Chenley Duffus' rendition of the William Bell soul ballad 'To Be A Lover', on which Duffus was joined by his brother Kenneth and his cousin Keith. Duffus had recorded a trio of unconvincing cover tunes for Perry earlier in the year, beginning with 'Sincerely', the rhythm of which Duffus said Perry built with Ansel Collins at Federal. Although the song failed to hit, Perry re-used the rhythm with Duffus again for sappy attempts at the often-covered 'Goodnight My Love' and 'At The End', both of which also failed to make an impact. But when Duffus voiced his version of 'To Be A Lover', it was clear to all present that the team had a hit on their hands. 'I did my biggest song for Perry, "To Be A Lover". We did that at Randy's studio. Only three musicians play that song: Tommy McCook play keyboards, Horsemouth play drums, and Lloyd Parks play bass. When Leroy Sibbles walk into the studio that day, he asked "Whose rhythm?" Upsetter tell him "It's mine," he said "It's a hit." It really hit! I was just coming off a tour from the States and I was crisp.' Tommy McCook was arranging much of Perry's material in this period, and it was partly his non-standard approach to keyboard playing that gave the song its shape, while Horsemouth's spacious drum pattern and Lloyd Parks' hesitant bass line gave emphasis to the inherent languor of the tune.

Though this proved to be the biggest hit of Duffus' career, he would virtually vanish from the recording arena shortly after. His earnings did not always reflect the hits he had made, so Duffus decided to concentrate on stage performances where payment tended to be more reliable.

Scratch later noted that the success of the song caused temporary friction between himself, Federal records boss Ken Khouri, and Coxsone Dodd: 'Coxsone was vexed when we were making "To Be A Lover", he was jealous. Downbeat didn't like what's going on, he think that me was with him, and me and Mr Khouri making hit tune and he was making none, so him get mad, come and start to fight. He was passing Federal to pick up him record and him hear Mr Khouri inside and Downbeat come in the office and say him want to fight.'

Meanwhile, Perry's close association with Max Romeo and Niney the Observer yielded further material in 1972 like 'Rasta Band Wagon' and 'Public Enemy Number One', songs that reflected a strong bond of friendship as well as the fruitful working relationship enjoyed by the trio. Romeo and Niney were then living in the same house, close to Scratch's home in Washington Gardens, and the three were often around each other in the studio, improvising and sharing ideas.

'Rasta Band Wagon' was Romeo's attempt to deal with the changing face of Rastafari. Not only were a growing number of 'baldheads' and some uptown folk proclaiming themselves to be Rastas, but Jamaicans who were not of African descent were also claiming to be part of what had previously been an exclusively black religion. The latter element was partly the result of efforts by the Twelve Tribes of Israel organization to broaden the appeal of Rastafari. Founded in Trench Town in 1968 by Vernon Carrington, a juice vendor who became known as the Prophet Gad, the Twelve Tribes controversially sought to emphasise the universal appeal of Rastafari, spreading its doctrine to all ethnic and social groups throughout Jamaica.

Though 'Rasta Band Wagon' was introduced by Scratch as being 'dedicated to all the imitation Rastaman', and a UK issue credited him as producer, Romeo was quick to point out that the song was a Niney production, issued first on his Observer label: ' "Rasta Bandwagon" was done for Niney, but it was being distributed for us by Upsetter because by then, Upsetter had this little distribution going so we decided to support it. We started to produce a few songs for that distribution and "Rasta Bandwagon" was one of those songs.'

Both 'Rasta Band Wagon' and its version side, 'When Jah Speak', used sparse instrumentation, notable for the absence of a drum kit. Romeo said this was the result of his frustration with the session's drummer, Leroy 'Horsemouth' Wallace, who was not giving the tune his due attention. 'I fired the drummer on the session, Horsemouth. It was the early days of Horsemouth, and every time we did a good take, he's off to the bathroom or somewhere, so I just fired him off that tune and said "Do it without a drum." At the end of the day, we just use the stick they use to beat the bass drum in Niyabinghi wrapped in a little piece of cloth, so we just touch the bass, boom!'

Niney noted that the lack of a standard drum kit changed the emphasis of the song. 'Because of the lyric that Maxie singing and the gimmicks, man don't have to play no drums. We would prefer to turn it into a listening song more than a dancing song.'

On the version side, credited to Murt, Turt and Purt, Perry slipped into another persona through a highly affected voice to proclaim how the very fierceness of Jah would kill, cramp, and paralyse His enemies, with Maxie and Niney shouting in unison with Scratch to give emphasis to certain words. As Niney remembered it, 'That was when me and Maxie and Scratch, we did have a group one time, we call ourselves Jeff, Mutt, and Turf. We were just producing; me producing, Scratch producing, and me and Maxie doing the same thing, so we never know who going to get the songs, because Scratch have a label, me have a label, and me and Maxie have a label, so we never decide. We just do a thing like that but that continue.'

Another Perry/Romeo collaboration from the same time period was 'Public Enemy Number One', on which Romeo fingers Satan as being responsible for a variety of social evils over another sparse rhythm with a wobbling bass line; its version side, 'John Public' (a.k.a. 'I Know Something'), had distorted vocals about poisonous dumplings and sweet sounds beneath a rhythm with an accentuated kick drum led by a bright and prominent organ riff straight out of a sci-fi horror movie. A couple of other strong Stingers tunes were also issued that year, though neither had the impact of 'Give Me Power': 'Preacher Man' spoke of how men of the cloth and Christians in general could be evil, while 'Forward Up' requested large amounts of weed over swinging horns, with a revving motorcycle engine adding to the song's aural realism.

Still feeling the loss of the Wailers, Perry reached back into his rhythm bag to begin recycling 'Keep On Moving'. He cut Dennis Alcapone onto an updated version of the rhythm with an added organ lead and percussion overdubs for 'Rasta Dub', on which Dennis sang the choruses as well as toasting and making cock-crow noises. 'Mooving Version' was a next toast of the updated rhythm cut shortly after by Big Youth, a former cab driver and hotel mechanic who was then the top deejay of Tippertone sound; after voicing this relaxed toast for Perry, he quickly shot to international prominence through work with Keith Hudson and young producer Gussie Clarke.

A number of other singles Perry issued in 1972 were strong and noteworthy efforts, although they failed to make much of a lasting impact as far as sales were concerned. One such number came from his faithful rhythm guitarist, Alva 'Reggie' Lewis: 'Natty Natty' was an excellent song that remains largely unknown, in which Lewis sang of the disapproval shown towards him by his girlfriend's parents because of his budding dreadlocks and lack of material wealth. Lewis said the song was based on true experiences: 'Me fool with a little girl. The mother used to like me and she know what a gwan, but the woman mother no know what a gwan. All of a sudden, the parents start resent me but me and she a gwan. She a left and take the train down to Manchester, go stay with my mother. Them mad at me now, 'cause she just pack up and make a move. So I write about it (in) the song "Natty Natty", "The mama no like I, poppa no want see I, they say me head natty natty and me can't buy a cup of coffee".'

Built around tightly wound drum rolls from Tin Legs, the song was again presented in an innovative way through a series of false endings, in which the rhythm is stopped for half a measure through the latter half of the song, adding to the feeling of fragmentation and disappointment of which Lewis sings.

One of the first issues on the Wizzdom label from early 1972 was 'Round and Round', a finely crafted harmony number by the Melodians, who were recording at Dynamic under a short-term contract with Byron Lee; although the song failed to make much impact, it shows Perry's uncanny strength in arranging vocal trios, and made good use of the All Stars rhythm section, now featuring Earl 'Chinna' Smith on rhythm guitar and percussion from Bongo Herman. Another such effort from later in the year was 'Whiplash', a tale of sexual frustration that also featured fine harmonic singing, credited to Wesley Germs – a.k.a. Wesley Martin of the Bleechers.

A somewhat more successful oddity Scratch issued that year was 'French Connection', on which Scratch himself provided a largely nonsensical toast over a chugging Upsetter organ rhythm. Though the title was obviously inspired by the hugely popular crime film, it is not clear how the title relates to the rest of the song, in which Scratch exhorts his listeners to dance to his hot new rhythm. He also slips in and out of a myriad of obscure personas on this disc, proclaiming 'My name is Kiba Wackie, better known as Killer Yackie . . . Kiba Wackie, Sukiyaki, Killer Yackie,' suggesting either ad-libbed nonsense, or more likely, concepts that he alone understood, perhaps inspired by film and television characters or creations from his own imagination.

'French Connection' was one of the first discs he mixed at King Tubby's studio at 18 Drumilie Avenue in the heart of the Waterhouse ghetto, whose tiny premises had minimal facilities but plenty of vibes and atmosphere. It was not possible to build rhythms in the one-room studio, but King Tubby's set-up was perfect for laying the odd vocal track or other overdubs and effects. Tubby then had only a two track recorder, but his home made mixing console could produce an interesting sound, and Perry began to use Tubby's skills with increasing frequency in the following months, particularly after Tubby had acquired the obsolete four track machine abandoned by Dynamic Sounds, which was again customised to better suit Tubby's needs.

Another early disc Perry helped shape at King Tubby's was 'Monkey Fashion'/'Fashion Monkey', a two-sided toast I Roy voiced at the studio for the singer Roy Cousins of the Royals, who had recently entered into self-production. Born on August 25, 1949, Cousins was raised by his mother, a domestic worker, in the Bread Lane area of downtown Kingston. His aunt was a member of a congregation on Waltham Park Road established by an American known as Bishop French, and it was at this church at the age of five that Cousins gave his first performance as a duo with a friend called Dennis. Attending Russeau school, located beside the Maxfield Park children's home in Chisholm Avenue, Cousins became friendly with future musicians Bernard Collins, Lloyd Parks, Ansel Collins, Wire Lindo, Eric 'Fish' Clarke, and Vic Taylor. When his aunt joined Claudius Henry's Coptic Church, she briefly removed Cousins from school to indoctrinate him into the movement until Henry was tried for sedition. It was while attending Tarrant School in Half Way Tree in 1962 that Cousins formed a group with classmates Garth Forbes, Granville Green, and Eileen Burnett to enter the Junior Festival held at the Little Theatre, but the group was not successful and disbanded.

By the time Cousins left school in 1965, he was living with his mother in Cockburn Pen, where he became friendly with local singing groups the Tartans, a quartet composed of Cedric Myton, Devon Russell, Lindburgh 'Preps' Lewis, and Lincoln Thompson (later known as Prince Lincoln but then known as Johnny Red Socks) and the Sheridons, featuring Winston Francis, Pat Kelly, 'a guy named Spirry and this guy Brammo'. It was while working at the New Yorker Garment factory making shirts that he met Keith Smith and his friend Trevor MacFarlane, who eventually formed a group called the Tempests with Cousins and his friend Bertram 'Harry' Johnson, the only person in the area with a guitar.

A few weeks after the Tartans recorded the smash hit 'Dance All Night' at Federal, Cousins' group attended their first audition at the studio with a song called 'House Up On A Hill', backed by musicians such as Ernest Ranglin, Ronnie Bop, and Hugh Malcolm. Unfortunately, Federal proprietor Richard Khouri stopped the session mid-way, ultimately causing Trevor to leave the group. Errol 'Tralla' Green took his place as lead singer for a subsequent audition at Treasure Isle, where the group recorded a handful of tracks, including 'We Are In The Mood'. When Duke held back issuing their material, Green left the group to be replaced by Errol Wilson, and the group then recorded a portion of songs for Matador at Federal with Boris Gardiner's band, including '100 Pounds of Clay', but Matador also kept these tunes in the can. Eventually, the group began attending auditions at Studio One, but Lee Perry turned them down twice and they were rejected a third time by Bibi Seaton, before Coxsone himself selected the group to record eight songs in 1967, backed by bassist Leroy Sibbles, drummer Phil Callender, guitarist Eric Frater, and keyboardist Jackie Mittoo, one of which was 'Pick up the Pieces'. Though the song would later prove to be a major hit due to its harmonic brilliance, Coxsone also declined to issue this material after failing to sell one of their songs on a dub plate, causing the group to split for a period.

Recognising the strength of 'Pick up the Pieces' himself, Roy Cousins decided to re-form his group as the Royals for a self-produced session at Dynamics in late 1971, partly funded by a co-worker at the post office named David Robinson; as Errol Wilson was then in Guantanamo Bay, Lloyd Forrester temporarily took his place. Session musicians included Geoffrey Chung and 'Gitsy from Binns Road, Waterhouse' on guitar, Lloyd Charmers on keyboard, Phil Callender on drums and Bertram Johnson on bass. As Johnson had no experience of the instrument, the singer Barry Biggs helped him shape a convincing line in the studio, resulting in the altered form of the new 'Pick Up the Pieces', which proved to be such a big hit when first issued on Cousins' Uhuru label that it prompted Coxsone finally to issue the original.

Not long after King Tubby acquired the four-track machine from Dynamic, Cousins took I Roy to the studio to voice him on his re-cut rhythm; according to Cousins, it was Lee Perry who gave I Roy's record its ultimate shape. 'Tubby and Lee Perry mix it, 'cause it's in King Tubby's we voice it. Lee Perry used to work up by Tubby's, and I and Tubby's was good friend. Tubby's had a four-track machine and a two-track, so when Tubbs mix it, and you hear where the organ used to go up, that was Scratch hitching up the organ. Scratch was a man who was very creative, one of the most creative minds to sound at the time. When you hear the organ, it was mixed that way before I Roy do him voice, and them days you used to do more than one cut to attract attention, so "Fashion Monkey" was the first take and "Monkey Fashion" was the second.' Scratch would later make selected use of the Royals' harmonies as backing vocalists for other artists.

Just in case he had been issuing too much serious and religious material, Scratch made certain to cut a couple of rude songs in 1972 to show that sex was still high on his agenda: 'Water Pump' was a blatant boast of sexual exploits to come, graphically illustrating his talented control of his phallus, while 'Puss See Hole' infused a sparse dub with sensual imagery through Perry's murmuring of folk sayings and nursery rhymes in a sexually suggestive manner. Some copies of the latter were pressed with Winston Groovy's 'Want To Be Loved' on the flip side, but this pop-reggae outing was a self-produced effort recorded by the London-based singer at Chalk Farm without Perry's involvement; it was one of a few tunes Scratch picked up from Pama for pressing on his label in Jamaica at this time. He also cut an updated version of 'People Funny Boy' that he again voiced himself in this period as 'People Sokup Boy', the rhythm of which was subsequently used for Dennis Alcapone's 'Backbiter', which featured another trombone overdub from Ron Wilson beneath Alcapone's toast.

Alcapone noted that all the work he did with the Upsetter was recorded in just a few sessions, with several tracks voiced each time. Although he found Scratch easy to work with, Alcapone claimed to have ceased working with him due to a lack of proper financial reward. 'I can't remember Scratch giving me any money, honestly. I can remember Scratch telling me to come for my money, yes, and me keep going . . . Pauline tell me Scratch not there or some shit.'

If Alcapone refused to work with him, Scratch was not particularly bothered as he had already found a replacement with one of Alcapone's protégés. Lester Bullocks was initially calling himself Alcapone Junior, but Scratch gave him the surname of another violent American mobster, John Dillinger. Born in Kingston on June 25, 1953, Bullocks was raised by his grandmother (a market-produce vendor) after his mother emigrated to America. Dillinger noted that his chief influences were U Roy, King Stitt, and Dennis Alcapone: 'I used to see them in the dancehall, listen to King Tubby's Hi-Fi that U Roy used to play, and Coxsone Downbeat, I used to listen to King Stitch. I used to listen to El Paso, listen to Dennis Alcapone. When I go in the dance and I hear all U Roy as a deejay, I used to ask him for the mike and do my thing. From there, the people them start to recognise what I do, that I'm a next champion.'

Alcapone recalled allowing the teenage Bullocks to express himself on El Paso sound: 'Dillinger used to come to my dance as a little youth from across the lane. Whenever the sound is playing, you have a lot of little youths who would gather around who is kind of interested, people like Dillinger, Trinity (Wade Brammer, a.k.a. Prince Glen), and a few others that was in the area at the time. Dillinger used to be very enthusiastic. Whenever we are playing, Dillinger always come right beside the amplifier, him always there. He wanted to be involved, so some time when I'm deejaying, I could hear him doing him own little thing. A tune was playing, you could hear him humming something, so one night him ask me fe give him a talk over the mike. I gave him the mike and I realised that he had potential, you could hear that there was something there. When I need a break, I want to go and lick two chalice or something like that, or go talk to a girl, I would give Dillinger the mike and make him gwan talk, him and Samuel the First (Samuel Philips) would be there, and that's how him come in. Him work himself in, because him go to Scratch and Scratch listen to him and decide to voice him.'

Dillinger noted that although he was eager to begin recording, Scratch was the only producer willing to gamble on him. 'I had a lot of songs that I did want to get on the market to record, so I was campaigning, visiting studios. On my way from studio to studio, I went to Dynamic Sound, and at that time Scratch was there recording. I talk to him and he let me do about two LP that night, straight through . . . due to you're young and greedy, you have a lot of inspiration and stress and anxiety to get it all out.'

To accommodate the high volume of Dillinger's material, Scratch dug deep into his back catalogue to voice him on cuts of 'Tighten Up' and 'Stranger On The Shore', as well as on current rhythms like 'French Connection'. As with Winston Prince's debut material, none of these releases was a hit, but Dillinger was also later to prove himself as a competent toaster with the Upsetter and producers such as Phil Pratt, Augustus Pablo, Bunny Lee, Joe Gibbs, and Alvin Ranglin, eventually scoring numerous hits in the latter half of the '70s at Channel One.

Aside from cultivating the careers of Junior Byles and upcoming deejays, 1972 also saw Scratch declining to appear in Perry Henzell's *The Harder They Come*, a film that would prove to be a pioneering cinematic work on many levels. Not only was the film shot and directed in Jamaica with an entirely Jamaican cast working with no written script and including some great reggae music on the soundtrack, but the plot's re-telling of the tale of 'Rhyging', the nation's original rude boy, implied that politically motivated criminal forces lurked behind every aspect of Jamaican society and were especially evident in the music industry. Scratch later said he chose not to appear because of the low payment offered.

> 'They offered me $5 to appear in it. That's all most of the others got paid. I told the man that $5 wasn't enough to fill my car with petrol, and he didn't offer any more money, so I didn't want to appear in the film – my time's too important!' [2]

In the early 1970s, Lee Perry's quest for the right set of recording circumstances saw him working in diverse places. Though he had become firmly entrenched in Dynamic from late 1971, his hunger for different and unpredictable sounds saw him making use of the less-equipped facilities of others, where sometimes a rougher or cruder mix better matched his sensibilities. When the four Hoo Kim brothers (Joe Joe, Ernest, Kenneth, and Paulie) opened the small Channel One recording studio on Maxfield Avenue in the middle of one of Kingston's roughest ghettos (on the site of a former ice-cream parlour they had previously used as a motorcylce sales shop), Perry was among the first to record there, though his use of the studio would prove to be minimal overall. He was still laying the odd track at Randy's, Studio One, and Federal, but most of his rhythms were being laid at Dynamic, with overdubs and effects tackled at King Tubby's. But while he was roaming around town in search of the appropriate recording spot, Perry was also nourishing a secret crucial dream: to build a studio of his own.

Though he was comfortable with his tenure at Dynamic, Perry felt increasingly constrained by having to rely on facilities controlled by others. Every aspect of record production in Jamaica was in the hands of a select few, and Scratch resented feeling unable to take charge of his musical destiny more fully. His muse was cramming so many ideas into his head that he really needed a recording space he controlled himself, somewhere that time constraints would not be a problem, where he could freely pursue the eclectic paths of his creativity.

After having settled in Cardiff Crescent at the start of the '70s, Scratch and Pauline had gradually salted away whatever surplus money they could with the express determination to build a studio, and by the spring of 1973 a considerable stash had been accumulated towards this purpose. Scratch scoured the Kingston area for a suitable location without success until a vision showed him the way.

In the small yard behind his house was a large *lignum vitae*, a tree with deep green leaves that releases a distinct odour at Christmas time. According to Pauline Morrison, it was while dozing beneath the tree one night that the spirits spoke again to Lee Perry, making it clear that he was resting at the exact spot on which his studio was to be built.

Scratch began work on the studio straight away, and added a fourth bedroom and extra bathroom to the house at the same time. He hired the guitarist and singer Bobby Aitken as chief contractor, and Aitken himself erected much of the masonry, while Leonard Dillon of the Ethiopians did the patterning on the cement walls of the surrounding compound, and a handyman known as Django provided general assistance. The building of the studio was a long, slow process that was ultimately expensive; completed towards the end of the year, it cost over £12,000 in total, a hefty sum by Jamaican standards of the day. By December 1973, Scratch was already recording material there.

Coinciding with the studio's completion was the arrival of Perry's half-brother Milton 'P-Son' Blythe, who had transplanted himself from the country life of rural Hanover to the unfamiliar ways of Cardiff Crescent; then just approaching manhood, P-Son spent much of his coming years assisting with the runnings in the Perry family yard.

From late 1972 to early 1974, while his studio was being constructed, equipped, and made operational, Lee Perry's work was becoming noticeably more radical. The instrumental was still his forté, and he would exploit its myriad potential to the fullest through a continual exploration of the dub and version genres while simultaneously remaining innovative with vocal and deejay formats. 1973 would see a number of important album releases, as Perry shifted his emphasis from the unblemished instrumental form more fully into the realm of dub, while a number of noteworthy vocal and deejay singles would also surface that year.

Meanwhile, Scratch was increasingly travelling abroad on business, often accompanied by Pauline. In London he was continuing to deal with Trojan and Pama, and began the odd collaboration with Larry Lawrence, the Creole employee who was branching out as an independent producer with the formation of his Ethnic label. As Lawrence recalled, 'Scratch always fly to London quite regular. This is where they used to base to do their (business). We become such good friends that when he comes to the airport I'll have to go and pick him up. We spend days and ends together, studio wise and everything, because by then we was moving like brothers. When he brings his tape over, "Beat Down Babylon" and all them records, it first comes into my hands because there used to be Revox recorders in my house. When they come, they come to me and listen to their music, take out what they want to give to their parent record companies. I would take them to their meetings and everything, if they want a good studio they come and ask me which are the best; I always know what type of music they are working on, like to transfer music and things. Then we start getting into the studios and start making records, with a girl called Silky Davis and some of the Trojan artists like Dandy Livingston and all these people. We used to take them into the studio with Scratch and make records for them.'

Larry also recalled helping Scratch to find much of the equipment that he would use in his studio: 'When he was building that studio, all those equipments that you saw in there, both of us bought them together with his money. Trojan gave him the cheque, but we drive around and look for those JBL speakers and all that was in there, we bought them and shipped them down there. We would drive down to Charing Cross Road to look for bass-drum mikes and all that.'

Some of the studio equipment that ended up in Scratch's hands is said to have come from less direct means, having been 'liberated' from a London studio that had closed down, though the exact circumstances surrounding this have proved difficult to ascertain properly.

From the early 1970s, Scratch was also travelling to New York to do business with various companies run by expatriate Jamaicans in Brooklyn and the Bronx, though he spent a lot less time there than he did in London. His first link in New York was with members of the Chin family, who had established American branches of the Randy's label there; he later established close links with Brad Osborne, owner of the Clocktower label, and Melvin 'Munchie' Jackson, who ran a small label called Aires.

By the end of 1972, Perry had assembled the *Cloak And Dagger* album, perhaps his most daring instrumental collection to date. According to Bruce White, Creole Records had arranged for Perry to travel to London towards the end of the year, but were later hit with further demands once the album had been completed. 'I can remember in the ninth hour when he's supposed to be flying in tomorrow, if we didn't send him another ticket for Pauline then the whole thing was off.'

Once Creole made the necessary arrangements, Lee and Pauline had their children deposited at the home of Perry's mother in Hanover, and travelled together to London, where they remained for some weeks. Two versions of the *Cloak And Dagger* album were pressed in London on this trip, one for release in the UK and the other for issue in Jamaica.

The UK issue of *Cloak And Dagger* appeared on Rhino, a subsidiary of Creole controlled by EMI; the cover showed Pauline emerging from Scratch's open leather cloak, appearing as a sort of black Avengers team. Ten of the twelve songs were presented as straight instrumentals, either horn pieces arranged by Tommy McCook, such as the title track (Scratch's version of the 'Joe Frazier' rhythm, first voiced by Burning Spear at Studio One), 'Rude Walking' (a version of Horace Andy's 'Skylarking'), 'Sunshine Rock' (loosely based on Otis Redding's 'My Girl'), and 'Iron Claw,' or organ pieces featuring Winston Wright, such as 'Hail Stone,' 'Liquid Serenade' (a version of 'The Liquidator'), 'Retail Love', and 'Creation'. 'Musical Transplant' was an instrumental rendition of Ernie Smith's 'Pitta Patta' done over in Upsetters fashion; 'Wakey Wakey' was the closest thing to dub on the album, a pared-down cut of the rhythm previously used for Dave Barker's 'Never Before' and Perry's 'Sons Of Thunder'. The odd track out was 'Caveman Skank', a thoroughly experimental and ironic dance number featuring toasting and vocal noises from Perry, along with running water, crashing cars and voices lifted from an American sound-effects record; the number opened with a Native American chief reading a portion of the Bible in Cherokee, and finished with the bustle of a public auction. Some of the live street-sound effects are said to have been recorded in the area surrounding Chalk Farm studio by Scratch and engineer Vic Kearey; Perry was bouncing around the street trying to get a reaction from the public.

If the UK issue of the album saw Scratch leaning more towards the outer limits of instrumental sound, the Jamaican Upsetter issue of the disc took things one step further by skating the fine line between instrumental and dub. 'Retail Love', 'Creation', 'Sunshine Rock', and 'Wakey Wakey' were removed to make room for 'Sharp Razor' (a dub of 'Cloak And Dagger'), 'Side Gate' (a dub of Lloyd Parks' 'Professor Ironside'), 'Version Ironside' (a dub of 'Iron Claw'), and 'Bad Walking' (a dub of 'Rude Walking'). The Jamaican pressing of *Cloak And Dagger* thus contained another exclusive Upsetter experiment: it was the first album to have instrumentals followed immediately by dub versions of the same rhythm, in what would later be known as the 'showcase' style used for presenting vocal tracks immediately followed by dubs. Both albums were also mixed in true stereo, with the lead instrument and voice overdubs in one channel and the unaltered rhythm in the other.

Cloak And Dagger sold rapidly in Jamaica but achieved little success in Britian. Perry later attributed its lack of sales to record-company disinterest, its absence of strings and unpolished rawness resulting in a lack of promotion.

'I gave that album to Rhino but at the time they were doing little things in reggae which the people didn't really like so they weren't really buying their records like they should then. A big company like EMI can't handle reggae people because they have so much at stake, they can't worry to go through that.' [3]

Bruce White felt it was more a case of Scratch's sound being too advanced for British ears. 'When it came to *Cloak And Dagger*, I don't think Scratch can say EMI didn't understand reggae. Maybe they didn't, but we were always there to push it in the areas where it needed pushing, and the main thing about having a company like EMI was their distribution. I think *Cloak And Dagger* might have been a bit before its time; perhaps the people weren't ready for it.'

Despite White's assertions about EMI's commitments to reggae, he and Cousins noted that the company eschewed its experimental side, and quickly established the independent Cactus label as an outlet for less commercial Jamaican sounds. 'We were getting to the stage of thinking we need a street label,' White conceded, 'because EMI aren't going to sell anything unless you get airplay.'

While making arrangements in London for the release of *Cloak And Dagger*, Scratch also crossed paths with his former toasting star, Dave Barker, who had been resident in the UK since touring Britain with Ansel Collins in 1971. When Scratch appeared in London on this visit, Barker was working with Creole under Larry Lawrence's supervision, and Perry got him to deliver another American-style soul toast on 'Sunshine Rock', which Creole issued as a single under the name Dave Collins. On the B-side, a Dave and Ansel Collins number called 'Hot Line' that seems to have been created for Winston Riley, Scratch overdubbed a ringing-telephone introduction and brief conversation with Pauline to enhance what was an otherwise ordinary tune.

1973 would see the release of a number of noteworthy singles, as Perry's recording techniques were becoming more refined. He was also maturing politically and spiritually in this period, and seems to have ceased his outside romantic entanglements – if only temporarily. Back in Jamaica, Perry produced a number of other strong songs with Junior Byles, who was still riding high on the popularity of their previous hit collaborations. 'Rasta No Pickpocket' was an attack on false Rastas who wore dreads but continued to rob and attack their brethren, issued with a reverberating bass-and-drum version on the flip side called 'Pickpocket Skank'. 'Auntie Lulu', issued somewhat later in the year, had Byles singing a series of proverbs over a lively rhythm given extra complexity by a melodica part and furious drum rolls from Tin Legs. Later still was 'When Will Better Come', in which Byles queried Michael Manley's failure to provide real change since being elected over a cut of the song that helped to elect him, Delroy Wilson's 'Better Must Come'; its version side, 'Ski Wa Wa', featured an odd scat vocal pattern by Scratch over a mix that placed emphasis on an overdubbed percussive wood block.

1973 also saw the release of one of Perry's most moving and enduring productions, 'Words Of My Mouth' by the Gatherers. This short-lived harmony group had formed on a Trench Town street corner the previous year, its loose line-up centring on singers Anthony 'Sangie' Davis, Barrington Daley, and Earl 'Bagga' Walker (later known as Errol Walker). The three teenage singers all hailed from the Trench Town area and had previously worked with other groups.

Earl George Walker, born in Trench Town on July 15, 1948, became known as Bagga after receiving the label from a schoolteacher as the pants he had inherited were excessively baggy; he received early musical training by players such as Ernest Ranglin, Lennie Hibbert, Roland Alphonso, and Tommy McCook. By 1962 he was singing with Barrington Daley, and later joined a group called the Graduates with Ken Boothe.

Born in Denham Town circa 1943, Anthony Davis became known as Sangie for his football skills, after a member of the Jamaican national team named Sangie Netty. Davis moved to Montego Bay and joined a group called the Melody Enchanters with Kingsley David and Basil Martin in 1959. Performing on the North Coast hotel circuit, they attracted the attention of Chris Blackwell, who brought the group to Federal to cut 'Crusaders' Ball' and 'I'll Be True', but the group disbanded shortly after. He returned to Trench Town in 1960, and spent many difficult years struggling to survive.

In the early 1970s, Sangie's singing talents and football skills began to be noted in Trench Town, where he was often found on Fourth Street, singing with Barrington Daley, Bagga Walker and a youth known as Jah Lenks. In 1972, the group made their recording debut with a tale of slavery called 'Right Now', backed by musicians including Peter Tosh, Family Man, and Tommy McCook, but producer Alvin 'One Foot Jimmy' Radway declined to issue the tune.

It was around this time that Sangie first became involved with the Twelve Tribes of Israel, whose teachings would have a profound influence on his lyrics. As Sangie explained, 'I was just learning to play guitar then, and that was about the same time me write a tune say "A man can live for a hundred years or more, for umpteen years and a score, not only by the words of him mouth, but the meditation of him heart . . . bring righteous praises to the King." That song "Words", it's me and Barry really write it; it was an inspiration that stem from among the whole of us, our actual trodding through life.'

Davis noted that a neighbourhood friend suggested the Gatherers approach Scratch with the song after seeing his success with the Wailers; the group thus went down to Dynamic with a number of acquaintances to present the producer with the tune. Scratch was so taken by the strength of their delivery that he recorded the group on the spot, creating one of his most enduring rhythms. 'About fourteen people did that song. Through you there

Trench Town them times, when you go studio, a lot of people come, so all who can sing, we just say, "Come in man, sing some harmony," and them sing the background part, "doobie doobie wah wah". Me play rhythm guitar and Barrington Daley play lead, Bagga play bass, Touter Harvey play keyboard, and the drums I think was Benbow.'

The resulting 'Words' placed Davis' high-pitched tenor voice over an extremely hard and competent rhythm built around a ghostly melodica riff from Augustus Pablo. Sangie related the necessity for a man to live not only by his words but with 'the meditation of his heart', praising God and all His wondrous works in a chilling delivery packed with the emotion of religious conviction.

'Words of my Mouth' would prove to be immensely popular almost immediately, and the durability of the rhythm would see Scratch re-using it countless times. Alternative cuts were issued shortly after the original, including 'Wam Pam Pa Do', in which the continuous scat vocal of the harmonic backing was presented without Sangie's lead, and 'Hot Tip', a searing deejay cut which not only featured a competent toast by a certain Prince Django, but also included a false start to the tune, interrupted by a studio argument between Scratch and an auditioning hopeful.

The second tune the Gatherers cut at the same session was the optimistic 'Start Over', led by Barrington Daley. Though hardly as noteworthy as 'Words of My Mouth', 'Start Over' showed the tightness of the Upsetter rhythm section, its beat propelled by rapid snare-drum rolls and rim shots. Unfortunately, the Gatherers did not record further as a group; though they eventually received the large sum of $(JA)1400 from Scratch for their efforts (which Sangie noted was divided 14 ways, leaving each contributor with $100), the group members went their separate ways: Sangie Davis took a long break from the music scene, becoming more closely involved in the Twelve Tribes organisation, though he would later become concretely involved with Bob Marley's work, partly through the recommendation of Scratch and Alan Cole. Bagga Walker became a leading session musician and backing vocalist, notably at Studio One, where he was featured on the earliest recordings of singers such as Dennis Brown, Johnny Osbourne, and Freddy McGregor; he also became a vocalist in the Boris Gardiner Happening by 1975. Though Barrington Daley faded from view and seems not to have furthered his singing career, Jah Lenks continues to record sporadically, though his material has remained somewhat obscure.

Another stunning 1973 Perry issue was 'Better Days' by Carlton and His Shoes, a trio formed in the mid-'60s by Carlton Manning with his brothers Donald and Lynford, both of whom were also in the Abyssinians. Known for their love songs at Studio One, 'Better Days' presented the harder and more religious side of the group. Singing in unison of the betterment coming to the black race, their voices reached searing choral heights over a typically solid Upsetter rhythm featuring *kette* drumming and piercing horns.

'Black Man's Time' by Neville Grant signalled a call for black equality on a rhythm that incorporated portions of 'Pop Goes The Weasel'; Perry also had the singer cut a new vocal of 'Sick and Tired' onto the 'Return of Django' rhythm at this time.

Stranger and Gladdy's boastful 'Conqueror' was another small gem issued on Wizzdom that year using a graceful rhythm fashioned by Gladdy and Scratch, while I Roy's update of Ansel Collins' 'Night Doctor' rhythm yielded 'Doctor Who', an homage to the British television time traveller.

Some of Perry's greatest innovations of this period came on 'skanking' dance singles, several of which incorporated obscure concepts or ironic jokes; most of these were mixed at King Tubby's studio. For instance, Perry's own 'Bucky Skank' was theoretically another dance tune with a frowning nod to the trigger-happy gunmen on the corner, but just what kind of dance could be done to a song with such peculiar movement is hard to picture. Perry's warped chanting and vocal noises are interspersed with Tin Legs' outrageously pounding drums, making the tune sound like the soundtrack to a demented cartoon. Its version, 'Yucky Skank', was less effective than it might have been due to a certain amount of the vocal track being perpetually audible in the background. 'Black IPA' and its version, 'IPA Skank', both featured horn sections so phased and mutated as to sound virtually unrecognisable, resembling outer-space creatures singing under water more than brass. Though Perry introduced the disc with the proclamation 'This is Black IPA, better known as the sniper,' the title does not refer to a radical Black Power organisation; 'Black IPA' is simply Rastafarian patois for black pepper. 'Jungle Lion' changed the melody of Al Green's soul classic 'Here I Am Baby' into a freaky Upsetter proclamation of Rastafarian roaring; its version, 'Freak Out Skank', gave excessive phasing to the horn section in a further permutation that seems to take the rhythm farther from the dancing arena. Though perhaps not instantly recognisable to the casual listener, Perry said that 'Jungle Lion' was a continuation of the themes explored on 'People Funny Boy':

> ' "Jungle Lion" is another record that's based on a man who claims that
> he's top and boss so I say right now I am the jungle lion. The people who
> I'm throwing my thing at know it's them I'm talking to.' [4]

If 'Bucky Skank', 'Freak Out Skank', and 'IPA Skank' were peculiar, 'Cow Thief Skank' was something else entirely. The lyrics of this duet by Charlie Ace and Scratch were aimed straight at Niney, who is referred to cryptically in the song as Moccasin, a name Scratch used to deride him at the time due to his sporting of unfashionable footwear. As Perry explained, 'The Italian is good in making shoes, so at that time they was making the Indian copies of these footwear and the cheap imitation named Moccasin.' Legend has it that Scratch learned Niney had stolen a cow in his youth and cut the tune to ridicule him, alluding to the notion that Niney had his finger and thumb chopped off as a result of the robbery. Ace taunts Niney as a 'raincoat tail' who will be left 'to pick up the pail' while Perry tells him to 'go back to Lucea', adding injury to insult by including absurd mooing sounds throughout the disc. Niney was keen to note that this was all in keeping with the playful spirit of the time, when such jokes were part and parcel of the healthy competition fostered by their close associations, which encompassed shifting rivalries and alliances. 'In those days we used to have "musters", but at the end of the day we is friends. I used to stay sometimes far from Scratch and Bunny and move around Joe Gibbs, and they will come and pick a fight with me and Joe Gibbs . . . Those times Bunny Lee gave me a bike and I left my bike at Bunny's, Scratch take the bike and lock it up in the shop and drive away. I say "Bunny, how Scratch have the bike?" Bunny look for Scratch and take back the bike, and deal with Scratch, so it's just like a muster those days, and we used to make song off each other. Bunny Lee make a tune Bob Marley sing, say "Hey! See the one Niney there, Mr Chatterbox!" In those days, we laugh at those things, and if we want to make back a song on each other we make it, but nowadays youth can't do that. They want to fire their gun in your face.'

Its insulting lyrics notwithstanding, it is the rhythm of 'Cow Thief Skank' that is truly noteworthy, as it marks another Perry first in the history of recorded sound. As seen more readily on the version side, '7 and 3/4 Skank', 'Cow Thief Skank' is a composite creation, splicing together three different Upsetter rhythms to create something unique beneath the toasting and mooing sounds. It begins with the rhythmic introduction to the Inspirations' 'Stand By Me', one of the earliest rhythms the Upsetter created as an independent producer, before alternating between dubbed-out portions of the 'Better Days' rhythm and a cut of 'Musical Transplant'. The cut-up technique employed by Perry on this tune was never really adapted by others in reggae, and pre-dates similar techniques that later appeared in new wave and hip-hop by many years – perhaps with a considerably higher degree of finesse than shown in most of the material created in other genres.

Another classic 'muster' tune from the period was 'Labrish', a gossiping duet between Scratch and Striker Lee. Over the plodding beat of a slowed-down Upsetter rhythm (which also helped to disguise their voices), the pair bemoan the trials and tribulations of being independent producers while taking passing swipes at friends and fellow producers Rupie Edwards, Clancy Eccles, and Niney. Though 'Labrish' was never destined for the charts, it captures the playful spirit of the era, and shows Perry's willingness to experiment continually with the extremities of recorded sound.

Although Rupie Edwards has said he never actually heard the tune, 'Labrish' managed to spark anger from Clancy Eccles, who was insulted in the song for having been used by the PNP. Eccles explained that there was some truth behind what was stated in the song: 'Of course I was used, but I'm a man of my word and I gave Manley my word. Financially, I went broke. I mashed up my two vehicle in the bandwagon for the People's National Party, a brand-new van and a brand-new car. At the end of the excercise I neither had car nor van, while some singers who went with me had an old car and got a better car, but it's just one of those things, it happens to the best of us.'

However, the wording of 'Labrish' got Eccles so angry that he decided to respond in kind, and recorded two insulting replies that have never been released. 'Then I made songs that I didn't publish. I call one "Big Gut Striker" and the other one "Bangbelly Chicken Scratch", and I told them some most derogatory things about their life. I thought it would be bad for me to put out things like that; I only did it to get them off my back.'

A further noteworthy hit that Perry created at King Tubby's studio in this period was 'Dub Organiser', voiced one evening with Dillinger, who had substantially refined his delivery since his debut session with Perry at Dynamic. 'Dub Organiser' was a salute to King Tubby, cut on the 'Cloak and Dagger' rhythm, in which Tubby's status is acknowledged and elevated. As Dillinger noted, 'In that era you find sound like Emperor Faith, sound like Tippertone, deejayed by Big Youth, and Ruddy's. A lot of sound, they used to go to King Tubby's for dub because he got the best dub in those days. Everybody have to see Tubby's, so the idea come, say well "Tubby's supposed to be the dub organiser for everybody come to him for dub." '

An obsession with the Chi-Lites' '(For God's Sake) Give More Power To The People' yielded further Perry innovations: the first was 'Station Underground News', a vocal Perry cut over Leo Graham's 'News Flash', one of the first songs Graham cut as a solo vocalist. Graham's number commented on Jamaica's worsening political and economic situation in the midst of the world oil crisis. Built around the refrain 'Everything crash, don't you hear the news flash?', Graham is partly attacking Michael Manley's failure to improve things for rich and poor Jamaicans since being elected, but Perry's version turned the song into a virtual news broadcast, with Scratch appearing as a roving reporter. In the middle of 'Station Underground News,' a line from the Chi-Lites 'Power To The People' was spliced in better to emphasise a point, using a primitive sampling technique many years before the sampler was invented.

Perry subsequently cut his own slow and heavy version of 'Power To The People' as 'Justice To The People', complete with crying babies, wailing adults, and rocking guitar lines, introducing the version side with a peculiar joke about a doctor having sex with his wife, making a mockery of the mores of upper class Jamaicans and others who were ruled by a hypocritical and repressed attitude towards sex.

As he increased his innovations on the 45-rpm single, so did his album innovations progress. In July of 1973, Lee Perry and Pauline Morrison made a brief return to London, joining fellow producers Clancy Eccles, Alvin Ranglin, and Bunny Lee; they were all doing business, pressing up new material, and hatching more innovative plans. Perry had compiled another Upsetter album which he cut stampers for on this trip: *Rhythm Shower*, issued in small quantities only in Jamaica.

Rhythm Shower was a proto-dub creation that attempted to continue certain themes explored on *Cloak and Dagger*, an album that had sold rapidly in its Jamaican incarnation. *Rhythm Shower* was foremost a collection of contemporary dubs in which the rhythms were presented in a fairly basic form, with the odd instrumental and a couple of deejay tracks left unaltered for good measure. The exceptions were Sir Lord Comic's 'Django Shoots First', presented in its original 1968 format but still sounding in place with Perry's 1973 creations; 'Double Power', an organ cut of 'Give Me Power' by Winston Wright; 'Rumplesteelkin', another instrumental mixed without the enhancing effects of dub, and a standard toast by Dillinger called 'Skanking'. The other tracks all fall under the dub category, mixed in a creative way to make the familiar less familiar and purge the music of its predictable qualities. The Mellotones' 'Uncle Charley' was also revived from 1968, but presented here to include less than half of its vocal track, while 'Connection', the dub of Dillinger's cut of 'French Connection' not only censored a portion of Dillinger's toast, but also included Perry barking instructions, captured on tape during a previous take of the tune. Other fine dubs on the album included cuts of 'To Be A Lover' and 'Words of My Mouth', here re-titled 'Kuchy Skank' in reference to the chalice or water pipe in which marijuana is ceremonially smoked. The album's tour de force came in 'Operation', a dub medley in which the Upsetter spliced together hard mixes of some of his strongest tracks of this period, including a cut of 'Whiplash' that revealed intricate piano and organ interplay over a crazed bass line, segueing nicely into a similar mix of 'Fever' with more previously inaudible piano work, followed by a heavily altered mix of 'Tipper Special' (a harmonica cut of 'Give Me Power' featuring blaring sirens and winding master tapes). A true cut-up of dynamic proportions, 'Operation' was a fitting end to what was another innovative Upsetter album release. No one else was daring to try such excessive techniques at the time, nor were his rivals assembling albums that remotely resembled *Rhythm Shower*. Like *Cloak And Dagger*, *Rhythm Shower* was far ahead of its time, and its innovations pointed towards more concretely challenging creations that were soon to emerge from the Upsetter's wizardry.

Meanwhile, the Wailers had broken as an international act through the *Catch A Fire* album, their debut for Island Records, which had been somewhat sanitised for non-Jamaican audiences through overdubs and mixing supervised by Chris Blackwell in London. Eager to cash in on Island's success, Trojan issued the *African Herbsman* album in July 1973, which contained all of the tracks on *Soul Revolution* except 'Memphis', supplemented by '400 Years', 'Small Axe', and two Wailers self-produced tracks, 'Lively Up Yourself' and 'Trench Town Rock'. When the album was issued, Lee Perry was credited as producer of all tracks, something that later drew anger from the Wailers; the group is said not to have known about the album's release, and blamed Perry for the use of their material without due credit or permission. Perry himself accused Trojan of acting improperly, claiming he had nothing to do with the track selection and laying the blame at the feet of Trojan's boss, Lee Gopthal, who had rejected the *Soul Revolution* album in the first place.

Towards the end of their month in London, Scratch and Pauline took in a concert by I Roy at the Battersea Town Hall, where the toaster was backed by an upcoming South London roots band called Matumbi, who had already established a firm reputation backing visiting Jamaican singers such as Pat Kelly. Bunny Lee and Larry Lawrence were also present at the event, which had been organised by sound system operator Lloyd Coxsone and promoter Castro Brown. According to guitarist Dennis Bovell, Pauline Morrison had been elected to introduce I Roy on stage, but made the unfortunate error of announcing him as U Roy; after a considerable uproar, an embarrassed Pauline re-appeared to deliver a more fitting introduction. Mid-way through the concert, Lee Perry made his way to the stage, where he was instantly recognised by the spectators; when he requested Matumbi play a song the group was unfamiliar with, he pushed their keyboard player out of sight and made a mighty noise by running his arm up and down the keyboard, much to the delight of the audience.

Earlier in the month, Scratch revealed some of his future plans to the British press, indicating boredom with the standardisation of reggae:

'I want to change the beat. The people are getting tired of hearing the same thing over and over again, and the musicians are getting bored with playing the same rhythms all the time. At the moment, I'm thinking of ways to make the beat more demanding, more powerful, more new.' [5]

Scratch also noted other ideas involving the transportation of rhythm tracks between Jamaica and the UK. An accepted practice among Jamaican artists and producers who were resident in Britain was to travel down to Jamaica to record rhythm tracks, bringing them back to the UK to voice and mix, often adding orchestration or a backing chorus. As this was the standard thing to do, Scratch was itching to try the reverse.

'I've seen so many artists from the UK coming to Jamaica to record backing tracks and bringing them back over here, so I wanna know what the difference is. If the studios are any problem or if the backing groups are any problem, I wanna test something. All being well, I plan to spend three or four days in Chalk Farm studios with Greyhound and The Cimarons recording the backing tracks for some original and standard items. Then I'll add girlie choirs in New York, because they can give me a much more soulful black sound there. The lead vocals will come last, when I get back home to JA, I shall use Annette Clarke and the

Silvertones, a fresh group that I think will make it. They already did a good version of Wilson Pickett's "In The Midnight Hour" and my record for being right about artists is pretty good.' [6]

The Cimarons were then the premier reggae backing band based in England, and Perry had been working with them sporadically when in London, though never on material that was voiced by the Silvertones. According to Larry Lawrence, Perry recorded some backing tracks at Chalk Farm in this period with a black band based in the town of High Wycombe, but these tracks were also not used for Silvertones material. Wire Lindo has spoken of a studio jam session he recorded with Perry in Cambridge around the same time, but it is not clear if the material was ever issued, and the session again seems to have no link with the Silvertones. Perry later issued material with Annette Clarke (including a cover version of 'Just One Look'), but the rhythm tracks seem to have been recorded in Jamaica. Although things seem not to have gone entirely as planned, Perry did begin work on an album with the Silvertones upon his return to Jamaica.

The Silvertones were originally a singing duo formed by Gilmore Grant and Keith Coley, friends who came to know each other while residing in East Kingston. Grant was born in St Mary on July 11, 1943, and moved to Kingston to live with his brother after finishing school. Coley was born in the town of Bow in St Elizabeth on March 7, 1944, moving to Kingston while still attending school. After singing together for a while in the mid-1960s, the duo met Delroy Denton, who gradually became their main lead vocalist through his guitar-playing ability and skills as a vocal arranger. Their debut for Duke Reid, 'True Confession' was an instant success, followed by another hit cover tune, 'Midnight Hour'. They continued to record for Duke Reid in the late rock steady years, also gaining a hit for Sonia Pottinger with an original called 'Guns Fever'. As rock steady turned to reggae, they made their first recordings with Perry, cover versions of Brook Benton's 'Kiddyo' and 'Endlessly'; they then worked with a variety of other producers. According to Gilmore Grant, the Silvertones renewed their connection with Lee Perry through hanging out at the Upsetter record shop. 'We know Perry from the record shop he had on Charles Street. That time he have an album named *Cloak And Dagger*. It sell in a plain plastic, he couldn't make the jacket fast enough to sell that album. We check him as Scratch, we said we'd like to make a few songs for him. In that time we had a tune named "Early In The Morning", "Sweet And Loving Baby", "Rock Me In Your Soul". Scratch said "Let's do an album", and we voiced that album in Tubby's studio, just a small little place. Each time we do a song, we would have to come outside and get some breeze and go back again.'

According to Coley and Grant, Perry laid all of the rhythm tracks of the album live at his partially completed studio over a period of weeks, working in tandem with the group. When the rhythms had been completed to his satisfaction, Scratch took the group to King Tubby's studio, where they voiced the material in one night-long session. Keith Coley recalled Scratch using old hands like Hux Brown and Ansel Collins for the melodies, with enhanced new rhythms coming from younger musicians like Ranchie McLean and drummer Anthony 'Benbow' Creary.

The resulting album, *Silver Bullets*, is indicative of a duality inherent in the Silvertones' overall work, in that it is half composed of cover tunes and half of originals, a duality typically inherent in Perry's productions as well. Although popular American songs like 'That's When It Hurts', 'Souvenir of Mexico', the Impressions' 'He'll Break Your Heart', and the Archies' 'Sugar Sugar' are covered credibly enough, the group really shines on the original numbers, particularly the spirited 'Soul Sister'. The religious 'Rejoice Jah Jah Children', (which was immediately followed by a fine reverberating version, 'Rejoicing Skank') was perhaps the best song on the disc, and Perry was keen to point out that the song was written by Pauline Morrison: 'She write it and ask me to make them sing it.'

Further to complicate what is already a divided release, the final cut on the album did not feature the Silvertones at all. As Larry Lawrence noted, the dub cut of Dave Barker's version of 'Are You Sure' was tacked onto the album's end in London when Perry found the ten tracks he had assembled was too short: 'I made that rhythm ("Are You Sure") with Jackie Jackson, Hux Brown, Winston Grennan, Ansel Collins, and those guys in Dynamic, and voiced Max Romeo on it and Slim Smith (on backing vocals). I voice the Dave Barker one over here (in London) using the same tape, that was made for Creole. I was in the studio over here one day, actually putting some crazy noise on top of it, Moog and all types of noise. Scratch was editing the Silvertones' *Silver Bullets* album the same day as I was doing my thing, and while he was in the studio mixing out, he said to me that he's only got something like nine tracks for the album, so he would take that one and finish the album. So I says "OK, fair enough." He had to go to the record company to do his business the next day, and he needed a track, that's the way we live. He mixed that cut himself off of my tape, this was in Chalk Farm studio.'

This peculiar add-on seems an odd choice, especially as Perry recorded other material with the group that he left unreleased, including a Gilmore Grant composition called 'I've Got This Feeling'. That said, the inclusion of 'Rejoicing Skank' meant that another dub did not seem entirely out of place in what was already a diverse collection of styles pointing in several directions at the same time.

When issued in Jamaica in early 1974 on a new label Perry controlled called Black Art, *Silver Bullets* had a totally different mix from that issued by Trojan, with the vocals again in one channel and the rhythm in the other; some songs featured alternative vocal takes or musical variations. Though hardly a ground-breaking album, *Silver Bullets* remained the Silvertones' sole LP for 25 years (a second was finally issued by Coxsone in 1999), and shows both sides of a group that remain sadly underrated outside Jamaica

By the end of 1973, Perry had compiled two further albums as his studio was nearing completion. One of these was *Double Seven*, which would prove to be the last of the mixed collections he assembled himself for Trojan Records. Besides the heavy soul influence shown on its predecessor *Africa's Blood*, *Double Seven* also showed traces of funk in the Upsetter mix. Portions of the album were recorded in London at Chalk Farm studio, including notable synthesiser overdubs by Ken Elliott.

Born in London in 1950, Elliott was the second of six children whose parents ran a furniture business. Growing up in Streatham, Elliott was exposed to reggae in his teens through the Jamaican community in nearby Brixton. After passing through local soul/rock bands the Next Generation, Secondhand, and Seventh Wave, Elliott eventually auditioned at Chalk Farm to play keyboards on a Dandy Livingston session, who was then recording under the alias Bobby Thompson. Along with Cimarons' organist Sonny Binns, Elliott became a regular session keyboardist at the studio, playing on numerous recordings for Prince Buster, Bunny Lee, and the Pioneers, with other musicians from the Cimarons and Greyhound. In 1971, Elliott bought one of the first synthesisers on the market, an ARP 2600, which he kept at Chalk Farm and used on an increasing amount of reggae material. A Mini-Moog was also purchased by the studio to use in conjunction with the ARP, giving a futuristic edge to many recordings; both machines were given great prominence in 1972 on an album called *Interstellar Reggae Drive* by the Vulcans.

It was partly Elliott's feel for the synthesizer that gave Perry's *Double Seven* album a thoroughly modern shape; the disc also employed a somewhat more sophisticated stereophonic mix than that of his previous albums, with much cross-channel fading of vocals and percussive effects.

The most clearly soul-influenced material included Perry's relaxed version of Sam and Dave's 'Soul Man', David Isaacs' version of the Chi-Lites' 'We Are Neighbors', and 'In The Iaah', said by some to be the Wailers but not credited as such. The relaxed and confident toasting on U Roy's 'Double Six' (a heavily rhyming cut of 'Auntie Lulu') and 'Stick Together' (over Leo Graham's 'Want A Wine') is contrasted by the more tightly wound tales delivered by I Roy on 'High Fashion' and 'Hail Stones' (both using sped-up Upsetter instrumentals). Using a continuous rain sound in the left channel, Perry's 'Cold Weather', like 'Hailstones', shows him trying to get to grips with the English climate, while Ken Elliott's Moog overdub makes 'Ironside' even more preposterous than it was in its previous forms. The odd track out is 'Just Enough,' David Isaacs' cover tune recorded some years earlier and sounding somewhat out of place, while dub cuts of 'Jungle Lion' and 'Justice To The People' (here re-cast as 'Waap You Waa') exposed the funky, soulful base of the

Upsetter's contemporary beat. The true gem of the disc is its opener, 'Kentucky Skank', a complex and beautifully arranged piece celebrating Colonel Sanders' secret chicken recipe with the sounds of a frying grill pan and a variety of other subtly startling noises; while singing about the effect of KFC's food on his music-making abilities, Scratch also manages to give passing reference to some of his previous creations, adapt biblical quotations, and throw in a few lines of Amharic (including 'Eshi-eshi wondemalem,' a favourite phrase that basically means 'OK, brother').

Though it may seem an odd source of inspiration, the song reflected the amount of Kentucky Fried Perry was apparently gorging himself on at the time: 'When I was up here the last time I eat so much Kentucky one of the time I feel like I was gonna fly.' [7] 'Kentucky Skank' would later be re-fashioned for other equally creative cuts, the most wacky of which was 'Bathroom Skank'. For this cut, Perry took the rhythm down to King Tubby's studio to voice a sensual duet with Pauline, giving instruction for the rhythmic scrubbing of various body parts over effects arranged by Tubby.

If *Double Seven* continued the natural progression shown on all the Upsetter collections for Trojan, the other album release Perry had assembled by the end of 1973 proved to be far more divergent and important. Released only in Jamaica in very limited quantity on the Upsetter label, *Upsetters 14 Dub Blackboard Jungle* – the original title of the album that came to be known as *Blackboard Jungle Dub* – was a virtual landmark recording, presenting the hardest of Perry's contemporary rhythms in their purest form.

Many have said that *Blackboard Jungle Dub* is the very first dub LP, and Pauline Morrison insisted this was the case. 'That's the first dub album that ever came out. I remember I pressed 300 in Jamaica, and I brought 100 with me to England . . . (Journalist) Chris Lane put in the magazine (*Blues and Soul*) that this is a classic album, this is dub that will go down in history!'

Whether *Blackboard Jungle Dub* is actually the very first dub LP remains open to speculation; Prince Buster's *The Message* and Clive Chin's *Java Java Dub* date from around the same time and it is difficult to be certain which was first. Even if it is not the very first, the album is certainly among the first, and remains as a classic and defining work of the genre. Part of what gives the disc its magic is that it was mixed at Tubby's studio, though Scratch himself has sometimes implied that Tubby's input was minimal or non-existent.

Whatever the case, *Blackboard Jungle Dub* showed the very power of dub to transform a piece of music, to radically alter any given composition through creative mixing and spatial representation. The first Jamaican issue, said to have been pressed in a mere 300 copies, collected 14 of the hardest Upsetter dubs of recent months, mixed in true stereo with definite channel separation; subsequent issues would select only twelve of these tracks, initially in stereo and more commonly as a monophonic mix.

The original pressing opened with 'Black Panta', an awesome dub of

'Bucky Skank' with flute and horn overdubs atop a phenomenal mix that blew Tin Legs' pounding drums into a disproportionate Sensurround dimension, while roaring sirens and wild guitar sounds increased the overriding tension. 'Black Panta' was liberally bathed in echo and delay, adding a surreal or ethereal quality to the rhythm, giving it a sense of timelessness or otherworldly feel. 'Version Panta Rock' was a trombone version of a slightly faster cut of the rhythm, presented in a somewhat more conventional manner with leanings towards the darker side of jazz. 'Kasha Macka' placed 'Hot Tip' in a stop-and-go mixing format; while the rhythm bumped jerkily along, a hidden piano line and various percussive licks were uncovered. The Hurricanes' 'You Can Run' was re-cast in a drum-and-bass mode as 'Elephant Rock', with a smattering of bright horn riffs left in to add a treble dimension to the mix. Junior Byles' 'Place Called Africa' was given the purest of drum-and-bass mixes as 'African Skank', with bursts of guitar and keyboard sneaking into one channel at odd intervals, occasionally reverberating into the other channel somewhat out of synch with the rest of the rhythm, with the Wailers' 'Dreamland' getting a similar treatment on 'Dreamland Skank'. Concluding side one was 'Jungle Jim', a swirling dub of Neville Grant's 'Black Man's Time' that emphasises the rhythm's reliance on the melody of 'Pop Goes The Weasel'. After a roaring introduction from Scratch, side two begins with 'Drum Rock', the eeriest cut of the 'Fever' rhythm, here presented with screeching sirens, the squeaking toy hammer, and odd percussive and vocal effects echoing around the solid drum, bass, and organ lines of the rhythm. 'Dub Organiser' left in enough of Dillinger's toast to salute the greatness of King Tubby as a dub creator, placing emphasis otherwise on clicking wooden sticks and rock-solid bass. Chenley Duffus' 'To Be A Lover' was stripped to its core of drum and bass to become 'Lover's Skank', with Tommy McCook's odd keyboard line springing in now and again to vary the texture. The Wailers' 'Keep On Moving' was dropped down to bass and drum for 'Moving Skank', with enhanced emphasis on cymbal and high hat, while 'Apeman Skank' was a transformation of 'Caveman Skank' that placed bass, drum, and percussion more at centre stage. 'Jungle Skank' was 'Water Pump' purged of its rude vocals, with only the bass line hinting at the song's former lasciviousness, while the Wailers' 'Kaya' mutated into 'Kaya Skank' through a fast drum-and-bass mix that fed in keyboard and guitar lines at random intervals.

Blackboard Jungle Dub had a continuity that previous Upsetter releases lacked, and is thematically united through dub to create a sense of natural wholeness. Although reggae scholars are still arguing over whether it was the first dub LP or not, it was clearly crucial in inaugurating the genre of complete dub albums, and greatly added to the validity of the dub format in general. Dub albums would gradually become more common in Jamaica, and would eventually be made off the island, its practices slowly filtering into other forms of popular music, but *Blackboard Jungle Dub* shows Perry again as a true innovator in his field. The original pressing remains as a classic of the genre, and is a true masterpiece of Upsetter engineering ingenuity. It also emphasises the highly skilled musicianship of the Upsetters, and shows just how creative Perry's approach to rhythm could be.

In the half-decade that had passed since he had established himself as an independent producer, Lee Perry had progressed dramatically. His skills as a hit-maker were renowned in Jamaica, and his peculiar outlook and odd musical sensibilities were already something of a legend. He was known overall for his experimentation, for a fearlessness in the aural realm and for a willingness to try what his peers and competitors would not. But if albums like *Cloak And Dagger*, *Rhythm Shower*, and *Blackboard Jungle Dub* seemed bizarre and excessively experimental, they merely pointed the way for the further innovations that Perry would unleash once his studio was fully operational at the end of 1973.

With the creation of what would eventually be known as the Black Ark, reggae music would be ushered into a new era, and the freedom brought by his studio premises would see Perry continuing to progress in his individual and unpredictable manner. With the advent of the Upsetter's studio, he was no longer chained to the whims of others, and this freedom would see his creative independence bear an abundance of increasingly strange fruits.

HURT SO GOOD:

Early Fruits of the Black Ark

The creation of the Black Ark studio began a new period of enthusiasm and optimism for Lee Perry. The studio gave Scratch a greater agency in his work, and added to the sense that he was finally beginning to exercise some control over the fulfilment of his destiny. Its proximity in the back yard of his home made it a natural extension of his daily life, and its situation within the familiar confines of familial domesticity saw him better able to tune in to his guiding spirit and focus on the channelling of his creative ideas.

Though recordings were being made at the Ark by December 1973, the studio was a rudimentary facility then, and the early works that surfaced from it are marked by the limitations of its minimal equipment. Much of the material created there in late 1973 and early 1974 made use of older rhythm tracks recorded elsewhere, to which new vocals and instrumentation would be overdubbed through the practice of 'bouncing'.

The Black Ark began as a four-track studio, and Perry had a quarter-inch four-track Teac 3340 for the recording of new material and a quarter-inch two-track Teac on which to mix down. As most Jamaican master tapes recorded in the 1960s and '70s have the vocal isolated in one channel when played on a two-track machine, it was easy to 'bounce' the rhythm track onto one or two tracks of a four-track tape and then overdub additional instrumentation or voice onto the remaining tracks, and this is mostly the method Perry was employing in the studio's early days.

The Black Ark's initial mixing desk was a silver Alice board, a small machine with limited capabilities Perry picked up on one of his trips to England. 'I don't think my mixer, the Alice, cost me even £35,' he chuckled, 'it was for radio station balancing or maybe like a PA system. You couldn't start a studio with that, but we were using them. Those were domestic machines; they weren't professional machines, they were only toys.' He had an electric piano and a cheap copy of a Clavinet, a Marantz amplifier and speaker for guitar or keyboard use and a small drum kit placed on a riser. He also had a Grantham spring reverb and a tape-echo unit for effects. A perpetual shortage of microphones meant that he was initially using an AKG drum-kit mike for voicing, and the room was not equipped with recording screens at this stage. Perhaps the most vital piece of equipment was a copy of the Bible, which not only served to consecrate the studio as a holy place, but could also be a source of inspiration for song lyrics.

Just inside the studio to the right of its door was an elevated control room, separated from the main studio by a wall of Perspex glass; as there was no audio link between the tiny control tower and the main studio, Perry would pound on the Perspex and shout instructions to the assembled musicians and vocalists – a situation that would remain constant at the Ark throughout all its years of operation.

The studio wiring was installed by Errol Thompson, one of Jamaica's most talented engineers who had worked with Perry on the Wailers sessions and a host of other material at Randy's, but Perry has adamantly insisted that he alone could make his studio work, and that Thompson was unable to comprehend the way it functioned despite having wired it up himself. 'Not even Errol Thompson who build the studio can't do nothing in there, he don't know what to do. Even the great King Tubby come in there and don't know what to do.'

December and January were always slow months in the music world due to the Christmas and New Year holiday period, so the studio's first few months were fairly quiet. The world oil crisis brought on by conflict in the Middle East had seen the price of vinyl rising rapidly, creating a further drain on Perry's limited finances, and his initial re-using of old rhythm tracks partly arose from the need to keep costs to an absolute minimum – though version always held a fascination for Perry that went far beyond mere economics.

Just as the studio became operational, Perry began issuing product on the Black Art label, the name of which again incorporated complex punning. Black Art was celebrating the creativity of African Jamaicans by clearly naming its product for what it was: art created by black people. Perry's product appeared on versions of this label using different illustrations (including one showing a smiling sun and moon with stars and another with intricate black lettering), but the scowling, hooded figure that lurked behind the stylised blood-red lettering of the most widely used form of the label again suggested the Black Art of Obeah, leaving the name open to a number of different interpretations.

Some say Perry was actively involved in Obeah, regularly visiting practitioners such as a man known as Capo in Waterhouse and another behind Hope Road in New Kingston; others claim Perry was even practising it himself, with one colleague suggesting he had painted his Jaguar purple – a colour associated with Obeah – to demonstrate this fact. Some of those closest to Perry suggested that Val Bennett first introduced him to an Obeah man in the late 1960s, and that the meeting marked the start of all of Perry's problems. Others say he, like Duke Reid, wanted to cultivate the myth that he was involved in Obeah so as to frighten enemies and potential foes into keeping their distance. It has also been suggested that the equation of Black Art with

Obeah made a mockery of mainstream Jamaica's perception of Rastafarians as 'Black Heart men', subverting the notion that the righteous were godless devil-worshippers who performed human sacrifices.

Perry himself has typically denied any involvement with Obeah. 'The whole of them things them say, like me deal with Obeah, that cannot be true,' Perry contested, 'because how could I deal with good and evil? I never have no contact with Obeah man, the person who say that are a goddamn liar. The only people I have contact with is righteous, spiritual people who know about God. Me want to know about things that happen in Africa, long time before we reach Jamaica – not idiot Obeah man, for me no need curse.'

His family also insist he stayed far from it, but acknowledged that some may have believed he practised it. In later years, he would speak of his music as part of a magical process, naming his creations as the only 'science' he employs: 'I don't have no other Obeah but the music.'

Many have attested that Scratch had a copy of the Macabee Version of the Bible, a forbidden text said to reveal the true supremacy of black people, though what he did with the book and whether it relates to his supposed practising of Obeah has typically been contested. Whatever the case, the Black Art label became a regular sideline to the ongoing Upsetter imprint. The label's name also led to the studio being alternatively referred to as the Black Art studio.

The Black Ark was apparently conceived as an antidote to the Caucasian myth of Noah's Ark; symbolically likened by Perry to the Ark of the Covenant, it was meant to be a sanctuary for black Rastafarians – somewhere joyful music could be made unto the Lord on unmitigated terms. As Perry would later explain,

> 'Black Ark studio, its original base is on the righteousness of fulfilment of Biblical prophecy, the Ark of the Covenant which Noah, who gain blessing and favour of the Lord to produce the mind of people who are clean, to produce and portrayeth life's positive dreams, to make it a reality, so the reason to call my studio the Black Ark, it means originally the Ark of the Covenant in . . . not interpreting but performing the works of the Holy Trinity of Love that firmament over our head above.' [1]

In December 1973, an overseas visitor appeared at Cardiff Crescent: Chris Lane, a young white English journalist who had a reggae column in *Blues and Soul* magazine. Born in London on January 13, 1956, Lane was the elder of two sons whose father was a police officer slowly rising in the ranks of the force. In the late 1960s, Lane became a fan of reggae, soul, and Motown as skinhead fashion pushed these music styles to the forefront of British working-class youth culture; by the time he heard the Reggae Boys' 'Mama Look Deh', he had developed what would be a lifelong love of Jamaican music.

Although American soul was still seen as an underground music form in Britain, it received a fair amount of space in the music press, but coverage of reggae was virtually non-existent; what little reggae content was being printed either mocked and ridiculed the music or re-printed verbatim the distorted claims of record-company press releases. To rectify this situation, Lane convinced the editor of the bi-weekly *Blues and Soul* to allow him a regular column in its pages, beginning one of the very first sources of favourable and accurate reportage on Jamaican popular music. Soon Lane was conducting in-depth interviews with producers and artists such as Bunny Lee, Keith Hudson, and Lloyd Charmers, giving a badly needed credibility to an art form that was still greatly marginalised in the mainstream press.

When Lee Perry travelled to London in July 1973, Chris Lane was one of the few journalists to interview him, and Perry was so taken with the young man's enthusiasm and knowledge of his music that he invited Lane to stay at the family home in Washington Gardens. Thus, after scraping together all the savings he could muster, Lane came to Kingston just after Christmas 1973, flying on the soon-to-be-bankrupt Court Airlines via Newfoundland.

A lack of street signposts in Washington Gardens meant that Perry's home was difficult to locate in the middle of the night, so after finding a costly bed in an uptown hotel, Lane went down to Orange Street the next morning to enlist the help of Bunny 'Striker' Lee. Striker indicated he would be happy to take Lane to Cardiff Crescent, but neglected to mention that he and Perry were having one of their periodic feuds, possibly due to Perry hoarding a number of Striker's microphones in his newly completed studio. 'What I didn't realise was they were at war at that moment, they'd fallen out big-time! Bunny Lee had just taken me out and fed me, taken me around town and introduced me to a few faces; then he's taken me up to Scratch's and he won't come in the house, they're not talking. Pauline's slagging him off something terrible, they were all having a row. Blackbeard that works up at Sonic Sounds now came in with me to act as mediator between Scratch and Bunny Lee, because Bunny Lee wanted his microphones back that he'd lent Lee Perry, and I'm there caught up in the middle of all this . . . but by the time I'd left Jamaica they were the best of friends again.'

Lane stayed in the Perry household for about a month, witnessing first-hand the voicing of some of the very first material to emerge from Perry's studio, most of it composed of a somewhat minimal sound that is notably sparser than the later Black Ark material.

Lane believes the studio had been operating for 'just a few weeks' before his arrival, and noted that former Bleecher Leo Graham was among the first to voice material there. Graham had left the Bleechers after backing vocalist Sammy tried to take over leadership of the group; after cutting a few solo tunes for Joe Gibbs, he approached Perry with an anti-Obeah tune called 'Black Candle'. 'Sometimes you're having times hard, give you some hard luck,' Graham explained in reference to the song's lyrics, 'so you believe that people messing around, trying something in your life.'

First issued on Perry's Judgement label (and later re-pressed on Justice League and Upsetter imprints), 'Black Candle' sold about 15,000 copies in Jamaica, making it a fairly strong issue from the new studio, and a number of further versions were cut on the same rhythm.

The sparse instrumentation of 'Black Candle' allowed Graham calmly to refute the black arts, while the version side 'Bad Lamp' had Perry quoting Psalm 1 to re-emphasise the points Graham made. An uncredited deejay cut, 'Big Tongue Buster', continued the attack on iniquity, furthered on a faster, alternative Leo Graham version called 'Doctor Demand' (a.k.a. 'Pampas Judas'), featuring snatches of an uncredited deejay's righteous rap, keyboard overdubs from Winston Wright, and wah-wah guitar from Earl 'Chinna' Smith (who had sought out the effects pedal after being inspired by the guitar sound of 'Poppa Was A Rolling Stone', Isaac Hayes' 'Shaft', and selected works of Johnny 'Guitar' Watson and Peter Tosh). Graham would later explore similar themes with Perry on the wonderfully executed 'Voodooism', and on a perplexing blank label issue that had a song about the false Rastas known as 'Semi-Nyah', (a.k.a. 'Dig Pit') backed with another number built around the refrain 'It A Go Hot'; other material Perry cut with Graham in this period included an adaptation of the nursery rhyme 'Three Blind Mice'.

Perhaps the most noteworthy version on the 'Black Candle' rhythm was voiced by Bob Marley as 'Keep On Skanking', the lyrics of which Lane himself had a hand in writing: 'I stuck a couple of lines in, just messing about at the studio.' Lane recalled that Marley turned up at Scratch's place with Bunny Wailer; he sank a few Red Stripes and voiced the song after feeling a vibe brought on by Scratch rolling his rhythms. The next day, Bob returned to voice 'Turn Me Loose', a new song cut on the 'Kaya' rhythm that changed its theme to that of a cinematic love fantasy come to life.

Lane noted that Marley and Perry were clearly on good terms, and that they seemed to have a kind of special bond. 'They seemed like good mates. They definitely had something, you could see there was a little spark between them, and I didn't see that between Scratch and Bunny. Bunny Wailer was sitting in the control room in the corner, smoking this little pipe, looking miserable.'

Lane also remembered Delroy Denton coming down to voice the religious 'Give Thanks' – credited on release to Delroy Butler as his baritone was similar to that of soul singer Jerry Butler. Perry dug up an old rhythm he felt was suitable for the lyrics and melody of 'Give Thanks', and had Ansel Collins blow a melodica riff to better enhance the rhythm. Denton was soon to leave the island for America, and his departure would see him replaced in the Silvertones by Clinton 'Tennessee' Brown, a singer from St Mary that the group encountered while working at Studio One. Horsemouth Wallace was around while Denton was voicing 'Give Thanks', and Perry had him record a toast he had written on the rhythm for 'Herb Vendor', a relaxed rap that showed an appreciation of the strong weed they were being supplied. Jah Lloyd had originally been asked to toast on the rhythm, but was unable to satisfactorily convey what Perry invisioned. As for the wisdom weed itself, Lane noted that Perry was not smoking it in excess, having just broken off a long period of abstinence. 'He said now and again he'd stop smoking (weed) for months,' Lane explained, 'and I think he'd just done three months without it. He was smoking some, but not continually.'

According to his brother P-Son, Scratch was smoking weed with moderation, retaining a general preference for cigarettes in this period: 'He used to smoke a lot of cigarette, that's further down in the '70s. I think Pauline is the one who smoke lots of herbs.' Perry has noted himself that marijuana always had a strong effect on his behaviour and thought processes. Though he would later find it irresistible, he was troubled by his early experiences of smoking it.

'It made me feel glitzy and I don't know what's happening. I want to say it took me on a trip, a strange trip. And I was no longer on this planet Earth. It take me into space and I want to come out of it. And I get out of it. I afraid of it and I want to say whatever it is, I try it again.' [2]

Around the same time 'Herb Vendor' was recorded, Chris Lane asked toaster Prince Jazzbo to come to Perry's studio, ostensibly to conduct an interview; as Lane was elsewhere when the deejay arrived, Jazzbo ended up voicing the songs 'Penny Reel' and 'Good Things' with Perry instead. Born Linval Carter, Jazzbo first became known as a deejay while chatting on a sound called the Whip. Coxsone Dodd began recording him in late 1971, enjoying a string of hits with the gruff voiced deejay's slow-paced delivery from his debut 'Crab Walking' (cut on the original 'Skylarking' rhythm). Though Jazzbo stated that he still feels Dodd is 'the best producer inna the whole reggae industry', Coxsone held back the bulk of material he recorded with the deejay, forcing Jazzbo to seek work with other producers such as Glen Brown and Bunny Lee. Like Lee Perry, Glen Brown was one of a handful of producers who were changing the face of reggae through unorthodox approaches to recorded sound, and Jazzbo said it was Brown who persuaded him to begin producing in 1972. 'Glen Brown is the man who give me a lot of encouragement about my future when I becomes a elder man, and what I should do to help the situation. He was the man who get me to be self-reliant in the music industry by sneaking me away from Downbeat to voice for him and giving me some rhythms.'

Though Jazzbo had already moved away from Coxsone's stable by the time Perry approached him to record, he remembered that it was his work at Studio One that had made an impression on Scratch, someone he had known since his early days as a downtown street urchin. 'Me know Lee Perry from me a little boy. Me was a street boy, me have parents but they call them rude boy them time there. Him just see me one day and respect me because them big man there love youth, so as a youth now where at Coxsone's studio I mash up the place, him just say "Jazzbo, I want you to come do something for me." '

Jazzbo's 'Penny Reel' was a slow motion re-working of a bawdy calypso laid on the 'Hail Stone' rhythm, embellished by a skanking melodica and percussive overdubs, while 'Good Things' was a cut of 'Retail Love' on which Jazzbo warned listeners to disregard Dennis Alcapone's message of dancehall ribaldry and go to school instead – though his toast peters out halfway through the song, as though he had run out of things to say or had difficulty riding the rhythm.

In addition to its adaptation on 'Good Things', the 'Retail Love' rhythm was also used for 'Jump It', a smooth love song by Leo Graham with a squeaking-door sound enhancing its sensuality (also issued by Graham as 'We Have Got a Date' on the Blue Jay label), and for the outrageous 'Burning Wire', an over-the-top toasting duet by Scratch and Jerry Lewis. A radio deejay of part-Indian extraction who was a close friend of Niney, Lewis favoured grossly exaggerated takes on the hep-cat American radio styles of jockeys like Wolfman Jack; Lane noted that he was also providing the odd keyboard overdub for Perry at this time. Another prominent radio personality Lane recalls seeing at the Ark was Uriel Aldrich, a deejay who would often turn up at the studio in his flashy Jaguar.

Clancy Eccles also recalled cutting a song at the Black Ark in its early days called 'Me Momma Yard'. Rupie Edwards heard the tune and sensed a hit, but despite an offer of $10,000 to handle it, Eccles declined to release it and has kept it shelved for over 25 years; the song's overdue issue has pesently been scheduled as part of an upcoming compilation of Eccles' material to be issued in Europe by Jamaica Gold.

While Perry was striving to create a major hit, his contemporaries were surpassing him in sales. Bunny Lee and Sonia Pottinger were particularly successful, though Pottinger occasionally relied on Perry's skills for her most interesting product. She had leased highly popular material like the Righteous Flames' 'Run to the Rock' from Perry, and recorded much of the Melodians' politically relevant *Pre-Meditation* album with him in the early days of the Black Ark – though it would not be issued until 1979, when it was pressed in limited number in London on the Skynote label. One of the album's strongest tracks, 'Survival Is The Game', was also versioned by Marcia Griffiths for Pottinger, a fairly strong hit when issued on Pottinger's High Note label. Lead Melodian Brent 'Porky' Dowe recalled Pottinger's presence in Perry's studio for the recording of such works, and detailed complications surrounding the *Pre-Meditation* disc: 'The whole album was done at Lee Perry's studio, except for "Little Nut Tree" and "Swing And Dine" which were done at Dynamic Sounds. The album was done for Mrs Pottinger, she was working at Dynamic most of the time but they were booked up, and at the time Lee Perry's studio came with a sound and she wanted to get some of that sound. Mrs Pottinger did more than one album over there, she recorded Judy Mowatt there and so on. At that time she and Perry was really together, they were grounded. You have a song named "Don't Get Weary" on that album, and we did these other songs, originals that we were doing over time. We work at Lee Perry's for a couple of months straight, but after we did all those songs for her, there was a broke-up. We left because it wasn't too financially strong; we didn't know that she would put out that album. The first song I did there was "Survival", I wrote that song and gave it to Marcia (Griffiths); I made the rhythm and did the arrangements and was in those background voices too.'

As with Pottinger's subsequent success with Griffith's version of 'Survival is the Game', other smaller producers were beginning to score serious hits with rhythms they had gotten from Perry. Some of Scratch's early Ark re-creations were thus inspired by hits his competitors had earned partly through his efforts, and the most notable of such scenarios involved re-cuts of 'To Be A Lover'.

The tremendous success of Chenley Duffus' original cut led to a series of belated other cuts issued on the same rhythm, several of which were created by other producers. Perry's former record salesman and runaround man Pat Francis had begun to issue deejay material under the moniker Jah Lloyd, and it was Francis who would issue the largest number of cuts on a label called Teem he established with his younger brother Vincent. Francis pointed to the success of Big Youth and Dillinger as inspiring him to switch from singer to deejay after his days as a salesman were over: 'I was a salesman for about five years, about two years at Rupie Edwards and another three years at Lee Perry. Then one day I hear a song on the Bob Marley '"Keep on Moving" (rhythm) and Big Youth do the toasting, and Dillinger do a few songs like "Bring the Cutchie Come". When I hear them voice I say, "Well, bwoi, look like I could deejay instead of sing now," because I sound like Big Youth too.'

Francis' production debut came with a cut of Horace Andy's popular cover version of Bill Withers' hit 'Ain't No Sunshine', voiced by Francis and singer Douglas Boothe: 'Me and Douglas Boothe do a song named "Ain't No Sunshine Girl" and one of the first deejay songs I do, "Zion Rock", and (trombonist) Vin Gordon do one named "Reggae Rock". When I put it on a dub plate, Pauline wanted to put it on the Upsetter label, but Vin Gordon said, "No, Jah Lloyd, you can't give that song, that is a hit song too. You should distribute it yourself, go out there and put out that song." I finally put it on my own Teem label and it do a lot.'

The Teem label was based at 36 Charles Street, site of the former Upsetter record shop. While based there, Francis kept up his close association with Scratch in his early days as an independent producer and deejay. When Perry had Francis voice 'The Lama' (a.k.a. 'Flashing Whip'), an ominous cut of the 'Kentucky Skank'/'Bathroom Skank' rhythm made eerie not only by Jah Lloyd's fearsome toast but also by the startling sound of a shrieking toy hammer or some other toy or unknown instrument, Jah Lloyd opted for a cut of 'To Be A Lover' as payment. He would re-voice the rhythm numerous times in quick succession, to yield the toasting cuts 'Zion Gate', 'Soldier Round The Corner', 'Ganja Crop', and a hilarious courtroom drama called 'Judge Natty'; he would also issue a fairly faithful (though less successful) vocal cover as Jah Ali on 'To Be Your Lover', as well as version sides such as Bongo Herman's 'Immortal Drums'. Francis recalled the circumstances of these creations: 'I do three songs for Scratch at 5 Cardiff Crescent, Black Ark studio. I do "The Lama", and he gave me that cut of the "To Be A Lover" rhythm for my payment. I do "Zion Gate", and when I put out that one and it sell so much, I take the same rhythm and do back "Soldier Round the Corner" and I also do "Ganja Crop" and "Judge Natty".'

'Soldier Round The Corner' would prove to be the most successful of all of Jah Lloyd's versions, his commentary on the volatile state of Jamaican society striking a note with its citizenry as the nation was hit with a series of curfews and states of emergency. 'The inspiration on "Soldier Round The Corner" is like anywhere you go you used to have state of emergency in those times. Everywhere you go it's soldier 'round the corner, sticking up people, hands up in the air, face against the wall, kick out your foot. Every move you make is a set of soldier coming, so I say "Soldier round the corner, curfew on ya, you've got put down your bucky," put down your gun I mean. Them stop you uptown, them stop you downtown, all around. Everywhere you go, it's soldier round the corner.'

The most successful cut of all would emerge from a certain Mr Fowler, a producer on the periphery of the music industry who is said to have gotten his cut of Perry's rhythm through Niney. Fowler voiced Delroy Wilson with a moving performance on 'Have Some Mercy', a song that topped the Jamaica charts at the start of 1974. Wilson's cut proved to be even bigger than Chenley Duffus' original take, so Scratch sought to make the most of the situation by cutting another version of 'To Be a Lover' with a different singer on the same original rhythm. As is notable from the version side, 'Loving Skank', Perry now embellished the original rhythm with keyboard overdubs from Winston Wright, bluesy guitar from Chinna, and sultry female backing vocals; the lead vocals on the new cut were handled by Earl George, whom Perry renamed George Earl for this release.

Born on July 6, 1946, in the Southeast Kingston ghetto of Rae Town, Earl was the second of three children; his father was a neighbourhood barber and his mother was a cook at a textile factory. By age 14 he was singing love songs at talent contests like Vere Johns' Opportunity Hour, and throughout the 1960s he performed regularly on live shows around the island. His recording debut came in 1968 with a cover version of an American soul song called 'See Me', one of a few tunes he recorded for Clancy Eccles that year. In the early 1970s, George ventured into self-production from premises on Charles Street, scoring a minor hit abroad with an original called 'There's A Train', which George said was clandestinely issued in England without his permission. George recalled that it was around this time that Perry first expressed an interest in working with him: 'When I had my little thing going down by Charles Street, he checked me there and asked me to do some work with him, but I didn't begin working with him right away, it was about a year or two after. First with Lee Perry, I did "To Be A Lover" as George Earl, he released it as a single.'

Though the deep tenor of George's delivery held plenty of soul, his first cut of 'To Be a Lover' made little impact, and Delroy Wilson's 'Have some Mercy' continued to keep the island captivated, leading to further instrumental cuts Fowler produced with Augustus Pablo and Tommy McCook.

Chris Lane mentioned that Perry voiced other material in this period playfully aimed at competitors who had versioned his rhythms. For instance, Augustus Pablo scored a big hit with an instrumentally re-created 'Dub Organiser', recorded with Family Man and Tin Legs for producer Clive Chin at Randy's; Pablo himself blew the melody line of Dillinger's lyrics on his melodica. To counter Pablo's unauthorised adaptation of the Upsetter's definitive version of this rhythm, Perry recorded 'Upsetter the Righteous Organiser", in which he taunted Pablo and Chin with lines like "Pablo a de miser, him copy the "Dub Organiser", Upsetter make it better . . . ' Issued only on dub plate, this version had more excessive vocal noises and toy-hammer effects. Another unrelated dub plate cut at this time was 'Stagger', a chanting scat vocal Scratch placed on his cut of the 'Skylarking' rhythm, in which the word 'stagger' or 'stammer' is spoken repeatedly.

Not long after Chris Lane's return to England, Lee Perry began to team up more solidly with Winston Blake for a series of records that did not achieve much commercial success, but which are still of noteworthy content. Blake is a complex character who has played a concrete role in the shaping of Jamaican pop through a variety of high profile and influential positions that have boosted Jamaica's home-grown music from the '50s to the present day.

The second of four sons, Winston Blake was born on November 19, 1940, in Morant Bay. His father, Winston St Valentine Blake, was a Grade I civil servant who sent Winston and his older brother Trevor to Kingston for their Schooling, and it was while attending the prestigious Marsnip Preparatory school that Blake first came to appreciate sound systems – an entity that would prove to become a most significant factor in his life. Changing buses daily at Cross Roads, the Blake brothers became enchanted by Sky Rocket sound system, run by a certain Mr Chin who ran the Shalanez restaurant. 'Sky Rocket in my mind was one of the early pioneer sounds, a sound that really did not get the credit that he deserved in the role that he played, probably because he was a Chiney man. He used to play out in the restaurant, R & B; sometimes we would miss the bus deliberately to hear the records he's playing. He said, "You guys like this thing? Why you don't get your old man to start something?" We always said, "It's a mad, man! Our old man send us from country to town, this

man's going to tell him we there listening to sound system?" In those days, for
you to say it's sound system that you're interested in, it's like telling a man
you're going to rob a bank: definitely no ambition. You had to be a doctor, an
engineer, lawyer, anything of the great professions. The funny thing is, I never
change my mind, because I didn't know what I wanted until I knew what I
wanted, and from I knew what I wanted, it was with music.'

Though Blake's father was earning a relatively comfortable wage in the
security of a governmental post, he found it difficult to maintain his sons'
upkeep and expensive education in Kingston, and he was forced to seek an
alternative source of ready cash through selling Phillips radios and amplifiers
in Morant Bay. He also unexpectedly chose to establish the Mighty Merritone
sound system in 1950, the first set to be based in the Parish of St Thomas;
Winston would buy most of the records for the set in Kingston, with his father
acting as selector and operator of the sound.

Initially powered by a Phillips 20-watt battery-electric amplifier,
Merritone was the unchallenged champion of St Thomas for several years, and
eventually began to attract interest from the Kingston sound systems. Tom the
Great Sebastian, Duke Reid the Trojan, King Edwards the Giant, and
Coxsone Downbeat all came to St Thomas to clash with Merritone, and
although Merritone was so poorly equipped that the Kingston sets always
blasted it out due to having so much more sheer power, Merritone's reputation
began to spread.

Winston Blake's mother died at the age of 29 in 1946, a few years before
the establishment of Merritone. When his father died at the age of 41 in 1956,
Winston and his brother Trevor continued running the sound, much to the
chagrin of older family members. In February 1961, Merritone was hired for a
dance held by a man from St Thomas who had become a police officer in
Kingston; the Beatniks' Ball was thus held in St Thomas with a large audience
of Kingstonians bused out for the occasion. The dance was such a success that
the policeman had them bring the sound to Kingston for part two of the
Beatniks' Ball, held in a place called Wembley near Rockfort in East Kingston.
The audience response at this dance was so positive that Blake knew there was
no turning back, and he and his brother moved the sound to Kingston in
1962. Initially operating from a section of the Allman Town area near Rae
Town, the sound soon became based in Frances Avenue in Vineyard Town.

Once established in Kingston, Merritone changed the landscape of the
sound system by attracting an audience from differing social strata. As Blake
put it, 'We transformed the music to link the bottom floor to the top floor.'
Before the arrival of Merritone, middle- and upper-class people avoided the
downtown areas where sound system dances were held, but the Blake brothers
began to attract people from the upper echelons of society through school
connections they had formed at Kingston College. Doctors and lawyers now
began mixing with ghetto people at sound system dances.

In 1965, the Blake brothers based Merritone at a club called the Copacabana in East Kingston, a popular venue where international artists such as Jerry Butler appeared. In 1968, they moved the sound to a posh venue called Peyton Place at Red Gal Ring in Stoney Hill, but the nightclub's isolated setting meant their audience began to dwindle as transportation back to town became problematic. After a brief residence at the Sombrero Club, Blake finally opened the Turntable Club on Red Hills Road in 1972, which would prove to be the permanent base for Merritone sound.

Although he had known Lee Perry since Scratch's days at Studio One, Blake noted that their friendship gradually developed through contact at the Upsetter record shop. 'Lee Perry used to be a side man for Coxsone. He used to be around Coxsone, produce and sing for Coxsone, and I met him through that, but our friendship didn't blossom at that time. When I really became close to Lee Perry was in the '60s, when we become so popular, we were the musical statement for the whole middle class and everybody wanted Merritone. When Scratch used to operate downtown at Charles Street, my aunt used to run a business in front of him. That was a little after the Tuff Gong period when everybody knew of my work; if you wanted to get a record (to hit), you knew that Merritone was a showplace. I used to go to his shop and get anything I want, so we developed a working relationship there and we became friends.'

Blake noted that once Perry's studio was operational, he found himself spending time at the premises and ended up contributing to some of Scratch's spontaneous creations. 'He moved down into Washington Gardens with his wife and his family, and we became very very close. I'd be in the studio, and he was doing some stuff and he'd give me a listen, so while nothing was going on, we'd do little things together, fooling around. Lee Perry is one of the most brilliant minds in terms of percussive productions, could put things in productions and really excite it. He was really a master at that. How those records came is that we had the rhythms, and people would come up with their different experimentations. We would be in the studio and he would say, "Winston, try this," and we would produce. Some of the stuff we did, we'd just put it on a track, and then not long after that, we'd just put that track out.'

Blake had already cut some deejay tunes for Lloyd the Matador as the Blake Boy, so it was not difficult for him to metamorphose into the fearsome Judge Winchester for a wild courtroom duet with Scratch on 'Public Jestering'. Using a percussive, modulated cut of the 'Skylarking' rhythm, the harsh Judge sentences Silvester the Public Jester from Manchester and his son Chester (both played by Perry) to 'indefinite detention' for being disrespectful – a sort of reversal of the 'Judge Dread' tradition that laid bare the inability of harsh sentences to deter crime and hinted at the social injustices that were at their root; as with the 'Judge Dread' saga, what sounded humorous on disc was a commentary on matters of great seriousness.

In March 1974, Michael Manley had introduced two of the most brutal acts of suppression in the face of a growing crime epidemic, much of which was politically motivated or linked to political sponsorship: the Suppression of Crime Act and the Gun Court Act. The latter saw the creation of the notorious Gun Court on South Camp Road, where possession of an unlicensed firearm or even the shell of a bullet could lead to indefinite detention. Such draconian measures were unexpected from the socialist Prime Minister, who had long supported the sanctity of human rights. Ironically, when the British Privy Council – the body that holds final say in Jamaican legal matters – objected to the Act, the maximum sentence was changed to mandatory life behind bars.

Though his father's position as a civil servant saw Blake raised in a middle-class environment, he has always retained elements of political radicalism and has been a rebellious defender of social justice. On 'Darkness Falls On The City', another Judge Winchester number, Blake furthered his socially motivated message over the updated 'People Funny' rhythm (this time featuring an overdubbed electric piano melody) by begging an end to the senseless violence that saw neighbours and even family members killing each other in the street.

Other Perry/Blake collaborations included another cut of 'Skylarking' voiced by Tyrone Taylor as 'Tables Turning', a pun about changing social forces that also made reference to Blake's club; though Blake says test pressings were cut and given a minimal issue on his Turntable label, the master tape may have been erased during the recording of 'Public Jestering'. Blake noted that when Taylor later re-cut the tune, he angered Perry by claiming its authorship. 'Tyrone did it over again, and claim he (wrote) it, and Upsetter was very upset with him when he did that. I said "Lee, this is the nature of the game. We don't deal with publishing and copyright and things the way we're supposed to. We just put on a record and that's it." '

Blake also had a hand in some of the new rhythms Perry began to build at the Ark, including 'Mumbling And Grumbling', a light-hearted number from Junior Byles with flute and trombone parts, 'Cutting Razor' by Byles' group the Versatiles (previously recorded by Peter Tosh as 'Stepping Razor' and said to have been written either by Joe Higgs or another unknown sufferer) and 'Lady Lady', a reworking of an American hit written by Eugene Record of the Chi-Lites; though its original Jamaican issue credited Cynty and the Monkees, while an alternative vocal pressed in the UK correctly credited the young Rasta singer Joy White, another beauty that garnered Perry's attention. 'Lady Lady' had some wah-wah guitar work and a crude synthesizer overdub, and even its vocal side was weighted heavily towards the bass; though a cover version of a soul song, it is far from the confines of the soul genre.

When Perry went down to Randy's with freshly pressed copies of the tune, he was in for a surprise: rival producer and freelance session musician Clive Hunt had arrived shortly before him with copies of an instrumental version of 'Lady Lady' he had recorded at Treasure Isle and pressed the same day on his Azul label. Laughing in retrospect, Hunt remembered the incident as being somewhat awkward. 'The day I recorded that song and I go in the record shop with the record, Scratch come in with a box of the same tune too. I didn't know Scratch was doing it and Scratch didn't know I was doing it. I see them buying from both of us, and I feel a little bad too, because I have Scratch like a big hero from long time.'

Born in Linstead, St Catherine, in May 1952, Hunt was the oldest of 18 children sired by a Rastafarian farmer who grew foodstuffs and herb. His unruly boyhood saw him sent to Stony Hill Reformatory School, where he initially trained to be a tailor. Joe Moore, one of the composers of the Jamaican national anthem, was the musical director at Stony Hill, and Hunt's mastery of the trumpet at age 13 so impressed him that Moore insisted Hunt pursue a life of music. Upon leaving Stony Hill, Hunt joined the army, where he played for many years in the military band. He also studied at the Royal Military School of Music in London, where a Ugandan friend re-named him Otim Azul, and Azul would be one of many aliases he would work under, Lizard and Clive Humpte being two others.

Back in Jamaica, Hunt began to play trumpet on sessions for the Fabulous Five, while his friendship with Geoffrey Chung of the Now Generation band saw him appearing on Lorna Bennett's *Breakfast In Bed* album for Harry J, for which Hunt often went AWOL from his barracks to make it to the recording studio. By the time he recorded his version of 'Lady Lady' (credited to the In Crowd but with most instruments played by Clive himself), Hunt was acting as musical arranger for Duke Reid at Treasure Isle studio in what would prove to be Reid's final days.

Some months after their dual issue of 'Lady Lady', Scratch would begin to use Hunt as a session musician, and Hunt would later use the Black Ark for some of his own productions, creating much of note there in 1975.

In addition to his general creative input, Winston Blake was also helping Lee Perry financially in the early months of the Ark, with the understanding that he would reap the benefits of any substantial hit that might emerge; unfortunately for Blake, none of the material he was involved with got very far. 'When he broke up with Bob and these guys he was going through a lot of trauma. A lot of stuff I did with him, I just give him some money as his friend. He's my brethren; I helped him regardless, expecting to have nothing in return. With all good intentions, he said, "Winston, if things happen, bwoi, me and you a brethren and brethren . . . " It just so happened that nothing really big happened in that time.'

Perry had been striving to create a hit at his new studio, but his lack of equipment and continued financial difficulties meant that the odds were initially stacked against him. Other events on the UK reggae scene added to his problems, as the two biggest reggae companies began to encounter difficulties.

Trojan executives were being vague about the future of the company, and it later became apparent that the label was beset with financial problems. Pama Records also had serious problems of their own: after Harry Palmer returned from a trip to America, he announced that a religious experience meant he was devoting his life to Christianity and abandoning the record business.

One of the last records Pama issued was DD Dennis' 'Woman and Money', another interesting composite Perry production. According to Dennis, Perry built the foundation of the rhythm in London in 1973 with Greyhound, a Brixton-based outfit that also recorded as the Rudies. He then brought the rhythm back to the Black Ark, where portions of the song were re-recorded by Jamaican musicians. Perry tried to voice the rhythm in Jamaica but was not satisfied with the result, and brought the rhythm back to London in 1974 to have Dennis voice it, leaving the screamed introduction of the first vocal attempt in place. 'He built the rhythm over here, finish it in Jamaica, then take it back for me to record. If you hear the beginning, someone scream, I don't know who it is. He took it to Jamaica, someone sing it and he didn't get the thing that he want so he take it back to England for me to do it. That's Lee Perry, he's a genius. I remember when we went in the studio, and I hear the intro, he said, "Sing this, mon!" I said "Sing what?" He said, "Riddle me this, and riddle me that: what is the two most dangerous things in the world that a man can't do without . . . " so I said, "Yeah man, that sounds good," and I just do it. He's the best producer I've ever had in my life, because he knows what he wants and he can feel it, he motivates you to do the things that maybe you think is no good.' For finishing touches, Perry had Ken Elliott of the Vulcans lay a Moog synthesiser on top of the rhythm, but Pama's collapse saw the tune make little headway.

With his ordinary outlets seemingly blocked, Perry began entrusting Larry Lawrence with his material, which was issued on labels Lawrence controlled from his base in Kilburn: Ethnic, which utilised EMI's distribution through Lawrence's links with Creole, and Fight, his own independent imprint; both labels would shortly merge as Ethnic Fight after Lawrence severed his ties with Creole and EMI. The first batch of Perry material Lawrence issued in the UK included George Earl's 'To Be A Lover', Leo Graham's 'Pampas Judas', Junior Byles' 'Mumbling and Grumbling', and Delroy Butler's 'Give Thanks'.

While in London, Perry went with Lawrence to Chalk Farm studio to voice some rude duets on the rhythm of 'My Heart Is Gone', originally a John Holt hit Phil Pratt created with the Soul Syndicate at Dynamic; Lawrence got a cut of the rhythm from Bunny Lee and scored a hit with a version of the song voiced by Tony Sexton. Lawrence had already recorded a deejay version of the tune as 'Kung Fu' with Jah Martin (a Jamaican based in London named Martin Williams who would later run the Mandingo record label), and it would be on the flipside of Martin's leg-flashing toast that Perry's duet with a

Chinese woman would be issued as 'Kung Fu Part 2' – with Perry drawling suggestive platitudes in English and she replying in Chinese. As Larry Lawrence recalled, this cut was one of several spontaneous creations thrown up by an unexpected studio encounter. 'Me and Scratch would always go way out to find different people to do different things. This Chinese girl, she don't know nothing about recording studio. Somebody introduce us to her at Chalk Farm studio and Scratch says, "Well why don't we record her?" I put on "My Heart is Gone" and said "Let's put it on that" 'cause we were putting some horns on it with Vin Gordon and Scratch was there. She went into the recording booth, and Lee Perry went in there and he was speaking to her, and she was answering him with her Chinese language. Then I done another vocal with him and an English girl on the same track, we call it '69'. It's Scratch speaking to her in a sexy voice, they're making love on the rhythm in other words.'

This alternative version which surfaced on a Fight 12-inch in February 1979 as 'Pussy Galore' was more blatantly smutty than the previous duet, leaving little to the imagination in its panting suggestion of lustful acts – made more laughable by Perry likening himself to Mark Antony and the woman to Elizabeth Taylor's portrayal of Cleopatra.

Other material that Perry had been involved with creating was being issued in the UK by Winston Edwards, initially on a label called Stop Point. Born on August 10, 1953, in Buff Bay, Portland, Edwards was raised by his grandmother on Mountain View Avenue in Kingston after his parents emigrated to the UK; he later lived with other relatives in Stony Hill. Edwards' maternal aunt was Joe Gibbs' mother, and though Edwards initially shunned the music business, the fact that Joe Gibbs was his first cousin would see him gradually becoming involved in it.

In the mid 1960s, Edwards was working at the family hardware store on Beeston Street when Gibbs returned from Guantanamo Bay and opened his record shop a few doors down. Edwards' family were staunch Labourites, and his secret ambition was to become the JLP candidate for West Portland, but as Joe Gibbs entered into record production, Edwards found himself being introduced to the mechanisms of the record industry. His friendship with Lee Perry stems from this period, when he observed that Perry was responsible for the most creative records to emerge on Gibbs' Amalgamated label. 'Scratch was a friend of mine even when I was not involved in the music industry. Scratch and Mr Gibson were very close friends, because in those days, Gibson wasn't the producer, Scratch was more or less the producer. He would come around and lend his talent to Gibson, so I know Scratch from those days, but I really get involved with Scratch when I came to England.'

Edwards first came to London to join his parents in the late 1960s, but spent most of the early '70s back in Kingston. By early 1974, Edwards was preparing to emigrate permanently to the UK to further his education, and decided to take his first serious stab at record production in conjunction with Scratch before he left.

Dennis Walks was a singer with a deeply expressive tone who had created a lasting hit at the start of the decade with 'The Drifter' for producer Harry Mudie, followed in 1973 by the calypso-influenced 'Margaret'. Hoping to score a similar success, Edwards arranged for Lee Perry to record 'Walks' with a version of the R & B standard 'Don't Play That Song' at the Black Ark. Edwards said that although he had an idea of how he wanted the song to sound, he left the actual producing to Lee Perry. 'I was not a producer then, I was the executive producer and Lee Perry was the man. I walk into the studio and I said to Scratch, "Listen, I want this thing to be so and so and so." He said "Winston, don't worry about it, I'll get some of the guys." I think Lloyd Parks was there, Geoffrey Chung and Gitsy (Lloyd Willis), those are the guys I can recall. I did that at Lee Perry's studio and maybe one more track with somebody else. I can't recall exactly, but I know I did that with Dennis in Lee Perry's studio.'

When Edwards returned to England to finish his A Levels, he issued the song from premises in the Southeast London neighbourhood of New Cross, where he would later establish the Joe Gibbs record shop and distribution service at 29 Lewisham Way. Although the song was not a strong seller, Edwards could see the potential of music to provide a form of income, and made arrangements to record more material in Jamaica which he would issue on Fay Music, a label he named after a girlfriend. 'I said to myself the easiest way to do my A Levels was to continue in the music business, so I decided to get involved in the music industry proper. I travelled back to Jamaica and I start doing bits and pieces.' Edwards would continue to work with Lee Perry throughout 1974, and it was Scratch's creativity that gave shape to the best tracks that appeared on a couple of dub albums Edwards would issue that year.

Relying on crucial contacts in Kingston, Edwards first assembled the album *Natty Locks Dub* from diverse rhythm tracks. Some were given to him by Tony Brevett of the Melodians, while others were created at Joe Gibbs' and Lee Perry's studios, with voicing and remixing occasionally undertaken at King Tubby's. The Jamaican rhythms then had horn parts overdubbed on them in London's Berry Street studio with trumpeter Michael 'Bammie' Rose and a saxophonist named Brown. The resulting *Natty Locks Dub* straddled the divide between dub and straight jazz, and remains as an interesting instrumental experiment. At least two of the rhythm tracks on *Natty Locks Dub* were created at the Black Ark: 'Jah Shakin Dub', voiced at King Tubby's as 'Wet Up Your Pant Foot' by toaster U Brown, and 'Well Charge', a cut of 'Don't Play That Song'; some of the other album tracks that originated elsewhere were re-worked or altered at Perry's studio.

Though Edwards had free use of Joe Gibbs' studio – a better-equipped facility than Scratch's place – he noted that he felt far more comfortable working at the Black Ark because of Lee Perry's creative vibes. 'I had one or two recording sessions in Joe Gibbs' studio, but the atmosphere at Joe Gibbs' was not the one I like, though I could have had the studio time for nothing. With credit, Scratch also gave me a lot of studio time for nothing. I think with the connection with myself and Joe Gibbs and him, studio payment was not important, it was more like a family thing. But the atmosphere of Scratch to me was much more what I really like. Joe Gibbs' studio was powerful, it was a bigger studio, it had a lot of sounds, it was probably even more equipped than Lee Perry's studio, but the man was so warm . . . I don't think it was because of the sound why I wanted to record at Scratch's place, I want to record there because the man was creative himself, and any ideas that I didn't have . . . I realise that he was more like 24 tracks going around, even if his studio was only four tracks at the time! I felt at all times he would assist me to give me that 24 tracks pleasure. So although Errol Thompson at Joe Gibbs' was again like a member of the family, Scratch was more like an uncle teaching a nephew, so I love the man. Upsetter's studio was more like a unique little place. When you go there, you're trying out things and the idea was always coming. It was out of what Scratch was saying to me that give me the ideas of the names. Scratch is a funny man, he would say, "You don't smoke, but you could cough," and you picked up a name straight away.'

Edwards followed up *Natty Locks Dub* with an album in the classical dub format: *King Tubby Meets The Upsetter At The Grass Roots Of Dub*. The album proved immensely successful on release, and would be directly responsible for establishing the popularity of the dub album format in the UK. *At The Grass Roots Of Dub* was presented as a mixing contest, pitting the Upsetter against the original Dub Organiser. Though the album purports to feature mixes by King Tubby on side one and mixes by Lee Perry on side two, Edwards admitted that this might not have strictly been the case. 'Five of the tracks were mixed by Scratch and five were mixed by Tubby, or maybe four tracks is Scratch and the other six were Tubby, but Scratch did a lot of work on that album. How that album comes about, I lay down some tracks in Scratch's place and a few tracks also at Joe Gibbs' studio. I had some of the tracks mixed at Scratch's studio and some mixed at Tubby's studio; some of them were also overdubbed at Scratch's studio and some overdubbed at Tubby's studio. In those days I have sound system like (South London's) Jah Shaka and (North London's) Fatman who I have to supply with dub plates, so I was coming back on the airplane and I thought, what should I name this album? I said, well some of the tracks were done at Upsetter's studio, and some were done at King Tubby's studio, so I'm going to name this album *King Tubby Meet The Upsetter* and that was the birth of that album, one of the best-selling dub albums in the UK.'

Several tracks featured trombone overdubs by Vin Gordon, allowing *King Tubby Meets The Upsetter At The Grass Roots Of Dub* to retain a jazz subtext from the edge of dub's abstractness, while the song 'Natty Roots' has vibrant hand-drumming Edwards said was overdubbed by Eric 'Binghi Bunny' Lamont at the Black Ark. Most of the rhythms are originals, adding to the overall feeling of abstraction through a lack of reference points, though a re-cut of Slim Smith's 'Born To Love' and a version of the Melodians' 'Come On Little Girl' (again provided by Tony Brevett) are instantly familiar.

Like *Natty Locks Dub* (but without the obviously non-Jamaican horn parts), *At The Grassroots Of Dub* is somewhat subdued, presenting the rhythms in a purer and less embellished form. What is supposedly the Upsetter's side has little of the panache and zest that is typically associated with Perry's dub works, but the concept behind the album was original and interesting, and the meshing of the two approaches makes for pleasant listening, even if the difference between the sides is not greatly noticeable. About the only distinguishing feature is that what is supposedly Tubby's side seems to have more reverb, and often features the unique equalising of treble sounds that only his customised mixing board has been able to create, while the so-called Upsetter's side relied more on delay, occasionally isolating an electric piano in the foreground of the music.

Back in Jamaica, Perry continued with his experimental innovations, but the hits were still not forthcoming. As the acrobatic fighting skills of kung fu films began to enthral black audiences all over the world, the influence of the Western began to wane, and kung fu emerged as Perry's new obsession. One of his earliest songs to show this influence was 'Fists Of Fury', cut on the updated 'People Funny' rhythm and issued on the back of Jah Lloyd's 'The Lama'. This abstract instrumental used crashing cymbals and rapid delay to try to capture the essence of kung fu itself, and makes direct reference to films like *The Five Fingers Of Death*. 'Enter The Dragon' took its name and inspiration from the classic Bruce Lee flick, with Scratch transforming the 'Lady Lady' rhythm into the platform for a musical journey inside the dragon, complete with a sliding whistle and burping sounds to add the realism of the trip. 'Black Belt Jones' had Perry grunting and groaning in emulation of the exaltation of a kung fu fight over another sparse rhythm, while Linval Thompson's 'Kung Fu Man' brought the obsession with martial arts into vocal focus.

A young singer with strength in the upper register, Thompson's expressive and confident delivery already held the defining elements of a new style of singing that would become popular towards the end of the decade, and though the subject matter may seem lightweight, Perry captured the best of Thompson's vocal abilities on 'Kung Fu Man'. As usual, the track had Perry renaming and transforming everything through a process of reversal, with the 'Kung Fu Man' also presented as 'Fu Kung' through Scratch's direction; even the shouting sound effects were apparently reversed, as Scratch later revealed.

'I turn the Kung Fu into Fu Kung. They make Kung Fu "ooh-haa!" in order to conquer everybody. So I go the other way, Fu Kung – "haa-ooh!"– so the conqueror cannot get me. I blow away the Kung Fu with Fu Kung.' [3]

Thompson was brought to the Ark by Phil Pratt, who had discovered the young singer at the Idler's Rest and was impressed by his vocal abilities; he had recently returned to Jamaica after living for a period with his mother in Queens, where he had been active in a group with William 'Bunny Rugs' Clarke. According to Pratt, he voiced Thompson's strong debut 'Girl You've Got To Run' at the Ark, and Perry had him voice 'Kung Fu Man' at the studio later the same day.

Pratt had first used the Black Ark some weeks earlier to record Al Campbell, another singer whose delivery was a precursor of the dancehall style. Born on August 31, 1954, in the Three Mile area of Western Kingston, Campbell's father was a preacher at the local Church of God. Al began his career singing sacred songs at church fundraising functions and performing at school concerts. His debut recording was 'Freedom is Equality', cut with Junior Menz from the Techniques at Treasure Isle, but the song was never released. He eventually formed the Thrillers towards the end of the rock steady period with his friends Michael Black, 'a youth named Sweet Pea and one named Buzzer'. Sir JJ wanted to record the group, but they chose to work for Coxsone Dodd instead, cutting 'Heart For Sale', 'Don't Run Away', and 'The Last Dance Is Over'. When the group split up, Campbell recorded some solo material for Coxsone, and intended to team up with Ernest Wilson of the Clarendonians and Freddy McGregor in a group to be called the Three Lads. In the end, Wilson and McGregor cut material without Campbell as Fitzy and Freddy, and McGregor and Campbell cut 'Saving My Love for You', 'When The Grass Is Green' and a cover of the Bee Gees' 'How Can You Mend A Broken Heart', all credited solely to McGregor. Campbell also sang backing for various artists at Studio One as a member of the Freedom Singers and Underground Vegetable harmony groups, notably on Dennis Brown's hit 'If I Follow My Heart' with Alton Ellis and Winston Rodney of Burning Spear. Campbell was also introducing fresh talent to Dodd in this period, notably bringing Jacob Miller to his attention.

When Miller opted to record for Bunny Lee, Campbell followed him to Orange Street one day, where he encountered an old acquaintance called Henry. Henry wanted to voice Campbell, and got a cut of Ken Boothe's 'Artibella' from Phil Pratt to accommodate him. Pratt ended up issuing the tune, and began to work closely with Campbell himself.

Al Campbell would enjoy a long partnership with Phil Pratt, and one of the first songs they recorded together was the stunning 'Where Were You', engineered by Lee Perry at the Black Ark. 'It is a true story,' Campbell admitted. 'I had this girlfriend, we broke up and she was coming back. That session was good because Phil Pratt sing harmony on it.'

It was Pratt's use of lesser-known musicians that partly contributed to the great sound of works he created at Perry's studio, and 'Where Were You' is a prime example of the strength of Perry and Pratt's musical partnership. Pratt's musical arranger was a keyboardist and melodica player from St Andrew named Bobby Kalphat, and Kalphat's keen ears provided the basic melody and overall shape of Pratt's material. For his rhythm section, Pratt was using underrated drummer Eric 'Fish' Clarke (brother of singer Johnnie Clarke) and bassist Sydney 'Left Hand' Guissine to create a different style from that used by other producers at the time. Pratt noted that Perry modulated the guitar sound of Campbell's hit by routing it through a four-band equaliser, resulting in another marked difference in the overall feel of the record.

Pratt recorded a handful of other songs with various singers at the Ark in this time, including 'Why Should You' by Roy Graham and the excellent 'Fire At Your Heals' (a.k.a. 'Run Come Feel') by Roman Stewart. The younger brother of popular singer Tinga Stewart, Roman was then at the start of his singing career, having cut some material at Dynamic for a small producer named Nemiah Reid, and it was again Roman's strength in the upper register that pointed the way to his later popularity in the dancehall style.

Phil Pratt enjoyed considerable success with material he cut at the Ark, but Lee Perry was still clamouring for a hit of his own. Though Perry's humour and adventurousness are evident on his karate material, many of his releases achieved little in sales and quickly faded from the scene. When a big hit finally emerged from the Ark, it came in a more accessible format: a cover version of an American hit voiced by a previously undiscovered female.

Born in St Andrew on November 2, 1951, Alison Anne Cadogan was the third of four children; her father was a Methodist minister from Belize, while her mother, Lola Cadogan, was a professional singer from the parish of St Anne whose sacred choral songs were issued on 78s. While Anne was attending primary school, she and her family lived in Belize; they returned to St Andrew at the end of the '50s, where Anne completed her schooling and got a job at the library of the University of the West Indies in Mona. Inspired by American artists like the Supremes, the Platters, and Ben E. King, Anne loved to sing in her youth but never dreamed of singing professionally until a school friend arranged for her to attend a recording session at the Black Ark late in the summer of 1974. Her debut release 'Love (of) My Life' was quite popular in Jamaica, though its UK issue on Black Wax would make little impact. Cadogan related the circumstances that led to its recording: 'I had a friend named Teresa Bryan. Her boyfriend, Jerry Lewis, was this disc jockey at JBC. He asked her to sing this song he had written called "Love My Life", so she said "Ask Anne because Anne loves to sing," so both of us were to do it. One Sunday we went down there and in the end I sang Jerry's song myself alone; Jerry Lewis play some of the instruments himself. When I was finished voicing,

Lee Scratch said "Boy, Jerry, lend me your singer now." He didn't even know my name.'

When Perry heard Cadogan voicing Jerry Lewis' song, he immediately knew what rhythm he wanted to record her on. The song was 'Hurt So Good', an ambiguous love song with hints of masochism that had been a previous success for controversial American soul singer Millie Jackson. Perry had recently built an instrumental shell of the rhythm, but previous attempts at voicing the tune with other singers had left him dissatisfied. Cadogan delivered exactly what Perry wanted: a sultry and suggestive vocal that retained the slightest hint of innocence.

Once Cadogan had committed her voice to tape, there was the matter of her name to deal with. 'I come by the name Susan compliments of Lee Perry, Lee Perry dubbed me Susan . . . After I sang "Hurt So Good", I came back inside the studio and he said, "So tell me, what's your name?" I said, "I am Anne Cadogan." He said, "Anne? No man! You mean Susan, that sound sexy!" Then he said he liked how I sing, and he wanted me to try some other songs. He gave me some tapes to learn and I took them home.'

The re-named Cadogan returned to the Ark the following Sunday and every subsequent Sunday for the next few months; by Christmas they had recorded over a dozen songs with Benbow Creary and Ansel Collins, occasionally assisted by keyboardist Glen Adams, with whom Cadogan was romantically linked for a while.

For the Black Ark version of 'Hurt So Good', Perry used the bass talents and arranging skills of Boris Gardiner, and it was partly Boris' ear for soul and foreign tunes that gave it such a pleasant and credible sound. Born on January 13, 1946, Boris was the youngest of three children born to a plumbing contractor and his wife. He lived in Rollington Town until he was thirteen, when he moved to Vineyard Town to be with his father after his parents divorced. At the age of 17, Gardiner was diagnosed as having the heart condition tachychardia, and spent a period of time in the hospital.

A tall young man with large hands, Boris Gardiner's build made him perfectly suited to be a bass player, but it was not as a bassist that he began his musical career. Within a year after being discharged from the hospital, Boris joined Delano Stewart, Richard Ace, and Richard Moss as a vocalist in a quartet called the Rhythm Aces. The group was soon performing at established venues on the north coast, including the Playboy Hotel, where they shared the bill with Jackie Edwards. In 1962, the group recorded 'A Thousand Teardrops' and 'Christmas' at Federal for Chris Blackwell, both of which were well received in Jamaica.

Though the Rhythm Aces were popular, lack of regular earnings saw their eventual break-up not long after their debut recordings. Boris then joined popular hotel band Kes Chin and the Souvenirs, a 14-piece orchestra that included saxophonist Val Bennett in its ranks. In addition to his singing duties, Boris played guitar on some numbers in Kes Chin's band, and began playing a little bass some months later. He also composed the songs 'Don't Speak To Me Of Love' and 'Memories Of Flora', Souvenirs songs that were included on a compilation album put together by the Red Stripe beer company.

When many members of the Souvenirs began to abandon the group to join the Caribs in 1964, Boris found himself being asked to join the Afro Jamaicans, a leading hotel band led by Panamanian trombonist and percussionist Carlos Malcolm; in addition to playing ska, the group was famous for playing theme songs from popular movies such as *The King and I*. At that time the group included Audley Williams on bass, steel guitar, and piano, Freddy Campbell on drums, Trevor Lopez on guitar, Carl 'Cannonball' Bryan on saxophone, Winston Turner on trumpet, and Derrick Harriott on lead vocals; Boris himself was singing, playing cowbell, maracas, and other percussion, and dancing the cha-cha-cha and bossa nova.

After Audley Williams left Jamaica, Carlos Malcolm temporarily took over the bass-playing duties. Unhappy with this situation, he persuaded Boris Gardiner to take a break from singing and begin playing bass full time. It was then that Boris began to learn to read music, soon becoming competent enough to sight-read. In 1966, the band went to the Bahamas, where they spent a year playing gigs between Freeport and Nassau. The band then went to New York, but when Gardiner learned the musicians were expected to get ordinary day jobs to supplement their meagre wages, he decided to leave the group. He went to Toronto in 1967 and joined keyboardist Leslie Butler in the house band at Club Jamaica, a night spot run by a Jamaican named Fritz Riley.

When the bleak coldness of the Canadian winter arrived, Gardiner returned to Kingston, where he formed a trio with a couple of older musicians to be the house band at a new club in Cross Roads called the Bronco. It was while leading the Broncos in 1968 that Gardiner began to attend sessions at Studio One, collaborating with keyboardist Jackie Mittoo and guitarist Filberto Callender on several enduring Jamaican rhythms.

Gardiner created a wealth of great bass lines at Studio One, as heard on material such as Marcia Griffiths' 'Feel Like Jumping' and the Heptones' 'Party Time'. He also played on Larry Marshall's highly influential 'Nanny Goat', which Gardiner said was originally built for an entirely different song by Jacob Miller; as Coxsone Dodd was not happy with his delivery, he asked Larry Marshall to come up with something else on the rhythm instead.

Moving over to Duke Reid's Treasure Isle, Gardiner crafted a few choice bass lines on material such as Dawn Penn's 'No No No' and Pat Kelly's 'You Don't Care'. He then became a general session musician, playing for Sonia Pottinger, Lloyd the Matador and Federal records, eventually providing the bass line for one of Harry J's biggest hits, Bob and Marcia's cover version of Nina Simone's 'Young, Gifted and Black'.

By this time, Boris has drafted keyboardist Keith Sterling and guitarist Hux Brown into the Broncos. The group was subsequently asked by Robert Lake Jr, manager of the posh Courtney Manor Hotel, to leave the Bronco club and work for him; once they were the hotel's new house band, Lake renamed them the Boris Gardiner Happening. Along with drummer Paul Douglas and vocalist Tinga Stewart, the group became one of the top live acts of mid-1970s, and their work for Federal and Dynamic was highly popular in Jamaica.

The musicians of the Boris Gardiner Happening were known for their professionalism and an ability to play a range of styles including calypso and soul. Boris Gardiner himself had the ability to play a wide range of styles, from the smooth bass lines of American soul to the rough and rugged riffs of hardcore 'sufferer's' reggae, and it was this versatility that would see Lee Perry make increasing use of his talents through the rest of the decade.

The melodic balance of 'Hurt So Good' was completed by horn parts provided by trumpeter David Madden and tenor saxophonist Glen DaCosta of Zap Pow, a group Madden formed in 1970. Though Zap Pow recorded infrequently as a group, their horn section was establishing a strong reputation at the time of 'Hurt So Good,' and Perry would also make regular use of their skills in the following years.

Though 'Hurt So Good' was possibly the most schmaltzy record Scratch had yet produced, he did manage to inject a rootsy sensibility to the tune through his sublime musical arrangement, which made good use of the heavily Jamaicanised rhythm section and original horn parts. Additionally, Cadogan's vocal style seemed influenced by the drawl of the American South, and her peculiarly seductive intonation greatly added to the record's overall appeal.

In contrast to her breathy vocals was the harmonic brilliance of the Diamonds, a roots trio composed of Donald 'Tabby' Shaw, Fitzroy 'Bunny' Simpson, and Lloyd 'Judge' Ferguson, singing their first harmony backing of another artist. Simpson had been in the Mediators with Pat Francis, and when the Diamonds formed in December 1969, Francis initially coached them. They had already made their recording debut for Rupie Edwards before being drafted in as harmony vocalists at the Black Ark, and their work at Perry's studio would prepare them for the stardom that they would find through material they were to record at Channel One studio in 1975. Tabby remembered the Black Ark as being a great source of learning for the group: 'With Lee Perry, it was like a music college. Me glad to go through those vibes there with him, because me learn 'nuff things towards the music. A so me get fe know about where Bob Marley originally come from – him start out from Lee Perry. I go inside the studio one day and I hear a music a play and I thought it was Bob that was singing but it wasn't Bob, it was Lee Perry, so I know say originally Lee Perry send on a vibe there from him through Bob. 'Round at Black Ark studio, them times there me a youth. We do harmony with Susan Cadogan on 'Hurt So Good', that song did come on and mash up the place at the time. (It was) the first harmony for him and the first harmony we did 'pon a music. He's a good music instructor, me a tell you. Me respect him.'

Initially issued on the new Perries label some weeks after Cadogan voiced it, 'Hurt so Good' was not initially popular in Jamaica. This is possibly due to an alternative version of the song being issued with another vocalist by a rival producer in the same time period, rendering Jamaican radio reluctant to promote Perry's version. However, pre-release copies given to Larry Lawrence saw an enthusiastic response to the disc in London in the summer of 1974; reactions to the record were particularly strong at the Notting Hill Carnival, a vibrant two-day street fair held in West London the last weekend in August in celebration of the Caribbean presence in Britain.

Larry Lawrence claimed that Scratch had promised to let him issue the first hit to emerge from his studio in the UK. Instead, he ended up entrusting the UK issue of 'Hurt So Good' to Dennis Lascelles Harris, an immigrant from Clarendon who established the DIP label in the Brockley area of Southeast London. Lawrence recalled that, although the situation caused him disappointment, he took it in his stride. 'He phoned me and says Boris Gardiner has arranged it and it sounds good. He send me up 2,000 (copies) of it, I play it through the Carnival and distribute it through the Carnival quite good. Then I went to press the record, got the label printed, stamper and everything, and then he sold it to DIP, so I wipe it from my catalog, and then it goes on to be a hit record. That's not to say that I'm upset with him or anything, that's just business. Maybe the guy's offered him some money, and I was giving him royalties, so maybe he needed to take the advance. At the same time I wasn't feeling no way upset about it, it didn't make no difference between us.'

When Dennis Harris was setting up DIP as a UK label that would carry Jamaican product, he received some initial assistance from Winston Edwards, who brought Harris to Jamaica in 1974 in the hopes of making DIP an outlet for Joe Gibbs' product. According to Edwards, the deal was foiled due to Harris' highly educated status – a quality that elicited significant mistrust from Joe Gibbs. But where Gibbs mistrusted Harris' intelligence, Scratch had the opposite reaction, and arranged for Harris to begin issuing his product in the UK. 'DIP was trying to launch himself in the music industry, trying to get some records and labels to start signing up, and we both were living in Southeast London. I was doing some work for DIP part time, and both myself and DIP went down to Jamaica. At that time, Joe Gibbs more or less appointed me to represent him in England and I wanted Joe Gibbs Records to do some business with DIP, but somewhere down the line, Gibson did not hit it off with DIP. Dennis Harris was a highly intelligent man, very articulate. He's an old student of Clarendon College and went to Manchester University in England. Dennis was an engineer, very clever academically, and Gibson never trust any man who is too sharp like that. Gibson is a very shrewd man and Gibson didn't like Dennis' fast talking, but Scratch and Dennis hit it off.

Scratch is such a man that he trust every man. He thought, "This guy can't damage me, he is such a nice guy," so Dennis and Scratch agree that DIP would control some of Scratch's things.'

DIP's version of 'Hurt So Good' had a different mix than the Jamaican original, with its version side, 'Loving Is Good,' sounding more dubwise with extra Perry percussion. DIP's issue of the song found far greater favour in the UK than Perry's previous Jamaican issue, striking a chord with a surprisingly broad section of the British public. When aspiring pop-music producer and mainstream record executive Pete Waterman heard the tune playing in a record shop, he realised its hit potential, and brought a copy of the song to the major Magnet label, who were promoting big-name commercial pop acts like Alvin Stardust and Guys and Dolls. Magnet approached DIP and licensed the single, bringing it straight into the UK charts in March 1975.

When rumours began to circulate that 'Hurt So Good' was getting popular in England, Cadogan's lawyer uncle pointed out that she should have something in writing from Perry regarding payment for the tune. When she approached Scratch, 'he drafted up some funny worded thing.'

Shortly after, Magnet's Michael Levy telephoned Cadogan to say that they were sending her to England. As Cadogan recalled, 'I was met at the airport by the PR from Magnet and Dennis Harris and his wife, they zoomed me off to the Holiday Inn like a big star. That was Tuesday, and Thursday I had to go on *Top of the Pops*, they got me a wig and contact lenses. After I did *Top of the Pops*, the thing jumped right to Number 25. The next week it jumped to 11, then to 4!'

When Scratch learned that his new discovery had flown the coop he was highly vexed, and flew to England to confront his budding starlet. 'My mother told me that Perry came up there the weekend and he was very annoyed to hear that I had gone. When I got the call from Magent, I asked them, "Should I tell Mr Perry?" and they said no, they had bought out the record, it's theirs. I think he had an inkling that something was going on, but Perry knew that he was signed to Trojan, and yet he made dealings with DIP, who went and sold out the rights of the record to Magnet. So it started a big confusion. Magnet said that they need me to sign this contract. They put me in a hotel, they did everything for me. I remember Perry coming to my hotel room, he walk up and down and ask if I sign anything with these people. I say, "No I haven't, but I have to sign something with them, they say they own the record." He said no, I'm not to sign it. I remember he held my wrist and said, "If you sign that thing I'm going to make sure you never get a cent!" and I was annoyed.'

As Magnet had paid for her air fare and were paying for her accommodation in London, Cadogan felt she had no other option but to ignore Lee Perry's demands and sign with Magnet. Being young and inexperienced, she signed a contract that was definitely not in her favour. 'I got £3000 on signing with Magnet, and every statement I ever got from them, they excluded "Hurt so

Good" from it. That one money I got, that was it, and out of all the royalties they were getting, they paid all my air fare, my hotel bills, my clothes, food, and everything, so I was always in debt. I remember Magnet bought Pete Waterman a Jaguar for finding "Hurt So Good," and they said that I couldn't drive so they wouldn't bother give me one.'

While Waterman cruised the town in his new Jag, forming his reputation on the back of the song she had voiced for Lee Perry, Susan Cadogan was not doing well financially. Her upfront payment of £3000 would be the only money she would get for recording the song until 1998, when her first royalty payment would reach her from the song's re-release on CD.

In June 1975 things really came to a head when Cadogan was summoned to Magnet's offices for a legal battle over who had rights to the hit. It would mark the end of her working relationship with Lee Perry, and would ultimately see her stardom begin to wane. 'I remember Magnet called me one day and said that they had to speak to me. When I went, there was this big conference table: Magnet was there with their lawyers, Perry was there with his lawyer, DIP was there with lawyer, even Warner Brothers was there, 'cause it was written by Philip Mitchell at Warner Brothers. It was one big table of lawyers and me alone! By that time I had signed Magnet's thing. Because of all the trouble they got into with "Hurt So Good", they froze all the money and didn't want Lee Perry's other stuff. I believe if they had released his stuff, I wouldn't have faded away as quickly as I did. At that point, they got Pete Waterman to produce me, and the material was just too lightweight in comparison to "Hurt so Good". On the Magnet album (called *Doing It Her Way*), it didn't have on the genuine "Hurt So Good", it was a re-recorded version; they'll never get back Perry's own again. Pete Waterman sings on "Would You Like To Swing On A Star With Me" in this chipmunk voice, and they had the London Symphony Orchestra . . . they just didn't have the bass beat. One thing I liked with Perry, in all the recordings I have done, and I have done so many, he just let me sing the way I want. He don't stop me and correct me and thing, he just let me sing.'

Although Perry had recorded over an album's worth of material with Cadogan by the end of 1974, he delayed issuing an album of her work until the furore with Magnet died down. The imminent collapse of Trojan meant that the UK issue of the album was further delayed, ultimately diluting its appeal.

Meanwhile, every time Magnet issued another Susan Cadogan single, Perry made sure to let off one of his own – though all failed to find the same success as her debut. The lacklustre 'Congratulations' aroused little interest, its stronger B-side 'Feeling Is Right' was totally overlooked, and her slow and sultry take of 'Fever' (complete with eerie flute) did not achieve the chart position it was due.

Perhaps one of the least challenging of Perry's creations, the *Susan Cadogan* album definitely has its moments, caught somewhere between throwaway pop and Upsetter experimentation. Besides capturing Cadogan at her freshest, with jazz and funk influences just below the surface of the material, the album shows the way Perry arranged material aimed at pop audiences in his particular unorthodox way.

The self-titled album surfaced in the UK in November 1977 on the new Trojan label controlled by Marcel Rodd's Saga Records after Cadogan had already issued her sub-standard pop album for Magnet which resulted in her rapid decline. Though the single 'Nice And Easy' (a.k.a. 'Do It Baby', featuring a mumbled backing vocal by Jimmy Riley) saw a brief reprieve, it was not enough to restore her favour in the fickle word of pop. Though she would still record sporadically in the 1990s, it was at the same library of University of the West Indies she worked in as a teenager that she would find her most steady form of employment.

Shortly after the recording of 'Hurt so Good', the Diamonds recorded the finely crafted 'Talk About It', a song about the disappointments of unrequited love. Further versions of 'Talk About It' show the playful experimentation Perry loved to indulge in: a seven-inch version on Pthe Perries label called 'Yama Khy' featured a cool scat-vocal toast from U Roy, double-tracked in places, while an absurd chant from Perry's children, Omar and Marsha, faded in and out of the mix; the version side, 'Dub Two', presented an alternative U Roy toast over the shrieking children, while a 12-inch of 'Talk About It' was later issued with a cut of 'Yama Khy' featuring the children alone.

'Yama Khy' was but one of a series of discs Perry cut with his children in late 1974 and early 1975. When Jimmy Riley recorded his version of the folk song 'Ram Goat Liver' at the Ark, Perry had his children Omar and Marsha try to voice their own rude take as 'Ram Goat Dub', which deteriorated fairly quickly into childish anarchy. More successful was Junior Byles' re-cut of a song called 'The Thanks We Get', a grudging tune about human ingratitude and labour exploitation that Perry had previously recorded on at least two separate occassions. The first version was created with Glen Adams and Family Man in the early 1970s and was apparently sung by the Versatiles; an alternative version later appeared with Lloyd Parks' bass line offset by a shaky xylophone melody. Though a UK pressing of the song credited the Heptones, members of that group could not recall recording it and it may have been mislabelled. On Byles' solo re-cut, Perry presented his voice in tandem with the children's yelping echoes of his chastising lyrics.

Omar Perry remembered being present when Byles voiced his new version of the song, and said it was his singing of it that led to his father voicing he and Marsha on the rhythm. Though their brother Sean would later join them for the recording of some material, their sister Michelle always opted out of such sessions; describing herself as a shy child who 'locked herself away' in her youth, Michelle noted that she did not even like to be photographed.

Marsha Perry remembered her and Omar's voicing of 'The Thanks We Get' as being part of their everyday life. With the studio in their back yard, they inevitably spent much time there, and becoming part of Scratch's creations seemed a natural part of growing up. 'We was in the studio the day, all running joke and all that. We were listening to people talk and my dad said "You know what? I'm going to let them do that song." ' Marsha also noted that the message of the song is one that has stayed with her, influencing her philosophical outlook. 'In today's world you have a lot of people that you do things for and they don't recall what you do, so the music pertaining to bad mind and grudgeful people.'

Some of the most interesting material Perry created in the early days of the Ark came through interaction with Glen Adams, who was then travelling back and forth between New York and Jamaica. Adams' keyboard work and arrangement skills made Perry's material that much more interesting, and their long years of close musical association lent an ease of communication to their work together. The re-cut of 'The Thanks We Get' is just one such creation, as is revealed more strongly on its version side: 'Ungrateful Skank' is a supreme example of rhythmic wizardry, its outlandish bass line pushed to the fore beneath Adams' spongy electric piano and a rising wall of thudding percussion.

It was another Perry/Adams collaboration with Junior Byles that proved to be the next monster hit: the sensitively rendered 'Curley Locks', a stunning antithesis to the militant 'Beat Down Babylon.'

Though 'Curley Locks' had a subtext of the contempt the 'baldheads' of mainstream Jamaica held towards Rastafarians, the earnestness of this very heartfelt love song saw its phenomenal success in Jamaica and the UK. After first being issued on the new Orchid label in Jamaica (distributed by Sonia Pottinger, who knew the song was bound to hit) and Glen Adams' Capo label in New York, it appeared on DIP (backed by the prophetic Byles vocal 'Now Generation') and was again picked up by Magnet in March, 1975. Over 250,000 copies are said to have been sold on UK pressings alone, but as with their issue of 'Hurt So Good', Perry said he made no financial gains from Magnet pressings; the true benefit of his link with DIP came in new equipment Dennis Harris shipped to his studio in Jamaica. 'What me make from "Curley Locks" is what me sell in Jamaica and DIP was supposed to have it in England, but after everything go caput with "Hurt So Good", he never organise himself proper and I lose everything; what I get from it was those equipment me could get for the studio, like the Soundcraft mixer. It was just a little domestic set that make "Curley Locks" and all those hit songs, and after DIP give me some advance to put out "Hurt So Good", we buy instruments instead with it, and he ship them down to Jamaica for me. That's how me get to change the Alice mixer to the Soundcraft mixer – he do that for me.'

A far more sophisticated board than the Alice, the Soundcraft would enable Perry to achieve a broader sound that was richer, fuller, more complex, and resonant with deeper textures. It was the most significant piece of new equipment, though other new elements would also see a gradual change in the shape of the Black Ark sound. The building of a drum booth was another notable modification, giving an added clarity and depth to Perry's rhythms, particularly where the kick drum was concerned. It was the drum sound that would come to be the most readily identifiable on Black Ark recordings, a sound that was instrumental in establishing the studio's reputation in Jamaica. Artex studio monitors and Yamaha headphones also helped Perry refine his creations.

As with 'Beat Down Babylon', the success of 'Curley Locks' spawned a number of further versions of the rhythm, some cut by other producers. 'Prince' Tony Robinson, an upcoming producer based at Slipe Road who had found some success since the early '70s with deejay material issued on his High School International label, scored a big hit with one of his re-cuts. 'Grow Your Locks', a vocal adaptation by Barrington Spence, initially made little impact, but Big Youth's 'House Of Dread' toast was a far-reaching success. It caused ripples in dancehalls from Jamaica to Britain, and elicited much anger from Byles and Perry in the process. Scratch was particularly miffed because he had helped establish Prince Tony's career by giving him a cut of 'What A Confusion', which Robinson used for Roman Stewart's 'Arab And Israelite', credited on issue to Roman Scotland; Prince Tony's success with 'House Of Dread' felt like a repeat of the 'Have Some Mercy' scenario with Perry's creativity becoming a platform for the success of another.

In retaliation, Byles and Perry cut 'Dreader Locks', an echoing alternative vocal cut that denounced Prince Tony as a 'phony' while praising Jah as the 'most high'; its version side, 'Militant Rock', had zany scat vocals from the pair. An acoustic guitar from Chinna and percussive bells were added for 'Golden Locks' and its version, 'Silver Locks', which surfaced in New York on Brad Osbourne's Clocktower label; Brad also issued 'Ital Locks' by Johnny Lover, a Rastafarian deejay who cut material for Prince Buster, Herman Chin Loy, and Joe Gibbs before migrating to the States. Lover's toast managed to reference the Vietnam War amidst a general confirmation of Rastafarian viewpoint. The version side, 'Ital Drums', had various piano and percussion overdubs – including that of a talking drum – enhancing what was already an unusual rhythm.

Another fine number Junior Byles created in this period with Perry and Glen Adams was 'The Long Way', a philosophical tune recounting the meandering journey of life. A minor hit in Britain with the immigrant community, 'The Long Way' continued to show the influence of kung fu visuals through reference to the television series *Kung Fu*, starring David Carradine.

It was around the time of 'Curley Locks' that Perry first began working with a group called Time Unlimited, then a quartet. The leader of the group

was a stocky young man named Junior Delgado, born Oscar Delgado Hibbert
Jr on August 25, 1954. Delgado was raised in the heart of downtown 'before it
was a ghetto' at 48 ½ Luke Lane, moving to Rockfort when the area became
too rough. His mother was a seamstress and his father a construction worker,
while his uncle, Lennie Hibbert, was a vibraphone player and percussionist for
Studio One.

Though Junior was initially following in his father's footsteps, his real
ambition lay in music, and his singing talents put him on a different path.
Delgado began performing on talent shows held at the Ward Theatre in his
youth, and later started Time Unlimited with friends Orville Smith and Junior
Marshall; they were eventually joined by Glasford Manning, a Studio One
vocalist from Trench Town whose brothers were in the Abyssinians and
Carlton and His Shoes. After rehearsing to a high standard, they were brought
to the Black Ark by producer Trevor 'Leggo Beast' Douglas and his friend Vill
for an audition with Scratch. 'The first song I sang was "Why Did She Cry",
we play it like R & B style. Then I sing "Warrior No Tarry Ya", he was the first
person I record that song for but it didn't release, and Glasford Manning sing
"African Sound", it came out on the Upsetter label. When we do the audition,
Scratch says, "We have to record this kid." He wanted to do it right there, same
night, because he's a genius, believe me. Don't let them tell you nothing, that
man is a genius. In the morning, we turn up early with our guitars, and well-
polished voice, because in those days you have to could sing; they have to hear
talent . . . You're facing the mastermind like Upsetter.'

In the following months, Lee Perry worked closely with the group,
coaching their vocal deliveries and greatly changing their overall sound.
Delgado stated that his whole approach to singing was significantly altered by
Scratch's influence: 'Scratch is a genius. He taught me how he want me to sing
the songs, because I used to have a more R & B type of singing, and he
changed that. I was kind of polished, and he want me to do this native
singing.'

It was not long before Time Unlimited became a prime roots harmony
group, and word of their talents began to spread on the ghetto grapevine.
Though Perry recorded plenty of material with the group in this period, very
little of it was issued. Their most successful release was 'Reaction', a soulful
number led by Junior Delgado that surfaced on Joe Gibbs' Reflections label; it
was Wire Lindo's inspired keyboard work that gave the song its overall shape.
Delgado noted the following particulars about some of their unissued work
with Lee Perry: 'Scratch have some real wicked songs, over two albums' worth
of stuff! I can remember "No Need to Buy Newspaper Any More", Boris
Gardiner wrote that one, and I can remember "Lying Lips", it goes:

> A lying lips is abomination unto the Lord high Jah,
> Speak the truth and speak it ever, cause it what it will,

WIRL publicity photo circa 1967 (courtesy of Heartbeat Records, photographer unknown)

The Upsetters in Randy's studio, 1969 publicity still.
L to R: Aston 'Family Man' Barrett, Carlton 'Carly' Barrett, Alva 'Reggie' Lewis, Glen 'Capo' Adams
(courtesy of J Collingwood, YALP)

Return of Django

Written by LEE PERRY

LEE PERRY leader of The Upsetters

1969 Trojan publicity shot (photographer unknown)

Photo-montage from the home of Perry's mother Ina Blythe — main photo: publicity still circa 1972; photo strip: publicity shots taken in London in 1987; small centre photo: Ina Blythe (centre), her sister (right), and daughter Lorna 'Miss Nell' Blythe (left) (courtesy of Ina Blythe, photographers unknown)

Top left: Outside the Black Ark, 1976 (photographer Kim Gottlieb-Walker). Top right: Perry with daughter Marsha (photographer Kim Gottlieb-Walker). Below: Perry with musicians, including Max Romeo (in white) and Clancy Eccles (with denim jacket) (photographer Kim Gottlieb-Walker)

In the doorway of the Black Ark (Photographer Dave Hendley)

Perry's mother, Ina Blythe (photographer David Katz)

Perry with children Mark (aka Omar) and Marsha (courtesy of Palm Pictures, photographer Adrian Boot)

Outside the Ark, 1977
(photographer Kim Gottlieb-Walker)

The Super Ape, 1977(courtesy of Palm Pictures, photographer Adrian Boot)

The Upsetters, circa 1978 including Hermann Marquis, Richard 'Dirty Harry' Hall, Lee Perry, Errol 'Tarxan' Nelson, Boris Gardiner, Felix 'Deadly Headly' Bennett, Winston Wright, Robert 'Billy' Johnson, George Faith, Junior Murvin and Cedric Myton (courtesy of Palm Pictures, photographer Adrian Boot)

The Black Ark, circa 1978 (courtesy of Palm Pictures, photographer Adrian Boot)

Perry in the Black Ark, April 1980
(photographer Jean-Bernard Sohiez)

Perry, April 1980 (photographer Jean-Bernard Sohiez)

He who hide the wrong he does, does the wrong thing still.
You should not lie, you should not lie.
Guys like Napolean, he was a butcher,
Christopher Columbus, them call him Come Bust Us,
Pirate Morgan . . . '

While Perry held back the bulk of their material, other producers began to express interest in them. Displeased with Scratch's over-protective tendencies, the group decided to cut some material for rival producer Rupie Edwards towards the end of the year, some of which was issued under an alias. 'People really admired Time Unlimited and we couldn't leave Scratch at that time. If we even want to go and do a song, it would get some argument. We decided to record three songs for Rupie, "Run Baldhead" led by Glasford Manning, "Rasta Dreadlocks", I lead that one on the "Skanga" rhythm, and another song (as) the Heavenly Singers because they don't want Scratch to know it's Time Unlimited.'

After their work for Rupie Edwards, the group recorded two songs for Tommy Cowan with arranger Warwick Lyn and musicians from the Third World band, but the songs were never issued and Time Unlimited disbanded shortly after recording them.

By the end of 1974, Perry felt quite settled in his studio, and he began to issue a plethora of material at a frantic pace. It was somewhat inevitable that much of this material would not hit, and a flood of material on the market could be financially counterproductive, as one of Perry's contemporaries noted. 'These guys just put out record after record after record with no business acumen. So one thing kills the other one and then one day the bottom drop out. Scratch would put out too much things at one time, and that's where a lot of producers lose a lot of their material, because if you put out five or six things, one sell or two; the other five don't sell.' But Perry was continually bursting with ideas, and was compelled to commit as many to vinyl as possible; his studio allowed him a greater unbridling of his creativity, and though he was not scoring many major hits, Perry's unique approach to recording meant that few of his creations were dull or ordinary, and many are worth mentioning just because of their sheer inventiveness.

Watty Burnett was living about two miles away from the Ark in this period, and he ended up spending a great deal of time there. As his friendship with Perry strengthened, he performed a number of tasks for Scratch, playing percussion on several sessions and creating original bass lines that would be adapted by whoever Scratch was using at the time. As King Burnett, he cut a couple of vocal numbers with Perry in late 1974, including 'I Man Free', notable for its use of a roaring siren and trilling horn section, and 'Babylon A Fall', a Rastafarian claim for equal rights over a sparse rhythm that typified the early Ark sound. Burnett noted that he and Junior Byles were treated like family members at the Ark, along with Bob Marley, who would occasionally pass through. 'We just sing all day and I didn't even go home. Junior Byles and I sleep in the studio, it's like we lived there. Sometimes Bob Marley come down in the middle of the night and just put on an acoustic track . . . it's like home. I'm with Scratch from around 14 years old, he's like my daddy. I go in the house, cook, go in the fridge, it's like my house. Junior Byles and I hang out, just having fun.'

Further creative moments from this period came with Jimmy Riley on 'Rasta Train', an adaptation of Ken Boothe's 'The Train Is Coming'; 'Yagga Yagga', an abstract concept record incorporating nonsense scat vocals and the 'Some Like It Hot' nursery rhyme; 'Kiss Me Neck', a startling phased-horn instrumental made more zany on its scat vocal version 'Da Ba Da' and 'Sons of Negus', a defiant groove made more humorous on a later cut called 'Stay Dread'. 'Cane River Rock' was a further sortie into abstract mayhem, with the 'Tighten Up' rhythm being updated for a dread motorcycle ride up to Cane River Falls, related in thick patois with motorbike sound effects and a wild Perry scat seriously cluttering its mix. Perry was backed on a couple of other humorous sorties by the Silvertones in this period, including 'Finger Mash' and the rude 'Dub A Pum Pum'. Both featured a heavily phased rhythm provided by members of the Soul Syndicate.

As word about the new studio spread, artists Perry had previously worked with who were embarking on their own productions began to approach him for studio time. Among the first to hire the studio was Doctor Alimantado, who had ventured into self-productions by late 1973, recording material as a singer as well as a deejay. The first things Tado voiced at the Ark were 'Ride On', a soulful number about the uplifting qualities of love, and the self-explanatory 'Oil Crisis', voiced on a cut of the 'Ain't No Sunshine' rhythm. Returning to the Ark in 1974, Tado voiced 'Can't Conquer Natty Dread-locks', an adaptation of Delroy Wilson's 'Trying to Conquer Me', and two more cuts of the 'Ain't No Sunshine Rhythm': 'Best Dressed Chicken In Town' and 'She Wreng Ep'.

'Best Dressed ChickenIn Town' made use of a highly creative toast, and it was the combination of Perry's approach to sound and Tado's inspired delivery that made the record so effective. Alimantado's idea was to have his toast remain continuous, and it was partly Perry's restructuring of the rhythm with multi-tracking and delay that would see Tado's concept realised. 'Best Dressed Chicken In Town' became a dancehall sensation when issued in Jamaica, and the song would eventually see Doctor Alimantado propelled to international stardom when it became the premier issue of the British Greensleeves label in 1978.

Alimantado noted that he liked to use the Black Ark studio for his productions because Perry was generous with allotting studio time, and his love of music would always see him making an extra effort to come up with a creative sound, as with that of 'Best Dressed Chicken'. 'If you go to him with an idea, he doesn't just handle it as though he's an engineer, he handles it as though he's a producer. He handles it as though it's his thing, so he puts his initiative behind it. Working in other studios like King Tubby's, there's always so much running after time, but with Mr Perry, if you book an hour or two hours, sometimes he will give you three or four hours on top just making sure you get the music right; with King Tubby, you go in for an hour and you have to come out within the hour, because there's always someone else who's coming in. Where the "Best Dressed Chicken in Town" is concerned, originally I was in Randy's studio making a master. I played the tape and the idea flash in my head and I turned to (fellow deejay) Jah Whoosh and said, "Jah Whoosh, listen to this . . . " That was how the idea came about. I went to Perry, we work and develop up, and add different voice filtering in to make it very exciting. Junior Byles was there and he wasn't really interested in that, he wanted to do a song on the rhythm. Later on, we let him do a voice on the rhythm, and maybe a year or so after, I gave it to him.'

It was also in 1974 that Little Roy hired Perry's studio to record 'Tribal War', one of the most moving and powerful songs of his career. Little Roy had been frustrated by the attitude of producers he had been working with, so he decided to gain better control of his product by venturing into self-production in partnership with Maurice 'Scorcher' Jackson, one of three brothers who lived in his neighbourhood. After cutting the song 'Mr T' at Randy's with Leroy Sibbles and Barry Llewellyn of the Heptones, the pair formed the Tafari label in 1973, finding some favour with their initial release 'Prophecy', a song Roy noted Lee Perry was involved in creating. 'The first song that we did was "Prophecy". The rhythm was laid at Harry J's studio by Blacka Morwell. He sold us the rhythm and Upsetter was the one who engineered my voice; we voiced it at Randy's before Black Ark was running.'

When Maurice Jackson dropped out of the runnings, his brother Melvin 'Munchie' Jackson became Little Roy's partner in Tafari, and the pair arranged to record two songs at the Black Ark in 1974: 'Tribal War' and 'Black Bird'.

A quietly emotional record celebrating a peace treaty between Kingston's warring political gangs, 'Tribal War' rapidly proved to be a hit. Though highly successful cover versions were later recorded by John Holt and a number of other artists, Little Roy's Black Ark original remains the definitive version, a tense and emotive recording that exposes the corrosive effect political tribalism had on the dwellers of the ghetto. Little Roy recalled the inspiration for the song reaching him after reading of the treaty in the news: 'It was the end of some war that usually be mostly carrying on over East (Kingston); it reach a time when the brethren them say them stop the war now. It came out in the newspaper, saying that the brethren them sitting down now and licking chalice, so it give me the idea, "Tribal war, we no want no more a that," because war rough stuff. I did "Tribal War" at Black Ark, Dennis Brown played the bass, Horsemouth Wallace played the drums, Pablove Black played the keyboards, and Roy Hamilton, a guitarist that usually be amongst Upsetters then, he play the guitar. That song was only four instruments.'

'Black Bird' was another serious and weighty number in which Roy used natural symbolism and predatory metaphor to relate Europeans' rape and pillaging of Africa, using the same musicians as on 'Tribal War' with the exception of the bass, played on the song by Alva 'Reggie' Lewis.

It was at this time that Munchie Jackson got some rhythms from Scratch, including instrumental cuts of the Inspirations' 'Stand By Me', Pat Satchmo's 'Goosey', as well as 'Ain't No Sunshine'. These rhythms would appear on the *Tribal War* album, issued on Tafari in 1975, but Little Roy said they were not voiced properly, and felt the album should not have been issued in its unfinished form. 'Most of the songs on that LP was some rehearsals that we used to have in a packing house. If you notice, most of the songs don't sound that clean. Upsetters gave Munchie some rhythms, and I'm rehearsing them in the packing house . . . Munchie had good songs recorded at a studio, put those songs with these that was just rehearsal songs, and released (them as) that album *Tribal War*, so I don't even count that as an album.'

The Upsetter rhythms used on *Tribal War* would find their way onto *Free For All* (a.k.a. *All For Free*), a dub album issued by Lloyd 'Bullwackie' Barnes, some with extra saxophone played by Baba Leslie. Another Upsetter rhythm that found its way onto the album was 'Action Wood', a rude song Perry's assistant Jubie had voiced with a deejay called Prince Williams in late 1973.

Barnes cut material for Prince Buster in the rock steady era, but found little success as a singer in Jamaica. After emigrating to the Bronx in the early '70s, Barnes set up a recording studio and numerous record labels. He emerged as a leading force in New York's reggae scene mid-way through the decade. Shortly after the recording of 'Tribal War'. Munchie Jackson also moved to New York, eventually basing himself at 775 Burke Avenue in the Bronx; his alliance with Barnes would see the above material surfacing on labels Barnes controlled, along with other material that made use of Upsetter rhythm tracks. These issues included 'The Bump', a fairly flat deejay cut of 'Stand By Me' with below-average toasting by one Jah Vill, and 'Revolution', a superb Heptones track voiced on the 'Tight Spot' rhythm at a small studio Winston Blake ran at Hagley Park Road.

Lloyd F. Campbell ran a popular printing establishment at the corner of Orange Street and North Street, printing record labels for many a vinyl release; he also ran his own small The Thing label, and voiced a notable one-off single at the Black Ark in 1974: the chilling 'Samfy Girl' by Keeling Beckford, using a rhythm Campbell had previously created for a Busty Brown tune. Beckford had already ventured into self-production by this point, but agreed to voice the rhythm because of the friendship he shared with Campbell, who would later succumb to an early death from heart problems; Beckford also noted that he had often been present at Black Ark sessions voiced by Junior Byles, but that 'Samfy Girl' was the only song he recorded at the studio himself.

In late 1974 and early 1975, the singer and producer Vivian 'Yabby You' Jackson also began recording material at the Ark, and the studio's evolving sound would prove perfect for his spiritually motivated music. Born into extreme poverty in the ghetto of Kingston 13 in 1946, Jackson experienced malnutrition by the age of 17. His father, a Garveyite PNP member originally from Clarendon, had difficulty supporting the seven children of the family, forcing Jackson to live on the premises of a giant furnace where he worked at age 12; his poor health would see him emerging from a long hospital stay with severe arthritis and crippled legs. Jackson also experienced a double form of social isolation through his religious beliefs: wearing locks and living among the Rastafarian community, he was naturally on the margins of Jamaican society, but his worshipping of Jesus and denial of Selassie's divinity saw him ostracised by many Rastas.

Jackson's physical difficulties and endless poverty saw him making a particularly slow ascent in music. In 1969, Jackson had an argument about religious matters with some of his Rasta peers, including members of the Gladiators and Brent Dowe of the Melodians. This resulted in his first concrete form of musical inspiration: 'You have some Rastaman who we call "steppers", man who locks them hair and go thief but they claim say is not them who thief. They say them take back some of what them father left the slave master. This day we were at the corner and I say "Jesus Christ say them things no right." The whole of them turn on me in a dispute, trying to show me which part of Rastafari is God. Everybody a lick chalice. Them keep saying to me, "Rastafari is the King of Kings and the Lord of Lords." I say to them, "The King of Kings is Jesus Christ." So now I hear this sound, the thunder roll. Me hear a voice, like a whole heap of angel, "Be you, yabby yabby you . . ." and me start to rehearse back with them. The men them get up and say, "Boy! This thing can turn into music!" Them say I should record it, and somehow I take it seriously.'

Jackson rehearsed the resulting song 'Conquering Lion' with Horsemouth Wallace, Chinna Smith, and Family Man, who agreed to record the tune with him for free. Jackson scraped together enough money to lay a rhythm track at Dynamic in 1971 by returning to work at the furnace that had made him ill, again with disastrous repercussions for his health. In 1972, he persuaded King Tubby to allow him to voice the tune with the Prophets harmony trio he had forged with Alric Forbes and Bobby 'Melody' Powell, and its initial release that autumn proved to be a success. Yabby You continued to issue strong Prophets material in 1972 and '73, eventually replacing Bobby Melody with another singer named Dada Smith.

The Prophets' harmony vocals contained all the power and glory of a deep-set religious faith, and most of their creations are marked by spiritual fervour. From late 1974, Yabby You recorded some very inspired songs at the Black Ark. Early material included the fearsome 'Jah Vengeance' (voiced at King Tubby's with Alric Forbes and Milton Henry on backing vocals), and the anthemic 'Run Come Rally' and chastising 'Carnal Mind', both voiced at the Black Ark with harmony by the Royals (then composed of Roy Cousins, Bertram Johnson, Errol Wilson, and Keith Smith). Yabby noted that the subtle power of the drum sound driving 'Jah Vengeance' was supplied by Benbow Creary, using elements adapted from the playing styles of other drummers. 'Sly (Dunbar) used to watch Horsey play, him start to imitate. Horsey tell Benbow about that style (know as "rockers"), and Benbow use that style and do "Jah Vengeance". Then we do "Run Come Rally" with Family Man.'

A later Black Ark session yielded the almost psychedelic instrumental 'Death Trap', with a horn section arranged by Tommy McCook, featuring his own very eerie lead flute echoing around the mix. Yabby also voiced the young Wayne Wade at the Ark in 1975 on 'Black Is Our Colour', an affirmation of the positive qualities of those of African descent.

Perry has said that he appreciated Yabby You's vision, and it is perhaps their shared eccentricities and very individual modes of spirituality that saw such fine work resulting from combined forces of the Jesus Dread and the Upsetter.

'Yabby You was trying to do something that him hear from the spiritual world which was OK. All the producers who was listening from the spiritual world and creating words what them hear through them ears from the spiritual world will have a chance, they will be saved in what world them think them believe in.' [4]

As Lee Perry was helping other individually minded producers and artists to refine their spiritually motivated creations, he was also gearing himself up to stretch the boundaries of his own work. Revelling in the freedom that the Black Ark now afforded him, Scratch was preparing for a next phase in which he would test the very limits of his creations. Though Perry was always hoping for a hit, he was less concerned with the conventional vocal than his peers; it was a song's overall sound that remained his chief obsession. While his competitors trod on firmly established commercial ground, the Upsetter thus continued to experiment, initiating a series of minimal instrumental albums towards the end of 1974.

ENTER THE DRAGON:

Black Ark Album Abstractions

The latter half of 1974 and early 1975 saw Lee Perry in another transitory phase, as he sought to consolidate the reputation of his upgraded studio and re-establish his status as a forerunner in Jamaica's music field; album releases from the period show him exploring two very different realms simultaneously. Though a couple of vocal albums with pop crossover leanings would surface in this period, the majority of his album releases were heavily abstracted affairs, as Perry continued his flirtations with the outer possibilities of instrumentals and dub.

The first official disc to surface was *DIP Presents the Upsetter*. The album was a collection of 12 Upsetter productions, most from singles issued by the label, released in a proper picture sleeve but pressed in limited number. As nine tracks were straight vocal cuts by various artists, and only three comprised the zany sounds of re-fashioned Upsetter instrumentals, it appeared as an inversion of the formula of the Trojan Upsetter compilation albums previously issued.

In addition to successful DIP singles including 'Enter The Dragon', 'Cane River Rock', King Burnett's 'I Man Free', the Silvertones' 'Dub A Pum Pum', and Linval Thompson's 'Kung Fu Man' (credited to Linval Spencer), the disc also included Leo Graham's ribald 'Jump It', a medley of Gaylads' hits as 'Have Some Fun' and a new number called 'Nature Man', a laughable re-working of Ken Boothe's 'Everything I Own' (originally a pop hit for Bread) as the distorted guitar melody of 'Jamaica Theme', and two very peculiar songs by Sam Carty, former lead singer with a group called the Astronauts. Carty's voice was high-pitched, and had a breathless, uncertain quality about it, while the subject matter of his material was ponderous. 'I Don't Mind' seemed to express the thoughts of a man condemned to death, while 'Life Is A Flower' used the imagery of nature to relate feelings of love.

Perhaps the disc's finest number was 'Time', a little known but outstanding song by the Gladiators, one of the most original harmony trios ever to emerge from Jamaica. Like many Jamaican vocal groups, the Gladiators have a convoluted history. The group's most constant member, Albert Griffiths, would eventually emerge as leader of the Gladiators, and it is Griffiths' distinctive voice and use of proverbs that has marked much of their best-known work. The youngest of seven children, Griffiths was born on New Year's Day, 1946, in St Elizabeth; his mother died when he was young and he was raised in poverty by his father between the ghettos of Kingston 11 and Trench Town. After learning the masonry trade, Griffiths worked alongside Leonard Dillon in the mid-'60s; their boss was Leebert Robinson, a contractor who began producing records in 1967 with the Ethiopians' 'Train To Skaville', which was backed by Griffiths' first recording 'You Are The Girl'. Griffiths then formed the first incarnation of the Gladiators with David Webber, who used to sing with the Webber Sisters group formed by other family members, and Errol Grandison, another friend from the neighbourhood. The group had a hit in 1968 with 'Train Is Coming Back', again financed by Leebert Robinson, before moving on to cut 'Live Wire' and 'Sweet Soul Music' for Duke Reid in 1969, the latter featuring additional harmony from Hopeton Lewis.

Moving over to Studio One that year, the group recorded the songs 'Free Reggae' and 'Soul Music', but Coxsone did not issue them. The group finally scored a number-one hit with 'Hello Carol' towards the end of 1968, a song Coxsone had initially rejected when Albert Griffiths and Nicky Thomas first approached him with it as 'Hello My Love'; after heeding suggestions from fellow singers Jacob Miller and Larry Marshall, Griffiths changed the song's title and refrain to 'Hello Carol', voicing the tune with Webber and Grandison for keyboardist and session arranger Richard Ace while Coxsone was out of earshot. The widespread success of the song would see the Gladiators gain Coxsone's reverence, and would lead to a long period of residence for the group at Studio One.

As David Webber succumbed to increasing bouts of mental illness, the group endured a period of instability just on achieving success. Griffiths briefly formed a side project with his girlfriend Thelma Taylor, his cousin Cassell MacPhearson and 'a brother named Austin', but found greater success with a revitalised Gladiators once Errol Grandison recruited Clinton Anthony Fearon as a replacement for David Webber.

The oldest of two children, Fearon was born in the district of Essex Hall, St Andrew in January 1951, and spent the first six months of his life there before moving with his father to Clarendon, where he spent another six months. Together with his father and stepmother Miss Louise, Fearon settled in a rural community at Mendeze, St Catherine, on the edge of the Cockpit Country, where the family cultivated a range of food crops. Clinton's father also worked on sugar plantations in Cuba, and briefly assisted parish politician Madame Rose Leon before becoming disillusioned with politics.

Growing up in the country, Fearon learned to harmonise in the local church, and built his first guitar out of the trunk of a cedar tree; he dreamed of becoming a successful musician, and left the country at the age of 16 to live with his mother in Kingston, where she had found work as a hat-maker.

Living in the ghetto of Kingston 11, Fearon formed a harmony group called the Brothers with two friends named Neville and Duke; though they auditioned before Gladdy Anderson at Treasure Isle, the group did not reach the recording stage and eventually broke up.

Fearon's deep tones gave a new depth to the sound of the Gladiators, and the group quickly scored hits for Lloyd the Matador with 'Freedom Train' and 'Rockaman Soul'. Errol Grandison then left the group to fulfil familial commitments, and Griffiths teamed up more seriously with Fearon, whom he taught to play bass guitar, making the Gladiators a duo for a brief period.

Feeling somewhat unbalanced as a duo, they recruited Gallimore Sutherland in 1970, another mason Griffiths had previously worked with, forming the most lasting and successful incarnation of the group.

Griffiths remembered being inspired by American singers like Elvis Presley and Tom Paxton in his youth, but it was Bob Marley who would prove to be his favourite singer and most significant vocal model. In their harmony singing, the Gladiators always strove for a sound that was different from that of the other trios, their voices merging in such a way as to reach exalting heights. 'We don't just sing to follow the meter,' Griffiths noted, 'we all create a little sound in the group.'

The Gladiators remained chiefly at Studio One for the next several years, recording a number of weighty Rasta-informed classics riddled with proverbs and religious references, including 'Bongo Red', 'Roots Natty', 'Jah Almighty', and 'Mr Baldwin'. Besides their singing talents, the Gladiators were talented musicians, and Griffiths and Fearon provided musical backing for a number of artists at Studio One. Griffiths mastered the guitar before he began his singing career, and was equally proficient at bass; Fearon began his session career as a rhythm guitarist, but soon became more proficient as a bassist. At Studio One, they teamed up with drummer Benbow Creary, keyboardist Pablove Black and bassist Bagga Walker to back artists such as Stranger Cole and Burning Spear.

According to Fearon, the Gladiators began working at the Black Ark from late 1974. They were brought to the studio by producer and singer Vivian 'Yabby You' Jackson to provide musical backing on 'Jah Vengeance'; they had come to know Jackson through mutual involvement in the Rightful Brothers, a Rastafarian group led by an acclaimed repeater player called Brother Joe. After impressing Scratch with their musicianship, the Gladiators arranged to return to the Black Ark to record two songs of their own. As Fearon recalled, 'Yabby You took the Gladiators to Black Ark and we did "Jah Vengence" for Yabby. The session was great: Scratch ask Yabby if he workin' Obeah 'cause no one supposed to come into Scratch studio and get them sounds except Scratch! Scratch liked the sound he heard and we came back later and did "Time", which is Albert's song, and one I wrote called "Untrue Girl". Me and Albert played guitar and bass and Hardley ("Orgie") Taylor was on keys. The session was a great one, although Scratch and Albert didn't hit it off – they were two strong personalities and obviously didn't see eye to eye on things; their spirits just didn't blend. Back then Scratch used to drink Tia Maria and he would get right into it! It was a treat watching Scratch mix.'

'Time' shows the extreme tightness of the Gladiators in this period, their strong harmony a fitting vehicle for Griffiths' reverent lyrics. The Upsetter's production placed the song in the same league as their best Studio One material, its unusual instrumentation including subtle ringing notes from a xylophone or struck bells. While 'Untrue Girl' showed that Clinton Fearon was a competent lead vocalist, its version side 'Real True Dub' again showed Perry's uniquely creative humour through a mix that repeatedly displayed a muted vocal pattern. Fearon would later cut the stunning 'Warning to the Nation' at the Black Ark, credited on release to Tony Fearon.

Though they recorded little of their own material there, both Griffiths and Fearon played on several Black Ark sessions for Scratch – particularly Fearon, who has fond memories of working at the studio despite a lack of proper credit. 'It was great. I met and worked with all kinds of different musicians over there and learned quite a bit about percussion from Scratch. Over all, it was like doing a day job – wake up and go to the studio, reach there ten o'clock and sometimes you don't leave 'til twelve or one the next night. I did that for about six months and sometimes we'd lay a whole LP, like twelve tracks a day! Scratch is one producer that get a lot of my bass work and I didn't get much money for it, but I don't feel anyway bad about doing those works as they were great works; the only thing I'm sad about is that I got no credit for any of them.'

A trio of abstract albums followed *DIP Presents The Upsetter*, two of which were issued as blank label pre-releases. The first was *Musical Bones*, an album of instrumental experimentation featuring trombonist Vin Gordon. Born on August 4, 1949, Gordon spent his infancy in the Jones Town area. His mother was unable to care for all of her eight children, so Vin was sent to the Alpha School for Boys at age five. Under the instruction of Lennie Hibbert, Gordon learned to play trombone and string bass, becoming friendly with older school-band members and other musicians such as Roland Alphonso. Upon graduating from Alpha in the mid-1960s, Gordon played trombone for a period in the Salvation Army Band in Montego Bay. He was then brought to Studio One by Roland Alphonso in the summer of 1965, playing with Alphonso and 'Deadley Headley' Bennett on the Wailers' monumental rude-boy tune 'Jailhouse' (a.k.a. 'Rudie'); it was at this time that Gordon first encountered Scratch. Vin Gordon remained at Studio One for several years, playing on hits for artists such as Bibi Seaton, the Heptones, and Bob Andy. Since the foundation days of early ska, when Don Drummond was crowned king of the trombone, no one had made such an impact with the instrument; Gordon's overall creativity with the horn thus earned him the title of Don D Junior.

By 1973, Gordon was working for other producers at Channel One studio and elsewhere, recording exceptional instrumental work with the Soul Syndicate for Keith Hudson. Having been impressed with his instrumental prowess, Lee Perry requested that Vin Gordon record a trombone-led instrumental album for him in the autumn of 1974. Gordon recalled the circumstances of the album as being very loose, with improvisation and experimentation being the order of the day; the album took about three weeks to complete, with a mixture of musicians swapping instruments to keep things fresh. 'I met Scratch when I first came to Studio One in the '60s. Scratch used to be the second guy to Mr Dodd, give the introduction to the songs, set up the mike and everything. After a while Scratch leave there, start his own studio called Black Ark, and he said he want an album, so I just go up there and do an album for him.

'He had some of the rhythms already, and some of the rhythms we put down live. I put down some of Don Drummond's solo track like "Far East", and some other songs that I make in Studio One, my own instrumentals, I just change them over, 'cause it's not hard to do with the right musicians. Wire (Earl Lindo) was the keyboard player, and I say, "Wire, I want it to go this way" and Wire say, "OK, it can go this way, change there." Wire was the one who arrange. It was musicians who play one instrument, but Scratch would say, "Try a next instrument" to see if it could work. He got Douggie (guitarist Radcliffe Bryan) on bass, Ansel Collins on keyboards, and some of the tracks mix up different musicians.'

The finished product, *Musical Bones*, was issued in England by DIP in extremely limited quantities – 300 copies are said to have been pressed in late 1974. Perry was tuning in to the sounds of jazz players like Stan Getz in this period, and it was the more melodic side of jazz that Perry sought to capture on this album.

Using sparse mixes of fresh Black Ark rhythms, *Musical Bones* borrowed heavily from the jazz tradition. On several numbers, Gordon recalled the spirit of his mentor, Don Drummond, through mutations of ska numbers like 'Real Rock' and 'Eastern Standard Time'; other purely original numbers dissolved into free-form jam territory. Over subdued wah-wah guitar, relaxed jazz drumming and didactic electric piano, Gordon's lead reminded that the trombone could express a lot on its own. Not since Treasure Isle's *Don Drummond's Greatest Hits* and Studio One's *100 Years After* had the trombone been presented in all its fiery glory; with Drummond dead and buried and Rico in exile in England, the instrument's profile had dropped.

The album also had one of the earliest examples of Perry's new mixing idiosyncrasy, in that one of the tracks had a series of false endings. After fading down to silence, the rhythm is faded back up again, only to repeat the process a number of times before the song actually ended. Perry occasionally employed this technique elsewhere in this period, most notably on a mix of 'Small Axe' that surfaced on Coxsone Dodd's *Best Of The Wailers* album.

Though *Musical Bones* ably demonstrated the trombone's expressive potential and highlighted Perry's mixing quirks, the small quantity of albums pressed saw the disc almost immediately unavailable and greatly overlooked. Gordon noted a negative consequence of the album's relegation to the underground: he never received proper payment for his role in creating it. 'I had a royalty arrangement with Scratch, and believe you me, that thing go to England and sold. Scratch came back down from England with a book, looking on it, saying that it's some royalty thing, and Scratch took out one pound and give me and say it's royalty! From that day 'til now . . . one pound!'

Perry was quick to deny Gordon's version of events. 'That's stupid, man. You have to laugh, you can't even vexed with them. If I would give a pound, that is totally rubbish – even a beggar on the street I give more than a pound. The money I was getting from all the music I sell, me pay back to the musicians at weekends and as this was the start of the album, he's going to get an extra advance over the rest of the musicians that play. When me go to London, if me give them maybe two albums' worth of songs, the record company give you something like £600 if you lucky; Harry J was getting big money from Trojan, but the smaller guys, it's small advance we get so some go bankrupt. What advance we get, we have to pay musicians and give them advance out of it but they eat it off; they're not fair enough to say "We were taking money all the time." ' To make matters worse, when the album was semi-clandestinely re-issued in Britain in 1997 by Ravensquire records, neither Gordon nor Perry received any payment, greatly tainting its long sought-after re-appearance.

Dennis Bovell, guitarist with Matumbi and selector of the popular Sufferer sound system at the time of this DIP release, recounted a serious incident indirectly connected with a track from *Musical Bones*. Bovell had left the tranquillity of the rural town of Rosehill in the district of St Peter, Barbados, to join his father in London at the age of 12 in 1965; already proficient on guitar, he joined a succession of school bands before eventually forming Matumbi. Bovell was also supplying sound systems with dub-plate specials he created himself using primitive loops and cut-up techniques, which partly led to his installation as Sufferer's selector in 1970. For several years, Sufferer had two regular engagements in West London on Friday nights, playing at the Metro club in Westbourne Park until 11 pm, and then carrying on to the early hours at the larger Carib Club in Cricklewood, located above a tailor's shop called Burton's.

On October 13, 1974, a three-way sound clash had been scheduled at the Carib Club, pitting Sufferer against rivals Lord Koos and Count Nick's; to counter Koos' supply of exclusive Bunny Lee dubs, Dennis Bovell went to the offices of Ethnic Fight in Kilburn to arm himself better on the day of the clash. Larry Lawrence had just collected Lee Perry from the airport with a pile of master tapes and dub plates he brought from Jamaica, including some of the freshly recorded Vin Gordon tracks and other material destined for DIP. It was the dub plate of Gordon's Black Ark re-cut of the 'Real Rock' rhythm that saw the crowd voicing unanimous support of Sufferer's superiority at the Carib, but the event was spoiled by an incident in which a fight broke out between spectators and police, who supposedly arrived at the venue in pursuit of a suspect. According to Bovell, the strains of 'Beat Down Babylon' being played on a rival's record deck saw violence increasing; when things turned ugly, Lee Perry turned up his collar, announced, 'I am the Upsetter!' and fled the premises. A total of 12 were arrested, with the most serious charge of Incitement to Cause Affray reserved for Bovell himself. His complicated and infamous trial, which lasted nine months and saw two juries unable to reach a unanimous verdict, resulted in a harsh and unjust sentence of three years' imprisonment. Bovell would ultimately serve six months in Wormwood Scrubs prison before being freed on appeal.

Lee Perry's other two DIP album releases to surface by the start of 1975 were more abstract experiments. *Return Of Wax* – another album issued only as a blank label pre-release – collected ten dubs, most of which were freshly recorded instrumentals. Some of these tracks may never have been issued in vocal form, though one was eventually used for 'Observe Life', one of Michael Rose's first recordings, and another for Delroy Denton's 'Different Experience', credited on release to Brother Roy. The most readily identifiable dub is a bass-and-drum cut of 'Curley Locks', again punctuated by subtle ringing bells; other rhythms are largely devoid of reference points.

The dubs of *Return Of Wax* are largely gimmick-free, presenting the raw rhythms of these early Ark recordings in their simplest form. Bass and drum have prominence, and percussion is one of the few embellishments to appear and disappear from the mix. The emphasis remains continually on rhythm, with slices of rhythm guitar and harsh electric piano chords shifting up and back, with barely a lead lick audible throughout. In keeping with Perry's latest mixing peculiarity, the trombone-led rhythm that would later become 'Different Experience' contained a series of false endings.

The final album of Perry productions handled by DIP was *Kung Fu Meets The Dragon*, a less abstract and oblique collection edging more towards the instrumental side of dub; it incorporated a more complex instrumentation and made use of an array of sound effects from Scratch.

Aside from a quasi-dub of Linval Thompson's 'Kung Fu Man' and a peculiar re-cut of Roy Shirley's 'Hold Them' with an over-phased harmonica (as 'Hold Them Kung Fu'), the album again presented dubs of fresh instrumentals, most of which were never issued in vocal form. But *Kung Fu Meets The Dragon* had far more melody than *Return Of Wax*; 'Theme From Hong Kong' and 'Scorching Iron' were led by a bright melodica; 'Fungaa', 'Black Belt Jones', and 'Iron Fist' had harsh synthesiser overdubs sprucing them up, while 'Skango' made used of a full horn section led by a swinging sax. The extremities were 'Heart Of The Dragon' (an alternative cut of which appeared on Larry Lawrence's dub album *Music Explosion* as 'Imperial Dub') and 'Flames of the Dragon', both manic attempts to interpret the visual imagery of kung fu films into the aural dimension, their frightful sounds again demonstrating a relentless urge to experiment.

Perhaps the visually suggestive sound of such releases shadowed Scratch's individual sense of humour and fascination with cinematic excess, a fascination that would occasionally manifest itself outwardly. When Lee Perry came to London towards the end of 1974 with master tapes of current material, he stayed in accommodation that Dennis Harris rented in the outer London suburb of Crystal Palace. Winston Edwards spent some time with Scratch on one such trip, and recalled Scratch's zany dress sense and peculiar sleeping habits: 'I remember he went into a coffin to sleep. He actually made a mattress like a coffin, put something over it, and went over to the West End, bought all these black clothes, looking like a vampire with his teeth like Dracula.'

In 1975, Perry forged new alliances with a number of evolving record companies in Jamaica and Britain, and his material would begin to surface on a variety of labels. In Kingston, Scratch strengthened his association with Pete Weston, a Jamaican of Indian extraction who had established Micron, a leading record-distribution company and label based at 14 Retirement Road in New Kingston – close to Joe Gibbs' new 16-track studio. Weston's partners in Micron were Ronnie Burke, an African Jamaican, and Mike Johnson, a white Jamaican of part-Syrian parentage who was distantly related to the family that founded the Johnson and Johnson cosmetics empire in the USA. Perry had first used Micron for distribution in late 1974, but continued subsequently to release his product sporadically through Sonia Pottinger's Tip Top Record Center as well as occasionally distributing product from his home. The more concrete link he established with Weston in early 1975 would see him relying on their services for much of the year, and would see him engineering a number of sessions that Weston and others would produce for Micron product.

Max Romeo's 'Revelation Time', a direct statement about the unfair treatment of Rastafarians in prison, was one of the earliest and strongest songs Weston produced at Perry's studio. In a lighter vein was Junior Byles' 'Lorna Banana', (humorously reworked by Byles and Winston Jarrett as 'Revolution Is For The Chinaman'); structured similarly to 'Best Dressed Chicken In Town', 'Lorna Banana' made use of delay to uphold a constant, double-tracked vocal line. Byles also made his first foray into self-production that year with his rendition of Ray Charles' 'Girl Next Door', recorded at the Black Ark and issued on Micron.

I Roy was then the top deejay on King Tubby's Hi Fi, and Pete Weston had him toast on a number of strong rhythms at the Black Ark with much success. The 'Revelation Time' concept was re-affirmed on 'Message From The Top', while 'Tea Pot' had the toaster chanting nursery-rhyme lyrics.

Leo Graham's 'Three Blind Mice' had seen a number of other permutations before I Roy laid a toast on the rhythm at the Black Ark. The most similar cut came in Dillinger's 'Ensome City Skank', which related a series of other nursery rhymes over the rhythm. Perry also placed himself and the Ethiopians on the rhythm for the insulting 'I Am A Dreadlocks', in which the Upsetter questions an auditioning baldhead who claims to be a dread. Leonard Dillon noted that the song was commenting on tension between those who wore locks and devout Rastas who did not. 'In those days, the majority of the Rastas were not dread, and the Ethiopian centre that we originate from, the Rastas did not dread, they are combsome. So we say"How come you no have a beard and say you're dread," and me a repeat "I am a dreadlocks," so it heartically dread, and you just hear in it one heart.'

Perry's religious faith came from within, and he saw no need to wear locks to demonstrate his conviction. As Leonard Dillon put it, 'He did not dread either at that time. To what we were defending, you could assume that the spirit was moving within.'

As with many other Rastafarians connected to Kingston's music scene, Lee Perry and his family were attending Sunday services at the Ethiopian Orthodox Church on Maxfield Avenue. As his son Sean remembered, 'We used to go to Ethiopian Orthodox Church over on Maxfield Avenue, Scratch used to carry we every Sunday. Bob Marley used to (be) there, and Tommy Cowan. More artists used to go to the Church then. We learn (a) different religion by going to church, the main concept was we are in oneness.'

The services were presided over by Archbishop Abuna Yesehaq. Born Laike Mandefro in Addis Ababa in 1933, Yesehaq had been sent to Jamaica in 1970 by Haile Selassie to spread the Ethiopian Orthodox form of Christianity and to quell the belief that Selassie was God. But Selassie's denials could not shake the faith of the Rastafarians, and though Baptism into the Church was technically dependent on a denouncement of belief in Selassie's divinity, many Rasta believers attended services there, and Yesehaq often found himself at police stations and prisons, trying to secure the release of Rastafarian innocents whose only crime had been to wear dreadlocks.

It was such police brutality that was the focus of Max Romeo's version of 'Three Blind Mice', using a new cut of Perry's rhythm featuring Soul Syndicate musicians voiced at King Tubby's studio some months after the release of Leo Graham's original. Instead of repeating nursery-rhyme lyrics verbatim as Graham had done, Romeo changed the theme to report on the police destruction of a ghetto dance, something U Roy said was a common occurrence at this time. 'The police used to brutalise people a lot in Jamaica. They always be shooting up dance, they don't like to see big crowd of people. If they're driving past and see this big crowd, they just stop and shoot up the dance, nothing done 'bout it. It's like poor people enjoyment wasn't really fun. While those people just cannot afford to pay this big money to go to Sheraton or to a ballroom dance, this little sound system dance is these people's enjoyment; these police just come by and shoot it up, and that's fun for them.'

On the version side, 'Three Times Three', King Tubby subjected the rhythm to extreme phasing and EQ, and though Tubby's sound was shortly to be destroyed by the same type of police action Max sang of, Romeo noted that Tubby was instrumental in establishing the popularity of the tune on his sound system. 'Scratch built the rhythm and King Tubby produced the vocal with me. I voiced it in King Tubby's studio and he mixed the dub. His sound was the first to play different versions of the song, he had all different type of cuts, with different things happening in various parts of it. He had about 14 different cuts of "Three Blind Mice" before it hit the street, and when it hit the street it was a hit!'

I Roy's 'Dread In The West' made use of Romeo's cut of the rhythm, this time re-viewing Psalm 23 through the red spectacles of Rastafarian socialism:

'If the Capitalist is I and I shepherd,
The higher high shall always want
They maketh I and I to lie down
Inna the sidewalk
Yet though I walk through the field
And the factories
I and I obtain no labour
Not even a favour . . .'

It was this kind of lyrical wordplay that made Perry happy to work with I Roy, a toaster he voiced considerable praise for when speaking to Carl Gayle of *Black Music* magazine in 1975.

'One must realise that whatsoever message you're sending to the people you must send it clearly, and I Roy is a guy who can send a clear message. He's one of the more stylish deejays.' [1]

The Micron link also yielded interesting product by smaller producers working at the Ark. Micron's Mike Johnson recorded excellent material there with a singer named Easton Clarke, using rhythms with plaintive melodica parts. The most outstanding of these was 'Bike No License', recounting the tribulation the singer experienced riding an unlicensed motorcycle in a curfew while laden with herb, while 'Mr Phong, Mr Wong, Mr Chin' voiced the dread's refusal to cut his locks to get work from Chinese Jamaicans who controlled much of the commercial sector.

The Micron connection also saw a number of records pressed on Perry's Black Art label in 1975 that were not recorded at the Black Ark, nor produced or enigneered by Scratch – in short, they were songs whose creation he had nothing to do with. Product that Perry and Micron had collaborated on was already being issued on both Perry- and Micron-controlled labels, and Micron began to issue other procuct unrelated to Perry on Black Art, either when their own stock of blank labels was short, or when they feared that the radio stations would avoid their material if it surfaced on one label alone. One such release was U Roy's self-produced 'The Right To Live', voiced on Cornel Campbell's re-cut of 'Keep On Moving' (itself produced by upcoming bassist Robbie Shakespeare using the Aggrovators band). Other material took the form of Pete Weston's productions for Micron, including 'Bang Bang Lulu' by Jackie Brown and portions of the vinyl feud between I Roy and Prince Jazzbo that was orchestrated by a record-shop owner in Toronto in 1975, including 'Jazzbo Have Fe Run' on a modulated cut of Niney's 'Beardman Feast' rhythm, and Jazzbo's return attack, 'Straight to I Roy's Head'. Johnny Clarke's 'I Need Someone', recorded for Bunny Lee, also appeared on Black Art through a lack of available blank labels, while the Morwell's self-produced 'Mother Long Tongue' found its way onto Perry's Upsetter label at this time.

Roman Stewart's great love song 'Man Of Dignity', produced by Enos McLeod at Channel One, was also issued on Black Art, and although Scratch was not involved in its creation, McLeod's connection with Micron would see another artist from his stable working at Perry's studio: Shorty the President, with whom McLeod had recently had a hit with 'Jestering', a clever re-cut of Carl Malcolm's 'No Jestering'.

Shorty the President was born Derrick Thompson in Trelawny on January 5, 1949. In his youth, he worked the land and sold produce with his mother at a weekly Kingston market before moving permanently to town at the age of 19. Settling in New Haven, near Duhaney Park, Shorty became active on a small sound system. The set, called Conquering Lion, was run by a Rasta friend called Bongo George. It was while chanting under a banana tree in the Conquering Lion yard that Shorty was discovered by Rupie Edwards in 1974, who turned him into an instant star with his first recording, 'The President Mash Up The Resident', voiced on a cut of the Uniques' 'My Conversation' that Edwards obtained from Martin Riley. Shorty continued working with Edwards until early 1975, when the British chart success of Edwards' novelty hits 'Irie Feelings' and 'Leggo Skanga' saw him spending longer periods in the UK. With Shorty left high and dry by Edwards' absence, Enos McLeod stepped in to continue the success of his chanting style.

Noting the impact of 'Jestering', Pete Weston hoped to replicate McLeod's success with Shorty on 'Love And Unity', a toasting cut of an original Micron rhythm that Shorty said was created and voiced at the Black Ark. Though Weston hoped to cut an album there with Shorty, 'King Pharaoh' was the only number they recorded, and it made little impact on release.

Shorty noted that before the recording of 'Love And Unity', he first encountered Scratch's contrary nature on Chancery Lane, a downtown gathering point for artists known as the 'Idler's Rest'. 'I always meet him on Chancery Lane. He would pass through, going to Randy's with some record or to pick up some money, but he wasn't a man who's coming around there often; when Scratch come on the corner, everyone pay attention to Scratch. He's funny, you would say something to him and he turn it around the other way. He just funny and serious, wasn't too much of a joker.'

Though he only voiced one tune there, Shorty recalled the Black Ark as a unique and individual place, and noted Scratch's lasting influence on Bob Marley: 'With Scratch's studio, it have a different sound, completely different from every other studio. You could see the beat that Scratch have, it was the same thing with Bob Marley's style, the top end is just a little different. It's a different little sound between them, but the beat and the timing was the same thing, same hit sound, so the inspiration was in Scratch and go right into Bob Marley. Black Ark studio is a different studio in Jamaica, the vibes and everything. You go to another studio, the engineer would be laughing but Scratch was serious. He don't have anything to talk back to you over there, so he make two sign, and you don't understand, but you can see that he's not pleased so you have to ready for him. It was no joke business when you go in the studio; with Scratch, when you come in, you come in to work. You would see men out in the yard but not too much in the studio. You do what you want to do outside, but when you come in, is a serious thing.'

Max Romeo said that the studio had a lived-in quality to it, making it seem more an extension of the Perry household than actual recording premises. 'If you go into Black Ark studio, you'd figure you're sitting in somebody's study with just a little component stock set in there. It doesn't look nothing like a studio until you hear it.'

Romeo and Scratch were still very close in this period, and after the successful result of the 'Revelation Time' single, Romeo returned to the Ark to record an album under Clive Hunt's direction for Sound Tracks, a label whose staff had high-ranking government connections: Pat Cooper, one of Michael Manley's public-relations assistants, was a chief label executive. Though Sound Tracks had arranged a lucrative distribution deal with President Records, the company ultimately was short-lived, and eventually folded due largely to overspending on production costs.

Tentatively entitled *Strictly Roots*, Romeo's album emerged at the end of the year as *Revelation Time* after the continued popularity of the single, and remains something of a landmark as the first Jamaican 'concept' album. 'The songs may not necessarily sound alike,' Max clarified, 'but if you listen to the words, it's like reading the Bible and just turning the pages.'

Along with the title track and 'Three Blind Mice', Romeo cut six new tunes at the Ark, some of which were written by Clive Hunt, expressing a Rastafarian view of the inadequacies of Jamaican society. In lyrics that were heavily loaded with the imagery of both religious and socialist doctrine, the album addressed the social injustices faced by the underprivileged black Jamaican masses on songs like 'No Peace', and 'Quarter Pound of I'Cense'.

The poppy 'Tacko(o)', which was issued as a single on Sound Tracks' Black World subsidiary, was a message to Rastas whose faith was dwindling in the face of reports that Selassie had been deposed in a Marxist coup. 'Tackoo was a slave who wasn't all that smart,' Romeo explained, 'so if one were to refer to you as a fool they call you Tackoo.' 'Warning Warning' was another single that used the prophecies of Marcus Garvey to comment on the growing chasm between rich and poor. The most effective numbers closed each side of the album in 'showcase' style, with the vocal immediately followed by a dub; 'Blood of the Prophet' made good use of the Black Ark kick-drum sound, while 'Open The Iron Gate' was a call for repatriation over a re-cut of the 'Iron Gate' rhythm originally recorded for *Cloak And Dagger*, a rhythm Romeo said particularly inspired him. 'I deliberately did that rhythm over because I liked it, it had a thing to it that catch you. We know that Babylon have an iron gate locked upon us as black people, locked in the form of inhibition. Freedom of movement is not in the West for black people, you need visas for here, you're being deported from there, so I'm saying, "Open the iron gate, let us go back to Africa. Free us!" '

Geoffrey Chung was one of the in-house arrangers for Sound Tracks, so his Now Generation band appeared on several of the album's tracks, along with members of the Soul Syndicate and Wailers bands. Romeo said the album was cut in 'a day and a half' with all tracks recorded live, again retaining a harsh and spontaneous edge that has given reggae music some of its best results.

Geoffrey Chung also produced one of the year's most original songs at the Black Ark for Sound Tracks. 'I Man A Grasshopper' was the debut recording by a young dread called Pablo Moses, and the song's symbolic lyrics and rock-music leanings seemed to point to the very future of reggae. The eldest of four children, Pablito Henry was born June 28, 1948, in Culloden, Manchester; at age eight, he settled in Vineyard Town in East Kingston, where he would eventually adopt the name Pablo Moses in rejection of his 'slave master's name'. After teaching himself to play guitar, Moses attended the Jamaica School of Music where he learned music theory and improved his guitar technique. While living in Vineyard Town, he became friendly with Mikey Chung, and the two would often jam together. When Mikey's brother Geoffrey eventually heard the 'Grasshopper' song Moses had written, he noted something different in its feel; sensing that the song would hit, he took Moses to the Black Ark to record him straight away.

Moses noted that 'I Man A Grasshopper' was inspired by the actions of a drunken lodger who was renting a portion of his mother's house. 'He was some captain in the army and he has this funny attitude. I'm always in my room practising my guitar, burning my spliff but I don't go where he is. I heard one day he went to the police station, reporting that I'm smoking herb and blowing it into these kids' faces. I (thought), "Why would a guy do something like that and I don't trouble him yet?" so that's why I wrote that song. I said

"That man saw I-man smoking I-man colly weed, that man should never call Babylon to spoil I-man irie." He was a drunkard too, come in drunk, so that's expressing, "That man loves sea and fish bowl, and that man loves to keep I and I soul" because a drunkard is like a fish in the fish bowl, it's like an abstract deal in a certain way. The song came off him specifically.'

Recorded with Clive Hunt on bass, Mikey Chung on rhythm, and Michael Murray from the In Crowd on lead guitar, plus Robbie Lyn on piano and Geoffrey Chung on clavinet, the superior musicianship of 'I Man A Grasshopper' paved the way for Moses' particular vocal delivery, scoring an immediate and lasting impact on release. Moses subsequently became a leading international artist, enjoying a widespread popularity around the world.

Other less successful Sound Tracks productions were cut at the Black Ark in 1975. Singles issued include 'Ethiopian Lament', a mournful Clive Hunt melodica instrumental, and the Black Traps' 'Kiss Me In The Rain', a slow love song with a choppy keyboard line produced and arranged by one Tesfa McDonald.

Scratch began cutting a range of material with singer William 'Bunny' Clarke in this period, much of which would surface under a variety of aliases. Born in Mandeville on February 6, 1948, Clarke was raised in downtown Kingston from the age of two. As his father was an Anglican preacher, religion naturally played a big part in the formative years of Clarke's life. On Sundays he was made to sit through three church services: those of his father's congregation, plus services his mother attended at the East Queen Street Baptist Church, and evening services his grandmother brought him to at the nearby Church of God. Though he was greatly impressed by the happenings at the latter, where 'people sing and fall down on the ground', his mother's attempts to get him to join the Baptist church choir failed, because Clarke was more inspired by the American soul music he heard on the radio.

In his teen years, he became determined to be a singer, and began hanging out with the street corner groups in his neighbourhood. Charlie Hackett and the Souvenirs was then the house band at the Kittymat Club, and Clarke became familiar with the group through rehearsals held behind his yard in John's Lane. By 1967 he was the group's resident vocalist, performing weekends at the Kittymat Club and other venues.

Clarke followed his parents to New York in 1968, and had a break from music for about a year. On his return to Jamaica towards the end of 1969, he joined the Inner Circle group, replacing lead singer Bruce Ruffin who had emigrated to the UK. In 1971, he quit the band and returned to New York, where he joined the Jamaican immigrant group Hugh Hendricks and the Buccaneers, playing Top 40 dance hits for weddings and other social events. Anxious to begin working on original material he had written, Clarke joined a group called the Bluegrass Experience that Glen Adams had formed in New York with guitarist Eric Frater and drummer Sparrow Martin. The group performed to West Indian communities throughout the East Coast, and although Atlantic Records expressed some interest, a contract did not materialise and Clarke again tired of life in New York.

When Clarke found himself back in Jamaica in late 1974, he went to all the studios in Kingston searching for a piece of the action without result – until Glen Adams brought him to Lee Perry's Black Ark around the time that Susan Cadogan was finishing the last of her material with Scratch. 'I walk to all the recording studios throughout Kingston, check out the vibes and see what was going on and the one that I fell in love with the most was Lee Perry's. For some strange reason I end up spending a year there, (late) 1974 to (early) 1976.'

'He didn't have a song to sing,' Scratch recalled, 'but he did have a good voice and he wanted to sing like a Jamaican, so I give him some tracks, find him somewhere to live, feed him, give him clothes to wear; me would have to treat him like me son, buy him herb and everything to get him cool.' Perry first used Clarke as a backing vocalist on Cadogan's material, placing the singer on her version of the disco hit 'Shame' and on the song 'I Will Keep On Loving You' – though he removed Clarke's voice from the latter track before its release. Scratch then teamed Clarke with singer Ricky Grant for a number of fine singles credited to Bunny and Ricky.

A nephew of late producer Leslie Kong, Grant's given name was Errol Kong, though he also recorded under the names Ricky Storme and I Kong; he had been a member of the Mad Lads trio in the 1960s, and was brought to Scratch's attention by Glen Adams.

Before Trojan's sustained economic problems resulted in their collapse, a few last singles of Perry's product were issued on their Attack subsidiary, the strongest of which was Bunny and Ricky's 'Bushweed Corntrash', which spoke of their difficulty in locating decent weed. 'Too Bad Bull', a song of romantic disappointment, was also credited to the pair on its Attack release, though the song features only one vocalist and was credited to Pat Simpson on its Jamaica Upsetter issue. The version sides of these singles showed Perry's dubs becoming ever heavier through modulated equalisations and increasing distortions of sound. Perry also had Bunny and Ricky voice the anti-tribalist 'Freedom Fighter' on the 'Beat Down Babylon' rhythm, a song that surfaced on the Birmingham-based Locks label, a subsidiary of the Black Wax imprint run by two Englishmen, Keith Thornton and Brian Harris; Harris was also issuing Perry product on his Mango label in this time through a link he had made with Pauline Morrison.

As the bottom dropped out of Trojan's bucket, the bulk of Scratch's material began surfacing in the UK on newer labels formed in the wake of its demise. One of the most significant to issue his product was Kilik, a label established in 1975 by former Trojan employees Joe Sinclair and Desmond Bryan (who had also set up the Muzik City chain of record shops in London), together with an associate named Larry Sevitt. Scratch says he had no direct dealings with the company, suggesting his material reached their hands either via Pauline or from their access to Trojan's liquidated stock.

Their fourth album release, *To Love Somebody*, was Perry's most commercial project to date, a collection of crossover material that he and others had recorded with Bunny Clarke. As with Dave Barker's *Prisoner Of Love* and Little Roy's *Tribal War*, Clarke noted the album was compiled without his consent, using tracks that he felt had not been properly executed. 'It's not really an album, you know. I used to go to Lee Perry every day and hang out, and then I'd do a little voicing. He eventually put the whole thing together without even my knowledge, I didn't know anything about it.' Worse still, Perry felt his typical urge to re-name the artist, and confusingly credited the album to Bunny Scott, much to Clarke's disatisfaction. 'I say "Why the hell you go to England and name me Bunny Scott?" He said "These people like Scottish names . . . English people like English names," so him name me Bunny Scott.'

Though the album relies too heavily on cover tunes to be truly original, *To Love Somebody* does have the odd moment of verve and creativity. Versions of Neil Diamond's 'I Am I Said' and 'Sweet Caroline' would have been eminently forgettable if not for their peculiar Upsetter arrangements, which put a warped harmonica line all over the latter and a choppy keyboard skank on the former. Sonia Pottinger had arranged for Clarke to cut a cover of the soul song 'What's The Use' at the Ark, which Perry included on the album after she decided not to issue it as a single. The Bee Gees' title track had long been a favourite with Jamaican audiences, and Clarke's update injected soulful new life into it, while his version of Bill Withers' 'Use Me' put a whole new slant on the tune. The re-cut of the 'Sick And Tired'/'Return Of Django' rhythm as 'Big May' saw it largely restructured through an updated drum part, continuing the legacy of Perry's most enduring creations, but by far the most noteworthy numbers are the original Clarke compositions arranged by Perry and Glen Adams.

The high point is 'Kinky Fly', a song that went against the grain of the popular Jamaican music of its day. Clarke noted that the song featured members of the Chi-Lites' backing band, who were then in Jamaica for a series of concerts, and their horn section greatly added to the soulful nature of the track. The song was one of the first recordings Perry made using a Conn Rhythm Box – pre-dating the standard use of drum machines by nearly a decade – and both the machine's ghostly tick and Chinna Smith's wah-wah picking heightened the eerie feel of this funky number, inspired by the 'Blaxploitation' images of *Superfly*. One of the earliest rhythm machines on the market, the Rhythm Box was a bulky studio component with a limited range of pre-set rhythms like bossa nova and cha-cha, and its sound graced several of Perry's creations that year. 'Second Avenue,' the other original, showed how well Clarke's voice was suited to American-style soul, again drawing its overall shape from the Chi-Lites' backing musicians.

Though *To Love Somebody* flopped on release, it indicates Perry's ability to produce a range of contrasting music styles, and has good examples of Clarke's powerfully soulful delivery. Clarke cut some stronger material for Perry that did not make it onto the album, including a fine rendition of William DeVaughans' 'Be Thankful' and the delightfully angry 'Move Out Of My Way', aimed at the obstructions of politicians. Clarke remembered that the keyboard sound on the former involved a concept Perry referred to as the 'conk': 'Lee Perry, as I tell you about the cat, he wasn't any great instrumentalist, but he would mess around the keyboards and get some sounds. He have a sound that he call the "conk", he would come up to you, take his finger and knock it on your forehead and say, "This is what I want to hear, the conk" . . . Lee Perry music, he has that keyboard sound that has a phaser sound on it, it comes and goes. Sometimes it's in the distance, sometimes it's upfront.'

Clarke indicated that Perry's creativity taught him a lot about the way music could have no limits, and noted that Perry's contradictory and intuitive approach is something younger producers could benefit from. 'It was so simple that it became complex, you know what I'm saying? The approach he has to music and to recording, I think the music nowadays lack that kind of intuition. He's somebody that would use a pliers and a screwdriver to create a percussion sound, he wouldn't hesitate to experiment and that was really good. He was a little . . . not crazy, but somebody with that kind of thinking must be somewhere else, in another zone sometimes, and he was really good. Even the early Bob Marley works that Lee Perry was involved with, you can hear so much of Lee Perry in the lyrical formation, the way Perry writes and the way Bob writes is similar, so simple that it becomes so fucking complex! That is what I learn from Lee Perry at the Black Ark.'

Despite the troublesome manner in which much of his material had been released, Bunny Clarke continued to hang around the Black Ark, hoping that Scratch would get him a significant record deal with a company more substantial than Klik.

Klik's next album release was *Negril,* a 1975 instrumental jazz-fusion album featuring American guitarist Eric Gale. According to drummer Paul Douglas, Gale and company recorded some material at the Black Ark that did not make it onto the album and presently remains unreleased. 'Scratch had a particular sound, everybody was fascinated by his sound. He had this way of putting things together and it was just his sound and it influenced a lot of people. A whole lot of people used to come down there. I've done so many things with Scratch, I've even gone to the Black Ark with Eric Gale for that *Negril* album, me and Val Douglas, Keith Sterling, Leslie Butler, Cedric Brooks, Richard Tee, an American (keyboard) player, and Eric Gale, of course. I remember myself and Val Douglas, we laid some tracks there, Eric Gale overdubbed stuff on there, but I honestly don't remember what happened to it. It didn't get on the album because all of the tracks were done at Harry J's; we were supposed to have done it at Federal but we end up doing it at Harry J for some reason.'

Around the time that *To Love Somebody* and *Negril* were released, other Perry material recorded in 1975 surfaced on Angen, a Klik subsidiary; the releases credited Pauline Morrison as producer, but were really produced by Scratch. These included Perry's zany 'Stay Dread' and the religious 'Many A(re) Call(ed)', credited to the Unforgettables; another Unforgettables number from the same session called 'Time' was issued only in Jamaica on Orchid.

Meanwhile, Scratch continued to create interesting material with a range of artists. Jimmy Riley spent a lot of time at the Black Ark in this period, cutting a superb version of Bobby Womack's 'Woman's Gotta Have It' and a desultory tune called 'Hypocrites', apparently aimed at Niney and Jerry Lewis; another strong issue was 'I Man Stand Still', on which Riley spoke of his frustration in the music business. When the Melodians temporarily broke up in 1975, Brent Dowe cut the excellent 'Down Here In Babylon' at the Ark, a song co-written by Dowe and silent song-writing partner Renford Cogle; over a characteristically rugged Upsetter rhythm provided by Boris Gardiner, Glen Adams, Winston Grennan, and members of the Gladiators band, a full chorus was provided by Melodians member Trevor McNaughton, Max Romeo, and Bibi Seaton and Maurice Roberts from the Gaylads. The Silvertones were still cutting the odd tune with Perry, of which 'Financial Crisis' was one of the best, while Dread Locks Fay (rude girl Fay Bennett) challenged the male hegemony of the deejay world on 'Back Weh'. Ronnie Davis and his partner Pat Scabba also used the Black Ark for Davis' excellent 'You Are The Fool', issued on the On Top label with a spacious, echoing Perry dub.

Upcoming producer Lloyd A. 'Spiderman' Campbell's collaboration with Scratch resulted in one of his most notable productions: 'Freedom' by the Inturns, recorded at the Black Ark in late 1975. The Inturns was another name for the Viceroys (a.k.a. the Voiceroys), a harmony trio formed in the rock steady era by Wesley Tinglin, initially with Lineal Williams and Daniel Bernard. The group would have a number of personnel changes, and used various spellings of either title at different periods of their career, eventually replacing Williams and Bernard with Neville Ingram and Norris Reid. They majority of their early work had been recorded at Studio One, with occasional output cut for Derrick Morgan and Winston Riley; they would later record notable material for Phil Pratt, Sly and Robbie, and Linval Thompson. The Viceroys are also said to have recorded a number of other titles at the Black Ark, including 'Trying Faith', 'Come on Over', and 'River to Cross', though the circumstances of these recordings remain unclear and it is doubtful the songs were ever issued.

Another singer who has mentioned working at the Black Ark in this period was Edmund 'Mike' Brooks, who recorded the song 'The Earth Is The Fullness' at the studio with a short-lived group called the Tots, featuring Norris Reid 'and a guy called Tony'. Brooks was a regular fixture at the 'Idler's Rest' on Chancery Lane until he landed a job building rhythms at Channel One with Skin Flesh and Bone. He then formed the Tots and recorded his Black Ark debut, issued on his Harvest label; he was brought to Perry's studio through a link with Jah Lloyd, whose Teem label Brooks was also involved with. 'I think it was '75,' Brooks noted, 'my first daughter Paula born that time. We did just one song, "The Earth Is The Fullness"; Carlton Barrett play drum, Family Man play bass, and I think Lester Sterling play horns on it.' The single made little impact on release, and the Tots subsequently disbanded. Brooks was also often present for sessions arranged at the Black Ark by Jah Lloyd, including the one that produced Barry Llewellyn's 'Meaning Of Life', pressed on the Morwell Esquire label; according to Brooks, the session featured Tin Legs on drums and Family Man on bass.

Perry also made a first foray into Gospel production by engineering several rudimentary tracks at the Black Ark for the Grace Thrillers' *I've Got a Love* album, issued on their Showers of Blessing label in 1975. Formed by Noel Willis in 1970, the group was based at the New Town Church of God in Kingston 12, and remained the most popular Gospel combo to emerge from Jamaica; the album featured contributions by notable session players such as keyboardists Harold Butler and Tyrone Downey and guitarist Lennox Gordon.

Meanwhile, Perry's own anti-barber 'Bury The Razor' hinted at a growing maturity lacking in some of his earlier solo issues, but the song itself was playfully constructed, using the melody line of an old Silvertones tune called 'Feel All Right'. Perry titled the single's version side 'Cheat Weston Head' as a dig at Pete Weston of Micron; who in 1976, he would thus chiefly use the former site of Beverely's records at 135 Orange Street as the outlet for his new product.

Though Lee Perry was creating much impressive material with a range of artists in a number of different styles, it was with Bob Marley and the Wailers that he continued to make the best of his exceptional creations in this period.

Scratch attended some of the *Natty Dread* album sessions at Harry J's studio in late 1974, and his presence influenced the final shaping of certain tracks. The engineer was Sylvain Morris, who had recently fled Studio One after Coxsone reneged on a promised pay rise – the first wage increase he was to receive after working for Dodd for five years. *Natty Dread* was the first Wailers album without Peter Tosh and Bunny Wailer; to fill the gap left by their absence, Marley used the newly formed I-Threes harmony trio, composed of Rita Marley, Marcia Griffiths and Judy Mowatt.

Though Rita had enjoyed popularity in the Soulettes and Judy in the Gaylets, it was Marcia Griffiths alone who had really established herself as a solo singer. Born in November 1951, Griffiths was the youngest of five children born to a carpenter and his wife in West Kingston. Though her family was poor, Griffiths grew in loving surroundings, receiving the proper nurturing that would help her to succeed and prosper. One of her neighbours in the tenement yard where she grew up was the girlfriend of Philip James from the Blues Busters, and when James discovered Griffiths singing one night in April 1964, he was astonished at the quality of the 12-year-old's voice. He persuaded Byron Lee to allow her to perform at an upcoming Easter stage show at the Carib Theatre, and her rendition of Carla Thomas' 'No Time To Lose' brought the house down. Ronnie Nasrallah became her manager, and soon had her performing Nancy Wilson songs on Jamaican television. She was then taken to Studio One by Lynford Anderson, where she created a string of hits through the rock steady and early reggae years; from 1969, she also built up a following in Germany through concerts and recordings arranged by promoter Harold Huber. It was while at Studio One that she came into contact with many important musical creators, including Lee Perry, Bob Marley, Rita Marley, and former Paragons member Bob Andy, who became her song-writing partner and long-standing companion. Griffiths and Andy subsequently enjoyed considerable success in the early '70s through recordings for Harry J as Bob and Marcia.

By the time of the *Natty Dread* sessions, Marcia Griffiths, Rita Marley and Judy Mowatt were long-time friends and singing associates. Griffiths and Rita Marley first sang together behind the Wailers on 'Baby We've Got A Date' for the *Catch A Fire* album; the trio also recorded with the group on Bunny Wailer's 'Hallelujah Time' for the *Burnin'* album. They had previously recorded as a backing trio on some of Horace Andy's material at Studio One, but it was not until Marcia Griffiths invited Rita and Judy to back her up at a 1975 performance at the prestigious House of Chen nightclub in New Kingston that the three decided to form a lasting harmony trio. Within a short space of time after their formation, Bob Marley requested the I-Threes' involvement on the *Natty Dread* album.

From the *Natty Dread* sessions, 'Talking Blues' and 'Bend Down Low' eventually surfaced in limited number as a single on Perry's Black Art label, reminding of concrete links between Perry and the group at this time. Some months after the *Natty Dread* sessions, Marley and Perry would combine forces more concretely for the execution of an interesting and challenging project.

In May 1975, Bob Marley began working with Lee Perry on an album with Martha Velez, an American singer of Costa Rican origin based in the hippie haven of Woodstock, New York; the album, *Escape From Babylon*, was being financed by Sire Records, a subsidiary of Warner Brothers. Sire had established their reputation by presenting the more experimental side of rock music, and a reggae-rock crossover album under Marley's direction was an inspired and original idea. When Marley heard some of the singer's rebellious lyrics on a demo tape, he agreed to the project and travelled to New York with his manager, Don Taylor, to finalise the deal.

As with *Natty Dread*, the album was recorded at Harry J's studio with Sylvain Morris at the controls. The Wailers band provided the rhythms and the I-Threes harmonic backing, supplemented on several tracks by the Zap Pow horn section, which then included trombonist Vin Gordon along with founding trumpeter David Madden and long-standing saxophonist Glen DaCosta. Though Marley was in charge of the overall project, it was Lee Perry that did most of the production work in Jamaica, and his musical versatility was a vital, enabling force.

An initial June session yielded a couple of tracks, with another six cut later in the summer; the songs were later overdubbed and remixed by Craig Leon in New York. The result was a subdued Wailers band at their most commercial bubbling beneath Velez's expressively melancholy vocals, its absence of foreign musicianship lodging the music closer to its reggae roots than rock. Wailers numbers like 'Bend Down Low', 'Get Up, Stand Up', 'Stand Alone' (as 'There You Are'), and 'Hurting Inside' (as 'Happiness') were presented in the middle ground between the two genres, while originals 'Money Man', 'Wild Bird', and 'Come On In' worked surprisingly well in the reggae format. The backing vocals of the I-Threes blend particularly well with Velez's deep timbre throughout, and Chinna Smith's bluesy guitar lead also enhanced some of the best numbers, but it was the percussion added by Marley and Perry that really gave the album its African-Caribbean flavour.

Sylvain Morris noted that Marley's extremely disciplined approach to the recording process resulted in the strong shape of the Wailers' rhythms, both on *Escape From Babylon* and on the Wailers' own work: 'When Bob started recording he used to use four musicians: the drum, the bass, the piano, the guitar. He used to lay those four tracks first, and it always impressed me that whenever they lay the tracks, they were always so solid from the beginning. That is what impressed me most, the basic tracks were so solid. Bob being an individual who is very firm also, there was a lot of discipline within his works.'

Such typically solid Wailers rhythms is what made the album work so well, and it is perhaps the most successful of the uncharacteristic crossover albums Lee Perry attempted. In addition to *Escape From Babylon*, Perry also worked with Bob Marley and the Wailers in this period on some of the most intense and exceptional works of their career.

With the *Escape From Babylon* project completed, the Wailers left Jamaica for an extensive and high-profile tour of North America, followed by four noteworthy concerts in England, one of which would be issued as the Wailers' *Live!* album.

Straight after their return, Bob Marley and the Wailers began working on the *Rastaman Vibration* album at Harry J's studio, drafting in Chinna Smith to make sure the sound was rootsy enough. 'When Bob and them come a Jamaica, them hear about artist named Dennis Brown, a dangerous singer. The man just a fret, "A who dat?" If you go to a dance, a pure Dennis Brown you hear and Johnny Clarke. Them days, through Bob a spend so much time a foreign, a different thing a gwaan, like "What About the Half", "Black Magic Woman", "West Bound Train", and "Cassandra", all those bad D. Brown tunes, D. Brown like fire! And Johnny Clarke, "None Shall Escape The Judgement" and all them tunes rock the world, and it's we who play the whole of them tunes there. So the man say "A which guitarist that?" because Bob, one thing me love with Bob, Bob is a man who check the sound, always curious, want to find out. So Skill Cole come check I; *Rastaman Vibration* was the next album so him reel in certain man.'

According to both Chris Blackwell and Chinna Smith, Scratch was present for some of the *Rastaman Vibration* recording sessions, and made certain concrete suggestions that helped shape the finished product. Two of the songs were re-cuts of material Perry originally produced, and it is likely that he assisted in their recreation: 'Who The Cap Fit' had initially been recorded with the Upsetter as 'Man To Man', and 'Night Shift' was an update of the *Soul Rebels* album cut 'It's Alright'. Additionally, 'Cry To Me' had originally been cut by the Wailers at Studio One when Perry was still working there. 'Crazy Baldhead' seems another likely candidate for Perry's input, as he later recorded his own version of the song, but the most clearly notable Perry influence can be heard on the song 'Rat Race'. Chinna Smith and others recalled Perry's presence in the studio when the song was being recorded, and noted his concrete involvement helped shape the work. 'Me arrange that,' Perry confrimed, 'that was about a politician affair.'

The Wailers would halt the *Rastaman Vibration* album sessions in September to collaborate with Lee Perry on what would be one of the most significant singles they ever recorded: 'Jah Live'.

When news reports reached Jamaica that Haile Selassie had died on August 27, 1975, the Rastafarian community was thrown into a severe crisis. Many would lose their commitment to the religion at this time, while others found the news creating unbearable turmoil in their lives. One such devotee was Junior Byles, who was unable to reconcile his belief in Selassie's divinity with the physical death of his earthly form; the news affected him so badly that he tried to take his own life, resulting in a long stay in Bellevue, Kingston's notorious mental hospital. Byles' lasting depression and drastic mood swings would see him prescribed prohibitive doses of medication with distinctly negative results, and though his career would be briefly reprised towards the end of the decade, he would never regain his full continence after Bellevue.

Others were less troubled by news of Selassie's death, interpreting the reports either as the false propaganda of Babylon or merely seeing the event as an opportunity to strengthen their faith in the certain divinity of the Emperor. Bob Marley was one whose faith could not be shaken, and he quickly felt the urge to demonstrate this to the world in song. Marley knew that there was only one producer whose commitment matched his own, so he summoned Lee Perry to Harry J's studio to record one of the most memorable songs of his career.

An unabashed affirmation of Selassie's divinity and proclamation of the Rastafarian belief in everlasting life, 'Jah Live' was supported by the very foundation of Marley's faith. It remains as one of the most stunning documents of his religious beliefs, a triumphant expression of the positive and unifying power of religious faith. As Marcia Griffiths noted, Marley went beyond his usual effort to give the song an extra sense of gravity. 'Bob was partially sad, concerned and questioning so that was one of the most serious sessions that we did. Bob does every single one of his songs with such conviction, but he was more forceful and firm that night than we have ever seen him. Whatever was being said, he knew Jah was alive, His Majesty was alive, come what may. That was the conviction that he did that song with.'

The version side, 'Concrete', is a finely balanced dub that shows off the tightness of the Wailers' rhythm section, Fams and Carly providing a solid wall beneath Chinna's wah-wah and 'Touter' Harvey's keyboards. The song begins with a vibrating yelp from Marley, apparently in a joking imitation of the manner in which Martha Velez would clear her throat before voicing.

When 'Jah Live' hit the streets in Jamaica, it found instant favour with the public; its international release, like Martha Velez's album, would be delayed until 1976. As evidenced by their intensely creative collaborations, Marley and Perry were certainly very close in this period, and though occasional differences might surface between them, they maintained regular contact when both were on the island.

Scratch's other album release of 1975 again headed towards previously uncharted dub territory. *Revolution Dub*, issued in the UK on Creole's Cactus subsidiary in November, was a dub album with a difference: the obtrusive sound of television reared its ugly head over much of it with overdubbed dialogue taken from the British sit-com *Doctor In The House*. The album also made more drastic use of cross-channel stereo fading, heightened the separation of the bass and treble elements, and trapped vocal snippets in a type of freeze-frame echoing action, with one word or syllable appearing from nowhere to echo over a dub's muted form. Such techniques could emphasize the potentially menacing qualities lying beneath a seemingly innocuous rhythm such as 'Woman's Gotta Have It', with by far the most frightening transformation involving Bunny Clarke's 'Move Out of My Way' becoming 'Kojak'. Over the barest of drum and bass rhythms, Perry uses a 'd(o)uble attack' loudly to inform us of his new persona as the bald, lollipop-sucking detective played by Telly Savalas, while Clarke's echoing voice is repeatedly frozen on the command 'move'; the overall result is a startling re-interpretation of disassociated brilliance. Junior Byles' 'The Long Way' leaves the realm of kung fu fully to embrace the stiff-upper-lip slapstick of 'Doctor On The Go', while the title track has Perry murmuring and grunting over another early Rhythm Box experiment. For the dub of 'Bushweed Corntrash', Perry adds fluidity to the rhythm by humming the absent melody line, muddying the distinction between the conventional dub and acceptable vocal.

Side two has Perry singing over a number of fresh dubs, moving the album farther away from the realm of dub towards that of the ordinary vocal. 'Dreadlocks Talking' hinted that rude-boy habits found their way into dread behaviour, with the voice of someone with a French accent appearing beside his own, while the autobiographical 'Own Man' had Perry's double-tracked vocals mentioning aspects of his personal ethos. 'Dub The Rhythm', a slow and ghostly dub re-cut of 'Feel The Rhythm', was punctuated by Perry's belching, transforming the rhythm into a celebration of dub indigestion, while 'Rain Drops' was another double-tracked number on which Perry warbled nonsense in a soulful style over the rhythm of Jimmy Riley's 'I've Never Had It So Good' (miscredited to Bunny Scott on later UK releases).

Revolution Dub is another dub oddity from Perry, lying somewhere between the extremities of dub and the ordinary vocal. It again shows Perry's perpetual quest to create music that was not ordinary, and reveals his inability to leave a recording in one particular form.

Lee Perry had spent 1974 and 1975 building up the reputation of his studio, refining his techniques within the new space, and giving input to the creations of other producers. As his own productions were gaining the added depth of additional dimensions, so was his religious conviction gradually deepening and becoming more solidified. He had come a long way in establishing himself as an independent production force, but a scarcity of hits meant he still had a long way to go. Tension was building in Kingston as an election year approached, and Perry sensed that further changes were in the air – though whether such changes would be positive or negative remained unclear.

By the end of 1975, Lee Perry had acquired a number of musical tools that would concretely change the overall sound he was shaping at the Black Ark. The earlier installation of the Soundcraft board was the first step away from the minimalism that characterised the studio's sparsely equipped early days, and the further acquisiton of new gadgetry would see his future material resonating with complex textures and greater depth. The slower and heavier sounds that Perry started to conjure up in the Ark in 1976 had the quality of aural molasses, undercut by a seething tension and subdued urgency – dread echos of what would prove to be a most chaotic period in Jamaica's turbulent history.

While passing through New York on his last business trip of 1975, Perry came across a demonstration model of a Mutron phaser effects unit that had not yet reached Jamaica. Once in use at the Black Ark, the phaser gave a dense, spongy quality to whatever instrument (or set of instruments) it was applied too. The other effects unit that began to alter his work with greater regularity was a Roland Space Echo (model RE 201), an analogue tape delay that gave a limitless quality to sound. The Space Echo would prove especially useful on vocal mutations for dub tracks, allowing a message or certain words or syllables to echo seemingly to infinity, as previously demonstrated on 'Best Dressed Chicken In Town'. But Perry did not limit his use of it merely for vocals on dubs: any instrument or musical element could be subjected to its alterations. He had long been experimenting with mixing techniques and equalisation, and the phaser and Space Echo gave him greater freedom to create the sounds he pictured in his head, making music that would always be vastly different from that made by his peers. 1976 would also see a gradual change in his keyboard sound, with the harsh quirkiness of the clavinet superseded by a more natural-sounding electric piano, later futuristically augmented through the occasional use of synthesisers brought to the Ark.

At the start of 1976, Pauline Morrison travelled to England with the first batch of Scratch's issues for the year. She established an important link with Daddy Kool records on this trip, then the only reggae record store in London's fashionable West End. The shop and Daddy Kool record label was the brainchild of life-long reggae enthusiast Steve Barrow, a working-class Englishman of Jewish descent born in London's poverty-stricken East End in 1945; finance for the shop was provided by Keith Stone, a fire-insurance claims assessor based in Soho. Among the material Morrison supplied the shop on this visit was Lord Creator's lewd calypso 'Big Pussy Sally', and two tunes by Winston Heywood and the Hombres: 'Back Biting', a reaction against Capitalist aggression, and 'Long Long Time', a song that also surfaced in the UK on Brian Harris' Mango label.

Other fine material from early 1976 included 'Four and Twenty Dreadlocks', a dread adaptation of 'Four and Twenty Blackbirds' by one Evans Jones; 'Come Along', a magnificently echoing chant about fleeing Babylon by two taxi drivers from Kingston 11 who formed a harmony duo called the Blue Bells; and harmony trio Truth, Fact, and Correct's 'Babylon Deh Pon Fire', which betrayed the influence of the radical thought of America's Nation of Islam over a charging rhythm driven by Niyabinghi-style hand drums. The first Black Ark creation to make a strong impact in 1976 was 'Roast Fish And Cornbread', a playful celebration of some of Perry's favourite sustenance using a loping rhythm provided by Albert Griffiths, Clinton Fearon, Benbow Creary and keyboardist Audley Taylor of the Gladiators band; the version side 'Corned Fish Dub' had some particularly quirky xylophone notes. Ironically, the hit rhythm was apparently created free of charge: ' "Roast Fish and

Cornbread" was a "broughta" – in other words, a bonus rhythm,' noted Clinton Fearon. 'We did eight rhythms that day but only got paid for seven; we didn't get paid for the last one, which was "Roast Fish And Cornbread".'

Other strong Black Ark material followed in the spring. The fiery 'When Jah Come' was issued in May, a stern warning to wrongdoers of the coming retribution cut on another hard-hitting Upsetter rhythm driven by Niyabinghi beats. It was sung by a light-skinned singer previously known as Bunny Gayle but re-named Devon Irons by Scratch on this occasion; the pair first worked together in 1971 on a song called 'I Am Sorry'. In September, Perry would issue the equally popular follow-up 'Catch Vampire', the strongest commentary yet on the 'false Rasta' phenomenon, in which Irons denounced impostors who wore locks as a cover for wickedness. Clive Hunt recalled being summoned to the Black Ark when Perry was arranging 'Catch Vampire', and noted the following particulars about the recording session: 'You never know when Scratch call you in those days, he have some different ideas. When Scratch call me I went with me trumpet, and he tell me to play bass, he just moved everyone around. Robbie Lyn play keyboard, Mikey Boo play drum, me play bass, and Fil Callinder from In Crowd play guitar.'

'Catch Vampire' captured all the ire and wrath that the true Rastas felt towards impostors, and it is partly Clive Hunt's spine-tingling bass line and the harsh phasing of Callinder's guitar that drove home the dark expressions of the tune. Though pressed in limited numbers, the song struck a note with audiences in Jamaica and Britain, where it surfaced on the Locks label.

Perry continued occasionally to act as an engineer for other producers in the first half of 1976, but was mostly concentrating on his own creations. Another stunning one-off Perry engineered for another producer was Prince Allah's 'Bosrah', voiced at the Black Ark for toaster and aspiring record producer David 'Tappa Zukie' Sinclair in early 1976. After a period in London where he voiced the acclaimed debut album *Man A Warrior*, Zukie acted as a bodyguard for Striker Lee, and began voicing cuts of Striker's rhythms. He then started building rhythms of his own, Prince Allah's 'Bosrah' being one of the first.

The rhythm of 'Bosrah' was based on Burning Spear's 'Joe Frazer', which Lee Perry previously versioned as 'Cloak And Dagger' and 'Dub Organiser'. Tappa's new 'Rockers'-style cut of the rhythm at the Black Ark proved to be the heaviest of them all, given greater weight through the surefire rhythm team of Sly Dunbar and Robbie Shakespeare, a clear horn section giving the tune added flashes of treble brilliance. The lead vocals were handled by Ras Allah, a tall singer from Greenwich Farm with a high tenor voice.

Also known as the 'Gentle Giant', Allah was born Keith Blake on May 10, 1950. He first recorded for Joe Gibbs in 1968 as a member of the Leaders with Milton Henry, later forming the Nazarines with Henry and Roy 'Soft' Palmer; Blake also recorded solo material for Gibbs in the same period.

Becoming a follower of Prince Emmanuel Edwards in the early '70s, Blake was out of the music scene for several years as he devoted his life to a religious existence at the 'Bobo Dread' camp in Bull Bay. In 1975, he began recording solo material as Prince Allah – so named because of his admiration for Muhammad Ali – also cutting tunes with Roy Palmer as the Vandells. On 'Bosrah', Allah was joined by Soft Palmer and Tony Brevett, who was recording a tune at the Black Ark with the Melodians on the same day. Allah noted that Perry greatly shaped the song during its recording: 'Lee "Scratch" Perry really did the arrangements. He is a man whe inna the spirit when him inna the studio, so him just hold the spirit and give the brother the bass line and get it nice. Lee "Scratch" Perry did a great part because he was a more advanced man, he know about music.'

The only song Tappa Zukie and Prince Allah ever recorded at the Black Ark, 'Bosrah' was also the first release to indicate Zukie's potential as a formidible producer, a potential he said was greatly enhanced by Lee Perry's assistance in the creation of the work. 'Lee Perry was not just an engineer, he also add to the production that was going on. I was a young producer then, but Lee Perry helped me structure that song; that's how my education start to expand from Bunny Lee's classroom. When I went to record that tune I didn't go there for just record – I go there to take in a lesson from Lee Perry.'

Another couple of strong numbers were cut at the Black Ark in this period by Rupie Edwards, who was then living in nearby Duhaney Park. Edwards would shortly become a permanent UK resident, but fashioned some rhythms at the Ark before his migration with drummer Fish Clarke and bassist Errol Carter (later better known as Flabba Holt). The result was 'Three 'Pon One A Murder', one of the most moving and politically relevant songs of Edwards' career, and a less successful love song called 'Baby It's You'; dub cuts of both songs were also issued as a separate single. Edwards later returned to the Ark to voice an alternative cut as 'Rise and Fall', which also featured Edwards' keyboard skills. Edwards also remembered recording a song called 'Natty Plant It' at the Black Ark in this period with 'a young deejay from Spanish Town' whom he named El Cisco Delgado, though precisely who the deejay was remains unclear.

The Cimarons also passed through the Black Ark in the spring of 1976, cutting some of their least commercial work there one afternoon. In 1975, the group ceased being merely a backing band and became a recording entity, fronted by a singer originally from St Catherine named Winston Reid. Their cover version of Bob Marley's 'Talking Blues' ended up being a number-one hit in Jamaica, so Tommy Cowan, former lead singer of the Jamaicans and head of the Talent Corporation booking agency and record label, arranged for the group to do a series of high-profile performances around the island. Of the five concerts they gave in Jamaica, their appearance at Kingston's massive Carib Theatre drew the biggest crowds, but an appearance in February at the Roots nightclub in Chela Bay – beside the grounds of the Playboy Hotel – was also well attended. The group remained in Jamaica for three and a half months, laying a number of tracks at Joe Gibbs and Channel One for what would be their second album, *On The Rock*; before the album was completed, Cowan brought them to the Black Ark to record the songs 'Paul Bogle' and 'Greedy Man' with Lee Perry as engineer.

A renewed link with Micron around the same time would see other interesting deejay versions of Scratch's rhythms cut in 1976, the most notable of which was Prince Far I's 'Psalm 53'. Born Michael Williams in Spanish Town, the well-built man was in charge of security at Studio One in the late '60s. He began his recording career as King Cry Cry in 1970, initially as a substitute for King Stitt; later work for Enos McLeod resulted in the moniker Prince Far I. 'Psalm 53', which used Perry's 'Mighty Cloud of Joy' rhythm, was one of ten Psalms Far I chanted over heavy rhythms on a Micron album produced by Lloydie Slim; the album, *Psalms For I*, remains a fascinating religious concept disc.

With the exception of Lord Creator's 'Big Pussy Sally', virtually all of the singles Perry produced in early 1976 had the particularly strong dubs that are associated with Perry's Black Ark sound, the Roland Space Echo greatly influencing their overall shape. The more extreme examples include 'Say A Prayer', the version side of 'Three 'Pon One', which used echo to enhance the recreated soundscape of Scratch's skilful freeze-frame mixing.

Perry had a pool of extremely talented musicians from which to draw, and the general competency of their musicianship greatly increased the quality of his output. His pristine and orderly studio was now entering a new phase of solidity, and in the coming months, Perry would find himself exploring the fullness of his capabilities as never before. The singles issued in the early months of 1976 show that Perry's evolving approach was reaching more solid footing, as improved equipment and greater knowledge of how to work his tools allowed him better to accomplish his musical goals. Scratch would shortly find himself at another significant turning point, where he would ultimately obtain the most concrete support for his product that he was ever to encounter in his career.

POLICE AND THIEVES:

The Golden years of the Black Ark

By far the most notable number to surface in early 1976 was Max Romeo's 'Sipple out Deh', a song that would become better known in a later form as 'War In A Babylon'. The word *sipple* means slippery, and 'Sipple Out Deh' captured the mounting tension that was slowly building in the run up to the 1976 general election, giving voice to the terror Jamaicans were faced with in the midst of the destructive factionalism that has defined the nation's politics from the end of the colonial period. It was a campaign year that would prove literally explosive, with many an innocent ghetto dweller caught in the partisan crossfire. 'Sipple out Deh' spoke of the disruption faced by the general populace as armed vigilantes controlled by the opposition JLP and ruling PNP – variously bolstered by police and soldiers – literally went to war in the street:

> 'War in a Babylon
> Tribal war in a Babylon
> It sipple out deh
> The policeman no like the dreadlocks man
> The dreadlocks man no like the policeman, no . . .
> Marcus Garvey prophecise say
> One must live ten miles away in this time
> I man satta 'pon a mountain top
> Watching Babylon burning red hot . . . '

The origin of much of the violence can be traced to JLP aggression, as attempts to oust Manley became increasingly extreme. Manley's direct links with Cuba and public overtures of friendship and support for Castro had frightened and displeased its larger capitalist neighbour, who did not take lightly to even the slightest suggestion of support for communism in 'America's backyard'. Many have suggested that Seaga and the CIA were orchestrating a concerted campaign to destabilise the country in a desperate effort to discredit Manley before Jamaica fully adopted policies of Cuban socialism, becoming a pawn of Castro and the Soviet Union. Though concrete evidence of such a campaign has not yet been publicly documented, JLP instigated violence increased throughout the year, with shootings, fire-bombings and other acts of 'sabotage being carried out with increasing regularity, often at the expense of the poorest and most vulnerable on the island.

The year began with a JLP hit squad storming into the PNP stronghold of Trench Town just prior to a Kingston convention of the IMF and World Bank – 20 houses were raised by fire bombs and a gun fight went on throughout the night, leaving several dead and dozens homeless. The next day, an anti-apartheid demonstration (ostensibly in reaction to South Africa's attendance of the convention) descended into anarchy, with widespread looting and shop burning resulting in further deaths, including those of four policemen. On May 19, another JLP gang attack left 11 dead and over 500 without homes through more explosions in a PNP ghetto. By June, over 160 Jamaicans had lost their lives in election-related violence, resulting in the instigation of a state of emergency.

It was under such a climate that Max Romeo and Lee Perry created 'Sipple out Deh', perhaps Max's strongest comment on the failures of Jamaica's politicians in its description of the battles raging in various Kingston shantytowns. Perry's musical arrangement provided a most suitable vehicle for Romeo's lyrics, with an intrusive lead guitar line supplied by Michael Leopold Williams (a.k.a. the Revered Mikey Zappow, normally bassist with the Zappow band), percussion from Clinton Fearon and Scratch's percussive wooden fish hinting at the tension in the streets. Romeo said that Perry's re-structuring of the song resulted in its particular hook: 'I had this song "War In A Babylon" where me say, "It wicked out there, it dread out there." I took it to him, said, "You like it?" He said, "Yeah!" with excitement, "but no dread and no wicked, it *sipple* out deh!" So I said, "Yeah, that have a ring to it," because sipple mean slippery, it's slidey out there. I said, "Fantastic idea: 'War In A Babylon', it sipple out deh," so I record the song. Scratch got $15,000 (JA) for producing the song. After production costs he gave me $2,500. That's the only money I get to date.'

Clinton Fearon also noted having an inadvertent hand in the song's initial creation: 'I was going to Scratch one Sunday morning to do a session and they just come in with these new Jolly buses and the seats were funny – you'd sit in them and slide off; not comfortable to sit on, in other words. There was a lady sitting beside me and we kept sliding off our seats and there was a verbal fight going on at the same time, and she turn around and said to me, "Everyting sipple this morning," so right there I got this idea for a song and the title would be "Everyting Sipple". Having this idea brewing in my head, I got off the bus, went by the studio and told Scratch about what happen and about my idea. We laid some tracks that day and the next day I went back to the studio in the afternoon and Max Romeo was there singing this song, "It Sipple Out Deh", so there went my idea!'

Scratch refuted both Romeo and Fearon's assertions, claiming he alone had written the song with Marley in mind as vocalist. Whatever the case, Perry chose to bolster the message of the song by having Barry Llewellyn and Earl

Morgan of the Heptones lay a resounding chorus of harmony vocals, and the pair's competence as backing singers would see them working often for Scratch in the following weeks. Earl Morgan noted that their close residence to the Black Ark made them an obvious choice for harmonies. 'I live in the area here and Barry nearby, so we pass through and get acquainted. We go there one night and he do "War In A Babylon" with Max Romeo and we just start hum a little thing behind him, "It Sipple Out Deh". He say, "Come do some work man" and we just start work 'pon that.'

Romeo recalled that many were impressed with 'Sipple Out Deh' in its early stages, most notably Bob Marley, who wanted to make the song his own. 'When Bob hear the "War In A Babylon" track he was ecstatic, he said, "Let me do this song." Scratch said, "No, this is Max Romeo's song, make him do it." So he went away and did "Three Little Birds", because it's the same (bass line).'

The success of 'Sipple Out Deh' led to further cuts on the same rhythm, including 'Fire Fe The Vatican', an alternative Romeo vocal against Catholicism, Jah Lloyd's version 'Leggo' which listed numerous behaviours to avoid, and 'Stop the War In A Babylon' by a deep-voiced deejay called James Brown (a.k.a. James Booms). Though these alternative cuts surfaced in the UK on Brian Harris' Mango label, they failed to achieve the levels of popularity generated by the original 'Sipple out Deh'. A further cut of the rhythm came through the renewed link with Micron on an album called *Micron Dub* (issued in Jamaica in small quantities and eventually re-issued as the confusingly titled *Reminah Dub* on Jah Whoosh's London-based Original Music label); other Perry-connected rhythms on the album included 'Jah Live' and a Black Ark re-cut of Bunny Wailer's 'Battering Down Sentence'.

Max Romeo noted that another important personality to be impressed by 'Sipple Out Deh' was Chris Blackwell, who was renewing his interest in Jamaican music after achieving commercial success with Bob Marley and the Wailers. 'Chris Blackwell came to the studio one day and Scratch played the song for him. He said, "Yeah, we can do an album with this artist" so we did the album then.'

In the early 1970s, Blackwell had turned his interests away from reggae music. He dissolved his partnership with Trojan's Lee Gopthal by selling out his shares in B & C, and recreated Island as a premier independent label for progressive rock. After finding far more commercial success with acts like Traffic, Free, and Jethro Tull than he had ever had with Jamaican product, it seemed unlikely that Island would ever return to reggae material until Bob Marley and the Wailers rose to international prominence after signing with the company in 1973. The emergence of Marley as an international superstar by the 1975 issue of *Natty Dread* saw Blackwell renewing his broader commitment to reggae with the serious promotion of artists like Burning Spear and Toots and the Maytals, and he was looking to increase his reggae roster in 1976.

Island had a reputation for presenting the more experimental side of rock music, and though Blackwell was mindful that reggae could be difficult to market in its rawest form, it was partly Scratch's experimentation that made his music so appealing to Island's boss. As the Wailers' first two Island albums – *Catch A Fire* and *Burnin'* – had included re-cuts of songs the group had originally recorded for Scratch, and as Bob and Scratch continued to spend a lot of time around each other in this period, Lee Perry seemed in many ways an obvious choice for Island to begin licensing product from. Blackwell had difficulty recalling exactly how he and Perry came to an arrangement, but noted that 'Sipple Out Deh' was the defining element of their connection. 'I have a feeling the first thing that brought us together was "War In A Babylon" with Max Romeo but I might be wrong. I can't remember how we initially got together at all, all I remember is spending a lot of time with him in the Black Ark studio; I sat in with him on a lot of sessions.'

Blackwell pointed out that Lee Perry's studio was very orderly at this time, a concrete indication of Perry's extremely disciplined work ethic. 'It changed a lot over the years but when I first went there the place was absolutely pristine. You waited at the gate and it was usually one of his children that would go and call him. He'd come out of the studio, walk you down, show you where to sit in the studio. He was very, very precise and clean, very meticulous in everything he was doing. If somebody was smoking a cigarette he would instantly put an ashtray under them to make it clear what they were to do with it. On the back wall of the studio was a whole shelf of tapes, and if you asked him about something that you'd listened to ages ago, he would be able to put his hand on it immediately.'

Once Perry reached an agreement with Island, he began working with a new drive and determination which would see him creating some of the finest work of his career. He began recording with a new diligence, his studio a constant hive of activity, with session after session stretching deep into the night. As his days grew shorter through increased musical activity, a series of superb albums was created for Island, their very uniqueness and experimentation resulting in widespread international appeal.

Both Blackwell and Perry have indicated that Island's working relationship with Scratch was a loose one, based more on the spoken word than on written contracts. 'There would always be an advance agreement, and basically we had a royalty structure in Island,' Chris Blackwell stated, 'we had no Jamaican contract.'

At the time, Perry stated a positive view of the bureaucracy-free relationship:

> 'It's loose, working man to man. We a do it with words and words are the greatest contract – you can tell me the truth with words, face to face, and I believe you. And when you feel me a squeeze you, you say "watch out man, you squeeze me" and it done. We don't have to fight and shout out and chain down one another like slave, 'cause slavery days over.' [1]

It was around the time that Scratch finalised his agreement with Island that Bunny Clarke decided to exit the Black Ark. 'Scratch eventually made connection with Chris Blackwell, who gave him some money, instruments or new equipment for the studio. We were all in Jamaica waiting on Scratch, he went away for about five months. He eventually told me that I have to start coming to the studio a little earlier, and I have to start dusting off the console, clean the instruments, sweep out the studio. I wasn't prepared to do that so I moved on.' Clarke returned to New York shortly after, where he would finally gain international recognition as Bunny Rugs by joining the pop-reggae band Third World, who already had a contract with Island. The group was composed of several members of his former band mates from Inner Circle, and after catching up with them one night at the Bottom Line nightclub, Clarke has been with the band ever since.

Once Island agreed to issue Max Romeo's album, Max and Scratch began working on it in earnest. Before its completion, Perry quickly put together a deejay album for the company to issue, as the style was gaining popularity abroad. His first choice for the album is said to have been Jah Whoosh, a deejay who had assisted Doctor Alimantado on some of the tracks he recorded at the Black Ark, but another toaster would ultimately tackle the task.

Jah Whoosh was born Neville Beckford in downtown Kingston on September 16, 1952. He began his career as half of the singing duo Neville and George, formed in the late '60s with George Daley (later known as Reggae George), but the duo failed their audition at Treasure Isle and never reached the recording stage. Nicknamed Whoosh after his propensity quickly to disappear from sight, his debut recording was 'Mean The World To Me' for Rupie Edwards, after which he decided to concentrate on being a deejay. By 1972, he was associated with the Prince Lloyd sound system based in Boys' Town, becoming involved with Sir Percy sound after Lloyd emigrated to America. He cut his first toasting sides, 'Angela Davis' and 'Mr Biah', in 1973 for independent producer George Bell, but it was his next release that hit: 'Try A Thing,' a cut of Little Roy's 'Prophecy' voiced for Blacka Morwell at Channel One. Subsequent hits followed for various producers including Clive Chin, Enos McLeod, Leonard 'Santic' Chin, George McLean, Keith Hudson, and Phil Pratt.

Though Whoosh was hot property by the time Lee Perry sought to put together a deejay album, Whoosh himself recollected that his initial hesitation resulted in Perry choosing to record the album with another deejay. 'Lee Perry did come to me and said he wanted me to do an album for him, but at the time I never ready. Personally, I never did too much like the tracks them at the time, so I kind of linger, linger with it, and hide out, until he used Jah Lion instead.'

In the end, Perry opted to work with a more reliable toaster with whom he shared a closer working relationship: Pat Francis, his old record salesman who was scoring hit singles as Jah Lloyd, but had no album yet under his belt.

Francis was often around the Ark, and had built up a strong rapport with Scratch; Perry knew that Francis could toast with originality on his rhythms, and would readily respond to his peculiar notions about sound.

Though Francis had built a name for himself in the toasting realm as Jah Lloyd, Perry chose to rename him Jah Lion for the album, in keeping with his need to re-create, alter, or reverse what is seen as acceptable or taken for granted. 'When I do as Jah Lloyd, Upsetter say, "Bwoi, you seem like a lion, so I'm going to call you Jah Lion." I was Jah Lloyd to him but he say, "I'm going to give you a new name." ' Causing greater confusion was the photograph of a grinning Lee Perry, standing in front of his neatly arranged shelves of master tapes, on the album's back cover; many incorrectly concluded that Jah Lion was Lee Perry under a pseudonym, and Island's early adverts supported the fallacy. The front-cover art by Jamaican Rastafarian artist Witter Dread was less ambiguous, its depiction of Rasta locks intertwined with the mane of a roaring lion framed by red, gold and green felt-pen lines and hearts suggesting the strength and devotion of the united dreads.

Francis stated that as Perry had already recorded the rhythm tracks on which he was to toast, the album was completed very quickly. 'Colombia Collie take about two weeks, recording three or four tracks a day. We no ramp them time, man bring a fire.'

In the mid-to-late 1970s, Colombia was probably exporting more marijuana than any other nation in the Western hemisphere. Colombian weed had a reputation for being strong and pleasant to smoke, becoming the contraband of choice for many potheads in America. As its fame spread throughout the Caribbean, Perry chose to name his debut deejay album production after the legendary herb.

Most of the album made use of rhythm tracks that pre-dated the creation of the Black Ark, but were voiced and mixed in such a manner as to be entirely in keeping with Perry's contemporary creations. Jah Lion's toasting is both relaxed and confident, his charged yet understated delivery perfectly suited for the complex stew of Perry's mix. Though most of the songs deal with the weighty matters of Rastafarian spiritualism, a few tracks break the heaviness through a humorous presentation of the lighter sides of life, making the message of Colombia Collie serious but not overbearing.

The opening track 'Wisdom' set the album's tone with an affirmation of Jah's everlasting life and limitless powers over a forceful cut of 'Words Of My Mouth'. 'Dread In A Jamdong (i.e. Jamdown)' provided a strong musical contrast in the shape of a fresh rhythm. 'Hay Fever' was a clever re-casting of the 'Fever' rhythm, a squeaking door emphasising its ironic new form. 'Flashing Whip' was a re-mixed cut of 'The Lama', its percussion moved to the fore, while the title track had Perry and Jah Lion discussing the merits of imported weed on a modulated mix of the Silvertones' 'Rejoicing Skank'. Side two began with another new rhythm, a bouncing re-cut of the oft-versioned R

& B standard 'Fat Man' (said to have been Fats Domino's first release in 1949), built around a disappearing bass line and making good use of the Ark's new keyboard sound. 'Bad Luck Natty', which was issued in Jamaica as a single, had Jah Lion bemoaning his poor lot over a strong cut of the 'Dub Organiser' rhythm with new percussion and keyboard overdubs, while the autobiographically titled 'Black Lion' double-tracked the toaster's interpretation of biblical events over an organ-led cut of Donny Elbert's 'What Can I Do' (covered by a certain Locks Lee for producer Clement Bushay with Perry's assistance). 'Litte Sally Dater (i.e. Daughter)' was a highly experimental mult-tracked toast of Chenley Duffus' original cut of 'To Be A Lover', on which frozen, echoing fragments of an unknown second toast are dropped into the mix. The closing 'Sat(t)a' was a chanting re-cut of the Abysinnians' Rasta anthem 'Satta Massa Gana', here again presented in a disjointed, fragmented manner on the rhythm Augustus Pablo also used for the brilliant cuts 'Pablo Satta/Silent Satta'.

Though *Colombia Collie* did not enjoy the degree of popularity afforded Dillinger's *CB 200* album, recorded at Channel One and issued by Island the week before Jah Lion's debut surfaced in late May 1976, it remains a highly creative disc that shows how strong the combination of Scratch and Jah Lion was at this time. Both were approaching the height of their powers, and each brings high levels of creativity to the album's construction. Jah Lion spoke fondly of Scratch's instructive command, despite the later arguments over finance that would eventually cause a rupture. 'Me enjoy working with Lee Perry because he knows everything about the music. He is very great, I rate him very much; I think he is a genius. Forget about the money part of it, but he's a genius; me and him do some nice work.'

Max Romeo's *War In A Babylon* album had been scheduled for a summer release, but would be held back by Island until September. From start to finish, the disc is a triumph, each track laden with venom and echoing with political and social relevance. It begins with a strong opener which Island issued as a single in June: 'One Step Forward', which Romeo said was a direct message to Michael Manley, urging him not to waver in his principles. 'It goes back to Michael Manley again. I said "Wait, we're taking one step forward and two steps backward because you don't know whether to suit Uncle Sam or to suit the people. One day you're a dreadlocks to hold up the rod of correction and the next day you're a bald head. Onward, forward and don't step backward, man, make we step out of Babylon!" That was straight to Manley's head.'

The next number, 'Uptown Babies', chronicled the different lives children were living on either side of the nation's social divide, while 'Chase The Devil' had Romeo seeking to rid the world of Satan's influence – a song he said he wrote in response to one of Perry's recurring pre-occupations.

'That song was written by me and Lee Perry. Lee Perry is a man who have some contention with the Devil. He's obsessed with doing something to the Devil, so he's always writing things about the Devil. He come up with this song about hanging the Devil, or cutting the Devil's throat and throwing him in the fire, so I said, "No, you don't have to do that. Let's just chase him out of earth and send him to outer space to find another race," and right away I just go into writing the song.' [2]

Romeo noted this was one of his original numbers that ended up being significantly re-worked by Scratch: 'In those days, you write a song and you take it to Scratch, no matter how good your song is, it's never good enough. You've got to debate it, and then take out that, put that in, and at the end of the day, you give him 50% of the publishing.'

Finishing out side one was the title track, a smoother mix of 'Sipple out Deh' with additional keyboard overdubs. Side two began with the tale of 'Norman', a true story about a friend that Romeo and Perry often played cards with: Norman Elliot, brother of disc jockey Desmond Elliot at JBC. Scratch's arrangement of the tune gave it an eerie quality, particularly through suggestive horn parts played by trumpeter Bobby Ellis, saxophonists Richard 'Dirty Harry' Hall and Herman Marquis, and trombonist Vin Gordon. The next song, 'Stealin', was aimed at devious preachers who used the cloak of religion to feed off the poor, while 'Tan And See' revived the 'Dub Revolution' rhythm for a particularly fine number laden with proverbs and religious symbolism, greatly enhanced by backing vocals from Marcia Griffiths, Cynthia Schloss, Earl Morgan, and Barry Llewellyn. 'Smokey Room' re-worked the themes of 'Feel The Rhythm' in relation to fine foreign weed, while 'Smile Out Of Style' remarked on the generally negative feeling permeating the nearly bankrupt nation.

War In A Babylon would prove to be the best-selling album of Max Romeo's lengthy career, and remains the best indication of his overall abilities as a singer and songwriter. But financial matters connected with the disc would leave Romeo bitter, and cause a certain tension between him and Scratch.

Once Island established a ready outlet for his product on an international basis, Perry shifted into overdrive mode. He rose early and retired late, spending the majority of each day ensconced in his studio. He would spend day upon day building rhythms, creating a virtual stockpile on which to voice artists. Other days would be spent entirely on mixing, with hours being devoted to one particular track. As Scratch stayed inside the Black Ark, delving deeper into a world where spiritual vision found an outlet in recorded sound, his behaviour began gradually to shift. The frightful power of strong white rum began increasingly to fuel his creations, sometimes in concert with ganja and sometimes on its own. The high percentage of alcohol in the pure sugar-cane spirit seemed to unleash hidden demons in Scratch – bringing up elements of the past he sought to repress, or perhaps even raising the confused emotions of a troubled ancestral past tainted by slavery. In time, his increasingly drastic behaviour would render him unrecognisable to those most part of his life.

It was around the time that Perry was completing work on *War in a Babylon* that he recorded, engineered, and mixed an album at the Black Ark called *Reggae in America* for a black American Rastafarian singer who went by the name of Lion Zion. In the early '70s, the singer had operated a record shop on the East Coast and was involved in the production of a small reggae magazine; in the mid-'70s, he became based in the city of Oakland, California, located just east of San Francisco. Pauline Morrison met him several times at Percy Chin's record shop in New York and encouraged him to come to Jamaica, but was quite surprised to see him turn up barefoot at the Black Ark in 1976, ready to record an album.

Together with bassist Lloyd Parks, drummer Benbow Creary, rhythm guitarist Filberto Callender, and keyboardist Keith Sterling, Perry created nine 'rockers'-styled rhythms for original songs the Rasta singer had written. The rockers style, based on the use of 'militant' drum patterns, was then seen as the most authentic comtemporary sub-genre of Jamaican roots reggae. The mix was augmented by horn parts from trumpeter David Madden, tenor saxophonist Glen Da Costa and trombonist Vin Gordon, with backing vocals by Barry Llewellyn and Earl Morgan on the most successful numbers.

The album was highly critical of the prevailing American values, with songs like 'American Revolution', 'Arise America', and 'Gas Guzzler' decrying the self-centred nature of the 'me generation' and exposing the hypocrisy and greed on which much of the nation had been founded. Perhaps the most damning number was 'Who Killed The Buffalo', giving vent to fury caused by the actions of 'Buffalo Bill' Cody, one of the supposed heroes of American history. Cody and his like slaughtered the once-plentiful buffalo that roamed the Great Plains, making them an endangered species while simultaneously destroying the civilisation of the Native Americans during the expansion west of the nation. The track was preceded by 'Buffalo Dub', another high-calibre Black Ark dub that showed Perry's mixing artistry in action, revealing also just how tight his session musicians were at this time.

Though all the album's rhythms are equally strong, they are sometimes let down by Lion Zion's somewhat amateurish and lisping vocals, his Americanised twang – often double-tracked – occasionally clashing with the rawness of the Jamaican rhythms (some of which are much closer to the conventional rockers sound than anything else Perry recorded). Although choral overdubs by the National Dance Theatre Singers of Jamaica and the Oakland Black Ensemble hinted at crossover potential, the album's limited issue on the singer's own House of Natty label meant that it was widely distributed. It would soon be a common sight in record-shop bargain bins throughout the San Francisco Bay area, and never enjoyed the widespread availability a larger record company could have ensured.

It was also around the time that *War In A Babylon* was being completed that Perry cut his other deejay album, Prince Jazzbo's *Natty Passing Thru'*. Issued on Black Wax in the UK in limited number in December, the album featured a full-colour drawing of a proud and confrontational dread, with religious invocations on the back cover.

If *Colombia Collie* had been created quickly, then *Natty Passing Thru'* definitely held the brevity of Jazzbo's wit. According to the toaster, the tracks were voiced in about 'one half hour' after Perry summoned Jazzbo to the Black Ark. 'Inna them time there I just love the music. Him play about 16 riddim tracks 'pon a tape, and me just start deejay on top 'til me reach at the bottom.' The resulting album is one of Jazzbo's strongest, his gruff, moaning delivery well suited to Perry's syrupy new rhythms.

In contrast to Jah Lion's *Colombia Collie*, the bulk of *Natty Passing Thru'* was cut on fresh creations laid by Boris Gardiner, Mikey Boo, Chinna Smith, and Keith Sterling. Only a few tracks stemmed from an earlier time, but Jazzbo's consistent delivery and Perry's custom mixing make them seem entirely in place with the rest of the songs. In his lyrics, Jazzbo generally stuck to the serious, giving the disc a pervasive gravity that seldom drops.

The opening track, 'Dread Locks Corner', was also issued as a single in Jamaica on the Truth and Rights label, whose illustration of a soldier harassing a dread represented the frightfully tense nature of the months preceding the 1976 general election. The album also had a fine cut of 'One Step Forward' as 'Ital Corner' and a powerful alternative take of 'Satta' as 'Prophet Live'. The anti-Catholic title track described the torturous journey of a Rastafarian through the Hell of Babylon, Jazzbo straining to express the dreads' tribulation over a stunning new rhythm driven by plaintive horns and Family Man's growling bass (originally recorded for a Dean Fraser vocal called 'Concrete Castle King', whose lyrics were written by Leroy Willis). The rhythm of the anti-greed 'Blood Dunza' seemed like an outtake from *Dub Revolution* in its use of some television dialogue, while 'Story Come To Bump' was a murmuring re-creation of Winston Heywood's 'Long Long Time'. Of the other old rhythms, 'Weeping and Wailing' was perhaps the most successful, with Jazzbo chanting proverbs over one of Perry's brilliant organ work-outs, while 'Live Good Today' and 'Life Is Gonna Easy' made interesting use of the peculiar songs 'I Don't Mind' and 'Life Is A Flower' that Sam Carty had cut for Scratch.

As *Natty Passing Thru'* saw release on Black Wax, it could never achieve in sales what the larger Island releases were capable of shifting, though its rougher edges initially found favour with black listeners in Britain. Its sustained appeal as a cult classic would see it re-packaged in America as *Ital Corner* for Brad Osbourne's Clocktower label in December 1979, and it would later enjoy further re-issues in a variety of formats.

In August, Island released what was by far the most complex Upsetter album in musical terms: *Super Ape* was a tour-de-force of Perry wizardry, weaving musical streams through the various pies Scratch had his fingers in during 1976 to form a startling organic whole of dub unity. Continuing the tradition initiated on *Cloak And Dagger* and *Dub Revolution*, *Super Ape* was a dub album with a difference, hovering somewhere between dub, standard reggae vocal, and experimental jazz. About half of the cuts are raw dubs presented in their purest form, the remainder being near-standard vocals or re-voiced dub tracks with serious jazz leanings.

Its original Jamaican issue surfaced in July as *Scratch the Super Ape* by the Upsetters, clearly naming Perry's latest symbolic incarnation as the frighteningly powerful ape of its title. As evidenced by the dripping lettering that graced Tony Wright's imaginative cover on Island's foreign issue, the Super Ape was straight out of some comic book or horror film; striding with authority through the mists of creation, uprooting trees and flattening all in his wake, the ape was powered by the fat spliff protruding from his hairy palm and the roast fish and cornbread in his stomach. In the top right-hand corner, letters on a square proclaimed 'Dub it up blacker than dread', and the album did not disappoint in the heaviness and strangeness of its mighty dub rhythms.

In addition to the solid rhythms laid down by Mikey Boo, Benbow Creary, Scully Sims, Boris Gardiner, Chinna Smith, and Keith Sterling, the album got much of its shape from the horn section of Bobby Ellis, Dirty Harry Hall, Vin Gordon, and flautist Egbert Evens, with vocals provided on several key tracks by Barry Llewellyn and Earl Morgan. Thus, the opening track 'Zion's Blood', appeared almost as an ordinary vocal tune, with the two Heptones presenting an affirmation of their African heritage over a thicker modulated cut of the 'When Jah Come' rhythm, now laden with searing horns and atmospheric keyboard overdubs atop its driving African beats. 'Croaking Lizard' edged closer to dub with an echoing outtake from Prince Jazzbo's album, a cut of 'Chase The Devil' on which the deejay toasted on diverse subjects, including the nature of the rockers rhythm and the untrustworthy face of Babylon (explored more fully on an Island single version). Like the album itself, the song was titled in reference to another of Scratch's many personas: in addition to being the Super Ape, he was also the Croaking Lizard, a mighty reptile from prehistoric times when dinosaurs roamed the earth, his very croak a form of music. 'Black Vest' was a fully reformed dub cut of 'War In A Babylon' with a fresh horn part, retaining snatches of James Brown's 'Stop The War In A Babylon' and Max Romeo's 'Fire Fe The Vatican' in the mix. 'Underground Root' placed a female chorus atop one of the Upsetter's most mysterious and bass-heavy rhythms, originally developed for a song called 'From Creation'. Cut in vocal form only on dub plate for Brixton sound system operator Lloyd Coxsone, 'From Creation' was incorrectly named as a Junior

Byles tune for many years, but had in fact been voiced by Clive Hylton, a strong tenor singer who also voiced a retribution song called 'Judgement Day' for Perry around the same time. In its re-structured dub form as 'Underground Root', Perry drew out the harshness of the 'From Creation' rhythm by focusing on Chinna Smith's wah-wah, creating spiralling treble patterns against Boris Gardiner's rock-hard bass. Closing out side one was 'Curly Dub,' a dubby instrumental on the edge of jazz on which the superb musicianship of trombonist Vin Gordon, saxophonist Dirty Harry, and flautist Egbert Evans formed a supremely heady backdrop to a religious scat by Scratch.

Side two began with 'Dread Lion', a psychedelic lick of the 'Natty Passing Thru'/'Concrete Castle King' rhythm, here made positively ethereal through melodica and flute overdubs, augmented by interjections from Scratch. Leading the way were the harmonies of Barry Llewellyn and Heptone's Earl Morgan and Leroy Sibbles, chanting 'The dread lion, king of the jungle, king of the forest, here comes natty dread.' 'Three In One' was another spacey vocal chant with vibrant congos from Scully and freaky keyboard licks, while 'Patience' was a fresh instrumental on which Chinna's guitar suggested funk and skanking horns held hints of jazz, but a ghostly toast from some unseen deejay meant that it could only be dub territory the whole project was grounded in. 'Dub Along' replaced the male voices of harmony duo the Blue Bells with snatches of a female chorus, while the closing title track used Barry and Earl's deep tones to express the overall theme of the album over a rhythm punctuated by blasts from Perry on some fife or toy whistle. 'This is the ape man, trodding through creation,' the pair chant, 'are you ready to step with I-man?'

If *Revelation Time* and *War In A Babylon* were reggae concept albums for Max Romeo, *Super Ape* was a dub concept album for Lee Perry, on which he relied on his rhythms to express his broader ideas about nature's powers of endurance. Perry grew in the depths of the country, where the spirit world was more readily acknowledged and his mother's Ettu dancing was one of the more direct reflections of the community's shared African heritage. As Perry entered his forties, such buried influences began to blossom in his work, as the link between man and animal was made symbolically explicit. In the creation of *Super Ape*, Lee Perry was reaching back to the primordial dawning of mankind, celebrating a more natural period when survival was the game, and the divisive destruction of racism and greed were virtually non-existent.

Max Romeo was present during much of the recording of *Super Ape*, and remembered a startled Chris Blackwell being perplexed by Scratch's lackadaisical approach to the primary master tape. 'The tape was hanging like an inch and a half from the reel. Chris Blackwell walk into the studio and said "Holy shit! I've never seen anything like this! That tape's hanging from the reel! Come on Scratch, what's that?" Scratch said "Man, this album is *Super Ape* so it's got to be on a super tape." '

To celebrate his successes with Island and further to proclaim his religious and spiritual beliefs, Scratch had the walls surrounding the studio decorated with huge, multi-coloured murals painted by Rastafarian artist Jah Wise (an associate of Tippertone sound system whose given name was Robert Van Campbell). A portrait of Haile Selassie was placed just above the door so that all would have to 'bow' to Jah upon entering or leaving; to the left of his head was Selassie in his feline form as the Conquering Lion of Judah. Another wall had a life-size mural of the Super Ape, tree and spliff in hand, while the inside of the studio depicted African ancestors in chains and Rastafarian tri-colour flags. As time passed, such images would be altered and re-cast as Perry sought to express different concepts; like the music that was coming from inside the studio, its illustrated walls would seldom remain static. He also erected a sign with a management order by the front gate, proclaiming that the premises included the site of a private house where women and children lived; all who sought to enter were to wait for official permission, and once inside were to refrain from using indecent language.

Though Scratch was concentrating on his own material, he continued to collaborate occasionally with others at the Ark. In May 1976, he voiced some extremely fine material with Dennis Brown for Niney, creating some of the most meaningful and enduring songs of Dennis' consistently strong career: 'Wolf and Leopards' and 'Here I Come'. Niney detailed the process by which the songs were created, using rhythms he had laid at Randy's: 'We voice and mix songs at Black Ark like "Wolf And Leopard"; me and Scratch and Dennis Brown write that song but Scratch write the most of it. I made the rhythm for Sang Hugh, the guy that sing "Rasta No Born Ya"; the song he singing still on tape but never come out. When Sang Hugh reach a certain part of the song it wasn't quite right so he said he want a different rhythm. Me and Scratch come up with the idea of "Wolf And Leopards", and we say Dennis Brown is the right one to sing it. I bring Dennis 'round Scratch, and then we write and voice the song, and one named "Broadway" (a version of George Benson's "On Broadway" mutated to "In Zion") and "Here I Come". "Here I Come" was my idea, I have that song from in my twenties, before "Blood And Fire"; I sing harmonies 'pon it because I know how I did want the song. That rhythm, it's Sly (Dunbar) play that drum, that is a wicked one-drop rhythm. Robbie (Shakespeare) play the bass, that time Robbie was rocking the bass. Those rhythm do at Randy's, but we come to Scratch to mix it. Scratch's studio was four-track but you could get a lot of track out of it; it's a Teac, but it's a different machine – if he hook it up a certain way he can get up to 12 tracks.'

Perry's skilful mixing greatly enhanced the tunes' overall impact, and helped 'Wolf And Leopard' go straight into the Jamaican charts; its UK issue was also highly successful. The popularity of 'Wolf And Leopards' saw I Roy cut a couple of versions onto the rhythm for Niney; 'Step On The Dragon' was an inpenetrable expression of Rasta faith, while 'Maggie Breast' was a quasi-rude bop that began with a limerick about Perry's insatiable sexual appetite: 'In the days of old when man was bold, and women were duly invented, man used to . . . go on quite contented, but in the days of soul when Neil Armstrong discovered the moon and girls were duly invented, man would have take his things and stick it with pins because Scratch could never be contented!" Dennis Brown subsequently broke from Niney for a period on the instigation of a more lucrative partnership with Joe Gibbs, so the issue of 'Here I Come' was delayed until January 1977. The mix on this single was all the more striking through its incorporation of a frothy phasing, while its version side, 'Head Shot', featured a plaintive trumpet melody from Bobby Ellis. I Roy also toasted the 'Here I Come' rhythm as 'Jah Come Here', his smooth delivery describing everyday runnings among Jamaican immigrants in London.

It was also in May 1976 that Junior Murvin first appeared at the Black Ark. Murvin Smith Junior was born in the town of Swift River in Portland some time after World War II. His father died when he was very young, so his mother put him in the care of his great-grandmother in Port Antonio before emigrating to the UK, where she found work as a nurse; one of his closest friends from boyhood days was Derrick 'Watty' Burnett. From the age of six, Murvin was fascinated by singing, and showed a surprising command of a range of vocal pitches from an early age. He used to imitate the deep baritone of singers like Louis Armstrong and Billy Eckstein, and could also emulate Nat King Cole and Sam Cooke, but it was the falsetto tenor of Curtis Mayfield that formed his greatest inspiration and vocal model. Though Murvin was a shy youth, encouragement from teachers at Port Antonio Junior and Senior Schools gave him the impetus to perform on local talent shows, and though singing did not seem a practical occupation, it remained his primary fixation.

When Murvin was 13, his great-grandmother passed away and he moved to his grandmother's home in Montego Bay. He began attending Montego Bay Technical School, training to be a mechanic, but his teachers and peers could see his true talent lay in singing, and encouraged him to pursue a singing career. After an aunt in the States sent him a guitar in the mid-'60s, he was taught to play by a friend named Raleigh and began writing songs under a tamarind tree in Glendevon. He also began performing on Christmas Morning concerts at Montego Bay's Palladium Theatre with Errol Webster (a.k.a. ET Webster). Seeking to further his musical career, Murvin left Port Antonio and moved to Kingston around 1967, ending up in the musical hotbed of Trench Town.

He passed through the Hippy Boys in their early formation, but left after a few performances with the group to sing for Derrick Harriott and Sonia Pottinger. He gave Harriott 'Solomon', the first song he had ever written, and Harriott's smooth rendition was a lasting success. Murvin voiced a number of other tunes for Harriott in this period as Junior Soul, including 'Big Boy', 'How Can A Man Have One Wife', and 'Chatty Chatty', and also wrote Harriott's Festival competition entry for 1968, 'Tang Tang Festival'; shortly after, he recorded 'Jennifer', 'Slipping', and 'Miss Cushy' for Sonia Pottinger. He then took a long break from recording, first upon joining the Falcons with fellow vocalists Dennis Brown, Noel Brown, and Cynthia Richards.

Along with the Mighty Vikings and Dragonaires, the Falcons was one of Jamaica's most popular live acts at this time, and Murvin gained much valuable experience in their ranks. However, Murvin gradually tired of the stresses of Kingston life, and eventually returned to Port Antonio in the mid '70s, where he joined a band called Young Experience. Led by trumpet player Bobby Ellis and featuring another singer named Carole Brown, the band toured Cuba and performed at high-profile events in Jamaica, including a birthday party of Beverley Manley, wife of Prime Minister Michael Manley.

When Young Experience showed signs of breaking up in 1976, Junior Murvin began devoting his energy to writing new songs. At the peculiar Folly ruins of a grandiose American banker's house perched above the peninsula east of Port Antonio, Murvin wrote much of his strongest material, in which he was now beginning to address the political and social upheavals that were clearly having adverse effects on Jamaica.

Junior noted that he knew that these new songs were ripe for recording, and made his way to the Black Ark after receiving curious or divine direction. 'While I was singing in Young Experience, I took time out from rehearsals. Sometimes I go by Folly ruins, sit by the sea, punch my tape (recorder) and sing what is happening, and when I come home, I put verses to it. When the band break up, I get a vision to carry me to Lee Perry in Kingston, because he was a very hard-core producer. I just get a vision and I went straight in with it.'

Though the Afro-hairstyled Murvin first appeared at the Ark with his guitar and a batch of fresh songs that May, Junior explained it was not the first time he had tried to convince Scratch to record him; nearly ten years earlier, he had sung for Perry in the yard of Coxsone's studio. 'I auditioned at Studio One with a song by Lloyd Price named "I've Got The Blues", and he told me all I needed was one more verse. He sent me to sit under a mango tree, and I got hungry and went away. In those days Peter (Tosh) used to play guitar and Bob (Marley), and Scratch was the audition manager.'

When he listened to Murvin's new material at the Black Ark, one song in particular caught Perry's ear. Like Max Romeo's 'Sipple Out Deh', Junior Murvin's 'Police and Thieves' spoke of the bloodshed and anarchy brought on by Jamaica's desperate social conditions, exacerbated by the tensions and upheavals of a particularly divisive election year.

'Police and thieves in the street
Fighting the nation with their guns and ammunition
Police and thieves in the street
Scaring the nation with their guns and ammunition
From Genesis to Revelation

The next generation will be, hear me
All the crimes committed day by day
No one trying to stop them in any way
All the peace makers turned war officers
Hear what I say . . . '

Though Perry felt the original lyrics needed slight amendments, he began to lay the rhythm straight away. As Junior Murvin recalled, 'He said he needed likkle more words, so we went and put in couple more words and Boris Gardiner lay the rhythm along with Ernest Ranglin and Sly (Dunbar), Keith Sterling on keyboards and Joe Cooper, an old friend from Port Antonio; he was a very good organist who usually play with the Mighty Vikings.'

In addition to the firm musicianship, harmony vocals by Barry Llewellyn and Earl Morgan again gave the song a particular texture, their wordless chorus helping to ensure its success. But it was the song's perceptive lyrics that made it stand out over all, its imagistic commentary on society's symbiotic parasites striking a note with listeners far and wide.

Everyone present at the Black Ark knew 'Police And Thieves' would be a hit, so Perry arranged for one of the 'big three' record companies in Jamaica to handle its initial release. The song's first Jamaican issue (as 'Police And Thief') thus appeared on Federal's Wildflower subsidiary. Backed with the appropriately named 'Grumbling Dub', which reduced the vocal to stabs of echoed murmuring, the single was an immediately strong seller in Jamaica.

Chris Blackwell recalled being struck by the topical nature of 'Police and Thieves', having first heard the song after passing through a roadblock. 'I remember going down to his studio one time and we just got stopped for no reason on the way, have an M16 shoved in our face by a young police guy. When I went in the studio, they were doing "Police And Thieves".'

Island Records issued the single in the UK in July, where it received widespread airplay and surprising critical accolades in the normally sarcastic music press; the song was also a hit in the USA, where it helped reggae to make major inroads in disparate parts of the nation, particularly in the more liberal coastal cities.

Part of the song's success in the UK was linked to the Carnival, the annual celebration of the Caribbean presence in Britain held at the end of August in the West London districts of Notting Hill and Ladbroke Grove. The Carnival was born largely from the tension that arose between black immigrants and their reluctant white hosts, many of whom sought to exclude black people from British society. The Carnival thus became a site of resistance and rebellion through its open display of traditions upheld by those of African descent in the Caribbean, contributing to an emerging hybrid culture through a dynamic transformation of the Dickensian drabness of London's streets. It would remain a source of conflict between an increasingly vocal black population and the hostile and repressive authorities who upheld specifically racist social policies; police and local politicians would repeatedly attempt to stop the Carnival once it began attracting a large number of participants, but their efforts to curtail the two-day street fair would be in vain. It remains at present the second-largest annual street festival in the world after the Rio Carnival in Brazil.

The earliest forms of public displays of Caribbean culture in London date back to Notting Hill's race riots of 1958, in which black residents were viciously set upon by gangs of white 'Teddy boys', resulting in the death of a black man, Kelso Cochrane. It was around this time that Caribbean immigrants began to gather annually in Saint Stephen's Gardens to sing calypsos and traditional songs on Marcus Garvey's birthday, largely in response to white racists who sought to render them invisible. Further public events were organised in the early 1960s by Trinidadian radical Claudia Jones, including steel-band concerts and costume competitions, in an effort to give black immigrants in London a more confident footing and validate Caribbean cultural expression. A community action group was running a local children's playground near Westbourne Park around this time, and a number of steel bands became based at the premises by the mid-'60s. One member of the community group, a white Englishwoman named Mrs Lazlett, decided to hold a street procession on the bank holiday weekend of August 1965, in which steel bands performed and children paraded in costume; this successful street fair marked the unofficial birth of the Notting Hill Carnival.

Between 1965 and 1972, the Carnival continued informally, with a leadership structure gradually established by some of the most prominent members of London's black communities; its growing popularity saw a crowd of about 3000 celebrants attend in 1972. In this early phase, the Carnival was geared largely towards the Trinidadian immigrant community; calypso acts and steel bands were the exclusive musical contribution of the festival, and its procession was modelled after the annual Easter Carnival in Port of Spain. It was re-structured to have a broader appeal to other Caribbean communities in 1973 – initially after a boycott by local steel bands – and attracted an estimated crowd of 50,000 participants after public advertising. Further diversification saw attendance jump to 100,000 the following year, as reggae acts like the Cimarons began performing. However, the increased popularity of the event came with a price, as an increasingly nervous and resentful establishment sought to quell this expression of black spirit. In 1975, the police responded to the Carnival's success by increasing their former presence of 100 officers to a full 10,000-strong contingent, and what many perceived as police hostility against black revellers culminated in small-scale disturbances.

1976 proved to be the most explosive Carnival ever held, with over-zealous police arresting and injuring participants with a virulent fervour, their destructive aggression laden with corrosive fear and hatred. It was against a backdrop of thousands of white police in riot gear obstructing and confronting joyous crowds of poor and downtrodden black people that 'Police And Thieves' was booming from every sound system in the Carnival, the confrontational mode of events transposed from Kingston to London with a startling similarity. It was the unfortunate reality of police suppression that made 'Police And Thieves' strike a chord with so many listeners in Britain, where it stayed in the Top Ten of *Melody Maker*'s reggae chart for 23 weeks in a row; in addition to being named as 'Reggae Single of the Year' in *Echoes*, it was also named as sixth-best single in any category in *NME*'s end-of-year chart.

The widespread popularity of 'Police and Thieves' made it inevitable that further versions would follow on the same rhythm, and before long Perry cut Jah Lion on the more overtly political 'Soldier And Police War'. This version began with Bongo Herman's laboured breathing in imitation of one who had been chased; the version side, 'Dub Of Justice', featured Herman's scattered congo drumming. Island issued Jah Lion's cut a couple of months later, backed with 'Magic Touch', an instrumental take led by the searing tenor saxophone of Glen DaCosta. When the song continued to enjoy popularity in the UK, Island eventually issued all four cuts on a 12-inch 45. Further cuts on the rhythm would follow in late 1976 and early 1977; meanwhile, Junior Murvin began cutting more of the material he had written at Folly ruins with Lee Perry at the Black Ark.

Around the time that *Super Ape* got its finishing touches, Perry also began cutting material with the re-united Heptones, who had done little recording as a trio since Leroy Sibbles' emigration to Canada in 1973. The Heptones were initially formed as a street-corner group around 1958 by Earl Morgan and Barry Llewellyn, then residents of Trench Town. Born in Jones Town in November, 1945, Morgan's father was a tailor and mother a higgler; from the age of four he lived in Trench Town, where he befriended Barry (born 1947) as a teenager. In the early 1960s, Leroy Sibbles (born 1949) had a rival street-corner group in Newland Town formed with two friends, Claire and Winston, and when the trio clashed with the duo in a street-corner contest, Sibbles was so impressed with Barry and Earl that he joined forces with them. A taller youth with something of a more readily identifiable voice, Sibbles started to become proficient on guitar through the guidance of Brother Huntley and Carrott, two Rastas who had a house in Trench Town, where the group would congregate to smoke herb and write songs. Sibbles gradually became leader of the Heptones, though all three members are lead singers who handle their own material.

In 1966, the Heptones were brought to Ken Lack by Sydney 'Luddy' Crooks of the Pioneers, and their debut single 'Gun Man Coming To Town' was fairly successful until Delroy Wilson's 'Dancing Mood' killed its popularity. Duke Reid and Leslie Kong showed no interest in the group, so they went one Sunday to Studio One – not long after Lee Perry had left Coxsone's stable

– for an auditon supervised by Ken Boothe and Bibi Seaton. They would remain under Coxsone's wing until 1971, recording some of the most popular and lasting material of the late rock steady and early reggae periods under the supervision of Jackie Mittoo.

After leaving Studio One, the group cut strong material for Joe Gibbs and subsequently recorded for various producers, first working with Lee Perry on a cover version of Billy Stewart's 'I Do Love You'; cut with the Soul Syndicate band, the song reached number four on the Jamaican charts upon release. Leroy's re-location to Canada would lead to a period of inactivity for the group, but in 1976 they burst back onto the scene with the strong *Night Food* album, cut at Harry J for Island Records.

Of the material they began cutting with Lee Perry in the summer of 1976, the first to be released was 'Sufferer's Time', a protest number led by Barry in which the 'sufferers' of the ghetto demanded their rights to decent housing and transportation. Though a slow and rootsy version of the song was issued first, a faster alternate version was also voiced at the same time, which Earl Morgan recalled was aimed at cracking the foreign market. 'Lee Perry is a man who swap everything. You do a thing and he say, "Hear me now, I don't like that one there, that one there likkle slow you know. Give me a likkle faster one, 'cause this one is for the foreign, that one is for local; give me a foreign one, upbeat," so we do two version of it: a foreign version and a local version.' In the end, Island declined to issue the fast vocal cut, making the odd decision to place the fast dub on the B-side of the slow vocal.

In Jamaica, Perry immediately followed up 'Sufferer's Time' with 'Sufferer's Heights', a clever deejay cut delivered in stuttering fashion by one Junior Dread; Perry also cut the toaster onto a fresh rhythm led by a spongy keyboard for a tale of the prolonged tribulations facing the ghetto populace called 'A Wah Dat'.

1976 was also the year that John Martyn appeared at Lee Perry's studio, the first of a few open-minded white rock artists to record there. Born in London in 1948, Martyn was raised in Scotland. He returned to London in his late teens to find work at a factory sorting parts; he was also playing folk music and writing songs. In the late 1960s, Martyn gave a performance at the Folk Barge, a floating club moored on the western edge of London at Kingston-upon-Thames, that impressed a talent scout named Theo Johnson. Johnson brought Martyn to the attention of Chris Blackwell, who made him one of the first non-Caribbean acts to be signed to Island Records.

By the mid-'70s, Martyn had switched to a more experimental form of progressive rock, resulting in a wider audience but also increased disillusionment with the music industry. Chris Blackwell suggested Martyn take a vacation, and brought the guitarist, his wife Beverley, and children Spencer, Wesley, and Mhairi to Jamaica in mid-summer, 1976; the family stayed at Blackwell's vast estate in Strawberry Hill, a tranquil oasis towering above the inferno of Kingston. Martyn was armed with his cherry-red 1965 Gibson SG and an Electro Harmonix phaser when Blackwell first brought him to the Black Ark; he had also been exploring the application of echoplex to guitar in his work. Martyn and Scratch thus had a certain affinity despite the vastly different spheres in which they operated; impressed by his guitar playing and genial demeanour, Perry requested that Martyn provide some fresh licks on his sessions. Martyn duly complied, structuring riffs around the loping beat supplied by Horsemouth Wallace.

Martyn remained in Jamaica a full eight months, dividing his time between Strawberry Hill and Negril; he was summoned back to Perry's studio on several other occasions. Martyn confirmed laying guitar riffs on a song called 'Oh Me Oh My' at one such session, though he had difficulty remembering who sang it; the song surfaced on an Upsetter single in 1976, credited to Bree Daniel. Martyn recalled adding guitar to a Max Romeo track, but could not remember its title; he also noted that the musicians were enthralled by his phaser sound, and several made desperate offers for the unit. Through their mutual connection with Island, Perry and Martyn would later collaborate on other creations outside Jamaica.

When *Sounds'* reggae specialist Vivien Goldman visited the Black Ark in October, she was astounded by the amount of material being created there. Goldman likened the studio to a 'conveyor belt for harmony groups', and described Scratch as being very focused and serious about his work; she also remembered evening screenings of kung-fu films and several still shots of Bruce Lee adorning the studio walls.

Though he could have a short temper when musicians failed to muster the sound he was searching for, Scratch would dance continually while in the control booth, relentlessly driven by the force of the music. Goldman also noted that although the studio was orderly and typically free from conflict, Perry often vented his spleen at the studio idlers who would loiter on the premises without purpose; as time went by, he would find their presence increasingly bothersome.

Perry created other strong singles in late 1976, including 'Mr Cop'. One of the strongest statements of Gregory Isaacs' career, the song directly demanded that over-zealous police cease their harassment of weed-smoking dreads. Overseas distribution by Micron the following year saw the song shift significant numbers in Canada, and the hit looked like the start of a firm musical partnership between the 'Cool Ruler' and the Upsetter. 'Mr Cop' also found its way onto Micron's *Extra Classic* album. Unfortunately, it seems to be about the only Isaacs number to have surfaced from the Black Ark, although another song called 'Set Back' is also said to have been recorded; despite laying the odd backing vocal on Perry's material in 1977, Isaacs was repelled by Perry's nightly screening of porno flicks and quickly quit the Ark due to 'too much fornication' on the premises. [3]

By far the most personally vindictive number Scratch cut in this period was 'White Belly Rat', a musical barb aimed at Bunny Lee after another of their numerous fall-outs. Perry initially asked Max Romeo to sing the tune, but Romeo had no wish to be in the middle of their quarrel and declined. 'I wouldn't, because it was singing about Bunny Lee. Bunny Lee is supposed to be the white belly rat. He and Scratch always have a feud, I don't know why, but even now, they are friends today and they are enemies tomorrow, friends the other day, and enemies the other day.'

When Romeo refused, Perry had a young singer known as Earl Sixteen have a go at the rhythm. Born Earl Daley in Kingston in 1958, Sixteen began his singing career by hanging out on Waltham Park Road in his teenage years, singing versions of Chi-Lites and James Brown songs. At 15 he entered a singing contest at the Bohemia Club in Half Way Tree, beating Michael Rose (later lead singer of Black Uhuru), Junior Moore (later lead singer of the Tamlins), Joy White, and Sabrina Williams with his version of the Chi-Lites' 'Peek A Boo'. While still at St Andrew Technical School, he joined a group called the Flaming Phonics, and eventually performed around the island backing Big Youth, the Mighty Diamonds, Burning Spear, and Dennis Brown in the early 1970s. The group laid the rhythm track of a song at Treasure Isle, but Duke Reid's gun antics frightened them off and they never returned to voice it; instead, they cut material for Herman Chin-Loy just before the group broke up in 1974. Sixteen went on to record solo material for Alphonso Bailey's Globe International label and for both Joe Gibbs and Derrick Harriott before joining Boris Gardiner's band, with whom the Flaming Phonics once shared a bill in Spanish Town.

When Earl Sixteen joined Boris' group, the Boris Gardiner Happening consisted of Boris Gardiner, Paul Douglas, Keith Sterling and Willie Lindo, with Errol 'Bagga' Walker also on vocals. Most of the group members were regularly used as session musicians at Lee Perry's studio, and it was while with the group that Earl Sixteen first came into contact with Lee Perry.

Though Sixteen respected Boris Gardiner's musical versatility and gentle nature, they were worlds apart in terms of political and spiritual outlook. Gardiner groomed his band to be distinctly uptown, while Sixteen was living in the ghetto and hanging out with revoutionary dreads, including Augustus Pablo's young protégé Hugh Mundell. When the band played a socialite nurses' ball at the prestigious Oceana Hotel, Sixteen eschewed his regulation Cariba suit for sufferer's flares and flying locks, and found himself fired from the band as a result. From late 1976, he was often present at the Black Ark, observing the runnings and hoping that Scratch would make use of his vocal talents.

When Scratch eventually gave Sixteen a try at voicing 'White Belly Rat', he was dissatisfied with the results, and chose to voice it himself in his own readily identifiable style. Although Scratch never issued the first voicing of the rhythm, Earl Sixteen remained a studio regular, and would later voice a couple of notable singles with Scratch that would greatly raise the singer's profile.

Though Island chose not to issue some of the singles Perry provided them with in 1976, like Junior Dread's 'Sufferer's Heights' or Devon Irons' 'Catch Vampire', they did issue the outrageously filthy 'Big Cocky Wally', an inverse re-cut of the 'Big Pussy Sally' calypso by Fay Bennett; though the song was too rude to have much impact, its heavy breathing and excessive dub showed that Perry had no plans to tone down his material for international release.

Perry was also engineering material in this period for the Meditations, an exemplary roots trio that would later work with Scratch on several stunning releases. Singer Highland 'Dobby' Dobson had been producing the group, and it was he who first brought them to the Black Ark for the recording of three songs that would appear on their debut album, *Message From The Meditations*.

The Meditations were three individual vocalists with exceptionally strong harmony skills: Ansel Cridland, Danforth Clarke, and Winston Watson. Born in Lambeth Pen, Westmoreland on February 11, 1951, Ansel Cridland had aspirations to become a jockey in his youth, but later concentrated on singing in the Kingston housing development called Majestic Gardens. He formed the Linkers with Oswald Grey in 1969, recording their debut 'Say Say' for Lloyd the Matador; when Grey quit, the group became a trio with Constantine Brown and 'another brother we call Peedo', cutting material for Sir JJ before splitting up around 1973. By this time, Cridland had become friendly with Danny Clarke, who then lived in nearby Madison Gardens – a notoriously rough ghetto patch known as Baktu. Clarke was well connected to the music scene: after recording for Lee Perry in the early '70s as a member of the Righteous Flames/Hurricanes, Clarke cut a few songs for smaller producers, none of which made much impact. When Cridland and Clarke began rehearsing together, Cridland was a partial member of Winston Heywood and the Hombres, one of the first groups to come out of Madison Gardens, while Clarke was trying to start something with Lloyd Forrester, who soon became a member of the Jays; Clarke had also worked with members of the Hombres on material cut for GG as the Meditations.

By 1974, Ansel Cridland and Danny Clarke were recording together, first on Cridland's self-produced 'Sitting On The Sidewalk'. It was around the time that Cridland was recording 'Bongo Man' that he and Danny came into closer contact with Winston Watson, a short young man with a distinctly high-pitched voice. Born in Trench Town on February 7, 1954, Watson's father was a stage magician. When the Linkers split up in 1973, a mutual friend brought Watson to Cridland, and though Cridland felt Watson did not have full control of his vocal abilities when they first met, he could see that his peer was capable of a unique and striking delivery. In late 1974, the three collaborated on Cridland's 'Woman Is Like A Shadow' at Channel One, but Joseph Hookim was dissatisfied with the song and initially held it back.

In early 1975, while Cridland's tune was still in the can, Clarke heard from his old friend Stranger Cole that Dobby Dobson was holding auditions at Federal. Dobson began recording material with all three singers, eventually resulting in the solidification of the Meditations with a string of hit single releases. Once their official formation was finalised, Dobson began compiling an album of their material and arranged for them to record three songs at the Black Ark: Danny Clarke's evocative 'Rastaman Prayer', Winston Watson's contemplative 'There Must Be A First Time' and Ansel Cridland's overtly political 'Running From Jamaica'. It was this latter song that proved to be the biggest hit.

Like Max Romeo's 'Sipple Out Deh' and many of the year's other hard-hitting songs, 'Running from Jamaica' took its inspiration from specific events connected to the upcoming 1976 election, as Ansel Cridland explained. ' "Running From Jamaica" is from election time in '76, when I see what was happening in Jamaica. I no believe in politricks, 'cause politricks is what them use to overthrow Jah, that's why I say the things them that I see. One party say, "Plant food" and one party say, "Don't plant food because you send your pickney a doctor" and all them things. The other party was trying to enlighten the people so that the people could read and write, but some want to keep people inna the same runnings so it cause a conflict. Now election coming up and people start to sell out and run away. I sorry at the time I didn't have two shillings, I could have a good home right now because I see some nice house that sell out for little or nothing, because them never want to stand up to the struggle. The way I really see it, to run left Jamaica and come inna any foreign land come live, it's slavery again and this is torment more than anything for your mind. In Jamaica you can dig a hole and plant food, cocoa in your back yard or callaloo and you can live, but up here (USA) you have nowhere fe plant nothing and everything you buy is a tax 'pon you. That is how the song come about.'

As ever, Scratch's skilful mixing and arrangement gave the songs an added edge. Mikey Boo's pounding rolls propelled the rhythms above Boris Gardiner's melodic bass, with the overall impact completed by interesting guitar riffs from Robert 'Billy' Johnson (brother of Tony Johnson, who had previously played keyboards with Burning Spear and Soul Syndicate); the songs helped ensure the long-lasting popularity of the disc.

Lee Perry also worked with Bob Marley on a few significant creations that surfaced towards the end of 1976. Among their collaborations were a couple of beatbox experiments that were cut at the Black Ark, though exactly when remains unclear; although the minimalist 'Rainbow Country' was pressed on dub plate for Jack Ruby's sound system in Ocho Rios around this time (also surfacing in England on dub plates obtained by Lloyd Coxsone and other sound system operators), it toyed with themes that were also used on Marley's 'Roots Rock Reggae' and was thus almost certainly voiced before the *Rastaman Vibration* album sessions.

'Rainbow Country' was a free and breezy affirmative number with a minimal rhythm driven by Family Man's powerful bass, embellished by blasts from the Zap Pow horns and subtle conga drumming. Similar instrumentation was used on Marley's early Black Ark cut of 'Natural Mystic', seemingly created at the same time. This early take was made more eerie than the later version on Marley's *Exodus* album by the inclusion of a haunting male chorus that Scratch overdubbed at a later session with the Meditations; Marley was not present when the harmonies were laid. Though never officially completed, clandestine issues of both songs surfaced from 1983 through Enzo Hamilton, a French record executive who obtained cuts of the songs from Pauline Morrison.

The most notable Bob Marley song to emerge from the Black Ark towards the end of 1976 was an alternative cut of 'Smile Jamaica', a song that would become the theme for a free concert the Wailers were going to give the Jamaican public on December 5; according to Judy Mowatt, Marley originally wrote the song at the request of the Jamaican Tourist Board. Many conflicting accounts have been given of the circumstances surrounding the concert, though various complications connected to it clearly had drastic repercussions.

In November 1975, the Wailers played a benefit concert at the National Stadium with Stevie Wonder for the Jamaican Institute For The Blind. After Wonder donated half his fee to the Institute, Marley began to think of organising a free concert for the people of Jamaica as a way of giving something back to the nation. The Wailers' busy touring and recording schedule meant that nothing was organised until October 1976, when some PNP heavies requested that the group play a free concert on December 5, sponsored by the Ministry of Culture; initially, the gig was to be held on the grounds of the Prime Minister's offices at Jamaica House, but was quickly moved to the larger National Heroes Circle to make its governmental links less obvious.

When the Wailers agreed to perform at the event, they had already cut two separate versions of 'Smile Jamaica'. The better-known official version, recorded at Harry J, was a slower and more rounded cut with the full Zap Pow horn section and a broader vocal arrangement, and it was this version that received widespread radio airplay in Jamaica, unlike much of the Wailers' more militant work. The other was recorded with Lee Perry at the Black Ark, a strictly up-tempo version driven by phased keyboards and modulated guitar, with some fine Niyabinghi congos peppering Carly's quick beats; mid-way through the song, Marley begins a scat over the punchy harmonies of the I-Threes. Like the fast version of the Heptones' 'Sufferer's Time', the Black Ark cut of 'Smile Jamaica' was raw and rootsy, its fast pace and minimalism setting it apart from much of the contemporary roots music then being made.

As Judy Mowatt pointed out, each work is noteworthy in its own right. 'The two songs sound different, and I think the different recordings are two great recordings in themselves. You can't say you like this one and you don't like that one, you just love both of them.' 'We respect Scratch for his expertise and his talent,' Rita Marley added, 'it was always exciting at his studio.'

Former Gatherers member Sangie Davis also noted that the circumstances of the Black Ark cut inadvertently led to his greater involvement in subsequent Wailers material: 'Bob did a version of "Smile Jamaica" at Harry J, but him come to me and say "Boy, me want to change it up." Me and him go down to Scratch with the idea and did the next one. When Scratch see me and Bob him say "Nice, Sangie!", him glad, and him tell Bob how me wicked, Bob must stay with me and me must stick 'mongst Bob. After that, I see Scratch late one night when a brethren go to Ethiopia and me and Bob out at the airport. Scratch tell Bob, "Stick with him, 'cause he can write couple tunes likkle good." Scratch and Alan Cole recommend me to Bob and in the later days of Bob, me and him used to move close. Me get to write few tune for him, even songs that never release yet: "Jingling Keys", "She Used To Call me Daddy" and "Babylon Feel This One".'

Depite the success of the 'Smile Jamaica' single and the generally positive concept behind the event, the PNP's immediate manipulation of the situation caused many to question its validity: not long after the 'Smile Jamaica' concert had been publicised, the government set the election date for December 15, a mere ten days after the music festival. The public was thus bound to equate the two events together, and see the Wailers' performance at 'Smile Jamaica' as a direct expression of support for the incumbent PNP. What was meant to be an expression of appreciation for the people was now taking a concretely political slant. As Family Man Barrett put it, 'We were asked for a day to give our people a nice show, because we usually spend most of the time touring. Shortly after we get our date – BOOM! – the campaign was set for the same time, so people been looking at the thing differently.'

It was particularly the opposition JLP who looked at the upcoming 'Smile Jamaica' concert with increasing displeasure, and when anonymous threatening calls were made to the Wailers' headquarters at 56 Hope Road in New Kingston, a group of PNP gunmen who called themselves the 'Echo Squad' were dispatched to stand guard at the premises for the week preceding the event. Many close to the group suggested they should wait to perform until after the election, but Marley insisted the Wailers appear as scheduled. The group thus continued to rehearse for the event as usual – with the exception of Marcia Griffiths, who used the pretext of a non-existent performing engagement to exit the island after Judy Mowatt spoke of an ominous dream in which a man was stoning three birds to death.

On the evening of Friday, December 3, Chris Blackwell passed through the Black Ark on his way to 56 Hope Road, where he was to meet a director to discuss the filming of the 'Smile Jamaica' concert. He found Lee Perry working on a powerful new song called 'Dreadlocks In Moonlight' (a.k.a. 'Big Neck Police'), which Perry said he had written for Bob Marley to record.

Using a rhythm that was stylistically patterned after 'Police And Thieves',' Perry sang in highly symbolic terms of the failure of police intimidation to deter the faithful from their chosen course of righteousness, his quiet delivery holding much emotion:

'A time to sow, why not time to reap? Yes my friend
The seed you sow that's what you shall reap
You light a fire to burn this niya but it no work out, you're
                                                    just a weak out
You send your big neck police friend fe come cool I up,
                                                    but it no work
For Jah Jah walk right in and cool up the scene, you get a jerk
For they that put their trust in Jah shall be like Mount Zion high
That shall never removeth but abideth forever
The knife that stick the sheep a go stick the goat, do you hear?
How you gonna feel when the knife is at your throat?
For sowing bring reaping, and reaping is harvest
The seed that you sow, that's what you shall reap
Jah is I light and salvation, whom shall I fear?
Jah the protector, Jah a firelight, of whom shall I be afraid?
Hypocrite in a broad day light, parasite in a dim light
Dreadlocks in moonlight, baldhead at sunrise . . . '

Though Perry's cut was meant to be a guideline for Bob, Blackwell was taken by the power of Perry's rendition, and offered to have Island release it as a single. Like 'Roast Fish And Cornbread', Island's issue of 'Dreadlocks In Moonlight' would not see much in terms of sales, Perry's individual vocal approach failing to find the broad appeal that Marley managed abroad, but the two songs remain particular favourites of Blackwell himself. Blackwell remembered with fondness observing Perry working on the track: 'I sat in a lot with him on sessions, a particular one was a major event in my life. I remember being in the studio watching him work. He is absolutely the master to me in terms of the production of Jamaican music, music which I think will have the most long-lasting value. The particular track came out as "Dreadlocks In Moonlight", he said it was a demo for Bob and I said, "You should do it yourself, I just love the way you sing it as it is. I think it's great, but I don't want to take it because I have to go to a rehearsal at Hope Road." For him to do a few mixes, they take hours.'

In the end, Blackwell decided to stay while Perry mixed the tune, possibly saving his own life in the process. When Blackwell went off into the night, Lee Perry returned to work on a Junior Murvin track with Earl Morgan and Barry Llewellyn; their session was interrupted when a friend burst in with shocking news. As Earl Morgan recalled, 'That night we was recording with Junior Murvin at Lee Perry's studio, somebody come in and tell we, "Them just shot Bob Marley." We had just finished voicing the tune and me and Lee Perry and Barry drive up to UC, look 'pon the man and say "Wha'ppen?" and him say, "Jah Live." It was an experience.'

Seven gunmen – said to be from the JLP stronghold of Tivoli Gardens – had sneaked into Hope Road during a break in rehearsals around 9 pm after all members of the Echo Squad had mysteriously vanished. They emptied an array of home-made bullets into various rooms from an assortment of weaponry, critically wounding Marley's manager Don Taylor; a bullet grazed Bob's chest and landed in his arm, while another lodged in Rita Marley's head. When Scratch and the Black Ark entourage came to the University College Hospital that night, they found Bob upright on a bench, wrapped in bandages and covered in blood. Michael Manley appeared and put Marley in the care of security forces, and Perry and other friends took their leave.

No one has ever been charged with the attack, and the circumstances behind it remain unclear. It is generally believed that JLP gunmen carried out the shooting, perhaps on direct orders by Seaga himself; some have suggested that the incident was meant to be a warning rather than a murder attempt, as the professional assailants wounded several but killed none. Others have linked it to a racetrack scam that various Tuff Gong associates were involved in, including Marley's former manager and close friend, Alan 'Skill' Cole; various other rumours also circulated involving ganja and cocaine rip-offs.

Whatever the actual cause of the events, most of the Wailers showed extraordinary courage and dedication by choosing to go through with the 'Smile Jamaica' concert a mere two days after the shooting – especially Bob, who as the main target was most vulnerable, and Rita, who appeared on stage in her hospital gown, having been discharged a short time before taking the stage. In following through with the 'Smile Jamaica' performance, Bob Marley gave the politicians and their lowly thugs a powerful message: he would not be manipulated by politics, even if the refusal to do so might kill him. He was born a man of the people and a free spirit, and so he would remain; though his siding with the sufferers may have seen him leaning towards socialism, his religious beliefs had him claiming to be apolitical. If the attempt on Marley's life was indeed a JLP ambush, it backfired badly; ten days after the event, the PNP won a confident majority in the polls, ending a prolonged and bloody election battle that had seen over 200 killed.

Not long after the 'Smile Jamaica' concert, the Wailers fled the country, beginning what would be a long period of self-imposed exile for Bob Marley. They spent a month in the Bahamas just chilling out, Marley cavorting with Cindy Brakespeare, his most prominent girl friend and then holder of the Miss World title. They then travelled on to London in early January 1977 to begin working on the *Exodus* album at Island's recording studio in Basing Street, located in the heart of Ladbroke Grove.

In the spring and summer of 1977, Lee Perry maintained a hectic recording schedule that saw releases flying thick and fast. It was the year the 12-inch extended-play format gripped Jamaica – confusingly known as the 'disco mix', in emulation of American dance music EPs – and while Perry was in Kingston testing the limitations of the format, Island was staggering his album releases abroad. Of the dozen or so songs he recorded with the Heptones, ten of the strongest were collected as the album *Party Time*, issued in the UK and USA by Island in March 1977. *Party Time* mixed Black Ark re-cuts of material they first cut at Studio One with some inspired originals, placing a couple of love songs between grave expressions of protest. Musically speaking, the album veered past the predominant rockers style to present an upbeat, guitar-based sound, with Willie Lindo's lead lines placed over Fil Callender's regulated rhythm (with Tony Chin providing rhythm on some tracks). 'Ronnie Bop' Williams, who had briefly returned to Jamaica after several years of residence in Britain, gave further augmentation on 'phased guitar'; shortly after working on the album, he emigrated permanently to Canada. Drummers Mikey Boo and Sly Dunbar kept the pace upbeat, and bassists Boris Gardiner and Mikey Zappow kept the rhythms heavy, while keyboard interplay between Keith Sterling and Winston Wright was virtually buried in the mix. Providing the swing on many of the tracks were David Madden, Glen DaCosta and Vin Gordon of the Zap Pow horns, with Scully providing Niyabinghi percussion at select moments. The vocal arrangements gave a passing nod to the funkier side of Philly soul, keeping the overall scope vaguely within the international appeal instigated by the *Night Food* album.

Of the re-cut material, the title track made far more use of all three Heptones' voices than either the Studio One original or Phil Pratt's re-cut, Mikey Boo's pounding drum rolls raising the tempo to fever pitch. The tormented love song 'Crying Over You', led by a mournful Barry Llewellyn, now used heavily phased horns and echoing keyboards to emphasise the protagonist's dread at his lover's departure; the song was picked up by Federal's Wildflower subsidiary, and issued as a single in Canada. Bob Dylan's 'I Shall Be Released' was completely revamped with an ear-catching horn part, each vocalist singing lines in turn, while Sibbles' 'Why Must I' was given the heaviest of contemporary Black Ark treatments. Most of the remaining new material dealt with contemporary issues, criticising destructive political policies and voicing the need for positive change. The affirmative 'Road Of Life' spoke of love's unlimited power, invoking the potential of unity, while 'Now Generation', 'Mr President', 'Serious Time', 'Storm Clouds', and 'Sufferer's Time' all pointed to the gravity of the age. 'Mr President' held particularly effective criticism, voicing the need for a cessation of the destructive overtures of mighty political figures from abroad.

In the spring of 1977, Perry cut a four-song Black Art Heptones Disco Dub EP in Jamaica, featuring extended mixes of 'Mr President' and 'Crying Over You' with forceful toasts by Jah Lion, plus dubbed-out mixes of 'Why

Must I' and 'I Shall Be Released'. The maxi was preceded by another inspired Perry disco with an 'extended domino mix' of Max Romeo's 'Norman', here issued with the sounds of a domino game and ensuing argument to emphasise the song's message, further embellished by another Jah Lion toast; the previously unissued 'Sexy Natty' had Romeo asserting a dread attitude to romance over a conga-peppered rhythm.

Junior Murvin's *Police And Thieves* album was issued by Island in April 1977, again composed of ten of the strongest tracks of the dozen or so he had recorded with Perry, about half of which had been completed by the end of 1976. According to Murvin, the songs were recorded over a period of months, and many had been written at Folly ruins. 'Along with "Police And Thief", I write "I Was Appointed", "Easy Task", and "Tedious" at Folly. We was working, so we take we time. Scratch don't rush: we voice some songs today, tomorrow we don't feel good so we leave that day. It was really a work more than a rush.'

As with its ranking title track, which was still highly popular a year after its initial release, most of the album dealt with the serious themes of black people dealing with the oppression that had been their lot for an age. 'Tedious' spoke of repatriation and Rastafarian unity, and also related in symbolic terms the potential Manley had to rebuild the nation. 'Michael Manley was Rasta-orientated,' Murvin eplained, 'his name was really close and very rhyming, so I just put it in.' Musically, Perry pulled out all the stops, subjecting the horns and even drums to ferocious phasing, and adding his own flashes of harshly hit cymbals. Issued as a single in Jamaica, it was exported by producer Gussie Clarke; Island later issued a particularly fearsome extended mix of the single on the B-side of a 12-inch EP. 'Rescue Jah Children' called on the powers-that-be to stop the wars of oppression that were causing endless strife for black people around the world, with a deliciously slow rhythm driven by phased horns and guitar, Niyabinghi conga drumming creating percussive movement. 'Roots Train' was a hard bop with horns and clavinet emulating railroad sounds; issued on a single in Jamaica with a hard Dillinger toast, the song showed Perry altering the harmony vocals through excessive doses of phasing and reverb. 'Solomon' was re-cut in a firm roots mode, with echoing guitar lines ringing throughout, while 'False Teaching' struck out against the educational brain-wash that greatly troubled Perry as a child. 'Easy Task' was Junior's commentary on the difficult nature of life, while 'Lucifer' was a particularly strong cut of the 'Catch Vampire' rhythm, calling for the collective death of the evil perpetrators of the slave trade. 'Workin' In The Cornfield' was another song whose Niyabinghi percussion emphasised the legacy of slave practices that lived on in modern Jamaican labour, while 'I Was Appointed' spoke of the negative role model presented by many in prominent professions.

Overall, the album gave evidence of the close working relationship that had grown between Murvin and Scratch, their mutual appreciation of each other's techniques resulting in exceptional creations. 'To work with Scratch is a great thing. He's the greatest producer I've ever worked with up 'til now. I never have problem working with him, I love working with him. He is a genius, you know? He feel the vibes. Sometimes he used to tell me, "Junior, you remind me of Bob Marley . . . Junior, 'Police And Thieves' will never die. Your talent, they can't stop you." He keep on guiding me like "Some of them guys, them no like you, watch them." He was a true man. When Perry sees a great talent, he don't like it to be destroyed, he love to push it to the fullest. That's how he is, spiritually.'

Other singles came out of this close bond in late 1976 and early 1977, including further versions of 'Police and Thieves' written by Perry: 'Philistines on the Land' attacked unscrupulous arms delears trading in nuclear weapons, its version side 'Bingo Kid' led by Chinna's bluesy guitar ramblings, and 'Bad Weed', an unbelievable re-structuring of the song in maximum disco-mix format, featuring booming baritone by Watty Burnett and percussion overdubs by Scratch.

Though it would be hard to surpass the greatness of 'Police And Thieves' as a single, 'Tedious' proved a strong follow-up, both in its music and lyrics. Island issued a thunderous extended mix of the song as a limited edition 12-inch in July, backed with a peculiar soul original called 'Memories'. The melodic structure of 'Memories' was patterned after the Impressions' 'Minstrel And Queen', which had been done over countless times in Jamaica as 'Queen Majesty', but Perry's mutation of the song and Murvin's fresh lyrics heavily disguised the rhythm's origins. Drum and bass are kept prominent throughout, and as with much of the *Police And Thieves* album, the rhythm is heavily phased; keyboard melodies drift in an out of the mix and a woman's ghostly laughter echoes in the dub portion. The follow-up disco, cut in December, was 'Closer Together', another Upsetter/Murvin re-structuring of an Impressions' favourite, here extended to incorporate portions of 'Gypsy Woman' which Junior sang in a surprisingly deep voice; the B-side was 'Dreadlocks In Moonlight', unfortunately in the same seven-inch format and far too short to be one side of an EP.

Augustus Pablo was also spending a good deal of time at the Black Ark in the spring and summer of 1977, blowing melodica and playing keyboards on Perry's rhythm tracks in exchange for studio time. One of their most noteworthy collaborations was 'Vibrate On(n)', a dense instrumental groove that was positively psychedelic, probing the outer reaches of reggae jazz. A version of Pablo's 'Java' was also cut as 'Lama Lava' in this time, using a style that went beyond the rockers mode; though unfinished, it would eventually surface on the back of the 'Rainbow Country' disco.

After singer Jacob Miller left Pablo's stable for greater fame with the Inner Circle group, Pablo concentrated on establishing a young singer named Hugh Mundell, the radical teenage son of an uptown lawyer. Two of

Mundell's best singles were cut by Pablo at the Black Ark in this period: the inspired 'Let's All Unite', driven by solid beats from Benbow, and the frustrated 'Why Do Black Man Fuss and Fight', on which a melodic bass line was provided by Chinna Smith. Pablo also arranged material at the studio for Everton Da Silva's Hungry Town label that year, playing string synth on songs such as 'Me Breda You A Go Feel It', credited to Hands and Hearts.

One of Lee Perry's outstanding productions to surface in the latter half of 1977 was 'Sons Of Slaves' by Junior Delgado. Perhaps the heaviest song of Delgado's consistently heavy solo career, 'Sons of Slaves' named the lowly history bestowed on Jamaica's African descendants, his declamatory message given solid vocal backing by the Heptones and Dennis Brown. The song was issued on seven-inch with a fierce dub and also on an extended 12-inch that revealed extra Niyabinghi hand drumming.

The flip side of the maxi featured Carlton Jackson's 'History', another heavyweight number. Jackson was a former civil engineer who voiced dub-plate specials for the Ethiopian Hi-Fi set in the early '70s. In 1973, the lyrics of 'History' came into his head while on a lunch break in the woods, but it was not until his friend Bunny Wailer found success with *Blackheart Man* that Jackson considered recording the song. He eventually made his way to the Black Ark, where Perry had the Diamonds give a wordless chorus to his relaxed 'History' monologue. Though a proposed album would never materialise, and other completed songs such as 'Jah Light' were never released, Jackson emphasised that he learned a lot by working with Perry. 'Scratch is a teacher. He teach. He wanted me to do an LP so I did a few more tracks for him, but because I knew nothing of the release of "History" until after it was published, I decided not to do any more tracks. Chinna Smith told me, "You have this nice tune," and when Scratch came back to Jamaica he told me about it; I was just a little upset.' To compensate, Perry gave Jackson a cut to release on his own, which surfaced with a different mix and dub on Jackson's Ital International label.

Other strong disco mixes to surface in the summer included an extended vocal cut of 'Vibrate On' as 'Reggae Music', featuring Hugo Blackwood from Time Unlimited and toaster Doctor Alimantado extolling the virtues of the 'music of the dispensation of time'; the A-side of this 'Upsetter Disco Jam' 12-inch was the duo's 'Rasta Train', a bouncing journey with excessive treatments in its extended section. Another fearsome Alimantado 12-inch, issued later in extremely limited number, had an extended cut of Devon Irons' 'Catch Vampire' with a haunting female chorus augmenting the vocal section; on the other side was an extended cut of Sangie Davis' 'Words'.

In contrast to such product was altogether different material from Earl George. It was eight crucial tracks that he and Scratch fashioned together in this period, all cover versions of American soul and pop hits re-done in a thick syrup of Black Ark rhythm. George noted that Perry suggested which songs to cover, hand-picking material he felt the singer would excel on; he then re-shaped the standard ballads into something entirely other through his individual visionary treatments. 'Scratch gave me these songs to do because I do covers so good. Scratch gave the musicians a lot of work; he's a very technical guy. You can be playing a drum pattern and he say "Play that upside down." His way of working is very unique. His rhythms have a different sound, the mix is totally different from everybody else. He does percussion different from everybody else too. He might bring the garbage pail, play a few instruments, then in a certain spot, he just kick that dirt bin. When he mix all the sound together, you get some way out kind of sound. You see, Scratch is a genius. Working with Scratch, you learn a lot of things too. Scratch is really the type of producer who was deep into the music.'

George also noted that time and energy devoted to this material was unduly long, resulting not only in several hit releases, but also in another name change for the singer. 'It take maybe about eight months, voicing it and the background vocals; the mixing take a long time too. It was taking so much time that he said to me, "Boy, you have a lot of faith. You should change your name to George Faith." I said "That sound all right," because faith move mountain. From there I just stick with that name.'

Island's first George Faith disco, released in July on their re-launched Black Swan subsidiary, was a new cut of 'To Be A Lover', which surpassed the popularity of all previous Jamaican versions. This Black Ark recording was a slower, heavier, and generally more creative rendition; powered by modulated horns and sliding bass grooves, Faith's vocals were more emotive and aided by unobtrusive harmonies. The Jamaican issue of this disco clocked in at near the 12-minute mark, with Perry toasting odd soliloquies about Rasta refusals to attend funerals towards the end of the song; Island's UK pressing, though shorter, inadvertently went one step further by leaving in some portions of Dillinger's toast to 'Roots Train', which had bled through one channel of the tape, highly distorted and out of synch. On the B-side, a swinging horn skank called 'Rastaman Shuffle' – an update of the Skatalites' 'Beardman Feast', which was based on American pianist Ernie Freeman's 'Live It Up' – two different strands of the same Dillinger toast accidentally appeared in stereo at the front of the song, resulting in a highly cluttered and unsynchronised mix. The situation most probably stemmed from Perry's tendency to re-mix material onto two tracks of a previously recorded four track tape in response to a perpetual shortage of available master tapes.

It was during the time such material was created that outside observers found Perry to be behaving oddly. After his initial pilgrimage to the Black Ark in late 1973, Chris Lane had briefly met with Scratch on a return visit to Jamaica in April 1976. He found the studio somewhat better equipped, and with a few visual adornments on the walls; otherwise, Scratch and his workplace were much as he had left them at the end of his first visit. But on a subsequent trip to Jamaica, Lane encountered the first hint of a noticeably troubling difference.

In mid-April 1977, Lane travelled to Kingston with his wife and John MacGillivray, founder of the South London record shop Dub Vendor, together with mutual friend Dave Hendley. Hendley was born on July 30, 1952 in Wood Green. His father was a tool maker and his mother a hospital accountant. Like Lane, his interest in Jamaican reggae and American soul began at school. As a teenager, Hendley landed a job as a messenger on *The Times* picture desk, where he taught himself the skills of photography. Between 1973 and 1975, his photographs were regularly featured in national news media, including *The Sunday Times, Time Out,* and *Let it Rock,* but Dave's love of music saw him quit the business to work in the Revolver Records shop located in Tottenham. It was here that he became closely acquainted with North London sound system operator Fatman and record salesman Mo Claridge, who was then working as a van driver for Creole. It was through Claridge that Hendley learned of a job vacancy at Contempo records, a specialist soul shop down the street from Daddy Kool in the West End, owned by John Abbey, publisher of *Blues and Soul;* while working at the shop in 1976, Hendley chose to revive the paper's reggae column, which Chris Lane had stopped producing after moving on to write for *Black Music* and *Melody Maker.*

These reggae aficionados made several visits to the Black Ark during their month in Kingston, where they found Scratch to be surrounded by a flurry of constant activity; they witnessed plenty of rhythms being laid but very little voicing. Scratch cut a few exclusive mixes for the trio of material he was to issue later in the year, including 'History' by Carlton Jackson (who Hendley recalled was doing odd jobs in Perry's garden), 'I've Got the Groove' by George Faith, 'Groovy Situation' by Keith Rowe (highly popular when released abroad in the summer), and a Rowe track tentatively entitled 'The World and Me' (later issued as 'Living My Life'). Hendley also remembered hearing the Heptones' 'Mistry Babylon' – recorded with Lee Perry at the Ark – the day after arrival in Jamaica, when Barry Llewellyn delivered freshly pressed copies to the Aquarius record shop.

Though Hendley recalled Perry as being fairly focused and together at this time, both he and Chris Lane remembered an occasion in May where his actions were somewhat difficult to comprehend. As Lane explained, 'That was the time when he was starting to act a little bit peculiar. He was drinking white rum, smoking and laughing maniacally, but no one else could work out what he was laughing at. He was talking nonsense, being odder than ususual.'

Though his troublesome behaviour waxed and waned in response to various stimuli, the person Lane and Hendley encountered on his trip to the Ark was a baffling precursor of what was later to blossom as a full-fledged new persona.

As Lee Perry's profile was raised abroad through well-publicised releases distributed and promoted by Island, the more forward-thinking members of the rock aristocracy began clamouring to work with him. The most distinguished couple seeking his production skills were Paul and Linda McCartney, who had Perry build some rhythm tracks at the Ark in June 1977 for Linda's projected debut solo album.

Paul McCartney's fascination with Jamaican music dated back to his days with the Beatles; he was specifically attracted to Perry's individual production style, and knew of Scratch's reputation for elevating unknown underdogs. The pair had met on several occasions in England, where a positive connection was established; the McCartneys thus sent Perry a demo tape of material they wanted him to re-create with his inimitable Black Ark sound, and Perry spent a week building three rhythms with Boris Gardiner, Mikey Boo, Winston Wright, and Billy Johnson. Despite reports to the contrary, Scratch pointed out that the couple never made it to his studio: 'Me meet Paul in London at this studio in Wembley and lots of other places, but he didn't come to my studio to do the songs. Chris Blackwell tell me that they want me to do something, so they send the music like it was originally, and said they want it in my style. Me have my musician them make it and me send it back to them and they voiced it somewhere else.'

Some of this material was voiced by the McCartneys in Scotland the following August, including the poppy 'Sandman', which featured phased guitar and a melodic bass line, but the project was then abandoned for nearly twenty years. In July 1998, while Linda was battling against cancer, the couple returned to these Jamaican creations, voicing the rockers-style cut of the Maguire Sisters' standard 'Sugartime' (a song that formed the basis of many a Jamaican dancehall hit in the late 1980s). Both tracks were eventually included on *Wide Prairie,* a posthumous collection of Linda's work issued after her death in the autumn of 1998.

It was also in this period that Robert Palmer undertook some ill-fated work at Perry's studio. Palmer had reached a stage in his career where he sought to draw on exotic music forms to lend a more cosmopolitan feel to his brand of rock and roll. He was already aware of some of Perry's outer-worldly productions – having been particularly struck by the flushing toilet that opened the 'Iron Gate' instrumental on the *Cloak And Dagger* album – and was optimistic of a positive result with Scratch. In helping to arrange for Palmer to record at the Ark, Chris Blackwell hoped to get viable crossover material for Palmer's upcoming *Double Fun* album.

Palmer remarked in a particularly frank interview in Grand Royal magazine that Scratch's position at the Ark was far beyond that of an ordinary producer; the man was clearly seen as a kind of spiritual leader at this point. 'His studio seemed to be the spiritual and political centre of the island. It was heavy, and it was all about getting this magic on the tracks.' [4]

Despite the rapport that developed between Palmer and Scratch, confrontation and hostility marked the week he spent at the Ark. Though Scratch seemed to be continually testing the singer, he accepted Palmer as an ally once his seriousness and experimental abilities were made clear. Links proved more difficult to form with some of the studio musicians, particularly Sly and Robbie, though Ernest Ranglin and Boris Gardiner were eminently friendly and well mannered. Palmer revealed that the harshest negativity emanated from the assembled dread idlers, who seemed to have nothing better to do than to try to disturb his concentration.

'These guys come around wearing robes and they've got magic wands and shit. I'm doing vocals and one stands in front of the mic and starts doing this weird dance. I thought it was fucking ridiculous, but I couldn't laugh because it would have been an insult. That didn't work, so they brought in another guy who stood with his back to me and pushed me with his shoulder blades into the microphone while this other guy did the magic wand shit. It was very strange, and Lee didn't do a thing to try and stop it. He was very amused by my reaction. When that didn't work, they brought all these friends who were dressed like military. They gave me the white boy routine: What're you doing here? And Lee's looking at me, grinning . . . he was like, I can't do anything about these hangers-on. I'm sorry, I think it's ridiculous too.' [5]

Regardless of the antagonism he encountered at the studio, Palmer had nothing but praise for Perry's recording techniques.

'I've been asked who was my favourite producer and it's definitely him. He used to do amazing things that were hard to accept unless you witnessed what he did. He used to record on a Teac four track and mix as he went, occasionally cleaning the head with his T-shirt . . . He was just this magnet for a scene that was the real musical cutting edge.' [6]

Despite such accolades, not one of the three songs he recorded at the Black Ark would make it onto the Double Fun album in their original form; instead, Palmer re-cut the material in less unpredictable circumstances in New York. Perry provided Island with a single mix of the track he felt was the strongest, 'Best Of Both Worlds', complete with dub version, but the single was not issued. The only song to surface from the sessions so far is the calmly emotional 'Love Can Run Faster', strengthened by a sweet female chorus, it was incompatibly cut on the back of Palmer's hard-rocking commercial cover of Moon Martin's 'Bad Case Of Loving You' in 1979.

It was at one of Robert Palmer's sessions that Perry first met Wayne Jobson, an aspiring singer and guitarist based in Ocho Rios who was brought to the Ark by Boris Gardiner. Jobson is from a prominent Jamaican family with close links to the Wailers: his cousin Diane was Bob Marley's lawyer and one of his closest confidantes; his cousins Dickie sporadically acted as the group's manager. Wayne noted that Perry pushed Palmer hard, striving to get original results. 'Scratch made him re-do a song for about eight hours straight until Robert Palmer was losing his voice.'

Jobson described other particulars of sessions he observed: 'He wanted a female vocalist so he called Pauline; she was in the kitchen mixing some dumplings with flour all over her hands, so she brush off the flour and come in the studio and sing the line, then go back in and mix up the dumplings again. In the studio he had a fan, and he put a pineapple in front of the fan, it was like scented air conditioning. On the walls was all these X-rated pictures out of *Hustler*, and I'm thinking "Is this a Rastaman with all this pornographic stuff?" It was wild. At the time, you could sense his genius, but it was this kind of madness that just changes every day.'

Like most white Jamaicans, Wayne Jobson has a mixed ethnic background. His father's side of the family had come to Jamaica from England four generations earlier, and then mixed with Spanish immigrants and Jamaicans of African descent. But Lee Perry took one look at him and had a different interpretation: he told the singer he would be happy to work with him because Wayne was 'an Arawak Indian' – the original inhabitants of Jamaica who were entirely exterminated by the Spanish in the 1600s. A baffled Jobson thus returned some time later to record a four-song demo with the nucleus of his band Native: bassist Sydney Bennett, drummer Ray Levy, keyboardist Peter Couch (later a member of the group Four), and Joe Higgs on percussion. The original songs they cut were 'Late September And May', 'Rockstone', 'Meet Mr Nobody' and 'In A Strange Land'.

Jobson was departing for England the morning after the session, where he would spend a year completing his law degree. Though he only paid Perry fifty dollars upfront – promising to cut him in on any ensuing record deal – Scratch stayed up all night mixing the material, striving to get the best out of what had been rapidly captured on tape. When Jobson played the demo to Johnny Rotten and Vivien Goldman in London, their publicised reactions had Jobson tipped to be the bext big thing; though the demo achieved the desired results and eventually landed Jobson a record deal, he would never manage to benefit again from Lee Perry's production skills.

It was also in this period that Lee Perry started working closely with the Congos on what was perhaps the most notable of a succession of significantly ill-fated musical projects. Under Scratch's guidance and direction, the Congos came together as a duo and then expanded to a trio. Each member has expressed differing tales of the group's genesis, and Perry and others have presented further conflicting versions of events, but the body of work that emerged from their formation remains as truly classic representations of the roots reggae genre.

Cedric Myton would eventually become the group's unofficial leader, and his strength and confidence in the upper register meant he often took the vocal lead. Born in St Catherine in 1947, Myton started singing in the rock steady era in the Tartans quartet with Devon Russell, 'Prince' Lincoln Thompson and Lindburgh 'Preps' Lewis; 'Dance All Night' was a massive hit for Federal in 1967. He and Devon Russell also cut some songs at Studio One in this period, though they were not released; it was while working on the material that Myton first came in contact with Lee Perry. Though Myton would eventually become involved in Prince Lincoln's Royal Rasses group, he was inactive as a singer for much of the 1970s.

Roydel Johnson was a tenor singer who provided a fitting counterbalance to Myton's falsetto. Though his vocal range was not so wide, some of the group's best lyrics came from Johnson's interpretation of biblical imagery. The impetus behind their original formation seems also to have stemmed largely from him.

As Johnson also hailed from Hanover, he and Lee Perry had connections that ran deep. One of twelve children, Johnson was born in Kendal on April 12, 1943; his mother was active in the local Holiness church. Like Lee Perry, he also attended Kendal School, and Johnson's mother was friendly with Perry's mother. Johnson recounted his early links with Scratch: 'I and Lee Perry is from the same district, and we used to dance together. Scratch used to be a good dancer, and I used to be a good dancer, so both of us would go out at the sound system dance in those days for contests in Hanover and Westmoreland.'

At age 16, Johnson moved to Kingston to live with an aunt. He began hanging around recording studios and was taught to play guitar by Ernest Ranglin, who took a shine to the youth because of their shared love of exercise; Johnson also received coaching from Gladdy Anderson and Winston Wright. Around 1964, events in Cuba prompted the US Peace Corps to recruit Jamaicans to work at the naval base in Guantanamo Bay, and Johnson was stationed there for a full five and a half years. In 1966, he heard about Selassie's impending visit to Jamaica, took some holiday time to make the journey home, and became a committed Rastafarian thereafter.

In the early 1970s, Roy Johnson was back in Kingston, hanging out in studios again and trying to persuade someone to record him. Though other producers were not prepared to record the youth as a vocalist, Lee Perry took the gamble in 1973 by having him attempt a song called 'Standing On The Hill'; when Johnson failed to achieve the desired results, Perry had the more seasoned Chenley Duffus voice the tune, and later voiced an alternative version himself. 'The first song I did was with Scratch was in Channel One before he had the Black Ark,' Johnson recalled, 'and then he did it over with Chenley Duffus. Those days we didn't do any more songs, and because it didn't work out, I decide fe just go into the guitar.'

Not long after this first thwarted effort, Johnson began playing in the Rightful Brothers, a Niyabinghi group led by a repeater player called Brother Joe who helped refine his hand-drumming skills. It was several years before he saw Scratch again, but when their paths crossed in 1977, it would prove to have fortuitous results. 'After I did that first song, I didn't see Scratch for about six years. One day I was at my home over Independence City, playing my guitar. I see this guy walk in through the gate and it was Scratch. He told me he was looking (for) a breadfruit tree to plant at his house. I said, "Yeah man, you can get a breadfruit tree, but what's going on in the music business?" He said, "I have a studio now, you know." I picked my guitar up and start to sing "Row Fisherman Row". Scratch said, "Shanti, you should come to the studio, make we record the song." '

Roy Johnson had gotten to know Cedric Myton through their shared involvement in a Niyabinghi order, and through mutual acquaintances such as independent producer Trevor 'Leggo Beast' Douglas and ranking toaster Big Youth. After selling their hand-knit tams and belts on the street, the pair began singing together, and when Scratch extended his invitation to Johnson in early 1977, they arrived at his studio as a duo.

The first song the Congos put together at the Ark was the same 'Fisherman' that Johnson had sung for Scratch – an adaptation of a traditional refrain with new lyrics that reflected their personal circumstances. Neither Perry nor the Congos thought the first take realised their full potential, so the group returned the next day to re-cut the tune with a different set of musicians, including drummer Paul Douglas and Geoffrey Chung on bass. Once 'Fisherman' was in shape, the group set to work on some of the other dozen songs they had written, completing several singles by the middle of June.

Over a period of weeks, the Congos recorded regularly at the Black Ark, laying the foundations of what would prove to be an exemplary roots album of the highest order: *Heart Of The Congos*. It was certainly the greatest album the Congos themselves would create, and was arguably the strongest album Lee Perry ever produced with a vocal group.

Part of the strength of the album lies in the song-writing skills of Cedric Myton and Roy Johnson. On songs like 'Can't Come In', 'Open Up The Gate', 'The Wrong Thing', and 'Solid Foundation', Myton imparted a visual quality to his words, painting a musical canvas that celebrated their African heritage while condemning the workings of Babylon and the divisive destructiveness of Christianity; on 'La La Bam Bam', 'Sodom And Gomorrow', and 'Ark Of The Covenant', Johnson related religious allegory in a way that was never stale or ordinary, re-casting Bible tales from a Rastafari viewpoint.

As Cedric and Roy were testing their ability, Scratch was reaching his artistic apex; when faced with material he was inspired by, he would re-shape and embellish the work into a less predictable and more satisfying product through unknown applications of technical wizardry and spiritual zest. With the help of Ernest Ranglin and Boris Gardiner, Scratch made sure the Congos had the inspired and original musical backing their devotional songs deserved. He had installed a Yamaha organ and a Gerhard acoustic piano by this time, and Winston Wright and Keith Sterling would provide the key melodic elements on these instruments, with Scratch's bursts of Africa-inspired percussion adding an extra difference.

Though the two Congos were both strong songwriters, Scratch felt their vocal deliveries occasionally to be weak. Scratch thus got Watty Burnett to use his deep baritone as a hefty balancing anchor on most of their songs, and the combination worked so well that he became a full-fledged member of the group by the time the album was completed.

Burnett had cut a few recent singles at the Black Ark, including the self-produced 'What A War' (on the 'Babylon A Fall' rhythm) and the obscure 'Rise And Shine' with Clinton Fearon (as Watty and Tony), but these had little impact. His big hit came with a cover version of Brook Benton's 'Rainy Night In Georgia', adapted at the Ark as 'Rainy Night In Portland'. The song was issued on a disco with one of Burnett's strongest originals, the declamatory 'Open The Gate'. Despite the popularity of these releases, Watty heeded Perry's advice and chose to stick within the Congos' ranks from the recording of the material that would make their debut LP. As Burnett explained, 'When "Rainy Night In Portland" became a hit, everybody's telling me I should stay solo, and Scratch is saying, "You can still go solo, but I would like you to join this group Congos." From there, I didn't do any more solo, I just involved in the group. I sung on seven songs on the album, but my photograph wasn't on it because I took a week off and went to Grand Cayman when the photograph shoot was happening.'

To round out the vocal sound further, Perry later had the Meditations provide a more general chorus on certain songs, along with Barry Llewellyn and Earl Morgan on 'Children Crying' and Gregory Isaacs on 'La La Bam Bam'. Roy Cousins and the Royals also provided backing on selected Congos songs at the Black Ark, and Cousins was keen to point out Perry's unequalled skill as a producer in this period. 'After we did the harmony for Yabby You, Lee Perry start to call we, he used to drive down to bring the group up to do harmonies. When Lee Perry was doing the Congos album, Meditations did most of the harmony with Heptones and we do bits and pieces, but what amaze a lot of people with Perry – even me and Joseph Hoo Kim used to talk about it – was the equipment Perry have wasn't professional, and Jo Jo, who did have a 16-track desk at the time, was amazed to see what Perry was getting out of unprofessional equipment. Perry was a clever overdubber and most of the producers them, they are just businessmen. Coxsone wasn't there when three quarters of Studio One was being recorded; it was Sylvain Morris who was doing most of the work. Joseph Hoo Kim, the whole of them man there is businessmen and then them want come and say they are producer. To me, the best producer reggae has ever seen is Lee Perry, second by Lloyd Charmers. Scratch was among the man who went to the studio with ideas of what he wanted and tell the musicians them to play; a lot of Scratch ideas, when Scratch put it to musicians, them say it is impossible! Because Scratch was paying them, them had to play what Scratch want and in the end it worked as Scratch right – no other man ever done that. You check the whole industry, no other man has ever done that but Lee Perry. The only man who might be second to him might be Prince Buster, who was creative, he tell the musicians what him wanted and how him wanted something to sound, but Buster never reach to the heights of Scratch; Scratch was a man who always have imaginery sound. I sit down and I watch him when him a work with Marley, when them a do "Rat Race"; I used to go to his studio when we do harmonies.'

As the Upsetter was helping to structure their music, the Congos were also having a gradual influence on Lee Perry's lifestyle. They would begin most mornings at sunrise collecting Perry and Watty Burnett for a run out to Hellshire beach, getting physically charged and clearing their minds for the tasks that lay ahead. Cedric and Roy spoke disparagingly of Scratch's rum-drinking and encouraged him to cultivate herb in the yard surrounding the Black Ark instead. They conducted lengthy reasoning sessions about the wonders of Rastafari, and brought Watty Burnett into the faith; they also elicited a greater outward religious commitment from Perry himself. It was the Congos who largely convinced him to 'locks up', resulting in the presence of the short nubs of dreadlocks growing from the Upsetter's head for the very first time in his life.

Lee Perry issued the first Congos singles in Jamaica early in 1977; their debut 'Fisherman' was followed by the upbeat 'Ark Of The Covenant' in April, while a stunning Upsetter Disco Cork with the religious 'Nicodeemus' and 'Solid Foundation' came in June, both songs complete with extended dub portions.

Shortly after Perry began working regularly with the Congos, independent English film-maker Jeremy Marre appeared at the Ark gathering footage for *Roots Rock Reggae,* a documentary later bought by the BBC. Marre's three-man film team captured a fully charged Scratch bouncing around the elevated control room in boxer shorts and a sleeveless tank top, pounding on the control-room glass and shouting orders. The Congos and the Heptones were in the voicing area, creating a delightful and impromptu reggae jam with Boris Gardiner and keyboardist Robbie Lyn, with Junior Murvin picking out a guitar riff on the floor. 'Play On, Mr Music' was especially created in honour of the film crew's appearance; though the song was never given a vinyl release in its Black Ark form (but was later re-recorded by the Heptones elsewhere), the footage of its spontaneous creation ultimately emphasised the fluid nature of Perry's work at the Black Ark. 'It wasn't a thing that we really arranged,' explained Earl Morgan, 'we just go in and play the rhythm and Barry just start (singing), "Play On, Mr Music, play on." Rhythm a play, something just happen: it's a groove.'

In addition to his more prominent, internationally oriented work with singers like George Faith, Lee Perry also cut strong material aimed at the local market with artists such as Eric Donaldson at the Black Ark during these summer months. A post-rockers version of 'Cherry Oh Baby' was issued in June as a disco 45, credited to Eric Donaldson and the Keystones; although the song did not really capture the glory of the original, its dub segment had a creative mix that showed off the talents of each of the musicians in turn. The little-known B-side, 'Say A Little Prayer', was stronger, a harmonic chant of praises to God that showed how much Donaldson had matured as a songwriter. A couple of other scarce but exceptional Donaldson singles that surfaced that year also addressed weighty matters: 'Freedom Street' was a particularly inspired song about the dehumanising aspects of slavery and incarceration, while the defiant 'Stand Up' urged people to fight for their rights. This latter track was submerged in delay and built around peculiar vocal treatments; its dub was a swathe of distorted echo that repeatedly proclaimed the word 'I'.

Meanwhile, Island continued to handle the cream of Perry's production crop overseas. In late July, they issued an arresting disco by the Congos, which was meant to be the first of a series of releases by the group on the label. 'Congoman' was a lengthy sombre chant over a beat-box rhythm with a free-form bass pattern skilfully executed by Winston Wright; its version was punctuated by ominous, echoing vocal fragments. Chris Blackwell was particularly struck by the songs and expressed interest in an album by the group at this time, though the single received a mixed reaction from the British press and would ultimately prove difficult to shift.

Much of the material Scratch was creating in this period was designed with Island in mind, and further George Faith discos found greater success abroad. While 'To Be A Lover' was holding strong in Europe, Island issued the equally strong follow-up in August, a driving version of the Ojays' 'I've Got The Groove'. Its intriguing instrumental arrangement, marked by echoing sax bursts from Taste Campbell and subtly phased guitar and keyboards, formed a suitable backdrop for Faith's subdued phrasing, his delivery helped along by wordless male harmonies. The disco's B-side, an absurd re-working of Paul Anka's 'Diana', somehow also worked well, Faith's voice floating above a virtual river of delay and reverb. The final Faith disco was an extended take on one of Perry's long-standing favourites, Wilson Pickett's 'Midnight Hour'. Not only did Faith's delivery do the song justice, but Perry's re-building of the song gave it a more dream-like quality, as though suggesting that the past will always be different than how we remember it. Its B-side was another Taste Campbell skank on an R & B standard, 'Turn Back The Hands Of Time'.

The pleasantly palatable cuts of psychedelic Jamaican soul that had proved so popular on these extended discos were shortened and put together with the slow and smoky 'Opportunity' and 'There's A Train' as George Faith's debut album, issued in Jamaica as *Super Eight*; Island's UK and American issues, cut in September, named the album *To Be A Lover* after the most successful single. Though some who bought the discos were disappointed by the lack of fresh material on the record, its sustained popularity saw the release of 'Opportunity' as a seven-inch the following February.

A final Black Swan disco, issued in August 1977, also provided another lasting hit for Island: Keith Rowe's 'Groovy Situation'. The song had a smooth, easy flow that prefaced the UK lover's rock craze of the early '80s; Perry enhanced the tune's romanticism through recurrent female laughter buried in the mix. The song marked Rowe's return to the limelight after a long period of absence from Jamaica, where he had previously found fame as half of the duo Keith and Tex.

Born in Franklyn Town on October 22, 1950, Keith Rowe is the second of three children whose father was a driver and preacher at the local Church of God; he learned to play the organ as a child, and was inspired to sing largely by exposure to popular music on the radio. While attending Kingston College, Rowe moved to the Marverley area in his teens, where he became friendly with Phillip Texas Dixon, a youth two years his senior who was an apprentice bookkeeper in the neighbouring district of Pembroke Hall; the pair soon began blending their harmonies and writing songs together, patterning themselves after the Blues Busters. In 1966, Keith and Tex were running the gauntlet of the Kingston music scene, joining the growing ranks of other hopefuls seeking to be recorded, but their initial auditions for Studio One, Prince Buster, and Treasure Isle were not successful. Derrick Harriott was then just venturing into production, and noted something special in their sound when they appeared at his record shop at 125 King Street; he agreed to record the pair, scoring instant hits with 'Stop That Train' and 'Tonight', both of which were particularly successful abroad. Keith and Tex stuck with Harriott for the next few years, hitting again with 'Don't Look Back' in 1968 and enjoying a high popularity in stage shows; Rowe was also concurrently a member of the Mighty Mystics with friends from Kingston College such as Val Douglas and Geoffrey Chung. In this period, Rowe settled in Washington Gardens, where he became friendly with neighbours that were also involved in the music industry, including Bob Andy, Marcia Griffiths, and Lee Perry.

Towards the end of the decade, Rowe's mother emigrated to the USA, and Keith joined her and the rest of the family in 1972, while Texas Dixon subsequently emigrated to Canada. Though Rowe joined the US Army shortly after his arrival in America, he remained active as a singer and musician, forming a band with former Mighty Mystics member Trevor Thompson. In the mid-'70s, he began working with a man named Frano, who ran an eight-track studio in Brooklyn called FNT; it was here that Rowe recorded the emotive 'Love On Aa Shelf' and the patriotic 'Out Of Many, We Are One' which won the first Festival Song competition held in New York in 1976, organised by popular radio disc jockey Ken Williams.

The contest prize was a flight back to Jamaica, enabling Rowe to travel to the island in the spring of 1977 for the first time since emigrating to the States; when he stopped by the Black Ark to visit Scratch, the producer immediately requested he set to work. Rowe recalled the particulars of the resultant session: 'He said, "Well, you're here, so let's work," though I'd never worked with him before. He called up (keyboardist) Robbie Lyn and some other guys and we went in the studio and start working. I did three or four songs, "Groovy Situation", "Living My Life", and another one. Those songs that I did for Scratch had a feel I've never had, there was a real down-to-earth-ness that permeated the entire situation of that session. The feeling was right, the mood was right – especially "Groovy Situation". I left Jamaica a couple of days later.'

Though 'Groovy Situation' enjoyed a long period of popularity, Rowe explained that circumstances prevented him from reaping much financial reward from his efforts. 'Scratch was supposed to deal with Jamaica and England and I would deal with America; he gave me a master tape, but my friend had it in his Volkswagen that got broken into and it got stolen. Then Scratch reneged on the agreement – he sent tapes to Brad Osborne in the Bronx, who put "Groovy Situation" out. That was the way the business went.'

For the rest of the '70s, Rowe was a member of the popular Realistics band with other Jamaican expatriates, such as Glen Adams, Pat Satchmo, and bandleader Ron Wilson; he later performed for military audiences in Germany and Hawaii, and would eventually join back with Texas Dixon for a series of performances and new recordings in the late 1990s. Of the other songs he recorded with Lee Perry, only 'Living My Life' has surfaced, credited on a 1977 Black Ark Disco Bum release to Keith Texon.

By the end of the summer of 1977, Lee Perry was back in London, ostensibly on his way to Nigeria to produce an album for Island with Ghanaian highlife trumpeter Eddie Quansah. Unfortunately, Perry had problems obtaining a visa, delaying the project to the point of abandonment; such circumstances not only robbed the Upsetter of a chance to explore the African motherland, but also robbed the music world of a potentially exciting collaboration.

Scratch remained in the UK to the beginning of October, but was far from idle in the weeks he spent hoping the bureaucratic obstacles would be cleared; besides furthering his negotiations with Island over the Congos material, Lee Perry also became involved in a number of adventurous side projects. Staying in a flat above the Basing Street recording studio, he spent much of his time in the company of Bob Marley, who was also unexpectedly in town, away from the rest of the Wailers and seeking specialist medical advice about a serious football injury. Besides working with the resting Tuff Gong on a few notable tracks in London, Lee Perry also found himself navigating the unknown channels of punk rock during his time there.

Scratch appeared in the height of punk's ascendancy, when the rebellious music of a disaffected white working class was causing a serious shake-up of the self-indulgent excesses of stadium rock, and the Upsetter rose to the challenge of the movement's rebellious spirit by agreeing to produce a single by the Clash.

Along with rival quartet the Sex Pistols, the Clash was the most important band to be thrown up by the UK punk explosion of 1976; the group the most successful to emerge from the genre, having a greater control of their own destiny and a wider range of ideas than many of their peers. While the Pistols built their career on shock and parody, flirting with Nazi symbolism and glorifying drug abuse (after having been fabricated and manipulated by manager Malcolm McLaren), the Clash concentrated on using their music as a vehicle to criticise society, and addressed racial and class-based inequality in many of their songs – though drug and alcohol problems would also plague the group.

One thing the Pistols and the Clash had in common was a shared love of reggae; lead Pistol Johnny 'Rotten' Lydon had long been inspired by the fiery music of the dreads, and the Clash also admired the daring and uncompromising stance of the rebel music. Bassist Paul Simonon drew the greatest inspiration from reggae; raised in Brixton, where Jamaican music was ever present, he was inundated with rock steady in his teens, and used the *Tighten Up* album series to teach himself bass melodies. Simonon remembered certain Lee Perry creations as outstanding works from his youth: he was struck by the baby crying on 'People Funny Boy' and awed by the unique arrangement of 'All Combine'. 'I see Lee Perry as the Ennio Morricone of Jamaican music,' Simonon noted fondly, 'his music is like the soundtrack to my childhood.'

Lee Perry may have seemed an unlikely choice of producer for a band who were then basing their songs around three chords, but it was with respect and admiration that the London punks approached Scratch, sending their manager Bernie Rhodes – a former reggae record-shop proprietor – to request his production skills for their upcoming third single 'Complete Control', which was issued in late September. Though Perry told the group they had 'ruined' Junior Murvin's 'Police And Thieves' with their musically inferior cover version, he felt enough of a connection in spirit to consider working with them – and the financial arrangement offered persuaded him to consent. The resultant 'Complete Control', recorded at SARM studio in Whitechapel, was a quickfire blast protesting against corporate manipulation. Though Perry's presence is not immediately detectable on the disc, he is said to have altered the shape of the single by insisting Joe Strummer and Mick Jones turn down their guitars in the studio; Simonon recalled little concrete input from the producer, but noted he complimented Jones by saying the lead guitarist 'played with an iron fist'. Scratch would later demonstrate his approval of the collaboration by giving their photograph a place of prominence on one of the walls of his studio.

Though Bob Marley is said to have initially shunned the self-mutilation and drastic dehumanism of punk's dress code, Scratch and Bob joined forces during this mutual time in London on 'Punky Reggae Party', a song that celebrated the commonalities of reggae and punk.

Tony Owens had been in contact with Lee Perry since Scratch made his first trips to London in the late 1960s, when Perry often stayed at the Owens family home; according to Tony, Scratch wrote the lyrics of 'Punky Reggae Party' on the way into London from Heathrow Airport. 'I picked Lee Perry up at the airport about three o'clock in the afternoon. We were talking about the big explosion of punk in London. By the time we got to the flat, he already wrote the song called "Punky Reggae Party". Bob Marley was staying in Earls Court, Scratch phoned him and said "Bob, I've got a song for you, come now," and Bob was there in about twenty minutes, with his guitar.'

Bob spent much of that evening reasoning with journalist Vivienne Goldman about why he did not believe in death; fellow journalist Neil Spencer of *New Musical Express* and aspiring film-maker Don Letts also joined in the discussion. That night, Marley and Scratch recorded 'Punky Reggae Party' with the handful of musicians that were present, including Angus Gaye (a.k.a. 'Drummie Zeb'), drummer with Aswad, then the premier reggae band in Britain, and Richard Daley, bassist with Third World. For backing vocals, Perry used Michael 'Ibo' Cooper of Third World and two women who were independently trying to get deals with Island records: Candy McKenzie, a singer and keyboardist from Guyana, and Aura Lewis, a South African singer who was then working with Jimmy Cliff.

Born on March 4, 1947, in the Western Native Township section of Johannesburg, Aurelia Msimang fled the denigrating policies of apartheid in the early 1970s by enrolling in New York's Hunter College; after marrying a jazz musician, she became known as Aura Lewis. Bitten by the reggae bug after seeing the Wailers at Max's Kansas City, she came to Jamaica in 1976 to attend the second Caribbean Festival of Arts. She then enrolled in the Drama Department of the Jamaica School of Arts and began working with United Africa, led by the gifted saxophonist and arranger Cedric 'Im' Brooks. One morning, Aura crossed paths with Jimmy Cliff, who drafted her into his band as a backing singer for a short West African tour in the summer of 1977. Before returning to Jamaica to work on Cliff's *Bongo Man* album, the band stopped in London just as Scratch and Marley were putting together 'Punky Reggae Party', as Aura happily recounted. 'One day, Jimmy took me to Island Records, it was during the time when Bob and Lee were doing "Punky Reggae Party" and "Keep On Moving". I went in the studio and Lee Perry says "I'm looking for a singer. We're doing something downstairs and we've got Candy McKenzie and we need another vocalist." Jimmy Cliff said, "Here's Aura, she sings with me and we just came back from Africa." The first time I saw him he said, "You look just like my daughter" and it's true, we have the same face. He had the Congos' *Heart Of The Congos* album, he had just been trying to make a deal with Island Records. I think I met the Clash at the same time, because

Lee was co-producing their album or something. It was a very interesting and exciting period.'

At the same session, Marley and Perry recorded a new version of Curtis Mayfield's 'Keep On Moving', working in a couple of bridges during which Marley sang salutations to his children and spoke of increasing African unity. Though the track was left unfinished and languished in Island's vaults for several years, it would eventually surface on the B-side of an extended mix of 'One Love'. Tony Owens noted that Marley and Scratch were also working on the lyrics of 'Babylon System' at this session, a song which would eventually be included on Marley's *Survival* album. Perry himelf was most excited about the message of 'Punky Reggae Party', but was unhappy with the performances captured on tape in London; he would significantly re-structure the song elsewhere before its eventual release.

During this visit to the UK, Perry again crossed paths with John Martyn at one of Chris Blackwell's residences in Reading. According to Martyn, the morning after his arrival at the property, Perry pontificated about the art of sex before Blackwell's assembled guests at the breakfast table; he used coffee mugs to illustrate his points. Scratch's wacky description of sexual union inspired Martyn, who was then working on his *One World* album; he thus wrote the song 'Big Muff', which Perry helped him record the next day.

Before returning to Jamaica, Scratch was interviewed by Linton Kwesi Johnson, who was then a freelance journalist as well as a playwright and poet; his experimental melding of poetry and dub was shortly to instigate the inventive reggae subgenre that became know as 'dub poetry' after Johnson's own description of the verbal artistry of Jamaican toasters. Johnson was born in Chapleton in the parish of Clarendon in 1952. His father was a baker and mother a domestic worker and he spent part of his childhood with farming grandparents in the district of Sandy River after his mother moved to Slipe Road in Kingston. At the start of the 1960s, she emigrated to the UK, and sent for Linton to join her in 1963; the experiences of racism he was confronted with in England would come to shape the bulk of his work. Johnson noted his long-standing admiration for Perry's creativity, and spoke reverently of their initial meeting: 'The first Lee Perry tune I was aware of was "Doctor Dick" by King Perry – a version of Kitchener's very risqué calypso. I think the first record by Scratch that I bought was "People Funny Boy" around 1968, when the music was changing from rock steady to reggae; in fact, it was one of the prototypes of the early reggae. What I found extraordinary about the tune at the time was this baby crying in the background, it was the first time I'd heard anything like that. Later on, Scratch used cows mooing and broken bottles and all kinds of weird sounds; after he started putting out those Black Ark records, I realised he is a special guy and I began to see him in terms of being like the Salvador Dali of reggae music with a sort of unorthodox approach. I met Lee "Scratch" Perry in 1977 at the offices of Island Records at St Peter's Square in

West London; at that time he was producing the *Heart Of The Congos* album. I remember saying to him, "You have a unique sound, you use the flanger and phaser," but he didn't want to let out his trade secrets. Most of the time he spoke in parables, about things like "the shadow that walketh underneath a man". It was an experience. The other thing that struck me about Scratch at that time was his shamanistic approach to music-making: he thinks like an Obeah man, and I think to him music is a kind of a magical act – an act of conjuring up things, whether they be evocative of Africa, judgement, Armageddon, or whatever; this is his basic approach.' Unfortunately, Johnson's interview was never published, due to the censorious editorial policies of London's music press.

After Lee Perry completed his business in the UK, he returned to Kingston immediately to set about embellishing the hollow shell of 'Punky Reggae Party'; he noted that the song had not been voiced properly, and felt its musicianship was under par. 'Bob caught up with me in England. Me write the song in England and think it could record at Chris Blackwell's studio but there was no life in Blackwell's studio to do it, neither Third World didn't have any energy to do it, so me take it back to Jamaica and re-make it in Joe Gibbs' studio with my musicians.' Scratch was particularly dissatisfied with the rhythm's bass and drum parts, and tried first to get something better out of Boris Gardiner and Mikey Boo, but the pair could not accomplish what Scratch had envisioned. Perry later brought the master tape back to Joe Gibbs' studio to have bassist Val Douglas of the Now Generation and drummer Sly Dunbar take a stab at improving the song, this time with more positive results. Further instrumentation was added in the form of bright blasts from the Zap Pow horns and keyboard riffs from Tyrone Downey, but the icing on the cake came in the form of further backing vocals from Watty Burnett and the Meditations: Burnett boomed out a *basso profundo* refrain of 'punky punky punk', while the Meditations made incredible oinking noises over Sly's thunderous beat. Perry's trademark bursts of crashing cymbals gave the rhythm further demarcation, and Glen DaCosta's tenor sax helped inject an essence of swing. All the song needed now was a proper lead vocal from Bob Marley, but the Tuff Gong still remained abroad, so Perry left the partially completed work temporarily on hold while concentrating on other material. Marley later summoned Perry to Miami, where the song was successfully voiced in one take at Criteria studio, resulting in a highly popular track released in various formats: it appeared in Jamaica as an extended 12-inch single on Perry's Black Art label and also on a Tuff Gong maxi; both cuts featured long scat vocal sections from Bob. In November, Island issued the song on the back of 'Jammin'', a single from the *Exodus* album; as with 'Police and Thieves', its release abroad would see a whole new generation of white fans tune in to the creations of Lee Perry.

Though the Criteria recording session went smoothly, Perry also noted that it was when Marley asked Perry to join him in Miami that he confronted the Upsetter with shocking news: doctors had planned to amputate his foot as cancerous cells had been detected in the unhealing wound obtained at a football match. As Perry remembered, 'He call me over and they were going to cut off him foot; if not, it was going to kill him long time, but before he die they say if him lose a foot him would live longer. Me write "Punky Reggae Party" and make him sing it – that's how I heal him. Me fly back to do it in Criteria studio in Miami, and that was the power that heal him from the foot. After the session, him feel a different vibration.' Varying information has been put forward about the situation regarding Marley's toe, but it was reported in the British press that Bob left London to have surgery in Miami on August 23; in charge of the operation was Dr William Bacon, the surgeon who had earlier repaired Don Taylor after the ambush at Hope Road. Instead of agreeing to the proposed amputation, Marley opted for a lesser operation in which a portion of his toenail was removed; after many weeks of recuperation, he was given a clean bill of health and plans were made to reactivate a thrice-postponed American tour.

Back in Jamaica, Lee Perry pressed on with other excessive 12-inch disco mixes, several of which were issued in record jackets bearing the legend Upsetters Disco Bum – so titled because the sound was explosive, like the booming of a musical bomb. Most of the jackets were green in colour, resembling an American dollar bill, though a few were also issued in gold and red to complete the triumvirate of Rastafari colours. One of the first he made upon returning to Jamaica from the visit to London that resulted in 'Punky Reggae Party' was 'Disco Devil', an inspired re-working of Max Romeo's 'Chase The Devil' that Perry sang himself. Scratch used the rhythm as a platform to repel the negative aspects of the disco dance craze, suggesting that the fashion-conscious 'Hustlers' give their unwanted cocaine to the Pope, instead of seeking to corrupt the natty dreads through licentiousness. The song was given a more rounded feel through harmony vocals from Full Experience, then a duo comprised of Aura Lewis and a black American dancer named Pamela Reed; the group would soon become a trio after Candy McKenzie appeared at the Ark to begin recording material slated for Island Records.

'Disco Devil' was issued in a plain white record jacket, illustrated by a ghoulish disco phantom; some of the sleeves were actually disused record jackets for a Maytones album Perry got from his old friend Alvin Ranglin, turned inside out for a second usage. Hidden away on the B-side was an extended mix of the Wailers' 'Keep On Moving', which began innocuously enough; aside from a few honking bars of Dennis 'Taste' Campbell's sax, nothing much seems amiss until halfway through the song, when the rhythm is stopped and abruptly re-started. Then out of nowhere, deejay Wong Chu, selector of Tipper Tone sound, bursts in through a wildly excessive haze of delay to deliver a bewildering toast about all things straight and twisted. When the rhythm runs out, Perry starts it up for a third time, to segue into a dub cut punctuated by echoing vocal stabs and horn blasts frozen by the infinite reaches of the Space Echo. This scarce nugget provided a rare glimpse of just how hard and 'rootical' the Wailers' rhythms could become when re-shaped by the words of a talented toaster, though as ever it is Perry's boundless mixing that really gave the disc its outstanding qualities.

One of the clearest indications of Perry's increasingly troubled frame of mind came in 'City Too Hot', a Black Ark disco from the same period on which his psychological anguish was all too evident. Though Perry sounded light-hearted and fully in control on the flipside 'Bionic Rats', he sounded close to tears and clearly on the edge on 'City Too Hot'. Lamenting the oppressive forces that were actively weighing against him, Scratch alluded to the political gang wars, harassment by police and soldiers, divisive Rasta in-fighting and 'tit for tat' mentality that had created an atmosphere far from harmonious in Kingston; the song suggested he would head for the hills to find some relief, though Scratch seems never to have found the time physically to retreat from the hell of the capital.

The Black Ark was in constant use in this period, with many of Scratch's peers seeking to use his facilities as no one else was capable of creating such an intense and unique sound. For instance, Earl Sixteen recalled contributing backing vocals with Bunny Rugs on one of Yabby You's hardest issues in early 1977, the archly defiant 'Chant Down Babylon Kingdom'.

A number of other fine singles had sprung forth from Perry's studio through the course of 1977, products of the conveyor belt of creativity that was perpetually rolling in the Ark. Although Perry was counting on Island to boost his profile internationally, he never compromised his experimental impulses to please them; he thus continued to cut a number of one-off singles that year with lesser-known artists, many of which were far too uncommercial for Island. Lloyd Robinson and Devon Russell's 'Wolf Out Deh' was one such issue, one of a series of singles on the tricolour Black Art Disco Bum label, its dub punctuated by echoing vocal fragments and thunder claps.

Around the same time that Augustus Pablo blew melodica on 'Vibrate On', Errol 'Bagga' Walker cut three great vocal tunes at the Black Ark. Though his solo vocal output has been slim, the work he did with Lee Perry in 1977 shows that his vocal talents and song-writing abilities are as skilful as his musicianship. Walker's most notable collaboration with Perry was 'Better Future', an optimistic single with suitably splendid Black Ark arrangement. Two other songs were cut around the same time, though they would not be issued for a couple of years until their inclusion on an Island anthology: the slow and broody 'John Public', which was also versioned by a deejay called Enos Barnes, and 'Summertime', a dread inversion of George Gershwin's standard from 'Porgy and Bess'.

A smaller producer based in Vectis Avenue named Sean De Laire also recorded noteworthy material for his Grass Roots label at Scratch's studio in 1977, beginning with the religious 'Look Around' by harmony trio the Roots. Issued just after was the Roots' finest single, a moving statement against iniquity called 'Mash Down' on which their harmonies were put to best use; a deejay version of the rhythm also later surfaced, 'All For One One For All' (a.k.a. 'Kingston Rock') credited to a certain Natty. Both versions were later issued on a 12-inch disco 45 by the Greensleeves label in England. De Laire also made an interesting re-cut of Slim Smith's 'What A Situation' at the Black Ark around the same time, credited to the Sons of Brave.

Of the slim amount of material other producers recorded at the Ark in 1977, Zap Pow's 'River' was one of the finest – a truly atmospheric slice of heady reggae jazz. Like many Jamaican backing bands, Zap Pow has a complicated history; the group was formed in 1970 by David Madden, Dwight Pinkney, and Mikey Williams out of the ashes of several other bands. Trumpeter David Madden was an Alpha graduate who spent four months playing in a gospel group in Las Vegas before recording with Cedric Brooks at Studio One; Dwight Pinkney backed the Wailers for the 1966 hit 'Put It On' and toured the Bahamas for two years as lead guitarist of the Sharks; Michael L. Williams had been a regular on the North Coast hotel circuit. Their debut, 'Mystic Mood', was highly successful in Jamaica, as was its humorous follow-up, 'Scandal Corner'. In 1972, the group found further success for Harry J with 'This Is Reggae Music', which Chris Blackwell issued abroad after overdubbing a string section and having Traffic's Jim Capaldi write additional song lyrics to broaden its appeal. It was shortly after that saxophonist Glen DaCosta joined the group; another Alpha graduate, DaCosta performed with Jamaica's military band in London in 1967 and later teamed up with trombonist Vin Gordon for session work for Coxsone Dodd and King Edwards prior to their membership of Zap Pow. By the time the group began recording at the Black Ark, their regular drummer was Cornel Marshall.

Though Zap Pow had a good track record for creating hits, it was chiefly as session musicians that its members were known on the music scene, and Scratch often made use of its members' individual talents. As with many of the best outside productions recorded at the Black Ark, 'River' was a bartered creation stemming from Scratch's inability to pay his session musicians in hard cash. As David Madden remembered, 'Me and Glen DaCosta and Vin Gordon were doing some things for Lee "Scratch" Perry over a two-week span, he was putting on horns for some Bob Marley songs. When we were supposed to get paid, Scratch didn't have any money, so he said to us, "The most I can do is give you some time to do something." I told (the group) that I had this song "River", we rehearsed it and went to the studio. At that time we had the keyboard player Tony Johnson, but he didn't come so I called Geoffrey Chung. I got Noel Seal to play the congos and the lead guitarist was called Roy. When we started to do it, Scratch said, "Wait, a no so my music go man. This kind of music, woah!" I said "Scratch, I don't care (about) your kind of music, this is my song! I do my song inna your studio." Then he eventually started to say "Rahtid! It sound good!" We did about three takes of it. When he was mixing, he had a phaser that you hear running through it and him say, "This is my latest sound, do you want me to put it in it?" I said, "If you feel that it could go in there, put it!" so he put the phaser in there. I really wanted to call it "Mamee River", after the place that I was born up in Gordon Town. The song gives me the feeling of where I was as a little baby boy in Mamee River, but we just say "River" though the guys were singing "Reggae River"; it was Dwight, Mikey, and one other guy that used to hang out 'round the studio that was singing.'

Mikey Williams added the following particulars: 'That was the mastery of Lee Perry, the Noah of the Ark, he was involved as a co-producer. He give us ideas. "River" was created at 1C Oxford Road, we turned the garage into a studio, padded the walls, and did a lot of writing there. When we recorded that at Lee Perry's Black Ark studio, that session was heavenly vibes because we had the great Leslie Butler on keyboards. That made the session very interesting, because we had a feeling together and he got in that sweet flow into the reggae river.'

Of all the product created at the Ark by bartering associates, 'River' is among the most noteworthy for the way its heavy phasing pushed the song even farther towards the depths of abstract jazz. A song that instrumentally captures a feeling of the wonders of nature, 'River' is certainly one of the finest instrumentals ever to emerge from the Ark.

1976 and '77 had seen Lee Perry in the midst of what many would describe as his creative peak, and he seemed destined for greater future rewards as his creativity continued to increase. The material he made for Island Records would stand the test of time, the albums remaining as classic representations of the broad and complex sound he was capable of mastering in such a small and technically limited studio; product he was fashioning with Jamaican ears in mind also saw him progressing by leaps and bounds, as he ever sought to push the boundaries of recorded sound into new realms and dimensions. Though he would go on to create a series of further stunning innovations at the Black Ark in 1978, many projects would prove to be abortive and counter-productive enterprises that would fill him with dread frustration and misery, ultimately pushing him over the edge.

CITY TOO HOT:

The Excessive Apex and sudden fall of the Ark

It was many months after Perry's first connection with the Congos that the first copies of *Heart Of The Congos* finally arrived in scarce quantities in Britain on import in early 1978; the album-cover margins of a number of this initial Black Art pressing were adorned with yellow stripes hand-painted by resident artist Jah Wise over the blue stripes printed on its cover. The first mix of this album was somewhat restrained, with few effects or technical embellishments: the vocals were left largely dry, with little delay or reverb added; Keith Sterling's piano had been placed to the fore on several tracks, and there was a general absence of the phasing that had defined his previous Island albums.

Chris Blackwell travelled to Jamaica with his lawyer, Tom Hayes, to negotiate the terms of the album; contracts were signed and everything seemed set for Island to give *Heart Of The Congos* an official release in the UK. Scratch put a lot of energy into creating an alternative mix of the album, though whether its instigation stemmed from Blackwell's reluctance to issue the album in its original form is unclear. In any event, Lee Perry completely re-structured *Heart Of The Congos*, rendering subsequent pressings radically different. He bathed many of the vocals, keyboards, and guitar in high doses of delay; the piano was made fainter; manic percussion and crashing cymbals were added, and several songs rolled into extended dub portions. Perhaps the most startling new element was a mooing-cow sound on several songs – a sound created by Watty Burnett using the cardboard centre of a roll of tin foil. As Burnett revealed, Perry recorded him making the sound during one session, and stored the effect on a master tape for future use. 'People say sometimes Scratch take a cow into the studio, well the cow is me. It's an aluminum-foil roll, I put my mouth in the cardboard part and I make a sound with a music in my throat. I won't tell nobody how I get that effect, but it's natural to me. I make the sound "Moo", and Scratch say, "Wow! Sample that." We did the first sample, Scratch have it on a quarter-inch tape; Scratch think it was funny and he use it on a lot of stuff.' The mooing cow first surfaced on 'Ethiopia Land', a beautiful repatriation number recorded in the latter half of 1977 by Waterhouse duo Peter and Paul Lewis. The sound remained a defining element of Perry's productions in 1978, baffling to both competitors and loyal fans alike.

As Lee Perry continued his regular association with the Congos, he was also beginning to have greater contact with members of the Niyabinghi Theocracy, a strict religious order that now had a regular presence in his studio. Also known as the Boboshanti, the order was centred on a congregation of Rasta burru drummers, Garveyites who held regular Niyabinghi grounations from 1960. Their leader was an elder Trench Town resident and master drummer originally from Manchester who was himself known as Boboshanti, affectionately addressed by the order as Pa-Ashanti; his elderly Princess (i.e. common-law wife) was similarly addressed as Ma-Ashanti. Other prominent members of the group included Bongo Chef, Jah Stone, Bongo Tawny, Jah Lion from Clarendon, and the elder Bongo Wake-I, but it was Jah Ned, the group's *funde* specialist and youngest member, with whom Perry became most friendly.

Ned Willacy was born into a musical family in Jones Town circa 1950. His father Seebert was a bassist in Val Bennett's band; his cousin Jackie was a guitarist and his grandfather a drummer. As a teenager, Ned's knowledge of Kingston's dancehall scene landed him a job as informal talent scout for Celebrity Concerts where he suggested which local act should open for visiting artists such as the Impressions, Sam Cooke, and James Brown. He was also learning the art of silk-screen printing in downtown premises shared by the Sheiks band, and his silk-screened labels were featured in stage outfits worn by the Blues Busters, Byron Lee, and Clancy Eccles. It was in the ska years that Ned first became aware of Lee Perry, whom he often saw shaking a grater with the Skatalites at their regular Sunday performances at Bournemouth Beach; Ned's work in the downtown area saw him becoming more familiar with Perry and other music industry personnel through contact made on Orange Street.

In the early 1960s, he was taught to drum at a young age by members of the Boboshanti in Back-O-Wall; when Seaga bulldozed the area to transform it into the JLP stronghold of Tivoli Gardens, the order moved their base to Marcus Garvey's former headquarters at Liberty Hall on King Street, and later established an office and permanent base on Church Street. In 1970, the group made their first devotional recordings, but lack of funds meant the songs were never completed. It was when the state of emergency was declared in 1976 that the group was galvanised into taking serious action, seeking to use their music to help bring urgently needed changes to Jamaican society.

The Black Ark thus gradually became a focal point and meeting place for the Niyabinghi Theocracy. Lee Perry was the most prominent producer making music that was relevant to the Rastafari cause; his records were consistently radical and uncompromising, and he was never afraid to express his religious beliefs. The brethren thus appointed him as their Minister of Music, heightening his role within their movement. As Jah Ned explained, 'Scratch is instrumental(ly) a representative of the Rastafari government; his musical contribution was enough weaponry for him to use to do his part.

Scratch was responsible for the musical development within the movement of
Rastafari itself, so Scratch was generally responsible for the music ministry of
our movement. He was the minister for that department; everyone was
looking forward to Scratch.'

Through the influence of the Congos and his interaction with the
Niyabinghi brethren, Perry turned his attention away from worldly things to
enact a more religiose lifestyle. However, he continued to decorate the inner
Ark with pornographic photos taken from *Hustler* and *Penthouse* – a reflection
of his view that sex is an essentially sacred and divine act.

As Lee Perry continued re-working the Congos' material to facilitate the
official release of their album, he also became involved in some other
problematic and ill-fated projects, the next of which involved Full Experience.
Aura Lewis and Pamela Reed had been working as backing vocalists for Scratch
on an increasing basis throughout 1977, and would appear on some of his best
solo work to emerge in 1978. While Scratch was working on the Congos
album, Candy McKenzie came to the Ark to record chart-aimed material
which was supposed to be issued by Island; tracks cut included a credible
version of Baby Washington's 'Breakfast In Bed' and a playful beat-box workout called 'Disco Fits', both issued on an Upsetter disco.

McKenzie's voice was strong, deep, and soulful, and her Guyanan
origins made her a perfect candidate for the Full Experience group. Aura
Lewis had conceived of Full Experience as a trio composed of 'women from
the three parts of the African diaspora: the continent itself, the Caribbean and
America', and McKenzie's arrival meant that her vision was made complete.
Scratch was impressed by some of the original material they presented him
with, and the presence of so many attractive women also appealed to his
amorous nature. He thus gave Full Experience the green light, and began
recording an album with the trio.

The group laid down 11 songs with Mikey Boo, Winston Wright,
Geoffrey and Mikey Chung, and Sticky, incorporating a range of styles into
the pervasive roots feeling of the Black Ark. The songs included a version of
Nina Simone's 'Young, Gifted and Black' re-cut as 'Young Gifted And Broke',
broken-hearted love songs like 'Can't See You', an R & B number led by Reed
called 'Let's Move', and an impromptu groove co-written by Scratch called 'At
Midnight'. The outstanding track was 'Full Experience' (originally entitled
'Strictly Roots'), a thunderous exploration of the concept behind the group
with a solid bass line from Boris Gardiner, an inspiring horn fanfare and
echoing sound effects from Scratch himself.

The Full Experience album had several elements of ground-breaking
originality. It was rare enough for a female harmony trio to be creating an
album of their own in Jamaica, and Full Experience had an added difference
reflected in the disparate origins of its members. The album also saw the first
instance of African traditional music done in reggae, versions of the Swahili

songs 'Malaika' and 'Haposamane'. Despite the overall strength and highly original form of the material, the Full Experience project eventually fell prey to external and internal sabotage in 1978. As Aura Lewis explained, 'We did this album in a wonderful environment, but in the middle of all this work, little aspects started coming in to create confusion. First there was Lee Perry's crush on Pamela; Black Ark was in the same yard as his house, and Pauline and the kids were there . . . Pauline was saying that (the album) was going to be a flop. Then Candy had a big crush on a certain musician that was creating a lot of havoc with the musician's family; also, Candy didn't want to do her songs because Island was going to back her to do an album of her own. A lot of bad vibes starting coming on the scene. Since I had been working with Jimmy Cliff, I asked Jimmy if he would help me pay for the master tapes and pay Lee like a producer. I don't think Lee Perry appreciated that, and from the moment I did that it was like I never existed. They made a deal between them, and I don't know what happened.'

Though singles were pressed on Cliff's Sunpower label in 1978 claiming to be 'Strictly Roots' by Full Experience, another group's music was substituted at the last minute, and none of their material was ever issued in Jamaica. Lewis never really learned what transpired between Perry and Cliff, but was distraught to discover that horns had been overdubbed on the tracks and the music remixed without the input or permission of the group; she also consulted a lawyer when Cliff refused to relinquish control of the tapes only to find that the contract she had signed with him was worthless. Eventually, Cliff allowed Lewis to retrieve a poor quality master tape with a mere five songs on it, which were issued in 1987 by the French Blue Moon label; the rest of the tracks remain sadly unreleased.

The start of 1978 also saw a number of strong Jamaican issues from Scratch; some of the year's best work would be recorded with the Meditations, with whom Perry was hoping to issue an album. Still smarting from Dobby Dobson's handling of the profits from their first two albums, the group was reluctant to consent to recording an LP with Scratch, but agreed to record a number of singles for the producer. The material they recorded together in early 1978 included Danny Clarke's 'Think So' (a.k.a. 'Much Smarter'), Ansel Cridland's moving 'No Peace', and a righteous Niyabinghi chant called 'House Of Parliament' that demanded an end to the Babylon system. According to Ansel Cridland, the trio also recorded a song that Perry had written at this time called 'Babylon Arrest', in which the security forces were instructed it was 'Time for police to go to jail', but the recording was not completed and remains unreleased.

Perry sent Island the Meditations' 'No Peace', along with the 12-inch version of Raphael Green and Doctor Alimantado's 'Rasta Train' and a remixed version of Augustus Pablo's 'Vibrate On', but Island declined to issue any of the material. They would, however, issue an extended cut of 'Much

Smarter' on the back of the Meditations' self-produced 'Life Is Not Easy', a blistering report on life's hardships recorded at Channel One; initially slated for release in France, record executive Erskine Thompson negotiated with the group for Island to handle its overseas issue. Cridland brought the masters to the Black Ark to transfer the song onto a tape for Island, and Perry placed his mooing-cow sound between the vocal and dub portions of its extended mix; unbeknown to Cridland, Perry also cut an alternative mix with excessive cow sounds and other effects resounding through much of the dub.

Much of the material recorded at the Black Ark in 1978 directly addressed the oppression and corruption that was then engulfing Jamaica. The nation was truly in a terrible state, with unemployment at an all-time high and food shortages more common; politically motivated violence had escalated as never before, and the highest-ranking politicians of both parties were being directly implicated in its propagation. At the end of the year when the two sevens clashed, Jamaica's anarchic state of affairs was directly exposed by a notorious incident that became known as the Green Bay Massacre.

Under the pretext of gaining access to automatic weaponry, 12 gunmen were lured to the Green Bay firing range in the early hours of a December morning in 1977. The rudies arrived at the spot in separate vehicles only to find themselves surrounded by members of the Military Intelligence Unit – a special branch of the JDF. The soldiers fired indiscriminately at the defenceless men; though most were killed instantly, a slim few miraculously escaped. Among the dead were the five leading members of the South Side Posse – a group of JLP gunmen who controlled the South Kingston ghetto known as Tel Aviv – and a number of lower-ranking PNP gunmen.

Public furore erupted as facts about the case came to light. Though Michael Manley claimed that those killed were leaders of ruthless criminal gangs that were terrorising the residents of his constituency, the word on the street was that the killings were the work of a renegade MIU faction, which implied that the government was no longer in control of its armed forces. The manner in which the men were slaughtered also brought widespread public condemnation: no attempt had been made to arrest the men; they were simply rounded up and eliminated.

This sad moment in Jamaica's increasingly discordant history would quickly be immortalised on vinyl, and Perry was one of the first producers to cut material commenting on the event. He had recently re-structured 'Dreadlocks In Moonlight' (now called 'Big Neck Police') by adding a Full Experience chorus in the mix, and placed a previously unrecorded deejay called Lord Sassafras (a.k.a. Michael Johnson) on the rhythm for the condemning 'Green Bay Incident'. Based in the Waterhouse ghetto, Sassafras deejayed for the Soul Expert sound in the early 1970s and later joined the Black Scorpio set; at the time of the Green Bay Massacre, he rode his bicycle to Perry's studio on a daily basis, begging Scratch for a chance on the mike.

When the government later refused to bring the eight soldiers who had carried out the killings to trial, Perry recorded Sassafras on a follow-up single called 'Green Bay Inquest', using the rhythm of 'Travelling', a minor hit by a little-known singer named Debra Keese. According to Earl Sixteen, Keese was another young hopeful that appealed to Perry's carnal instincts. Her song about the personal journey of joining the Rastafarian faith garnered favour with many of the dreads, but 'Sweat Suit', a weak answer to Althea and Donna's smash hit 'Uptown Top Ranking' (credited to Sonny and Debby) was unpopular; Perry chose not to issue a follow-up single called 'In These Last Days' and Keese quickly faded from the scene.

Perry cut more critical commentary on the first vinyl sides to feature radio-technician-turned-disc-jockey Michael Campbell, a.k.a. Mikey Dread. The tall and charismatic Campbell was an old friend of Watty Burnett from Portland whose four-hour after-midnight spot aired on JBC five nights a week was then the only show on the island to feature nothing but home-grown Jamaican music, earning him the love of the common people and the loathing of the station's controllers. Campbell used to hang out at the Black Ark, gathering exclusives from Perry to air on his show, and eventually cut a number of toasts for Scratch, of which the first to surface was 'Home Guard', cut on an abridged version of 'Free Up The Prisoners'; the disc sarcastically attacked the government's Home Guard scheme, an early version of the 'Neighbourhood Watch'. Campbell's follow-up was 'Dread At The Control', another cut of 'Big Neck Police' that venerated dreads and cursed baldheads, while a further Black Ark recording was 'School Girls', using the rhythm of the spirited 'Elaine' by the group Mystic I.

Often miscredited as the Mystic Eyes and sometimes a Mystic M, Mystic I was a trio based at the Rastaman camp in Selassie Drive, close to the Ethiopian Orthodox Chruch in Western Kingston; the street was so named because Selassie walked there on his 1966 state visit and established an Amharic school nearby. Lead vocalist and chief songwriter of the group was Les Clarke, a furniture-maker with short dreadlocks who lived for many years in Canada; harmony was handled by a nightclub chef from Maxfield Avenue named Balvin Fials and a singer from Trench Town called Anthony Johnson, who also occasionally sang lead. Johnson was the only group member with previous recording experience, and it was his contacts in the industry that led to the establishment of the group.

Born on Christmas Day, 1957, Roy Anthony Johnson was the sixth of ten children raised by a market higgler; his father was a waiter at the popular Sombrero Club on Molynes Road. Johnson grew in an environment where roots music dominated, as the family home at 15 James Street was also the site of the only dancehall yard in Trech Town, owned by an Indian from Cuba named Mr Biah; top sound systems like King Tubby's and Emperor Faith regularly appeared there. Many of the country's best singers were Trench

Town residents at this time, and Johnson drew much inspiration from local artists such as John Holt, Slim Smith, the Heptones, and the Gaylads, but his greatest influence was Dennis Brown, whose singing style he would largely emulate. Johnson spent much of his youth in Alton Ellis' nearby yard on White Street, marvelling at the singer's talents and learning the rudiments of guitar and drums from Alton's nephew Aston.

As Johnson reached his teen years, tensions were rising in the neighbour-hood as political rivalry led to increased police harassment of Trench Town residents. Johnson thus spent a period in Montego Bay, living in the yard of Alton Ellis' younger brother Irving in Glendevon. Known as Nine-Finger due to a missing digit, Irving led a popular steel-pan band that Johnson joined as a singer, gaining much experience through hotel performances.

Johnson later returned to the Kingston area, but moved to a new home in Portmore – a dilapidated area west of the city that then had a few speculative properties built on a swamp; the PNP would later re-develop the area by building a large, low-income housing estate in an attempt to ease Kingston's chronic overcrowding. A close friend of Johnson in Portmore was the performer Carl Bradshaw, who was establishing himself as an actor and comedian on the North Coast hotel circuit; Bradshaw thus had Johnson join his backing band for regular weekend performances in Negril.

It was in the mid-'70s that Johnson began attending studio sessions with a friend from Trench Town named Horace Grassett (better known as the singer Badoo), trying to find someone willing to record him. Studio One was always too busy and Federal was losing popularity, so Johnson began spending more time at Dynamic Sounds, where he became friendly with Vic Taylor and Keith Lyn of the Dragonaires. He eventually made Bunny Lee's acquaintance, and voiced a tune with the Soul Syndicate band named 'Free Black Man' for the producer, but Striker apparently declined to issue it; he did, however, persuade the singer to drop the first name Roy from his moniker, as Anthony Johnson had a better ring to it. Striker was then working with Linval Thompson, and Johnson made Thompson's acquaintance at the same session; Thompson would later produce several singles with the singer, the strongest of which was 'Africa'.

After his abortive debut for Bunny Lee, Johnson subsequently recorded for the Hookim brothers, who allowed him to choose an acoustic guitar from Randy's shop after one of his recordings was an early success for Channel One abroad (though Johnson himself could not recall its title).

Though Johnson's official residence was in Portmore, the singer found himself spending an increasing amount of time at the Rasta camp on Selassie Drive in 1977, smoking a chalice, reasoning with the other brethren, and being greatly inspired to write more songs. It was here that Johnson became friendly with Les Clarke, who had already written many songs of his own, and Balvin Fials, who was always ready to provide further harmony. The three singers thus came together as the trio Mystic I.

According to Johnson, the group first approached Linval Thompson, who agreed to record an album with them at Channel One; though they received a small advance for the material, they heard nothing further from the producer after its completion. It was only years later when Johnson came to England that he learned Thompson had issued the tracks as an album called *Mysterious* on the Burning Sounds label; its outstanding track, 'Judgement Time' (a.k.a. 'Perilous Time') was a strong success abroad on Thompson's Strong Like Sampson label.

Johnson said it was after the album had been completed that the group made their way to the Black Ark, where they were introduced to Scratch by Johnson's cousin Cleveland, who had known the producer since his days at Studio One. The group thus recorded three strong songs for Scratch during an afternoon session at the Black Ark in late 1977 or early 1978, the strongest of which was 'Forward With Jah Orthodox', issued on a Black Art seven-inch. This militant number had the group inviting the faithful to stone the Devil by demanding an end to taxation; the fearsome rhythm, punctuated by skilful Niyabinghi percussion from Scully, formed a strong contrast with the group's uplifting harmonies. Their harmonic skills were also put to good use on the spirited 'Forward With Love' and on the aforementioned love song 'Elaine', but Scratch held back issuing this material, which was later pressed on discos in the UK.

Another single from this period to comment on how difficult life had become in Jamaica was 'Economic Crisis' by Jackie Bernard of the Kingstonians (re-named Jack Lord by Scratch for this release). Bernard's emotionally laden delivery captured the desperation of the people, while Perry's quiet sound effects suggested the growing anarchy in the streets. Conversely, one of the few songs to emerge from the Ark that was not concerned with social commentary was Earl Sixteen's 'Cheating', a fairly successful love song that Perry issued with two different mixes in quick succession.

'Cheating' was one of a handful of songs that Sixteen voiced at a Black Ark session; of the other songs, only 'Freedom' was ever released. As Sixteen remembered, 'I did "Cheating" and one called "Do Good", it never came out. I did "Bird In The Hand", the vocal never came out either; he's got the rhythm on the *Return Of The Super Ape* album. "Cheating" and "Bird In The Hand", those two were played by Boris Gardiner, and "Bird In The Hand" was written by Fitzroy Martin, he played saxophone in Boris' band. "Freedom" (written by a friend called Clive Jeffries) and "Do Good" were played by drummer Albert Malawi and (guitarist) Dalton Browne; that was the first time that Steelie (keyboardist Wycliffe Johnson) came to the studio as well.'

As most artists recording at the Black Ark continued to draw attention to the harsh reality that formed the basis of ghetto existence in Kingston, some positive changes were surprisingly brought to such communities at the start of 1978. In the aftermath of the Green Bay Massacre, the Niyabinghi Theocracy had a crucial involvement in bringing a year's worth of tranquillity to the streets of Kingston; though their achievements relied largely on the participation of Bob Marley, Lee Perry also directly contributed to the winds of change that blew a peace treaty into the war-torn streets of Kingston in January 1978.

The unexpected truce was called by two of the highest-ranking political gunmen: Claudie Massop and Bucky Marshall. Claudie 'Jack' Massop was first commander of the greatly feared Shower Posse, the ruthless JLP gang that controlled Edward Seaga's Tivoli Gardens constituency; Aston Thompson, a.k.a. 'Bucky Marshall', was one of the leading members of their most prominent enemies, the PNP-backed Spanglers posse. The gangs had a bitter rivalry that dated back to the late 1950s, but which intensified under their political alignment from the mid-'60s onwards.

In the days before political sponsorship resulted in the rudies being heavily armed, the Spanglers were followers of Duke Reid's sound based in the Western Kingston slum of Back-O-Wall. When Seaga bulldozed it and the neighbouring area, known as Rema, to build Tivoli Gardens, Jamaica's first government housing development, he housed JLP supporters in the area and armed the Tivoli Gang to make sure residents remained loyal to the JLP; by the end of the decade, the Tivoli Gang had evolved into the Shower Posse. Once Seaga's gang controlled his constituency, the Spanglers became aligned with the PNP and moved to a new base downtown in Matthews Lane (known in the Kingston vernacular as Matches Lane). Besides keeping their areas politically 'pure', the gangs launched an endless series of attacks on each other, particularly in election years; along with their butchery of rival gang members, countless innocent ghetto residents were often senselessly killed.

At the start of 1978, Bucky Marshall found himself in the same jail cell as some JLP gunmen. Contemplating their shared captivity, they began to realise they were mere pawns in a politicians' game in which common ghetto folk would never be winners; much like the gunmen who had been rounded up and obliterated at Green Bay, they were certainly expendable in their role as 'enforcers', regardless of political affiliation. They thus began to speak of unity as the only solution to Jamaica's seemingly endless spiral of self-destruction.

After being released on January 9, Marshall made contact with Massop to discuss a peace treaty; Massop agreed and the 'rankings' held a reasoning session through the night in the Tel Aviv ghetto of South Kingston attended by members of the Niyabinghi Theocracy. At the next day's dawning, they announced an official peace treaty from the corners of Beeston and Oxford Street – the official boundary line between JLP and PNP areas. They then began making arrangements for the One Love Peace Concert, a live-music event which would help publicly cement the peace and raise money for the impoverished communities that had been destroyed by decades of political factionalism; their proposed headliner was Bob Marley, the island's biggest international star.

The concert is said to have been Massop's brainchild, but he felt unable to approach Marley directly due to his membership in a JLP gang, as the JLP were widely believed to have ordered the attack in which Marley was shot before the Smile Jamaica concert. Massop and Marshall thus enlisted the help of the Twelve Tribes of Israel to act as intermediaries, after speaking to Marley by telephone from the Church Street office of the Boboshanti.

Members of the Twelve Tribes went to visit Bob Marley in Miami to gain his consent to headline the event, but Marley requested clarification from Massop that he would no longer be a target for JLP bullets. Massop and Marshall offered to come to Miami to speak with Bob directly, but Marley did not want gunmen around his family members, so a meeting was arranged to be held in London in February. Massop, Marshall, and Marley spent a week in London making negotiations, along with the higher-ranking PNP cadre Tony Welch; after Marley was assured of his safety, the concert date was set for April 22.

One of the first people to issue a song applauding the Peace Treaty was Kiddus-I, another prominent member of the Peace Movement; though he had previous studio experience, the Black Ark recording 'Security in the Streets' ended up being his first release. Born Frank Dowding in St Mary in 1954, his father was a bookkeeper and mother a potter; he adopted the name Kiddus, which means Blessed One in Amharic, after becoming a Rastafarian. This quiet, thin, and thoughtful dread operated a Rastafarian commune and crafts centre at 1C Oxford Road since 1971 with the goal of establishing a wholesome and self-sufficient Rastafari community; its location at the juncture of Uptown and Downtown meant that persons from all social strata could meet in a harmonious atmosphere, making the compound a unique entity in a city starkly divided by social class. As some of the best ital food could be found there, and as Rastafari was the main focus, it naturally became a congregation point for musicians, and the Zap Pow band eventually built a rehearsal room on the premises.

Besides being a community leader, Kiddus-I was also a fine singer; his pleasant, deep voice has a distinct and slightly nasal timbre. In 1972, he recorded his first self-productions with Family Man at Joe Gibbs' studio, 'Careful How You Jump' and 'By The Sweat', but lack of funds meant the songs were never released. A few years later, Gregory Isaacs began reminding Kiddus of the value of his voice, resulting in Jack Ruby recording him in 1976 with the song 'Graduation In Zion', which would eventually feature on the soundtrack of the movie *Rockers*.

Once the Peace Treaty was in full swing, Kiddus-I went to the Black Ark to praise the efforts of 'Brother Claudie, Brother Bucky, and Brother Tony' on record with 'Security In The Streets', the most moving of all songs celebrating the truce. This extended disco mix issued on Kiddus-I's Shepherd label featured bursts of clavinet from Wire Lindo, harmony vocals from Tyrone

Downey, timbre blasts from the Zap Pow horns, a smooth guitar line from Chinna and throbbing bass from Robbie Shakespeare; its flip side, 'Too Fat', used another extended rhythm to point a guilty finger at the greedy. Kiddus-I also recorded the politically censorious 'Crying Wolf' at the Ark in this period; all three songs are marked by an air of majesty and seriousness. Though his later work would deal with equally serious issues, it would lack the lush and attentive mixing lavished on these tracks by Lee Perry, and would ultimately make less of an impact.

On February 26, 1978, Bob Marley returned to Jamaica for the first time since fleeing the country after the Smile Jamaica concert in December 1976. Around 2000 people are estimated to have pushed past police barricades to swarm the plane when it came to a halt on the runway – the largest public gathering at the airport since Selassie's visit in 1966. Several functions had been organised to coincide with Marley's return, which also marked the 50th anniversary of Garvey's UNIA: the National Heroes' Circle had been given over to a Rastafarian rally, at which Bob Marley gave an informal performance in the evening, followed by several of the island's emerging dub poets, including Mutabaruka, Oku Onoura, and Mikey Smith; flanked by body-guards, Marley then went on to join Lee Perry and the rest of the inner city's most devout brethren for a night-long grounation held by the Niyabinghi Theocracy in Matthews Lane.

The grounation was one of a series held by the Boboshanti after the peace treaty had been announced to motivate the people towards embracing its philosophy; they were historic events in that the government granted permission for the grounations to be held, and the brethren were able to chant and drum without the ever-present fear of police harassment that blighted so many of the events, particularly when held in Kingston.

After repeater player Jah Ned had a vision that the city was decorated in red, green, and gold, the brethren made tricolour sashes to mark off the area of the Niyabinghi, draping what had been streets of bloodshed with the presence of His Majesty. When Bob Marley arrived at the grounation after his brief performance at Heroes Park, he was overcome with emotion at seeing so many formerly at war gathered in a spirit of oneness; then, mid-way through the proceedings, Kingston was shaken by an earthquake as though in acknowledg-ment of the magnanimity of the event.

Although Marley was busy making preparations for the One Love Peace Concert and spent many days visiting ghetto areas to help bolster the peace, he also found the time to lay the foundations of a couple of new scorchers with Scratch one Sunday at Dynamic. Recorded in front of an array of onlookers that included Claudie Massop and Bucky Marshall, 'Blackman Redemption' and 'Rastaman Live Up' were optimistic proclamations of righteousness, harder than the bulk of Marley's recent *Kaya* album; the rhythm of the historical 'Buffalo Soldier' was also laid at the same session. Scratch's influence is readily apparent on the first two songs, particularly 'Rastaman Live Up', which contains a favourite refrain of his about Daniel slaying the Philistines with a donkey jawbone.

After the basic rhythm tracks had been laid with musicians such as Chinna Smith and Robert 'Billy' Johnson, Marley and Perry set about voicing and re-structuring 'Blackman Redemption' at Aquarius studio with engineer Murvin Williams; Bunny Wailer was a silent observer at the session. To give the songs an added harmonic difference, Perry sent for the Meditations, who arrived at the studio around seven o'clock. Though Perry had retroactively placed their backing vocals on some of Marley's earlier material, Bob had never actually met the trio; happy to be working with them, he told the group of the strong impact their 'Woman Is Like A Shadow' had on him in London. According to Ansel Cridland, Scratch lengthened the 'Blackman Redemption' voicing session to get the best from all assembled; he was not satisfied with Marley's vocal performance until well after midnight. The Meditations' harmonies were also used on 'Rastaman Live Up', and though they took a stab at harmonising 'Buffalo Soldier', the voices of Rita Marley and the sister of Junior Tucker were eventually used instead.

Despite his hectic schedule in these weeks, Bob Marley spent a fair amount of time around Scratch. Later in the year, the old cronies would join forces for another couple of impressive tunes; for the moment, Marley had other commitments to fulfil.

The One Love Peace Concert turned out to be a truly historic event. The National Stadium was filled to capacity, the unusually low ticket prices allowing the common citizenry to see some of Jamaica's top acts at the peak of their form. Peter Tosh delivered an expletive-strewn lecture aimed at the island's wealthy few; he also implored Seaga and Manley to take up the principles of the Peace Movement and stop victimising the poor. But by far the most incredible moment came at the climax of the Wailers' triumphant performance, when Marley managed to get Manley and Seaga to join hands on stage – an event that would have been unthinkable until Marley precipitated it.

It was around the time of the Peace Concert that Bob Marley's mother, Cedella Booker underwent her official conversion to Rastafari. As a further expression of her new-found faith, Bob had the idea that his mother record a gospel album of spiritual hymns. He thus made arrangements for her to begin recording at the Black Ark. As Mrs Booker remembered, 'Bob told me he want me to do a gospel album, he make arrangements with Scratch and send me there. We did "Enter the Lord's Anointed" and about three other gospel songs. Scratch was a good director, he tell the man them what they're doing wrong and how they are to work with me.'

A few weeks after the concert, Bob Marley and the Wailers left Jamaica for the start of a world tour. Cedella Booker went back to Miami, leaving unfinished the work she began with Scratch at the Black Ark.

It was also in this period that Perry became involved with another tainted Black Ark project: *Monama*, an album recorded with 'Seke' Molenga Mosukola and 'Kalo' Kawongolo Kimwangala (a.k.a. Buffalo), two Congolese musicians from Zaïre. Though conflicting information has been put forward about how the pair ended up at the Black Ark, Roy Johnson stated that they were brought to Perry's studio by Nadette Duget, a record executive then working for CBS France. When Duget brought the pair to Kingston, she was seeking to exploit the burgeoning reggae and African markets in France by creating a hybrid crossover; to keep costs to a minimum, she recruited the two semi-professionals who had only recently backed up Tabu Ley for a brief period in France on guitar, saxophone, percussion, and backing vocals. Although the album was originally meant to be cut at Dynamic, the pair ended up at the Black Ark, where they began the slow process of laying tracks with Perry and his crew.

The duo recorded a total of 12 songs with Perry, ten of which were sung in Lingala, creating an unprecedented blend of Jamaican reggae and Zaïrean soukous. Perry co-wrote a final couple of songs with them in English: 'Bad Food', based on their experiences in Kingston, and 'African Root', a reflection of the links between African and Jamaican culture.

At some point during the realisation of their project, Nadette Duget and her assistants realised that Seke and Kalo were somewhat inexperienced, and that her plan to cut corners was backfiring. According to Roy Johnson, Duget's team became more interested in the Congos after observing the highly professional and rapid manner in which they worked. 'Some white people working for CBS France came down to Jamaica, they was recording these African guys in Scratch's place. They see us do three-four tracks a day, and when those guys come, they can't finish one track for a day. One day they say, "Shanti, you know where we can get some congo drums?" I took the lady to get some drums and she asked me, "Would you like to do something with us? We would like to do some business." '

As Lee Perry continued to work with the African amateurs, his connection with the Congos was severed. Lured by the promise of a more lucrative arrangement, the group left Perry's camp to work with Duget after a bitter parting with their former mentor towards the end of 1978. It was at this point that Perry trimmed off his budding locks, rejecting their view that his inward belief in Rastafari must be manifest through visible dreadlocks on his head.

Though conflicting views have been put forward by group members about the circumstances of the rupture, all agreed that it stemmed from Island's failure to issue *Heart Of The Congos*; though the company issued publicity of its upcoming release in April, they ultimately chose to keep it on the shelf. The master tape Perry initially presented to the company had been recorded at a low-fidelity slow speed on a re-used four-track master tape that had Fay Bennett's 'Big Cocky Wally' still present in another two channels –

hardly the ideal format for album mastering, though whether this had any influence on Island's decision is unclear. As the album would never cease to be in demand, would be repressed on at least seven labels in four nations, achieving a high volume of sales when lovingly re-issued by Blood and Fire Records in 1996, Island's refusal to issue the Congos' debut is difficult to understand in retrospect.

Roy Johnson suggested that Island feared the album was too strong, and would damage the sales of Bob Marley's albums, which they were chiefly concerned with promoting. 'Leslie Palmer used to work in the A & R Department in Island, so he know what's going on. He said to me, "When that album come from Jamaica, we have meeting for a month straight about who we was to put the promotion on: Bob Marley or the Congos." ' Max Romeo has made similar claims about *Reconstruction*, his self-produced follow-up to *War In A Babylon*, which he felt suffered from a lack of promotion at Marley's expense. 'I realised that they sign all the artists that was a threat to Bob Marley and put them on the shelf so they can send the King ahead and crown the King. We were all victims, all sacrificed to make the Marley empire, but we thank God for it because the world would hear reggae music.'

Roy Johnson further noted that tension had already been growing between Perry and the group after Cedric Myton's son started a rumour that Scratch deliberately fed him pork, the most taboo of meats for Rastafarians. However, his suggestion that Perry asked Blackwell to block the album is clearly misguided, as Perry himself was greatly angered by Island's refusal to release it. 'Cedric's little boy go and tell a lie that Scratch cook pork and give him to eat. Scratch get vexed; maybe he tell Chris, "Just keep that on the shelf." When we did *Heart of the Congos*, it stay so long to surface, for Chris Blackwell have it there doing nothing with it, Scratch have it there doing nothing with it.'

Watty Burnett recalled the pork incident, but said that the real friction stemmed from Perry's view of Roy's vocal abilities. 'There was no pork cook in that house, but Roy and Scratch had a feud because Scratch always say Roy couldn't sing, and Roy knew he didn't have a great vocals so he take it offensive. It start from that, and Cedric is easily led. When they had the feud, I was very upset because I didn't want to leave Scratch. It really fuck me head up until now; I sleep and I dream about it. When CBS took us, I didn't want to leave Scratch. Scratch feel a way badly, Scratch take it very hard too.'

When asked about Island's decision not to issue *Heart Of The Congos*, Chris Blackwell hesitantly stated, 'I remember at the time thinking that there was one great track and the rest of it was weak.' However, he was quick to deflect claims that he venerated Bob Marley at the expense of other artists. 'People think a guy like me does an incredible job to make and break artists, but you don't at all, you're around to try and help the artists you're working with make it. The main role is to help guide, to try and be a friend, help develop choices and open doors. I didn't push Bob above anybody else, Bob just had more going for him than anybody else; I honestly believe that is the case. I pushed Burning Spear, I pushed Toots – I love Toots, I've known Toots much longer than Bob – but I just wasn't able to get him across. Lee Perry, like most reggae artists, was embraced more by the press than by the radio; the press gives you credibility but radio is really what sells records, so Lee Perry never sold a lot of records in the same way like how Bob sold a lot of records. Songs like "Roast Fish And Cornbread", these are absolute masterpieces, but we weren't able to make them hit singles at that time.'

When Island refused to issue the album abroad, Perry cut the second foreign mix in Jamaica just as the rupture was approaching. When the split happened, the Congos were given master tapes with a cut of the second mix, which they would use to re-press the album on a number of occasions. Watty Burnett was also given master tapes of his material, as well as a cut of Earl Sixteen's 'Freedom' (a.k.a. 'Right Yow'), which Burnett had funded and produced.

With the Congos out of the picture, Scratch continued working with the Zaïrean singers; though CBS France had abandoned the project, Perry was inspired enough by the cross-pollination of African and Caribbean music to continue working with them under his own steam. With the Congos' album, Perry sought to capture the essence of Africa that was buried deep inside all black Jamaicans; now two Africans straight from the heart of the Congo had appeared in his midst, the very language of Africa on their lips.

He eventually sent Island Records a rough mix of the *Monama* album, along with four extended Lingala grooves for an additional disco 45. Again, the mix was sent on a very poor-quality tape, which only added to the bad impression the album made on Island's executives; though they would consider releasing the album at several points, they have kept it under wraps to the present day.

When the Congolese vocalists left Jamaica, Kalo Kawongolo was given a rough mix of six of the most finished tracks by Scratch, which were subsequently pressed on the French Sonafric label in 1979 as the self-titled debut *Seke Molenga And Kalo Kawongolo* album; the remaining tracks have yet to be released.

While Perry was completing his work with Seke and Kalo, he was also recording an album with the Jolly Brothers, a harmony group based in the Edgewater area near Hellshire beach. The trio of Winston Edwards, Lennox Miller, and Willis Gordon – occasionally augmented by Hendrick Nicholson – had been brought to the Black Ark towards the end of 1977 by their friend and musical coach Mattis, who oversaw the recording of two original numbers called 'Colour' and 'Conscious Man'. It was the latter song that proved to be the strongest, its catchy harmonic chorus and use of biblical allegory to explain the romantic etiquette of men hinting at commercial potential. Scratch also applied a new technique to the song's lead-guitar line, and the rapid see-saw effect helped give a greater sense of movement that would ultimately increase its popularity.

Perry's old London connection Tony Owens had come to Jamaica in this period, seeking material to license for a label called Seven Leaves he was in the process of establishing in the UK, and Scratch agreed to give him a helping hand by allowing him to issue the song abroad. When Owens brought the tape back to London, he arranged instead for it to be issued on the newly-formed Magnum label, which benefited from major distribution by Pye; the label was run by Mo Claridge, who had established the Mojo Distribution company and Bam Bam record label in West London after breaking away from Creole in 1976.

In early 1978, Mojo created the Ballistic imprint through a licensing deal with major label United Artists; the label would greatly raise the profile of reggae in Britain and Europe in the late '70s. 'Conscious Man' was one of the first singles to appear on the label, re-packaged in a picture sleeve, and Ballistic's widespread distribution and promotions network helped the song quickly to become a hit in Britain, where it eventually peaked at number 45 in the pop charts; they would also ensure that the song was a hit in Europe in 1979 through the release of an extended disco mix.

When 'Conscious Man' entered the British charts, Tony Owens returned to Jamaica to assemble a Jolly Brothers album under Lee Perry's guidance, finding Scratch in the midst of work with Seke and Kalo; the Africans were thus enlisted to play guitar, congas, and saxophone on some of the Jolly Brothers' new material, and the Jolly Brothers were used for backing vocals on part of the African project.

The Jolly Brothers recorded around eight more topical songs at the Black Ark, often singing in unison over Perry's spongy rhythms, but conflict between Tony Owens and Ballistic saw the release of the material delayed by several years. While their disagreements continued, Claridge enlisted Waterhouse producer Lloyd 'Prince Jammy' James to record an album of love songs with the group at Channel One and Harry J, subsequently issued on Ballistic in 1979 as *Consiciousness* (which included the Black Ark hit single as its opener). The rest of the more socially relevant and musically innovative Black Ark material was left on the shelf until the early 1980s, when a few disco mixes would appear in the UK on Seven Leaves; the remaining songs would not be cut until 1993 when Owens issued the album *Conscious Man* on his Roots Records imprint.

Before his rupture with the Congos, Lee Perry was putting the finishing touches on two albums of his own material. *Roast Fish Collie Weed And Cornbread*, issued in late April, was the first album entirely to feature Perry as a vocalist, and though some have felt that singing was not his strong point, the album showed that Perry could excel on inspired material written and produced by himself. In addition to the remixed title track (with added cow sounds), the revamped 'Dreadlocks In Moonlight' (with full chorus as 'Big Neck Police'), and a re-cut of Junior Byles' 'Curley Locks' (with crashing cymbals, sung by the Upsetter himself), the album had seven strong originals addressing a variety of topics.

Several of the tracks were fairly humorous: 'Soul Fire' had a double-tracked Perry wailing the lingo of soul over a thick Upsetter mix of mooing cows, echoing percussion, funky guitar, and mournful sax; 'Throw Some Water in' used automobile upkeep as a metaphor for taking care of the human body over a militant rockers drum line; 'Yu Squeeze Me Panhandle' (a.k.a. 'Mr DJ Man') requested that radio jockeys help his new material to become a hit so that his family could eat properly, and the self-explanatory 'Favourite Dish' used a large quantity of sound effects to give the song a third dimension; over a post-rockers rhythm with plenty of off-time percussion, babies bawled and cows mooed while Perry sang of the food he loved and how nature made sure his manhood needed no chemical stimulants to perform properly. The more politically motivated 'Ghetto Sidewalk' requested more light for the sufferers, while 'Free up the Weed' was an optimistic plea for the legalisation of herb. But the track that most indicated what would increasingly become Perry's frame of mind was 'Evil Tongues', an ominous and vindictive number that verges on paranoia:

> 'There are some hypocrites around me
> Who pretending to be my friend
> Little did they know that I saw them coming
> Saw them coming around the bend
> Evil eyes and wicked heart
> I saw them coming from afar
> Coming coming to play their part
> You want the lion's share, but Jah Jah know that no fair
> Wicked tongue and evil heart
> By the sweat of your brow you shall eat bread
> Then how you want to live off the next man head?
> You too lazy, you can't leave you bed . . . '

'The song based upon the Congos,' Scratch would later say in an interview on London's Capital Radio, 'their attitude . . . dreadlocks, vampires, sorcerers. People who hold people's progressive works and nature to ransom.' [1]

Whether he was directing the song specifically at the group at its time of writing is not clear, especially as the Congos are shown on the back cover of the album along with the Full Experience, Lee Perry, and his young son Omar; a harmonic image of happier times before Perry fell out with those present.

At this time, Perry was negotiating with Island for an 'Upsetter Revue' tour to be assembled; the planned package would bring the Congos, Junior Murvin, George Faith and Scratch's ace session players to UK audiences in the summer. The dazzling spectacle of such an array of high calibre talent could only have raised Perry's profile to a higher level, but the tour unfortunately proved to be another Utopian project that was not to be realised.

The outer walls of the Black Ark were now heavily adorned with painted handprints, while an inner wall had a portrait of Scratch that proclaimed him to be 'The Mad Scientist.' Even present at his studio console, Perry completed the somewhat more experimental *Return Of The Super Ape* by July; the disc was a mixed bag that transcended category in the manner of several earlier album releases. Though most of the ten songs had lead vocals of some sort, the jazz experimentation employed on the album saw it veering into dub territory, with the vocal tracks far from typical reggae hits of the day.

The opening number was 'Dyon Anaswa', roughly based on Roy Richards' 'Freedom Blues' (adapted from a Little Richard hit), but restructured so drastically as to be barely recognisable: a Full Experience chorus in African language formed the only words, and echoing percussion that seemed out of time was pushed to the fore. The title track was a mutation of U Roy's 'OK Corral', sounding entirely in place many years after its initial recording through additional percussion and jazzy sax breaks (possibly provided by Cedric Brooks); it was followed by the least abstract track, a laughable version of Rufus' 'Tell Me Something Good' sung by Perry himself. 'Bird In Hand' had a quavering Amharic chant by an unknown vocalist, set to a sparse Black Ark rhythm with ringing bells; the song becomes a beautifully simplistic dub halfway through. Concluding side one was the oddly titled 'Crab Yars', a dubby jazz instrumental with rather magnified percussive effects at centre stage.

Most of the songs on side two had lead vocals by Scratch, though his subject matter is difficult to follow in places. 'Jah Jah Ah Natty Dread' denounced the Pope for being a baldhead, and is delightful for the inclusion of the sound of Perry sneezing in its middle; 'Psyche & Trim' dismissed the godless 'top rankings' with a spanking, while 'The Lion' recycled the Hombres' 'Africa' rhythm to elevate the righteous dreads above the heathen. 'Huzza A Hana' was a mumbled scat vocal over another jazzy dance riff driven by a great sax line, while the closing 'High Rankin Sammy' was a slow skank with a double-tracked Perry vocal that saluted the protagonist of its title.

Both *Roast Fish* and *Return Of The Super Ape* are certainly fine achievements, and mark a high point of Lee Perry's career as a self-produced solo artist. They are complex and dense experimental works on which Perry's individual personality comes through quite strongly, and are indicative of how far his creations were from reggae's mainstream. Since the middle of the decade, Jamaica's biggest hits had been based on re-cuts of classics from Studio One and Treasure Isle; Bunny Lee's early dominance in this do-over field with his Aggrovators was later superseded by Channel One re-cuts with the Revolutionaries, who in turn gave way to a series of re-done hits created at Joe

Gibbs' 16-track studio by the Professionals. Throughout it all, Lee Perry avoided the trend, preferring to stick with originals or sometimes to mutate an American standard; on the few occasions that he did base his work on what had previously been a Studio One hit, he would completely re-structure the song into an entirely different entity. But the price of such uncompromising originality was that Perry's work was not achieving much mainstream popularity in his native land; though he had a fierce reputation as a sound originator and was noted as the most vocal of producers espousing the Rastafari cause, his productions were simply not ramming the dancehalls or generating the sales of his chief competitors – circumstances that would become increasingly frustrating to Perry with the passing of time.

  Roast Fish Collie Weed And Cornbread and *Return Of The Super Ape* are certainly unique works that illuminated the strength and originality of Perry's new directions. But Island Records were beginning to give Perry mixed messages about his unconventional material. Their policy seemed to be shifting, though no official declaration had been made.

  Perry's link with Island had given him the greatest exposure yet outside Jamaica, helping to establish him as a cult figure with an entirely new audience. As with the *Super Ape* album, Perry felt particularly proud of the work he created on *Roast Fish* and *Return Of The Super Ape,* and issued both albums in Jamaica soon after they were completed. When Island chose not to issue either of these albums, it would prove to be the final straw. He was frustrated by their refusal to handle his strongest and most complex creations, and his relationship with Island was effectively over.

  Chris Blackwell had difficulty remembering the exact sequence of events, but admitted that Perry's break with Island stemmed from Blackwell's refusal to release the albums he had presented to them. 'I think around that time he got pissed off with us because we didn't issue some of his records, and it must be that I didn't think they were great. I can't remember specifically, but that would probably be the reason.'

  The long hours of work were beginning to take their toll on Perry, and the endless series of disappointments heightened his dissatisfaction and confusion. Perry's behaviour was becoming increasingly extreme, especially when fuelled by rum, but still the tapes kept rolling. Though a large number of his creations from this period would never be released, the music that sprang forth showed an overloaded genius at the peak of his powers.

  The bartering arrangements established with Augustus Pablo yielded further results in 1978 on some of Pablo's most timeless work: portions of Pablo's *East Of The River Nile* album were recorded or remixed at the Black Ark, with Perry's trademark phasing giving tracks like 'Upfull Living' a very special sound. Further unissued melodica-based instrumentals were also cut in this period, possibly enough to make up an album; track titles listed on master-tape boxes include 'Soul Too' and 'Colombia Gold Dust'.

Wall painting at Black Ark, April 1980 (photographer Jean-Bernard Sohiez)

Black Ark, April 1980
(photographer Jean-Bernard Sohiez)

Perry, live in Paris, November 1987 (photographer David Katz)

Perry with Earl 'Wire' Lindo and Family Man, London 1987 (photograher David Katz)

Perry with Tyrone Downey, London 1987 (photographer David Katz)

Perry with Mario Caldato Jr (left) and Beastie Boy Adam Yauch, New York 1997 (photographer Ricky Powell)

Perry with Linton Kwesi Johnson, Switzerland 1991 (photographer Victor de Bros)

Perry with Syd Bucknor in the background

Augustus Pablo, London 1997 (photographer David Katz)

Winston Jarrett (left) and Leo Graham, Kingston 1998
(photographer David Katz)

Vin Gordon (left) and Glen DaCosta, Kingston 1998
(photographer David Katz)

George Faith Kingston 1998
(photographer David Katz)

Cleopatra Perry and Sandra Cooley, Harrow 1999 (photographer Adrian Thomas)

With Mireille Perry, Switzerland 1989 (photographer Robert Kuypers)

Mark 'Omar' Perry, London 1997 (photographer David Katz)

Marsha Perry, Blue Mountains 1998 (photographer David Katz)

Marvin 'Sean' Perry, Cardiff Crescent 1998
(photographer David Katz)

Above and below; The Black Ark, 1998 (photographer Adrian Thomas)

Among the wealth of significant late-'70s creations that would never be released was a second Junior Murvin album, recorded with the nucleus of the band that is now known as Axx of Jahpostles just before Perry severed his ties with the Congos. As Murvin explained, 'Scratch told me to get a band. These young kids were living in Norwich, so I started training them as Junior Murvin and the Apostles Band. I carry them to town and we did an album which wasn't released, Scratch still have it there. The second album, we rehearse it for two weeks straight, just went straight in and do it. That was Leslie Mowatt on organ, Lynford Richards on guitar, Devon Bradshaw on bass, and Tony Bradshaw on guitar, Rocky on drums, and I think Roy from the Congos is playing congos. When Lee Perry was supposed to start the album, he put the Congos in my space; I don't know if that caused Chris Blackwell and him to (fall out), because when Chris wanted the second album he didn't get it.'

Junior Murvin also sat in on several other Black Ark sessions, recording a few odd tracks that surfaced as singles. One of the most notable was 'Crossover', an impromptu studio creation on which Scratch's young son Sean tried to play a keyboard part; the song was first issued in Jamaica that March. 'We was in Lee Perry's studio fooling around and it came up. I was playing the bass, Lee Perry's son play the piano, and Watty Burnett from the Congos play the drums.'

George Faith also recorded a second Black Ark album, completed by the end of 1978, of which precious little would be released. '*Working On The Guideline*, that's another album for Lee Perry,' Faith explained, 'I don't know what happened to that one. It was ten (songs), it took maybe about nine months or a year (to finish). He use musicians like Robbie Lyn, Winston Wright, Sly, and Mikey Boo, but he switch round the musicians along the way.'

In late 1978, Perry issued the arresting single 'Guideline', which was meant to be the title track of the album; a 12-inch version also later surfaced in New York through Munchie Jackson on the Andre label, named after Jackson's son. Driven by a highly modulated keyboard line from Winston Wright, the vocal performance on 'Guideline' showed that Faith could be just as successful with original material as with the cover versions that were always foisted on him. The only other song yet to surface from these sessions was 'Don't Be Afraid', initially issued as an Upsetter single and later on a 1979 UK disco by Mo Claridge's Warrior Records.

Other strong one-offs to surface in the latter half of 1978 include the atmospheric 'Land Of Love' by the otherwise unknown Sons of Light, the condemning 'Mr Money Man' by a certain Danny Hensworth, and 'Brother Noah', a harmonic re-telling of the biblical flood by the Shadows – three singers named Sam, Don and Errol. Also noteworthy was 'Free Up The Prisoners', a vocal magnum opus from Perry himself, cut on a peculiar 'Disco Prisoner' 12-inch single at 33 rpm. Issued on his new Conquering Lion of Judah label with a beautiful picture sleeve, 'Free Up The Prisoners' was nearly

13 minutes of Scratch listing the many reasons why those in captivity should be freed over a relaxed and rolling re-cut of 'Feel the Rhythm'; two versions of the single were issued, the second made notably different through its inclusion of a prominent piano riff. As the song progressed, a crescendo of sound effects emerged, with sine waves and electric see-saw sounds gradually overpowering the mix; the sobering B-side, 'Chase Them', spoke of non-Rasta elements, such as income tax and birth control, that needed to be chased away.

Towards the end of the year, Perry was contacted by an American punk group called Scratch who wanted their namesake to produce them. The Upsetter was pleased by the album they sent him, and agreed to work with the group, but it was another project that would not be realised; however, Pauline was sufficiently inspired by their version of Dusty Springfield's 'I Only Want To Be With You' to record a version of her own at the Black Ark, ironically recorded just before significant upheaval would blight her relationship with Scratch.

As on previous occasions, some of the year's best work was created with Bob Marley and the Wailers – though the creations would ultimately prove to be a source of friction. When the Wailers returned to Jamaica mid-way through their *Kaya* world tour, Marley soon found himself back in the Black Ark for the recording of two monumental numbers that would not be issued for over 20 years: 'Who Colt The Game' and 'I Know A Place'. Details of the recording session that produced these songs remain obscure, though lead guitarist Chinna Smith supplied the following likely particulars: 'I think it was Mikey Boo, Scratch's resident drummer; I don't think it was Family Man on bass, if it's not Boris (Gardiner) it would have to be Winston Wright because Winston Wright used to play a wicked bass too. Billy (Johnson) might be the next guitarist.'

According to Clancy Eccles, Scratch had written the basic lyrics for 'Who Colt the Game' in the late 1960s, though certain adaptations were made when Bob Marley recorded the song. ' "Who Colt The Game" was written at West Indies Records, some years before Bob Marley sing on Scratch's own productions. Friday night everybody meet and gamble, play 21, and one Friday night Scratch, Lynford Anderson and Bill Garnett was playing domino down by WIRL and the song come up. Ten years later he give that song to Marley.'

'Who Colt The Game' used domino metaphors to query the injustices of Babylon; Natty Dread was revealed to be the innocent victim, while Baldhead was the guilty party who cheated. The rhythm was a slow, shuffling one-drop skank, spiced up by plenty of wah-wah riffs from Chinna, and piano and organ licks that Chinna suggested were overdubbed later. Scratch also overdubbed male harmony vocals onto the song at a later session, though who sang them is unclear; the Meditations would have been likely candidates, but each member stated plainly that they did not sing harmony on the tune.

Though never properly finished, the symbolic humour of 'Who Colt The Game' certainly equals the best of Marley's symbolic deliveries. The other unfinished masterpiece to emerge from these sessions was the truly heartfelt 'I Know A Place', in which Marley sings of a Utopian locale where he could escape the world's hypocrisy and hatred. Over a thunderous, optimistic rhythm that included a highly distorted guitar line shaped by a finger slide, Marley and the I-Threes sang with an intense passion that is present on only their finest works.

Though conflicting statements about the exact circumstances of this recording session continue to emerge, the songs would definitely cause a serious conflict between Marley and Perry. It is also truly unfortunate that the songs were left unfinished and unissued for so long. The rough demo versions that were eventually released somewhat clandestinely by Jet Star Records in 1998 did not include the male backing vocals and were of questionable fidelity; other higher-quality recordings with backing vocals exist elsewhere, and will hopefully be given the bona-fide release they deserve in the future.

The same distorted guitar sound that was so prominent on 'I Know A Place' was also featured on a humorous though incendiary Perry vocal called 'Baffling Smoke Signal', one of the final solo singles Perry would release in this period. This provocative jingle had Perry's double-tracked voice commenting on the controversial election of Pope John Paul II after the mysterious death of his predecessor on September 28, 1978; the disc was initially cut at the low-fidelity speed of 33 rpm. The song spoke of the endless black smoke that blew from the Vatican chimneys while the authorities deliberated about who would be the new Pope, interpreted by Perry to be a representation of the black supremacy claimed by radical Rastafarian theology. Recorded around the same time was 'Captive', another double-tracked Perry proclamation; the song revealed the continual enslavement of black people in the West, and called for mental and spiritual liberation.

It was in this time that Scratch began to concentrate on recording Niyabinghi material, completing a frutiful collaborative work with Ras Michael and the Sons of Negus. Ras Michael Henry came from a Rastafarian community in St Mary, where he learned to play the repeater drum as a youth. In his teens, he moved to Kingston and linked with a set of Rastas based in Waterhouse. Gathering in the yard of an elder drummer and carpenter named Solomon Wolfe, Ras Michael began playing with elder *funde* players such as Brother Jack and Brother Martin (a.k.a. I-Marts), with bass drum beaten by Sidney Wolfe, Solomon's oldest son; Lloyd Brevett and Tommy McCook often attended their sessions, giving the players musical coaching.

Committed to spreading the Rastafarian faith, Michael formed the Sons of Negus Churchical Host, cutting Niyabinghi music for his Ziondisc label in the mid-1960s; he also provided vibrant hand drumming on a few sessions with Jackie Mittoo for Studio One. The proceeds of these works were used to fund *Lion of Judah Time,* a Rastafarian radio programme broadcast on JBC. In

1974, Michael reformed the group as Ras Michael and the Sons of Negus, mixing their Niyabinghi drum core with the electric instruments of session players for a broader musical focus. In their new form, the group recorded a series of highly experimental and varied albums with a variety of producers.

Ras Michael knew Lee Perry from Scratch's early days in Kingston, but the two never worked together until Michael played percussion on some of Scratch's sessions with Junior Murvin. Present at the Black Ark for some of Bob Marley's sessions in 1978, Ras Michael and the Sons of Negus then made arrangements to record an album with Scratch, which would eventually surface in America as *Love Thy Neighbor*. 'That album was done by Lee Perry,' clarified Sidney Wolfe. 'It's a funny thing, an adventure. Same time Bob was doing "Who Colt the Game", we were there and then we came to agreement with Scratch to do that album at Black Ark.'

The Sons of Negus completed over ten songs at the Black Ark, with the resultant *Love Thy Neighbor* a definite high point of their career. It was the application of extreme levels of reverb and delay that gave *Love Thy Neighbor* such an awesome sound; fragments of instruments and voice burst forward at unexpected moments, heightening the menacing quality of these serious works. 'Don't Sell Daddy No Whisky', 'Wicked Got To Go', and 'Hear River Jordan' are among the most powerful works Ras Michael has ever recorded, while 'Time Is Drawing Nigh', 'Little David', 'Perfect Love', and a re-casting of the nursery rhyme 'London Bridge Has Fallen Down' are strong presentations of Rasta optimism. Perry also ensured that the album was one of the more successful blends of Niyabinghi drums and electric studio instruments through skilled direction of his session musicians. Boris Gardiner, Santa Davis, and Mikey Boo all helped give added texture, and Hux Brown's expressive blues licks greatly enhanced the overall melody of the work.

Brown had recently returned to Jamaica after a long absence, having just completed a brief tour of Nigeria, Senegal and Sierra Leone with Toots and the Maytals. The harshness of life in Jamaica had affected him badly in the mid-'70s, culminating in a low period where he often sought solace in drink; he thus emigrated to the USA in 1976 in an attempt to straighten himself out. After his 1978 West African tour with Toots, Brown spent a month recording in Jamaica. His work with Ras Michael was the last he ever recorded on the island; once permanently in America, he would be less musically active.

Hux Brown was not the only one to succumb to the pressures of Kingston living in this period. Among the other casualties was fellow guitarist Alva 'Reggie' Lewis, who developed an alcohol dependency from which he would never fully recover. After his glory days as a session player faded, Lewis began a new existence as a vagabond, later to be saved from a life of destitution by Rita Marley, who gave him an informal job as gatekeeper at Tuff Gong.

Leo Graham was also feeling distressed. Earlier in the year, the singer recorded 'My Little Sandra' at the Black Ark, a pleasant love song that was as good as any of his previous hits; shortly after, his repeated financial frustrations and various other pressures caused an emotional breakdown, effectively ending a long and brilliant singing career.

And then there was the troubled mind of Lee Perry himself. It was during the completion of the *Love Thy Neighbor* album that Scratch's behaviour became resolutely drastic. He entered a new phase that centred on graffiti, painting cryptic proclamations on the walls of his studio. Shortly after, he began placing the letter X over certain letters of his proclamations, as though to erase or blot out the cipher; later still, whole words would be covered with X's. In time, entire walls would be covered with nothing but the letter X, or completely overwritten by a series of words or statements scrawled in paint or magic marker. As Sidney Wolfe explained, 'During that period of time, he got a little bit upset, or probably got mad, some people would say. He was writing up a lot of X's and shit like that around his place, and refuse to do any more record. That was about the time that Black Ark studio started to get demoralised.'

Fortunately for the Sons of Negus, Scratch allowed them to retrieve their master tapes before things totally disintegrated. On their emigration to the USA, they allowed Delroy Wright to issue the album on his Live and Learn imprint. The original issue did not include 'Perfect Love' or 'London Bridge' (listed on the sleeve and included on all subsequent pressings), but had three unlisted extra tracks: the powerfully historic 'Long Time Ago' and 'Do You Know', plus the praise song 'Jesus Christus is the King'. Further incomplete and partially mixed tracks from the sessions were also included on Ras Michael's 1981 *Disarmament* album.

Love Thy Neighbour was one of a few last great recordings to emerge from the Ark in 1979. An exceptionally strong release was Leroy Sibbles' 'Garden Of Life', whose dub Perry re-structured to include blasts of mechanised rhythm; its flipside was the playful 'Jah Fari On A Pinnacle', which mutated melodic themes of the Maytals' 'Monkey Man'. These tunes were issued in Jamaica on a cryptically named Big Spanner Ajax disco – Ajax again alluding to the cleansing powers of the letter X. The B-side of this single later surfaced in the UK on Warrior Records, one of several late Black Ark discos that appeared on the label in the autumn of 1979.

A number of late Black Ark Heptones gems were also issued abroad around this time: A disco mix of 'Party Time' surfaced on VP's Love label, backed by 'Come On Into My World', a throbbing love song led by Niyabinghi beats; a peculiar re-working of Steam's 'Na Na Hey Hey' appeared as 'Babylon Falling' on VP's Roots From The Yard imprint; and an extended version of 'Mystery Babylon' was cut in the UK on Count Shelley's Third World label.

Further notable 1979 album material had Black Ark origins. I-Kong recorded some of his debut album *The Way It Is* at the Black Ark with Geoffrey

Chung, but most of the disc was laid at Harry J and was entirely remixed at Dynamic. Another mysterious album release was the Slickers' debut *Breakthrough,* issued in New York on the Tad's label. Initially formed by Sidney Crooks' brother Derrick (known as Joe), Roy Beckford and Winston Bailey, the group scored one of the biggest selling reggae hits ever with the anti-rude boy 'Johnny Too Bad' in 1972. In the late 1970s, Bailey was replaced by Abraham Green, who wrote much of the album's best material. Like the I-Kong album, *Breakthrough* had several tracks that had been initially laid at the Black Ark, later embellished and remixed elsewhere; Ark rhythms include 'Marcus', 'Every Wolf', and 'Black A White'.

Meanwhile, other roots aficionados were trying to copy the Black Ark's legendary sound. A concrete example is 'Stand And Look', a tale of dread tribulation by a Waterhouse trio called the Fantails, led by a certain Dad Brown; the song was pressed as a seven-inch on the Boss label in Jamaica, and cut as an extended mix on a Trojan Attack disco in the UK in 1979. When North London sound system operator Fatman heard the group singing on a street corner, he built a rhythm for them at Joe Gibbs' studio, which the group then voiced at King Tubby's; according to Fatman, he requested that Tubby make use of a phaser in an effort to emulate Perry's Black Ark sound.

While the records noted above were gradually surfacing abroad, Lee Perry was spending much of his days writing on the walls of his studio, building junk-sculpture fetishes in the yard, and antagonising all who would appear there, after tensions arose during a new religious project initiated with members of the Niyabinghi Theocracy. 'Me decide that me want to close the reggae factory because reggae is a dog,' Perry later explained, 'a monster dog. Me decide to close the reggae shop and open the ears, close the reggae campaign. The reggae people didn't have nobody else to live off of, vampire always want something so me decide to close it, then Niyabinghi is a church me start now.'

Scratch had been strengthening his bond with the group after they increased visible displays of musical and social activism; in truth, they were planning a revolution together that would usher in a new era of theocratic government, and part of the motivation behind Perry's declamatory graffiti seems to stem from his prolonged involvement with the group. The Boboshanti are said to have taken the linguistic code of Rastafari I-words to even more radical heights, placing great importance on letters and sounds as well as on the more standard Rastafari word usage; Lee Perry adopted their methods with an incessant fervour, seeking another vehicle with which to express himself. 'Even now in Jamaica, certain words to the Rastaman don't right,' explained his brother P-Son, 'so it's a vibes like that. I think in his mind, he was back to school studies. I think it was just inspiration and the good from the bad, like you have X stand for the Devil, D for Death.' Jah Ned explained the process more succinctly: 'The realisation came to Scratch that certain words did not belong to His Majesty, some words really belongs to Satan.'

The Bobshanti held a 30-day Niyabinghi from Marcus Garvey's birthday on August 17; Scratch then funded a forty day Niyabinghi from late September, initiated just before the death of Pope John Paul I – which more radical members of the order claimed was caused partly by the energies released at their Niyabinghi.

It was some time after these non-stop drumming sessions that Perry made more regular use of the Boboshanti drummers on specific new works for an album tentatively entitled *Niyabinghi Slaughters the Dragon.* Though some of the material was captured on the four-track Teac, Perry noted that some sessions were taped later on a half-inch eight-track Tascam recorder, which he indicated was given to him some time after the Congos' album sessions by Chris Blackwell, who hoped to broaden Perry's musical horizons by doubling his recording capabilities: 'Chris Blackwell bought me an eight track, it was like a birthday present. He never tell me what was happening, but he send down a surprise for me: an eight-track Teac from Island. I think the machines break down after this Congos sessions, they was over-worked so I want to change them, so then when the four-track no carry so strong, Chris Blackwell buy the eight-track. He say, "If four-track sound so good, imagine eight-track," because me experiment and him hear the songs me do on the Teac four-track, it let him know that if that was sounding so good, and now they have another advanced machine – because it was the same Teac now come as Tascam – him think this would be fun. Him have a surprise for me and him send it, but I didn't ready for using it yet.'

Scratch had difficulty confirming exactly when the Tascam arrived, but noted there was a long delay before it was put to use. He specified that he did not use the machine on any George Faith, Heptones, or Junior Murvin songs, and that none of his releases from the 1970s were recorded on the machine; he believes it was not functioning until 'long, long after' his work with Ras Michael, but others involved suggested the Niyabinghi recordings date from the same era, and the exact chronology has proven difficult to ascertain. Prior to these album sessions, Scratch had sporadically recorded the group when their Black Ark assembly coincided with the arrival of certain artists whose music he felt would benefit from their percussive contribution.

The Niyabinghi are said to have initially asked Scratch for financial backing of a musical stage play called *One Hundred Drums*, but further details of the supposed theatre piece have not emerged. Jah Ned detailed the gradual process by which they came to work together: 'Scratch was the one who had changed the whole phenomenon of the music, because Scratch was the one that brought everyone to the path of singing about His Majesty. We were doing some live recording at the Niyabinghi that we had in the city, and then we decided to add a portion of studio recordings; Scratch was responsible, because he was the General responsible for the music ministry for the movement. After the One Love concert, I had taken full duty with Scratch, strictly for doing recordings now to make funds to help do what we want to do. We did quite a number of recordings but Scratch never release; it was an ongoing thing. Sometimes we were here and other musicians came and we go in the studio and we did something, sometimes an instrumental, sometimes a vocal. We had Santa on drums and P-Son sometimes, Mikey (Chung) on bass, Gladstone Anderson, Headley (Bennett), Cedric Brooks.'

The group appears to have undergone a period of ostracism from the end of 1978, along with the other dreadlocked Black Ark regulars, whom Perry castigated and rebuffed in a series of hostile confrontations. Though the Black Ark gates were generally closed to visitors from this time, with the premises becoming increasingly marked by declamatory words, members of the Niyabinghi Theocracy would later be admitted at key intervals, and were present at the studio as late as April 1980; unfortunately, the album was never completed and the master tapes were eventually mislaid.

While Perry was undergoing his linguistic transformation, 'Blackman Redemption' was creeping up the Jamaican charts, peaking at a number two position in September. 'Rastaman Live Up' would make a similar impact, reaching a number-three Jamaican chart position the following February. But by the end of 1978, Lee Perry was under a tremendous amount of pressure from a variety of sources and had reached a breaking point.

As Ansel Cridland explained, some of the most serious pressures involved increasingly threatening financial demands from a variety of sources, including disgruntled musicians, studio idlers, and members of the Boboshanti. 'After "Blackman Redemption" came out, a lot of people used to be down there during the day, asking for money from Scratch. Musicians, people that work for him, everybody come for money.'

Police and soldiers are also said to have had a regular menacing presence at the studio, and Earl Sixteen noted that Perry was being extorted in this period by known and feared gang members – perhaps the most significant of all his pressures. 'I hung out in the studio all the time. Heptones come and did Party Time album, and Bob Marley did "Blackman Redemption", until Perry started drinking too much rum and smoking at the same time. Then there was this elder dreadlocks who used to come across and preach a lot, and he used to get on Perry's nerves. I don't know what happened, Perry went on this trip; he was getting focally rich, really rich: companies used to come from America and would want to film the studio, and Perry would take their money and kick them out, literally. Then there was the bad boys called Spanglers, who was coming up for money every day, they wanted weekly-paid protection money, and Perry didn't need that. He was building up the studio, Jah Wise came and painted up the studio all nice, did some nice stuff leading right into the Ark; Perry just tripped out and started making X on all the A's and E's.'

Conversely, P-Son explained certain of these negative elements in a somewhat different context. 'Spanglers and all the guys from town who follow music used to come and beg a money, lots of people from each side. Scratch would talk to them, he'd say, "Put down your gun, cool off," try to stop them from the bad ways they're doing, killing people. They would listen to him; he do a lot of work. Police will come but is friend; they sit in the studio and listen to music, no problem. More time the road hot and they would take a little drive and come have a drink. It was good vibes.'

Furthermore, Perry's extended family continued to look to him as the breadwinner. In addition to Pauline and children Michelle, Sean, Omar, and Marsha, Scratch was providing for his brother P-Son and nephew Enoch on a daily basis; his mother regularly relied on him for money, as did his sister Girlie, who lived in town with plenty of other children, and he and Pauline had other outside children that he would sometimes be called on to support.

The financial pressures were an ongoing source of worry, but other elements also had a decisive impact. As a faithful servant of His Majesty, Perry was chiefly concerned with using his music to elevate Rastafari, but had begun to take issue with the wearing of dreadlocks following his rupture with the Congos. His anti-dread sentiments were shortly to intensify, and would remain a negative focal point for decades to come.

As the pressure brought on by various conflicts continued mounting, achieving peace of mind was a necessity, but also an impossibility in Kingston. If Scratch had followed the direction of his spirit guide and gone to the tranquillity of the Blue Mountains or some other unspoiled country retreat, he may have been able to clear his head and find a practical solution to his troubles. Unfortunatley, Lee Perry did no such thing. As he had regularly done for the last five years, Scratch remained deep in the bunker of the Black Ark, immersed in his creations day and night, hardly stopping to eat or sleep; the most regular forms of sustenance were herb and alcohol.

As Perry's behaviour became more drastic and less predictable, Pauline Morrison began to feel the strain. When Scratch had been earning good money from Island, he had spoken of buying a house for her in the tranquillity of Beverly Hills in uptown Kingston, but she is said to have feared isolation and never sought out a property. She had suffered a variety of indignities at Scratch's hands over the years, particularly regarding his adulteries: she has spoken of him frequenting an illicit Hanover Street night spot in the early days of their relationship, and of enduring several prolonged affairs (though some say Pauline was also known to be promiscuous). 'Scratch was so wild, he had so many women when I was with him. I beat up some, I broke up some, and I broke him up too. It's kind of disturbing, so I said I want to leave that part of my life behind.' They also came into conflict over her decision to keep the dreadlocks she had started to grow in 1977. But it was Perry's extreme behaviour that finally became unbearable. 'Even now, it kind of marvels me. It put me in a state of mind where I'm saying, "What's this guy saying?" If you see our house, this guy write all kind of shit on the wall, on the fence . . . He used to build sculpture into the wall! I spent years of that, wondering if I'm going to go insane until I finally just went "Rah!" It just take me by surprise, and I couldn't be a prey to Scratch's stupidity. If I was, probably I would be in the asylum.'

Pauline has claimed she was preparing a meal one afternoon when she noticed an odd smell coming from the kitchen. When she checked the pot, she found that Scratch had emptied the simmering contents into the mud of the yard, substituting a pan full of rocks in their place on the fire. He had also taken a week's worth of newly purchased groceries out of the refrigerator, and thrown them to perish in the mud. As Kingston was hit by harsh flood rains towards the end of 1978, Pauline knew she had to make a change to retain her sanity; she thus started spending nights away from Cardiff Crescent, beginning an affair with Danny Clarke of the Meditations.

Clarke recounted the genesis of their relationship: 'Scratch was kind of going out of his head. I don't really know what happened; he was all right, and the next thing I know he start marking up the walls and making all kinds of X's. I used to live over by Central Village, up near Sufferer's Heights. When Meditations were working on the *Guidance* album, Pauline came up by Three Mile Market and we spent the whole day in the studio. Pauline said she couldn't take it any more, she was finding some way to get out, because if she stayed, she might go crazy too. After two weeks I hadn't seen her, so Ansel takes her by my house one night, buses stop running so she have to spend the night. That's how we really get hooked up. I was just coming out of a relationship of two years so I was all by myself then. After that I stay away from Cardiff Crescent because there was a lot of vibes going around, people saying I take away from Scratch and I drove Scratch crazy and all that shit.'

As the affair began under such problematic circumstances, their relationship would take time to blossom and would prove to be generally problematic. Despite efforts to keep it secret, the grapevine that is the Kingston music scene soon spread news of their liaison as Pauline was more frequently away from Washington Gardens; she eventually rented a room of her own in the suburb of Cherry Gardens. Shortly after, she moved to a larger space on the other side of the suburb in an upstairs property where barefoot poet Mutabaruka and his family also rented quarters; she sent for her children to join her once in the space.

Despite her departure from Cardiff Crescent, such was the bond between Isha Morrison and Lee Perry that the pair found it difficult to sever their ties with one another. The couple were also mindful of hurting their children's feelings, and tried to keep their escalating conflicts hidden from the kids, who were often back and forth between both addresses – as was their mother.

Sean – who greatly idolised his father – was worried that Scratch was not caring for himself properly, and he and Omar gradually began to spend more time keeping an eye on him at the Ark as the weeks passed; their sisters would later follow suit, and all four children would move back into Cardiff Crescent by the end of the following summer. By that time, Pauline Morrison had gone to New York to visit her mother, seeking advice on how to repair her ruptured life.

As Pauline was in and out of the Ark, Perry's grasp of the line between reality and fantasy gradually deteriorated. He told certain key people that he was not really crazy, that he was just enacting an elaborate charade to rid himself of unwanted attention, but at some point the charade seems to have superseded his control. Many close to him have testified that he underwent some sort of breakdown, though even this is disputed; others insist his behaviour is simply an elaborate act. In any event, a chaotic new persona emerged to take charge of his actions; though his perceived 'madness' would wax and wane from this point onwards, he would never quite be the same again.

Though he did not want to admit it, Pauline's betrayal and departure greatly affected Lee Perry. She had long handled much of his business affairs and provided some badly needed stability in his life. That she would take up with one of the musicians whose career he had helped build hit him hard; that the man was a dreadlocks was worse still.

Scratch soon found fault with almost everyone around him, and took drastic measures to shake them off. Danny Clarke noted some of the elements that contributed to the enactment of Perry's surreal charade: 'Scratch was a Rastaman from way back. At the time you have Ras Michael and the Sons of Negus used to go by Scratch, you have the Niyabinghi people them used to come and sit down, and everybody come want money, everybody always looking money, money money money! So them drive Scratch to zero, take Scratch to country, say they're going to kill the Pope and them shit, so all those things just kind of get to Scratch. Because Scratch is a scientist, Scratch just come with something to get rid of these people.'

Max Romeo recounted certain incidents that occurred as Perry struggled to shake off the predatory idlers who congregated daily at his studio: 'He had a Rastafarian church he started with a bunch of dreads. I don't know what happened, but these dreads fall out of grace, so he wanted to keep them off him. He put a pound of pork on his antennae, and rode around town until it rotted and maggots were falling from it, claiming that he don't want no Rasta 'round him because Rasta come give his kids lice. After he put the pork on the antennae, the dreads was still coming, so he wrote on his car back, "I am a batty man." [2] That's when the dreads run in all different directions! His situation continue a little further with the game: he had a nice orange Pontiac, took the bonnet off, planted flowers in and was driving around. The dirt lodges in his carborater, so the car can't go no further.'

Though Perry concretely denied these assertions, he agreed that his car broke down and confirmed he has never driven since – though the car in question was in fact a blue Chrysler Charger. 'It was never nothing like what

Maxie say, but no problem, give them a joke,' he said when told of Romeo's statement.

George Faith added other memories of Perry's changed behaviour. 'At one stage, I was supposed to go on a tour. Scratch was supposed to make the arrangements with Island, but he went away and when he came back he was a changed person; he started to deal with something else. For instance, equipment or anything in the studio that had the letter R, he would throw it outside because it represent Rome, and he begin his routine of making X all over the place. I didn't think anything was happening to him, I think, "That is just Lee Perry" because when you're working with him he do some strange things too.'

By the end of January 1979, the Black Ark was entirely devoid of visitors. Though the mixing desk and tape machines were still connected, the studio became little more than an abandoned shell covered in words; despite retaining a basic functionality, it had virtually ceased to exist.

THE RETURN OF PIPECOCK JACKXON:

The partial Rebirth and ultimate Destruction of the Ark

While Pauline was seeking some perspective on Scratch's actions and the chaos of Cardiff Crescent, Lee Perry ensconced himself in a lonely solitude. He spent his days re-arranging items in the compound, building abstract sculptures and painting more declamatory graffiti. Though he had barred the premises from dread outsiders, he was still occasionally voicing previously recorded rhythm tracks on the old Teac four track, but his severed ties left him with no real outlet for his work and his antisocial outlook meant he was not actively seeking new avenues.

In late January, a trio of foreign visitors appeared at the Black Ark gates: Dave Hendley, Mo Claridge and David Rodigan. Hendley had recently been hired by Marcel Rodd as an A & R man for Trojan, but was already planning to establish his own Sufferer's Heights label and was gathering material to release. Rodigan was then the pre-eminent radio disc jockey in England through his weekly show on Capital Radio, and this was his first visit to Jamaica. Claridge was continuing to license material for the Ballistic and Warrior labels, notably with the Royal Rasses, with whom Ballistic was shortly to enjoy a widespread success with their debut album *Humanity;* it was, in fact, the group's lead singer Prince Lincoln Thompson who brought the three Englishmen to the Ark on this occasion, though Claridge had first visited the studio with Roy Cousins on an earlier trip.

Dave Hendley remembered being shocked and saddened by what he found there: 'By this time, Scratch was totally transformed. We went up once and there was no one around, we peered through the railings and you could see he had covered the place, scrawled absolutely everywhere. That's the first thing that hit you, all the little crosses on the walls and all the elemental stuff. First time we went up there we couldn't find him. When we eventually linked, he was just talking virtually non-stop, talking all the time, even if he was talking to himself a lot. Everybody had gone, nobody was coming 'round there any more. I thought he looked in really bad shape, there was a certain tragedy about it to be honest. There were moments where he would make sense, and I remember him saying "No one comes by any more, they've taken everything they can off of me." The board was still set up, he had the Teac and it could still play tapes, but all the tape boxes were scribbled over; they were just lying around everywhere. There wasn't one surface that he'd not written on, and the amount of time that he must have spent just writing that stuff is phenomenal. He must have been so alone when he was doing that, it's very solitary stuff and the tiniest of things like the staple gun had been written on. Even the little polaroids had writing everywhere, and eyes were crossed out on people's pictures.'

Though Perry seemed in no mood to do business with his foreign visitors, he was secretly waiting for some sort of divine intervention to show him the way forward, and the next foreigner to appear at the Ark ultimately helped initiate his next phase of creation.

Henry W. Targowski's Polish parents met in England during World War II after miraculous escapes from Nazi aggression, and Henk was born in Nottingham on May 31, 1947. His father Frank had been an air force pilot, but became a cinema projectionist after the war; when the family relocated to Chicago, he was unable to retain the profession and became an electrician. After hearing of the horrors of war, Henk became a pacifist in his teens, and hopped freight trains to get to San Francisco in April 1967, where he became involved in the Diggers collective and other underground groups. In 1970, he relocated to the more permissive climate of Amsterdam, joining a growing community of bohemian American expatriates.

As with many other American and European enthusiasts, it was the Wailers' debut album for Island Records that sparked Henk's interest in reggae; as his knowledge of the music and culture of Jamaica deepened, he began to make regular trips to London to import reggae pre-releases. In 1978, he formed the Black Star Liner distribution company and record label with the express purpose of issuing product by the best producers in Jamaica, and Lee Perry was at the top of the list of those he sought to work with. The company's main financial backer was Bill Bradford, an African-American from Northern California who had made a fortune through an international import/export business; other silent partners included Sicilian friends Santo and Fred.

After a few trips to London to import British pressings of reggae material, Targowski made his first trip to Jamaica in April 1979 – not long after Claudie Massop's murder by JCF officers ruined the year-long peace treaty, ushering in a return to 'tribalist' violence. Upon arrival, Targowski checked into the Terra Nova Hotel – a former family home of Chris Blackwell – and took a taxi straight to the Black Ark, where he received an ominous reception.

In 1981, Targowski wrote a detailed account of this initial meeting in an article published in the Dutch magazine *Vinyl*, relating some of the obscure concepts and motivation behind Perry's troublesome preoccupations:

'No dreads (were) in the yard, only children playing; at the end of (the driveway) stood Lee "Scratch" Perry, the Upsetter himself. You can imagine my great surprise when Scratch greeted me with the words "I've been expecting you." How that could be was a mystery, since I had neither previous contact with Scratch, nor had I told anyone of my visit who could have warned him. Scratch made it seem like a fore-ordained event – apparently, Scratch had anticipated someone showing up from outside Jamaica, someone to help him with some master scheme . . . Scratch invited me to follow him into the inner sanctum of the Black Ark. The colourful paintings which had decorated the outer wall of his studio were all gone; Scratch had covered them over with splotches of ugly green and shit-brown paint. Black graffiti had been scribbled in felt-tip over everything. When I entered the studio, the inside decor proved to be an ever greater shock: The place was a disaster area. Bits of equipment lay scattered around the room; shelves had been torn down. Boxes of recording tape lay strewn in a jumbled heap in the middle of the floor . . . tape ends, unravelled from their reels, had spilled out in a tangle of confusion. The mouldy rug onto which they had been carelessly thrown was soggy wet from rainwater which leaked through holes in the roof . . . The inside walls had become a wild montage: The previous art had been painted over with the same green and brown as outside; Scratch had also glued records, metal stampers, tapes and other assorted objects to the walls – layers upon layers of paint and posters and book pages, a chronological history of Scratch's mental state. The overall atmosphere of the place was oppressive . . . .the horrible smell coming from an overflowing septic tank added to the feeling of discomfort. After carefully noting my reactions to all this, Scratch proceeded to give me his rap: he was the "Lord Thunder Black" and his black footprints of Time trod upon the Rainbow. Scratch went on about his mission on Earth, how he had been entrusted with the job of protecting the "original Jah Soundtrack", guarding it from violation by the profane. Scratch was fond of using props to illustrate his conversation: an upright piano stood in the room, painted entirely yellow including the keyboard; Scratch explained that it represented the Golden Harp of David. A bass guitar symbolised the female element, while the drums stood for the male. Scratch had developed a metaphysics which linked nature to music. Every so often he would ask me a direct question like "Do you know who Jesse the Hammer is?" When I inevitably answered no, he responded with some revelatory statement like "Jesse the Christ, get it?", then burst into a mad cackle of laughter – the mad professor instructing a neophyte, asking test questions to ascertain if his teaching had penetrated. The thought that Scratch had gone off the deep end was hard to supress, yet I sensed a method in Scratch's madness.

'Somehow, Scratch created a feeling of conspiracy. He was weaving spells and forming a vast cosmology – and all of it was directed towards the accomplishment of some clandestine goal. In the beginning was the Word which is sound. Thunder crashes and lightning strikes the earth, causing an X-shaped crack in the surface, out of which life forms emerge – Mother Earth giving birth. Scratch applies the alchemical elements of Earth, Air, Fire and Water into his music; he balances these into a nature track. Symbols of these elements are seen in the three nature trees: Coconut, Banana, and Marijuana. The coconut contains distilled water, which is necessary to operate a battery . . . it is the medium which allows the spark to form. Black banana water is a tonic rich in iron, it represents the earth and also the ink used to write the words. Marijuana smoke is air, the medium through which sound travels. Lee Perry was releasing the product of his explorations through "King Solomon's Mind"; by tapping into the "Stone Age Scull Cap Of Wisdom", Scratch hoped to unravel the secrets of Jesse the Hammer who is Love, thereby creating a philosophy of "Love Universal Automatic Vibrations". The console wizard had become the magician of words, operating out of his "Raja Faith Sound Magentic Power Station". His aim was to bring tidings of Great Joy by loosing the "Seven Seals Of Love" with sound power. "Taget 9" was to Hijack the Earth with music . . . But I was still confused. Why was there no music? And why were his tapes, those magentic archives of Upsetter music, getting irreparably damaged on the floor? I ended my first meeting by asking Scratch if he could use my help in straightening out the tapes. He accepted my offer and I agreed to come by the following morning.

'Bright and early the next day, I arrived to find Scratch walking around outside. When I announced my readiness to begain the day's work, he told me to wait a while until he was finished with what he was doing: Scratch was performing his ritual. He'd pick up an object, hold it in the sun, walk with it, touch it to other objects or to certain words, wave it through the air with a brisk movement of his arm, then do a tornado spin so fast that the eye only caught a blur, and walk off again. The same actions were repeated many times. Scratch would suddenly grab a felt-tip pen, hold it in front of him, then go and scribble some cryptic words and phrases on any available surface – casting a magic spell, tuning into the ethers, establishing contact with the elemental forces. When I asked him what he was doing, he said that he was "Declarating the Rights and Executing the Wrongs".

'The recurrent phrases which appeared on walls, tape boxes, instruments, mixing panel, pieces of paper and whatnot were mantras. Scratch felt that his studio had been used by negative people; he was performing an exorcism to remove the bad vibes . . . As part of his Declarating ritual, he recemented the walkway in front of the Black Ark so that only new clean footsteps should pass through . . . Eventually we went into the studio to start clearing up. We carefully rewound all the loose ends back onto the tape reels, and then stacked the boxes into neat piles.' [1]

Targowski briefly explained that he wanted to distribute some of Perry's back catalogue in Europe through Black Star Liner; drastically short of money, Scratch was pleased to hear of the plan. For the remainder of the six weeks Targowski spent in Jamaica, he travelled to the Ark most evenings after conducting business with other producers, including Augustus Pablo and Yabby You, whose material he also hoped to issue. Targowski gradually started to win Perry's confidence, and a friendship developed, based partially on metaphysical conversations. As their plans began to take more concrete shape, Targowski noted a gradual shift in Perry's method of decoration: 'After cleaning the place up, Scratch was still "declarating" but it started to get more colourful, more creative, more artistic. The whole place started becoming an artwork: the garden, his house, the studio. It was quite an exhibition in more ways than one.' Before Targowski returned to Amsterdam with pre-releases he obtained from other producers, he received a verbal agreement from Scratch for the first Black Star Liner releases of his material.

Another notable visitor who was allowed inside the confines of the Ark was Wayne Jobson, who re-appeared at the gates in May 1979. Jobson landed a contract with Arista Records in late 1978 based on the strength of his Black Ark demo, and went back to Jamaica the following January to form the band Native in Ocho Rios. After three months of rehearsals, they were ready to work with Scratch, but found him much changed upon being re-admitted to the Ark.

'At this stage now, he was saying that bananas were God,' Jobson explained. 'Every time I went to see him, I had to carry a big bunch of green bananas, he would kneel down and pray to the banana. Then he would say that he had to X a wall, so he would take a whole day just to X maybe three feet square.'

Perry told Jobson he would be happy to work with him, but that his equipment was faulty; he noted that he was now working with some people from Holland who were planning to refurbish the studio. Jobson made subsequent visits to the Ark every few weeks to see how things were progressing, but typically found Perry more concerned with decorations than creating new music, and eventually recorded the album without Perry's involvement at Dynamic.

In July, more foreign visitors were admitted to the Ark: Vivien Goldman, who came with photographer Adrian Boot. They found Scratch wearing a straw hat, hitting metal poles with a hammer and speaking of a plan to 'Hijack Earth' with music; he also named his daughter Marsha as 'the reincarnation of the Queen of Sheba'. Bob Marley had recently told Goldman that he felt Lee

Perry was a genius, and that he was willing to work with Scratch again at any time, but Perry told Goldman he could not work with Marley due to Bob's wearing of dreadlocks: 'I love him as a brethren but I wouldn't agree with the dread situation he's portraying.' [2]

He further explained that the dreads had placed a 'dread lock' on the Earth, which Scratch himself was going to undo with the assistance of Pipecock Jackxon – apparently a new name for the Almighty, but also seemingly the name of Perry's startlingly excessive current persona. It was from this point that Perry would blur the line between himself as a servant of God and himself as some sort of component or extension of God; after all, it was Pipecock Jackxon who was 'X-ecuting the wrongs' in his human form as Lee Scratch Perry.

Dave Hendley and Mo Claridge also returned to the Ark that month, again brought to the studio by Prince Lincoln. After the European success of the Jolly Brothers' 'Conscious Man', Claridge was hoping to license more material from Scratch, but the pair again found communicating with Perry was difficult. As Hendley recalled, 'Mo was trying to get a couple of tracks for disco 45s like Leroy Sibbles' "Rastafari", he was trying to do a deal with Scratch on that. Scratch seemed to be having a kind of three-way conversation with Pipecock Jackxon; at times he *was* Pipecock Jackxon and at other times Pipecock Jackxon was over there with some other character. He told us to come back tomorrow and we'll talk about it, but when we turned up at the gates he just ignored us altogether. I remember later driving around Kingston with Scratch in our hired car, and nobody wanted to sit next to him; I got lumbered with it. He had a large stone and a piece of wood, and I was thinking "I hope he's not going to hit me." He was just talking complete nonsense, and you had to humour him; whatever you asked him, he'd come back with something that was totally somewhere else. In the main studio room where the musicians would play, there was nothing in there but half a drum kit, and he'd dug a hole under the drum about three foot square with water in it, but it was boarded over; that was back to this thing with the elements, to get the sound of water. Scratch would talk about the hole and how the water was there to get that sound. When it come down to working out the deal with Mo, I remember being in the control room and Scratch had been talking complete bollocks for about an hour, but he was able to land back on earth to work a deal out with Mo for "Rastafari".'

Claridge also successfully licensed Mystic I's 'Forward With Love' and 'Elaine', George Faith's 'Don't Be Afraid', Bunny Scott's 'What's The Use', Jimmy Riley's 'I Never Had It So Good' (miscredited to Bunny Scott), and Mikey Dread's 'School Girls' on this trip, all of which were subsequently released on Warrior discos in the autumn of 1979.

When Henk Targowski returned to Jamaica that August, he found that Pauline Morrison had returned to Kingston, but things were visibly strained between her and Scratch and they were generally avoiding each other. When Isha learned that Targowski was planning to issue Black Ark material in Holland, she offered to supply him with whatever tracks he wanted, but Targowski declined to deal with her, explaining he had already made exclusive arrangements with Scratch. In February 1978, Morrison issued a Jah Lion toast of 'White Belly Rat', Junior Delgado's 'Sons Of Slaves', the Congos' 'At The Feast' and a disco of Leo Graham's 'My Little Sandra' on a label called PM she established in London; now she was preparing to issue Black Ark tracks in New York. Her own 'Be With You' appeared on Wackies' Village imprint (credited to Isha Inerman), and she also cut the single in Jamaica on Black Art, along with an Orchid disco featuring a previously unreleased Winston Watson track called 'Dispensation' complete with an enigmatic toast by Dillinger called 'Lion Rock'. As Dillinger noted, it was the last song he ever recorded with Scratch. 'The last one I recorded at Black Ark studio goes "This is the dispensation lion rock, the power of the pipe, the power of the cock, the power of the Lord RaJah," me and Scratch write the lyrics. These times he was marking up the studio and do all kind of crazy things; people was afraid of him. One day Bob Marley come 'round there for some of his tracks, Scratch was there marking up all the walls with paint. I went to him and he said he want me to record the song, but I didn't hear it after that.'

Another Morrison production that surfaced as an Orchid single was Locksley Castell's excellent 'Jah Love Is Sweeter', voiced at King Tubby's over a cut of Black Uhuru's 'Let's All Unite' that she obtained from Prince Jammy in the spring of 1979.

At the end of the year, Morrison would travel to Ghana with a Ghanaian national named Sammy, cousin of her friend Pepe Judah – a dread from Western Kingston who had run the Nationwide and Student labels in England with his brother Burt. Born Frank Warren on July 24, 1949, Judah was a regular figure on Orange Street through much of the early '70s, though he spent the bulk of each school year in London after joining his mother there in 1962. Judah made his first trip to West Africa in 1977, and it was partly his tales of the lifestyle that inspired Pauline Morrison to go there. Her first weeks on the African continent would greatly change her outlook on life, but would ultimately be the cause of further tension between herself and Scratch. 'When I came back the guy cussed me every day,' Pauline noted bitterly.

Perry initially requested that Black Star Liner issue *Roast Fish Collie Weed And Cornbread* and *Return Of The Super Ape*, the master works that had been scorned by Island, but as copies were already available in Europe on import, Targowski asked that something older be substituted instead. Perry thus supplied the master tapes of *Cloak And Dagger* when Billy Bradford came to Jamaica towards the end of Targowski's stay; he also handed over tapes of 'Cane River Rock', 'Dread Lion', Jah Lion's 'Leggo' (issued as 'The Earth Is

The Lord'), Max Romeo's 'Norman The Gambler' and 'Sexy Natty', the Heptones Disco Dub EP, plus 'Baffling Smoke Signal' and 'Captive'.

Once back in Amsterdam, the crew facilitated the repressing of the album, and the other tracks on four disco 45s, all of which would surface by the end of the year; they also began making arrangements to return to Jamaica to become involved in producing new music with Scratch. When Island Records learned that Black Star Liner had issued cuts of material from the Heptones' *Party Time* album, they issued a written demand that the company stop pressing the disco as they claimed exclusive rights to the material. Black Star Liner challenged Island to provide proof, but received no response from the company and thus continued to handle the material. Island staff were then compiling the *Scratch on the Wire* album from some of the late Black Ark material they had been sitting on; the disc was issued the following October, reputedly without Scratch's sanction.

Perry was generally pleased with Black Star Liner's handling of his material, but took issue with the colour red being present in the red, gold, and green cover of *Cloak And Dagger*; blue was thus substituted on all subsequent pressings. It was on his second trip to Jamaica, Targowski hear several partially completed works initiated before the studio went into decline. 'He played me about nine tracks in various stages of completion, he had sort of given up on them because he needed new equipment. There were some technical flaws but I still quite liked the stuff and asked him if we could put some of it out. "Babylon Cookie Jar A Crumble" was one of them, and there was one called "Black Cinderella". He had a song about the 72 names for the Almighty where he rattles off quite a few of them, another song was "Jesse The Hammer", his name for Jesus Christ. We made arrangements to work on the most finished pieces.'

Targowski also noted coming across strange new sounds from within the wreckage of the Ark: 'One time I heard a bass sound coming out of the studio, Scratch said "It's the heart of the palm." He had stuck wires into the soil of a palm tree and somehow got this pumping bass sound out of it. Then he got into this whole philosophy about how the bass and the drum is Mother Earth and the sky and everything else.'

On another occassion, Targowski was present when a young group of aspiring musicians approached Scratch with a song that Perry consented to record on his somewhat damaged equipment. 'He still had that old drum machine of his, there was a kind of funky drum set and a keyboard, but everything was slightly out of tune; it wasn't really prime equipment for a studio and it wasn't working very well, because he'd been pouring baby oil on it and stuff like that, but it did work because a young set of kids came in to do a record. They weren't professional in any way, and they asked Scratch if he would let them record this song. He did, and it sounded lousy until he started fiddling with the knobs; he added some effects and corrected when things were out of tune by adding reverb with this strange connection that he had. When I first heard it just the way it was played it was dreadful, but when he played it tuned up and effected, it had possibilites.'

Targowski returned with Bradford in the autumn to make arrangements for the recording of new material and plan the re-construction of the partially completed tracks Perry played him. Scratch initially spoke to Winston Wright and engineer Errol Thompson, but no sessions were arranged at this time; he then specified that he wanted to work only with white musicians. The Black Star Liner crew were opposed to this idea, and got Perry to compromise by allowing certain non-dread Jamaicans to make up the rhythm section; his eventual choices would include guitarist Dwight Pinkney and drummer Cornel Marshall of Zap Pow along with Don Grant on bass and Tony Johnson on keyboards. In a three week period, the musicians laid a number of rhythms with Scratch on the eight track Tascam – the very last material to be recorded on the machine according to Scratch.

On Targowski's fourth trip to Jamaica, he and Billy sensed that Scratch would benefit from a break from the stresses of Kingston, and took him to Negril to relax for a few days. Perry let off steam with some local beauties, and spent an afternoon gathering boulders in a duffel bag; when the trio flew back to Kingston, they had to pay for an extra seat on the light aircraft to accommodate Scratch's rocks.

Scratch had discussed a feature film concept with Black Star Liner, and Bill Bradford arranged for a film crew from Canada to spend a week in Ocho Rios capturing Perry's ideas on 16mm celluloid. Provisionally entiteld *Nature Survival* and later referred to as *Sea Bat Cloud 9,* the film was to star Perry himself as 'Doctor Sea Bat', a 'nature defender' apparently related to Pipecock Jackxon. 'We was going to make a movie,' Perry explained, 'it was sunshine and moon and star, and we base part of it in Ocho Rios with the waterfalls. It would look like everything would be with the Ark, the Flood, the Judgement.' As with a great many other grandiose creations instigated in this period, the film was never completed as Perry and Black Star Liner shifted their focus to other projects.

Towards the end of the year, the company brought Lee Perry to Amsterdam in anticipation of an Upsetter tour of Europe scheduled for later in the year, billed as 'The African Jungle Safari'. Word of his arrival had circulated, and Scratch was greeted at the airport by a large contingent of followers, some of whom made banners to herald his arrival; their enthusiasm elicited an impromptu reception at the Black Star Liner offices, located near the Vondelpark at Vondelstraat 90.

Scratch spent most of the first month of the new decade attending interviews and overseeing the auditioning of white musicians and backing singers for the proposed tour and accompanying album project. One of the first European musicians recruited was GT Moore, an English guitarist and reggae enthusiast who had come to know Henk Targowski when Henk was working in the bakery of Amsterdam's famed Melkweg venue. Born May 2, 1949, in Reading, Gerald Thomas Moore comes from an English family that has some Irish roots. The first of three children, Moore's father was a truck driver and his mother an employee of the National Health Service. In his teenage years, he fronted a popular band called the Memphis Gents and was brought to the attention of Peter Eden, manager of the folk singer Donovan and in-house producer for Pye records. In the mid-1970s, Moore recorded what was probably the first reggae album by a white artist at Delane Lea studio in Wembley under Eden's direction; the disc was slated for release by Island until a conflict with executive Dave Betteridge saw the company pull out. Moore eventually landed a contract with Charisma, who released the albums *GT Moore And The Reggae Guitars* and *Reggae Blue*. As the New Wave movement began to change the face of rock at the end of the decade, Moore made some guest appearances with the group Curved Air, featuring drummer Stuart Copeland. When Copeland quit to join the Police, Moore assembled a related group called the Rhythm Tramps with a number of London-based Texan musicians; as the band found greater success in Amsterdam and Den Haag, they subsequently moved to Holland.

Moore's audition and first meeting with Scratch took place in late December 1979 at the offices of Black Star Liner, the walls of which Perry had covered with felt pen statements such as 'Free the weed, free the airwaves'; though the audition went smoothly enough, Moore was shocked to find Scratch had defaced one wall in a thoroughly unpleasant manner. 'When I did the audition, he'd written something like "White blood suckers, stop sucking the black man" and he'd smeared his own shit on the wall. Basically, the whole media gang were waiting to meet him, so he did a little number to shock everybody and writing on the wall was part of it. It's like masturbating in a Los Angeles toilet: a bit distateful, but it works. He also said that Europe was the antithesis of his culture, but what was good about Europe was that you could have peace and quiet compared to Jamaica.'

Perry later confirmed Moore's assertions, explaining that his excrement was used for a protective ritual: 'I don't pay police protection, I don't pay gunmen protection; I believe in my shit, so why shouldn't I plant my shit on the wall in Amsterdam? My shit is my lawyer, my barrister, my attorney, my "scientist" and my Obeah man; anyone fuck with me, why should I hire a gunman when I have my shit?'

Along with GT Moore, other successful recruits included a German singer named Jutta Eichhorn and Martiniquan singer Jocelyn Beroard, who would later find fame with the Zouk group Kassav; musicians later added to the entourage included former Rhythm Tramps keyboardist James Lascelles and saxophonist Bud Beadle, a former member of Geno Washington's Ram Jam band. To familiarise the musicians with his material, Scratch provided the group with a rehearsal tape recorded with his Jamaican backing band, which included 'Soul Fire', 'Big Neck Police' and 'Baffling Smoke Signal'.

Meanwhile, word reached Perry's ears via the international media that the Japanese government was seeking to impose a heavy penalty on Paul McCartney after the singer was caught bringing a large quantity of herb into the notoriously strict nation, which he was visiting to give some live performances with his band Wings. To counter their stringent policy, the Upsetter had Black Star Liner dispatch the following telegram on January 21, 1980, to the Minister of Justice in Tokyo:

'I Lee Pipecock Jackxon Perry would love to express my concern over your consideration of one quarter kilo to be an excessive amount of herbs in the case as it pertains to master Paul McCartney. As a creator of nature's love, light, life and all things under the creation sun, positive feelings through songs, good times and no problems, I find the herbal powers of marijuana in its widely recognised abilities to relax, calm and generate positive feelings a must. Herbs is his Majesty's. All singers' positive directions and liberty i-rations; please do not consider the amount of herbs involved excessive. Master Paul McCartney's intentions are positive.

(Signed) Baby Blue Green Star Pipecock Jackxon Lee "Scratch" Perry, Banana Eye I Pen, Jamaica, Nature's Love Defender.'

In February, Scratch travelled to London to reclaim the master tapes of *Revolution Dub* from Creole records. He caught up with Paul and Linda McCartney – now free from their Japanese caper – and discussed Paul's participation in the 'Jungle Safari' tour; plans for future collaborations were mooted. Perry also appeared on Capital Radio to give deejay David Rodigan confusing statements about his frame of mind and motivations:

'It is a pleasure being for one to say that I am mad, because it mean that the individual are doing something different from the massive crowd. I am glad to be mad because I am to son of William Shakespeare, Marcus Garvey, Rajah the Conquering Lion of Judah. He order me to rest and leave all the hypocrites out of the studio which is the moon base, the Black Ark, the painted bird . . . I am clean crystal, I am Crystal Chris, Jesse the Hammer the Royal Iron Fist . . . I am the rootsman of creation, I am the dust of Marcus Garvey's ashes . . . '[3]

When Scratch checked Tony Owens, he found his colleague was actively getting his Seven Leaves label off the ground; he had cut his first Black Ark discos in late 1978, with 'Such Is Life' by Lord Creator and Hendrick Nicholson's 'Brotherly Love' being among his inaugural releases. After completing his business in London, Perry went back to Amsterdam, where he delivered the master tapes of *Revolution Dub* to Black Star Liner, and made further arrangements for the refurbishment of his studio. Scratch had initially been staying in a spare room at Bill Bradford's place and was later housed by Black Star associates Bert and Eleanore in their apartment on Churchilllaan in the southern outskirts of the city, but would eventually be moved to a nearby hotel after defacing the apartment walls with more graffiti.

Shortly before returning to Jamaica, Perry voiced some of the fresh rhythms he had brought from Jamaica at Ballad Sound studio in the country town of Vuren – a studio he noted was 'surrounded by water'; his ad-libbed lyrics were based on notes he had written (or dictated for others to transcribe), and the sparse rhythms were mainly powered by GT Moore's guitar licks. It was at this session that an eleven minute jam he recorded on the eight track with Zap Pow was shaped into the rude 'Bed Jamming', featuring a female chorus by Jocelyn Beroard, Jutta Eichhorn and Karen Harvey (an American singer active in the Melkweg house band Sail); a slower, spooky rhythm became the inscrutable 'Easy Knocking'. Scratch revealed these creations as the only material to be released that were recorded on the eight track Tascam: 'When I start to use the Tascam, making some tracks with musicians, it sound extremely good, excellent. The Teac was in there as well, it never move out yet; on some sessions I was using the Teac and the Tascam. I don't think I used the Tascam for long, and I haven't put out any record off it, except those rhythms we done on it and carry to Amsterdam to voice like "Easy Knocking"; all the other songs that record on that Tascam machine, I don't see them – like we have a whole Niyabinghi session, can't find one of the tapes even now.'

GT Moore noted that the session players ingested hallucinogenic psillicibyn mushrooms on the day of the Ballad Sound session, but that Perry avoided the substance; however, the guitarist would later encounter the widespread rumour in Jamaica that Scratch had lost his senses after drinking mushroom tea brewed in Green Island. A related rumour put Perry's subsequently agitated behaviour down to his having taken LSD in Amsterdam, but Scratch has denied ever taking the drug; though he admitted an addiction to spliff and a former alcohol dependency, Perry scorns all notions that he has ever ingested hard drugs. 'In Jamaica somebody was trying to say me was taking cocaine with Bob Marley, but if I was taking coke I would get addicted to it. If I was taking LSD I would get addicted to it, because once you get involved in those things . . . it's like with the herbs: I was trying not to smoke it so much, and I was smoking too much. I love it so much that I don't want to be without it; I did want to smoke up for knowledge, for a spiritual vibration, and I get to the point that I was smoking one spliff after another. Then it get to a next point where Pauline was making my spliff, and when I discover what was going on, I wonder what was she putting in my spliff? At that point I stopped it before it can go further. The only thing I was getting addicted to is herbs, Wincarness wine and beer; that's what I was getting addicted to that is really destruction, but not LSD, 'cause once you start you can't stop.'

Henk Targowski also insisted that the rumour is entirely unfounded. 'I don't think it ever happened, and we were with him all the time. He was smoking a lot like he usually does and when he drank he was impossible to deal with, but to the best of my knowledge, he never took LSD or other hallucinogens – not intentionally nor unintentionally.' In later years, Lee Perry would variously be debated as a schizophrenic or acute sufferer of the neurological disorder Tourette's Syndrome; though both are equally plausible descriptions, neither adequately explains the daily reality experienced and lived by the Upsetter.

Upon Scratch's return to Jamaica, Black Star Liner sent a construction worker to begin repairing the studio; known as Sampson the Iron Man, the expatriate American Dave Sampson used to repair houseboats in Amsterdam. While the work was being carried out, Scratch and his children were housed in apartments at the luxurious Casamonte Hotel in Stony Hill, though Scratch was quick to return to Cardiff Crescent; once she learned that Black Star Liner was footing the bill, Pauline Morrison also installed herself in a room at the hotel – sometimes with Danny Clarke in tow – enjoying a lengthy residence at the company's expense. Once the major portion of the construction work had been completed, the kids moved back to Cardiff Crescent, but continued to go for meals at the hotel; the Perry family thus sought to glean the maximum possible from the generosity of their foreign hosts.

In late March, a set of musicians was sent to Kingston and also installed in the Casamonte; the first to arrive were GT Moore, James Lascelles, who came with his wife and children, and Bud Beadle, who also came with his wife and child. Though the money brought in by Black Star Liner was instigating a new renaissance at the Black Ark, Perry was still angry with the majority of his dread peers. GT Moore recalled that Scratch was in the process of once more ejecting the resident Jamaican players – presumably the musicians of the Niyabinghi Theocracy – the very day that the European session team arrived, which would ultimately delay their recording schedule. 'He had this commune of dreads that he was using as a band, they had something to do with the Congos. When I arrived, they had just got the sack; they were all moving out, piling their gear into this Volkswagen Bug. There was a lot of talk of Rastafari, so you got the feeling that Scratch did his ravings to get rid of them. They'd had an argument and Scratch had told them that he had the greatest players in the world that he had flown out to play for him and he didn't need these Rastafari yagga-yaggas. When I told Black Star Liner that there was no band, they told us to get into the vibes and go on holiday, so we went to Negril for two weeks.'

When the European players returned to Kingston, they found Scratch no nearer to having recruited replacements for the musicians he had fired; according to GT Moore, he was more interested in stating proclamations and decorating his compound than in finding any other Jamaican session men.

'Nothing was really happening, though the studio was completely set up. He had this guy called Artist (Jah Wise), so he would say "Artist, paint me the Pope" and Artist would come running up with his little natty dreads and he'd start painting a classic picture of the Pope with a golden papal hat. Then Scratch would prognosticate, enact some quasi-ritual where he would expound something like "Rastafari, the sun, the earth, my mother, Lee Perry" and then Artist would write those words on the artwork. The studio was all set up; it had this incredible rainbow carpet that was deep and full of fleas and there was a painted ledge that went all the way around the top and pigeons and doves would fly up there. It was a really happening place, but he didn't have any musicians; everything was painted and he had the minimal equipment but it all worked. In the control room he had the Teac, the reverb out of a Fender amp, and a bio-phase analog tin effects unit that had phase and tremolo, it's marvellous and a lot of his sounds were coming from it. He had the old, out-of-tune upright piano which he'd painted red, gold and green, an Ampeg bass amp and an old Gibson semi-acoustic bass guitar which had the deepest, wickedest sound, and he had some kind of drum kit and drum booth but they couldn't get a drummer – for weeks they were talking about Mikey (Boo), "Mikey's going to come," but what I didn't know was that Scratch had more or less got it that no one would play with him any more, and that's why he was getting people to fly from Amsterdam. One day we went up to Tuff Gong because (Wailers guitarist) Al Anderson is from Texas and he moved a little bit with my Texan band, and James Lascelles knew Junior Marvin, so we went up to see them and the I-Threes said, "We all heard that you were coming, how's it going with Scratch?" They were taking the piss, but I didn't realise it at the time.'

Eventually, a drummer who lived in the ghetto near Roosevelt Avenue was recruited to play on the sessions, while Moore arranged for former Curved Air member Colin Gibson to be flown out from England to play bass.

It was a chaotic start to what would be six weeks of anarchic mayhem, as work began on the album in earnest. Though Jutta Eichhorn and Jocelyn Beroard would later travel to Jamaica to become more closely involved in the project, Colin Gibson found the chaos too difficult to deal with, and left the island after three weeks; Eichhorn's American boyfriend was asked by Scratch to fill in for Gibson, but had little command of the bass. GT Moore detailed the unfocused nature of the sessions, which were frequented by a few stellar Kingston musicians who were still in Scratch's good books. 'We were recording every day, all day. There was no real organisation, but there was a great order in the chaos. What we had to do was come down and start a rhythm, and Scratch would be around the house and more or less ignore us; he'd be walking around declaring, and when the rhythm was irie, Scratch would come in and toast, but sometimes we would play a rhythm for 45 minutes and he wouldn't come in. It was an effective way of controlling the band without saying a word, while also leaving us with the freedom to play as we wanted. Dwight Pinkney and the keyboard player "Snapping" (Theophilus Beckford), they played all the time and a lot of people were hanging around just for meal times, like Dillinger. Joe Higgs was there, he sang one time and Scratch said they were going to arrange something, and Max (Romeo) used to hang out and check the vibes; when Scratch was holding court, they were his buddies. Rico came 'round and Pauline went off with his car to Negril and did some kind of herb deal: she got $40 from me, she got some money from Bob Marley, some from Danny (Clarke) and some from another guy we called Teeny Bop, and she said she'd be an hour and she was gone five hours and Rico was cursing her. Scratch said about Rico, "Me have him in a dunce cap, mon," because Blackwell had signed him and put him on ice. Scratch said to Rico "Why does he have the island on the record label? Because every time the record go round, he can control the island." Scratch also had a cardboard box of these little reel to reel tapes of rhythms from the '60s or '70s; sometimes he would just stick a tape on the Teac and then do dubs on top of it. A typical thing was "Disco Devil" on Max Romeo's "Chase the Devil", he would take it out, whack it on and voice it up with a cow bell or something, or then he'd want the horn to do something on it or the singers to do it with him. Some of the time we'd lay a track, and then sometimes we'd just dub over these tapes. The best tune we did was "Baffling Smoke Signal", I played a new guitar line through all of it. "Disco Devil", we learned the bass line, turned it around and he did a new version of it. Another tune we did was "Pipecock Jackson", I don't know if that ever came out; that was one of the tunes that he'd written and was into at the time.'

Moore also noted that although the eight track Tascam was still around, Perry showed no interest in using it. 'He still had the four track and he didn't like the eight track. He'd got a system of mixing where he put the bass and drums on track one – sometimes the bass and drums on track two as well but with a lot more bass – all the music like the chops, the brass, and the vocals on track two, and then he'll use tracks three and four to dub. If he's got something he wants to voice up, he'll just keep the bass and drums on, have a rap with a cow bell or something, and because he's using a percussion instrument with his voice, that makes an acoustic link with the drums. You can't do that with eight tracks because it's a different mentality, I would say a Western mentality: every track is separate and almost equal.'

The musicians were chiefly meant to be rehearsing for the upcoming tour, on which Scratch wanted the group to be billed as Pipecock Jackxon and the Corner Stones. Moore related a few problematic incidents that had come up in the course of the rehearsals: 'He had herb plants growing in the front garden; the police came one day and pulled them up and Scratch went nuts and started cursing them, that was in the middle of the sessions. It produced a hitherto unfelt solidarity in the camp, as the kids and people hanging around the yard thought the police were cheeky. We Europeans were reminded that despite our obvious different culture, we had something in common, so it gave the whole camp a sense of solidarity. Then I got sacked one day by Scratch because he got drunk one night and knocked over my amp. Scratch very rarely got drunk but he smoked a lot; he would be the last to go to bed at night and he was the first up in the morning, so he was fit, but he got drunk and knocked my amp over and I said "Look man, be careful, that amp's been with me a long way" and he said "Fuck off you blood claat guitarist, fuck off back to London!" The next morning, everyone's hung over, and Billy (Bradford) says something like "Well Scratch, what are we going to do about GT?" and Scratch just said "What are you talking about?" Another thing I remember involved Poppa Son. I was giving herbs to Poppa Son and he became like a brother, and I was going to go out with him to a disco in New Kingston. Like most of the people hanging out there, he hardly had a penny to rub together; they were impotent socially, and Scratch was a despot – everything that they ate and drank came from him, so no one challenged him. Poppa Son got all dressed up in a pastel green outfit and as we were about to go, Scratch said that Poppa Son had to dig the garden. He was so humiliated, and he got his green disco clothes dirty, and I went right off Scratch then.'

As April turned to May, the chaos wore on and the album seemed no nearer to completion, though the band was getting tighter despite the personnel changes, and looked forward to what they felt was bound to be an electrifying run of stage shows. In their spare time, some of the European players began moonlighting, occassionally at the request of Pauline Morrison: GT Moore thus played on a session with Sly and Robbie at Channel One, cutting songs such as 'Irie Irie' as the Originals, while Bud Beadle played flute on the Majesterians' 'So Many Times' (mixed at the Black Ark by band member Phil Matthias) and added a flute riff to the Silvertones' 'Give Praises' for her. Moore also organised sessions at Harry J with Zap Pow, which were initially to be funded by Black Star Liner; though he began laying tracks on May 2, the material was never completed.

Meanwhile, Sampson the Iron Man was continuing to fix the Black Ark roof, and make whatever structural alterations Scratch deemed necessary. The most individual of these involved the studio's new drum booth, now fully adapted to allow for the presence of water birds. GT Moore recalled the process by which Scratch explained the design to Sampson: 'Billy had a place in Red Hills, he was there with his wife. I was up there with the Zap Pow band, we were working out my lines with James and Bud Beadle. Scratch was there and we're having a meal, and Billy said 'David's going to build you a drum booth, Scratch, what do you want? How do you want it built?" David was sitting there with a pen, and Scratch started to prognosticate. The first thing he said was "Egg", and then something like "Aqua", then we got "the Earth", "Rastafari", and "Metal". David looked at it for a while and said "Egg, could you make that out of concrete?" and Scratch says "Irie". Then David went "Aqua is water," he was beginning to get it. It was a magical process the way the scheme of the drum booth formed in David's mind, so he said "Earth, can you have sand?" and "Metal, what do you think of chicken wire, Scratch?" and Scratch said "Irie" and that was it. So he built this booth that had a fantastic sound, it took three or four days and in the end it had a wooden floor and underneath was sand. There was a large hole in the wooden floor in the shape of a Star of David and there was water in the hole. Above it was wood up to the halfway mark and then glass, and there was chicken wire on the top. It made all the high sounds have this kind of metallic ring that was partly the glass and partly the wire slightly vibrating, and the bass drum and low toms had this dull thud which was a combination of the wood and the sand. It had an incredible sound and it was very much the Scratch sound, very punchy and psychedelic.'

Scratch later revealed the motivation behind the building of the pond within the drum booth:

'The heat itself and the energy that was coming, the heat was so strong that we were going to need water to cool it. It get too powerful and might be exploding, so then I need birds, because the birds is the power of the air, and the water . . . it work because when you're not playing drum, then duck would be swimming around and having fun, and when you're playing drums, then the duck could go outside and rip up plant.' [4]

While GT and the other musicians were busy with other projects, Black Star Liner was arranging for new tape recorders to be installed, along with top of the range Quad amplifiers and a new mixing desk. Unfortunately, the machinery would never be made operational, and its abortive installation would mark the end of Perry's connection with Black Star Liner. Scratch detailed the circumstances of the rupture: 'Billy buy up to date machine, up to date mixer, and was ready for everything to go but it couldn't happen. Billy buy tape recorders and Sampson bring me two transformer from the ship, specially made; we had a new booth from Amsterdam and new mixer and we turn on and ready to go but we hear a "Pish!" We set up and start and after we turn on it was an explosion. The engineer who setting up didn't have any idea and set up things wrong; they have some guy who make the (electrical) connection, maybe he was an amateur and he blew up the machine. The heat go through some of the things they bring here and something never go right, then me say "No, leave it. Take up everything back." We just set up and it go "Whoosh!" and that was it. I was so mad about it, I throw out the new board same time, me give it to Errol (Thompson) and Errol must have sent the mixer to Bunny Lee. We was trying to get the machines working and I just get mad and say "No, forget the whole thing." That's when Billy crashed the tour – musicians stayed three weeks and nothing happen, so I didn't want to go on the tour. I tell Billy "Take back the things them because I don't really ready to rebuild and I don't want to do it" – I just didn't want to replace the studio when he want to replace it.'

These unfortunate circumstances saw Scratch leaving the album unfinished, forcing the white musicians to return to Europe around May 9. After the tour was cancelled, he is said to have poured sand in the Quad amplifiers, and he would go on gradually to dismantle what had been painstakingly rebuilt, beginning a new cycle of destruction mirroring that which had begun towards the end of 1978. But Scratch was keen to point out that he still retains respect and appreciation for Bill Bradford, whose concrete support he readily acknowledged: 'Me and Billy never had no problem. One guy me can say, don't care what happened, I will never say nothing bad about Billy; I am sure Billy somebody really fucking special. If I said "Billy we need this," Billy said "Let's go to the shop and choose the best you want, choose all you want." If I say "Billy, give me $10,000," him give you instantly without any argument. He would give me every fucking thing; even what Chris Blackwell wouldn't do, Billy would do everything to see that you were comfortable. I can take Billy for his word; if Billy saying he's going to do something then he's fucking going to do it. Him get into some trouble, and when I see him again, he said "Lee, I bring back some tapes from Amsterdam and leave them at your house." Billy did have so much tapes and after things go bad him bring them back to my house, like "Bed Jamming" and "Easy Knocking". Nothing him ever said to me him didn't do.'

Without the motivating forces of solid financial backing and a concrete goal to work towards, Scratch drifted back into a period marked by depression and mental anguish. He continued to shun contact with outsiders, and would gradually empty his studio of its contents.

The saving grace for Perry and his family came through the arrival of Vicky Nelson – an impressionable young singer with a big heart who became concretely involved in their lives shortly before things went wrong with Black Star Liner. Born March 2, 1952, in the town of Grantham in rural Clarendon, Vicky was one of ten children born to a farmer and tailor who was also a minister in the local Church of God. She moved to Kingston as a teenager to complete her schooling, and began performing in talent contests as a singer. By the end of the decade, she was singing in hotels on the North Coast, regularly performing gospel as well as pop. In 1979, she made a concerted effort to begin recording, which eventually resulted in her making the acquaintance of Dennis Brown.

Brown suggested Lee Perry as a potential producer, and brought her to the Black Ark one afternoon, but Perry was away on that occasion. After experiencing a later vision at her home in Duhaney Park, Nelson made her way to the Black Ark to meet Lee Perry for the first time. Though Scratch seemed to be expecting her, Vicky noted the ominous emptiness that permeated the Ark in this period. 'At that time he wasn't hardly seeing anyone, like when somebody gone into exile. He welcomes me very good and the kids were there, then my heart reach out, definitely. I told him I'm a singer, so he got some musicians and I did a 45 with him, "Black People You've Got To Know Yourself" with musicians like Family Man and Easy Snapping; I don't know what happened to that song.'

With the subsequent upheaval and eventual demise of the studio, Scratch never got around to releasing Vicky Nelson's song – or anything else he had been working on. But Nelson became a frequent visitor at Cardiff Crescent, forming a strong and lasting bond with Perry's children. Before the cancellation of the European tour, Nelson was already caring for them regularly; a few months later, Scratch asked her to take her things and move in with them, and though Nelson had to break up with her boyfriend and would be greatly ostracised by her family, she was unable to decline Perry's request. Thus, his children gained something of a step-mother for a time, and her nourishing care also soothed the savage beastliness of Scratch himself. 'I was a part of whatever he was doing,' Nelson recalled, 'my foot would be in paint, I would get rocks and all those nature things, and I remember we go about three days with no sleep. Whatever he was going through, I would be there.'

Pauline Morrison briefly returned to Jamaica but finally left the island for a new life in New York, where she initially planned to launch a career as a record producer; Danny Clarke had moved there some months previously, but their relationship remained tenuous and unstable. Pauline had cut more material in Jamaica, including the Orchid single 'Ethiopia' by singer Carol Cole, voiced at King Tubby's over the rhythm used for Winston Watson's 'Dispensation'. While passing through London, she arranged to cut material on the Black Ark International label in conjunction with Starlight – a Harlesden record company set up by former Trojan executive Desmond Bryan. Flat mixes of late seventies rhythms with obtrusive synthesizer overdubs surfaced towards the end of the year as the misleadingly titled *Black Ark In Dub* album – part of which was not recorded at the Ark, and which lacked the attentive mixes of Lee Perry. Along with dubs of late Ark work by George Faith, Watty Burnett, Danny Hensworth and Scratch himself was a cut of 'Dreadlocks I' (a little-known single by the singer Ras Keatus) and other unknown instrumentals, plus a Tubby's dub of 'Jah Love Is Sweeter'. Starlight also issued a previously unreleased Junior Murvin disco, comprising the original 'Crossover' and a romantic cover tune, 'I'm In Love'. The Murvin disco was also released by Morrison on Orchid in New York, along with a disco of Watty Burnett's 'Open The Gate', backed by 'Lion A De Winner', Scratch's wild vocal version of the 'Words Of My Mouth' rhythm.

Meanwhile, Black Star Liner issued the *Return of Pipecock Jackxon* album in an attempt to gain back some of the fortune they had spent before winding down the company (estimated at $65,000), but the disc had not been finished properly, did not benefit from a final Perry mix-down, and was an uneven mix of old and new material. Along with the fresh 'Bed Jammin', 'Easy Knocking' and the skeletal 'Untitled Rhythm' (possibly planned as the title track but never properly voiced) were several out-takes from the *Roast Fish* period: the delightfully paranoid 'Who Killed The Chicken' (complete with cow sounds and Full Experience chorus), 'Babylon Cookie Jar Aa Crumble', 'Some Have Fe Halla' and 'Give Thanx To Jah', another number featuring distorted guitar, recorded at the time of 'Baffling Smoke Signal'. Perry later expressed a general dissatisfaction with the album upon learning of its release.

> 'That's a bad movement. They were in a haste to catch a flight which isn't ready. Them trying to rip me off but them are fools . . . If I have an album, I have to be there, I have to mix my album. They come with the idea that they want to do an album with me, but they don't find the money. And so many demands they make upon the album, the cover and everything, so I told them I wasn't interested. So they figured that's it now, and put the album out, so it's a bad spell me a cast 'pon them – them fall into the twilight zone.' [5]

At Cardiff Crescent, Perry remained in chaotic solitude, enacting rituals and again partially dismantling the Ark; his dramatic outbursts and self-destruction symbolically mirrored that of the nation, as Jamaica was tearing itself to pieces in the most violent election campaign the nation had ever seen. Since the abolition of the peace treaty, orchestrated violence had plummeted to new depths of depravity; the kidnapping and torture of citizens was becoming commonplace. The M16 was now the weapon of choice, and bombs were going off downtown; politicians were being killed and Manley himself was shot at while on the campaign trail. The election battle was nothing short of a civil war, as Jamaica was fought over by clashing ideologues that sought to align the nation with America or Cuba. In the end, Manley's unrealistic ideals could not match the greater powers of American strong-arm tactics, and the PNP suffered a crushing defeat at the end of October. But by the time Edward Seaga came to power, around one thousand Jamaicans had died in election related violence; Kingston had been transformed into a hellish inferno where tranquillity was an impossibility.

Inevitably, friction again grew between Lee Perry and some of his closest peers during these volatile months. Clancy Eccles recounted witnessing a physical attack on Striker Lee and King Tubby: 'Bunny Lee, Tubbys and I went to Scratch when Marley was on tour, and Scratch went for a hammer to bust up Bunny Lee and Tubby's head; they jump in the car and left me. Bunny Lee is a friend, but anything you do, tomorrow morning Bunny Lee say it's him do it. Tubbys is another copy man again so Scratch didn't like none of them.'

On the same occasion, Eccles found Perry railing against Bob Marley, who had raised Perry's anger through the circumstances of what would be his final departure from Jamaica in the summer of 1980. Scratch named the initial cause of the friction as stemming from Marley's failure to loan Scratch a small sum to fix his broken-down Chrysler: 'Bob Marley promised to lend me $1000 (JA) to buy a car part, the part wasn't expensive. When I have money, Bob Marley couldn't want; he didn't have nowhere to live and I give him house, I didn't charge him any rent, but when my car did caput, money wasn't in sight. I only need a thousand Jamaican dollars to get the new parts for it; somebody go up to America and bring it back for me. I was invited to come at one o'clock, but (Marley) tell me lie, because when I come at one o'clock, him gone. He didn't tell me he was going on a tour and he didn't have it in mind to give to me. Those times he have Claudie Massop and all those rude boys, too much money to give them, so I said "That stupid idiot, they didn't tell me never to come, fuck this". I couldn't get the parts that was here for me car, and the next thing you hear is that Bob dropped down on stage.'

Scratch's brother P-Son noted that Marley and Perry had been on good terms before Marley left Jamaica. 'Bob was going on a tour with Commodores, and they were talking about how the music was changing and what they're going to do with the music, they're going to change it to chanting, keep on a reggae level. Bob say him is like Selassie-I, and Scratch is like Marcus Garvey.'

Unfortunately, the fact that Marley departed without honouring his pledge raised a bitterness in Scratch that was never alleviated, as Ned Willacy noted. 'Scratch went to Bob to ask for Bob's assistance which Bob did not give him; Scratch said that Bob is going to die, 'cause him ears hard.'

While the Wailers were in New York, preparing for three upcoming shows at Madison Square Gardens with the Commodores, Marley met with Ansel Cridland, who was then often travelling between Jamaica and New York. In a last-ditch effort to retrieve "Who Colt The Game", and "I Know A Place," he asked Cridland to try to obtain the tapes from Scratch. As Cridland recalled, 'When he held onto the song 'Who Colt The Game", Bob send me to him. At the time the board giving him problem; Scratch throw paint in the board and start acting a way to get people off of him. When I go, Scratch said "No, I nah let off nothing," 'cause something was wrong with him car and him go to Bob and say him want some money to fix the car, Bob never give him. So when I go to Scratch, him nah give him, and Bob never really get back the song.'

Scratch later complained that masked gunmen demanded Wailers master tapes from him, but he has never discovered exactly who was behind the attack, and further details of the incident have not emerged; whether the tape in question was 'Who Colt The Game' or another tape has also not been clarified. 'One night me was there sleeping and three guys come inna the house front, theif trying to rob me and all them things. Them say them come for the Wailers tape. I don't know if he was involved, 'cause I don't think he would send no bad man to me for tapes. Even if he was involved that doesn't matter to me because me don't see Bob would really want to hurt me. He is a person me really love, and it is my belief and when you love a person they can't hurt you, don't care what they do.'

In September, Bob Marley collapsed in Central Park, as the cancer that entered his bloodstream through his foot wound now spread throughout his body to his brain. He was gravely ill, and his days on earth were numbered. Although Scratch and Bob had some unresolved issues, Lee Perry was still held in high regard by the rest of the Marley family and the Wailers crew – so much so that Rita Marley had Scratch mix of a dub of a religious groove called 'That's The Way' she had put together with Grub Cooper of the Fabulous Five; Perry's thumping dub mix was cut at Tuff Gong in December 1980 and issued on a Trident disco in the UK.

Scratch then left the island at the start of 1981, leaving his children in the care of Vicky Nelson and their uncle P-Son. He was in bad need of a change of scenery as well as a source of income; New York thus seemed as logical a place as any to venture to.

Chris Blackwell arranged a prime place for Scratch to stay in the Big Apple, putting him up at Perry Henzell's apartment on Irving Place and Seventeenth Street in Manhattan, initially with Kiddus-I; after Kiddus left town, Scratch continued to exercise his compulsion of writing declamatory graffiti on the walls. He soon made contact with Max Romeo, who had recently relocated to New York after gradually spending longer periods there. Romeo had endured a portion of ostracism from Scratch some time after *War In A Babylon,* culminating in the writing of 'Judas' over the photograph of him that hung in the Black Ark, but Romeo noted that he took such incidents lightly, knowing that Scratch could easily be offended by what he took to be disloyalty. 'During his transition to the heights that he's in, we rarely meet, and when he don't see me, I think some times he feels that I'm a traitor by not tracking him down,' Romeo explained. 'He used to play that game with me in the studio: he doesn't see me for a month, you go in the studio you see all my pictures marked "Judas". Then here I come, everything's come down, new pictures go up. I disappear for another month, you go in there, "Max Romeo – Judas," Max Romeo this, Max Romeo that.'

On their reconnection in New York, Romeo took Scratch out to Brad Osborne's premises on White Plains Road in the Bronx, where the pair discussed the further issue of Perry's material on Osborne's Clocktower label; Clocktower had been issuing Perry singles since the mid-1970s, and had re-issued Prince Jazzbo's *Natty Passing Thru* in an altered form as *Ital Corner* in December 1979. The pair now discussed a re-issue of *Blackboard Jungle Dub,* which would surface in an altered form in April.

Romeo noted that Perry took a large pirate's chest with him when visiting Brad, which he said would kill anyone who looked in it; when Osborne and Romeo insisted he open the chest, they found it contained a large stone about the size of a television set, several bags of dirt and bottles filled with unidentifiable liquids, plus a number of children's toys. Romeo also noted that Perry's dress sense was gradually shifting in this period: influenced by the shocking attire of punk, Scratch began wearing studded bracelets and a Nazi SS cap, much to the displeasure of the Jewish staff of a camera store that Perry sought to patronize. On each subsequent visit to the apartment, Max Romeo found more graffiti on the walls; eventually, Scratch would cover the ceiling, bathroom tiles, shower and toilet with words, and even begin writing on the fire escape; 'Let me tell the world about women' was one prominent bathroom proclamation.

Lee Perry was not long in New York when good things began happening for him, and his departure from Jamaica brought a generally more positive mood. He quickly forged a romantic link with a striking blonde model named Brynn Lacey, and spent much time in the company of Stevie Wonder's brother Larry, himself an aspiring musician. Island Records coordinator Rema Marx, a black American woman who produced the b-side of the Slits' first single, also had designs on Scratch, but Perry sensed she was more attracted to his fame than to him personally, and generally rebuffed her advances. Perry also came into contact with Stiff records salesman Phil Fox, who was also selling T-shirts and trying to form another record label. Fox had strong links in the music industry, and introduced Scratch to David Lass of the San Juan music company, who subsequently made a lucrative lisencing deal with Scratch for his *Soul Rebels* era Wailers productions, prompting a worldwide dissemination of the material on cheaply made album collections, mastered from a poor quality cassette.

On March 7, Fox brought Perry to a concert at Isaiah's, one of the first Jamaican dance halls in New York, at which Roland Alhponso was the star attraction. For his first set of the evening, Alphonso was backed by Jah Malla, a band led by one of his sons; he was then backed by a white reggae band called the Terrorists for a second set, after the band presented some of their own material. Perry was so inspired by the band's blend of reggae and New Wave that he leapt on stage mid-way through Alphonso's second set, grabbing the saxophonist's microphone while unceremoniously kicking him backstage; he then launched into an impromptu rap with the group, beginning a brief period of collaboration.

The Terrorists was formed in November 1977 by drummer David Ostrowe (a.k.a. Dro), bassist Gary Schiess (a.k.a. Gary Buildings), singer and guitarist Ray D'Angelo and keyboardist Frank Covello; D'Angelo and Covello were replaced by singer John Collins and guitarist Mark 'Steady' Levi in 1980. Perry first met Dro and Schiess at Brad Osborne's place in the summer of 1977, when they were the rhythm section in a band called Tribesman (with saxophonist Baba Leslie), and this previous association helped cement their re-connection in 1981.

Scratch's New York arrival coincided with an awkward period for the group, as their rhythm guitarist had left the band and they were having trouble finding a reliable replacement; nevertheless, they were delighted by the prospect of working with Perry, whose work had long inspired Dro and Schiess. Plans were quickly made for the recording of new material, but as the group had already been booked as the opening act for an upcoming concert by Culture at Irving Plaza on March 27, they had just enough time to arrange one rehearsal with Scratch on March 16, at which songs such as 'Soul Fire', 'Roast Fish And Cornbread' and 'Babylon Cookie Jar' were reconstructed. Dro also mentioned to Scratch that he had read about an unreleased Black Ark song called 'Pipecock Jackxon' in an article by Vivien Goldman, and Scratch happily taught the band to play it, making it part of their growing repertoire.

At Irving Plaza, the Terrorists were temporarily aided by the presence of Christine Church, rhythm guitarist of a White Plains reggae-rock band called Beast. Scratch joined the group in an outlandish space costume after their own initial set, drifting between ad-libbed new mutations and fairly faithful versions of what had been rehearsed; it was a strong and promising first performance for Scratch and his new band. The three Congos watched the entire set from one side of the stage, along with Cedric Myton's brother Patrick, who was soon to establish the Electric Dread studio on Tenth Street; though the Congos greeted Scratch after the event backstage, they received only the scantest of responses from the Upsetter.

In the weeks Perry worked with the Terrorists, a friendship formed between Scratch and Dro. The drummer would go to Perry's apartment most mornings to wake him up, and Scratch would then perform a daily ritual: after turning on the gas stove in the kitchen, he would put his hands over the burner, heating up the rings he wore on each finger to give himself more power. In Perry's pirate trunk, Dro recalled seeing five or six reels of 16mm film footage from the unfinished *Sea Bat Cloud 9*.

As Perry continued rehearsing with the band, Dro witnessed other inscrutable actions, the most startling of which involved the squandering of a very fat cheque from Island on an antique silver dining set. As Dro recalled, 'I loved doing music with Scratch and the main impetus was for me to learn, to touch his genius so to speak. The other half of the story, which I barely even saw, was the side show that was his personal life. I had a lot of time on my hands, so I used to go to Scratch's every day and hang out with him, every day was some kind of a trip. One day Scratch said he needed to see Chris Blackwell because Blackwell owed him back money; Island was selling all kind of Perry productions and he was collecting his quarterlies or whatever, so we went to the offices of Mango Records on Madison Avenue. He did a graffiti design on the wall with a black Magic Marker, and some of the people at Island seemed a bit freaked out, though (Mango founder) Lister Hewan-Lowe was having a great time with it. It was around that time Scratch got the check for $20,000 and spent most of it on a beautiful antique silver serving set that would serve ten people which he brought into his apartment. Before he went to Island he was talking about getting it, in fact I think he wanted to get the money so he could buy it.'

Blackwell confirmed that Scratch blew a large sum of money he got from Island in this period, and noted that it further soured their relationship, as Blackwell hoped Scratch would use the money to get his studio back in shape. 'It was $25,000,' Blackwell clarified. 'I know the studio was rebuilding and I figured he wanted to start back; he wasn't asking me for money, I might have been encouraging him to get something back together again. I heard all kinds of stories, he took the money and bought silverware, that kind of thing. All I know is it didn't happen. It was a long shot and I don't resent it.'

Perry explained that he bought the antique for investment purposes, with money related to Marley material he had worked on that Island controlled. 'They did have a plan, I don't know what. They give me an advance on some royalty, I don't know which of the songs they give me off of, but when me say that me didn't have no money they make sure that they give me money for some of the Marley tune that they were taking away, like "Blackman Redemption" or "Kaya". They give me that $25,000 and I buy some material and cloth and sterling silver. When you go on a treasure hunt, you must want silver and gold to make sure, because when these (paper) money won't value any more, the silver and gold will. Silver and gold worth more important than paper money, so I wanted to have a selection of silver, because silver represent immortality.'

Meanwhile, Phil Fox arranged for Scratch to make a second appearance with the Terrorists in April at Tramps – a blues joint owned by Irish American night club impresario Terry Dunn – but the gig was somewhat less successful due to problematic circumstances. The band was again without a rhythm guitarist, which rendered them somewhat imbalanced, but the real problems began when they finished their warm up set and played their version of the Silvertones' 'Rejoice' to usher Perry onto the stage, only to find that he had gone missing. To keep the momentum going, the band allowed a white Rasta deejay known as Lizzy Dreadess to toast over the rhythm before taking a break to locate Scratch, who had left the venue and was said to be back at his apartment.

After making a hasty exit from the stage, Dro rushed over to Scratch's place to find him administering some harsh discipline to Fox. 'Scratch was standing there, repeatedly slapping Phil Fox's face, because Fox didn't come together with the money,' Dro recalled, 'Scratch thought he was trying to make a fool of everybody and he was fucked up on drugs. I told Fox to take a hike and got Scratch to come back to the club with me to finish the gig.'

Later in the month, Perry undertook some studio work with the Terrorists. The group planned to use a large 24 track studio in Manhattan, but Scratch brought them instead to the eight track Sunshine Sound studio in the Bronx to impart a roots feel to their music; it was still a rudimentary facility, lacking basic components such as reverb. The studio had been set up by

Munchie Jackson, whose partnership with Lloyd 'Bullwackie' Barnes had been dissolved after the pair had a harsh falling out; Jackson had spent a good few years in jail, and is said to have held Bullwackie partly responsible for his conviction.

Though Scratch built three rhythms with the Terrorists, only the rollicking 'Love Is Better Now' was voiced, which Perry versioned as the rambling 'Guerrilla Priest', 'white smoke signal' seemingly about God's many powers, delivered by Scratch in the form of 'Smokin' Joe, Joseph the Hammer'. These latter two tracks were issued as a twelve inch on Phil Fox's Splif Rockers label in May, making a fair impact on both sides of the Atlantic; *Black Music and Jazz Review* named the release 'Singles pick of the month' in September, while *NME* placed it at number eight on its Reggae Hit Parade.

Before the recording of 'Guerrilla Priest', Scratch had already voiced several tracks with Munchie. Largely ad-libbed metaphysical diatribes and rambling declamatory rants, the material was firmly in the mode of *Pipecock Jackxon* and varied only in its overall presentation of heaviness and light. Tracks such as 'Hi-Jack', 'Atlas Road Map', 'Cockroach Motel' and 'Calamooch' all reflected the optimism he had come to in New York, while others conjured a darker mood, particularly the black magic declarations of 'Seven'. Though two albums' worth of material was rapidly captured on tape, scheduled to be released as a double album in the summer, Jackson's involvement in the music business began to wane. Some say he became more concretely involved in the sale of cocaine, and was eventually shot dead by his son Andre in a drugs-related incident in the mid-'80s; Andre's gun was allegedly fired in self-defence. The material Scratch voiced with him was thus neglected until 1994, when some of it surfaced as the VP album *Smokin'*.

Cocaine was an insidious presence on the New York music scene in this period, and its destructive powers would soon also make a strong, negative impact in Jamaica. Phil Fox is said to have offered cocaine to Lee Perry, only to find that he took the stash and rubbed it all over his body, entirely wasting the expensive powder. Though his bouts of drinking still brought on destructive behaviour, and though he perpetually consumed large quantities of spliff, Scratch would increasingly voice displeasure at those who used cocaine or other hard drugs.

As Scratch continued working with the Terrorists, Pauline Morrison made a brief re-appearance in his life, spending time with him in the apartment on Irving Place. Though Perry had been greatly angered by her ongoing liaison with Danny Clarke and by her issuing of Black Ark material, their relationship seems to have undergone a brief reprieve at this time; he even gave her a substantial portion of the money he received from Island Records. 'Me give Pauline $6,000 out of it,' he explained, 'she was going to buy a car in New Jersey. Me see the car and everything, but I never knew she was taking coke. I give her $6,000 and they coke it out, but I did save.'

It was around the time that the Terrorists' EP was recorded that Dro accompanied Scratch to Brad's Record Den in the Bronx, where Perry's ire was raised through the discovery that Brad Osbourne had issued a compilation album called *Scratch And Company Chapter 1* on his Clocktower label. As Dro remembered, 'He wanted to go see Brad so we took a trip up to the Bronx and Brad was so happy to see him; Brad loved Lee Perry, he was an Upsetter freak! Brad used to get tapes from Scratch, and he had a four track Teac A3340S that he'd keep upstairs in his office; he'd spend hours listening to the stuff. He idolised Scratch and was really happy to see him, but Scratch got real angry when he saw *Scratch And Company Chapter 1* for the first time. *Chapter 1* is the result of Brad going through tapes that Scratch sent him over different periods of time and compiling the tracks, and I think that's what pissed him off; Brad compiled it without asking "Should we put these tracks together with these tracks" or "Can we release this track right now?" Brad was kind of making excuses; he gave him some money, but only small change. Scratch ripped the album open, drew all over the cover and ripped it up. He took a bunch of them with him and a bunch of the *Blackboard Jungle Dub* and *Ital Corner* albums. Later on at his apartment, he had drawn something like "I hate Brad" or "This is the devil" on a picture of Brad.'

Perry's third gig with the Terrorists was at the Mudd Club on May 1, where the band was joined by organist Jah T and a rhythm guitarist called Ronnie, both Jamaican session musicians who had played on their Sunshine studio sessions; the live mix at the club was provided by Munchie Jackson. Backstage at the Mudd Club, Scratch explained his desire to work with white artists and spoke of why he had abandoned his studio.

'I want to change my life. I work with the black so long and they give me a hard fight. I want to live a cool life, no problem, easy going . . . the studio, it's being remodeled for a new future with some cleaner people, honest people worthy to step into the Ark of the Covenant to sing. I have locked it away from parasites and vampires. All I see in the business is singing parasites, singing lies, singing something which they don't mean. It really bothers me, it really get me mad . . . They kill you, the vampires and bloodsuckers, take away your diamond, stab you in the back and take away your girl. They kill the prophets, one by one, because every prophet come to tell the truth. But tell them they can't kill *this* bloodclot because him can't dead.' [6]

He later named the greed and envy of those attatched to the Black Ark as the reason for his drastic transformation:

'Me have black man, they try to deliver the message years ago, but them was so much interested in money, they wasn't clean inside to deliver the message. All them was seeing is money, and them was being corrupted, because one horse can't serve two masters. Them was working not because they want to work with me but because they want to get me idea. I couldn't deliver the message because the music them play be corrupted like them mind; they were poisoning and stifling the music so I had to change quick and come and toy with the white to straighten meself and no stay down in the dungeon with them. That's when them get trick, that's when me play mad because me no want them to come around me any more, and me no want them to follow me anymore. Me want them to think me mad, done with the music, and me finish and run out of idea.' [7]

On another occasion, he mentioned the Terrorists as helping him realise the plans of his latest emerging persona, which was chiefly concerned with administering justice:

'I am hiding from parasites and pulling myself together with some new youth. I am working with white men. They are the Terrorists and I am Doctor Sea Bat, here to bless the good and to curse the evil. Pipecock Jackxon, he took a rest. He was the Executioner, that is another form of him. He's a man in exodus, he's changed form. He has four million billion trillion different faces, that's a lot of faces, ha ha ha! I left Jamaica to come to New York and find some crooks . . . things will get better when people get justice. I am the Black Arkean general, now is my time to collect, how about that? My music is roots music, I am not one of the reggae fanatics. I am the supreme creator . . . saying to the people love and truth, it's the key to eternity, so I am asking the people of the Universe to stop stealing, stop telling lies, stop being hypocrites, stop being parasites. That's a special message and a special warning. Stop being deceivers and deniers. When they do all that, they will get the blessing of the Most High.' [8]

Just as things began taking off with the Terrorists, Perry decided to ditch them after an ill-fated concert in Boston at the Spit club on May 11. The concert was organised by Mike Cacia, a promoter who had arranged for Culture to play at the Irving Plaza show at which Scratch had his debut with the Terrorists; Cacia made arrangements for the Boston gig through Phil Fox. According to Dro, the Terrorists decided to cancel the performance at short notice due to the unclear financial arrangements surrounding the concert, and because the band again found themselves with no rhythm guitarist. However, the group was pressurised into fulfilling the engagement by the well-connected Cacia, who suggested their popularity in Boston would suffer should they fail to appear. The band thus chose to drive to Boston against their better judgement (while Scratch himself was flown over), with vocalist John Collins drafted in as rhythm guitarist – an unfortunate choice, as the singer could barely play a note.

It was during the soundcheck that a laughing Cacia broke the news to the band that Bob Marley had died. 'Cacia said "Guess what I just heard on the radio: Bob Marley just died," ' Dro remembered. 'He looked at Scratch and said "Well, what do you think?" and Scratch said just one thing: "I am the teacher, Bob Marley was the student." That was his first verbal reaction.' According to Dro, the news cast a pall over the evening, culminating in the group's all-time worst performance.

Though the Upsetter made disparaging comments about Bob Marley on a radio broadcast recorded after the soundcheck but preceding the performance, the news was also clearly upsetting to him. He would subsequently continue to be haunted by Bob's absence and the lack of closure afforded their final arguments. Perry later offered the following comments about the actuality of Marley's passing:

'When Bob Marley die I was in Boston and there was an instant telephone call saying he dead. So I said "OK, he got away. When he was alive he had problems, now he has no problems." Me love him still, and me still see him at night. But he dead because he would not repent.'

Disgusted and with saddened spirits after the gig, the band drove back to New York; Scratch went back to Mike Cacia's place to receive his pay, and spent the night in a spare room. In the early hours of the following morning, Cacia was awakened by Scratch with the news that the police had arrived. 'Do you know this guy?' asked an incredulous policeman. 'Some of the neighbours called, he was dancing around with butcher knives on the street. Do me favour and just keep him inside.'

That same day, Cacia showed Scratch a video of Bahama Mama, a white band from his home town of Rochester, New York that played a mixture of reggae and calypso; the video was recorded at an informal performance given in the back room of Rochester's Record Archive. It was *Catch A Fire* that first sparked the band's interest in Jamaican music; originally called the Putz Brothers, they became Bahama Mama in 1977. Shortly before Scratch's arrival in Boston, core members Ron Stackman, keyboards and guitar (born June 20, 1954), Jim Schwarz, bass (born January 7, 1952) and Louis LaVilla, drums (born November 13, 1952), had regrouped as the Majestics. Greatly inspired by the video, Perry broke ranks with the Terrorists and made the Majestics his new backing band.

Cacia made arrangements for Scratch to spend a couple of weeks at a farmhouse owned by a friend of the Majestics in Victor, New York at the end of May to rehearse for upcoming performances and possible studio work. Bahama Mama guitarist Jim Kraut had become disillusioned with playing in a band, so Cacia arranged for Chris Wilson to join the group on rhythm guitar.

Wilson spent much of his youth in Kingston, where he was born in the early 1950s; he also spent formative years in Cuba and England. As a Member of Parliament under Lloyd George, Wilson's grandfather was a progressive force in British politics; his father was more conservative, serving in the British Legation in Washington. In the mid-1960s, Wilson's father became a businessman in Jamaica, promoting live shows with Byron Lee and staging cricket matches; Wilson himself became fascinated by Jamaican music after being exposed to ska by the gardener who lived on the family property, located near the top end of Shortwood Road in Arcadia, an exclusive district close to Cherry Gardens. In 1969, Chris Wilson moved to America to begin attending University, returning regularly to Jamaica to visit his parents. In 1979 he joined the I-Tones, a Boston-based band who toured the island of Aruba in 1980; they would later release an album, *Something We Share*, and have a minor hit with their cover version of Dionne Warwick's 'Walk On By'.

Wilson was managing one of the Strawberry chain of record shops when Mike Cacia brought him into the Majestics' line-up; he quit the job to join the group, hastening the break-up of his marriage in the process. Though nothing much came of Wilson's short-lived membership in the Majestics, the early connection he formed with Lee Perry during the farmhouse rehearsals would ease the realisation of later projects he was to initiate with Scratch.

On the appointed day of his arrival, Scratch failed to turn up at Rochester Airport, though Pauline Morrison insisted she had placed him on the correct plane that morning; eventually, he was traced to Syracuse, where he had gotten off the plane in error. When Cacia and company drove the many miles to Syracuse to collect him, they found Perry surrounded by trinkets he had bought at the airport shop, including model airplanes that he was waving around in the air. A few days later, Pauline arrived herself, and the two returned to New York City together at the end of the rehearsal period.

Perry's rehearsals with the Majestics were typically unstructured, and involved long free-form jams more than anything else. Scratch was initially mistrustful of the group, and requested they did not record the rehearsals, but in time a stronger working bond was established. One of the odder pronounce-ments he made to the group involved his nickname, which Perry now placed within a scatological framework. 'My new name is Piss, Poop, Shit and Spit,' he told the baffled musicians, 'I want to rest the Scratch for a while.' Like Nigeria's jazz rebel Fela Kuti, the post-Pipecock Lee Perry sought to normalise the more taboo elements of nature; the realities of human sexuality and defecation would be increasingly expounded on. On another occasion, band members were cooking stew in a large pot after an all-day session, prompting Perry to remark 'If all the pots of the world were just one pot, what a great pot it would be'; he then had the musicians create a new tune around the concept.

As rehearsals progressed, Scratch accompanied the Majestics to one of their engagements at a club called the Haunt in Ithaca. Though he insisted he would not be performing at the venue, the band fired his inspiration that night and he took the stage to deliver an energetic and spontaneous set. 'About one a.m. he came on a killed everyone,' Ron Stackman remembered. 'I don't think the crowd had any idea what they were witnessing but they knew it was something special; Lee was awesome and the people went wild.'

In the midst of the farmhouse rehearsals, Scratch was contacted by the Clash, who were arranging a series of June performances on Broadway at Bond's International Casino, a former clothing store. The band was booked for ten nights in a row, and sold out every date at the venue; extra engagements were subsequently added when the Fire Department said the venue was overcrowded. The Clash had two bands opening the show each night, and requested that Perry and the Majestics take the prime opening spot just before them for the Friday and Saturday night shows on June 5 and 6.

When Jim Kraut learned the Majestics were to perform such high profile live dates with Lee Perry, he asked to be included in their lineup; Chris Wilson was thus removed while Kraut momentarily returned to the fold. However, the first of the Bond's performances did not go very smoothly, with Scratch's on-stage arrival delayed by a minor incident.

'The first night,' Ron Stackman remembered, 'he asked us to tell the audience that "Pipecock Jackstone will be out in a minute" and to vamp on the chords of "Give Thanks to Jah".' It was meant to be the first of a four-song set, the other numbers selected by Scratch being 'Roast Fish', 'Pipecock Jackson' and 'Soul Man'. The band complied with his instructions, and took the stage while Perry was putting on an outfit in a dressing room located at the side of the stage; when an automatic door rolled up, exposing Perry in the midst of changing his pants, he hid backstage for a quarter of an hour while the Majestics continued jamming before the crowd.

Unfortunately, Perry's belated entrance did not signal an end to difficulties, as Ron Stackman detailed. 'When he finally came out he spent another several minutes placing artifacts around the stage, and then marching up to each musician and saluting. We never got past "Give Thanks To Jah" that night, it went on for maybe forty five minutes. I recall a stagehand yelling at me from the wings to get off the stage – as if I was going to interrupt Scratch's thing; they finally cut the power and we skulked off. We impressed upon Lee the need to have endings for the tunes and to shorten them up a little; we had an onstage rehearsal the next afternoon at Bond's and Lee devised his ending cue: he'd raise his outstretched arms perpendicular to his body and clench his fists. That was our cue to end the tune, and the second night we got through the entire set.'

The second set included 'Give Thanx To Jah', 'Babylon Cookie Jar A Crumble', 'Soul Fire', 'Roast Fish And Cornbread', 'Psyche And Trim' and a number of new creations; it was strongly received by the capacity audience of 1800 people, who were later treated to a duet between Perry and the Clash on their rendition of Junior Murvin's 'Police And Thieves'.

By the time of these performances, Lee Perry had done so much damage to Perry Henzell's apartment that the manager of the restaurant downstairs threatened to sue Henzell, prompting Perry's eviction from the premises. He stayed briefly at an apartment where a friend of Rema Marx lived, but Marx's distress at the situation caused him to leave. Pauline Morrison then arranged for Scratch to stay with Danny Sims at his plush Fifth Avenue apartment shortly before her own departure to Jamaica.

Sims was trying to gain control of the material Perry had produced with Bob Marley, but was unable to persuade Scratch to let him have it; instead, Perry began re-decorating Sims' posh space with fresh paint, marking the walls and even Sims himself with crosses. After Scratch had significantly defaced and altered the premises but was no nearer to handing over any of the desired material, Sims brought Scratch back to Jamaica, his departure hastened by domestic and financial complications.

Perry had been sending money regularly to his children through Joseph Hookim at Channel One, but had given a large sum to Pauline on hearing she was travelling to Kingston. When Pauline's departure was temporarily delayed, she sent the money to Channel One, where it was collected by her first born son Derrick (now known as Everton). When Vicky eventually told Scratch that Derrick refused to give any money to the kids at Cardiff Crescent, Perry quickened his departure from America; on arrival in Jamaica, he found that Pauline had tried to re-install herself at Cardiff Crescent, causing further upheaval at the disrupted family home.

Having been given no notification of Perry's exit, the Majestics were thus forced to cancel a twenty city US tour that included West Coast bookings after Perry failed to appear at the Casablanca Club in Rochester for a scheduled performance on July 15. It was at this point that Jim Kraut also made his permanent exit from the group after its members lost their day-jobs due to the long period of absence the tour required.

When Lee Perry first entered New York, he was given only limited entry visa, which he overstayed; he would subsequently be barred from performing in America for over fifteen years. His absence from the nation would have wider repercussions, as he left a number of precious items behind, including the valuable silver service set, which had been placed in the care of his old associate Keith Chin in Brooklyn. As Chin would later meet his death in Puerto Rico, the fate of this and Perry's other personal items is unknown.

Not long after Lee Perry's return to Jamaica, Mike Cacia subsequently relocated to Kingston in the autumn of 1981. He quickly renewed his acquaintance with Scratch, taking his children on frequent outings to video arcades and the zoo. By December, Cacia had made arrangements for the newly formed Heartbeat record label to fund an album of new Scratch material, and had them send down the three Majestics for ten days of recording with Scratch in January 1982.

Lee Perry and Mike Cacia both hoped to have the album recorded at the

Black Ark, but the Majestics found it in too much of a dilapidated state to work there; the space was filled with empty record sleeves, while much of the painted equipment and master tapes were being stored in the house. 'He wanted to record in his house,' recalled Ron Stackman, 'that's where a lot of instruments from the Ark were. Everything was painted – cymbals, piano keys, tubes – everything. There was also a breezeway chock full of master tapes.' 'All the recording equipment had been removed,' added Jim Schwarz. 'Scratch still had the original Ampeg B-15 amp that he used on most of his recordings in his house; there was junk littering the control room and hundreds of Scratch album covers on the floor.' 'We all convinced Lee that it'd be tough to get all that stuff working and we'd better to go over to Dynamic,' Stackman concluded.

The band thus laid the core of their rhythms with Don Grant on guitar and Scratch on vocals and percussion at Dynamic (with two songs later given piano overdubs by Gladdy Anderson); other sessions were later arranged at Aquarius studios for multi-tracked vocal overdubs.

The resultant *Mystic Miracle Star* album was conceived entirely in the studio, with Perry directing the band and scrawling the outlines of his lyrics on empty record sleeves (particularly of 'Free Up The Prisoners'). Ron Stackman described the overall process: 'He would have us play a few chords and then things would develop. Sometimes he would ask for a specific bass line or guitar lick. We'd jam on each rhythm for quite a while; most of the time Scratch would be singing, then we'd go back and add more keyboards and guitar. Don Grant was there for all the sessions – a very nice man and a great guitarist who had worked with Scratch plenty and knew the programme. Scratch's sons Mark and Marvin and his daughter Marsha were around all the time; in the studio Mark sat next to me at the Hammond B-3, operating the Leslie speed control for me when I nodded to him. They were really nice kids.'

Though the music he created with the band during the farmhouse rehearsals bordered on hard rock, the songs they recorded in Jamaica had a pervasive roots reggae feel, with the exception of 'Chalice Ablaze' and 'Music Breeze', which were lodged in the rock end of the spectrum. The album was a vehicle for Perry's stream of consciousness raps, which touched on a range of subjects: 'God Bless Pickney' mentioned some of his magical powers between a series of comments on the Cosmos; 'Radication Squad' was a twelve minute jam that saluted Seaga's repressive new solution to Jamaica's crime problem; 'Pussy I Cocky I Water' named sex as a vital force of nature (and was later featured on the soundtrack of John Sayles' *Brother From Another Planet,* a film about a black alien who visits earth).While waiting for Scratch to arrive at Dynamics for the first of these album sessions, the Majestics recorded a Ron Stackman composition called 'Word Sound And Power'. When Perry arrived mid-way through its recording, he volunteered to place a new lead vocal on the song, but it was not properly completed and was left off the album – despite being a straight-forward number that might have garnered college radio airplay in the States had it been issued as a single.

As with *The Return Of Pipecock Jackxon* and his recent work with Munchie, Perry employed certain devices on this disc that would often be repeated in future works, including the recitation of the alphabet and the musical Sol-Fa scale; double-tracked vocals also gave the impression that he was having a conversation with himself.

The Majestics recounted witnessing a few incidents during their time in Jamaica. First there was a minor confrontation with Bunny Wailer, who was recording at Dynamics in the same period – typically during the day, while Perry and the Majestics would occupy the studio from around 9 p.m. On one occasion, Perry and the band arrived to find Wailer still recording in the studio, sparking anger from Scratch. Jim Schwarz recalled the confrontation: 'We arrived at Dynamic for a session and Bunny was still recording, so we had to wait 'til he finished. Scratch gathered small pieces of wood and built a small fire on the ground outside, directly in front of the door. When Bunny and his band were getting ready to leave, Scratch positioned himself behind the fire, facing the door, with his arms folded. Anyone who wanted to exit the studio had to negotiate both Scratch and his fire. I remember being surprised at how small Bunny was and how timid he looked as he tried to get through the door without disturbing either Scratch or his fire.'

Schwarz also recalled Perry's failed attempt to claim outstanding payments from Federal records in this period: 'One night Scratch took us to Federal studio to collect some money that was owed to him. I remember him knocking on the door and a small window opened, speakeasy style; word were exchanged – with Scratch yelling "What is this, a jailhouse?" – but no money. I guess that Scratch thought having three white guys backing him up would increase his chances of getting paid, but he was wrong.'

In negotiating an advance payment from Heartbeat, Scratch asked Mike Cacia to supply him with a video camera, which he quickly became fixated with. He would set up the camera at any given opportunity, and was obsessed with filming images reflected in mirrors, particularly when a passenger in a moving car. Jim Schwarz recalled witnessing a time when Perry ran out of blank video tapes, and thus filled his camera with dirt instead; miraculously, the machine was not destroyed and continued to function thereafter.

After the Majestics left Jamaica and the album had been completed, Mike Cacia took Scratch and his three youngest children to Negril for some rest and relaxation; Perry spent much of his time filming the sea and its environs. One evening, he stood on a sink while trying to film something reflected in the bathroom mirror; the sink broke loose from the wall, flooding the apartment.

Before the initiation of the *Mystic Miracle Star* album, Lee Perry started working on a different album at Joe Gibbs' studio with Errol Thompson and the Professionals house band. He typically brought his children to the sessions, which focused on adaptations of Bob Marley material, including 'Rainbow Country/Roots Rock Reggae', 'Nice Time' and 'Keep On Moving'. After Marley's death, Scratch made a series of contradictory statements about his formerly close associate; though Scratch would sometimes bad-mouth Marley in public, the music he was recording at Joe Gibbs gave evidence to the positive feelings he retained about Bob and the work they had created together – mirroring positive statements he sometimes made about Marley in private.

Scratch was filmed at the studio during one such session, voicing a bright and optimistic adaptation of the spiritual 'Daniel Saw The Stone' for a special edition of the *The Tube* programme, broadcast on England's newly created commercial station Channel Four; on the same programme, rock musician and television personality Jools Holland interviewed Scratch at the gates of the Black Ark, where Perry memorably explained that an electric toaster was impaled on the iron gate because he himself was a toaster, and not a boaster.

Midway through the chaotic Joe Gibbs sessions, work on the material was halted – possibly because Scratch had run up a large studio bill. In early 1982, the partially completed version of 'Daniel Saw The Stone' was cut on a Joe Gibbs disco as 'Jah Road Block', but Scratch expressed displeasure at its premature release and retrieved the rest of his master tapes for completion at a later date.

Meanwhile, Pauline Morrison was arranging for more Black Ark material to be pressed by Starlight in London on her Black Ark International label. In May, Bunny Rugs' 'I Am I Said' and 'Let Love Touch Us Now' were cut on a disco with Bunny and Ricky's 'Freedom Fighter'; an album called *Black Ark Volume 2* was later issued, placing several of Morrison's 1980 Jamaican productions (including the Originals' 'Iry Iry', Inamans' 'How Deep Is Your Love' and Carol Cole's 'Ethiopia') along with the earlier Upsetter material issued on the disco, plus the Silvertones' 'Rejoice' (with Bud Beadle's flute overdub) and Junior Byles' 'Mumbling And Grumbling' (miscredited to the Silvertones).

Around the same time, Tony Owens returned to Jamaica to attend his grandmother's funeral. Owens had re-cut some of the Jolly Brothers' tracks on UK discos in 1981, and had further plans to issue more of Perry's productions. After paying a customery visit to the Perry household, he made arrangements to issue an authorised collection of Black Ark tracks in the UK on Seven Leaves, counteracting those clandestinely cut by Morrison. *Heart Of The Ark*, which surfaced in September, had a range of strong vocal material, spanning from Bunny Scott's 'What's The Use' and Evans Jones' '4 & 20 Dreadlocks' to George Faith's 'Don't Be Afraid' and Leroy Sibbles' 'Rastafari'. Owens maintained a strong connection with Scratch, and would later facilitate a number of related releases.

Life at Cardiff Crescent continued to be chaotic in 1982, falling prey to the ever-changing whims of Lee Perry. When Carl Bradshaw and friends brought a small film crew to Scratch's home in July to gather footage for a proposed Bob Marley documentary director Gary Weiss was assembling for Island, they found him enacting more peculiar rituals. They filmed him loudly pontificating about obscure concepts, spinning around with boulders on his head, and walking through the flames of a fire that had been lit in the kitchen, perpetually anointing himself with baby oil; he also placed his tongue and hands over the burner of the kitchen gas stove. The walls of the kitchen and several appliances were now also covered by graffiti. Scratch had Sean present a number of hand-drawn diagrams to the film crew, including one where a penis labelled 'Globe' was penetrating a vagina labeled 'Selassie I', above which was written 'Sex World Fuck Live Life Hot Plate'. Perhaps the strongest images captured were on objects outside the house: Scratch altered a stop sign mounted below the roof to read 'Scratch stop them all', while the brick wall next to his front gates bore the painted message 'Satan the Devil live here'.

The children were filmed singing a rude song in the shell of what used to be the studio, now empty save for small piles of rubble; the remains of a drum set and a partly ruined bass were the only visible instruments. An unplugged keyboard and components such as an eight track mixing desk and echoplex unit were captured on camera in storage at the house, and dozens of master tapes were also filmed in safe storage, stacked neatly in boxes against the wall of an inner room. In the yard was a framed photograph of Perry in the control room of the Black Ark in its untarnished heyday – a startling contrast to the present state of the space. Unfortunately, this documentary was never completed, but Perry was one of those featured the same year in Channel Four's *Deep Roots* series, assembled earlier by Howard Johnson with Pepe Judah's assistance.

In December 1982, Vicky Nelson left Jamaica when her mother sent for her to join the family in Canada; she would be away from the island for just over a year. Her departure would see another reign of chaos and depression at Cardiff Crescent, with Perry's unstable frame of mind bringing bitterness and bile to the centre of his daily domestic life. By this time, Scratch's adopted daughter Michelle was heavily pregnant.

In earlier days, Michelle – or 'Yawnie' as she was affectionately known – kept a watchful eye on her younger siblings, dutifully reporting any wrong doing to her parents. Now that Michelle was approaching womanhood, her somewhat strict mother was overseas (where she was shortly to give birth to the first of two children fathered by Danny Clarke), and the equally strict Scratch was more pre-occupied with things of cosmological importance. With no parental figure to tell her otherwise, she began a relationship with a dancer named Wayne Campbell, who held a day job at the Ray and Nephew plant; once pregnant, she stopped attending Edith Dalton Secondary School.

When Michelle gave birth to a first child named Lasanno on February 4, 1983, Scratch began strongly to express disapproval. It was then that he hit her with the shocking fact that he was not her father – something she had long suspected, but which was still greatly hurtful to the young mother, who had only recently turned seventeen. When friends and neighbours used to remark that Michelle looked nothing like her siblings, Scratch used jokingly to state that 'she favour her father'; now that she was confronted with the news that he was not her dad, she found that no one would tell her who her biological father was. She felt low and rejected by Perry's treatment once she was pregnant, and tension would increasingly grow between the two – particularly after Campbell moved in with the family at Cardiff Crescent.

Throughout this period, Lee Perry was haunted by mixed feelings about the Black Ark. His overall plan was to re-open it, but he was still bitter about the treatment of many he had worked with in the past, and nursed a festering mistrust of his former associates. He was also plagued by drastic mood swings, particularly when drinking rum, and lacked the concentration and ready cash needed to oversee the proper reparation and refurbishment of the Ark. It thus remained in its partially dilapidated and dismantled state, cleared of all recordings and most of its equipment. Then, in the early hours of a summer morning in 1983, the studio received a baptism by fire, in which much of it was totally destroyed.

The cause of the fire is still disputed, and it remains unclear whether it burned by accident or by Perry's design. As with the speculations on Lee Perry's sanity, whether he torched the Black Ark has been fiercely debated. The rumours circulated would reach truly epic proportions, and contradictory statements by Perry himself would lodge the fire firmly in the realm of legend.

The family members who were on hand to witness its destruction all claim it was an accident that stemmed from an electrical fault, and have stated that Perry himself fought desperately to contain the blaze. Sean Perry described the tragic scene: 'One morning me wake up and see the whole studio catch a fire. When me fly out of the house, you can't out it, because it burn fast. I was sleeping, so I couldn't tell you say is a man light a fire there. But the alleyway, it's there the fire start, beneath the control room, go into the rehearsal room, the boards catch a fire, the whole place light up. Scratch say "P-Son! Come fe the fire!" The fire just a build, never go away within the space of an hour. By the time the fire brigade come, the top just lick off! Blown super high like a volcano lava, so we couldn't out it, because of the heat alone that come off of it, we couldn't go near it. Scratch a call we to help him put out the fire. I couldn't tell you is him start it definitely 'cause I didn't see it and I don't tell lie.'

P-Son added the following particulars: 'I was in the room where Bob Marley used to stay, and I wake up and see it like six in the morning. He tried to out it with water. When it burned, some of the stuff like the mixing board, and all the tape was out because no work was going on in there. It was an accident, an electrical fault.'

'I know for a fact that it was electrical problems,' said Marsha Perry authoritatively, 'because one time we was in the studio and saw smoke coming from the meter, so maybe the electrician did not drop the chord. Whenever two negative meet, you know you definitely have to have a negative; positive and negative clash, so we see smoke coming from there and everywhere. But this thing that they're saying that my dad burned it down, that's a lie. It was definitely electrical problems.'

Perry himself has given conflicting accounts of the fire, and despite claiming responsibility for it most of the time, we are unlikely ever to be certain of its true origins. The closest thing to a believable confession first came a couple of years after the fact in *NME*.

'For weeks and months the pressure had been building up. I was getting no money, just pressure, pressure, pressure. I got up that morning with turmoil in my heart and went to the bottom of my garden, the studio y'know. I love kid's rubber balls. They are air, trapped. I love that and I collected many of these balls. Anyway, I have one favourite, it came from America and I kept it on the mixing desk. Some one had taken it when I got to the studio and I was just filled with anger. First all the pressure, the thievery, and then this . . . I destroyed the studio. I smashed it up and then I burnt it down. Over.' [9]

Could Perry really have destroyed his studio because someone took a child's rubber ball from it? On other occasions, he has strictly denied lighting the fire that caused the final destruction of the Ark. 'If the government or whosoever try to find out if it's me who try to burn out my studio, they'd make a big mistake because it's not I who burn down my studio,' Perry later said on a French radio broadcast. [10]

In May 1999, I hoped to clear up the situation once and for all by asking Perry directly what had happened. Did he burn the studio himself in a deliberate act, or was the fire the result of an accident or electrical fault? 'Of course it's me who burn it,' Perry insisted with absolute seriousness, 'who else could burn it? I was just working morning noon and night for musicians and singers, and I did want to be a singer. And then that ball was there for concentration, and nobody should go inside the studio when I leave there; somebody was messing with my energy, so it wouldn't be clean anymore, so I throw gas in there and light it. I didn't hold no insurance on my building, I only hold life insurance for me; I cannot get a money from it, so it was mine to do what I want to do. When the fire light, the only time me try to put it out is when me see the (electric) light wires start to burn off; the fire was going out, so when it come to those places, that's when I was trying to get it out.' I asked Perry how he felt about the fire all these years later, to find if he had any regrets or felt he had done the right thing; 'Good thing I did that!' was his simple and immediate reply.

After the fire, Scratch was held by police for several days in Hunt's Bay Jail while an investigation was launched into the cause of the blaze, only to be released without charge due to lack of evidence; contrary to popular myth, he spent no time in Bellevue mental hospital or any other sanitarium, and as his master tapes were stored elsewhere, none perished in the fire.

While Perry was languishing in captivity, Tony Owens returned to Jamaica for a ceremony connected with the first anniversary of his grandmother's funeral. When Scratch was eventually freed by the police, Owens presented him with plans for a new vocal album and made further arrangements to issue more of Perry's back catalogue in England. Though Perry disagreed with some of the songs Owens had chosen for him to cover on the album, the pair went to the newly opened Music Mountain studio in Stony Hill to lay a half-dozen backing tracks with the Sagitarius band; Scratch laid basic guide vocals on the material, some of which would eventually be re-voiced in England. Scratch was greatly impressed with Music Mountain's location, and its panoramic vista of Kingston proved greatly to inspire his delivery.

When Tony returned to England, Scratch inevitably continued to live a reclusive existance. Most musicians and music industry personnel gave him a wide birth, with the exception of Family Man, who lived nearby and would often come to check on him and the kids; Ned Willacy was also a frequent visitor, the only member of the Niyabinghi Theocracy still welcome – particularly after he trimmed off his locks. Most of the time, it was only an unproductive and anti-social Scratch at Cardiff Crescent with his children.

It was in the early months of 1984 that Vicky Nelson returned to Cardiff Crescent, again bringing some badly needed stability into the life of Lee Perry and his family. When she first returned to Jamaica in December 1983, she avoided Kingston entirely, spending time with her family in the country near Montego Bay. But she felt it was her duty to provide some support to Perry's motherless children, and found it difficult to deny Scratch's charismatic pull. She again became a member of the household, and tried to persuade Scratch to become involved in music once more. 'I didn't really want to go back but I couldn't resist, I have to go back, 'cause it's like my job wasn't finished, somehow I wanted to reach out and help. He was trying to hide away from the music business because of some rough times he had, the whole issue with Bob Marley and other musicians and people, he was very hurt deep down, so getting him back into music was very hard.'

Nelson noted that on her return, several instruments and other pieces of ruined equipment were still stored in the house, but later on the items were removed – sent on a one-way journey to the stinking depths of Perry's toilet pit. Scratch revealed that the eight track Tascam met a similar fate, though precisely when is unclear; after experiencing continued financial difficulties, he chose to destroy the equipment rather than allow perceived foes to reap from his misfortunes. As Perry explained, 'Me take out the instrument them, like drum kit and guitars, and the eight track Chris Blackwell bought me; all of those, I throw them in the toilet pit. All the drums them, me throw them in the toilet pit just like that; they are there still now. Bunny Lee want me to sell the Tascam to his friend Jammys – that's when me decide me have to throw it in the pit. Him send somebody that wanted to buy and me don't have no money; the Tascam was there and Bunny Lee come with something about Jammy want my mic to buy. Bunny go into the studio and take my mic, so I throw them all in the pit – run it off before I have to send it to Bunny's friend Jammy. Those are bad vibrations.'

Since the Joe Gibbs sessions of late 1981, Lee Perry created virtually no new music, save for the tracks initiated at Music Mountain. Tony Owens continued to issue collections of his late Black Ark creations – eventually cutting a second volume of *Heart Of The Ark* and two volumes of *Megaton Dub* – but Scratch himself was largely inactive as a producer or recording artist, concerned more with destruction as opposed to creation. When he finally returned to work towards the end of 1983, it was partly through the encouragement of Vicky Nelson; she and Perry approached Chris Blackwell together to see if Island would be interested in funding another album of new work. Though Blackwell was still upset about the money Perry had squandered, he agreed to bring Scratch to the new Compass Point studio he had established in the Bahamas, to complete the album that would become *History, Mystery, Prophecy*.

Perry came to Nassau on November 29 with the master tapes of the tracks he had been working on at Joe Gibbs. He worked at the studio for one month solid and was back in Jamaica on New Year's Day; he subseuqently returned to the Bahamas for another two weeks of work in mid-February 1984. At Compass Point, Perry revamped the Joe Gibbs rhythms with synthesizers, drum programming and fresh vocals with the assistance of engineer Steven Stanley; John Martyn and Robert Palmer were both at the studio, working on material of their own, and Scratch had them put down fresh guitar and bass on his evolving tracks. Some new songs were also created at the sessions, including a rambling word association called 'Funky Joe' and an alternative cut of 'Bed Jamming'. Though several songs addressed frivolous topics, the disc's most politically motivated track was 'Heads Of Government', in which the song's protagonist claimed not to believe in God, but only in money and luxury. Scratch's personal favourite was 'The Ganja Man', a loose update of 'I Am the Upsetter'.

History, Mystery, Prophecy occupied an uneasy space between a highly commercial sound influenced by disco rhythms and an experimental form of language poetry; its failure to fall into category would see a UK release vetoed by Island records; they would, however, issue the disc in America in September 1984, where it was aimed at Perry's younger New Wave fans who bought the *Mystic Miracle Star* album; it also formed a strong contrast to the classic Ark material issued around the same time on Island's *Reggae Greats* collection. In early 1985, Perry would have Tony Owens issue *History, Mystery, Prophecy* on a UK branch of his Lion of Judah label with a far superior front cover, showing a close-up of Lee Perry with blue body paint covering his face; though not achieving much in terms of sales, the album was fairly well received by the UK press.

John Martyn recalled that Scratch was still a hard task master, being very particular about the sound he wanted on these sessions. He also witnessed the transformation of Perry's apartment, which began with his customary graffiti and continued to be altered through other perplexing acts. 'The cooker was on all day,' Martyn reported. 'He had metal coins on one burner, a dead fish and flowers on the other.' One morning Martyn awoke to find Scratch cuddling trees in the compound. 'People say you're fucking mad,' the guitarist challenged, 'what are you doing?' The Upsetter looked John Martyn straight in the eye and whispered quietly 'I'm keeping them away from me.'

While working closely together on this album, Martyn began cooking for Scratch, who insisted on paying him for dishes of ackee and saltfish and curry goat. At one point, Scratch was robbed by a local youth who used to run around town toting a rifle; when the burly Scot confronted the brash youngster, he promptly returned Perry's money.

Though Scratch had accepted Blackwell's offer to use his studio, he was still harboring grudges against the Island boss, particularly over recognition and cash he felt was being denied him from the Marley material he helped create. The deepness of this bitterness is evident in his refusal to work with members of Talking Heads on material discussed at Compass Point. The adventurous East Coast new wave group had been recording at the facility since 1978, and the husband-and-wife team of Chris Frantz and Tina Weymouth had property in the nation; the pair had hoped to gain Perry's assistance with their first Tom Tom Club side project, recorded at the studio in 1981, but Island deemed the fee he demanded too expensive. When Scratch was working on *History, Mystery, Prophecy,* Frantz and Weymouth were preparing a follow up disc, but despite cordial interaction with the couple and their children, Scratch chose not to get involved because of their Island connections; he also had lengthy conversations with Talking Heads' lead vocalist David Byrne, but ultimately avoided a collaboration.

When Scratch returned from the second of his brief trips to Nassau, it soon became apparent that little was happening for him in Jamaica. Just as the final destruction of the Black Ark had marked the end of an era for Jamaican music, it had also formed a boundary line in Lee Perry's career; he had no desire to work with Jamaicans, and had no space in which to try his own independent experiments. In April, he obtained a multiple-entry non-immigrant visa, which would allowed him to visit but not work in the USA; however, Scratch did not have the available cash to make the journey and was mindful of his previous immigration problems there.

His lack of ready income and anger at Island also saw him approaching Rita Marley for money at this time. 'Scratch asked her for some funds, because Scratch was not getting any royalty from the music he and Bob had done together,' Ned Willacy explained. 'Scratch had a lot of music to release and him wanted some new machines in the studio, so he say "Well Rita, I want some money, $5,000,000 would be a good start." She told him he would have to go to England to see Chris Blackwell.'

When it became clear that Scratch planned to continue his period of unproductive limbo and would not make music in Jamaica, Vicky Nelson spoke to Tony Owens about sending Scratch to do some business in Britain. Perry initially expressed anger at Nelson's plan, as he had not instigated it himself, but when Owens offered to pay for an airline ticket, Scratch consented. Thus, on September 26, 1984, Vicky, Jah Ned, P-Son and the kids accompanied Lee Perry to the airport, escorting him to the beginning of a long period of life outside Jamaica.

I AM A MADMAN:
years in England

When Tony Owens brought Lee Perry back to London, he initially installed him in a spare room of the flat he occupied with his Bajan wife Barbara and their three children in a government housing block at Lansbury Close on the notorious St Raphael's estate – a sprawling warren of interconnected buildings squeezed between industrial corners of Harlesden and Neasden, just behind the perpetually congested North Circular Road. Once Scratch had his London feet back on, he again became involved in creating music. He found that Joe Gibbs was in town, and quickly linked with Gibbs and Winston Edwards; the pair came with Scratch and Tony Owens to Ariwa studio, where Perry voiced the rhythms he and Owens laid at Music Mountain in 1983.

The Ariwa studio and label was established in 1979 by Neil Fraser, a recording engineer better known as the Mad Professor. Fraser was born in Georgetown, Guyana, on March 20, 1957; both his parents worked at the local hospital, where his father was a laboratory technician and his mother a nurse. He was first exposed to reggae in his youth through a Saturday night radio show hosted by the Groove Governor on BVI, a radio station broadcasting from the neighbouring Virgin Islands; exposure to the productions of Prince Buster, Bunny Lee, Byron Lee, and Federal Records thus sparked an early interest in Jamaican music. In 1970, Neil joined his parents in London where they had found work at Charing Cross Hospital. After they divorced and his mother returned to Guyana, Neil decided to remain with his father in the South London suburb of Tooting. In London, his love of reggae intensified through exposure to the Studio One and Treasure Isle stables, to the work of deejays like U Roy and Dennis Alcapone, and to the heavenly sounds Lee Perry was creating with the Wailers.

As Fraser's passion for reggae grew, so did his knowledge of electronics. By the time he left home, he had built a mixing desk, and found work as a technician at Reddifon Radiofusion. He later worked at Soundcraft – the company who had built the main Black Ark mixing desk. In 1979, he built a studio in his home at 19 Bruce Road in Thornton Heath, initially equipped with a four-track Teac 3440; he named the studio Ariwa, which means 'Communication' in the Yoruba language.

Shortly after opening, the home studio was upgraded to eight-track, becoming 16-track within a year. Early issues on his Ariwa label were by previously unknown local artists such as Rockaway and Sister Audrey; as the label's output increased, it would be divided between the smooth sounds of lover's rock, conscious roots reggae, and Fraser's own creative dub material. The studio would also be a focal point for visiting Jamaican artists in the 1980s after Congo Ashanti Roy and Mikey Dread recorded their own productions there at the start of the decade.

In 1982, Fraser moved the studio to larger premises in the basement of 42 Gautrey Road in Peckham. As his 16-track Ampex MM1000 recorder was too heavy to take downstairs, Fraser sold it and bought a lighter Aces recorder. One of the first artists to work at the upgraded 24-track facility was Johnny Clarke, whose Ariwa album showed Fraser's strength in the realm of roots.

By the time Lee Perry, Joe Gibbs, and the rest of Scratch's entourage turned up at Ariwa in September 1984, Fraser had just installed an Ampex 1100 recorder acquired from the Barge studio of Virgin boss Richard Branson. The first tracks Perry voiced at Ariwa were 'Judgement in a Babylon' and a version of the Wailers' 'One Drop'; the songs would surface on a Lion of Judah 12-inch issued in early 1985 through Seven Leaves. According to Professor, both songs were engineered by Perry's old Studio One associate Syd Bucknor, and featured the backing vocals of Akabu, an all-woman reggae band featuring Valerie Skeete and Vyris Edghill (the latter a mother of one of Family Man's many children).

'Judgement In A Babylon' was an incendiary number aimed straight at Chris Blackwell's head, in which Perry made some incredible statements he has continued to claim are 'nothing but the truth':

> 'I saw Chris Blackwell in Nassau
> Drinking the blood of a fowl from a rum glass
> At his new studio in Compass Point . . .
> He offer me a cup of fresh blood.
> Chris Blackwell is a vampire
> Tom Hayes his lawyer is a vampire
> His secretary Denise (Mills) is a witch . . .
> They believe in cult voodoo and Obeah
> Chris Blackwell is a vampire
> Sucking the blood of the sufferers
> He killed Bob Marley and take away his royalty
> He killed Bob Marley because Bob Marley was speaking the truth . . .
> Chris Blackwell came to Jamaica want to sign up all the artists
> Because he want to control Jamaican music
> Then he can take the black man music and promote his white artists
> But Jahoviah Jah Rastafari say it won't work . . .
> He give Bob Marley cancer, he couldn't find the answer
> He take away his riches, he take away his wealth
> Chris Blackwell is a vampire . . . '

Thus, Lee Perry dared to speak on record things that others would mutter under their breath or whisper behind each other's backs. Though many artists have acknowledged a great debt to Blackwell, others have expressed resentment of the control he has exercised over the dissemination of Jamaican music, and the great wealth its success has afforded him. Yet, had Perry gone too far by naming Chris Blackwell as a vampire? Would the Island boss really have been sipping chicken's blood from a rum glass at the opening of Compass Point?

'Well, that's true,' Blackwell hesitantly admitted. 'It's part of a custom in Jamaica, and I'm from Jamaica: when you build a building, you kill a chicken and mix the blood with rum in your mouth – just a little bit – and drop it on the four corners.'

Although Blackwell thus consented to having sipped fowl's blood from a rum glass, he was understandably angered by Perry's other accusations in 'Judgement In A Babylon', taking particular exception to the notion that he was 'sucking the blood of the sufferers'. 'I don't agree with it, but if he felt that way at the time, that must have come across to him,' Blackwell explained. 'Hopefully what I do is introduce and help promote his stuff.'

Shortly after voicing these Music Mountain tracks, Scratch began voicing fresh material on rhythms Mad Professor had created with his house band, then featuring a multi-instrumentalist known as Black Steel. According to Professor, Perry would spend much of the day in his studio, often accompanied by a young black woman named Martine with whom he had a brief liaison; she was barely out of her teens, and the relationship did not last long. Dozens of tracks were voiced in a matter of weeks, eight of which would surface in 1989 as the *Mystic Warrior* album; others remain unissued at present. Professor noted details of these early sessions: 'Scratch would come in from twelve o'clock and stay 'til midnight. Scratch loves the studio, he loves recording. When he finished with his tracks, he ended up voicing a load of tracks for me as well; some of them came out on *Mystic Warrior*, but there was at least another two albums that never came out, with tracks like "Hippy John". Between Scratch and Syd Bucknor, I learned a lot from them guys; soon after these sessions I started making really good hits.'

The eventual *Mystic Warrior* album had Scratch chanting over stylistically diverse rhythms. Though held back for four years, the album sounded entirely contemporary on release – unlike the Music Mountain material, which quickly became passé through its reliance on Syndrums and synthesised horns. There were several more adaptations of Marley material on the disc, including 'Crazy Baldheads', 'Put It On' as 'Feel The Spirit', and 'Natural Mystic' as the title track, but the most effective numbers were originals cut over eerie Ariwa rhythms, on which Perry unleashed some of the anguish of his tortured soul. For those who listened closely enough, '25 Years Ago' contained more shocking statements, this time in highly revealing self-referential claims:

'This is Madman Scratchy
You better watch it
He draw matches and the place go "boom!"
I've been working for 21 years and I ain't got a cent
I've been working in the studio all my life
And I don't have no fucking money
This is Madman Scratchy with his episode
This is Madman Scratchy who is getting rid of his heavy load
Five years ago I-man bend down low
Bend down in the earth
I want to change my shirt
Bow down in the earth
I even eat the earth
Sometimes I eat my shit
Sometime I drink my piss, why?
Because the food is the shit, and the water is the piss . . .
21 years ago, I been working night and day
Ain't got nothing to show, because the wicked take it away . . .
25 years ago I been working like a slave in the ghetto
Never earn a cent,
Neither praises for the work that I have done so . . . '

The ambiguous confession at the start of the song alludes to the burning of the studio, but does not make clear whether the fire was accidental. The overall message is one of frustration, with years of work resulting in neither financial nor aesthetic reward. And what are we to make of the middle lines, when Scratch describes how, post-breakdown, he eats his own excrement? Is this the raving of a madman, or the bluff of one who wants the world to believe that he is mad? If we think of these words in another sense, we may find Lee Perry tapping into an ancient link with nature through the utterance of such a taboo. The lines are not so different, for instance, from a chant recited by tribal Asmat fishermen in the unblemished wilderness of Irian Jaya:

'Shrimp are in the river
Shit is in the river
Piss is in the river
The shrimp eat the shit
The shrimp drink the piss
We eat the shrimp.' [1]

While Lee Perry continued to record with Mad Professor, Tony Owens was arranging a UK tour for November and December, with subsequent engagements planned in mainland Europe and Scandinavia. He paired Scratch with the Sus band, a black West London outfit with a full horn section and backing vocalists, including Hopeton McClean; Mad Professor was drafted in as live engineer for all dates.

The tour was to commence on November 22 at Dingwalls nightclub in Camden – what would be Perry's debut performance in the UK as a vocalist. Owens ensured many advance tickets were sold by having Scratch appear with Desmond Dekker on *Rockers FM*, the weekly reggae show on BBC Radio London, hosted by Tony Williams; Perry used the airtime to lambast Chris Blackwell and to state how much he missed Bob Marley. He also stated he had come to London 'to prove that I am not crazy and that I am not mad, but I am sober and madder', adding that his eccentric behaviour stemmed from being 'half human and half machine; I am a computer, also I'm skin, flesh, and bone'. [2]

The Dingwalls engagement was a sold-out performance that was well received by a crowd of adoring fans. The Sus band was tight, giving Scratch adequate backing on both new and old material. The set included 'Mr Music', 'Nice Time', 'One Drop', 'Pipecock Jackstone', 'Soul Fire', 'Big Neck Police', and the surprise of the evening, 'People Funny Boy'. Much to the delight of the audience, Scratch introduced himself as a madman, playing on his dubious reputation; less popular was an interjection about toilet etiquette. Perry seemed genuinely worried that the audience were not enjoying themselves, and asked if he was boring them at one point; their demand that he return for an encore made clear their overall enjoyment.

It was at this performance that Lee Perry met Sandra Cooley, a young admirer with whom he began a lasting relationship. Born Sandra Theed in the North London suburb of Wealdstone on July 23, 1963, Sandra was the oldest of two children born to a lorry driver and his wife, a shop assistant who later ran a café. There were periods of financial difficulty for the family during her childhood, so Sandra grew up partially with a great-aunt; when their circumstances improved, she later moved back with her parents in Kenton, close to where she was born. At the age of 15, she began dating Paul Cooley, an unemployed builder five years her senior who identified with punk and heavy metal. The pair were married in the spring of 1980, and produced a daughter named Sharon in February 1981. By the end of the year, the marriage was faltering, and Sandra soon found herself a single mother. Though she found it hard caring for a child by herself from the age of 18, she revelled in her new-found freedom with a place of her own, free to re-discover the reggae her parents had exposed her to as a child.

When the Dingwalls gig was over and most of the audience cleared out, Perry emerged from backstage to be approached by Sandra, decked out in high heels – one of several females seeking his attention that night. She made her way backstage to offer him a spliff, and Scratch asked directions to her place. 'I said I lived in Middlesex, so that kind of tickled him,' Sandra recalled. 'Some girl had given him her address and she lived in Surrey, so he said, "If I go to Surrey I'll be sorry, but in Middlesex I'll be OK."'

Sandra did not intend to have Scratch spend the night, and when he did, she assumed she would never hear from him again. But Perry returned the next day, and began gradually spending more time with her, occasionally bringing boxes of his possessions; he eventually brought over the video camera he had taken with him from Jamaica, and a box of video tapes – many of which were of Perry himself making ominous proclamations. 'We would talk about the things we liked and I said, "Nature, I love the sky." He said, "Oh, I've got some videos of the sky" and he brought a load of videos, but they were videos of himself chatting. That's when I thought things were a bit strange. Up until then, there were a couple of eccentricities that you'd sort of allow, like writing on my wall. I was decorating; the upstairs had been done and the living room hadn't. He started with one or two things on the top, just writing his name.'

Before she knew what hit her, Sandra Cooley found that Lee Perry had moved into her council house at 15 Waghorn Road; before long, sculptures began to appear in her front and rear gardens. Sandra was then 21 years old, less than half his age by several years.

Though Perry was not troubled by their age difference, he was sensitive to the notion that he was growing old. Ever fit and with the boundless energy of a youth, Scratch took notice when Sandra remarked that his glasses made him look older; he subsequently abandoned them altogether, preferring blurred vision to an elderly visage.

When Lee Perry was living at Tony Owens' place, he normally telephoned Jamaica every Sunday and spoke to his children on the telephone of their next-door neighbour. Sandra Cooley had no phone when he moved in, so Scratch had one installed, but gradually contacted his children on a more sporadic basis.

The mid-1980s saw a shift in British immigration policy, as the Conservative Thatcher government increased restrictions imposed on the citizens of its former colonies. Jamaicans came under specific scrutiny after the island became a centre of cocaine-smuggling during Seaga's reign; many of the former political gangs used their espionage techniques to propagate the drug trade abroad after Seaga came to power. The presence of such violent Jamaican drug gangs in Britain – the so-called 'Yardies' – resulted in a pathological mistrust of Jamaican immigrants and visitors, and Perry thus received a foreboding visit from a pair of immigration officers shortly after he moved to Waghorn Road; they wanted to confirm his correct address was on their records, and made it clear his movements would be monitored.

Meanwhile, Perry's performance schedule progressed at a fair pace. The Dingwalls debut was followed by a series of concerts in other parts of the country: Scratch and the Sus band played the Sheffield Leadmill on November 29 and St Albans City Hall on December 1. They were filmed in Newcastle performing 'Mr Music', 'One Drop', and 'The Ganja Man' for Channel 4's *The Tube*, broadcast on December 7, played Manchester's famed Hacienda

Club on December 13, and gave a final performance on December 15 at Leeds Polytechnic – a concert at which Perry broke with the band. 'Sus were doing their own set first,' remembered Mad Professor. 'They were playing very good and very strong, getting a very good response. Then Scratch come on and start to cuss the band, start to tell the people that the band trying to steal the show.'

It seems Scratch was jealous of the tightness of their opening set, which formed a stark contrast to his own performances, which could drift into rambling and unfocused interludes. After the embarrassing public rebuking before the audience and ugly scenes backstage the band was fired; Mad Professor wisely chose not to become involved, making a hasty exit from the premises instead. He would not see Lee Perry again for nearly two years, and the recordings they made together would remain neglected while Professor found greater success with lover's rock artists like Sandra Cross.

After the Leeds Polytechnic performance, Scratch and Sandra Cooley were brought to the town of Clitheroe by BBC Raido Lancashire disc jockey Steve Barker; the couple stayed overnight with Barker's family so that Scratch could make a special guest appearance the next day on Barker's *On the Wire* programme. Born in the Northwest of England in February 1948, Barker was first exposed to reggae while working with homeless people in Ladbroke Grove in the mid-'70s. His journalistic training led to freelance radio work for the BBC in 1978, where he was an early champion of reggae music, and the *On the Wire* programme was eventually established in September 1984.

On this occasion, Barker's co-host was Roger Eagle of Eric's nightclub in Liverpool, who brought in some of the rarest of his Lee Perry collection to elucidate comments from Scratch on the works. During the three-hour session, Barker drew some illuminating responses from Scratch, with whom he built up a strong rapport; portions of the interview were later worked into the song 'Scratch on the Wire' by Sir Freddy Viaduct and the Flying Vicars, issued on Barker's *Bugs on the Wire* compilation by Leghorn/Skysaw records in 1987. Barker noted that Scratch did not seem in peak physical condition at this point: 'Lee was like an old man with low energy levels. Through a lot of that period he was drinking horrible stuff like bottles of sherry; I think he came together later in the middle '80s, got his body together, and everything. Roger was showing him tunes he'd done and he'd forgotten them, then Lee got a ballpoint pen and was ticking them. At that time he wasn't as obviously obstructive and quasi-mystical; when people started paying attention to him, he got more spooky. When he stayed at our house the kids loved him, he stood on his head for them and he'd bring crystals out and drop them in glasses of water before he drank them.'

After Perry broke with the Sus band, an Englishman named Ron stepped into the fray to try to take over his management – another in a long line of aspiring managers who were to find out the hard way that Scratch is virtually unmanageable. Towards the end of December, Ron brought Perry to a community recording and rehearsal facility called Pyramid in Hackney, East London. Perry saw a group called World Service rehearsing there, and chose to make them his new band; a brief UK tour was subsequently organised, beginning with a previously scheduled date at Dingwalls on January 31.

The Dingwalls concert was recorded for broadcast on Capital Radio – the first commercial radio station in London – but Scratch said such negative things about the station during the performance that the concert was never aired. Pop-reggae act Amazulu were then just reaching the height of their popularity; after attending the concert, they requested Scratch produce their music, but nothing concrete ever came from this connection. Scratch had previously been approached by Buster Bloodvessel – the overweight leader of white ska revival group Bad Manners – who had invited Perry, Sandra Cooley, and Ron to his place for a New Year's Eve party; Bloodvessel wanted Perry to produce his group, but Perry stipulated that they would have to change their name to Good Manners if they were to benefit from his production assistance.

In February, Scratch appeared with World Service in Folkestone, Manchester, Portsmouth, Bournemouth, and at the Albany Empire in Deptford; they gave a final concert together on March 29 at Walthamstow Town Hall for an event sponsored by the Greater London Council as a showcase for Pyramid Arts. World Service was a mixed band with black and white musicians, but their music was rooted in rock, funk, jazz, soul, and blues, and was far from the reggae standard. As Scratch himself was seeking a new direction, he was happy to adapt his vocal rants to their non-reggae style, but many audience members came expecting Perry's reggae classics, and the concerts received generally poor reviews. Scratch was also disappointed with the size of the venues they were playing and the meagre transportation arrangements, having been used to travelling in a luxury coach with Tony Owens and Sus – arrangements that meant Owens was often out of pocket. Perry thus dismissed Ron's focus as being 'too local', and simultaneously broke with his management and the band; Ron would eventually find success as manager of electro-dub duo the Orb.

A driving force behind World Service was lead guitarist Steve Marshall, a multi-talented musician, singer and songwriter who was closely involved with Pyramid Arts. Marshall kept in touch with Perry, and eventually persuaded Scratch to mix one side of his first solo single in December 1985. 'Lightning Strikes Twice', credited to Steve Marshall and the Dangerous Drivers, was issued on Marshall's State of Emergency records in August 1986; the song was a smooth blend of funky R & B, akin to the mellower side of Prince, but its issue drew little attention. Scratch also voiced a rhythm Marshall had built called 'Black Cat' on this session – which he re-named 'Elephant Rock' – but the song was left in the can and never issued.

It was not long after Perry's dismissal of Ron in the spring of 1985 that Waghorn Road was rocked by the news that Sandra was pregnant with Perry's child. The pregnancy was unplanned, and both parties had some initial reservations about the event, as it was unclear how long Scratch planned to live in London. Though the couple gradually grew to have positive expectations of raising a family, their anticipations were cut short when Sandra had a miscarriage in May.

Meanwhile, Lee Perry was searching for another backing band. One day he was walking down Portobello Road with Tony Owens when he was approached by a long-standing fan; the admirer was Mark Downie, a rhythm guitarist, songwriter, and graphic artist who was then working with a band called Studio Six. Born in 1959, Downie was raised in Stevenage, a small country town north of London. The first record Downie ever bought was Dave and Ansel Collins' 'Double Barrel' in 1970, and he remained a reggae enthusiast thereafter; he even joined the Merchant Marines to travel to Jamaica in 1977.

Downie later came to Waghorn Road to play a demo tape of his band for Scratch, prompting him to travel to Stevenage for a few informal rehearsals with the group. Though the rehearsals drew inconsistent results, Perry and Downie developed a working friendship, based on a shared love of the wonders of nature and artistic experimentation. Scratch eventually appeared with Studio Six on a couple of low-key gigs in Hertfordshire: the first was at a pub called the Bell in the town of Cotticutt, the second before a larger crowd at Stevenage College.

After these performances, internal friction about the band's new direction saw Downie and keyboardist Russ Cummings breaking away to form a new multi-ethnic band called Dub Factory, with bassist Mark 'Spike' Kolodzinski, Anglo-Jamaican drummer Kenneth 'Peng' Smith, and Tarlok Mann, a lead guitarist of Indian descent. In November 1985, the new group fleshed out ideas with Lee Perry at three days' worth of rehearsals; Scratch then took them into the studio to record what he claimed would be a dub album.

Perry had recently entered into negotiations with Trojan Records, who claimed the rights to much of his back catalogue. In the early 1980s, Trojan had changed hands yet again; it was now being run by Colin Newman of Receiver Records and his associate, Frank Lee – a relative of one of the founding members of Midlands rock group Slade; both men are alleged to have strong underworld connections. The new executives furthered Marcel Rodd's policy of keeping Trojan as a re-issue label, knocking out cheaply compiled packages which inevitably included Lee Perry's historic material; a pleasant exception was the tastefully assembled *Upsetter Collection*, compiled by Dave Hendley and Chris Lane in 1981, subsequently used as a blueprint for Heartbeat's 1985 collection *Some Of The Best* (which used several tracks sub-licensed from Trojan). As Perry entered into negotiations with the company, Trojan was preparing to re-issue *Africa's Blood, Double Seven,* and the scarce *Rhythm Shower* as a three-album box set with extensive liner notes by Steve

Barrow; the set was highly praised in the media and saw a high volume of sales on release in December 1985.

While seeking to straighten out the situation of his back-catalogue royalties, Perry was persuaded to provide Trojan with two albums of new material by Patrick Meads – a record executive with pop-industry contacts who was then seeking to breathe new life into the hackneyed Trojan label.

Meads arranged for Perry and Dub Factory to record at Thameside studio, a small 16-track facility on the edge of the Thames in Rotherhithe, then a particularly squalid corner of Southeast London, home to many squatters, and suffering from urban decay. Thameside was run by a gifted engineer and keyboardist named Jerry Tilley, the first white man to play in Fats Domino's band; the Pioneers and Boris Gardiner had recently cut material in the studio. As Mark Downie recalled, about 15 songs were recorded over a three-day period; the band even slept in the studio, only taking short breaks. Thus, the foundations were laid for an album that would surface the following June as *Battle Of Armagideon* (*Millionaire Liquidator*).

With the album partly completed, Trojan quickly issued one of the most commercial tracks as a single in time for the approaching Festive Season: 'Merry Christmas, Happy New Year', incongruously backed by the original 'Return Of Django'. Verging on overkill, they also issued a remixed cut on a disco, along with an alternative Lucifer-castigating anti-abortion take as 'Happy Birthday', plus a modern adaptation of 'Return Of Django' as 'All Things Are Possible' (with Val Bennett's sax solo embarrassingly imitated by Mark Downie's voice). Patrick Meads also used the 12-inch as an opportunity to boost the career of Sandra Robinson – a singer he drafted in for backing vocals whose delivery Scratch did not rate very highly.

After the initial three-day session, Scratch returned to Thameside on various occasions over the next four months to re-work the material, sometimes with Downie and other band members in tow. Patrick Meads brought in trombonist Trevor Jones and saxophonist Lloyd Clarke, Jamaican members of the Ipswich-based band Jah Warrior, to play on certain tracks; others were given multi-tracked vocals and other re-arrangements by Scratch. It was at one such session that Scratch first met Rudy Mascoll and his wife Jennifer, a couple whose involvement in Perry's affairs would become increasingly significant.

Born on October 18, 1955, in Bridgetown, Barbados, Mascoll moved to London when he was ten. Members of his mother's family formed part of the Bajan elite; his great-grandfather was chief of police, and his maternal grandfather controlled a chain of national newspapers in Barbados and Grenada, including the prestigious *Herald*. When Mascoll first met Lee Perry, he was working the night shift at a bakery in Wood Green; he also worked as a mini-cab driver to make ends meet. Jennifer was born in London on March 29, 1959, the first of four children Max Romeo's mother bore in England after marrying Clement Lambert, a Jamaican immigrant from Clarendon who worked as a set builder for the BBC. Jennifer began her singing career as Sister Jane, but later changed her stage name to Jennifer Romeo to heighten the family bond with Max. In the early 1980s, Jennifer worked closely with West London reggae band Undivided Roots; she also had links with the Ruff Cut band and Akabu, and she and Rudy had close ties to the Southall band Misty in Roots, being actively involved in their co-operative label, People Unite.

When Lee Perry first met Jennifer Romeo at Thameside, she was voicing 'You Can Wake Up With Me' with Sydney 'Luddy' Crooks of the Pioneers. The song was an answer to Boris Gardiner's hugely successful pop-reggae crossover 'I Want To Wake Up With You'; Romeo's version was issued on the Pioneer International label by Jet Star – the new name for Pama Records – and distributed by EMI. When Scratch learned Jennifer was Max's sister, he was ecstatic; he hailed Max as one of his key stars and said that Jennifer was to be his new star. As time went on, both Jennifer and Rudy would become increasingly involved in Perry's work and personal life.

By the end of March 1986, the *Battle Of Armagideon* album was entirely completed, but Perry's ongoing dispute with Trojan over royalties meant its release was delayed until the end of June. Along with the material noted above, the album had a couple of tracks that played with reggae's past: 'Show Me That River' was a loose adaptation of Prince Buster's 'Wash Wash', while the ditty called 'Drum Song' adapted the melody of 'Norwegian Wood', as had some of Ras Michael's creations. The album had a number of strong points, including its autobiographical opener 'Introducing Myself'; the peculiar 'Grooving', which placed a chant of international banking over references to zodiac signs and heathen activity; a cockney meditation on the Devil called 'The Joker', built around the sol-fa scale; and the eerie 'Time Marches On', which featured Scratch's percussive banging on an electric fire (pictured on the back on the album atop his head). The weakest track was 'Sexy Lady', a failed attempt at disco-funk, while the album's most popular and notorious track was to be 'I Am a Madman', another autobiographical work with a complicated history.

Like '25 Years Ago', 'I Am A Madman' is an ambiguous comment on Perry's sanity that is open to interpretation. But before too much emphasis is placed on the title, it is worth noting that the song was originally called 'The Cuntist' – Lee's tribute to the female sex organs from which all humans are born and of which he is so fond; it was transformed into 'I Am A Madman' after Perry altered the lyrics at a later session when the rest of the album had been completed. 'Obviously, you could never print "I Am A Cuntist", on a record,' Mark Downie clarified, 'that's how "I Am A Madman" came about.' Perry was later to note that the song's title and repeated refrain referred to a reaction to his vision of repentance: 'When I tell people in Jamaica to repent, then them say me mad, so me just compete with what they say . . . I didn't say I am mad, they say I am mad, so if they say I am mad then I say yes, I am a madman!' [3]

When *Battle Of Armagideon* was released, Trojan issued a press release with the outrageous claim that Scratch had been drinking petrol while recording 'I Am A Madman'; Mark Downie insisted that he witnessed Perry sipping petrol at a particular session, but noted that the event in question involved 'Time Marches On', and not the 'Madman' track. 'Spike and I went to the studio one day with Lee. We stopped at a garage and Scratch bought a container and filled it with petrol; he was in the back of the motor, sniffing it. We thought, what's he doing? But with Lee Perry you just accept that kind of thing. We got to the studio and he had some rum and blackcurrant, and he took the lid off the petrol so the fumes were circulating. Then he ran out of rum, so he said, "I've got to try the petrol." He was drinking petrol and blackcurrant, actually drinking it – not very much, but how much could you drink? The fumes were all over the place, it was like sitting in a petrol station; we were trying to create the rhythm to go with "Time Marches On" and Spike fell asleep and I was dozing, but Lee was vibrant. Jerry was going, "Oh, my God, what's happening to my studio?!" '

Other tracks were left off the album, including a re-cut of 'The Ganja Man' and a love song called 'This Girl Is Mine', which was somewhat reminiscent of Michael Jackson and Paul McCartney's 'The Girl Is Mine'. 'May Sound Funny' was an adaptation of Prince Buster's 'Waiting For My Rude Girl' (itself based on the R & B standard 'Sitting In A Ya Ya') in which Scratch related how visits from a genie who appeared in his toilet would result in his accumulation of wealth; the genie has been named by Perry as Eenie Meanie Tekel. 'Pipecock Jackxon' was also recorded for the LP, but Perry was unhappy with its outcome, and had a dreadlocked toaster named Zebbie lay a religious chant over the tune to liven it up; this cut was subsequently vetoed because Perry did not want 'any more Bob Marleys' on his records.

Along with Perry's creative vocals and individual arrangements, part of the success of *Battle Of Armagideon* can be attributed to its album cover, designed and illustrated by Mark Downie from Lee's instruction. 'Lee said to me, "I want a ghost smoking a spliff wearing a crown sitting on a Bible throne," and that's my interpretation.' The album was a fair success in Britain and the USA, where it drew widespread airplay on college radio, largely through 'I Am A Madman'.

Live dates had been organised in the UK to support the release of the album. A brief UK tour was to start on July 10 at Gaz's Rock 'n' Blues – a weekly club night held at Gossip's by Gary Mayall, estranged son of blues guitarist John Mayall. However, by the time the album was issued, a few weeks before this engagement, internal divisions had brought disharmony to Dub Factory – who were now being billed as the Upsetters. The musicians had signed no contract before working with Scratch, and none of them would see a penny from the disc, except for Mark Downie, who received a nominal fee for his cover illustration. When Trojan refused to pay the band, the rhythm section quit, forcing Downie temporarily to recruit the bassist and drummer of Studio Six, brothers Gary and Mick Lewis. In the end, the Gossip's performance was marred by the band's internal friction, and disparaging reviews prompted Perry to fire the band.

Patrick Meads then arranged for Jah Warrior to back him for a performance at the first 'Reggae Seasplash' in Cornwall on August 16, where Perry shared the bill with Misty in Roots. Scratch then appeared with Jah Warrior at the Wag club in London's West End; unhappy with the group's handling of his material, he subsequently fired the band.

In the autumn, Trojan tried to string out the buzz generated by the album through the issue of further singles. 'Sexy Lady' and 'All Things Are Possible' were released in late November without much impact, followed by yet another cut of 'Merry Christmas, Happy New Year' that had been remixed by the Mad Professor at a session conducted without Perry's knowledge or permission. The song was also issued as a 12-inch Trojan disco with Professor's inspired cut-up mix of 'I Am A Madman' on the flipside; both songs featured melodica overdubs supplied by Mark Downie at Ariwa. Professor had recently moved the studio back into his home in Thornton Heath after a burglary in Peckham; he seriously considered exiting the music business at this point, but ultimately chose to persevere, moving Ariwa to its present-day location at 34 Whitehorse Lane shortly after.

By this time, Lee Perry had already become involved with other projects. He returned to Thameside to begin recording an album with core members of Misty in Roots, including bassist Tony Henry, drummer Bumpy Peters, guitarist Dennis 'Chop Chop' Augustine, and keyboardist Tawanda, but the album would unfortunately be plagued by a number of difficulties, mostly stemming from contractual arrangements. Mid-way through these sessions, he began working on a side project that would prove to be a strong commercial success that greatly revived his popularity: an album collaboration with inventive English producer Adrian Sherwood, proprietor of the On-U Sound record label.

Adrian Maxwell Sherwood was born in London in January 1958; he was the second of three children, but his siblings did not survive past infancy. Sherwood's father owned a couple of hotels in the South London suburb of Streatham, one of which was the large Liam Court; his typist mother was set to become a member of the George Mitchell Singers until the responsibilities of motherhood ended such aspirations. In 1960 the family moved to Slough where his father became seriously ill; his subsequent death in 1963 saw the family endure much hardship. Eventually, his mother re-married and the family moved to the town of High Wycombe in Buckinghamshire.

Sherwood's long involvement in the UK reggae scene stemmed from an early exposure to the music during school days through a friend whose parents played a mixture of reggae, soul, and calypso at their parties. Soon the young

Sherwood was hanging out at the Newlands club, High Wycombe's premier venue for reggae, becoming a regular deejay there in his early teens.

The club was run by Joe Farquarson, a friend and business associate of the Palmer brothers. Through his link with Farquarson, Sherwood began working for the Pama record company during his summer holidays, first by promoting their soul releases in nightclubs in the North of England and then by working in their Soundsville record shop on Craven Park Road in Harlesden.

In 1975, Farquarson and Sherwood formed the J and A distribution company with partners Anil Kanna and Chips Richards. Focusing on the Northern and Central regions of England, they handled independent UK reggae labels such as Ethnic Fight, Klik, Grounation, and Trojan; when Virgin began issuing reggae, their releases were also distributed by the company. Sherwood and his partners soon had a fleet of four vans and their own record shop, and a logical next step was the licensing of Jamaican material for their own Carib Gems record label.

Joe Farquarson had family connections with Dickie Wong who ran Kingston's Tit For Tat club, and Chips Richards had extensive connections through his days at the Trojan and Vulcan labels, so the company was able to secure prime material by rising artists such as Black Uhuru, Dillinger, and Trinity. One of the first albums to appear on the label was Prince Far I's classic *Psalms For I*, obtained from Micron proprietor Pete Weston; when Sherwood subsequently met the toaster in Birmingham with Flabba Holt and Eric 'Fish' Clarke, a strong friendship developed and many collaborations followed.

By 1977, J and A was heavily in debt, some of which was secured against the mortgage on Sherwood's mother's house. Though it would take him years to clear the debt, he quickly set up the similar Creation Rebel imprint, operating from an office in the back of Pama's shop. The team voiced notable material with toaster Jah Whoosh on the label, starting with a cut of Al Campbell's 'Gee Baby' that Whoosh obtained from Phil Pratt; Whoosh's *Marijuana World Tour* album was voiced in an evening over a pre-recorded dub album and issued in small quantity on the label.

Sherwood's next proper vehicle was Hit Run, which issued several hard-hitting Prince Far I productions and other strong material in 1978. Sherwood also began to influence the shape of Far I's current material, mixing all four volumes of his *Cry Tuff Dub Encounter* series and working closely with the toaster on his *Message From The King* and *Voice Of Thunder* albums; Sherwood also produced the *Starship Africa* album by a London studio band he named Creation Rebel in this period.

When Hit Run also fell prey to detrimental financial difficulties, Sherwood was briefly involved with the short-lived 4-D Rhythms label before he formed the more lasting and self-contained On-U Sound.

Though Sherwood did not have a direct link with Scratch, some of

Perry's rhythms turned up in altered forms on the *Psalms For I* and *Marijuana World Tour* albums, and one of the strongest 1979 Hit Run discos also featured a Black Ark backing track: Thomas White's 'Ivory Girl'.

White was born in Clarendon in 1958 and moved to London in 1972; the haunting 'Ivory Girl' was his debut recording and positive reviews in *Echoes* seemed to point to a promising career, but lack of airplay meant his subsequent recordings would not be issued. The song was voiced at the Crypt studio in Hertfordshire for producer Carl 'Stereo' Fletcher on a cut of Jah Lion's 'Dread In A Jamdown' that Fletcher had obtained from Scratch in Jamaica.

A member of the Twelve Tribes organisation, Fletcher worked with an outfit called Still Cool in conjunction with other Twelve Tribes members such as Pablove Black and Freddy McGregor; based in Weymouth Drive in the heart of Washington Gardens, he was often present at the Black Ark from the days of 'Curley Locks'. While in the UK in 1979, a link Fletcher made with Adrian Sherwood saw the 'Ivory Girl' disco pressed in a limited quantity of 500 copies. Sherwood himself would later name Lee Perry as a major influence, noting a particular preference for the work Scratch created between 1973 and '77.

The start of the 1980s saw Adrian Sherwood headed in a new direction, due largely to financial considerations and prior negative experiences. 'He used to get a lot of pressure from the man them,' explained Jah Whoosh, 'so he kind of back out and started him own little thing; he go into the studio and do his own little rhythms.'

In 1981, Sherwood established the On-U Sound label to present some of the more interesting of the underground artists in Britain. Early acts included the New Age Steppers (a reggae-influenced project led by former Pop Group member Mark Stewart) and the London Underground (a post-punk mix of Gaelic soul with rock and reggae hues). As the label grew, the mid-'80s saw Sherwood presiding over several loose collectives, taking the best from top Jamaican session players to merge with elements from his cutting-edge British crew. Singers and Players was one such amalgam, used to back artists like Congo Ashanti Roy, Bim Sherman, and Mikey Dread; an inverse group was African Head Charge, a vehicle for the music of transplanted Jamaican percussionist Bonjo Iyabinghi Noah, subjected to extreme sound treatments by Sherwood, who also occasionally played bass under the alias Crocodile.

Though Sherwood can recall a chance teenage meeting with Lee Perry in Pama's Soundsville shop, it was Steve Barker who first suggested that Perry collaborate with On-U Sound; the Lancashire disc jockey had been one of the label's earliest supporters, and retains a close friendship with its boss. A meeting between the pair of musical innovators was thus arranged in the spring of 1986. 'Steve Barker said that Lee should be cutting with On-U Sound and working with me on a record,' Sherwood noted. 'I was originally going to be working on some rhythms he'd built, like a re-cut of "One Drop" he'd done with a little crew south of the river, but when I played him a couple of Dub Syndicate rhythms that were heavily processed, he said, "This is great, give me a mike," so we parked what he'd been doing and literally flew straight into the *Time Boom* album.'

Dub Syndicate was another On-U conglomeration using Jamaican and British musicians, centring on drummer Lincoln 'Style' Scott (a.k.a. Rotterdam) of the Roots Radics band. Just as the Black Ark was entering into its demise, the Roots Radics were formed from the remainder of the Morwells group; they subsequently became the most popular Jamaican backing band of the early 1980s. Sherwood often used its core members for Dub Syndicate rhythms he and Style put together when the band was present in London; the rhythm tracks he presented to Lee Perry thus featured bassist Errol 'Flabba Holt' Carter, guitarists Eric 'Bingi Bunny' Lamont and Dwight Pinkney, and keyboardist Wycliffe 'Steely' Johnson atop Scott's drumming. To this Jamaican core was added bass by Doctor Pablo and Evar, guitar by Martin Frederick Harrison (a.k.a. Martin Frederix, former guitarist with the London Underground), percussion by Bonjo-I, and keyboards by Sherwood's then wife, Kishi Yamamoto.

In the autumn and winter of 1986, Perry voiced a number of Dub Syndicate tracks at Berry Street and Southern Studios, laying the foundations of what would emerge as the album *Time Boom – De Devil Dead.* Sherwood reported that most of the work went quite smoothly, despite Perry's eccentricities. 'I heard he was off his head and found him not to be. He's a lot more eccentric than your average (person), but he's very inspirational to work with. He's very talented with timing, and he's got the energy of a kid. I wouldn't say it was difficult, but nothing that's good comes easy.'

In November, when the bulk of the album was finished, Scratch made an appearance with Bim Sherman, Mark Stewart, drummer Keith LeBlanc, and other On-U stalwarts aboard the *HMS Elizabethan*, a riverboat that was hired for an event billed as 'The On-U Sound Annual Conference'. While floating down the Thames past the Houses of Parliament, Scratch sang over backing tracks from his upcoming album, accompanied by live hand drumming and percussion. Adrian Sherwood recalled the chaos connected to the anarchic excursion: 'We had 280 tickets, which sold within hours at Rough Trade; about 500 other people were begging to be let on. I had just gotten back from Poland, and Lee came over to our house in East Ham on the day of the gig; we weren't watching him and he drank a whole bottle of Polish vodka. He was trying to climb up this shelving unit in the front lounge, screaming; then he got really ill and says we've got to get some weed and ended up comatose on the floor. We cleaned him up and got him to the gig and he was welcoming everybody on to the boat, then he got a mike and was doing karaoke, singing on his back on the floor. There was a lot of spliff and drugs on the boat and after about two and a half hours, the police were trying to stop us, so Scratch was hurling abuse at the police with a megaphone, saying "Fire on your head in the River Thames! Back off Babylon!" and cursing "Blood clot". It was the maddest night, great fun, and I'll remember that for ever.'

Sherwood also recalled a minor act of shamanism enacted at his East Ham dwelling in this period. 'We had a Prophet 2000 keyboard, my (ex) wife Kishi said Lee had a cooking pan with three pebbles in it, he'd got them underneath the Prophet in the lounge, and he'd got the kiddie's watering can. She said, "Lee, what are you doing?" and he looks up at her without blinking and goes, "I'm watering the stones at the foot of the prophet." Make of that what you like, but that always struck me as a fantastic thing; he's always thinking of something that will cause some magic. The thing with him is he's a one-off completely, cut from a different cloth.'

When Sherwood went to master the *Time Boom* album the following January, he found that the songs 'Blinkers' and 'Allergic to Lies' would not cut properly because of a problem with their vocal tracks. 'Initially I was trying to make the voice really acute, so it's got a real edge to it,' Sherwood explained. 'Apparently I did it so much that it couldn't cut.' Further sessions were thus organised for February 22 at Southern studio, in which the offending tracks were amended in a 12-hour session. *Time Boom* was thus a complete entity, ready to be given a final mix-down and then to be unleashed on the public.

The *Time Boom* material was easily the strongest work Lee Perry had created since the demise of the Black Ark. It was partly the complexity of the rhythm tracks that so suited his delivery; the Roots Radics core was solid and familiar enough for him to feel comfortable singing over, while the On-U augmentations and Sherwood's sonic treatments resulted in a thoroughly modern sound that Scratch was seeking – a sound both unique and broadly appealing.

As is typical of Perry's post-Ark canon, his lyrics were all over the map. The opening 'SDI' caught him at his most critical, protesting against the needless Cold War being perpetrated by the Superpowers. Though the closing 'Time Conquer' spoke of the overall insignificance of man, he spoke of his own supernatural powers on 'Kiss The Champion', 'Jungle', and the title track, while 'Blinkers' saw him hailing 'the return of President Abraham Perry and his holy hands', making additional comments on the necessity of passing waste over a rhythm filled with the sounds of collapsing buildings, electric drills, and breaking glass. 'Music And Science Lovers' was a rambling excursion over a spirited saxophone-led rhythm, while 'Allergic To Lies' provided a catchy chant that stuck in the mind – despite being the track Scratch said he was least pleased with.

Perhaps part of the success of *Time Boom* stems from the fact that the rhythms had already been built before Scratch's involvement; he was thus freed from the constraining process of explaining his wishes to the musicians, and could get on with his vocal delivery and structural re-arrangements. Sherwood was also adept at providing Perry with the sounds and treatments he envisioned, as seen, for instance, in the inclusion of a vocal bridge using the sol-fa scale included at the end of 'Blinkers'. Overall, *Time Boom* was the result of a strong combination between two independent thinkers with keen ears, fast hands, and plenty of ideas.

While Adrian Sherwood was mixing down the *Time Boom* tracks and making arrangements for the album's upcoming release, Lee Perry returned to concentrating on the fresh material he had been creating at Thameside with the core members of Misty in Roots in the latter half of 1986. When not occupied with the On-U tracks, he spent much of the autumn and winter in the studio, which he was gradually in the process of taking over, much to the dismay of Jerry Tilley; Scratch was covering the walls with paint and Magic Marker, and placing champagne bottles filled with his own urine at strategic points around the space. A Turkish fan was also a regular visitor at Scratch's sessions, sitting quietly in the corner or dancing to the music; he would often ingest magic mushrooms while observing Scratch at work.

Jerry's brother John became Lee's manager in this period, another in the long line of those who briefly sought to represent him. John had previously managed a heavy metal group called the Desolation Angels, but had left the music business to run a construction firm; his involvement with Lee marked John's brief return to the industry. Scratch did not have much confidence in John, and used him chiefly as a chauffeur between the studio and his home on the other side of London; Rudy Mascoll also often provided transportation. When a passenger in a moving car, Scratch continued his obsession with filming whatever he saw in the rear-view mirror, later overdubbing different sounds and spoken conversations onto the audio track.

Material completed in early 1987 included an explosive version of Marley's 'Exodus' that lasted over 13 minutes; the lyrics were changed to speak of 'flying Scratchy the flying Apache', mixing 'Exodus' with the 'ashes and dust' to which Bob had returned. Perry later had a jogger he encountered on the river bank bring his Alsatian into the studio, overdubbing the dog's ferocious barking at the start of the song. A new version of 'Duppy Conqueror' was also cut, in which Perry scolded his 'bad friends' for their wrongdoing, and he had another crack at 'The Ganja Man', which he gave new lyrics to proclaim himself 'the King of Poop, Shit, Piss, and Spit'. By far the most beautiful number was a song co-written by Jerry Tilley called 'Sitting By The Seaside', which held a fine harmonic balance in its presentation of the more contemplative side of Perry's nature.

At many of these sessions, Scratch videotaped himself singing and mixing, or overdubbing tuneless keyboard lines and percussion; on several occasions, he placed rocks inside the video monitor. He also blew reefer smoke directly onto the moving master tapes of tracks he was altering (on a machine located just below a No Smoking sign), and treated the studio machines as though they were living beings. In addition to his video fixations, Scratch was developing an obsession with being photographed, seizing every opportunity to be snapped in a variety of peculiar poses; it was as though each flicker of a camera shutter could freeze any of his limitless personas in time, capturing the momentary emergence of a fragmentary splinter of his being. Photographers and onlookers would thus be required to burn through endless rolls of film, and prints presented to the Upsetter would typically be given a talismanic function through being pasted to the wall, worked into sculptures, or glued to the surface of instruments.

As Perry was completing what was meant to be his Trojan follow-up to *Battle Of Armagideon*, growing tension on a number of fronts worked to spoil his mood. His unhappiness with Trojan was worsening, largely due to continued uncertainty about his royalties. Through John Tilley, Lee Perry began using the services of Tim Spencer, LLB, a knowledgeable solicitor with the firm Compton Carr who specialised in business law. Spencer began the tortuous process of unravelling the legal particulars of Perry's complicated past dealings in conjunction with publishing company Westbury Music; a barrister was engaged and a lawsuit was pending, but such efforts would result in little gain after Perry changed his mind at the eleventh hour by refusing to acknowledge their representation.

Trojan employee Patrick Meads was also getting up Scratch's nose by meddling with the Thameside material. He brought in rock musicians for overdubs without prior consultation with Perry, and often mixed down Scratch's work without permission. Scratch would generally disappear when Meads arrived at the studio, taking barefoot walks in the snow along the river or building sculptures in the kitchen until Meads left; he would then work late into the night, spending hours undoing the changes.

Meanwhile, his home life was shaken by the news that Sandra was again pregnant with Perry's child. As on the previous occasion, the pregnancy was unplanned, and there were again initial reservations about the event, though both would be delighted when the baby arrived in the summer.

Though Scratch was quite content to have taken over Thameside studio, he was less happy about John Tilley's management, and gradually began requesting increased assistance from Rudy Mascoll. Tilley sensed the potential earnings Scratch could generate, and spoke of schemes to fall back on if his music failed – like having Perry paint a limited number of abstract works on canvas, to be sold at extortionate prices. He was perhaps naïve as to the drastic nature of Perry's temperament, and lacked a basic understanding of Scratch's past. But he was still trying his best to revive Perry's career, and arranged for another Dingwalls performance at the end of February. However, a miscommunication resulted in the show being advertised with a performance date of January 22; though an announcement was subsequently made with the correct date, Scratch dutifully appeared at the venue in January to apologise to any fans who might have come to see him, and ended up performing three unrehearsed numbers with a British reggae band called the Nomadix.

As at so many of his public appearances in Britain, Scratch was drunk by the time he took the stage, and the booze infusion brought on strange behaviour. He spent much of that evening grabbing electric light bulbs with his bare hands while blowing a whistle, or blowing weed smoke through a wooden recorder that he placed in alternate nostrils. It was also the occasion that Lee Perry first met the author of this book, and after reading an article I had written about him in San Francisco's underground magazine *Wiring Department*, he appointed me 'Ghost Writer' a few days later after an initiation ceremony involving 13 stones and a silver death's-head ring.

To prepare for the actual Dingwalls performance on February 23, Scratch began rehearsing with a new band composed of London-based Jamaicans, led by bassist Larry 'the Professor' Silvera; Jennifer Romeo was to open the show and also rehearsed with the group at Thameside. At Dingwalls, Perry played the strongest tracks from the upcoming *Time Boom* album and highlights from *Battle Of Armagideon*, plus versions of 'One Drop' and 'Exodus'; live mix was provided by Adrian Sherwood, who helped shape the sound with an Echoplex unit. Scratch appeared on stage wearing a pointed hat, entirely covered in tin foil, with bits of greenery poking out of the top; he sang through his own personal microphone, which had several talismans attached to its handle, hidden behind a wall of silver duct tape.

It was at this performance that Perry was approached by a publicity agent named Jenni Francis, a Grenadan who ran a small firm called Net Working in West London. Though Francis never generated a great deal of publicity for Scratch, she did provide him with a brief romantic diversion that spring – despite the child he was expecting with Sandra Cooley.

On February 28, Rudy Mascoll accompanied Scratch and Adrian Sherwood to BBC Radio Lancashire for another radio broadcast with Steve Barker; Scratch again stayed overnight with Barker and his family, who now lived in the city of Blackburn.

By the time of this second broadcast, Adrian Sherwood had already been approached by singer Mick Hucknall of Simply Red, another committed reggae enthusiast who hoped to have Sherwood and Perry remix some of the group's work. Sherwood and Hucknall have long-standing links: when the singer was still in an outfit called the Frantic Elevators, Simply Red's future rhythm section were playing in an On-U act called the Mothmen; Adrian was also an old friend of Mick Hucknall's then manager. On their first meeting, Scratch had a positive impression of Hucknall, equally pleased by his straightforward attitude and soulful pop style. Perry thus consented to the project, and a mixing session was scheduled for later in the month.

Other groups to approach the Upsetter that February were not so fortunate. New York hip hop artist Mantronick failed to impress Scratch with his 'technotronic' sound, and an offer to collaborate was thus declined after Scratch witnessed an uninspiring London live performance. Former Clash guitarist Mick Jones' Big Audio Dynamite also got the thumbs-down from the Upsetter, his decision possibly influenced by the group barring him from joining them on stage at a concert at the Brixton Academy. Californian Heavy Metal experimentalists Faith No More also approached Scratch through an intermediary around the same time – their drummer and bassist being long-standing fans – but he was not inspired by their debut album *We Care A Lot*, and declined to work with the group.

Lee Perry had a busy schedule for the rest of 1987. Much of his time was spent in recording studios, creating literally dozens of tracks of which only a handful have been released; he also had frequent rehearsals for live perform-ances with a variety of short-lived backing bands. There were also occasional social functions to attend, such as a public appearance at the Radio London Reggae Awards on March 7.

By the time of this presentation, John Tilley had been fired, with all management duties now the responsibility of Rudy Mascoll. On March 25, Perry and Adrian Sherwood fulfilled their pledge to Simply Red by remixing the group's version of Bunny Wailer's 'Love Fire' at London's Southern studio, where the singer overdubbed certain vocal lines Perry thought could be improved; Perry then added his own additional vocals and other effects. Despite – or perhaps because of – such playful enhancement from Scratch, the group's major label Warner Brothers chose to relegate the remixed 'Love Fire' to the B-side of the 'Infidelity' single, thus diminishing its overall impact; a second song remixed at the same session was left unreleased.

On April 1, On-U Sound issued the first pressing of *Time Boom* in Europe and North America; its British release was scheduled for July, but would be further delayed as Sherwood entered into negotiations with major label EMI. Two days after the foreign release, Scratch travelled to Manchester to perform at the International club. The entourage that made the journey in a luxury coach included Perry and 'Professor' Larry's band, live mixer Adrian Sherwood and assistant Martin Frederix, opening act Jennifer Romeo and her three brothers, manager Rudy Mascoll, lawyer Tim Spencer, publicity agent Jenni Francis and her son, and the mother-to-be of his next child, Sandra Cooley; Perry also brought a number of stuffed animals with him. Roger Eagle spun discs at the nightclub, which attracted a mixed crowd with a high proportion of skinheads in Ben Sherman shirts and bovver boots; Scratch appeared on stage in a track suit, holding a bare electric light bulb on a long extension lead, generating a positive response with a similar set to the previous Dingwalls event.

Two days after the Manchester performance, Max Romeo came over from New York to spend a week in London, visiting his family and organising business. Max's presence greatly lifted Scratch's spirits; he became highly energised once his old spar was around, and the pair began planning to issue a 'confrontation'-style album. One of the first songs they voiced together was 'The Queen Can't Shit', recorded at Thameside studio over the rhythm of 'Show Me That River' after Scratch learned that the Queen Mother wore a colostomy bag; the offensive duet was not completed properly and remains unreleased.

It was during Romeo's visit that Perry fired the band led by 'Professor' Larry. Plans were underway for a summer European tour, which would include a date with Curtis Mayfield in Austria; requests also came through for an appearance in Germany and at the Reggae Sunsplash held in Zimbabwe. Scratch thus began rehearsing with another band composed of ex-patriate Jamaicans, to which he added an Australian female horn section. When the musicians demanded upfront money for rehearsals, Scratch fired several members on the spot; the keyboardist later returned to the rehearsal premises with a gun, demanding £50 expenses from Rudy Mascoll; a rubber cheque was duly issued to the upstart. Scratch then drafted in musicians he knew were more reliable, including rhythm guitarist Locksley Gichi and keyboardist Sonny Binns from the Cimarons, plus a lead guitarist known as Trevor Starr, who had worked with Scratch in Jamaica and was a main player in Jimmy Cliff's band. Unfortunately, circumstances saw the cancellation of the above engagements, as Perry continued to be plagued by bureaucratic difficulties.

In mid-May, lawyer Tim Spencer left Compton Carr to work for Polydor; he announced he would no longer be Lee Perry's legal representative. Gone too was Jenni Francis, whose controlling efforts had drawn considerable displeasure from Scratch.

At the end of May, Perry began recording with Jennifer Romeo and the Cimarons at Southern Studio with resident engineer Trigger, typically on 12-hour sessions. On the first day, he recorded Romeo's original composition 'Music'. He then re-voiced 'Drum Song', first changing it to 'King of the Punks', but was unhappy with this version and wiped the vocal the next day. Dissatisfied with the Dub Factory rhythm tracks, he had Sonny Binns add new keyboard parts, which he explained were to capture the sound of 'the stinger of the African killer bees'; he also added new guitar parts and permeated the song with the sound of crunching glass after making a sample by breaking the two bottles of wine he consumed. He subsequently recorded a new vocal on the rhythm, now addressing 'Poor People Rights'. On the third day, he brought a singer from Brixton named Simian – sister of Pauline Catilin of lover's rock trio Brown Sugar – to join Jennifer Romeo in providing backing vocals on 'Poor People Rights' during another 12-hour stint; by the end of the session, the singers were fainting with hunger, while Perry became more and more energised; he had been anointing himself with baby oil before his portable heater to gain more power, and eventually poured the oil directly onto the heater, releasing a cloud of sickly-sweet smoke. Though the singers and engineer fled in horror, Perry remained in the smoky room; he became further energised by inhaling the noxious gases. After dropping off the backing singer in Brixton, Scratch stopped at a kebab stand for refreshment; he demanded free samples, and asked the frightened staff if they were serving rat and cat.

In June, Perry began working at the Brent Black Musicians Co-op – a relaxed community recording facility in Willesden, close to the hub of Northwest London's Jamaican community. With engineer Syd Bucknor, Scratch put the finishing touches to Jennifer Romeo's 'Music', and began mixing down the album he had been working on for Trojan.

As Perry's dissatisfaction with the company grew, he began making disgruntled noises. First he vowed only to let the company have the worst of the dozen or so tracks he had recorded; the best of the bunch he would issue himself. He then began saying they deserved nothing, and that he would issue all the work himself.

Trojan had scheduled the album release for the summer of 1987; once they had fired Patrick Meads, Enzo Hamilton began overseeing the project. Hamilton was a Frenchman who had dealings with a number of dubious reggae companies; Scratch referred to him as 'the vampire from Notre Dame'. Hamilton inquired why it was taking Perry so long to complete the album, and demanded he surrender its master tape and track listing. Eventually, two master tapes were delivered to Trojan with the following song titles:

1. I Am the Upsetter
2. Yes Me Friends
3. Boom Cannibals
4. Fire Wankers
5. I Win the Revenge
6. Pal Bad Breath
7. This Time It Is Different
8. Eye for Eye
9. Tooth for Tooth
10. Surprise.

Though Scratch continued to be vexed about Trojan's handling of his back catalogue, he certainly had the last laugh on this release, as the tapes sent to Trojan were blank.

With Trojan thus thrown off his scent, he continued to alter the material, recording and mixing at Matrix and BBMC in June and July; he ran into Winston Grennan at the latter studio, and had the drummer give some of his material a new beat.

Despite the excesses of 'Judgement In A Babylon', Perry was still invited to the 25th anniversary celebrations held by Island Records at Pinewood film studios, where he spent much of the evening toasting over the PA system. Scratch later revealed that his presence seemed to unsettle Chris Blackwell, who trembled slightly when shaking Perry's hand: 'He approach for a handshake, and it's body shake he get.'

On August 13, Sandra gave birth to Cleopatra Perry to the delight of both her parents, though Sandra's subsequent post-natal depression would see her prescribed strong medication that did not agree with her temperament. Cleo was the first child Perry fathered with a white woman, and her creation marked a shift away from the excluding mind set of Black Supremacy Scratch championed in the latter days of the Ark; her arrival also strengthened his resolve to stay in Britain, as he had little desire to return to Jamaica. Sandra became pregnant again shortly after Cleo's arrival, but was advised not to have the child as the medication she was taking could lead to birth defects; a subsequent miscarriage would see her hospitalised overnight in the autumn.

A couple of weeks after Cleo's birth, Scratch appeared live on the back of a float in the procession of the Notting Hill Carnival with Adrian Sherwood, Keith LeBlanc and Akabu; the truck was hired by EMI as promotion for the *Time Boom* album. Continually rapping, Scratch wore an army cap decorated with SS regalia, a spiked wristband and masses of rings and necklaces, holding a hammer in one hand and a microphone in the other. Perry was meant to perform at Portobello Green that evening, but never made it to the stage; instead, he toasted on the float until the very end of the event.

It was around the time of Cleopatra's birth that Scratch and Rudy Mascoll set up the Arkwell label, distributed through Jet Star; their first release was Jennifer Romeo's 'Music'. Hidden on the B-side was one of the tracks he had recorded with the musicians of Misty in Roots; mis-credited as 'Music Well' by Jennifer Romeo, the song was in fact an inspired new version of 'Keep On Moving' by Scratch himself, built around melodic keyboard riffs from Tawanda. Unhappy with the overall sound of 'Music', Scratch remixed the tune for a second pressing that made his few lines of toasting more prominent; it was issued with another Romeo original called 'Dance', recorded without Lee Perry's involvement. Unfortunately, neither version found favour with the public, and a lack of promotion saw both discs quickly deleted.

The next Arkwell release hinted at occasional tension that waxed and waned between Scratch and Adrian Sherwood. Scratch's mistrust of outside influences was beginning to surface again, spurred on by members of Perry's entourage who were not fond of the On-U crew and partly exacerbated by factors involving race. 'Adrian is a white man who wants to steal my power,' Scratch proclaimed in this period. 'Would I give my power to a white man? I would never do that. I would rather die than do that.'

As the UK release of *Time Boom* was further delayed, Scratch was becoming impatient. He had also learned that select Black Ark singles were changing hands at ridiculously high prices, and sought to cash in on the phenomenon by repressing Devon Irons' 'When Jah Come' (re-titled 'First Judgement') on an Arkwell/Upsetter disco, featuring a label designed by

Sandra Cooley that depicted Scratch as a monkey with wings. The other three tracks on the disco – titled 'Water Genesis', 'Second Judgement', and 'Fire Revelation 22' by Jesus Rainford Perry – were actually the first three tracks from the *Time Boom* album, with mumbled interjections Perry had overdubbed at a drunken studio session; deluded statements such as 'I give and I take what is rightfully mine' shows an overarching and unfounded mistrust.

Such impertinent reactions turned out to be a little premature. Just before Peter Tosh's murder in Jamaica on September 11 – which Scratch hailed as an act of retribution – EMI released the single 'Jungle' on their Syncopate subsidiary. The single was cut on three formats (with a seven-inch 'Radio Plate', ten-inch 'Disco Plate', and 12-inch 'Big Hot Plate' simultaneously issued), and given a massive publicity campaign through huge posters of zany portraits by noted rock photographer Bleddyn Butcher. The campaign was co-ordinated by Amrick Rai and Paul Smith, former Blast First executives whose Daisy Sounds company was linked to independent label Mute records; friends of Adrian Sherwood, the pair had helped arrange the *Time Boom* album deal with EMI.

As the hype surrounding the singles and the approaching UK album release escalated, Scratch quickly assembled a pick-up band of Harlesden musicians (including guitarists Locksley Gichi and Trevor Starr and saxophonist Lascelles James, formerly of Boney M and Spear of Destiny) for a sold-out performance at London's Town and Country club on September 22 – the most notable of Scratch's live appearances in England to be mixed by Adrian Sherwood. Scratch appeared in a thoroughly outlandish costume, wearing a facial mask that had cat's whiskers and an umbrella on his head; he also distributed lollipops to the heaving crowd. This was the first performance to benefit from the presence of dancers Eve Peters and her friend Christine, whom Scratch had discovered while buying clothes at the Hyper Hyper market in Kensington; Eve was a Trinidadian clothing designer and Christine an Anglo-Jamaican runner who would later be a candidate for the British Olympic team. Scratch did four songs from *Time Boom*, 'Nice Time' and 'Roast Fish And Cornbread', plus a version of 'Mr DJ Man' dedicated to David Rodigan; though occasionally giving an anarchic performance, Scratch received a strong audience response.

The day after this concert, Perry was interviewed at his home by MTV, but the footage would languish in their vaults and was not broadcast. His next live performance on September 28 at the Kensington Town Hall formed a stark contrast to the Town and Country gig, although the set and players were basically the same; also appearing on the bill was Brother Resistance, the Trinidadian pioneer of the blend of rap and calypso known as Rapso. The gig was a benefit concert for the family of Michael Galvin, a white resident of Ladbroke Grove who had been murdered at the Carnival, but a lack of publicity surrounding the event meant it was attended by less than 300. Based on the invented testimony of a paid police informer, a young black man was convicted of Galvin's killing, said to have been triggered by the price of a can of soda; the police were using publicity from the case as an excuse to ban the Carnival. However, the informer later admitted the tale was entirely fabricated, and that the man convicted was needlessly imprisoned; it later emerged that Galvin was a drug dealer who was killed by a more established dealer who felt Galvin was encroaching on his turf.

In late September, Scratch was also contacted by Patrick Jammes, a young French promoter proposing a debut Parisian performance in November at the Elyseé Montmartre venue; the concert would be filmed for a home-video release. After Jammes came to London to negotiate a fee in person, Perry began assembling a reliable backing group that included Akabu on backing vocals and Pauline 'the Rhythm Queen' on keyboards. On October 10, Scratch brought Akabu to Ariwa to record a new version of 'Small Axe', but the song was not completed to his satisfaction.

French rock critic and cartoonist Bruno Blum of *Best* magazine came to London to interview Scratch at the offices of Mute records in mid-October, just as *Time Boom* was finally issued in the UK. The interview was to generate some pre-concert publicity in France, and Blum brought his girlfriend to film the event on video. However, Perry was rapidly bored by his questions, and elected to liven things up by exposing himself to the camera; he also flashed his organ at Jane, the office secretary. Blum played Scratch a demo of a reggae-flavoured pop song he'd been working on, and asked Perry for production assistance, but the request was politely declined.

Time Boom received highly complimentary reviews in the music press, and helped introduce Perry's work to a new audience with sales in excess of 50,000 copies. However, the Upsetter was displeased with elements of its release – particularly its long delay in reaching the UK – and had an angry confrontation with the staff of Daisy Sounds in the offices of Mute Records (witnessed by Stephen Mallinder of avant-garde group Cabaret Voltaire). He also began issuing public proclamations that painted Adrian Sherwood in a highly negative light:

> 'Who is Adrian Sherwood? He is one of the past, he is not one of the future and I don't want to hear about him any more! He is finished, totally finished, he is wiped out! He asked me to do him a favour, I didn't ask him to do me any. I don't need Adrian Sherwood, he is copying Lee "Scratch" Perry, he is doing what Lee "Scratch" Perry used to do 25 years ago. Adrian Sherwood needs Lee "Scratch" Perry but Lee "Scratch" Perry does not need Adrian Sherwood . . . He is a good copy artist, but I like people original . . . I see him as a pagan, next to a vampire. Bloodsucker. Trying to steal other people's birth right . . . '[4]

Familiar with Scratch's volatile countenance, Sherwood viewed such criticism as a less important aspect of Perry's character. 'Well, he's not called the Upsetter for nothing,' Sherwood explained. 'It was my turn then, but Neil Fraser also got slagged off for several years, and so did Chris Blackwell. It's not confined to us either; it's like producers, and everybody else.'

Meanwhile, the enormous popularity of *Time Boom* led to several other requested collaborations. The first came from subversive pop-rocker Zodiac Mindwarp, who asked that Perry remix his single 'Backseat Education'; the singer was particularly fond of Perry's 'Bed Jamming', and thought his similarly risqué single could benefit from the maestro's magic touch. On November 3, Scratch thus joined Mindwarp at Matrix to add keyboards, Syndrums, water sounds, and vocals to the tune in another 12-hour session, for which he was paid £500 by Phonogram; JAMU founder Bill Drummond and Dave Balfe, his former partner in the Teardrop Explodes, were also present, passing around a bottle of whisky. Unfortunately, a drop in the popularity of the original single saw Phonogram veto Scratch's remix, which has thus remained unreleased.

The day after mixing this single, Scratch awoke in a foul mood, as bitter memories from the past came back to haunt him. When Rudy Mascoll picked him up at the start of the next day's business, Scratch went straight to an off-licence to buy a bottle of Overproof Rum – a clear liquid with a startlingly high alcohol content. He began drinking the spirit as though it was water, but each swig seemed to intensify his bitterness. He was carrying a small sampling keyboard with a built-in microphone; over a mechanised rhythm Perry sampled himself repeatedly stating, 'I don't like dreadlocks' until he had built an echoing wall of sound around the phrase.

By the time he arrived at rehearsal premises several hours later, he was drunk and angry, his keyboard statement firing his rage. He was snapping at the musicians, who failed to muster a plausible version of 'Duppy Conqueror', but in the midst of this rehearsal, Family Man and Wire Lindo appeared; they were in London with the rest of the Wailers band preparing for a concert at the Astoria Theatre. At Scratch's request, Wire stepped up to the acoustic piano and banged out the melody of the tune, an act that immediately brightened Scratch's mood; the mere sight of Wire and Fams had a strong impact on his behaviour, prompting him to wipe the stored message on his keyboard. 'I change the spell,' Perry proclaimed, and recorded a new message: 'I love dreadlocks!'

Family Man went to Waghorn Road during this brief London visit, where Perry gave him money to deliver to his children at Cardiff Crescent; he had sporadically sent cash through his local bank, but was happier to have it delivered by his reliable neighbour. Though his brother Carlton had recently been murdered by his wife and her lover, Fams was still concentrating on the positive; he also spoke with Perry of finishing a project he had started with the brothers some years previously. 'After we finished the *Legend* tour in 1984, I and my brother were supposed to meet back with Scratch in Europe to do something,' Fams explained, ' 'cause I help him to finish up an album at Harry J studio and we start an album together at Tuff Gong. All the rhythm tracks are just there, unfinished, waiting on Scratch.'

As advance promotions had sold out Perry's Parisian debut, a second show was added a few weeks before Scratch's arrival – an excessively optimistic move that would cost the novice promoter dearly. Then, less than a week before the gigs, a conflict led to the firing of Akabu; Scratch quickly drafted in a replacement band featuring bassist Franklyn Dunn and guitarist Locksley Gichi from the Cimarons, saxophonist Lascelles James, plus keyboardist Stefan Lumsden, drummer Gary Duncan, and a rhythm guitarist called Vassel; backing vocals were handled by a trio called African Pearl.

As rehearsals were being organised, Perry was asked to remix 'Sign Your Name' and 'If You All Get to Heaven', two hit singles by mixed-race American pop singer Terence Trent D'Arby – a vocalist Scratch somehow likened to Dave Barker. D'Arby's star was on the rise, and Perry arranged the high fee of £1,000 per day to remix the songs for CBS at Matrix. On November 14, he altered the shape of both songs by adding the cries of his daughter Cleopatra, new keyboard parts, and water sounds; as he did not have Watty Burnett's cow sound to hand, he used a Chinese novelty toy that imitated a cow when turned upside down further to enhance the tunes; he also drank so much rum that he could barely stand at the end of the session, and had to be escorted home. Scratch returned the next day to mix down the material, but D'Arby expressed dissatisfaction with the result, requesting a dubbier mix; Scratch thus returned for a third session to give the tracks a sparser feel, subsequently issued on a CBS ten-inch EP in the UK and a white-label 12-inch in the USA.

On November 18, Scratch and the band flew to Paris after only two rehearsals. On arrival, they went straight to Radio Nova – an adventurous commercial-free station with a multi-cultural focus founded by Jean-François Bizot in 1979. Scratch toasted live on the air over his productions for a couple of hours, interviewed by Bizot mid-way through; they spoke of the Frenchman's visit to the Black Ark a decade earlier, of Selassie's visit to Jamaica in 1966, and of the protection Lee Perry feels he receives from spliff.

As the concert on November 19 had been added late, it was somewhat undersold; Lee Perry and Jennifer Romeo thus appeared before a crowd of nearly 1000 people. Despite his pre-gig nerves, Scratch waited until after the concert to get drunk, and thus gave a highly competent performance; the new material and version of 'Duppy Conqueror' – transformed to 'Yuppie Conqueror' to castigate the negative influence of young urban professionals – received particularly strong responses from the crowd.

The following night's performance was perhaps his strongest ever since leaving Jamaica; too hungover to drink, the Upsetter was stone-cold sober, sipping nothing but Perrier the entire night. He appeared in a black cape and top hat – looking like a cross between a chimney sweep and an undertaker – and kept the capacity crowd hanging on his every note; the musicians also made an extra effort to keep it a memorable performance, climaxed by an unrehearsed encore of 'Put It On', delivered as a frantic ska duet between Scratch and Jennifer Romeo.

Before leaving France, Scratch gave a revealing interview to small community station Tropic FM, in which he expressed dissatisfaction with societies he had lived in, and a resolute desire to remain outside Jamaica:

> 'The achievement I achieve living in the UK is learning the ways of evil people . . . not the UK alone, the whole world is evil, but certain part of the world, you have good people . . . If I have to go back to Jamaica, then I will but I wish I don't have to, and that's my final answer.' [5]

Though the Parisian shows had been an aesthetic success, the late addition of the November 19 date meant that promoter Patrick Jammes lost money; Perry took pity on the youth and returned some of his fee after the performances. Unfortunately, the video footage was never issued, after Jammes and the video team became involved in a financial dispute. Jammes would later find greater success as manager of Swiss electro trio the Young Gods.

When Jammes deposited Lee Perry and his band at the airport for their return to London, they found themselves delayed for many hours due to an incident on the incoming aircraft. Scratch was decked out in military garb, with a magnifying mirror hanging from his neck, plastered with an Ethiopian decal; he was carrying an electric guitar in one hand and a duffel bag of magic objects and master tapes in the other. When he finally went through the metal detector to board the plane, Scratch set off every alarm nearby; perplexed airline staff kept their distance and declined to search the man.

However, Lee Perry was interrogated by an immigration officer upon arrival at Gatwick Airport; the officer pointed out that Perry had overstayed his visa by a long period. When asked how long he intended to stay this time, the Upsetter looked the officer straight in the eye and said, 'Don't know, could be a day, could be a thousand years.' Rudy Mascoll intervened, explaining that Perry lived in London with his common-law wife and their new-born child; he pointed out that the performer had been working in France, and indicated the working visa obtained for the concerts.

Scratch was eventually given restricted entry to Britain, under the condition that he return to Gatwick the next day to discuss the situation with immigration officers. When Perry complied with their request, he was told he would have to leave the country, and that he was to obtain the necessary paperwork to be granted the correct status upon re-entry.

The officials suggested he return to France, as it was the country he had last entered Britain from, but Scratch had no desire to linger there while waiting for bureaucratic red tape to be completed. On November 30, he thus boarded a flight to Kingston, where he was planning to stay for less than a week; he was due to return by December 6 to give a performance at London's Mean Fiddler.

His few days in Jamaica would prove to be tense, though his children and P-Son were very pleased to see him. Vicky Nelson recalled Scratch's unexpected return to Cardiff Crescent: 'Early in the morning I saw this big coach drive up. When I looked it was just Scratch alone came in this big bus, and we were all glad to see him and everything, 'cause I was worried. I wasn't hearing from him all this time, and I was worried and depressed not knowing if anything happens to him, but we were all glad to see him and just welcome him right there.'

Scratch found that his sons had dropped out of St Joseph's High School in Half Way Tree as they did not have enough money to pay the school fees; Michelle was living at the home of the boyfriend Perry disapproved of, and thus kept her distance from Cardiff Crescent; Marsha was attending Fitz Henley's Secretarial Institute in New Kingston, and was set to graduate the following June.

When Vicky Nelson learned Scratch was planning to return to England, she told him she was leaving Cardiff Crescent, tired of waiting for him to return, but Perry managed to persuade her to remain there, and her close bond with his children meant she felt unable to abandon them. 'I told him that my time is up and I don't think I can stay there any more, because I want to see if I can get my life together. I didn't hear anything for all this time, to be honest I was pissed off really. He was saying that Marsha, which is his little queen, if she as a girl child to be left all alone, what is going to happen? Then he tell me that everything will be fine after a while and we would all be OK, and he's just going up there to make the way but that wasn't so . . . anyway, I promise him I'll stay until Marsha graduate from school, and I did keep that promise.'

Vicky also recounted that Scratch's departure from Kingston was as unexpected as his brief return had been. 'He send me to get something and when I ask where he is, he's gone to the airport – gone; he went back to England, he leave me just like that.'

Though Perry's exit from Cardiff Crescent may have seemed abrupt to Vicky Nelson, a mix-up with airline tickets meant he returned two days after he was supposed to appear at the Mean Fiddler; the expectant crowd assembled at the venue was greatly disappointed when the Upsetter did not appear as billed, and the loss of revenue meant that no future date was scheduled. Perry was given the most minimal of entry clearances on arrival, allowed to remain in the UK only until the end of January.

Rudy Mascoll thus sought assistance from Tim Spencer – who was acting as a legal consultant after being made redundant when Polydor merged with

Polygram – but Spencer was reluctant to represent Perry directly, due to a heavy workload and to fees outstanding from previous work for Scratch. An application was eventually made to the Home Office, resulting in a phase of uncertainty as Perry's passport was scrutinised by the bureaucrats.

Perry's ongoing visa problems meant he did not achieve much in London at the start of 1988. He made a final appearance at Dingwalls on January 6, with opening act Phil and Diana (led by former Vibrators guitarist Phil Ram and featuring Ginger Baker's son Kofi on drums). Perry drank heavily before the show, decorating the walls of the venue with black crosses after the sound check; he also fought with Rudy Mascoll and Jennifer Romeo after delivering a sloppy performance in which he insulted the band on stage.

The Mascolls were already miffed with Scratch for taking numerous liberties. He had ruined their fish tank and relieved them of an electric organ which he covered with photographs of himself, only to sink it in the mud of his back garden, where it was destroyed by rain; several master tapes had also been placed beneath the earth in this period. Though Perry's wrath was not normally directed at Mascoll and his wife, the alcohol that Rudy was unable to stop Scratch from imbibing brought on a tirade at Dingwalls that resulted in a period of mutual avoidance between the couple and Scratch.

With his visa expiring and paperwork still unsecured, Scratch travelled on February 5 to New York, where he would spend a month working with Max Romeo and Lloyd 'Bullwackie' Barnes at Wackies' studio in New Jersey; he also recorded material at Coxsone Dodd's studio in New York. As Romeo noted, the original idea was for the pair to record the 'confrontation' album they had planned when Max was in London: 'The whole idea was to do an album, Max Romeo meets Lee Perry, I'm going to do one side of the album and he's going to do the other, but when he flew over to New York, the plans change: he ended up doing two albums for the company, and I end up doing one, which is *Transition* – he didn't really do anything else (on the album) other than be in the studio. By the time that session was done, that studio had to be re-painted; he was scrawling all over the bloody ceiling!'

Romeo and Perry collaborated on a couple of duets before devoting their energies to individual projects. A fresh version of 'Keep On Moving' was the most successful creation, and Wackies quickly issued it on a disco, complete with a toast by Major Irie. The pair also voiced 'Maccabee Version' – loosely interpreting elements of Romeo's early hit – which was included on the *Transition* album along with an alternative take of 'Keep On Moving'.

By the end of the month, the bulk of Scratch's album *Satan Kicked The Bucket* was complete. Its July 1988 release on Wackies in America and Overheat in Japan would reveal it as another strong album, perhaps not as memorable as *Time Boom*, but a competent issue nonetheless. The largely digital rhythms leant closer to the contemporary Jamaican dancehall sound, but were given a greater depth through the creative constructions of the

Wackies crew; the exception was 'Ooh La La', a money chant which resurrected the rhythm of 'Tight Spot'/'Revolution' (recorded at Randy's, though incorrectly listed as a Black Ark rhythm on the sleeve). Along with 'Keep On Moving', Scratch mutated a version of Marley's 'It's Alright', turned the Techniques' 'Love Is Not A Gamble' into 'One Horse Race', and re-visited themes of 'Grooving' on 'Bank to Bank', but the strongest tracks were pure originals like the title track (which contained another snipe at Island), the eerie 'Sweet Dreams', the soulful 'Day Should Turn To Night', and the positively freaky 'Bat Bat', in which Scratch announced he would shoot Margaret Thatcher with fuel from his rectum.

As Scratch left New York before the album's completion, he had little control over its general shape, and was largely not involved in the creation of its dub companion, *Satan's Dub*. Unused and poorly constructed tracks initiated at the sessions, on which Scratch's vocals are typically off-time and often out of key, would be cobbled together with alternative vocal takes of earlier tracks as the 1990 Rohit album *Message From Yard* – a poor execuse of a disc whose premise is perhaps best summed up by the song 'Money Me A Deal With'. The album had a few successful moments, such as a multi-voiced re-cut of 'The Joker', and certain tracks contained amusing lyrics (with bold statements such as 'I am the President: if you don't like that, drop dead' retaining a bitter humour), but the bulk of it is best described as filler material, marked by haste and sloppiness. A follow-up release on Tassa, *The Dub Messenger*, made further use of the same lousy out-takes by placing greater delay on Perry's substandard vocals.

A more positive musical endeavour to surface from Scratch's time at Wackies studio was his appearance on three tracks by Japanese dub combo Mute Beat. The group was led by trumpet player Kazufumi 'Echo' Kodama, an established figure on the Tokyo club scene of the early 1980s, who strove to incorporate reggae and jazz influences in his music. Born on January 29, 1955, in Fukui Prefecture, Kodama's first musical experience came through singing Christian hymns in his childhood. At age 13, he learned to play trumpet in a junior high-school band, and was playing in jazz and rock groups by age 15. In 1973, Kodama went to Tokyo with the intention of pursuing a career in music, but became more interested in art and decided to devote his creative energies to painting. It was not until the punk explosion of the late 1970s that Kodama became interested in music again, and exposure to alternative forms, including reggae, led him to pick up his trumpet once more, resulting in the formation of Mute Beat in 1982. It was just before the group's foundation that Kodama was exposed to the work of UK artists such as Matumbi, Linton Kwesi Johnson, UB40, and Ian Dury; this led to an enthusiasm for Jamaican originators including the Wailers, King Tubby, Augustus Pablo, the Skatalites, and Lee Perry, whose album *Super Ape* was the first Upsetter work the trumpet player encountered. Kodama found such music highly inspiring: 'I took reggae as the music of musics,' he explained. 'Discovering the instrumentals and dubs of reggae is just like discovering the horizon which I have been looking for but never found yet.'

Another key member of the group was talented drummer and programmer Gota Yashiki. Born in the village of Ayabe in February 1962, Yashiki gained classical drum training at the annual village rice-harvest festival in his youth; he was also exposed to Western pop music through the eight-track cassettes his father rented from the family restauarant and coffee shop. In 1979, Yashiki saw a televised broadcast of the Wailers' 1977 concert at London's Rainbow Theatre and was so stunned by the power of Carlton Barrett's drumming that he did not touch a drum for over a year, but when he moved to Kyoto in 1980 he decided to pick up his sticks again. He then moved to Tokyo in 1982 where he joined Rude Flower, a band playing cover versions of Latin music; he also became heavily influenced by dub music, particularly the work of King Tubby. After Kazufumi Kodama joined Rude Flower, he and Yashiki discussed their dissatisfaction with playing only cover versions of Western songs; they thus established Mute Beat to create original material by blending jazz and reggae influences with Oriental melodies.

As Mute Beat's popularity grew in the mid-1980s, Yashiki became involved with other projects. The group had been supporting hip hop/techno band Melon at Japan's largest nightclub, and Yashiki travelled to London with the band in 1985 to record an album for Sony Japan; he subsequently spent longer periods abroad, and had already begun producing other artists by the time of Mute Beat's 1988 collaboration with Scratch. He would eventually settle permanently in London, where he would help shape some of the biggest hits by artists such as Soul II Soul, Sinead O'Connor, and Simpy Red, as well as concentrating on solo work – though his departure from Mute Beat would hasten their eventual demise.

It was Bullwackie's connection with Overheat records in Japan that led to Perry's re-structuring of Mute Beat's material, re-worked with Bullwackie and Sonny 'Sabwackie' Ochiai at sessions for which Mute Beat were not present. Overheat president Shizuo Ishii – a major figure on the Japanese reggae and dub scene who would later manage Jamaican singer Thriller U – had the idea to release a Mute Beat dub album, and had gone to Jamaica with Mute Beat master tapes in September 1988 to arrange for tracks to be remixed by Fatman and King Tubby at Tuff Gong. In February 1988, Ishii sent more Mute Beat master tapes to Wackies studio for Scratch to remix; when Scratch heard the material, he immediately began to sing along with the backing tracks, and quickly voiced three of the rhythms.

The songs Perry created on the Mute Beat rhythms were very much on par with his other Wackies recordings; his largely ad-libbed vocals, though somewhat repetitive in places, gave a certain flair and panache to the group's strong rhythms, resulting in a highly satisfying combination. The most jazzy of the Mute Beat tracks, 'After The Rain', became the haunting 'Day Should Turn To Night', included on Perry's *Satan Kicked The Bucket* album; the slow skank of their 'Beat A Way' became the autobiographical 'Thread Mill Of Life', while an adaptation of Gershwin's 'Summer Time' ('Frozen Sun') was transformed to 'Yackety' through ad-libbed warbling aimed at Lionel Richie and the Clash.

The latter two tracks, remixed by Scratch and Bullwackie, were subsequently issued in May 1989 on *Mute Beat Dubwise* by Tachyon, along with the tracks mixed by Fatman and other tracks remixed by Mute Beat's live mixing engineer and percussionist Izumi 'Dub Master X' Miyazaki in Tokyo. The album led to a highly successful tour of America by Mute Beat the following September.

After the 1988 Bullwackie sessions, Lee Perry returned to London on March 3, glad to be away from New York, which had 'too much poverty people' for his liking. He spent a couple of weeks becoming re-adjusted to London life before returning to Matrix studio to work on the album he had left unfinished in 1987. He spent a couple of days re-working a few tracks, including the resurrected 'Time Marches On'; working on his birthday on March 20, he was joined in the studio by Sandra Cooley, her daughter Sharon, and the sleeping Cleopatra Perry. A few days later, he was joined in the studio by Adrian Sherwood, who was obviously back in Perry's good books. Sherwood was shortly to include a rocking Lee Perry track on the second of his *Pay it All Back* compilations: The previously recorded 'Train To Doomsville' (voiced on a 1984 Dub Syndicate rhythm called 'The Show Is Coming') had Scratch predicting the death of several record companies, including Trojan, Island, CBS, and EMI; the song also featured the voices of Emily and Zara Mascoll, young daughters of Rudy and Jennifer. An alternative cut of the rhythm was also voiced as 'Rolling Poland', a one-off recording made for Sherwood's friends Jurek and Wordek in Warsaw, early establishers of the Polish reggae scene; never given an official release, the track was broadcast by the pair on Polish radio.

Lee Perry spent much of May and June in Matrix studio, re-working and remixing his partially completed album with assistance from engineer Tom-Tom. It was basically finished at the end of June, but Scratch was unhappy with its mix; the unpaid bills he had chalked up at several studios made it difficult for him to continue with the work. He also had no real outlet on which to issue his material, and refused to entrust it to any other company, despite lacking the funds and drive to issue it himself; it thus remained unissued and was virtually abandoned from this time.

Lee Perry renewed his link with Steve Marshall in June, who assisted Scratch with several projects at Mark Angelo's studio. Scratch was requested to mix a track for a group called The Neighbourhood who had signed to EMI; after completing the task, he began recording material of his own at the premises. Marshall arranged a guest spot for Perry at a fund-raiser for Pyramid Arts, headlined at the Hackney Empire by African Headcharge on July 16; Scratch performed a version of 'Train To Doomsville' with Marshall's State of Emergency band, accompanied by a dance troupe led by Marshall's partner Debbie Baddoo. The boozed-up maestro also mumbled over an extended mix of 'War In A Babylon' that he had embellished at home with water sounds and various effects until an Empire assistant escorted him off stage.

In August, Perry returned to Mark Angelo's to record a number of fast-paced, hard-rocking tracks with Marshall and engineer/bassist Lindell Lewis. The lengthy 'Masters Of The Universe' utilised a cartoon soundtrack; its cluttered and heavily overdubbed beat was a platform for Scratch's baffling commentary. 'AD Vendetta' was more in the mode of straightforward rock, on which Scratch sang of the 'lady Upsetter' and an alligator; similar titles recorded at the same sessions include 'Teddy Bear', 'I Am God', and 'French Connection'.

Though Marshall and Perry met with executives from a major record label in September, nothing concrete came for the connection, prompting Marshall to cut 'Masters Of The Universe' and 'AD Vendetta' as an Arkwell disco, issued through Jet Star in February 1989; as with the other Arkwell releases, this disco was issued without much publicity or promotion, and was soon made unavailable.

On September 2, Marshall brought Perry to a low-key performance of a short-lived band called Mystery Train at a London pub called the Crown and Castle. The band was the new vehicle for Pete Holdsworth, former lead singer with the London Underground, and the keyboard player was the author of this book; Perry drew a mild inspiration from the music, and joined the band on stage to deliver some impromptu vocals.

September 1988 also saw Hurricane Gilbert give the island of Jamaica a severe battering, killing 45 and making half a million homeless. Worried his family had been affected, Lee and Sandra telephoned the next-door neighbour at Cardiff Crescent and spoke to his children, who were thankfully unhurt; a care package of items was duly assembled and dispatched.

Besides the commotion caused by Gilbert, much of the autumn of 1988 passed calmly, with Perry spending the majority of his time with Sandra, Cleo, and Sharon. However, there were times when he was beset by frustration, and would become uncommunicative; pacing around the house, he would murmur to himself or record cryptic statements on cassette. Sandra also continued to suffer from post-natal depression, and found it difficult to cope with Perry's moods; she was also too much in awe of him to insist he curb the mess he was making.

It was in this period that Lee Perry dictated the following proclamations, to be included in this book, which he initially wanted to be called *The End Of The Universe*:

I. HOT NEWS

This is an interview from Lee 'Scratch' Perry to the outerviewers of the modern world. The First World and the Second World live, but the Third World is finished because I, Lee 'Scratch' Perry, knows the head of the IMF – the IMF big boss, the Bank of England big boss, the Midland Bank big boss, the International Giro Bank big boss.

Mr Lee 'Scratch Westminster Bank' Perry is my new name. IMF must see I, is a compulsory, 'cause is me got the world paper money book that is missed upon the future – I lock it away in the past.

Hot news! World news, international news; it's not the Hot Plate label; it's Hot News label this time. Hot news! I, Lee 'Scratch' Perry is the King of the Jews. Hot news! Worldwide news message from Lee 'Scratch' Perry to the Third World: the First and Second World, King Alpha, and Queen Omega, live, but the Third World finish, so them better start feed on spinach like Popeye, because I, Mr Rainford Hugh Perry, own the sky, and all the bank must come and see I, 'cause it is I who work the SDI and hide the world paper money book, and zap the 100 cash index.

My stingray gun, sunshine supersun – sunshine supersun, my supergun. Time boom, X29; de Devil dead on cloud nine. IMF must call I, the Bank of England must call I, the Bank of Egypt must call I, and the Bank of India must call I, and the Swiss Bank must call I because I am the asset and I am the cassette, and I am the basket, and I am the boss kid Flash, the Sundance Kid; the Tree of Life, history life given, Mr Music.

Live and direct: rain check, air check, breeze check, lightning check, thunder check, brimstone check, and fire check, and blood and fire. Confidence of Rastafari: burning fire in the bush. Coosh coosh, push push. The Jungle Book, the Jungle King, the Jungle Lion, the Jungle Lord, the jungle yard; the graveyard, the cemetery, the grave; the box and the ghost in it. The death angels sing, angels flap their wings; the death angel sing the sweetest song I ever heard: Lee 'Scratch' Perry on the wire, Lee 'Scratch' Perry ball of fire.

De Devil dead, God live. De Devil Dead! God Live! God take and God give, God son and God save. X29, Master of Time; X29 Master of Time, Isaiah 9 from the Holy Book of Life, calling all his 300 wives, 900 concubines to powder his behind, and 144,000,000 angels from the Bird Laws Squad, with the Sea Bird Squad, the Jungle Squad, and the Jungle God.

The Third World drawn in. The game blocked; the road block, the lane block, and the street block, so who can't see good better see them eye specialist and take a good look upon the road. The road blocked; all roads are blocked.

This is a supernatural black magic spell from Lee 'Scratch' Perry, the Upsetter, that is done and it cannot be undone until Thy kingdom come, oh Lord, Rastafari.

I, Lee 'Scratch' Perry hold the key to the past, the present, and the future, 'cause I don't use gunmen to fight my war. I am the Duppy Air Ace Marshal; I run a Duppy Squad and it is legal. I am the boy of the Royal Air Force. When I clap my hand, duppy appear to me from coast to coast, flying through the night post and through keyholes. Sometimes they melt the key, if the key is in the keyhole, in a puff of smoke – Pffffffff . . .

When I cut a stench, it so loud that it bring up volcano lava, and is more dangerous than a hurricane, so beware: it liquidates cocaine, kill instantly, and take away pain – a painless killer.

I am a spirit, and I am a sleep walker, a sleep talker, a sleep flyer, and a sleep swimmer; they call me Mr Grimmer, the Grim Grim Grim Reaper, and his Desolation Angels of Destruction in a Babylon.

Mr Perry and his ganja gun that cannot be touched or conquered by the evil hand, 'cause my sword is Psalms 1, the holy hand, and Love Fire, writing on the wall of Babylon; Meanie Meanie Tekel.

Behold! I conquer Hell with my Merry Christmas bells. I am Santa and my toys; me and my reindeer, my rainbow and my sledge, and my pledge, my sea, and my bed, my box of fire on my head. I am Charles Atlas, with the world on my head, A to Zed.

Zebra say 'de Devil dead.' Cobra say 'de Devil dead.' Abba say 'de Devil dead'; robbers, don't touch my head because I am the triple red, the massive red, and I'm a walking, talking time boom. Once I was dead, but now I'm alive, and the light of the world is Jesus: sweet loving Jesus, massive Jesus, sexy Jesus: Cocksman Jesus, the Mighty Fucker; Jack Lightning, Pipecock Jackxon, President Abraham Lee 'Scratch' Perry.

Emperor Haile Selassie, the overthrower, exterminator, dissolver, executioner, TNT H-boom, boom Hell with a bad, bad spell called 'Poor People Rights'.

I pen tax, and I pen VATs. No more of that! No VATs, Third World rats! No more VAT and no more tax! Tax the rich, and tax the witch, Margaret Thatcher; they can afford it, poor people cannot afford it. Tax Reagan, behold pagan, who is a close resemblance to Satan, the old dragon from Hell bottom with his spell of dooms; Reagan the doom-maker, Thatcher the Queen-fighter. Thatcher who want to overthrow the Queen with her criminal government team . . . Ministers of crimes and governors of wrongs, killers of animals, and eaters of flesh, which is known as the cannibal (we call them the Cannibal Squad, name given unto them by God), scum of the Earth, blood suckers, cock suckers, and mother fuckers; wankers and skankers; robbers and thief. The big stealing from the small; the heathen face Paul. Paul John, the rougher don; Dandelion the King of Zion; piss the cramper, vampire slayer.

Vomit worm and shit maggot; old witch Margaret Thatcher, she vomit worm and shit maggot. I'll save the Queen and her country and see that you rot in Hell, old witch Margaret Thatcher from the FBI and the lady spy. I am the 'Spycatcher' the book write about; I catch spies with my eye and hand them over to the sky for a death sentence, life detention, an instant execution without mercy, without pity and without consideration. Instant execution of wrongs and declaration of rights.

Animal rights come first, not human rights, because we were all animals before we became humans on this planet Earth. If you don't believe me, ask the Earth, wind and fire, ice and snow, heat and cold weather; Mr P the weather bee.

God and the Seven Sea present the big breakdown; Hot Plate and Syncopate; cue plate and thumb plate, and tongue plate and hot plate; tongue fate, the fatal boom. I boom Death and I boom debts, and I bust bets and I win bets, and I sin Death, and I kill Death with my fate lock. I tick and I tock, and I open the lock, and I kill some cock with my Kryptonite rock.

X bank. Sell all you've got, Richie Rich, and give it to the poor, and take up your fuckin' ragged cross and follow me to Tombsville where I get my train, where I say 'Be still!'

I am the Hebrew king, executor of sin; Super-Chin from Castle Gray Bed; spooky Scratchy on Blueberry Hill, where I get my thrills, saying 'Be still' by skill. Say 'Hi' to the lovers of Christ and 'Bye' to the lovers of the Devil, 'cause I kill the Devil with my spiritual level MXR Armagideon war. Electric machine, computer man, the mighty Upsetter, the ghost in the machine. Mad Perry, lightning headmaster, breaker of doom, Dr Fu Manchu. Boom! Boom! Boom! Boom! Boom! Boom! Boom! Boom! This is a musical curse: blessed are the poor and cursed are the rich. Hick hick, hock hock, yak yak. It finish, yak yak.

II. THE RETURN OF THE GRIM REAPER

Back to our conversation with Mr President Abraham Rainford Hugh Perry: At last, Lee 'Scratch' Perry the Upsetter saying in a loud voice: repent, ministers of crimes, repent, governors of wrongs, and this is my brand-new song, coming from the sea and sun, Jamaica, the island in the sun. Emperor Haile Selassie I, lightning and thunder, hailstone, brimstone, and fire, music whirlwind, hurricane and tidal wave judgement; mixed by Earthquake, the ambassador, produced by Flood.

Jesus Christ's blood on the cross, while a piece of shit stuck in Moses' ass when he was writing the Ten Commandments, as well as in transfiguration of Jesus Christ on Mount Sinai, lightning flashing out of his eye, riding his white horse. Lightning, thunder, ball of fire, 1980 and 8 future; Mosiah Zodiac, the weather interpreter, Pipecock Jackxon, Jack Lightning, Jesse the Hammer, Magnetic Abajah Perry.

Push Bush alight, 'cause it is Lee 'Scratch' Perry who control all the American assets and world economic structure: The 100 cash index, all millions, trillions, zillions of dollars, and all millions, trillions, and billions in pounds hijack and kidnap by Jesus Christ – my sweet prick who piss, and rain come; shake his cock, and lightning flash; fart, and thunder roll. God, the

Upsetter, Him that sent I, music sceptre, Conquering Lion of the Tribe of Judah, Elect of God, Light of the World, Earth's rightful ruler, evil cooler, INRI.

I am the 'He' that sent I to scorch with lightning and burn with ball of fire, through the heart of this world, Selah. Selassie-I All, Ali-Kali-Eye. Seven seas and seven seal, Neptune world, nose code. I am the future – and all who doubt it, go and ask Satan: Lucifer, de Devil, Phantom Pluto, Lex Luthor, the arch-criminal from Krypton (Phantom Zone Jail), where he escape in a pail of shit by drinking acid and turning into mercury, in Oblivion, but I came and I saw and I conquer. I came to London, England, Britain, and conquered. I capture Lex Luthor with my teddy bear, my hair, and my invisible chair, and my 144,000 Mosquito Angels what sting with lightning, pssssst!

I am carrying a personal feeling for BBC radio and BBC television, because they fight against the truth. And that's why they don't want to play my records for the public, because they know my words are the truth that represent the true and living God's predictions of prophecy and things that must happen on Earth, written from Heaven by Moses' law: 'An eye for an eye, and a tooth for a tooth.'

I, Pipecock Jackxon, Jack Lightning, Jesse the Hammer, Lee 'Scratch' Perry (Perry Lee: £ for pound, $ for Scratch, and 'D' for Daniel Dandelion the Lion); Jah, Jehoviah, Jah Rastafari the Crumbler; black supremacy, black music; the ghost of King Arthur and his sword, Excalibur (the oath of the King: 'death before dishonour') put a curse on BBC radio and television, and BBC government, that they can never overcome or undo until they repent and start playing Mr Perry records morning, noon, night, and day, and around the clock – tick tock.

Tick tick toe. Big Ben de time clock is my headmaster. Together we interpret disaster for the popes, de deacons, and de pastor, for all who don't piss, shit and poop, and spit and fuck (makin' love like it is), hold up them hand and God will strike them with lightning, 'cause He know that they will be committing a sin, that their grandfather and grandmother did in the beginning, tempted by sin.

'I am the flying fish' says Scratch; prophecy by Bob Marley, the big fish's crotch, in 'Trench Town Rock', his first hit when he leave Scratch with Family Man and the lot. 'And the Lot's wife that turn a pillar of salt' says A to Zed. Heavy asphalt; aspects of dog mess, puss mess, all mess; rats, roaches, flies and lizard, frogs and mosquitoes, birds and bees, trees, dew water come from the sky, and water, and flowers, and plants by night.

Angels sing and God smile, for the angels sing the sweetest song God ever heard: Lee 'Scratch' Perry legalise ganja. De devil dead. Lee 'Scratch' Perry legalise Kali, internationally. Lee 'Scratch' Perry legalise ganja, universally. Lee 'Scratch' Perry legalise cannabis, and it globally. De devil dead. Kill it with lightning head.

17 million BC. Waterfall and water-rise. Tarzan and the Jungle survive. The Master is in full control. God never lose a war, and from the beginning, God was black like tar, and all who think God white, tell me what colour them think them shadow have. Stand up in the light, and they will see a shadow transfer from their body, and tell me what colour the shadow have, is it black or white?

Highty tighties, mighty mighties; Jah is mightier. Jah is wicked, wickeder than the wicked. Jah is strong, stronger than the strong. Jah is right, righter than the wrong. Jah is evil, eviller than the evils, 'cause it is He, Jah, who creates the good and evils, and it is He, Jah, who create the good and bad. Jah is cruel, crueller than the cruel. Jah is mean, meaner than the mean.

Jah Eenie Meanie Tekel nick hell riches, nick hell wealth, nick hell fortune, and nick hell fame; nick hell moneyum and cashum with opium, onion, garlics, scullion, and thyme. AD Vendetta, the Upsetter, riding the alligator as the Grim Reaper: Killer of thiefers, butcherer of traitors, exterminator of vampires, liquidator of robbers, and the exterminator of the IMF, and the liquidator of the rich, and presenter of the poor, for the rich shall be poorer, and the poor shall be richer. It is a switch connection, coming from Buddha, from Oblivion, where He sits in Infinity.

The great Ball-of-Fire, volcano lava. Marcus Garvey, God horse. Lightning and thunder, first class. The first aeroplane without engine, that president George Bush mention on television, this is it: it name Lightning and Thunder, God's riding horse. Garvey made it.

Black Moses, the honourable Marcus Garvey, the Prophet. Words that live for ever, the God incomparable words that bring rain from the sky, flash lightning, and roll thunder; that change the weather, and make the weather cry, whipping them from the sky with the Holy Mystic Eye. Thank God for Jesus Christ: Marijuana, Kali, ganja, tampy, lambsbread, sensimillia, black hash, rocky, time weed.

Tick cop, tut-tut cop. I am the mop who don't shoot; I chop, and who I don't run through with my sword, I slew them with my rod. At last, road map, A-Z. Haile must kill the Son of Light, Tree of Life, Book of Rules, Bag of Tools, Table of Stone. God on His throne in His rainwater rainbow crown: crowned by rights, crowned by nights, crowned by days, crowned by weeks, crowned by months, and crowned by years, crowned by breeze, and crowned by trees, crowned by air, and crowned by hair, and walking on an invisible chair.

Lee 'Scratch' Perry, the man who goes around with an invisible chair on his bottom (called Ethiopian swastika); the man who stick Hitler bomb and defuse it in them face, and defeat Hitler race, and put them to disgrace, and wipe them out of space with his drum and bass, guitar, piano and organ, horns, trumpet and trombone, baritone, tenor sax and alto sax; cricket and bats, Peter Piper and his pack of rats.

Washing machines, water pipe, tops, mops, fridges, freezers, Caesars, geezers. Gilders, yen, German marks, sterling; pounds and dollars, pence and pences, cents and senses; munch and munches, dime and dimes, half and quarters. Uncle Sam Sharp return with him harp, with ice and sickle, his hammer and pickle. Ashes to ashes, dust to dust; six foot six, and 666; Mixiplix.

This is a magic potion name VoomVATa, and it have a name BoomTax-a. Voom VATters and Boom Taxers. And as for you Locksers, repent, before I cut another stench and defuse thee with my shit-pipe, hot-pipe. Ha ha ha ha ha ha ha ha ha ha ha ha ha!

Voice of the Master, laughin' in the echo chamber. I repeat: I break the spell, and I undo what the wicked have done. I now turn the Table of Life, and make the rich poor and the poor rich. All that a rich man have will be taken away and given to the poor, and if them argue about it, we will shoot them in this full-scale glorious revolution of our Lord and Saviour, Jesus Christ.

Super Ape firmament; Ten Commandments. Death to liars. Death to heathens. Death to pagans. Death to vampires. Death to thief. Death to robbers. Death to rulers of sins and commanders of murders in cold blood. An eye for an eye, tooth for a tooth; that day gonna be a blood bath, soon.

Words from the Almighty: God in the Moon, Africa baboon, balloon man, Marcus Garvey (seven mile of Black Star Liners). Water and flood, blood fe blood, fire fe fire; thunder vex and slew de Devil in his Echoplex.

'The time has come,' says Elijah. Time Boom present the Return of the Grim Reaper: Death riding on a horse in the cloud with 144,000 Death Angels to conquer Egypt, and slew the first-born of every royal family. History repeat itself. The book is unfold, the mystery untold. Miracles by the score, with a natural mystic blowing through the air, and if you listen carefully, you will hear the news, and you will see the news.

BIG NEWS FLASH:
Lee 'Flash Gordon' Perry with the Kits of Life and the Key to the Future: heaven galaxy of stars, and Saturn, Jupiter, and Mars; Atlas A-Zed, Lee 'Scratch' Perry and the electric fire on his head say Merry Christmas, Happy New Year, De Devil dead, amen.

III. THE RETURN OF THE GOD OF THUNDER

Lee 'Scratch' Perry on the wire, with the Hammer of Justice, re-changed from a record producer to a newspaper editor and magazine expert. To establish the life of Lee Perry in this magazine called Upsetter magazine, I resign from the recording business. I don't want no part of it any more. It fill with grief, thief, robbers, scoundrels, heathens, pagans, vampires, and scum of the Earth.

Record business now becomes a pain and headache, stinkard and stink, a positive waste of time, waste of energy, waste of knowledge and waste of wisdom. It stinkier than shit, it ranker than piss. It's like dog vomit, a rat race, and a cut-throat affair in the dog-eat-dog world.

Thinking of the future, education comes first, so this is where I see my magazine could be a second episode of the great and mighty William Shakespeare, who write the Holy Bible, the Word of God that we are living on today, word of wisdom, knowledge and understanding. So I'd rather to waste my money in books, education to teach people knowledge than to waste it in recording industry to feed pagans and vampires, and entertain bad manners people. I refuse to do so any longer in the Year of Our Lord Nineteen Hundred and X29, Selah.

Selassie-I, His Majesty the Emperor of Ethiopia; lightning teleportation, a positive education. Ha ha ha ha ha ha ha! Life guarantee, cat collateral and security is education, not in music. Music is good to cheer the spirit up, but too much of it could distort your mind, and make you live in a World of Dream, of negativity, next to madness and a low profile where there is no way out. The only way out is Boot Hill or madhouse, or poorhouse, graveyard and cemetery. So see God before it's too late, or Judgement might catch up on you in the dancehall, or in the club, or in the pub (rubbin' dub where the mighty lightning flash and the mighty thunder roll), and all electric wire catch a fire, and the big blaze is on and the big panic start, and all the doors jammed – people runnin' to and fro, stampede in high speed; people climbin' over each other's back, heading for an exit that is jam-packed. 'Where will they run to?' says the Rock, the God of Lightning, Pipecock.

This vision is for the Wicked who deny God and say there is no God, and 'It won't be long, it will be soon' says the moon, the stars, the sun, the clouds, the rain, the rainbow, the birds; and the animal from the jungle that speak through the wind say, 'Vengeance is ours to take revenge, and the cannibals that eat our flesh . . . ' As for the bird hunters, it worse, and as for the animal killers, they get a permanent curse.

Catch a fire, vampires, and burn yourself out, but there is no antidote to remove the poison of the animal flesh from the cannibal's throat. Conquer-Worm from the Earth and Maggot-Flies soon sort them out and get even with them that kill the animals and shoot the birds for their selfish pleasures. 'Enjoy death,' says the dead birds and 'Enjoy death,' says the dead animal.

'The curse of the animals is on the cannibals, the curse that can be cured by no doctor, no scientists and no psychiatrists,' says Fire, Jahoviah, Jah Rastafari on the wire; Blabba Blabba, Abba Abba. Death to all robbers.

TEABREAK AND EARTHQUAKE, RATTLE AND SHAKE
Back to the truth, words from the root. Reggae music finish and diminish. Reggae music is a curse. It breed death and hatch cancer, and I Lee 'Scratch'

Perry say reggae music is no good. It breed bad men, it breed bad woman, it hatch gunmen. It creates violence, and encourage sin from deep within. It is the evillest music that ever come on the face of the planet Earth.

God turn his back on reggae music and said: 'I know it not, neither them that deal with it. It is a total destruction, and I have no lot that part with it.' The name itself is a doom, create by an evil scientist called Dr Doom, who live in an iron coffin; Death himself, in person. Reggae breed death, gangsters, gunmen, bad men, thief, liars, hypocrites and parasites, liars, robbers and dumb scull, nincompoop. It trigger off a violence so stink, stinkier than stink-boom.

Jesus Christ, Son of God, see it and ban it out of Earth planet, so I wonder what all the reggae singer, reggae producer, and the reggae artist going to do now that reggae finish. God don't like reggae music; he tell me, Lee 'Scratch' Perry, that in a dream, so all reggae music producers and all reggae artists doomed with reggae music.

Reggae music is a curse, the ultimate destruction. The reggae artists and producers, them so ugly and horrible-looking, that when decent people's children look upon the jacket sleeve, it give them nightmare for days and bad dreams to change the children them into horrible monsters and bad manners brats, look at that!

Logical Fox, solid-state logic. Words coming from my lip, words from my tongue of fire: Obadiah, the one and only chapter in the Bible; Obadiah I, who says reggae music is a curse, kill Bob Marley. It kill Peter Tosh, and Bunny Wailer is next to be wipe out by reggae music, according to History, Mystery, and Prophecy from Jerusalem school room.

Ancient King Solomon's tomb; Marcus Garvey, the man in the Moon. Seven Mile of Black Star Liner; Theocracy, Black Supremacy. Shit rule us all; Piss design it. Pisces the King Fish; Jack Lightning. President Abraham Rainford Hugh Perry, His Imperial Majesty Haile Selassie-I in the skies as the executioner.

Battle Axe, Small Axe, Dr Syntax, Professor Pentax; Olympius, the Slayer of VAT, who says 'No Poll Tax and no VAT for the VATicans who kill them own white men and impersonate Jesus Christ.' I am sure Jesus Christ is black, 'cause Jesus Christ is my sweet cock. Any girl I fuck, compulsory must say these words: 'Lord, Jesus Christ! Fuck me!' and when them discharge, them must say 'Oh God!'

Lee Perry says his music represent God, the living air, in my interpretation of poop, fart (also called stench), the Most High Stinky-Poo. It have nothing to do with reggae. The only reggae music I ever make is 'Punky Reggae Party'. My music is spiritual background: Heaven Churchical Order that bring rain and form flood, flash lightning, roll thunder, form earthquake, volcano lava, whirlwind, hurricane, tidal wave, heat wave, and bring hailstone from the sky, and form ice and snow at the wintertime.

My music represent Time, the Master Himself, 'cause I am the son of

Mother Nature, and I can destroy anybody I don't like just by lifting a finger, just by casting my spirited tarts telepathically, or using my X-Ray vision, John I.

Repent and be Baptised by water or you shall be burned by fire. Fire gun and fire boom; fire bass and fire drum; fire guitar and fire organ, 'cause I am the fire gorgon and I am de bull backer, and I am de Duppy Conqueror. I wrote them all, and I am the same John Paul.

My Father is the Sea and he is very salt and Peter, and dreader than dread, rougher than rough, tougher than tough, badder than bad, crueller than the cruel, wickeder than the wicked, eviller than the evil, madder than the mad, badder than the bad who slew King Pharaoh with the rod, who make Nebuchadnezzar the King of Babylon eat grass like a horse, and broke a stick in his ass, and kill de Devil with the iron cross.

Ha ha ha! We laugh. Everything wreck, everything finish, so we want to start over again. You have to start from Scratch, whether you like it or not. Who want to start have to start from Scratch, whether you like it or not, 'cause Scratch is the beginning and the end of all things. So I am lucky to have that name because I am Scratch, so who love Scratch will live, and who hate Scratch will die.

Words that fill the immortal sky, the Almighty Eye. Now as I live, I swear I will never tell a lie, neither lick molasses nor catch a fly, 'cause my eyes is the light, and the light is in my eye.

The moon, the stars, the sun, the clouds, the world, the globe, the universe, the equator, the galaxy, everything is in my eye. I kiss the Earth and thunder roll. This is the truth and nothing but the truth, so help me true and living God.

My bat-bat holy third eye, Cyclops: I've got three eyes, two on my face and one on my bottom: my bat-bat hole, the third eye, Cyclops. My head is the pillar of sky, and my two hands are fins that change into wings, because I am a Pisces, and I change into a bird and fly, change into an eagle, the flying fish.

*   *   *

Shortly after dictating the last of these utterances, Scratch renewed acquaintances with those he had cast aside. On October 23, he joined Mark Downie at the small Second Sense studio near Queensbury to toast over some fresh rhythms Downie had been constructing with a friend; he sang a version of Bob Dylan's 'Mighty Quinn' as 'Mighty Chin', and cut a fresh version of 'Keep On Moving' over a lone beat-box rhythm. He subsequently abandoned the project as Rudy Mascoll re-established contact after being approached by a noted reggae promoter called Simon who wanted Perry to share a Parisian bill with Dennis Brown on November 10 at the larger Mutalité; Mascoll convinced Scratch to commit to the performance, but did not mention Dennis Brown was on the bill as he feared Perry would refuse to perform before the dreadlocked singer. Another pick-up band was quickly assembled, composed of drummer Trevor Fagan, bassist Lenny Mead, guitarist G. Simpson, keyboardists Steve Kelly and G. Asing, plus saxophonist Lascelles James.

In the days leading up to Perry's return to France in November 1988, he and Rudy Mascoll went to Jet Star to see about some business. It was there that Lee Perry first met Mireille Campbell, a striking Swiss woman who had a peripheral involvement in the reggae industry and a rather colourful past.

Born Mireille Ruegg on November 30, 1959, she was an only child, born to a Swiss couple that ran a restaurant and guesthouse. Leaving school at 18, she planned to become a psychiatrist but could not endure the boredom of years of medical studies, and eventually obtained a counselling qualification after attending night school, but never practised as such. Instead, she began pursuing her interests in the paranormal and psychic and spiritual phenomena.

A love of reggae led to the subsequent establishment of the Fire Music record shop and booking agency in Zürich – later known as Lion Star promotions. She began to spend an increasing amount of time in Jamaica, where she eventually bought a house in Montego Bay.

In 1983, a Jamaican fathered her first child, Collette, and moved with her to Switzerland; however, the relationship broke down after Mireille had an affair with Max Romeo, whose Swiss concerts she had organised and promoted. In 1987, she married a certain Mr Campbell,[6] who fathered a son named Noel the same year, but the relationship faltered while Noel was still an infant and the couple went their separate ways. In this period, Mireille began working with Michael Hesemann, a German expert on UFOs and publisher of the magazine *2000*; she assisted with distribution of his publications and audio cassettes, helped arrange their international conferences and organised trips to Egypt for UFO enthusiasts, in addition to her music promotions. She also established the Institute for Humanistic Therapies in Zürich, which employed a healer and two assistants specialising in the alternative practices of rebirth therapy, body massage and shiatsu.

Mireille Campbell and Rudy Mascoll had worked together on several occasions in the 1980s, as Misty in Roots, Max Romeo, and Jennifer Romeo had previously performed at Swiss concerts Campbell had organised – all of which involved Mascoll's co-ordination and assistance.

When Mireille stumbled upon Lee Perry and Rudy Mascoll in Jet Star, she was buying stock for her record shop and initiating an upcoming tour with Dennis Brown. She recalled the memorable details of this brief first meeting: 'I always liked Lee "Scratch" Perry's voice, but I didn't really check who he is and what he is. When my first two children were very small, there was this album *Time Boom* and they used to love the song "Jungle", they always used to sing along when I play that song in the car. When I was in Jet Star to buy records wholesale and organise this Dennis Brown tour, I was with some dreads who work with me, and they introduced me to Lee; he was wearing a little red plastic coat with a black collar – something funny, like an imitation fur, and he had a little toy radio in his hand. I said my name and he gave me his hand, and then he hold my hand by saying "Hello" at least for about three minutes. I said "Eh? What is this?" but that was it; they asked me if I was interested to book a tour with him, but I said I have to finish the other one first.'

Lee Perry found their initial meeting quite intoxicating, though neither party was then aware of the important role she would subsequently come to play in his life.

A few days later, Scratch and his band travelled to Paris. At Heathrow Airport, he was surprised to see Dennis Brown stepping onto the same aeroplane, but quickly engaged in friendly banter with the singer; Mascoll's fears of potential animosity were revealed to be entirely unfounded.

Perry's pre-performance nerves saw his usual excess of drinking; his tipsy set contained the usual mix of *Time Boom* and *Roast Fish* material, plus versions of 'Duppy Conqueror', 'Keep On Moving', and the surprise of the evening, Millie Small's 'My Boy Lollipop', delivered in a tortured wail.

On his return from this performance, Perry experienced more immigration problems. He was again interrogated at the airport, where he was reminded that there were certain procedures he had not complied with; he was initially denied entry, forcing Sandra Cooley to appear in person to plead for his release. 'I had to go and explain to them I needed him to come in because I was on anti-depressants for post-natal depression as things were getting to me then,' she recounted. 'For a while, he got a reprieve but he had to go back out. A friend of mine drove me up there, and on the way back Lee was saying to everybody how we were going to have a big wedding . . . '

With no right to remain in Britain, Lee Perry thus returned to Jamaica in late November 1988, with the original intention of returning to England within a couple of weeks; once in Jamaica, other paths would be taken by the Upsetter, and this departure would mark the end of his residence in Britain.

THE SECRET LABORATORY:

A Base in Switzerland

Lee Perry returned to Jamaica just as the winds of change were blowing towards the island again. Seaga's nine years as Prime Minister had practically obliterated any sense of optimism left in the country at the start of the decade through the implementation of a series of restrictive policies that proved more disastrous than Manley's naïve Democratic Socialism; CIA-ga's pandering to the Reagan administration saw the country controlled by the wishes of Uncle Sam, and the weight of the hefty loans secured from the IMF was more than the country's faltering economy could bear. Worse still was the culture of fear and anarchy propagated by the former 'enforcers' of party loyalty, who now controlled massive international networks overseeing the production and distribution of crack cocaine. The widespread availability of the highly addictive drug saw negative changes sweeping across Jamaican society: young people were blowing their minds by smoking the combustible coke derivative, and street wars were erupting over control of its sale; likewise, Jamaican music was now driven by a harsh, aggressive beat, with lyrics often glorifying the violence of the drug 'posses' and the 'Dons' who headed them.

Somehow, Scratch managed to be absent from Jamaica for much of Seaga's reign; when he came to England at the end of 1984, the first of a series of major strikes was about to be waged in protest at Seaga's policies, which would see more than half the island's populace living below the poverty line. By the start of 1989, the people of Jamaica were thoroughly disgusted by the failed rhetoric of 'Seaganomics', and returned the PNP to power after a surprisingly peaceful election on February 9.

Scratch experienced mixed emotions on his initial return to Jamaica. He was surprised to find how good it was to be there, and how natural it felt to be in such familiar surroundings – despite a lack of available funds that saw the electricity and water supply disconnected at Cardiff Crescent. He found himself feeling reluctant to return to London, though his home life in Kingston was far from conflict-free, with various elements contributing to tension, despite the pleasure his children expressed on his return.

Vicky Nelson had been true to her word and stuck by Marsha until she completed her course the previous June, but had eventually left Cardiff Crescent for a new home at 25½ Constant Spring Road, from which she ran a restaurant; Marsha also lived at the property for a period, and assisted Vicky in the running of the place. Although Marsha obtained high marks in most subjects at Fitz Henley's Institute, a low grade in maths prevented her from graduating fully, and she would eventually join her sister in turning to hairdressing as a main source of income. Once she learned that Scratch was back at Cardiff Crescent, Marsha spent a few solid weeks with her father, cooking for him and making sure his clothes were clean.

His sons Sean and Omar were still living at Cardiff Crescent with their uncle P-Son; they had plans to break into the music business and had begun to videotape weddings and sound system dances with borrowed equipment. Sean had a daughter named Nakeesha, born on February 19, 1987; though his relationship with the child's mother did not last, they remained friends and he often spent time with his daughter, who lived nearby.

Though Marsha and the boys were on fairly good terms with their father on this visit, receiving a fair amount of positive feedback, each held their own unvoiced resentments that would later erupt without warning. The most direct confrontation arose between Scratch and Michelle, the daughter he adopted as a baby but virtually disowned as a teenager. She now had a second young son, Lauren 'Buzz' Campbell, from her partner Wayne, of whom Scratch so disapproved. Michelle herself held bitterness towards her surrogate father for his unfair treatment of her once he split with her mother, but her very face reminded the Upsetter of Pauline's betrayal, and he found it difficult to be around her. Harsh words were eventually exchanged at the house, culminating in his demand that she leave the premises as she was not of his flesh and blood.

Though Perry's original plan was to stay in Jamaica for a couple of weeks, arrange for the proper paperwork and return to London, time passed quickly for him on the island, where he found himself to be surprisingly content, despite the above domestic incident. As there was no phone at Cardiff Crescent, he asked Sandra Cooley to telephone his neighbour once a week so they could discuss the progress his legal representative was making with the necessary formalities, and to determine when Perry would be able to return. When the legal process proved slow and cumbersome, Scratch suggested Sandra Cooley come to Jamaica, but her fear of flying meant she never made the journey, despite an offer from Perry that tickets be sent for a friend to accompany her on the aircraft. In later conversations, Perry's vagueness hinted at a rising indecisiveness as he fell back into the Jamaican way of life. Scratch again felt himself to be living out what was destined, and was watching for the signs of divine intervention for deliverance.

Soon after Lee Perry returned to Jamaica, he found Coxsone Dodd on the island, and began voicing more of Dodd's rhythms at Brentford Road; dozens of tracks are said to have been voiced at this time, possibly as many as 40. Ned Willacy related the following particulars about certain sessions:

'Myself and his two sons went to studio, they was supposed to do harmony. At that time Mr Dodd and Perry decided they were going to revive the music business because it was kind of going down and they wanted a new lieges, so we decided to use some old rhythms with new lyrics to make an uprising for the music. We did a number of songs for an All Star (release), with Tony (Brevett) of the Melodians and a brother that was there with Scratch. "Mighty King, Reveal Yourself", myself and Scratch did that together as a duet but it never came out.'

It was in the midst of these sessions in February 1989 that Scratch received an unexpected visitor at Cardiff Crescent: Mireille Campbell, who had returned to Jamaica to finalise arrangements for Dennis Brown's European tour. When she heard that Scratch was in town, Campbell experienced a powerful compulsion to visit him, but found it difficult to find anyone willing to take her to his address. 'From the moment I heard he was in Jamaica I get a feeling I have to go to see him, but it took me about ten days because everyone was afraid. They were all saying he has broken bottles on his gate and a TV on the roof, and I should not go there because he is crazy. Finally I had three dreads in the car and I was driving, and one guy who used to hang out on the corner by that record shop on Parade decide he's going to take us there. We went to his house and he came out of the gates and said to the guys, "Oh, come out," and they said, "No, no!" and locked the car door! I came up and he said he was telling people in England to get in touch with me; he said he was waiting on me.'

As the dreads drove off, Lee Perry escorted Mireille to the inner courtyard of his home, where she took a seat on the low cement wall to the right of the property. She was startled by the mess and chaos of the place, but had a positive interaction with Perry and his children nonetheless. 'Those times he had a lot of pigeons in a cage, everything was messy and his shorts and T-shirt were full of holes. The three kids came and was very pleasant, but said they are suffering: they have nothing to eat and their father doesn't give them no money.'

As the hours passed and the evening came, Lee Perry had something to show Mireille, which they both accorded a minor mystical significance. 'I had a white miniskirt on and a belt, both with yellow stars on them. In the evening, Lee said "Come, let me show you something," and take me in his bedroom. He pulled away the bed and show me a poster of Princess Diana, with a yellow crown in white clothes with some white stars, and there was a bow and arrow on top of it (the symbol of the Sagittarius zodiac sign). He said "What is your sign?" and I said, "Sagittarius." Then he said, "Look here," and on the wall was written "SOS, calling for help." He said "What? Sagittarius? I was expecting a Sagittarius, but I never know it was a woman!" '

When Campbell's friends returned to bring her back to the Pegasus Hotel, Perry asked her to clarify exactly why she had come to see him. 'He said, "What do you really want?" and I said, "I just have a feeling I should come, and

I don't know nothing about your life, but actually I want to be involved in everything that you do." He said "Yes, really? Sure, arrange it!" I said "OK, I can make a management contract by my lawyer," and he said "Write anything you want to write and I'll sign it." '

The next day, Perry accompanied Mireille Campbell to the offices of noted music lawyer Lloyd Stanbury, and had a management and personal contract written up that would renew itself every three years; Perry agreed to grant Mireille 20% of his business gains, and allowed her to take charge of all proposed future projects and engagements.

Once the contracts had been signed, Mireille came back to Cardiff Crescent to spend the evening smoking weed and talking. She was supposed to attend a party with Yellowman, but changed her plans when Scratch initiated amorous activity; the couple thus retreated to the luxurious privacy of the Pegasus where they spent the first of many passionate nights together.

In the morning, Campbell bought Perry a new wardrobe; returning to Cardiff Crescent, she made a list of clothing items to buy for his three offspring. Some days later, she returned to the property she owned in Montego Bay, making arrangements for Scratch to join her shortly after. But when Perry arrived at the property, he found Mireille in the company of another man – a musician she had met at a hotel in Barbados on a recent holiday with her two children. Though the man intended to marry Mireille, and was making arrangements to join her in Switzerland, Scratch made his intentions perfectly clear and had the man ejected from the bedroom – initially to the guest room, and shortly after, out of the property.

For the next few months, Lee Perry and Mireille Campbell were inseparable in Jamaica. Towards the end of their time on the island, they went swimming with Mireille's children in the dramatic setting of Joseph's Cave in Negril, where a diver found a starfish while searching for Mireille's misplaced sunglasses; Scratch took it as a sign and presented Campbell with a serious request: 'You have to give something to get something, so let's make a baby.'

As had already been hinted at their first meeting in London, the chemistry between the couple was as exceptional as it was immediate. From their first carnal union in Jamaica, Lee Perry was entirely smitten; the child they conceived in Negril further solidified what would prove to be the most lasting of his post-Ark relationships. After basking in the new-found glory of their budding love, he then accompanied her to Switzerland in May, beginning a most enchanted phase of existence in another foreign land.

Mireille was accustomed to extravagance, and made a point of living life to the fullest. She had a large property overlooking Lake Zürich in an exclusive suburb of the capital known as the Goldküste, or Millionaire's Row; her live-in servant Weetus kept the place clean, looked after the kids, and made sure the family and their dog Schatzi were well fed, while her Jamaican bodyguard Bobby ran errands for her and made sure her business ran smoothly. She had a large Jeep in which to get around, and plenty of attractive friends; she also had a cellar that she eventually allowed Scratch to use for his Secret Laboratory – a space he began referring to as the Blue Ark after decorating it with blue paint.

The life Lee Perry came to in Switzerland brought shape to the dreams he had long been discussing with his magic genie, Eenie Meanie Tekel. There was the elusive wealth that had so long been denied him, the great sex that he could never get enough of, and the peace and tranquillity that had been so hard to find. In London, as in Kingston, he had been surrounded by disrespectful greedy people who meddled in his affairs, trying to run his life. Such tense, unhealthy atmospheres brought on destructive behaviour, as the demons he was haunted by drove him to drink. On the contrary, the Goldküste was far removed from the madding crowds of most capital cities, and was entirely devoid of music-business personnel with their disheartening attitudes. Most notably, Mireille managed to wean him off alcohol, bringing a dramatic change to his countenance; she also encouraged him to change his diet, and he eventually became semi-vegetarian. Though he missed his young daughter Cleopatra, there was no question of returning to life with Sandra in London – his new life in Zürich with Mireille Campbell was just too good to give up.

Though they may outwardly have seemed an odd couple, the inward connection between Scratch and Mireille was very strong, and their temperaments and tastes had overlapping elements. She was an ardent herb smoker, and shared Perry's strong belief in UFOs and life on other planets; she was against taxation, rejected conformity, and held an individual view of spirituality. Perry also adored her two children, and referred to them as angels in the literal sense; he had long discussions with Collette about a 'money tree' that grew currency, and loved to chase Noel around the garden.

In the summer of 1989, Scratch and Mireille came to London to organise some of the chaotic affairs he had left behind. In late July, he was back in the Ariwa studio with Akabu, having another go at 'Small Axe', but the track was not completed properly and still remains unreleased. He broached the topic of the material he had cut with Professor in Peckham, but the Ariwa boss was evasive, and nothing concrete was arranged; a number of other record companies were approached on this visit without the desired results.

There was also an inevitable confrontation with Sandra Cooley, who received an unpleasant shock one evening when Scratch and Mireille appeared at Waghorn Road to collect a few of Perry's possessions. Having been unable to reach him in Jamaica for several weeks, she already suspected that Lee had become involved with someone else, but the reality of the couple's fleeting visit filled her with despair. 'I got this phone call at my mum's saying he'd be arriving at about 7.30, so I thought "He's coming home!"; the house was clean and there was a meal under way. The last couple of months I couldn't get a hold of him, they said he was at the studio, which was a way of being polite. The phone bill was nearly £800, so I said to one of the boys, "Tell your dad if he isn't there on Friday, this is the last time I will ever be phoning, because I'm not in the habit of chasing people." He was only meant to be gone two weeks, and I had said to him, "If you've met somebody, tell me." It turns out he was at Mireille's house, apparently they'd been together about three months. He didn't say much at all; I said "Come and see the child," he hadn't seen her for eight months. Mireille come marching up the stairs like it was her house, and I said, "What the hell do you think you're doing, who do you think you are? You're carrying on like you're his woman." That's when she dropped the bombshell: "I am his woman!" My jaw hit the floor, "What the hell is going on here? If I'd have known about this situation, you'd have come through the door, I'd have offered you a cup of tea, it would have been fine." I think he was a bit taken aback by my reaction, but I think he was also a bit shocked to come back and find that everything was exactly as he left it.'

Their business in London completed, Lee Perry and Mireille Campbell returned to Zürich just as the Mad Professor was preparing to issue *Mystic Warrior* and its obligatory dub companion, entirely mixed by Professor. A few months after the albums were released, Professor and his wife visited Perry in Zürich on their way to a holiday in Neuchâtel. 'By that time he had moved to Switzerland. I thought, "I'm sitting on this stuff, I need to change the direction," so I brought up the concept and decided to put it out swift. He hear about the album and gave me his address, so I went there with my wife to give him some money, and from then on, whenever I see him I fix him up with more money. I think at that time we had sold a few thousand copies, and he got £1500; we've got standard royalty rates, it works out about eight per cent retail.'

Scratch later noted he was unhappy about the release, which he felt was incomplete and required many changes, though he was pleased to receive Professor's payment for the work.

'He is another man who is trying to hustle as usual, because we done (those tracks) when I was a little bit addicted to alcohol, so I didn't take advantage of it because I know that them tape not ready to put out. I ask him to give me (them) back and him play sick the day and disappear, him wait 'til me leave England and go and put it out. The people them love it but it no done yet, but it's all right, him can't spoil my name.' [1]

Though *Mystic Warrior* was thus somewhat unauthorised, it was a fair sight better than a number of other albums issued that year which bore Perry's name but had nothing to do with him, and from which he received no reward. Such releases are many and varied, and had dogged him on a number of occasions in the past, beginning with *The Good, The Bad And The Upsetters* in 1970 and furthered in 1980 by the Bunny Lee production *Val Bennett and the Upsetters*, issued by Carl's records in New York, and by *King Tubby Upset the Upsetter*, a collection of non-Perry dubs compiled by Count Shelley.

Once Perry was out of the UK in 1989, many unauthorised collections of his earlier product began to be issued, mostly without his knowledge or agreement and for which he was typically not paid – though some money was occasionally put forward at a later date when Perry confronted those responsible in person. Such practices would continue unabated through the 1990s, often with product that beggars belief.

Material that surfaced in 1989 included several new Trojan collections, Seven Leaves' *Excaliburman*, and *Magnetic Mirror Master Mix* and *Turn And Fire*, two albums issued by Henk Targowski on his new Anachron label. The one to anger Scratch the most was *All The Hits*, a Rohit collection of late '60s and early '70s material, licensed to the company by Bunny Lee, who had acquired a number of Perry's master tapes; the release subsequently appeared as *News Flash* on Enzo Hamilton's Esoldun label .

In June, word reached Scratch and Mireille that Coxsone was planning to cut some of the material the Upsetter had voiced with him in Jamaica and New York. As the tracks were unfinished and controlled entirely by Dodd, Scratch sought to block the release, which did not appear beneficial. His legal representative Lloyd Stanbury thus arranged a public press conference at the Pegasus Hotel at which Scratch threatened Dodd with litigation; the project was therefore temporarily halted due to negative publicity generated by the Jamaican media.

Among the more questionable material cut in England in 1989 were several collections of Channel One dubs by the Revolutionaries, mislabelled as Perry material, including Jah Whoosh's *Sensi Dub 1 and 2*. *Blood Vapour*, issued by Laurel Aitken from master tapes Mike Brooks obtained from Jah Lloyd, had more late '70s Revolutionaries dubs from Channel One; many of the tracks had previously been issued in a different form as *Goldmine Dub*, mixed by Prince Jammy. Brooks would later concede that the album was packaged misleadingly, as Scratch did not oversee the recording or mixing of many tracks, but continues to insist that Perry was involved in some of the initial recording sessions from which these dubs were taken. He also said some of the Channel One dubs from the set were mixed down by Perry at the Black Ark, though he admitted the entire album was remixed in the UK before release. The album was also re-pressed in 1993 by Rhino as *Hold Of Death* with bonus tracks from an early '80s Sly and Robbie session, recorded without Perry's involvement.

The worst offender for falsely labelled product in 1989 was definitely Phil Pratt, who attempted to pre-empt Perry's Ariwa material by issuing two volumes of *Lee Perry Meets The Mad Professor In Dub* on his Angella label – albums that featured the work of neither Perry nor the Mad Professor, and which were later re-issued in various forms by a number of other companies (including Esoldun in France and the UK's Orange Street; Delta Music's despicable 1997 low-budget issue, *A Serious Dub*, added insult to injury through the use of pirated photographs and near-plagiarised liner notes).

'That is a fiction,' Pratt later said of the material. 'Scratch never have nothing to do with it, neither Professor. Those were the people who were selling, so in order to survive, that's what I did. I made them here at Easy Street with Drummie (Angus Gaye) from Aswad, the bass from Aswad (Tony "Gad" Robinson), and Bubblers (keyboardist Carlton Ogilvie). Professor was angry, but Scratch, we have an understanding: We have to survive.'

Professor noted that his confrontation with Pratt had little result. 'He just shrug his shoulders and say, "People have to eat bread." It's the kind of thing Pratt and Bunny Lee do to wind up the opposition.' Unable to get Pratt to take his falsely titled product off the market, Professor was forced to label *Mystic Warrior* as 'The only genuine' release. Pratt later issued two further dubious collections as *Lee Perry Meets King Tubby In Dub Confrontation*, supposedly recorded by Scratch and Tubby at the Black Ark in Kingston between 1986 and 1988 – an impossibility, given that the Black Ark was ruined and that Perry was resident in the UK. These discs formed part of the flood of questionable issues cut in King Tubby's name after the mixer's brutal murder at his Kingston home in February 1989.

Once Scratch was settled in Zürich, he began hankering to create new music, but had no network of studios or musicians to draw from, unlike those he was solidly connected to in Kingston, London, and New York. To find some sort of link and instigate an outlet for his musical aspirations, Mireille Campbell sought advice from Marc 'Nof-Nof' Tortchaninoff in Neuchâtel, the first promoter of reggae music in Switzerland; Campbell met him during Prince Far I's European tour of 1982. Promoting reggae since 1978, Nof-Nof had contacts with many musicians in Switzerland; he was the first to bring Steel Pulse, Sly and Robbie, and Rico Rodriguez to the nation, and was involved in the concert that resulted in Dennis Brown's acclaimed album *Live In Montreux*.

Scratch and Mireille thus came to Neuchâtel to meet with Nof-Nof and discuss a proposed European tour; he suggested Perry use the Zürich-based Ganglords band, but Perry was unhappy with the group and turned them away. Nof-Nof also mentioned a friend called Fizzè who had a studio in the village of Jenins, and his description of the musician's open-mindedness and avant-garde approach sparked Perry's interest. Fizzè was duly summoned to Zürich in July, and Scratch was pleased by his easy-going manner; he thus arranged to work at the studio shortly after, and made his first journey to Jenins in early August.

Fizzè had a great deal of musical experience behind him, stretching long before his first meeting with Lee Perry. He was born Victor de Bros in Basel on September 4, 1952, the youngest of seven children born to a chemical-industry public-relations clerk and his pianist wife; his nickname Fizzè is a corruption of the pronunciation of Victor in the dialect of the Berne region.

Fizzè had been tutored by American blues pianist Eddie Boyd, opened

Neuchâtel's Jazzland club and record shop in 1976, and became involved with avant-garde group Débile Menthol in the early '80s; their drummer, Gilles 'Dizzi' Rieder, has provided him with a lasting, collaborative alter ego. In 1986, Fizzè issued his debut *Kulu Hatha Mamnua* album on the Mensch Music label, followed by *Manœuvres D'Automne*. Work with a Swiss reggae group called the Heart Beat Band prompted Fizzè to travel to Jamaica in late 1987, where he proposed that trombonist Rico Rodriguez come to Switzerland to collaborate with the group. In April 1988, Fizzè arranged for Rico to travel to Zürich, while he stayed in Kingston to alter Swiss rhythm tracks at Music Works studio with Dean Fraser, Robbie Shakespeare, and Scully – the first of several such sessions that Fizzè would arrange on the island for his *Peeni Waali* project. Back in Switzerland, Fizzè began working with dub poet Linton Kwesi Johnson and Dennis Bovell, with whom he has enjoyed a long working relationship and close friendship. In April 1989, Fizzè altered his material further in Kingston with Horsemouth, Deadley Headley, and others.

When Lee Perry and Mireille Campbell first made the hour's drive to the Mensch House in Jenins at the beginning of August 1989, Fizzè was in the midst of re-working these skeletal tracks for eventual inclusion on *Peeni Waali*. Fizzè lived alone in a large, comfortable house, and gave Scratch the opportunity to occupy a guest room; Perry thus spent the greater part of the month in the studio, going home for a few days each week to take a break from the work and spend time with his new family. Scratch eventually became so accustomed to the journey that he travelled to the studio alone by train, making his way to the premises while Fizzè was out.

By the end of the month, Fizzè and Scratch had built ten tracks using largely mechanical rhythms; the vocals were delivered in Perry's raving, stream-of-consciousness style, often multi-tracked, and seemingly about whatever came into his head at the time. Highlights from the sessions include a love/sex chant built around the phrase 'I Am The Dub Machine', and an impenetrable rant called 'I Am The Government'; another track, 'The Party', threw more rhyming abuse at the Pope.

Fizzè recalled some particulars about the sessions, which he noted were loose, unstructured and largely unplanned: 'It was a rhythm box and a little percussion and loads of overdubs: percussion and samples of animals and machine guns. He was just working, then after a while he would say "'Give me another track." It was one 30-minute reel that just went on; Scratch was not working on a concept.'

Though most of these sessions went smoothly, Fizzè noted that Perry's mystifying behaviour could also be trying at times. He insisted that a microphone be placed outdoors to record the sounds of the country while they were working, and when Fizzè protested that the equipment would get wet, Scratch built a little 'shaman's hut' for the implement; he would also roll around on the ground for no apparent reason, and pissed in empty bottles of the beer-like Rivela, which he placed at strategic points around the studio. 'I think he's a big con man, a big jester,' Fizzè surmised. 'He would always take a probe at me and check out just how much I would go for it. Sometimes he would squeeze orange juice over the electric plugs, so I said "Hey, I don't want no pop star fried in here"; I was very provocative with him, so of course we got along.'

In the middle of August, Linton Kwesi Johnson returned to Fizzè's studio, where he had worked the previous January. He spent some thoughtful days in the tranquillity of Jenins, constructing rough demos with Fizzè of material he was to re-record for the *T'ings And Time* album. As Johnson had much admiration for Scratch, Fizzè contacted Mireille to request that Perry join them in the studio, where they had another brief exchange – though Scratch was apparently reluctant to acknowledge their previous meeting. 'When I was re-introduced to him by Victor, he sort of acted as if he didn't know who I was,' Johnson noted, 'so I started to sing "Jane Ann a who pick the pumpkin", and he said, "Oh, that's why them call you Crazy Johnson, you remember me before I do." '

By the end of the month, Scratch was basically finished with the ten tracks he had created with Fizzè; in his own words, the material was 'nothing serious'. Before exiting the Mensch House, he gave a more successful voicing to one of Fizzè's previous creations, after awakening early one Sunday morning with a craving for something to puff. 'At six in the morning he wake me and say, "Victor, give me something to smoke now." Luckily I knew someone right here, close to Liechtenstein where I live, so we got a piece and on the way back home I explained what Liechtenstein is, the smallest country, and I did a little detour just to show him the place; I explained that everyone's been stashing their money there. When we came back he said 'Let me voice a track for you now,' so I brought out the track ("C'est loin" from *Manœuvres D'Automne*) and he voiced it.'

Having heeded Fizzè's driving commentary, Scratch voiced what would later be issued as 'Licht & Stein,' a comical, half-sung chant about Franken-stein stashing his cash in Liechtenstein over a rhythm that was stripped down to the balafon patterns at its base. The song would be left untouched for quite some time, though it would later undergo a metamorphosis and eventually became part of the *Peeni Waali* project.

In September, Scratch returned to Zürich, taking his master tapes with him and leaving Fizzè only with 'Licht & Stein'; Scratch never issued any of the material he recorded there and is reported to have buried the master tapes in his garden at the Goldküste. A gig was scheduled at the Mutualité in Paris for November 25, but was later cancelled; though he was planning a European tour for the following spring, he began to speak of retiring from the music business, seeking a life of tranquillity through creating art that would not involve music any longer. At the end of the year, he telephoned Fizzè with a command that none of his product be released, but not because of retirement: he had just signed a new album contract with Island Records and was mindful of breaking its restrictions.

Lee Perry spent much of the 1980s swearing vengeance on Island, predicting the label's downfall, and hurling insults at its staff. He also issued a number of defamatory statements against Adrian Sherwood in the aftermath of the *Time Boom* release. It may thus seem surprising that Lee Perry returned to London towards the end of 1989 to voice a second album with Adrian Sherwood, to be issued the following year by Island's Mango subsidiary, but those close to the man may recognise such actions as totally in keeping with his logic. Perry has eventually fallen out with the majority of those he has worked with, but he is capable of making amends if the offending party demonstrates their loyalty. He has also been known to swallow pride if the price is right, and has occasionally been swayed by popular opinion. Perry later indicated that the latter element greatly influenced his decision in this instance, though Sherwood's direct and upfront approach must also have made the project seem less daunting.

Though the resultant *From The Secret Laboratory* had a greater complexity than *Time Boom*, it was perhaps also somewhat more disjointed. Several of the rhythm tracks had been built at Kingston's Mixing Lab by Style Scott with Flabba Holt, Binghi Bunny and Steely; others were constructed by Sherwood and company at the Manor in Oxford and London's Matrix studio, lending a varied and perhaps unbalanced feeling to the set. Ultimately, time constraints saw limitations placed on Perry's vocal delivery, which Sherwood noted was due to the low budget afforded the project. 'Island were saying to us the budget is very small, so we did the voicing, overdubbing, and mixing of that album in eight days. Scratch was pissed off with me because we hadn't finished it; I'm getting all the gyp but I actually only got paid a £2,200 Akai sampler for producing that album and giving it to Island, that was it – and David Harrow ended up getting the sampler!'

Despite such drawbacks, the combination of Sherwood's imaginative On-U melange and Scratch's off-the-wall ad-libbing again resulted in unusual successes, with both artists reaching into previously unexplored territory. There were moments closer to the current Jamaican dancehall sound than anything either had ever recorded, most notably the exceptionally executed title track and the rocky 'You Thought I Was Dead', in which Scratch castigated Michael Manley, Edward Seaga, and others who had shown him disrespect. Unfortunately, excessive dancehall re-constructions of 'I've Got the Groove' and 'Vibrate On' only heightened the strength of the originals, and were further devalued by a mediocre vocal performance. The rest of the album touched on a curious mix of subjects: Perry's enduring love of cartoon characters was noted on the playful 'Inspector Gadget'; his most abstract performance of July 1988 was referenced on 'African Head Charge in the

Hackney Empire'; and he spoke of himself as an outer-space alien on the minimal 'African Hitch-Hiker' – the first of many official proclamations in which he named himself as a celestial being.

Though Sherwood's pool of musicians gave the album a multi-faceted sound, with rock pyrotechnics from Tackhead guitarist Skip McDonald, futuristic computer programming from David Harrow, and keyboard licks from Carlton 'Bubblers' Ogilvie augmenting the sharp rhythms of the Roots Radics, some tracks seemed somewhat mismatched or lacking in continuity – and Scratch's wavering, semi-spoken delivery was occasionally off-key. However, the machinery of Island Records would see that the album was a widespread success, aided partly by an excellent album cover depicting Perry in his new guise as the King of Switzerland. Nevertheless, Scratch would still express dissatisfaction with some of the material, railing against elements of its creation when it was issued.

'I am mad about this album, because the album mix behind me back, singers singing where they shouldn't be singing, what wasn't my plan . . . Me have me destiny to fulfil, so me fulfil me destiny, but me have a better album than this that me do one year before . . . It won't have 'pon it no Adrian, it will only have mixed by Lee "Scratch" Perry written on it. I asked him if he get some white girls for me to sing with "Inspector Gadget" and he fuck around the plan before it finish, and I won't be pleased of it. I'm fucking mad about it, you understand?' [2]

When he finished voicing the album, Scratch went to visit his young daughter Cleopatra at Sandra's place; the former couple were briefly reconciled, though she expressed her displeasure at Perry's previous actions.

Back in Zürich, at the start of the new decade, Perry began making plans for the creation of new material and, though heavily pregnant, Mireille continued solidifying his further business arrangements. Anticipating the need for assistance when the baby arrived, Scratch sent for his daughter Marsha, who flew over from Kingston to join the family in Zürich on January 27; on February 2, the child arrived, a daughter named Shiva Elaine Sharon Perry. Mireille also opened the Conoshimi Institute at this time, another centre for humanistic therapies in Zürich.

Marsha remained at the Zürich household for three months, and although she was pleased to spend time with her father, the experience ultimately proved to be trying, as her difficulty with the language and dislike of the cold weather exacerbated her perceived alienation. There was also a growing tension between herself and Mireille, who was beginning to resent the financial support she had continued to provide for Marsha and her brothers in Jamaica; a series of quarrels eventually took place, and Marsha decided to leave.

She subsequently went to England to visit a pen friend and to meet her sister Cleo, whose photograph she had seen in Jamaica; she thus stayed with

Sandra Cooley for a few months before going home, giving Sandra some additional freedom by caring for Cleo and Sharon.

Towards the end of Marsha's time in Switzerland, Robert Kuypers came to Zürich to make arrangements for the re-issue of the six Black Ark tracks by Seke Molenga and Kalo Kawongolo released on Sonafric in 1979. The son of a wealthy Belgian boat-builder, Kuypers was closely involved in the reggae and African scenes in Belgium and Holland, and met Kawongolo through contacts in the Zaïrean immigrant community in Brussels. Kuypers made several visits to Zürich in 1990, bringing Dutch journalist Karl Michiels with him on a number of occasions. He eventually released the six songs Kawongolo had given him on cassette as *From the Heart of the Congo* in 1991 on his Tropical Sounds/Jolly Zaïre label, complete with photos of the singers and Scratch obtained from Tony Owens, whom he had previously assisted in releasing *Excaliburman*.

In the spring of 1990, Perry was busy creating material at Zürich's Power Play studio with a group of Swiss musicians, including drummer Christoph Beck, bassist Felix Mueller, keyboardist Andy Mueller, and guitarist Marc Portmann, plus backing vocalists Miriam Rousseau and Claudia Boggio. Most of the material made use of Black Ark rhythms, to which the musicians added new melodies and beats; the heavy Ark foundations were thus covered by a mutant collage of rock and disco elements. By the time Perry embarked on his first European tour at the end of April, an album's worth of material had been assembled, which would be issued in the summer by the independent Black Cat/Sound Service label.

The first three songs to surface were issued as the *Moonwalk* EP, featuring Scratch's poppy paean to the gliding steps American pop star Michael Jackson adapted from the techniques of James Brown and Fred Astaire. The song's original rhythm had been built in Jamaica under Mireille Campbell's direction before she met Lee Perry; used on one of a series of sound system dub plates voiced by Yellowman and other deejays, the rhythm was her attempt at copying the phrasing of Perry's 'Jungle', but ended up sounding closer to J.C. Lodge's dancehall hit 'Telephone Love'. The B-side of the disco had 'Spiritual Healing', which made use of the rhythm track of Jackie Bernard's 'Economic Crisis', successfully updated to a pleasantly contemporary Perry romp (on which Mireille's children Collette and Noel repeatedly stated, 'Lee's coming to save the world'), while 'Cross My Heart Babush' was a disco rant that leaned on the heavily buried rhythm of 'Lady Lady', over which Scratch related a series of magical upsets in England.

The *Spiritual Healing* album had a re-structured title track with an alternative vocal line, with 'Babush' also re-voiced to explain how Perry's powerful farts would make the Pope flee. 'Sex Vibration' was another rocky cut of 'Vibrate On' that was greatly inspired by Mireille, as was the lusty excess of 'Sexy Boss', which recounted the history of their relationship. Pablo's 'Lama

Lava' was turned into the rocking dance number 'Come On And Dance'; another late '70s rhythm became the scatological 'Mr Dobberman' and 'Vendetta' was an alternative cut of the 'AD Vendetta' track created with Steve Marshall in England.

Though divided between 'Spiritual' and 'Dance' sides, what truly differentiates the material is the amount of pseudo-sexual groaning on side two; though hardly among his strongest work, it remains as another of the unique creations assembled by the Upsetter in this period.

When Lee Perry and Mireille Campbell first began planning his debut European tour, the use of a Jamaican band was considered. Mireille suggested the popular Blood Fire Posse, but Perry was unhappy with the choice; he gave more serious consideration to the Sagittarius Band and Chalice. After arrangements were made for the recording of Secret Laboratory, a tour was organised on which Scratch was to be backed by the Dub Syndicate, prompting Style Scott and other musicians to travel to the UK. Unfortunately, Perry's required fee was not deemed acceptable and he belatedly cancelled the tour, organising a smaller number of European dates backed by the Revolution band, featuring Secret Laboratory programmer David Harrow and former Public Image bassist Jah Wobble. Though not as masterful as the mighty Dub Syndicate, the Revolution was one of the most competent live bands Scratch had worked with since leaving Jamaica; their concerts presented a range of material from the *Roast Fish* era through to *Spiritual Healing*, including tunes from *Battle Of Armagideon*, *Mystic Warrior*, and both *On-U* albums; even 'Radication Squad' was revived. The tour included a return to the Elyseé Montmartre in Paris on March 11 and April 28, and a German debut at the Metropol in Aachen on May 7. Further dates were organised in the UK for the end of May, but Scratch broke off the engagements without explanation and subsequently stopped using the band.

Paris reggae kingpin Simon organised a further date at the mid-sized Bataclan in Pigalle on June 1, so Scratch started hunting around for a new band to back him on the night. It was while finalising the arrangements for the release of the *Spiritual Healing* album a couple of weeks before the gig that Perry was introduced to a group called the Limit by Power Play studio boss Higi Heilinger. Composed of drummer Lukas Bernays, keyboardist Jeannot Steck, bassist Robin Halley, and guitarist Micha Lewinsky, the Limit was a teenage jazz-rock band whose members knew little of reggae and were entirely unfamiliar with Scratch – a situation that suited the Upsetter perfectly, as he was seeking to dissociate himself with reggae and edge closer to pop and dance music. Together with the female backing vocalists from the *Spiritual Healing* album, the Limit rehearsed with Scratch a couple of times in late May, forming loose interpretations of the selected tracks they had been presented.

Unfortunately, the Bataclan performance was marred by a late start after Perry and Mireille missed their scheduled departure due to a quarrel with airline check-in staff; the promoter turned the situation to his advantage by charging an excessively steep door price for the massive crowd of people without advance tickets who were forced to stand outside in the rain, waiting for the hall doors to open. Eventually, Scratch arrived and rushed to the stage in haste to perform lengthy funk adaptations of 'Introducing Myself', 'Sexy Lady', 'Happy Birthday', 'Jungle', and 'Bank To Bank'; just as he seemed to be warming up, the lights were switched on and the audience was forced to exit, as the Bataclan's position in a highly populated residential area meant all performances had to cease by midnight.

It was shortly after this concert that Lee Perry was filmed in his home by journalist Karel Michiels for a video that would eventually be issued in limited quantity by Jet Star as *The Unlimited Destruction*. Though too short and low-budget really to capture the essence of Perry's life, Scratch's commentary has some revealing moments, and his antics were visually exciting. For instance, when Michiels tells Perry it is a shame he destroyed the Black Ark, Perry's defensive reply is 'Tell me what I can't destroy'; other comments on his working methods are equally illuminating. More documentary footage of Perry was shot in Zürich on July 4 and 5 by John Corbett, a theorist of popular culture at the Art Institute of Chicago; the contact would lead to a lengthy examination of Perry œuvre in Corbett's 1994 book *Sounding Off*.

In the autumn of 1990, Scratch was again contacted by Fizzè, who had completely re-structured 'Licht & Stein' with additional instrumentation from Dennis Bovell, recorded that September; he had also added trumpet and trombone work from Hans Kaemmerle and Gerhard Lampert, credited as the 'Horns of Liechtenstein' – though Fizzè was later to learn the pair were Austrian. Fizzè was preparing to issue the song on the *Peeni Waali* album, and came to Zürich to obtain Perry's permission for its inclusion on the release; a term was negotiated, and Fizzè was allowed to issue the track. The *Peeni Waali* album was first pressed on CD in early 1991 by Mensch Music as a limited edition of 500 copies; he later arranged for an American issue by Shanachie records, which appeared in 1992. Though an alternative mix was created for the company, they went against his wishes by re-issuing the original, and there were subsequent discrepancies involving royalty payments – an unhappy outcome for an inspired and original project.

Scratch and Mireille returned to Jamaica in October 1990, bringing their children to Montego Bay for a period of relaxation. It was while on another excursion to Negril that the couple had their first significant rupture, stemming from a purported infidelity with Sandra on a visit to London earlier in the year. It was Scratch's continual denial that anything had transpired – more than the actual event itself – that greatly unnerved Mireille, who had what she felt was concrete proof of the event; she thus left in a huff back to Switzerland, leaving Perry on his own in Jamaica.

After Mireille's departure, Scratch went to Kingston to hook up with his old spar Niney the Observer, who had recently re-activated his production career after a long hiatus abroad. Niney proposed that Scratch voice an album for Heartbeat, with whom he had recently been dealing; Chris Wilson now had a prominent role in the company, and came down to pay the pair an advance when Scratch consented to the project. The *Lord God Muzick* album was thus voiced in December at Channel One.

As a producer with a great deal of experience behind him, Niney's rhythms were somewhat more imaginative than the majority of the younger dancehall producers who used nothing but machines to make their music. Though the core of the *Lord God Muzick* rhythms was electronic, Niney made sure to include a number of live instruments to give the tracks a greater depth and texture.

While in Kingston working on the album, Scratch painted new messages on the walls of Cardiff Crescent, where it was clear his children were finding it difficult to make ends meet; a good chunk of Heartbeat's money was used to replace the roof of the house, which had been badly damaged by Hurricane Gilbert. Marsha had moved back into the property, and had the most ready source of income through her hairdressing, but her salary was far from regular; they were all short of clothing, with Sean and Omar looking particularly scruffy.

Scratch's sons had been trying to make a name for themselves as the Upsetters Junior, partly through the family link with Caveman sound; in addition to videotaping Caveman dances, they produced two songs by artists associated with the set: the anti-drug 'No Stocky Shop' by Shorty Rankin' and 'We Want Some Money' by Nardo Ranks were recorded at a studio in Mountain View and issued on the Upsetters Junior label, but received little response from the public, despite promotion by radio deejay Winston Williams. In time, they would release a last self-production, the original 'Positive Vibration', which featured lead vocals by Sean – who sounded just like Scratch – and harmony by Omar and Marsha, with musical backing by the Food Clothes and Shelter band. They would later give a performance at the beachside Coney Island amusement centre in St Catherine, but ceased creating music as a unit shortly after.

Scratch could see that his children needed guidance, and tried to persuade Vicky Nelson to move back in to keep an eye on them, but this time she refused. 'He was trying to tell me I shouldn't leave the house,' Nelson recalled, 'and then he tells me, "You are the only black queen I have" and all this stuff, but I'm not in that crap.' However, she decided to comply with the request that she provide backing vocals on selected tracks of *Lord God Muzick*, together with the Upsetters Junior.

The album's most controversial track was a re-cut of Bob Marley's 'Who Colt The Game', now aimed squarely at Bunny Lee's head in response to Striker's unauthorised licensing of Upsetter material. Scratch went so far as to croak 'Everything Bunny Lee Touch Die,' citing protégés Slim Smith and King Tubby as examples. (Unfortunately, Perry's censure seems to have ultimately backfired, as Striker subsequently issued a series of Aggrovators dub collections through Creole records falsely attributed to Scratch.)

Other strong album tracks include the opening 'Free Us' and its version 'Happy Birthday Marcus'; the vitriolic 'Hot Shit', cut over a Yami Bolo rhythm and dedicated to Chris Blackwell; plus the amusing autobiographical numbers 'Angel Gabriel and the Space Boots' and keenly harmonic 'Supersonic Man'. Unfortunately, a number of lesser works were also included, such as 'Reggae Emperor', which had an inconsistent vocal delivery, and 'Collie Ruler', a mediocre re-cut of the 'Real Rock' rhythm. The weakness of these tracks may be partly attributed to an increased alcohol intake while away from Mireille's watchful eyes. According to Chris Wilson, Scratch drank a great deal of Dragon stout before voicing, and burned through a quantity of spliff.

Some out-of-place adaptations of older songs also broke the continuity of the disc, including 'Lee The Upsetter', on which Scratch mumbled nonsense over the original 'I Am The Upsetter', and 'Lee in the Heartbeat', an ill-fitting snippet of a late-'70s rhythm, which would surface in its entirety a few months after the release of *Lord God Muzick* on Heartbeat's *Soundzs From the Hotline* – an excellent collection of rare Perry material from the Black Ark and Dynamic, taken from master tapes the company obtained from Alvin Ranglin, who is said to have acquired them as surety for a loan that was never repaid. (To confuse matters further, *Lord God Muzick* was later re-packaged by Niney as *The Reggae Emperor*, issued in the UK by Rhino in 1996.)

Perhaps the track from *Lord God Muzick* with the most personal significance was 'Lightning And Thunder Flash', which Scratch gave to his son Omar to send to Mireille by express mail on an unmarked cassette immediately after having voiced it; the song's cryptic message would soothe her anger, and heal the rift that had been formed in Negril.

Another notable 1992 Heartbeat issue was *The Upsetter And The Beat*, comprising 12 of the tracks Scratch had voiced for Coxsone in New York and Jamaica – released despite Perry's previous threats of litigation against the Studio One boss. The concept behind the album was an inspired one, with Perry adding his wit and wisdom to classic Studio One rhythms, but the incomplete feel of the abandoned project and intermittent lacklustre deliveries ultimately meant it did not live up to its dynamic potential. The opening 'Welcome Aboard' sets the tone of the disc, with Scratch warbling above the Wailers' 'Rudie' anthem; his disorienting, off-key ad-libbing seems at odds with the rhythm, and may ultimately detract from it. A similar situation is also evident on the Wailing Souls' prime nuggets 'Back Out With It' – now transformed to 'Don't Blame The Baldhead' – and 'Mr Fire Coal Man', here changed to the stuttering 'Twiddle With Me'. Perhaps somewhat more successful are Scratch's handling of Coxsone's new digital rhythms, as heard on the tracks 'Big Apple Coconut' and 'There Is A Place For Us', while mutations of 'Freedom Blues' as 'Love Power' and Ken Boothe's 'Just Another Girl' as 'Coming In From The Cold' are perhaps not so obtrusive; unfortunately, the Bassies' great 'Things A Come Up To Bump' is given a nonsensical re-working as 'Holla And Bawl', and the Heptones' 'Why Did You Leave Me To Cry' is similarly downgraded on 'Making Love'. Like so many of the Perry albums issued from the end of the 1980s, *The Upsetter and the Beat* is ultimately lacking in the care and attention Scratch lavished on his own independent work, and this lack of devotion would often achieve such disappointing results.

After completing work on the *Lord God Muzick* album, Perry returned to Zürich in early 1991. For much of the coming decade, Scratch lived something of a nomadic existence; though based in Switzerland, he often moved between Jamaica and Europe, travelling throughout the continent and occasionally farther afield when live dates or studio work beckoned. These years also had long periods when domesticity took precedence over music, with Scratch and Mireille devoting the majority of their energies to their children.

In May, Mireille travelled to Tucson, Arizona, to attend another UFO conference. It was there that she heard a presentation by Vitko Novi, a.k.a. Vlado Kapetanovic, a Yugoslavian who spent the majority of his life in Peru. Novi claims to have been abducted by aliens and taken to the planet Apu on eight different occasions between March 1960 and January 1961, and names a variety of historic figures as originating from the planet, including Moses, Jesus, Pythagoras, Martin Luther, Karl Marx, Leonardo da Vinci, and Robin Hood. Impressed by his words, Mireille made a licensing deal for the German-language publication of his book *170 Horas Con Extraterrestres*,[3] which Lion Star subsequently published in a limited quantity as *170 Stunden mit Ausserirdischen*.

In the autumn, Scratch made a few significant European performances with Adrian Sherwood and the Dub Syndicate. The most notable was his debut performance in Belgium at the Leffinge Leuren festival on September 15, where Scratch appeared with his eyes outlined in white paint and a white cross drawn on his forehead, clutching his latest talisman: a small red electric guitar (which would eventually be decorated with glass and other objects, much like the crown he was wearing on his head). As Perry had cancelled every previous engagement secured in the nation for the past five years, the performance was greatly anticipated and proved to be highly successful – particularly renditions of 'Roast Fish' and 'Soul Fire', which had the rapt audience bellowing for more. 'That's one of the best gigs I've ever been to in my life,' Adrian Sherwood remembered proudly, 'I saw about ten people crying at that gig, it was that good. That band was only Bonjo-I, David Harrow with the computer, (London session player) Reuben on bass, and maybe one guitarist; I had all the sounds so it sounded like a record, dubbing up exactly in time. That was one brilliant gig.'

It was also in the autumn that Scratch and Mireille attended the annual spiritualism conference in Basel, at which a key speaker was their friend, Michael Hesemann. At the conference, a number of peculiar events transpired: first, a healer with a divining rod proclaimed that Lee's energy gave her stomachaches and headaches due to conflicting elements that were mixed up inside him; an onlooker then approached Mireille to deliver a spontaneous message: 'You have to marry this man,' he said, indicating Scratch. Michael Hesemann was standing close by, near an exhibit on the Hare Krishna movement, and immediately agreed with the stranger: 'Yes, Mireille, marry Lee "Scratch" Perry, we're going to have a big party, Hare Krishna, Hare Krishna.'

Thus, on November 30, 1991, Rainford Hugh Perry and Mireille Ruegg Campbell were married before 12 guests in an intimate ceremony conducted at a Hare Krishna temple in Zürich; Adrian Sherwood was brought over to act as Perry's witness. 'I was really honoured, I think they were even going to pay for my air ticket but I just got my own. It was a very spiritual wedding in a Krishna temple; it was incredible and I had a brilliant time. We went 'round the lake in a boat with Mireille's friends, and we ended up in this hotel, eating and having a party all night. It was truly excellent.'

The rest of 1991 and much of 1992 passed quietly, with Perry creating little new music and performing infrequently; live dates that year included a return to Paris' Mutualité in March, and a gig at the Vooruit club in Ghent, Belgium, using a 'pick-up' band of London-based Jamaicans led by guitarist Renford Bailey; along with more standard material, 'Curley Locks', 'I am the Upsetter', and 'White Belly Rat' were revived for the latter performance. Meanwhile, Perry's scattered Jamaican productions were still finding issue on a variety of outlets, notably through Tony Owens' Roots Records, a new record label and distribution service. A CD single with extended mixes of the Jolly Brothers' 'Conscious Man' and 'Brotherly Love' was an early issue on the label in 1992, followed by the long-awaited *Conscious Man* album in 1993 and further re-pressings of the *Heart Of The Ark* and *Megaton Dub* collections, with bonus tracks.

The most significant new musical project of 1992 would see Scratch and Mireille travelling to Japan in June for his first live performances on the Asian continent, backed by Adrian Sherwood and the Dub Syndicate, who now included Style Scott, Skip McDonald, Bubblers, Reuben, and Rennie Bailey. Organised by Ray Hearn, an Australian music promoter who runs the Geo music agency in Japan, the tour had engagements in Tokyo, Osaka, and Kyoto, where Scratch and Mireille enjoyed one week's holiday when the tour was finished. 'In Osaka, Lee Perry did the whole gig with a flower pot on his head, standing on one leg,' remembered Skip McDonald. 'He had a mirror he'd taken off the wall and was shining the light in the audience, and was baptising everyone with water.'

In Tokyo, Scratch appeared at the World Music Festival on June 12, held at the Shibuya 'On Air' venue. It was after this appearance that Perry first met Kazufumi Kodama, the former trumpet player and bandleader of Mute Beat, who was backstage with a demo tape of the debut solo album he was working on for Sony Japan, *Quiet Reggae*. Scratch was taken by two of the tracks, and agreed to voice them a few days later; he thus joined the trumpet player and his collaborators at the Echo House studio in the Roppongi district of Tokyo. Kodama related the particulars of the brief session: 'When he came into the studio, I said, "I am sorry that there is no herb" because I heard he wouldn't work without herb, but he said, "What are you talking about?" and ignored it. He placed many candles around a microphone and lit them, put the Bible on a sheet-music stand, and made up the studio just like his own room. He asked his wife to write down the lyrics he had been preparing and sang them impressively. With the two songs, he produced his own world instantly; he looked happy and relaxed all the time, just like a great master of the art. During the rough-mixing, he seemed to want to play the small strange electric guitar he brought along. He asked if he could do dub mixing, but unfortunately it was impossible because the master tapes had been mixed in stereo. He was disappointed, but I had to organise everything in minimum condition. After finishing the session, he shook hands with all the staff and me and put guitar strings around a duct pipe in the studio before leaving with his wife Mireille.'

Though much of *Quiet Reggae* was composed of trumpet interpretations of mellow grooves popular in Jamaica – such as the traditional 'Greensleeves', 'End Of The World', and Max Romeo's 'We Love Jamaica' – the album also had a few Kodama originals, and it was two such tracks that Scratch chose to voice. 'Open Up The Japanese Door' pitted the usual Scratch meandering over a melancholy rhythm, while the more dancehall-oriented 'Japanese Rock' had a series of cheap rhymes involving rock and clock. Ultimately, time constraints meant the collaboration was not quite as successful as that of *Mute Beat Dubwise*, though Perry's voice shifted the emphasis of the tracks he appeared on; though his involvement in the project was minimal, his presence on the disc was used as a major selling point in Japan, where Scratch's mystique had gained a growing following.

Back in Switzerland, Scratch took a break from making music for the rest of the year, which would continue for the greater part of 1993. The most momentous creation was a son with Mireille, named Gabriel Merlin Zay Perry, born on December 26, 1992. Mireille also opened the Alpha and Omega health and beauty clinic in Zürich at this time. Scratch kept a fairly low profile in the months preceding and following Gabriel's birth, and did not make any new music until the summer, when he became involved in a project that ultimately did not follow its intended course.

It was while in a music shop in Zürich in May that Scratch was surprised to find he recognised a staff member: Jeannot Steck, the former keyboardist of the Limit band who had backed him up at the Bataclan three years earlier. Steck told Scratch that the Limit had split up, but he was recording an album with a band called the Roundabouts, together with drummer Lukas Bernays; the pair were also developing their own project through the creation of electronic dance rhythms at a small studio called SHS. Scratch rented SHS for a series of sessions in collaboration with Steck, who later brought Bernays in to add electronic drumbeats to the material. For their collaborative work with Perry, Steck and Bernays ultimately took the name X-Perrymental.

Scratch worked in SHS with the pair every two or three weeks, voicing dozens of tracks over the course of the summer months, some of which would eventually be issued in a highly altered form as *Technomajikal*, an album ultimately plagued by miscommunications and trickery. Lukas Bernays explained the genesis of the project: 'He and Jeannot met each other again and decided to make something, because at this time Lee was a little bit bored and very greedy of making new things with new people. He was impressed by this new techno scene and wanted to jam with us, so we made about twenty or thirty sessions, sometimes with people playing instruments, sometimes with keyboard programs, and sometimes Scratch just had his microphone and was spelling out his fantasies on the machine.'

X-Perrymental had initially planned to form a label and concert agency in conjunction with Scratch and Mireille, but were disappointed when Scratch entered into separate negotiations with CBF Management Agency in Zürich. By early 1994 it was clear that X-Perrymental did not have the funds or international contacts to establish such an enterprise on their own; seeking the guidance and support of an experienced professional, they thus wrote a letter to Dieter Meier with details of the project.

The son of a wealthy Swiss banker, Meier was a former law student and professional gambler who formed the trend-setting dance outfit Yello in 1979 with a former truck driver, television repairman and synthesiser specialist, Boris Blanc. Yello's early use of sequencers and synthesised dance beats proved enormously popular, and Meier's great wealth allowed the group to indulge their creative whims without fear of commercial failure, ensuring a consistently individual approach. As X-Perrymental had no previous link with Yello besides a shared Swiss identity, they figured it was a long shot requesting Meier's involvement. However, Meier was sufficiently inspired by the project, and thus came to see the team in Switzerland.

In June, X-Perrymental informed Perry of their plan to re-work a few of the SHS tracks for a proposed limited-edition maxi-single on Meier's Solid Pleasure label, and Scratch faxed his basic consent to the duo for three tracks to be remixed. Arrangements were eventually made for Bernays and Steck to spend a few days in Meier's Soundproof studio in Malibu, California, in October to re-work the SHS material, but Meier specified that Scratch was not to make the journey. The material was thus re-worked without the involvement of Lee Perry or the absent Dieter Meier, gaining sitar, flute, and didgeridoo overdubs in co-operation with Martin Kloiber (born on March 19, 1966 in Kusig, Austria), a sound engineer and music producer who had overseen the completion of Soundproof's construction. Due to Meier's perpetually demanding schedule, the material was then left in limbo for the rest of the year.

Though Scratch had recently fathered his second child by Mireille, there were definite signs that he was physically slowing down in 1994; though he still retained his high degree of physical fitness and had a generally undiminished level of energy, his beard was turning greyer by the day and his voice thinning.

Besides a live engagement at L'Elysée Montmartre in Paris on April 2 – mixed by the Mad Professor – Scratch made few public appearances that year. One notable exception was a spring appearance with Mireille on the *Daily Talk-Täglich*, a television programme broadcast on the Tele Züre station that details the lives of politicians and artists in the area. Interviewed by station owner and noted media personality Roger Schawinsky, Scratch was uncharacteristically subdued; Mireille was thus left to do most of the talking herself.

He returned to Jamaica for a few weeks in June, where he was filmed at the Black Ark by Don Letts and Steve Barrow for an archive project funded by Island Records, but his brief time in Kingston was far from tranquil, particularly where domestic matters were concerned. As ever, Marsha was keeping herself together best, and seemed to retain the strongest bond with her father; she had recently moved to Portmore with her fiancé, Prince Robinson, a custom-auto builder she met on a trip to Canada in 1992. His brother P-Son had moved round the corner after his girlfriend became pregnant with their first child, though he still spent much time at Cardiff Crescent; for much of the 1990s, his main source of employment was as a road technician for Lloyd Parks' We the People Band. Michelle, who now had a young daughter, Leticia Campbell, along with her two sons, had moved back into the property, but was told to leave by Scratch after another angry confrontation; she thus left the house and moved to Forest Hills. It was a particularly difficult time for her, as Wayne Campbell subsequently emigrated to America, leaving her in Jamaica with three children to care for and little chance of earning enough to support them.

Scratch's sons also felt the force of his censure on this brief trip. Although Sean still idolised his father, he was singled out for particular criticism, as he had become an intermittent user of crack cocaine. The drug later took a hold on him he has not been able to shake off, and he was arrested in connection with the substance towards the end of the year, only to be rescued from a jail term by Pauline Morrison, who returned to Jamaica for the first time in many years just at the right moment to make the necessary intervention.

Pauline had long lived apart from Danny Clarke, who had left New York in 1987 to move to Arizona. Pauline herself eventually spent a period in Los Angeles where she performed as a singer and imported African fabrics; she returned to Jamaica in 1994 to arrange for Taffia and Macheela, her two children from Clarke, to be schooled in Kingston, and subsequently moved to London, where she would spend the better part of 1995 and '96. It was in this period that Pauline made deals with an array of record labels for further clandestine issues of Lee Perry's material – sometimes providing one label with DAT or cassette copies of master tapes she had previously sold to another, other times sanctioning unauthorised collections culled from vinyl, and occasionally pressing her own productions, using rhythms that had a Black Ark foundation that had been altered abroad.

Unlike his older brother Sean, Omar was more in control of his life during Perry's upsetting 1994 visit, though tension between him and Scratch would ultimately see Omar draw closer to his mother. He would subsequently pursue more concrete engineering experience through a series of apprenticeships at Kingston studios; the first came at the eight-track Track Star studio, and he later learned about equalisation through work at Boris Gardiner's 16-track facility. By 1995, he was working at Junior Reid's 24-track studio, engineering work by veterans such as Big Youth and Tyrone Taylor, as well as upcoming artists like Terry Ganzie.

Regarding recorded material, Scratch was effectively in a semi-dormant state for much of 1993-94; however, product associated with the man continued to be issued at an escalating pace, each with varying degrees of authenticity. On-U Sound's *Echomania* was about the most genuine, with the songs 'Dubbing Psycho Thriller' and 'Dub Addisababa' making use of Perry's previously recorded *a cappella* statements. 'The samples we used, they date from the late '80s, or early '90s,' noted Adrian Sherwood, 'we paid him a bit of money for the usage and he said "Cool." Sometimes he says better stuff away from a record than he does on a record, so I'd pick up on ideas, write down things he was talking about, almost interview him and make him enlarge on the idea. I actually have a couple of reels of tape, just *a cappella*.' VP's *Smokin'* was a genuine Perry album, though it was not made clear on the disc that the material dated from 1981. Seven Leaves/Roots Records' *Phoenix Of Peace* by Earl Sixteen was more misleading, as it claimed to be a Black Ark album produced by Scratch; though it featured Black Ark rhythms, no mention was made of the fact that all but one of the tracks were voiced in London in 1993 without Lee Perry's involvement. Downright ridiculous was Esoldun's grossly mistitled *Lee Perry Meets Mafia and Fluxy in Jamaica*; despite its modern sound, the album purported to be culled from a 1976 session – a good decade before the England-born rhythm team ever set foot on the island. If Mafia and Fluxy ever did meet Lee Perry in Jamaica, the results of the meeting were certainly not captured on this album. Equally absurd was Rhino's *Lee Scratch*

Perry And The Upsetters Meet At King Tubby's, which featured Tubby's and Jammy's dubs produced by Bunny Lee; *Guitar Boogie Dub*, comprised of Earl 'Chinna' Smith instrumentals produced by Bunny Lee at Tubby's, and *Lee Perry Presents Gregory Isaacs*, which repackaged *Extra Classic* with unrelated bonus tracks.

When it was suggested to Creole executive Bruce White that Scratch may not have had anything to do with this material, his insistence that Bunny Lee had assured him of Perry's involvement proved definitely less than convincing: 'As far as we know, it's Scratch; I don't think Bunny Lee's hungry for falsifying the situation. They worked on a lot together; they were like brothers at one time.'

Rhino would continue the onslaught in 1995 with *Lee Perry The Upsetter Presenting Dub*, composed of Channel One Aggrovators tracks previously issued on the Clocktower albums *Heavy Metal Dub* and *King Of Dub*, interspersed with Augustus Pablo material. *Bunny Lee & The Aggrovators Aggrovate Lee Perry & The Upsetters* featured 12 genuine Upsetter dubs (along with 14 Aggrovator dubs), but the Perry tracks were lifted from a badly scratched vinyl copy of *Blackboard Jungle Dub* and re-titled to suit the release.

While such releases continued to flood the market, Lee Perry remained pre-occupied with building new material. Towards the end of 1994, the Mad Professor contacted Scratch proposing he voice another Ariwa album; as Perry's popularity was continuing to rise with a generation of new fans, Professor was certain of high sales, and offered 'a huge advance, several thousand pounds – the biggest I've ever paid anyone'. Mindful of Professor's penchant for brandy and attractive females, Mireille had a couple of stipulations to assert before consenting to the plan: there was to be no alcohol and no girls. 'Before I came,' Mireille explained, 'Professor could give Lee a bottle of brandy, have him sing on the mike for many hours and Lee would not even remember, but Professor would just put out things. Suddenly those things couldn't work, because I was there observing his plans.' With her conditions agreed to, Scratch and Mireille thus came to London just before Christmas, and booked into the Hilton Hotel for a long weekend, during which a startling volume of material was created, some of which would eventually be issued as the *Black Ark Experryments* album.

'He come Thursday, finish by Monday,' the Mad Professor recalled, noting the incredible speed at which they worked. 'Myself, a guy named William, and a guy named Nolan, we put together the basics of those tracks; three guys, none of us who you would say are musicians, we put together the album but we had to move fast. We sequenced some tracks and some were played live and then afterwards overdubbed.' As usual, Scratch felt the urge to decorate while he was working; 'The whole studio was a mess after that,' chuckled Professor.

Despite the great haste in which this material was created, *Black Ark*

Experryments was the most complete and coherent album Perry had been involved with for years. The lyrics may have been largely ad-libbed in his inimitable word-associative style, but were somehow more captivating than on much of the material he had issued since *Time Boom.* The multi-dimensional rhythms – part-computer durability and part organic roots – also greatly enhanced the album's feel, resulting in a consistently strong work.

Among the most notable tracks was 'Open Door', in which Scratch spoke of the musical doors he had opened for a wealth of amateur collaborators but closed on insulting upstarts like Bunny Wailer. Another strong number was 'Heads Of Government', which was largely an autobiographical ramble through Perry's twisted ethos, while the heady title track – nicely complemented by a lilting flute melody – spoke of miraculous periods in his life, from early days crushing boulders in Negril to the present at the Secret Laboratory in Switzerland. In the best reggae tradition, Professor also left in studio conversations between Perry and the session musicians on the introduction of 'Super Ape In A Good Shape', though the originally vile and possibly libellous insults levelled at a host of former peers was thankfully left off the track.

After finishing off this material, Scratch made a fleeting visit to his daughter Cleo, though he did not see Sandra on this occasion, as she was working in Greenford; he did, however, meet Sandra's current partner, a calm and responsible man, who had become Cleopatra's surrogate father.

By the time Lee Perry returned to Switzerland, the Mad Professor had already mixed dub versions of much of the material they had worked on for what would be the *Experryments At The Grassroots of Dub* companion, and though Perry 'came along and turn a few knobs' during these initial mixes, his involvement in the dub disc was minimal. Professor also threw together outtakes from the sessions, which he would issue just before the *Experryments* album as the largely unlistenable *Super Ape Inna Jungle,* an opportunistic collection of unused Perry vocals remixed in the hyper-mechanical jungle style that was then sweeping London; further snippets would also appear on the Ariwa *Rupununi Safari Steaming Jungle* album.

On his return to Zürich, Scratch was contacted by Lukas Bernays of X-Perrymental, who arranged a meeting on January 11 between Dieter Meier, Perry, and the group at Meier's Zürich residence; though the meeting was ostensibly to clarify future plans for the material that had been re-constructed in California, Scratch has stated that no particulars were mentioned; instead, Perry and Meier briefly exchanged ideas while drinking tea together after listening to the re-constructed tracks. Meier later noted being struck by Perry's forceful drive: 'It was an extraordinary meeting with a man who had a clear vision of who he was and what he wanted to do. He had a hat with various antennae to tune in to the artistic and spiritual vibrations – he seemed to listen, but was very involved in his personas; it was as though he was listening from another world. I've never met a guy who seemed to operate on this planet but was so very involved in his own artistic vision.'

Instead of issuing the planned three-song maxi-single, Meier later asked X-Perrymental to send further rough mixes from Switzerland, which were duly provided some weeks later, though Perry has said he was unaware of such actions by the group. Martin Kloiber also arranged for Los Angeles-based remix artist Rich Sihillig to provide further mixes of selected tracks, aimed at the hard-core trance and ambient crowd, again without Perry's knowledge. Sihillig planned to organise an album's release on independent dance label Eye-Q Music, but the deal ultimately fell through; there then followed a long period of silence, during which the project was seemingly abandoned.

Meanwhile, the Mad Professor was putting the finishing touches to the *Black Ark Experryments* album; he secured live dates for Perry in France and the UK for the coming spring, and brought Scratch and Mireille back to London to attend rehearsals and to re-voice a few album tracks in late February.

It was while in London that the couple's relationship was given a concrete test through a domestic incident. Scratch had spent the majority of a Friday and Saturday working on the *Black Ark Experryments* tracks at Ariwa; on Saturday night, he went out on the town with Nolan and William, arousing the anger of Mireille when he returned to the hotel very late. An argument ensued the next afternoon, and the obscure dispute turned violent; Mireille was injured by Scratch in their hotel room, resulting in her hasty exit to Switzerland alone. Mireille recounted the scenario: 'He licked me on the head with these long, hard exercising sticks. You know why? Any time somebody else come around, Lee want to play important. He change completely; he's not the same as when he is with me alone . . . so this argument started. When Lee came back to the hotel, he hit me on the head, and it burst – blood was all over.'

A traumatised and angry Mireille telephoned Professor to inform him of the situation, but when Professor and assistant Eddie Brown arrived at the hotel, they found Mireille had already been taken to a hospital by hotel staff. While Brown went to the hospital to check on Mireille, Professor took an agitated Scratch back to Ariwa to calm him down.

Used to the high standards of Switzerland, Mireille was displeased by the overcrowded and run-down appearance of the hospital; once her wound was no longer bleeding, she thus returned to the empty hotel room, packed her bags and vacated the premises, taking Perry's passport with her. She stayed overnight in another hotel, and left for Switzerland the next day, having evaded Scratch and the Ariwa posse.

When she arrived in Zürich late that evening, a private surgeon told her it was too late for stitches, but that the wound was likely to heal itself in time. Although the cut now posed no serious threat to her health, Mireille was deeply angered by the incident; she thus sent a fax to Ariwa a couple of days later with a list of harsh personal demands Perry would have to fulfil should he wish to retrieve his passport.

'He was essentially stuck here,' Professor recalled. 'I put him up in a house I've got at Thirsk Road, right across the road from Ariwa, and ended up baby-sitting him for about a month.' Perry had a dozen tour dates to fulfil in France in April, and was preparing for the performances despite his lack of travel documents. He spent the majority of his time rehearsing with the Robotics and voicing rhythms with Professor – possibly enough to fill two new albums; he was also slowly trashing the property at Thirsk Road.

Scratch also crossed paths with his former partner Pauline Morrison in this period, and incredibly took her to Sandra Cooley's home to meet his daughter Cleopatra; though their meeting was amicable enough, he would later be furious with her for further disseminating unauthorised versions of his creations. Among the first to surface in 1995 was Starlight's *Black Ark Almighty Dub Chapter Three*, which had a few of Perry's rhythms with crass synthesiser and guitar parts grossly overdubbed onto them in New York; also issued that year was a 12-inch with a previously unreleased version of 'Soul Alimighty' featuring a duet between Lee Perry and Bob Marley.

Despite Perry's missing travel document, Professor was determined to bring him to France to fulfil the live engagements, and eventually found a way surreptitiously to spirit Scratch across the border. 'It comes back like a nightmare to me,' Professor confessed. 'How do you get someone into France without a passport? We got him into France, did about 15 shows in March and April, and got him back into England; he was staying across the road, and I was giving him food and money.'

The performances Scratch gave with the Robotics were fairly consistent, due to a previously rehearsed set from which the band never deviated; in addition to the usual Black Ark, Thameside, and On-U favourites, 'Open Door' and 'Heads of Government' became mainstays, as did re-structured versions of 'Bucky Skank' (blended with elements of 'Papa Was a Rolling Stone') and the Staple Singers' 'Come Go with Me'. There was still plenty of room for vocal improvisation, but the revue-style presentation of the material saw the band keeping a lid on too much rambling excess. When Scratch did opt for scattered vocal interludes, Professor would often apply a 'doppelgänger' effect to his voice; the other-worldly nature of his rants and chants would thus be heightened. 'You cannot go there expecting a show like you see with Perry Como or Andy Williams,' Professor insisted, 'but it is a very set and orderly show, yet very spontaneous at the same time.'

It was after the French performances that Perry somehow made his way to Switzerland, accompanied in a car by Eddie Brown, only to find that Mireille had frozen the 30,000 Swiss francs in his bank account. Hoping to resolve the situation, Scratch and Eddie went in person to his former home, only to be chastised and castigated by a ferocious Mireille, who demanded they disappear.

Once back in England, Scratch voiced a few tracks towards the end of April with Akabu and 'Bubblers' Ogilvie at the On-U Manor in Walthamstow, the studio Adrian Sherwood opened in the early 1990s. Sherwood himself was largely absent from the sessions, which were run by engineer Andy Montgomery and assistant Maggie Apostolu; the singer Bim Sherman was frequently among the assembled onlookers. The songs voiced included a version of Curtis Mayfield's 'It's All Right' incongruously mutated to 'Voodoo Economic'; another song that incorporated a chant of 'Hare Krishna' from Akabu seemed to be a plea to Mireille to start again (though Scratch insisted it described a fictitious situation); the third centred on a chant of 'Revolution – Boo Tax, Boo VAT.' As with much of his creations in this period, these tracks were not properly finished, and remain unreleased at present.

On April 28, Scratch performed 'One Drop', 'Crazy Baldheads', and 'Roast Fish And Cornbread' as an unscheduled surprise guest with the Robotics at London's Town and Country club; the gig was a benefit for the family of D. Elmyna Davis, a.k.a. Sister D, a Rastafarian film-maker who tragically contracted fatal malaria while filming a music event in Ghana. The Rastafarian community was well represented in the audience, and Scratch's sober, calm performance befitted the gravity of the event.

However, the weeks apart from Mireille had made him thoroughly depressed, and he continued to destroy the Thirsk Road dwelling as the melancholy weeks dragged on. 'We later spent about £4000 re-decorating,' Professor indicated. 'Every possible surface was painted – even the light bulbs – with words, drawings, all kinds of things.'

In early May, Scratch went back on the road with the Robotics for a few live dates in Belgium and Holland. It was at one of the Dutch performances that the pair had a public reconciliation – incredibly, the day after Scratch had berated Mireille on stage at the Amsterdam Paradiso on May 3. As Professor recounted, 'Scratch was feeling lonely and pissed off, and I guess he missed her as well. One night we were in Amsterdam and she called me on my mobile. He was on stage saying not the most pleasant things, and then she called him and they're on the phone about half an hour and he said, "I sort it out with Mireille." We arranged for her to reach the gig at Tilburg the next day and they had a reunion, and if you hear the two shows it's quite incredible: One night he's saying the worst things about his wife, then he's saying she's the best thing, the only one who could understand. We did another few gigs, and then they went home together; I guess they resolved all the arguments.'

At the end of the month, Scratch gave his only official UK appearance of 1995, headlining the first Reggae All Dayer at the annual Essential Music Festival in Brighton on May 29; Scratch was in fine form, and received a strong audience response, though the presence of U Roy and Max Romeo backstage had mildly unsettled him.

Further live dates had been arranged in the US independently of Professor, originally scheduled to take place in August 1995. However, the engagements were cancelled at the last minute, and though rumours circulated that a lack of sufficient funding had sullied the deal, in reality it was Perry's previous American visa problems that led to the cancellations.

Meanwhile, public attention was being focused on Scratch as never before. The many retrospective re-issues had brought a thorough examination of his back catalogue, and the genius of his innovations was being belatedly acknowledged on a wider scale. Younger, more mainstream artists were now also naming him as an inspirational force. In July, East London jungle combo Spring-heeled Jack even released a poppy jungle disc named 'Lee Perry' on Rough Trade in tribute to the man's dub techniques. Scratch was also increasingly lauded in print, with David Toop's *Oceans Of Sound* following John Corbett's *Extended Play* as notable music theory books to praise him. But perhaps his most notable name check came on a Beastie Boys record called 'Sure Shot' on their *Ill Communication* album: 'Like Lee Perry, I'm very on; I rock a microphone, then I'm gone.'

Formed by three white, middle-class toasters/musicians from New York in the early 1980s, the Beastie Boys' first release was the punk-oriented *Polly Wog Stew* EP in 1983. After cutting the obnoxious rap 'Cookie Puss' in 1984, they were picked up by hip-hop label Def Jam and eventually signed to Colombia for their 1986 album debut, *Licensed To Ill*. Though originally classed by much of the popular music press as wimpy rap impostors with foul mouths, the group's blend of punk and hip-hop proved enormously success-ful: *Licensed To Ill* became the biggest-selling rap album of all time, partly through their innovative use of rock samples which saw a broader appeal to the adolescents of white America. Their second album, *Paul's Boutique*, gained favourable reviews but was commercially less successful, while subsequent discs drew widespread acclaim as the group's sound became more complex. By the early 1990s, the previous press criticism that had dogged the group was replaced by near-universal praise; they had been transformed in the eyes of the media to the epitome of cool.

The Beasties would later name Lee Perry as a major influence, though as with many of their generation, their exposure to his music was retroactive. As Mike Diamond (a.k.a. Mike D) explained, 'All three of us are all really inspired and influenced by Lee Perry's music and production. I think of it in terms of opening up truly infinite possibilities of sound and music; by manipulating sounds through using the mixing board and every outboard effect and every potential tape speed to achieve sounds you might have in your head, to make those a reality. More than anyone else, he was the example of that for us, though I would say I became aware of his music unwittingly, probably first through the early Bob Marley and the Wailers stuff he did, and in a way from the Clash – I was a big Clash fan when they had that cover of "Police And Thieves", and I later realised he was the guy behind all this stuff. Then Adam Horovitz (a.k.a. Adrock) really got into it and started making a lot of tapes, like "Best Dressed Chicken In Town", and our co-producer Mario Caldato Jr is a huge Lee Perry fan, so that, of course, had an influence.'

Born in Brazil to an Italian father and Brazilian mother but raised in Los Angeles, Caldato is an engineer and musician who has played a central role in the creation of some of the Beasties' more adventurous works; he had long been inspired by reggae in general and Perry in particular after listening to Rogers Steffens' and Hank Holmes' Reggae Beat radio show on KCRW, and a subsequent trip to Jamaica strenghtened his love of the music. It was he who introduced the group to some of Perry's more experimental material, including the *Revolution Dub* album. Caldato also introduced the group to the Mad Professor, who did several remixes in the Beastie Boys' Los Angeles studio while they were working on the *Check Your Head* album in 1991; unfortunately, the material was never edited properly and remains unissued.

As the albums they released became more varied, the group also diversified their creative activities to form the Grand Royal clothing line and eclectic record label, and launched *Grand Royal* magazine in 1994 with a first issue focusing on Bruce Lee; the second issue, slated for publication later in the year but delayed until the summer of 1995, concentrated on Lee 'Scratch' Perry.

Grand Royal's 24-page spread on Scratch was the most comprehensive magazine coverage devoted to the man to date. Editor Bob Mack (a former MTV staff member who first met the Beasties to conduct an interview for *Spin* in 1992) had an extensive international team who presented an impressive range of material; nevertheless, the delay of the project, which far outstripped its budget, would see Mack ejected from his post after destroying an office in a temper tantrum, resulting in the unfortunate inclusion of a number of errors in the piece that would later spark Perry's ire. Worst among them was Mack's entirely spurious claim that Scratch's 1984 version of 'Bed Jamming' resulted in 'rumours of incest circulating around Kingston' due to a line in which Perry proclaims he wants to 'pop' his 'daughter's water'. This slanderous untruth stemmed from Mack's low command of Rastafarian patois, in which all females are typically labelled with the term 'daughter'; the daughter referred to in the song was certainly not a family member. Also unacceptable to Scratch was the inclusion of a quote from Pauline Morrison in which she claimed responsibility for the building of the Black Ark and the mixing of *Blackboard Jungle Dub* – absurd statements that were presented in an isolated quotation with no contextual explanation, ultimately giving credence to her unauthorised issuing of Black Ark material (in particular, the curiously mistitled *Original Blackboard Jungle*, a bootleg CD re-cut of the Clocktower edition of the album, mastered from a badly scratched vinyl album copy).

Such errors aside, the *Grand Royal* magazine feature raised Perry's profile in America as never before, with the Beasties' sanctioning of his genius instigating a whole new wave of interest among their young fans.

The second half of 1995 passed rather uneventfully, with Scratch and his family taking another break from the music scene, though an appearance on Channel 4's *Baadaass TV* kept him in the public eye; despite his punkish purple hair and newly pierced ears, Scratch seemed fairly subdued on the programme, chatting amicably to co-celebrity Ice-T and delivering an impromptu rap over an instrumental cut of the Heptones' 'Party Time'.

At the start of 1996, Blood and Fire's lavish re-issue of the Congos' *Heart Of The Congos* album placed widespread media focus back on Scratch. Such attention would see the further issue of cheaply packaged collections of dubious dub material cut in Lee Perry's name, including Rhino's *Lee Perry Meets Scientist At The Blackheart Studio*, a set of basic Sly and Robbie rhythms that seems to lack the involvement of either mixer mentioned in its title; the release further contradicts itself by stating in the fine print that it was 'recorded at Striker Lee Studio' with engineer Newton Williams. The London-based Graylan company issued other supposed Black Ark collections on their Hit Squad label that year, such as *The Great Lee Perry King Of Dub* (which had only tenuous links with Perry through a cut of the Wailers' 'Keep On Moving' with overdubbed percussion, plus dubs of two rhythms that were used on the *Lord God Muzick* album) and *Scientist Upset The Upsetter* (which stemmed mostly from '70s and '80s Aggrovators material, and had little to do with Scientist or Lee Perry, though the final track is a dub of Niney's 'Mutiny', which is said to have been voiced at the Ark on a Channel One rhythm). As such product continued rolling forth, Perry himself was galvanised back into musical action through a number of notable projects and performances, though his personal life would clearly suffer for it.

Perry and Mireille returned to Asia in late January for more live dates with Adrian Sherwood and the Dub Syndicate. The first took place in Hong Kong's Sub Zero club on January 19 – part of a series of artistic events staged in reaction to control of the territory passing back to mainland China the following year.

After the well-received concert, a birthday party was thrown for Adrian Sherwood at a large Hong Kong venue, attended by noted rock stars such as the Foo Fighters and the Beastie Boys, who were introduced to the maestro for their first face-to-face meeting. However, the event was sullied by a dramatic quarrel between Scratch and Mireille that would almost finish their relationship for good. As the argument escalated, Mireille's anger was raised as never before. She left Hong Kong immediately, and filed for divorce on her return to Switzerland.

Directly after Mireille's furious departure, Scratch made his triumphant return to Japan for another set of live dates with Dub Syndicate; they were travelling on the same aircraft as the Beastie Boys, for whom Scratch was to open at a newly built sports stadium in Kawasaki. Though the audience grew restless towards the end of Perry's set, he would return to the stage to deliver an impromptu rap on a portion of the Beasties' 'Sabrosa'. Scratch then performed to capacity audiences on his own dates at the Quatro Club in Osaka and Tokyo's Liquid Room on January 26 and 27.

At the end of the Japanese tour, Scratch stayed briefly at Adrian Sherwood's London home, but his behaviour soon brought conflict to the dwelling. A change in his personal circumstances had seen Sherwood recently move into a new flat in Finsbury Park, and when Perry buried Sherwood's expensive television set in the back garden, he decided that Scratch would have to make other living arrangements. Sherwood thus suggested that Lee Perry return to Jamaica, and Scratch readily complied with the request.

It was not long after his return to Kingston that the Upsetter attempted to instigate a most serious mission: the re-building of the Black Ark. Though Scratch continued to be plagued by mixed emotions towards his children and by what the Black Ark had come to represent, he had long been toying with the idea of rebuilding the facility – though he had told Linton Kwesi Johnson in Switzerland that his days behind the mixing desk were basically over. It was Adrian Sherwood's encouragement that acted as the strongest catalyst, prompting Perry to make a pact with his estranged son Omar, pledging to re-build the studio with his involvement.

In the latter days of the Black Ark, Scratch had repeatedly referred to his children as the hope for the music's future; he thus joined together with the son who retained greater control over his life to begin re-sculpting the house and surrounding yard. In the weeks he spent in Jamaica, a portion of work was instigated, with new plumbing and windows put in; materials were purchased, and concrete plans were laid. Much of the money for materials Perry had brought with him from his tour in Japan; other funds came from Coxsone Dodd, who had been re-issuing Scratch's material in New York. 'Him don't show me the list of the records them that he press up, but somebody tell me Dodd was pressing my record in America, and him did get some money towards that and give me,' Perry explained. 'Me take it and buy some material, I was maybe going to replace the Black Ark studio. It was $8,000 US he get, but he have to take a certain percentage according to what him have, so me take maybe $6,000 and buy material; me bring back money me get in Japan too, and me send to England for money.'

The money from England came from his renewed link with On-U Sound, which bore more vinyl fruit through the issue of *Voodooism*, a strong retrospective collection of Black Ark material cut by On-U's re-issue subsidiary Pressure Sounds. Though culled entirely from rare vinyl, it was one of the few collections to gain Perry's sanction prior to its release, and was thus a keen antidote to the flurry of bootlegs that continued to surface in his name – though the inclusion of Zap Pow's self-produced 'River' on the disc would see the company pay a fine after David Madden instigated legal proceedings.

Towards the end of March, Perry returned to London via New York to rehearse with Dub Syndicate for upcoming live engagements, including an appearance in May at the Essential Music Festival in Brighton. When Adrian Sherwood and Steve Barker went to collect him at Heathrow Airport, they found Scratch being held by customs officers who had discovered a small amount of ganja glued to the toe of his boot; the battery compartment of his foot-long flashlight was also found to be full of herb seeds. Though such an offence usually results in a nominal fine, the officers decided to release Perry free of charge after learning he had reached his 60th birthday a few days earlier.

Due to the previous television incident, Scratch found his former host at *On-U Sound* reluctant to house him in London. Neil Fraser thus came to Adrian Sherwood's home after Perry's return, and discussed ways that On-U and Ariwa could form an alliance to cater best for Perry's needs; Professor then housed Scratch for a couple of days at one of his South London dwellings. Scratch was clearly in low spirits; he greatly missed his family in Zürich, and was resolved to return to them directly.

Arrangements were thus made to take Scratch back to Switzerland; he eventually made peace with Mireille, who retracted her divorce proceedings and allowed him to return to their home in Zürich. As Adrian Sherwood had been caught in the crossfire of their differences, Mireille held him partly responsible for their domestic troubles and made sure that links with him were entirely severed; Sherwood and Scratch have thus had no communication since Perry's return to Zürich, though Pressure Sounds were later to issue another strong collection of authorised Upsetter material, *Produced And Directed By The Upsetter*. Despite the rupture, Sherwood was keen to speak of his reverence for Scratch: 'I understand I got stuck between Lee and Mireille and that's my stupid mistake, but that's neither here nor there. When me and him have worked together, we get on well. I love him, I actually think he's one of the most important music figures of the 20th century. I can't speak highly enough of him as a talent, and as a man, he's great company, really good fun. I like working with him more than anybody, though he can be awkward as well – but who wouldn't be?'

Scratch soon returned to the UK for the performance at the Essential Music Festival on May 27, second on the bill below headliner Burning Spear; as he had broken contact with On-U Sound, he again appeared with the Mad Professor's Robotics. Dressed in lurid silver Spandex, he shocked those in the crowd whose ears were sharp enough to understand his words with a favourite sexual joke that equated his penis with Jesus – highly provocative behaviour, though later reports circulated on the Internet that he had exposed himself were grossly exaggerated. He also made a public acknowledgment of Mireille, who was watching from one wing of the stage.

In the summer of 1996, Scratch returned once more to Jamaica with Mireille, where he was filmed at the ruins of the Black Ark by a BBC television crew for the *Dancing in the Street* rock-and-roll documentary series; Scratch would appear on the punk episode 'No Fun', which incongruously also included Bunny Wailer; other unused footage was also shot with Scratch and drummer Hugh Malcolm at another Kingston studio. Unfortunately, the work he had started at the Black Ark had been undone, with many of the materials stolen or sold off; he held Sean largely responsible, as the youth was feeding his crack habit by any means necessary.

Scratch visited his mother in Hanover, ending a 13-year period of silence that began when she told him he was crazy after the burning of the Black Ark; mother and son had an emotional reunion, and siblings Sonny, Sitta, Lloyd and Miss Nell were also pleased to see him. Though now over 80, Miss Ina was still planting yams on her plot of land, working the bush with a machete; she also continued to perform Ettu at the annual Mento Yard festivities, and had even travelled to USA to perform at a televised event. Scratch offered to put some plumbing in his mother's home, but Miss Ina could see no need for running water; she did, however, eventually allow him to install electricity.

Before leaving Jamaica, Scratch again made plans to reactivate the Black Ark, despite warnings from Mireille that things were unlikely to happen as planned if Perry was absent from the country. Nevertheless, workmen were hired to clear the space and begin making the necessary preparations to lay new foundations; on departure, Perry left a substantial sum of money in Omar's care with specific instructions to be implemented.

Exactly what happened to this cash is fiercely contested by family members. The general consensus is that Omar disappeared with it, but others may have raided some of the money; in any event, little building work was carried out after Perry's departure and the Ark was left in limbo. 'It couldn't work with the Omar project,' Perry lamented, 'it's like it wasn't to be, no way.'

When several months passed and Scratch did not re-appear, Omar decided he had waited long enough and chose to join his mother in London in November 1996. On arrival, he became involved in product she was issuing, such as the misleadingly titled *Upsetter Meets the Upsetress In Dub Around The World*, the first of several such releases handled by Bibi Seaton's Sprint label; like Starlight's *Black Ark Almighty Dub Chapter 3* and Fotofon's *Dub Net Philosophy*, the album had a few of Scratch's rhythms (such as 'Evil Tongues' and 'Dyon Anasawa'), buried under guitar and synthesiser tracks overdubbed in New York. Some songs would later be re-titled for inclusion on Graylan's *Lee Perry & The Upsetter(s) Meet Scientist At Black Ark Studio* (which also included a dub of the Wailers' 'Keep On Moving' along with 12 Bunny-Lee-produced Aggrovators dubs). Omar Perry subsequently accompanied Pauline to a new home in The Gambia, where she based herself after marrying a West African; he had since gained considerable local fame as presenter of the Saturday-night *Roots Rock Reggae Showcase* programme on The Gambia's premier station, Radio One FM.

Meanwhile, Sean still dreamed of his father's return, and remained at

Cardiff Crescent waiting for him; unable to shake off his dependency on crack, he wandered the streets at night like a duppy, begging for change outside nightclubs in New Kingston after smoking the proceeds of rent gained from a stream of lodgers at the house.

After returning to Switzerland for a few uneventful months, Scratch contacted the Mad Professor in the latter part of the year, asking to work on a new album; though Professor was sitting on plenty of Perry material, he readily consented, and Scratch and Mireille were duly dispatched to London. Professor had recently opened a second 24-track studio near Thornton Heath railway station, ambiguously titled Are We Mad, and it was in this studio that Perry and Professor set to work; specifically designed for the recording of live instruments, the somewhat larger new studio held much of Professor's older equipment.

According to the Mad Professor, he and Scratch put together a strong roots album with drummer Drumton Ward and other Ariwa stalwarts in a matter of days, provisionally naming the disc *Underground Roots*. However, Scratch was beginning to resent the control his collaborators exercised over the finished product of material he had initiated; *Spiritual Healing* was the only album to surface this decade that was truly of his own creation and production. Perry's growing frustration combined with his pervasive mistrust of outsiders, which again re-surfaced with negative consequences: the unfinished album was subsequently shelved, beginning a period of animosity between Scratch and the Mad Professor. 'We ended up doing this album *Underground Roots* and having a bust-up. It was wicked roots tracks, all brand new, with a new version of "Curley Locks". We done the album in about four days, and he wanted to take the tapes and finish them in Switzerland some time. I didn't want him to take the tapes because it's my studio time and I paid for everything, so I said "No!" He stormed off angry and sent me some strong fax: he tell me he's an Obeah man and he'll do this, so I tell him my father's an Obeah man, and I give him the same. I'm from the West Indies as well, so Obeah's not out of the question; I fired him back and then we didn't speak for months.' Though the album remains unreleased at present, Professor has aired certain tracks in public on some of his solo live dub performances.

To compensate for the shelving of *Underground Roots*, Professor issued *Who Put The Voodoo 'Pon Reggae*, a collection of songs voiced by the Upsetter during his weeks in the Professor's care in the spring of 1995. Thematically similar to *Black Ark Experryments*, the album was another stream of continual words from the Upsetter, striving to express the minutiae of his particular world vision over electronic Robotics rhythms: he thus saluted his new-found Japanese popularity on 'Megaton Bomb', warned romantic rivals on 'Don't Touch My Shadow', spoke of his bad habits on 'Messy Apartment', on which he also named himself as Selassie's twin, and made oblique references to Mireille on several tracks, notably 'Go And Come Back'. Unfortunately, much of the rambling material seemed to lack focus, and no track was truly outstanding, though the album was bonded by a certain continuity and had several finely constructed rhythms.

Back in Switzerland, the Perry family was growing quickly, prompting a move at the start of 1997 to a larger property in a village on top of a mountain in the middle of the country. It was shortly after the move that the couple received a surprising request from Island Records, who were arranging to issue a high-profile retrospective collection of gems from the Black Ark.

In the aftermath of the hype generated by *Grand Royal*'s focus on Scratch, Island decided to have a triple-CD boxed set compiled of Perry's back material. From April to December 1996, tracks were dug up from the Island vaults, selected and annotated; now all the company needed was Perry's consent to the release. After some predictable haggling about money, Perry agreed to the project, and came to London towards the end of January 1997, to be subjected to a feeding frenzy of journalistic interviews – some of which drew uncharacteristically candid remarks from the Upsetter; additional publicity footage was shot by Don Letts and Rick Elgood on Island's behalf. Scratch also toasted on the mike at Anokha, a weekly club night held at London's Blue Note venue; the club's proprietor, tabla player Talvin Singh, had recently signed to Island, and their executives organised the event.

Technicalities saw the release of *Arkology* delayed until July, allowing Island to throw their publicity machinery into overdrive. The strength of the material, which was all taken from master tapes and included many previously unheard tracks, drew widespread acclaim and ranks as one of the finest presentations of material from Scratch's Black Ark heyday.

The hype generated by *Arkology* was possibly greater than that brought by the *Grand Royal* issue, and Don Letts made use of the situation to create a 30-minute documentary on Scratch by supplementing the *Arkology* promotional footage with archive material; titled *The Return Of The Super Ape*, the documentary was aired twice on Channel 4. Though too short to detail the magnanimity of Perry's creative output, the film made fascinating viewing, its archive material showing Scratch at his most manic, shortly before the final destruction of the Ark.

After Scratch's brief appearance before the press in London, the Mad Professor was able to heal his rift with Perry by engaging a lawyer to rectify Scratch's American visa problems, thus enabling him to perform in the States for the first time since his untimely departure from New York in 1981. 'I told him I've got two dates for you in America,' Professor recalled, 'very good cash in hand, so he said, "All right, let's go." ' The concerts thus took place at San Francisco's Maritime Hall on April 4 and 5, where Scratch appeared before a capacity audience draped in an American flag, backed by a Robotics backing band composed of bassist Fitzroy Brown, drummer Sinclair Seales, keyboardist Noel Salmon, and guitarist Errol Nicholson.

On the first night, Scratch took the stage at 11pm, carrying candles and incense; he was full of energy, roaming the stage and providing plenty of between-song commentary. He took a break at midnight for a costume change, only to return for the better part of another hour, much to the delight of the crowd.

The first night's set included a mutant version of Marley's 'I Shot The Sheriff' and an extended take on 'Roast Fish And Cornbread', which Perry punctuated with a bicycle horn; highlights from the similarly lengthy second night's set were subsequently issued as the CD *Live At Maritime Hall* by the newly formed 2B1 records, together with an accompanying video release – the first products to showcase Perry's abilities as a live performer. The rapturous applause that was showered on Scratch both nights showed the strength of his following in the region, and these successes would pave the way for future appearances in America.

Back in Switzerland, Scratch was itching to cut some new material, so he had Mireille contact Fizzè in May to discuss viable ideas for a maxi-single. Fizzè had moved to the village of Weite, where he set up a 24-track digital home studio – though he still retained his 16-track machine for more organic projects; he was now a family man, with a wife and young child living at the premises.

When Scratch made the journey to Weite, Fizzè was in the midst of compiling *The Return Of Peeni Waali*, another composite creation using tracks recorded in Switzerland and Jamaica, this time featuring luminaries such as Leroy 'Horsemouth' Wallace, Earl 'Chinna' Smith, Studio One keyboardist Pablove Black, England-based instrumentalists Steve Gregory, John Kpiaye, and Michael 'Bammie' Rose, plus Georgie Fame and American blues singer Taj Mahal. Determined not to repeat the abortive folly of their earlier sessions, Fizzè supplied Scratch with some opening lyrics for an oompah/ska hybrid he was working on called 'Nice Time', in which Scratch narrated a firefly's journey 'from the cockpit of Peeni Waali'; the rest of the lyrics were improvised by Scratch.

Perry returned to the Mensch studio a number of times over the ensuing month, working on his own material; he had Fizzè build him some hip-hop rhythms and eventually voiced three tracks. He subsequently asked Fizzè to build a ballad for him, but the note Fizzè sent with a rough mix of the rhythm evidently caused inadvertent offence, prompting Scratch to abandon angrily the project. As Fizzè explained, 'I sent him a beautiful ballad, and I wrote, "I will give the song to you, all you have to do is find lyrics that make sense" and he must have taken offence at that. He called me and said, "I've never met a man like you that tell I what fe do. Lee Perry is the originator. Make sure you nah release none of my riddims." '

As with the other ten tracks he had voiced at Mensch, none of the three hip-hop tracks would find a release, though Scratch's voice would feature on the 'Nice Time' track that opened the Swiss pressing of *The Return of Peeni Waali*, issued in 1998. When a baffled Fizzè contacted Mireille to inquire what had led to Perry's unexplained outburst, she informed the Mensch boss that Scratch was tired of collaborating with humans, and wanted now to work only with machines; Fizzè thus suggested Scratch contact his friend Boris Blanc, the creative force behind Swiss technological pop group Yello.

Scratch never made a link with Blanc, but it was ironically just after Fizzè's suggestion that Rich Sihilling arranged the release of the X-Perrymental tracks through ROIR as *Technomajikal* in June 1997 – ultimately a very different product from that envisioned by X-Perrymental and Scratch, and one tainted by a lack of authorisation from Perry. According to Martin Kloiber, he and Sihilling had been disheartened by a lack of interest in the album, and agreed to ROIR's small advance (circa $3000) in an effort to recoup the expenses incurred in its creation; the disc's subsequent low sales meant no royalty payments have been generated.

An exasperated Lukas Bernays spoke of his overall disappointment with such arrangements. 'After the meeting in January 1995, I had several phone calls with Dieter Meier about a possible release with Island Records, then I never heard anything. Rec Rec Music in Switzerland told me it was released and I had to buy copies of the record in a shop for myself and all the other musicians. To this day, no royalties have been paid to Scratch nor X-Perrymental. The album had a totally different cover, and it's not a new Lee Perry album because it's a co-operation between Lee Perry and some electronic rhythm builders. Since the beginning, the project was supposed to be called "X-Perrymental Featuring Lee 'Scratch' Perry" and I had no chance to make these things right. We tried to make a combination of electronic and acoustic instruments together, but had a very short time to make this record, and although there are some good moments on the CD I'm not really satisfied with the result.'

Lee Perry would later express his disgust with the circumstances of the disc's release: 'I hired the (SHS) studio and Jeannot was the keyboard man, he use machine drums and all those things, and call his drummer Lukas to see what he can invent. I paid six thousand Swiss francs for the studio time, then he said this studio place was leaky or something like that, so he disappeared to another studio and that was the last time me see that tape. Jeannot took the tracks like techno to Yello, and Yello was so stupid to release it without my signature; I don't know how him do that and that is piracy, it released without my permission. I've never heard (the album) and it's a shame to put out an artist without the artist's permission.'

Though billed as a Lee 'Scratch' Perry release, the Upsetter is little more than a visitor on much of *Technomajikal*, and its ambient and trance mixes of certain tracks drew maximum usage from minimal material. The opening 'Maxi Merlin', a '90s stew of organic and mechanised sounds that referenced 'I Am The Upsetter', is about as good as it gets, though 'Crazy House' has a certain musical clarity, and 'UFO Attack' makes good use of a sitar and a didgeridoo. The remainder sounds largely unfinished, and there are moments when Perry's voice clashes with the largely re-constructed rhythms.

Adding to the absurdity of the release – subtitled 'Genetic Mutations Of The Super Ape' – was a sticker bearing the legend 'Dieter Meier Presents Lee Perry'; although adapted at Meier's studio, the pair did no work together, and Scratch had been recording music for nearly 20 years before Meier ever set foot inside a studio. ROIR's press release, which claimed that Scratch 'refused to enter the studio but stayed on the outside lawn with headphones on and a microphone in hand', was completely untrue, according to both Dieter Meier and Lukas Bernays; this was merely a clever way of covering up the fact that Perry never made the journey to Soundproof studio.

Another interesting issue to appear in America around this time was Shanackie's *Megawatt Dub*, a collection of Black Ark and King Tubby dubs compiled by Watty Burnett; the Black Ark material was taken from master tapes given to Watty by Scratch when the singer left his stable with the Congos.

Meanwhile, Perry was voicing more new tracks in the spring of 1997. In May, the Mad Professor brought Scratch back to London for a few days to voice what would become the *Dubfire* album, issued on Ariwa nearly one year later. The pair had long discussed updating some of Perry's classic oldies, and Professor pre-built most of the rhythm tracks before the Upsetter's return to Ariwa studio. When it finally surfaced in April 1998, *Dubfire* was a puzzling issue, a sort of studio translation of his live sets with the Robotics in that chestnuts from the past were excavated for mutative purposes, familiar foundations re-used as a platform for Perry's complicated vociferation. Though the songs held interest, largely because the listener could not predict where Perry's new ramblings would lead, the album verged dangerously close to self-parody at moments, such as Scratch's imitation of a baby on the title track, and in the excessively filthy delivery that spoiled the new 'Doctor Dick'.

Similarly, cracks at Junior Byles' 'Place Called Africa' and Marley's 'Soul Rebel', 'Satisfy My Soul' and 'Duppy Conqueror' somehow lacked the depth of feeling imparted to their original versions, though their new lyrics were certainly original and somewhat humorous. The most successful numbers were perhaps those on which Scratch deviated so completely as to induce a new creation; for instance, 'Favourite Dish' no longer spoke of food, but dealt instead with the magic powers Perry used to Obeah the Devil, while 'Keep on Skanking' became an autobiographical dance number, touching on various subjects. Perhaps best of all was the melancholic new cut of Junior Byles' 'The Long Way', which concluded the album, now transformed into a broken-hearted song of romantic devotion.

However, like *The Upsetter And The Beat*, *Dubfire* ultimately had the unfortunate effect of reminding how great the originals were in the face of these somewhat inferior re-cuts; though technically well structured, the rhythms simply lack the furnace-hot vibe of their Kingston-built predecessors.

According to the Mad Professor, Scratch also voiced a number of tracks on 'trip-hop'-style rhythms during these sessions, recording enough material for yet another album that Professor is still currently sitting on.

Scratch and the Robotics were subsequently brought to New York by the Milarepa Fund – a non-profit ogranisation founded by the Beastie Boys, working to free Tibet from Chinese occupation – for a high-profile appearance at the second Free Tibet benefit concerts held at Randall's Island on June 7 and 8. Scratch again wore an American flag and had a hat made out of currency; his face was decorated with gold paint and his hair was had been dyed a streaky mix of blonde and pink. His performance of 'Heads Of Government' from this engagement was eventually included on the *Free Tibet* double album, featuring highlights from various artists at the gig. Backstage at the event, an MTV crew was preparing to film an interview with Perry, but quickly abandoned the idea after he frightened onlookers by exposing himself during another on-camera interview.

Another significant live engagement that summer saw Scratch billed to appear on the second day of a spectacular festival at a ski resort on the side of Mount Fuji in Japan, along with Massive Attack, Horace Andy, and the Prodigy on July 27. Backstage at the picturesque location, Scratch and Horace mumbled dark prophecies on the wrathful nature of God as the elements unleashed their fury in the shape of Typhoon Rosie; the drastic weather conditions gave Fuji such a battering that the second day's events were cancelled.

Scratch then returned to London to headline the Roots Day at the first Essential London Weekender, held at Finsbury Park on August 3; though backed by the Robotics as usual, Scratch seemed distracted and delivered a poor performance; younger opening artists such as Cocoa Tea, Yami Bolo, Everton Blender, Anthony B, and Horace Andy thus seriously upstaged him. During one interlude, Scratch dumped some pent-up angst on the crowd, screaming 'I say fuck you police and fuck you soldiers!' at the top of his lungs. Further dates were undertaken in Europe, including an appearance at Lokeren in Belgium, where Scratch wore a feather in his hair and baggy purple trousers.

At the end of October, Perry began an extensive one-month tour of North America with the Robotics, performing on 19 separate dates in the US and Canada. The tour began on October 28 at the 9.30 Club in Washington DC, directly followed by three nights at Wetlands. The Beastie Boys were then working on a new album with Mario Caldato Jr in a makeshift studio they had set up in the basement of a building in Greenwich Village where Sean Lennon has an office, and decided to ask Scratch if he would be willing to voice a rhythm they had created a couple of years earlier. The track was led by an Upsetterish organ and peppered by Niyabinghi beats; unlike anything else the group had created, the rhythm was reminiscent of 'Mr Brown' and seemed perfectly suited for Perry.

Caldato and Mike D thus went to Wetlands early on October 30, hoping to catch Lee Perry at his sound check, but Scratch was not on the premises and the duo left a message for him with Mad Professor. The next day, Professor confirmed Perry's interest, and when the group made a call to his hotel room at the World Trade Center Hilton, Scratch cut short a conversation with Mireille about financial particulars to request he be picked up and brought to their studio.

As it was Adam 'Adrock' Horovitz's birthday, he had a previous engagement and disappeared, as did Mike D; Adam 'MCA' Yauch and Mario Caldato Jr thus brought Scratch and Mireille to the studio to transform the aforementioned rhythm into the humorous 'Dr Lee PhD'. According to Caldato, Scratch got into lyrical flow as soon as the tape was rolling. 'Before we started he went to the mixing board, put his hands on top of it and bowed his head, banged his head on it a couple of time, blessing it. Then he started with the lyrics – he had a poster in his pocket of the gig with his lyrics already written on it. After about 30 seconds of listening to the track, he said, "OK, let's record this." Then he said, "Let's do it one more time," he did it better and that was it. Then he goes, "Give me a background track again," and he did two background tracks with cow sounds and coughs, they were great. Then I said "Lee, I love the way you play percussion on your old recordings," so he got maracas, tambourine, cowbells, and chucked them on the floor in front of the mic, said "OK, let's go." There was this picture of Bruce Lee in front of the console and after we finished the session, I said, "Can I post you up there? I'll put you up with Bruce Lee," but he said, "I-man no go next to a Chinee man, put me on top," so we put his picture on top of the Bruce Lee picture. He said "Make sure it doesn't come down for a long time." '

Once the percussive track had been captured, Scratch needed to leave the area quickly to fulfil his final engagement at Wetlands, but the Greenwich Village Halloween parade made it impossible for a taxi to reach the area. Scratch and Mireille were thus forced to travel to Wetlands with Caldato and Yauch by subway, though the appearance of costumed revellers meant that Perry blended naturally with the crowd. 'It was the one night of the year Lee Perry could walk down the street and no one would give him a second look,' explained Mike D. 'His clothes had mirrors all over them, painted everywhere; every potential surface was covered with something, but no one gave him a second look.'

After the Wetlands performance, Scratch made his Canadian debut at Toronto's Phoenix Theatre on November 4, followed by an appearance at Detroit's Majestic Theatre the next night and a memorable evening at Chicago's Cubby Bear Lounge on the 7th (where a number of people bowed down in prayer before the stage); he then played the Fox Theatre in Boulder the next night and the Coach House in San Juan Capistrano on the 10th, followed by appearances at the Belly Up Tavern in Solana Beach, the West Hollywood Billborad, Palookaville in Santa Cruz, San Francisco's Maritime Hall, the Reggae on the River Festival, Eugene's WOW Hall on the 18th, Seattle's Foenix Theatre, Vancouver's Sonar Hall, and a final date at San Francisco's Maritime Hall on November 22.

Another quiet period followed the tour while the ball of releases and publicity rolled on without him. Towards the end of the year, Scratch's attention was called to an unofficial website devoted to his work that had been set up by a certain M. Chevalier, a.k.a. Mick Sleeper, a 28-year-old Clash fan and radio disc jockey on independent station CJSR in Edmonton, Canada, whose highly visual Lee Perry site first appeared on the Internet on August 16, 1996. Though incorrect information was occasionally posted on the site, its visual presentation and textual pizzazz made a strong impression on Scratch, who contacted Sleeper through an intermediary to address the world via two telephone interviews with the webmaster. The first was conducted in December 1997, and had Scratch waxing lyrical about why he abandoned reggae, alluding to conflicts with his son Sean and others he had worked with in the past; he also claimed he was building a White Ark and that he would no longer perform live with black musicians. After Scratch and Mireille spent another month in Jamaica, returning to Switzerland in mid-January 1998, Sleeper conducted a second telephone interview in February, elucidating candid comments on a variety of artists.

Scratch's extensive touring with the Robotics continued in 1998, starting with live dates in France that April to support the release of *Dub Fire*; the highlight was an appearance at the 22nd Spring Festival in Bourges, where Perry performed to a crowd of 5000 on a bill shared with Linton Kwesi Johnson. On April 23, he and the band travelled to Eugene, Oregon, to kick off a two-week, 15-date US tour concentrating on the West Coast; highlights included a return to San Francisco's Maritime Hall on May 1, another Cubby Bear performance in Chicago on May 7 (which again drew praying fans before the stage), and two final nights at New York's Wetlands on May 8 and 9. After his performance at the Fenix Club in Seattle on April 25, Scratch was approached backstage by former Black Ark session player and current Seattle resident Clinton Fearon for their first meeting in many years. Fearon noted the following particulars of their brief exchange: 'I reminded him who I was and we were excited to see each other again – it had been maybe 15 years or more since I last saw Scratch. Scratch said to everybody else in the room "This is a bad bass player; he come from the hills, from nowhere come play several hits like 'Curley Locks'." I tried to correct him and say it's "Roast Fish And Cornbread" but he was still saying "Curley Locks". At one point him turn to his wife and say "Give him a $50 for me," then him scratch him head a little bit and said 'OK, give him $100.' She wrap up some bills and put them in my hand; I thought it was 100 bucks but found out later it was just 50 bucks, so now I can say I got $50 royalties from all those past works! I don't know what happened to Scratch, I heard all kinds of different stories. At one point he was actually walking around as though something had really happened to him in the head, which left everyone thinking that Scratch was mad. But in those same times, I happened to talk with Scratch and Scratch was sound to me. I thought maybe Scratch was covering something up, or intentionally fooling the public. I always think that Scratch is more of a genius than a madman.'

Back in Europe at the tour's end, the Upsetter appeared at the Essential Roots All-Dayer on May 25, second on the bill to South African singer Lucky Dube; as the Brighton Festival had grown too big for its original site, the concerts were moved to the cramped indoor venue of the Brixton Academy in South London. In high contrast to the previous year's Finsbury Park success, the Academy event was unfortunately something of a shambles. It started late, was overcrowded, dirty, and poorly lit, had poor sound quality throughout and was so overbooked that many artists had their sets cut drastically short, most notably Augustus Pablo, who was dragged off stage after only a few numbers. Scratch's performance itself was somewhat lacking, perhaps stemming from the chaotic atmosphere; he yelled more than sang on most numbers, though two trip-hop style rhythms proved popular with the audience.

During his brief time in London, the Upsetter went to Harlesden to check Phil Pratt, a colleague he had regularly visited over the years, often in the company of Adrian Sherwood. On this particular occasion, Perry was displeased to find Bunny Lee in the vicinity, and made disparaging remarks when Striker passed.

In the summer, Scratch and the Robotics played selected dates in America, with a notable performance taking place at San Francisco's famous Fillmore venue, where he informed the audience that 'Jesus was a hippie'; he also baptised the electrical wires on stage before a version of 'War In A Babylon'. He was second on the bill below Alpha Blondy at the 12th annual Reggae On The Rocks festival in Morrison, Colorado on August 23, and gave a further notable performance at the end of the month at the Reading Festival in England, where he once again shared the bill with the Beastie Boys, a fitting combination, as the group's *Hello Nasty* album had been freshly issued, with great media interest placed on Scratch's appearance on 'Dr Lee, PhD'. Other summer performances were made in Holland, where Scratch and his family also relaxed on vacation; though their touring schedule was often hectic, Scratch and Mireille always made space for their children, taking them to various amusement parks in Europe and America.

In September, Scratch returned to Jamaica where he spent some time in Montego Bay with Mireille before travelling to Kingston to do business. He renewed his links with Coxsone Dodd, who had returned to the island after the death of his mother; Dodd was in the process of refurbishing Studio One, and

Scratch came to meet him at the studio on several occasions, where he also encountered such Studio One regulars as King Stitt, the Silvertones, and Winston Jarrett. Scratch and Downbeat discussed plans for future work together, and devised schemes to help Perry gain greater control over his back catalogue, though little was actually arranged.

At the end of the month, Scratch re-appeared at Cardiff Crescent, and immediately kicked the lodgers out of the house. He had come with the precise intention of re-building the Black Ark, but knew the work could not be completed while Sean still lived at the property; he thus persuaded his errant son to find some space elsewhere.

Although he had made efforts to reduce his crack consumption, attending a drug-treatment centre in Half Way Tree, Sean was unable to break his addiction and continued to live a problematic existence; shortly before his father's arrival, Sean had his arm slashed by a tenant in a fracas at the house.

To demonstrate his solidarity and loyalty, Sean dyed his hair a similar shade of orange to that now sported by his father, but the gesture failed to impress Perry senior. Nevertheless, a tenuous peace was established with his troublesome eldest son, and Scratch again issued directions to construction workers once Sean had vacated the premises and Jah Ned was appointed guardian of the property.

His daughter Marsha eventually visited him at Cardiff Crescent, though she found him somewhat guarded and reserved on the afternoon they spent together; she was continuing to support herself through hairdressing, and from the rent obtained from the bottom half of the property she occupied with Prince, whom she married at a church ceremony the previous March.

In contrast, Michelle chose to avoid Mr Perry, having retained too much unhappiness about the past. Unable to support herself in Kingston, Michelle had placed her children in the care of others – including Marsha, who took charge of her eldest child Lassano – and went to work as a hotel hairdresser on the wealthy neighbouring island of Grand Cayman in 1996. She returned to Kingston a few months before Scratch turned up in Washington Gardens, and was trying to raise enough money to try her luck on the Turks and Caicos Islands.

After engaging builders and issuing instructions, Lee Perry again left Jamaica to return to Switzerland before much substantial work had been carried out at Cardiff Crescent. Back in Switzerland, further upsets were shortly to reach the Upsetter through further pirated tracks. In the run-up to Christmas, 1998, Jet Star issued a box set of Perry material as *Lost Treasures Of The Ark*, much of which was taken from cassette and DAT copies of master tapes Pauline Morrison had previously sold to another company. The true gems in the set were Marley's 'Who Colt The Game' and 'I Know A Place', though other tracks overlapped with previous collections (including Jet Star/ Charm's oddly titled *Original Super Ape*, a 1997 re-issue of *Return Of The*

Super Ape, whose bonus tracks were re-cut on the boxed set). Despite the strength of much of its contents, the random track order and generally poor-quality packaging – which included an unauthorised use of photographs and other pirated images – rendered the collection as an inferior imitation of *Arkology*, though it was certainly among the most lavishly packaged issues ever released by the company. When Scratch found out about the boxed set in early 1999, he was understandably furious, and had an angry confrontation with Carl Palmer by telephone; the Jet Star boss thus cut Pauline out of the deal and began making payments to Scratch.

In mid-February, Scratch returned to the USA, spending a week relaxing in Orlando on vacation with his family before what was billed as the 'Fat American Tour' with the Robotics; it covered 13 dates in two and a half weeks, mostly concentrating on the East coast. Notable engagements included gigs at the House of Blues venues in New Orleans and Chicago – where Perry exposed himself on stage despite the cold weather – and a return to Irving Plaza in New York.

After completing his US tour on March 8, he returned to Jamaica for a three-week period to continue rebuilding the Black Ark, again planning to house the studio inside the main building at Cardiff Crescent.

Back in Switzerland in April, Scratch planned to change his future live act by employing a Jamaican band featuring his old bassist Family Man, but changed his mind after a CD Fams sent him jammed his CD player. He then consented to appear with the Robotics on an 11-date North American tour beginning June 14; other summer and autumn festival dates were secured for France and Spain, and debut appearances in Australia and New Zealand scheduled to take place in October.

In early May, Perry spent a few days in Düsseldorf going through a draft of this book; he then returned to Jamaica on May 18 to spend another three weeks supervising construction at Cardiff Crescent, though whether the studio will ever be functional again is anyone's guess. Scratch is reported to have spent over $30,000 (US) on his last attempt at re-building, and exactly what he plans to do with the space seems to be changing with the passing of time. In September 1998, he insisted he would make sure the studio be completed, specifying that the new Black Ark would now be a pop-music facility at which no reggae could be created: 'What was is what was, and reggae is what was, but now I'm coming back with pop music.' On returning to the premises in May 1999, Perry had P-Son build some outdoor fish tanks and begin the creation of an area for turtles, and now spoke of what was being constructed in abstract, cinematic terms; his wife suggested the space may emerge as a 'museum' or some kind of 'holy house', while Scratch described it as a 'seat of power' he was obliged to construct due to his destruction of the original: 'I'm going to buy another house for myself, because what I re-build, I won't be living there. Because I burn it down, I overstand that I was wrong; I couldn't take those people, what those guys want me to take, so I say I commit a sin and burn down the Ark, so I am out there now, working to re-build back that Ark . . . It looking to a movie or film house, because the film was filming from the beginning of time; God did make original film and whosoever here to play the part, we play it now and me reach Revelation which is the Judgement: It will finish off poor America, because if they fuck with my passport I'm going to fuck with their goverment and mash them down with Judgement. Me know me working fe God, but other people working for money or working for the Devil . . . It won't be a recording studio, it will be a government to rule the world, the universe, the globe, and the equator straight from there with rain, thunder and lightning, hailstone, brimstone, and fire, hailstone and ice and smoke, with the blood of Jesus – with Jesus Christ's blood bath.'

The exact shape of Perry's future – both musical and otherwise – thus remains unfathomable, or perhaps simply unknown, but as the Mad Professor has so poignantly noted, Scratch is too spontaneous to plan really ahead, preferring to blow where the wind blows him, or to act on the directions of his ever-changing secret spirit guide.

As we cross the threshold of a new millennium, Lee Perry is approaching what the Western world normally deems an appropriate age for retirement, but it is difficult to imagine that Scratch would cease creating music while still a living being on this earth. His glory days as a music producer may have given way to a focus on the spectacle of live performance and spontaneous, disjointed collaborations, but Scratch continues to exercise the musical shamanism and ceaseless innovation that has characterised the previous four decades of his career. As further retrospectives place a greater focus on the past Perry so desperately seeks to forget, the public continues to overlook the fact that the Upsetter is living in the future; as a true appreciation of the genius of his work has typically arrived a good 20 to 30 years after the fact, the passing of time may see an illumination of the innovative nature of his more recent creations. Whatever form such future creations ultimately take, they are assured of being unique, and will certainly continue to be futuristic in character. 'Mr Perry is an enigma,' says Sean of his famous father, 'but, trust me, he is way ahead of his time; it's we who have to try and catch him up.'

And what does Scratch envisage for his future at this point? I leave the closing words of this tome to him who should best know: Rainford Hugh Lee 'Scratch' Perry, the mighty Upsetter, visionary artist and musical originator:

'A message: I'm going to re-organise Africa with my music government. In England, I must caput the Queen, caput the taxes; I am going to, no problem, knock out the Queen government, re-build African government, and show them in Jamaica who me responsible for. An eye for an eye and a tooth for a tooth, the law of Moses: you be good to me and I'll be good to you, you be bad to me I'll be extremely bad to you; if you be wicked to me, I'll be wickeder to you. The Upsetter present the end of the Heads of Government, because the 2000 is here, and I represent the year 2000, I come before my time and they respect me. For the future, I see that Jesus Christ is black and God is also black, so the Pope and the Bishop wrong: Jesus Christ wasn't white, so I black the future of all the politicians and all the government – black it with the Black Ark; I black the future as Super Man, Super Ape. Me know have no mercy any more, I'm cold as ice. When the children must exist, children don't exist in fear; you have to upset them . . . (when) them rediscover the spaceship, they will see it is the Ark of the Covenant, and the right solution. That must go in the book, let people know what is going on: I am here to prove that God is black and that Jesus Christ is black, that's why I'm here with the Black Ark. The game black, cannot be opened after me. Lee Scratch Perry is in God's spaceship.'

◆

Notes to the Text

CHAPTER ONE

Introducing Myself: *From Kendal to Kingston*

1 Danny Kelly, 'Lee Perry' in *New Musical Express*, 17 November 1984, page 6.
2 Interview with Bruno Blum, Zürich, May 1994.
3 Kelly, op. cit.
4 ibid.
5 ibid..
6 Blum, op. cit.
7 ibid.
8 ibid.
9 Kelly, op. cit.
10 ibid.
11 Blum, op. cit.

CHAPTER TWO

Chicken Scratch: *The Studio One Years*

1 Interview with Steve Barrow, Kingston, March 6, 1994.
2 Blum, op. cit.
3 Interview with Steve Barrow, Kingston, March 1994.
4 Blum, op. cit.
5 Chris May, 'Starting From Scratch' in *Black Music*, Volume 4, Issue 47 (October 1977), page 13.
6 Blum, op. cit.
7 May, op. cit.
8 ibid.

9 Bob Mack, 'Downbeat the Ruler Reflects Upon His Prize Pupil' in *Grand Royal*, Issue 2 (1995), page 78.
10 May, op. cit.

CHAPTER THREE

Give me Justice: *The Upsetter Emerges*

1 Kelly, op. cit.
2 Jean-François Bizot, 'Jamaïque: Reggae, Colts et Cubans' in *Actuel Almanac des Année* 1980, page 256.
3 Ray Hurford and Geoff Sullivan (1987), 'Dennis Alcapone – The First DJ Cup Winner' in *More Axe*, Ray Hurford, ed. (1987)
4 Blum, op. cit.
5 Carl Gayle, 'The Upsetter' in *Black Music*, Volume 2, Issue 14 (January 1975), page 10.
6 Thomas Markert, 'Grand Royal Interview' in *Grand Royal*, Issue 2 (1995–1996), pages 68–69.
7 Markert, op. cit.
8 Gayle, op. cit.
9 Kelly, op. cit.
10 Blum, op. cit.
11 May, op. cit.
12 Helene Lee, 'Lee "Scratch" Perry, le reggae aux portes de la folie' in *Hors Série L'Affiche* Number 2 (1996), page 71.
13 Barrow, op. cit.

CHAPTER FOUR
THE RETURN OF DJANGO: *International Success*

1 Blum, op. cit.
2 Barrow, op. cit.
3 Interview with Karel Michiels in *The Unlimited Destruction*, Jet Star Video, 1990
4 Carl Gayle, 'Blood Brother' in *Black Music*, Volume 2, Issue 15 (February 1975) page 20.
5 Carl Gayle, 'The Upsetter (Part 2)' in *Black Music*, Volume 2, Issue 15 (February 1975).

CHAPTER FIVE
SOUL REBELS: *The Upsetter and The Wailers*

1 Interview with Daddy Ernie, Choice FM London radio broadcast, May 13, 1999.
2 Blum, op. cit.
3 Interview with Bruno Blum, October 18, 1997, Reims.
4 ibid.
5 May, op. cit.
6 Barrow, op. cit.
7 Gayle, op. cit.
8 ibid.
9 Blum, op. cit.
10 ibid.
11 Gayle, op. cit.
12 ibid.
13 ibid.
14 ibid.
15 Interview with Bruno Blum, May 1994.
16 Gayle, op. cit.
17 ibid.
18 Blum, op. cit.

CHAPTER SIX
BEAT DOWN BABYLON: *Building the Ark*

1 Gayle, op. cit.

2 Chris Lane, 'Starting From Scratch' in *Blues and Soul*, number 115, August 3–16, 1973, page 27.
3 Gayle, op. cit.
4 ibid.
5 Lane, op. cit.
6 Rob Randall, 'Lee Perry: Reversing The Trend' in *Melody Maker*, July 7, 1973, page 52.
7 Carl Gayle, 'The Upsetter' in *Black Music*, Volume 2, Issue 14 (January 1975), page 10.

CHAPTER SEVEN
HURT SO GOOD: *Early Fruits of the Black Ark*

1 Interview with Tony Williams, BBC Radio London broadcast, November 1984.
2 Doug Wendt, 'The Return of the Upsetter' in *High Times*, January 1998, page 66.
3 Ashley Heath, 'Jesus is a Soul Man' in *The Face*, April 1997, page 130.
4 Crispin Taylor, 'Return to the Ark' in *Straight No Chaser*, Number 40, spring 1997, page 47.

CHAPTER EIGHT
ENTER THE DRAGON: *Black Ark Album Abstractions*

1 Carl Gayle, 'The Upsetter Part 2' in *Black Music*, Volume 2, Issue 15, February 1975, page 42.

CHAPTER NINE
POLICE AND THIEVES: *The Golden Years of the Black Ark*

1 May, op. cit.
2 Interview with Steve Barrow for Reggae Archive project, March 1994.
3 As stated by Isaacs to Ray Hurford, *Small Axe* magazine, 1979.
4 Interview with Bob Mack in *Grand Royal*, Issue 2, 1995, page 81.

5   ibid.

6   ibid.

CHAPTER TEN

CITY TOO HOT: *The Excessive Apex and Sudden Fall of the Ark*

1   Interview with David Rodigan, Capital Radio, London, broadcast February 23, 1980.

2   That is, a homosexual.

CHAPTER ELEVEN

THE RETURN OF PIPECOCK JACKXON: *The Partial Rebirth and Ultimate Destruction of the Ark*

1   Henry W. Targowski, 'Lee Perry: Genius, Madman, Magician' in *Vinyl* No. 7, 1981, pages 14–15.

2   Viven Goldman, 'Lee Perry has found God, and His name is Pipecock Jackxon' in *Melody Maker*, July 21, 1979.

3   Rodigan, op. cit.

4   Interview with Pieter Franssen, VPRO Radio 3 broadcast, Holland, April 4, 1990.

5   Richard Grabell, 'Curse of the Vampire,' in *New Musical Express*, July 25, 1981, page 24.

6   ibid.

7   Interview with Robert Kuypers and Karel Michiels, Zürich, April 10, 1990.

8   Author unknown, *Talk Talk*, Vol. 3 No. 4, June 1982, page 20.

9   Kelly, op. cit., pages 57–58.

10 Tropic FM radio broadcast, Paris France, November 6, 1988; interview conducted November 1987 by Mary Nnankya and Florent Drouet.

CHAPTER TWELVE

I AM A MADMAN: *Years in England*

1   As told by Tobias Schneebaum at 'Art of the Asmat' presentation, September 10, 1998, San Francisco.

2   Interview with Tony Williams, BBC Radio London, November 1984.

3   C. Gordon, *The Reggae Files*, 1988, page 99; interview conducted November 1, 1987.

4   ibid.

5   Drouet and Nnankya, op. cit.

6   The man in question is not Mikey 'Dread' Campbell, as has been inaccurately reported elsewhere.

CHAPTER THIRTEEN

THE SECRET LABORATORY: *A Base in Switzerland*

1   Kuypers and Michiels, op. cit.

2   Franssen, op. cit.

3   i.e. *170 Hours With Extraterrestrials.*

selected albums discography

LEE PERRY PRODUCTIONS, PLUS PERRY VOCALS AND DUB ALBUMS

1969

THE UPSETTER
[Trojan (UK) TTL 13]
Tidal Wave/Heat Proof/To Love Somebody (Busty Brown)/Night Doctor/Soulful I/Big Noise/Man From MI5/Dread Luck/Kiddy-O (Muskyteers a.k.a. Silvertones)/Wolf Man/Crying About You (Busty Brown)/Thunderball.
Note: Night Doctor produced by Ansel Collins. Re-issued 1996.

RETURN OF DJANGO – The Upsetters
[Trojan/Upsetter (UK) TRL 19]
Return Of Django/Touch Of Fire/Cold Sweat/Drugs And Poison/Soulful I/Night Doctor/One Punch/Eight For Eight/Live Injection/Man From MI5/Ten To Twelve/Medical Operation.
Note: Night Doctor produced by Ansel Collins. Re-issued 1996.

CLINT EASTWOOD – The Upsetters
[Punch (UK) 21/PSP 1014]
Return Of The Ugly/For A Few Dollars More/Prisoner Of Love (Dave Barker)/Dry Acid (Sticky)/Rightful Ruler (U Roy with Count Ossie & Peter Tosh)/Clint Eastwood/Taste Of Killing/Selassie (Reggae Boys)/What Is This/Ain't No Love/My Mob/I've Caught You (Sticky).
Note: Re-issued 1980 by Jet Star as BEST OF LEE PERRY & THE UPSETTERS VOL. 1 (PTP 1023).

1970

MANY MOODS OF THE UPSETTERS
[Economy (UK) & Upsetter (JA) SECO 24]
Exray Vision/Can't Take It Anymore (David Isaacs)/Soul Stew/Low Lights/Cloud Nine (Carl Dawkins)/Beware Fade/Serious Joke/Goosy (Pat Satchmo)/Prove It/Boss Society (Pat Satchmo)/Mean And Dangerous/Games People Play/Extra.
Note: 'Extra' included on Jamaican release only. UK version re-issued by Jet Star in 1981 as THE BEST OF LEE PERRY & THE UPSETTERS VOL. 2 (PT 1026).

SCRATCH THE UPSETTER AGAIN – The Upsetters
[Trojan/Upsetter (UK) TTL 28]
Bad Tooth/The Dentis(t)/Outer Space/One Punch/Will You Still Love Me (Dave
     Barker)/Take One/Soul Walk/I Want To Thank You/Mule Train (Count Prince
     Miller)/Touch Of Fire/She Is Gone Again (Alva Lewis)/The Result.
Note: Re-issued 1995 in combination with EASTWOOD RIDES AGAIN; solo re-issue 1996.

THE GOOD, THE BAD AND THE UPSETTERS
[Upsetter (JA) TTL 67]
Same Thing All Over/It's All In The Game/Big Ball/If You Don't Mind/Dracula/ It's
     Alright/Man To Man V-3/Soul Rebel V-4/Must Reach You/Equalizer/Down The
     Road/Some Sign/On The Rock/Same Thing V-3.
Note: Issued in sleeve of Trojan (UK) TBL 119, stickered with different track listing.

EASTWOOD RIDES AGAIN – The Upsetters
[Trojan (UK) TBL 125]
Eastwood Rides Again/Hit Me/Knock On Wood (Untouchables)/Pop Corn/Catch
     This/You Are Adorable/Capsol/Power Pack/Dollar In The Teeth/Baby Baby (Val
     Bennett)/Django-Ol' Man River (a.k.a. Django Shoots First, Sir Lord Comic)/Red
     Hot/Salt And Pepper/Tight Spot.
Note: Re-issued 1995 in combination with SCRATCH THE UPSETTER AGAIN; solo
     re-issue 1996.

SOUL REBELS – Bob Marley & the Wailers
[Trojan (UK) TBL 126 & Maroon/Upsetter (JA)]
Soul Rebel/Try Me/It's Alright/No Sympathy/My Cup/Rebel's Hop/Corner Stone/400
     Years/No Water/Reaction/My Sympathy.
Note: Re-issued 1988.

PRISONER OF LOVE – Dave Barker Meets the Upsetters
[Trojan (UK) TBL 127]
Shocks Of Mighty/Build My Whole World Around You/My Cup/Love Me Baby/Set
     Me Free/Blowing In The Wind/Prisoner of Love/I Was Wrong/One Little Lie/
     Skanky Chicken/Never Before/The Same Game/Runaway Child.
Note: Re-issued 1996.

1971

SOUL REVOLUTION – Bob Marley & the Wailers
[Maroon (JA) TTL 65/Maroon LOP TTL 65 & Upsetter (JA) TTL 65A/TTL 66A]
Keep On Moving/Don't Rock My Boat/Put It On/Fussing And Fighting/Duppy
     Conqueror V-4/Memphis/Riding High/Kaya/African Herbsman/Stand Alone/Sun Is
     Shining/Brain Washing.
Note: Many Upsetter label copies issued in SOUL REVOLUTION PART 2 sleeves. Re-
     issued 1988 by Trojan as part of SOUL REVOLUTION I & II (TRLD 406).

SOUL REVOLUTION PART 2 – Bob Marley & the Wailers
[Upsetter (JA) TTL 65B/TTL 66B]
Keep On Moving/Don't Rock My Boat/Put It On/Fussing And Fighting/Duppy
     Conqueror V-4/Memphis/Riding High/Kaya/African Herbsman/Stand Alone/Sun Is
     Shining/Brain Washing.

Note: All tracks are instrumental. Re-issued 1975 by Tuff Gong (JA) on Upsetter as RHYTHM PART 3. Re-issued 1988 by Trojan as part of SOUL REVOLUTION I & II (TRLD 406).

AFRICA'S BLOOD – The Upsetters
[Trojan (UK) TBL 166/Upsetter (JA) GWL 3]
Do Your Thing (Dave Barker)/Dreamland/Long Sentence/Not Guilty/Cool And Easy/ Well Dread Version 3 (Addis Ababa Children)/My Girl/Sawdust/Place Called Africa Version 3 (Winston Prince, a.k.a. Dr Alimantado)/Isn't It Wrong (Hurricanes)/Go Slow/Bad Luck/Move Me/Surplus.
Note: Re-issued 1985 as part of THE UPSETTER BOX SET (PERRY 1); solo CD re-issue 1996.

1972

BATTLE AXE – Various Artists
[Trojan (UK) TBL 167/Upsetter (JA) GWL 4]
Battle Axe (Upsetters)/Place Called Africa (Jr Byles)/Cheerio (Upsetters)/Picture On The Wall (Ras Darkins, a.k.a. Carl Dawkins)/Cool Operator (Delroy Wilson)/Knock Three Times (Upsetters)/Pop-A-Pop (Andy Capp)/Earthquake (Upsetters)/Don't Cross The Nation (Mark & Luke, a.k.a. Little Roy)/Dark Moon (Upsetters)/Rough And Smooth (Upsetters)/Groove Me (Upsetters)/Easy Snapping (Upsetters)/I'm Yours (Delroy Wilson).

BEAT DOWN BABYLON – Junior Byles
[Trojan (UK) TRL 52/Dynamic (JA) WIZZ 5001/3]
Da Da/I've Got A Feeling/Don't Know Why/Demonstration/Coming Again/Beat down Babylon/A Place Called Africa/Joshua's Desire/A Matter Of Time/Poor Chubby.
Note: Re-issued 1987 by Trojan as BEAT DOWN BABYLON THE UPSETTER YEARS (TRLS 253) with altered track order and bonus tracks: Fun And Games/ Motion Dub/Pretty Fe True/Pretty Dub/King Of Babylon/Pharaoh Hiding/Hail To Power. Original album re-issued on CD by Sprint (UK) in 1998 (UP 3) with bonus tracks: The Thanks We Get/Rasta No Pickpocket/Curly Locks/Now Generation.

AFRICAN HERBSMAN Bob Marley & the Wailers
[Trojan (UK) TRLS 62]
Lively Up Yourself/Small Axe/Duppy Conqueror/Trench Town Rock/African Herbsman/Keep On Moving/Fussing And Fighting/Stand Alone/All In One/Don't Rock The Boat/Put It On/Sun Is Shining/Kaya/Riding High/Brain Washing/400 Years.
Note: Lively up Yourself/Trenchtown Rock produced by Bob Marley. Re-issued 1988.

1973

CLOAK AND DAGGER – Scratch the Upsetter
[Rhino (UK) SRNO 8002]
Cloak & Dagger/Hail Stone/Musical Transplant/Liquid Serenade/Retail Love/Creation/ Iron Claw/Rude Walking/Cave Man Skank/Pe We Special/Sunshine Rock/Wakey Wakey.

CLOAK AND DAGGER – Scratch the Upsetter
[Upsetter (JA) SRNN 7001]
Cloak & Dagger/Sharp Razor/Hail Stone/Musical Transplant/Liquid Serenade/Side
   Gate/Iron Claw/V-S Iron Side/Rude Walking/V-S Bad Walking/Caveman Skank/Pe
   We Special.
Note: Issued in plain sleeve. Re-issued by Black Star Liner (NL) on Black Art (BSLP
   9001) in 1979 and by Anachron (NL) in 1989 (TSLP 9001).

RHYTHM SHOWER – Upsetters
[Upsetter (JA)]
Tighten Up (Dillinger)/Django Shoots First (Sir Lord Comic)/Uncle Charley/Sokup/
   Double Power/Lover Version/Rumpelsteelkin/Skanking (Dillinger)/Kuchy Skank/
   Connection (Dillinger)/Operation.
Note: Re-issued by Trojan 1985 as part of THE UPSETTER BOX SET (PERRY 1).

UPSETTERS 14 DUB BLACKBOARD JUNGLE (a.k.a. BLACKBOARD JUNGLE
   DUB)
[Upsetter (JA) SCR LP 1]
Black Panta/V-S Panta Rock/Khasha Macka/Elephant Rock/African Skank/Dreamland
   Skank/Jungle Jim/Drum Rock/Dub Organizer/Lovers Skank/Mooving Skank/
   Apeman Skank/Jungle Skank/Kaya Skank.
Note: True stereo mix, original pressing of 300 copies, blank sleeve. Re-issued by
   Coxsone (US) in 1990 on Upsetter as BLACKBOARD JUNGLE DUB with
   incorrect track listing. Alternative pressing with amended track listing and different
   mix issued on Upsetter (JA), on Clocktower (US) in 1981 (CT 115), by RAS (US) in
   1988 as part of SCRATCH ATTACK, by Jet Star/Orchid in 1994 (ORCHCD 1) as
   'ORIGINAL' BLACKBOARD JUNGLE DUB (re-issued as budget price release
   1998) and with altered titles by Rhino (UK) in 1996 (RN 7015) as part of BUNNY
   LEE & THE AGGROVATORS AGGROVATE LEE PERRY & THE
   UPSETTERS.

SILVER BULLETS – The Silvertones
[Trojan (UK) TRL 69 & Black Art (JA)]
I'll Take You Home/Early In The Morning/Sugar Sugar/Souvenir Of Mexico/Rejoice
   Jah Jah Children/Rejoicing Skank/That's When It Hurts/Soul Sister/Rock Me In
   Your Soul/Sweet And Loving Baby/He'll Break Your Heart.
Note: Jamaican pressing has different mix from UK release; UK version re-issued 1996.

1974

DOUBLE SEVEN – The Upsetters
[Trojan (UK) TRLS 70]
Kentucky Skank/Double Six (U Roy)/Just Enough (David Isaacs)/In the Iaah/Jungle
   Lion/We Are Neighbours (David Isaacs)/Soul Man/Stick Together (U Roy)/High
   Fashion (I Roy)/Long Sentence/Hail Stones (I Roy)/Ironside/Cold Weather/Waap
   You Waa.
Note: Re-issued 1985 as part of THE UPSETTER BOX SET (PERRY 1); solo CD re-
   issue 1996.

RASTA REVOLUTION – Bob Marley & the Wailers
[Trojan (UK) TRLS 89]

Mr Brown/Soul Rebel/Try Me/It's Alright/No Sympathy/My Cup/Duppy Conqueror/
Rebel's Hop/Corner Stone/400 Years/No Water/Reaction/Soul Almighty.
Note: Material recorded 1970.

1975

DIP PRESENTS THE UPSETTER
[DIP (UK) DLP 5026]
Enter The Dragon (Upsetters)/I Don't Mind (Sam Carty)/Cane River Rock (Upsetters)/
I Man Free (King Burnett)/Jamaican Theme (Upsetters)/Time (Gladiators)/Jump It
(Leo Graham)/Life Is A Flower (Sam Carty)/Have Some Fun (Gaylads)/Nature Man
(Gaylads)/Dub A Pum Pum (Silvertones)/Kung Fu Man (Linval Thompson,
miscredited as Linval Spencer).
Note: Re-issued 1999 as BLACK ARCHIVES by Ravensquire on Justice League (JL
5005) with Dub A Pum Pum & Kung Fu Man removed, plus bonus tracks: Vampire
(Upsetters)/Dub In Time (Upsetters)/Stand Up (Eric Donaldson)/Dub Fe Yu Right
(Upsetters)/Down Here In Babylon (Brent Dowe)/If The Cap Fits (Upsetters)/
Perception (Divine Brothers)/Perceptive Dub (Upsetters).

MUSICAL BONES – Vin Gordon
[DIP (UK) DLP 6000]
Coco-Macca/Fly Away/The Message/Licky-Licky/Labrish/Quinge-Up/Raw-Chaw/5
Cardiff Crescent/Four of a Kind/Voodoo Man.
Note: No track listing on original release. Re-issued 1997 by Ravensquire (UK) on
Justice League (JL 5002) with above titles, CD has bonus tracks: Nah Go Run (a.k.a.
Nuh Fe Run Down)/Mek It Soon (a.k.a. Iron Claw)/Breddah's Dub (a.k.a. Brotherly
Dub)/Matches Lane Affair (a.k.a. In The Valley)/A Wise Dub (a.k.a. Kuchy Skank).

RETURN OF WAX – The Upsetters
[DIP (UK) DLP 6001]
Last Blood/Deathly Hands/Kung Fu Warrior/Dragon Slayer/Judgement Day/One
Armed Boxer/Big Boss/Fists Of Vengeance/Samurai Swordsman/Final Weapon.
Note: No track listing on original release. Re-issued 1998 by Ravensquire on Justice
League (JL 5003) with above titles; CD has bonus tracks: Difference Experience
(Delroy Butler, a.k.a. Delroy Denton/Brother Roy)/Living My Life (Keith Rowe,
a.k.a. Keith Texon).

KUNG FU MEETS THE DRAGON – The Mighty Upsetter
[DIP (UK) DLPD 6002]
Theme From Hong Kong/Heart Of The Dragon/Hold Them Kung Fu/Flames Of The
Dragon/Scorching Iron/Skango/Fungaa/Black Belt/Iron Fist/Kung Fu Man.
Note: Re-issued 1995 by Ravensquire on Justice League (JL 5000); CD issue includes bonus
tracks: Exit The Dragon/Rockstone Dub/The Dragon Enters/23rd Dub/Rebels Dub.

TO LOVE SOMEBODY – Bunny Scott (a.k.a. William 'Bunny Rugs' Clarke)
[Klik (UK) KLP 9004]
What's The Use/I Am I Said/Kinky Fly/To Love Somebody/Use Me/Big May/Let Love
Touch Us Now/Sweet Loving Love/Sweet Caroline/Second Avenue.
Note: Re-issued by Tabou 1 (Fr) in 1999 (CD 19) with bonus tracks: Be Thankful/
Hip Harry/Hip Version/I Never Had It So Good (Jimmy Riley, miscredited to
Bunny Rugs).

REVOLUTION DUB – Lee Perry & the Upsetters
[Cactus (UK) CTLP 112]
Dub Revolution/Womans Dub/Kojak/Doctor On The Go/Bush Weed/Dreadlocks
   Talking/Own Man/Dub The Rhythm/Rain Drops.
Note: Re-issued by Black Star Liner in 1979, by Anachron in 1989, by Lagoon (FR) in
   1992 (LG 1083), by Rhino (UK) in 1995 (RN 2120) and by Orange Street (UK) in
   1998 (CDUB 2).

1976

NATTY PASSING THRU' – Prince Jazzbo
[Black Wax (UK) WAX LP 1]
Dreadlocks Corner/Story Come To Bump/Natty Pass Thru' Rome/Hold My Hand/
   Prophet Live/Ital Corner/Bloody Dunza/Weepin' And Wailin'/Live Good Today/
   Life Is Gonna Easy.
Note: Re-issued in altered form on Clocktower (US) in 1981 as ITAL CORNER (CT 103).

COLOMBIA COLLY – Jah Lion
[Island (UK/US) Wildflower (JA) MLPS 9392]
Wisdom/Dread Ina Jamdong/Hay Fever/Flashing Whip/Colombia Colly/Fatman/Bad
   Luck Natty/Black Lion/Little Sally Dater/Sata.
Note: Re-issued 1994 (RR47).

WAR IN A BABYLON – Max Romeo & the Upsetters
[Island (UK/US Wildflower (JA)) ILPS 9392]
One Step Forward/Uptown Babies/Chase The Devil/War In A Babylon/Norman/
   Stealin'/Tan And See/Smokey Room/Smile Out Of Style.
Note: Re-issued 1990 (RR23).

SCRATCH THE SUPER APE – The Upsetters
[Upsetter (JA) LP 8108]
Dread Lion/Zion Blood/Three In One/Curly Dub/Patience Dub/Super Ape/Croaking
   Lizard/Black Vest/Underground Root/Dub Along.
Note: Alternative mix and track order to UK issue below.

SUPER APE – The Upsetters
[Island (UK/US) ILPS 9417)]
Zions Blood/Croaking Lizard/Black Vest/Underground/Curly Dub/Dread Lion/Three
   In One/Patience/Dub Along/Super Ape.
Note: Alternative mix and track order to above JA issue. Re-issued 1990 (RR13).

1977

PARTY TIME – The Heptones
[Island (UK) ILPS 9456 & Mango (US) MLPS 9456]
Party Time/Crying Over You/Now Generation/Mr President/Serious Time/I Shall Be
   Released/Storm Cloud/Road Of Life/Why Must I/Sufferers Time.
Note: Re-issued 1990 (RR14).

POLICE AND THIEVES – Junior Murvin
[Island (UK) ILPS 9499 & Mango (US) MLPS 9499]

Roots Train/Police And Thieves/Solomon/Rescue Jah Children/Tedious/False Teachin'/
   Easy Task/Lucifer/Workin' In The Cornfield/I Was Appointed.
Note: Re-issued 1994.

SUPER EIGHT – George Faith
[Black Art (JA) ILPS 9504]
I've Got The Groove/Opportunity/The Hand Of Time/There's A Train/Midnight
   Hour/To Be A Lover/Diana/So Fine.
Note: Alternative track order and title to UK release below.

TO BE A LOVER – George Faith
[Black Swan (UK) ILPS 9504]
Midnight Hour – Ya Ya/To Be A Lover (Have Mercy)/Opportunity/So Fine/I've Got
   The Groove/Diana/All The Love I've Got/Turn Back The Hands Of Time.
Note: Re-issued in altered form 1994, quickly deleted.

HEART OF THE CONGOS – The Congos
[Black Art (JA) LP 4049]
Fisherman/Congoman/Open Up The Gate/Children Crying/La La Bam Bam/Can't
   Come In/Sodom & Gomorrow/The Wrong Thing/Ark Of Covenant/Solid
   Foundation.
Note: First mix of album, lacking cow sounds and various effects on later editions. First
   pressing has printed blue stripes, some copies with hand-painted yellow lines over
   them; back cover has typographical errors.

SUSAN CADOGAN – Susan Cadogan
[Trojan (UK) TRLS 122]
In the Ghetto/Nice And Easy/Hurt So Good/Congratulations/If You Need Me/Lay
   Down/I Keep On Loving You/Don't You Burn Your Bridges/Feeling Is Right/Fever/
   Shame.
Note: Material recorded 1974.

1978

ROAST FISH COLLIE WEED & CORNBREAD – Lee Perry the Upsetter
[Lion of Judah (JA) LPIR 0000]
Favourite Dish/Free Up The Weed/Big Neck Police/Mr DJ Man/Roast Fish &
   Cornbread/Soul Fire/Throw Some Water In/Evil Tongues/Curly Locks/Ghetto
   Sidewalk.
Note: Re-issued 1985 by Jet Star on Upsetter and 1995 by VP (US) in 1996 (VP 1000).

RETURN OF THE SUPER APE – The Upsetters
[Lion of Judah (JA) LPIR 0001]
Dyon-Anaswa/Return Of The Super Ape/Tell Me Something Good/Bird In Hand/Crab
   Yars/Jah Jah Ah Natty Dread/Psyche & Trim/The Lion/Huzza A Haha/High
   Ranking Sammy.
Note: Re-issued 1986 by Jet Star on Upsetter, on CD by VP (US) in 1996 (VP 1001)
   and on CD by Jet Star/Charm (CRCD 67) in 1997 as budget price ORIGINAL
   SUPER APE (re-issued 1998) with bonus tracks: Bag Of Collie (Dillinger)/Down
   Here In Babylon (Brent Dowe)/Shoulder To The Wheel (Flying Sensation)/Earth A
   Go Wheel (Flying Sensation)/Weak Heart A Go Feel It (Shaumark & Robinson).

HEART OF THE CONGOS – The Congos
[Black Art (JA) KLP 5]
Fisherman/Congoman/Open Up The Gate/Children Crying/La La Bam Bam/Can't
    Come In/Sodom & Gomorrow/The Wrong Thing/Ark Of Covenant/Solid
    Foundation.
Note: Second mix of album with added cow sounds and other effects. Front cover
    stripes are black and back cover typographical errors have been corrected. Repressed
    on Congo Ashanty (JA) in 1978 (DRS 8408/8155), on Jah Live (FR) in 1979
    (14101), on Go Feet (UK) in 1981 (BEAT 2), on Sunfire (JA) in mid-'90s, on VP
    (US) in 1994, and given a definitive re-mastering by Blood and Fire (UK) in 1996
    (BAF 9) with bonus tracks: At The Feast/Nicodemus, CD edition with further bonus
    tracks: Congoman (12" mix)/Congoman Chant/Bring The Mackaback/Noah Sugar
    Pan/Solid Foundation (Disco Cork mix).

1979

SCRATCH ON THE WIRE – Various Artists
[Island (UK) ILPS 9583]
Vibrate On (Augustus Pablo Meets the Upsetter)/Soldier And Police War (Jah Lion)/
    Diana (George Faith)/John Public (Errol Walker)/Bird In Hand (vocalist unknown,
    miscredited to Lee Perry)/Big Neck Police Man (Lee Perry)/In These Times (Errol
    Walker)/No Peace (Meditations)/Soul Fire (Lee Perry)/War In A Babylon (Max
    Romeo).
Note: Material recorded 1976–78.

SEKE MOLENGA AND KALO KAWONGOLO – Seke Molenga & Kalo Kawongolo
[Sonafric (FR) SAF 5008/SD 13]
African Roots/Bad Food/Moto Ya Motema/Mengieb/Nakoya/Guipimbu Gienu.
Note: Material recorded 1977. Re-issued on Tropical Sounds/Jolie Zaire (BE) in 1991
    (TSLP 1) and on CD by Runn Netherlands (NL) in 1993 (RN 29) with liner notes
    by Steve Heilig and bonus track Love Can Run Faster (Robert Palmer, miscredited as
    Zap Pow's River Stone).

1980

THE RETURN OF PIPECOCK JACKXON – Lee 'Scratch' Perry
[Black Star Liner (NL) BSLP 9002]
Bed Jammin/Untitled Rhythm/Give Thanx To Jah/Easy Knocking/Who Killed The
    Chicken/Babylon Cookie Jar A Crumble/Some Have Fe Holla.

1981

SCRATCH AND COMPANY CHAPTER 1 – The Upsetters
[Clocktower (US) CT 114]
Scratch The Dub Organiser/Who You Gonna Run To (Johnny Lover & the
    Towerchanters)/Tighten Up (Lee & the Blue Bell)/A Serious Joke (Val Bennett)/
    Little Flute Chant (Brad Osborne & the Towerchanters)/When Jah Come (Devon
    Irons)/Scratch Walking/Come Along (Lee Perry & the Black Arks)/Bushweed
    Corntrash (Ricky & Bunny)/Curly Dub.
Note: Material recorded 1967–76; some tracks later remixed or altered in New York by

Brad Osbourne. Compiled & annotated by Brad Osbourne. Re-issued by RAS in 1988 as part of SCRATCH ATTACK.

THE UPSETTER COLLECTION – The Upsetters & Friends
[Trojan (UK) TRLS 195]
Cold Sweat/Return Of Django/Check Him Out (Bleechers)/Django Shoots First (Sir Lord Comic)/Kill Them All/The Vampire/Drugs And Poison/Sipreano/Black IPA/ Bucky Skank (Lee Perry)/Words Of My Mouth (Gatherers)/Tipper Special/Cow Thief Skank (Lee Perry & Charlie Acc)/French Connection (Upsetters)/Better Days (Carlton & His Shoes)/Freak Out Skank.
Note: Material recorded 1969–73. Compiled & annotated by Chris Lane & Dave Hendley. Re-issued on CD 1988.

1982

MYSTIC MIRACLE STAR – Lee 'Scratch' Perry & the Majestics
[Heartbeat (US) HB 6]
Holy Moses/God Bless Pickney/Radication Squad/Mystic Miracle Star/Chalice Afire/ Pussy I Cocky I Water/Music Breeze.

HEART OF THE ARK – Lee 'Scratch' Perry
[Seven Leaves (UK) SL1]
I've Never Had It So Good (Jimmy Riley, miscredited to Bunny Scott)/What's The Use (Bunny Scott)/Don't Be Afraid (George Faith)/Forward With Love (Mystic Eyes, a.k.a. Mystic I)/Rasta Fari (Leroy Sibbles)/Rasta Fari (Combination Two)/4 & 20 Dread Locks (Evans Jones, miscredited to Prodigal)/Nuh Fe Run Down (vocalist unknown, miscredited to Lee Perry)/Elaine (Mystic Eyes, a.k.a. Mystic I).
Note: Material recorded 1975–78. CD re-issue 1992 with bonus tracks: Reggae Music (Preacher)/Brotherly Dub (Lee Perry).

1983

MEGATON DUB – Lee Perry
[Seven Leaves (UK) SL2]
Dem No Know Dub/Conscious Man Dub/Such Is Dub/Corn Picker Dub/Rasta Dub/ Freedom Dub/Megaton Dub/Dreader Dub/School Girl Dub.
Note: Material recorded 1977–78. CD re-issue 1992 with 1976 bonus track Simon The Sorcerer (Upsetters).

HEART OF THE ARK VOL. II – Lee 'Scratch' Perry
[Seven Leaves (UK) SL3]
Such Is Life (Lord Creator)/Freedom (Earl 16)/Dread Dreader (Jolly Brothers)/Brotherly Love (Hendrick Nicholson)/Them Don't Know Love (Twin Roots, miscredited to Righteous Vibes)/African Freedom (Brotherhood)/Cool Down (Jolly Brothers)/Jah Say Love (Twin Roots)/4 & 20 Dread Locks (Evans Jones, miscredited to Prodigal).
Note: Material recorded 1977–78. CD re-issue 1992 with bonus tracks.

1984

MEGATON DUB 2 – Lee Perry
[Seven Leaves (UK) SLS]
Travelling In Dub/Fisherman Dub/Zion In Dub/Groovy Dub/Dub Crisis/Green Bay
  Killing (featuring Lord Sassafrass)/Big Neck Dub/Living In Dub.
Note: Material recorded 1977–78. CD re-issue in 1992 with bonus track Groovy
  Situation (Keith Rowe).

REGGAE GREATS: LEE PERRY
[Island (UK) ILPS 9792 & Mango (US) MLPS 9792]
Party Time (Heptones)/Police & Thieves (Jr Murvin)/Groovy Situation (Keith Rowe)/
  Soul Fire (Lee Perry)/War In A Babylon (Max Romeo)/Wisdom (Jah Lion)/To Be A
  Lover (George Faith)/Roast Fish & Cornbread (Lee Perry)/Croaking Lizard (Prince
  Jazzbo)/Dreadlocks In Moonlight (Lee Perry).
Note: Material recorded 1976–77. Compiled by Trevor Wyatt, annotated by Doug
  Wendt. Re-issued 1990 (RR10).

HISTORY, MYSTERY, PROPHECY – Lee 'Scratch' Perry
[Mango (US) MLPS 9774 & Lion of Judah (JA/UK) LP 1]
Mr Music/The Ganja Man/Nice Time/Tiger Lion/Funky Joe/Heads Of Government/
  Daniel/Bed Jamming.
Note: UK pressing has slightly different mix. US version re-issued 1994.

1985

THE UPSETTER BOX SET
[Trojan (UK) PERRY 1]
Note: Re-issue of AFRICA'S BLOOD, RHYTHM SHOWER and DOUBLE SEVEN.
  Annotated by Steve Barrow.

1986

BATTLE OF ARMAGIDEON (MILLIONAIRE LIQUIDATOR) – Mr Lee 'Scratch'
  Perry & the Upsetters
[Trojan (UK) TRLS 227]
Introducing Myself/Drum Song/Grooving/All Things Are Possible/Show Me That
  River/I Am A Madman/The Joker/Happy Birthday/Sexy Lady/Time Marches On.
Note: Recorded in London.

SOME OF THE BEST – Lee Perry & the Upsetters
[Heartbeat (US) HB 37]
People Funny Boy (Lee Perry)/Da Da (Upsetters)/Shocks Of Mighty (Dave Barker)/Set
  Me Free (Dave Barker)/Live Injection (Upsetters)/Freedom Train (Ernest Wilson)/
  Finger Mash (Lee Perry & Silvertones)/Duppy Conqueror (Wailers)/Upsetting
  Station (Dave Barker).
Note: Material recorded 1968–74. Compiled & annotated by Bill Nowlin. Re-issued on
  CD with bonus tracks: The Thanks We Get (Jr Byles & Omar Perry)/Fu Man
  Version (Linval Thompson)/Kiss Me Neck (Upsetters)/Keep On Skanking (Bob
  Marley). Re-issued 1995 as budget price REGGAE'S GEATEST HITS VOL. 3.

1987

TIME BOOM X DE DEVIL DEAD – Lee 'Scratch' Perry & Dub Syndicate
[On-U Sound (UK export) ON-U LP43 & EMI/Syncopate (UK)]
SDI/Blinkers/Jungle/De Devil Dead/Music + Science Lovers/Kiss The Champion/
     Allergic To Lies/Time Conquer.
Note: Produced by Lee Perry & Adrian Sherwood in London.

1988

SATAN KICKED THE BUCKET – Lee 'Scratch' Perry
[Wackies (US) 2740 & Overheat (JP)]
Bank to Bank/Once I Had A Dream/Sweet Dreams/It's Alright/Ooh La La/Keep On
     Moving/Satan Kicked The Bucket/Bat Bat/One Horse Race/Day Should Turn To
     Night.
Note: Produced by Lee Perry & Lloyd 'Bullwackie' Barnes in New Jersey.

GIVE ME POWER – Lee Perry & Friends
[Trojan (UK) TRLS 254]
Sick And Tired (Neville Grant)/Rasta No Pickpocket (Jr Byles)/Don't Cross The
     Nation (Little Roy)/Give Me Power (Stingers)/Give Me Power Version 2 (King
     Iwah)/News Flash (Leo Graham)/Flashing Echo (Upsetters)/Justice To The People
     (Lee Perry)/Verse Two (Upsetters)/Babylon's Burning (Maxie, Niney, Scratch)/Ring
     Of Fire (Upsetters)/The Thanks We Get (Upsetters)/Dig Your Grave (Upsetters)/
     Public Enemy Number One (Max Romeo)/Mid-East Rock (Dillinger)/Forward Up
     (Stingers)/Hot Tip (Prince Django)/To Be A Lover (Chenley Duffus).
Note: Material recorded 1970–73. Compiled & annotated by Steve Barrow.

SHOCKS OF MIGHTY – Lee Perry & Friends
[Attack (UK) ATLP 104]
Pound Get A Blow (Soul Twins miscredited to Upsetters)/No Bread And Butter
     (Milton Henry)/The Tackro (1st, 2nd & 3rd Generation Upsetters)/Set Me Free
     (Dave Barker)/Shocks Of A Mighty (Dave Barker)/Dark Moon (Upsetters)/
     Civilization (Classics)/Black Man's Time (Neville Grant)/Three Blind Mice (Leo
     Graham)/Three Times Three (King Tubby & the Upsetters)/Be Thankful (Bunny
     Clarke)/Dubbing In The Back Seat (Upsetters)/Woman's Gotta Have It (Jimmy
     Riley)/Gotta Have Dub (Upsetters)/Move Out Of My Way (Bunny Clarke)/Move
     Out Dub (Upsetters).
Note: Material recorded 1969–75. Compiled & annotated by Steve Barrow.

WHEN WILL BETTER COME – Junior Byles
[Trojan (UK) TRLS 269]
Fever/Auntie Lulu/When Will Better Come/The Thanks We Get/Mumbling And
     Grumbling/Curly Locks/Dreader Locks/The Long Way/Bur-O-Boy/Run Run/
     Tubby's Want The Channel/King Of Babylon/What Kind Of World/Weeping/Can
     You Feel It/I Ah Feel It Version.
Note: Tracks 1–8 produced by Lee Perry; tracks 9–16 produced by Niney the Observer.
     Material recorded 1972–76. Compiled & annotated by Steve Barrow.

1989

MYSTIC WARRIOR – Lee 'Scratch' Perry
[Ariwa (UK) ARI LP 54 & ROIR (US) A 184]
Dub Those Crazy Baldheads/Pirates (Black Plastic)/Kung Fu Fighting/25 Years Ago/
   Mystic Warrior/Feel The Spirit/Good Lucky Perry/Jazzy Lady.
Note: Produced by Lee Perry & Mad Professor in London. Material recorded 1984.

MYSTIC WARRIOR DUB – Lee 'Scratch' Perry & Mad Professor
[Ariwa (UK) ARI LP 55]
Dub Them Crazy/Broken Antennae/Black Art/Dub The Past/Mystic Warrior Dub/Dub
   Reggae Soca/Dub It Scratchy Dub It/Jazzy Dub.
Note: Produced & mixed by Mad Professor in London.

VERSION LIKE RAIN – Various Artists
[Trojan (UK) TRLS 278]
Want A Wine (Leo Graham)/Stick Together (U Roy)/Double Wine (Upsetters)/Fever (Jr
   Byles)/Hot & Cold Version 1 (Augustus Pablo & the Upsetters)/This World (Milton
   Henry)/Fever (Susan Cadogan)/Influenza Version (Upsetters)/Beat Down Babylon (Jr
   Byles)/Informer Man (Jr Byles & Jah T)/Outformer Version (Upsetters)/Babylon's
   Burning (Maxie, Niney, Scratch)/Beat Version (Upsetters)/Freedom Fighter (Bunny
   & Ricky)/Iron Wolf (Upsetters)/Bet You Don't Know (Chenley Duffus).
Note: Material recorded 1972–76. Compiled & annotated by Steve Barrow.

OPEN THE GATE – Lee 'Scratch' Perry & Friends
[Trojan (UK) PERRY 2]
Words (Sangie Davis & Lee Perry)/Vampire (Devon Irons & Dr Alimantado)/Babylon
   Falling (Heptones)/Version (Upsetters)/Mistry Babylon (Heptones)/Version
   (Upsetters)/Garden Of Life (Leroy Sibbles)/History (Carlton Jackson)/Sons Of
   Slaves (Jr Delgado)/Open The Gate (Watty Burnett)/Talk About It (The
   Diamonds)/Yama-Ky (Upsetters)/Cherry Oh Baby (Eric Donaldson)/Rainy Night In
   Portland (Watty Burnett)/Ruffer Ruff (Horace Smart)/Ruffer Dub (Upsetters)/
   Nickodeemus (Congos)/Know Love (Twin Roots)/City Too Hot (Lee Perry)/Bionic
   Rats (Lee Perry)/Bad Weed (Jr Murvin).
Note: Material recorded 1976–79. Compiled & annotated by Steve Barrow.

MAGNETIC MIRROR MASTER MIX – Scratch & the Upsetters
[Anachron (NL) AAS 9003]
Voodism (Leo Graham)/Voodoo Dub (Upsetters)/Wolf Out Deh (Lloyd & Devon)/
   Shepherd Rod (Upsetter)/Better Future (Errol Walker)/Future Dub (Upsetters)/
   Bafflin' Smoke Signal (Lee Perry)/Captive (Lee Perry)/Dub Cap (Upsetters)/Different
   Experience (Brother Roy)/Living My Life (Keith Texon, a.k.a. Keith Rowe).
Note: Material recorded 1974–78. Compiled by Henk Targowski.

TURN AND FIRE – UPSETTER DISCO DUB
[Anachron (NL) AAS 9004]
Disco Devil (Lee Perry & Full Experience)/Norman (Max Romeo)/Sexy Natty (Max
   Romeo)/Why Must I? (Heptones)/I Shall Be Released (Heptones)/Mr President
   (Heptones)/Crying Over You (Heptones).
Note: Material recorded 1976–77. Compiled by Henk Targowski.

1990

FROM THE SECRET LABORATORY – Lee 'Scratch' Perry
[Mango (UK) MLPS 1035]
Secret Laboratory (Scientific Dancehall)/Inspector Gadget/The Groove/Vibrate On/
    African Hitch-Hiker/You Thought I Was Dead/Push Push/African Head Charge In
    The Hackney Empire/Seven Devils Dead.
Note: Produced by Lee Perry & Adrian Sherwood in London.

SPIRITUAL HEALING – Lee 'Scratch' Perry
[Black Cat/Sound Service EFA 14998]
Spiritual Healing/Babush/Sex Vibrations/Vindetta/Sexy Boss/Com'on And Dance/Mr
    Dobberman.
Note: Produced by Lee Perry & Higi Heilinger in Zürich.

SATAN'S DUB – Lee 'Scratch' Perry Meets Bullwackie
[ROIR (US) A 178]
Satan Dub/Come Home Dub/Ooh La La Dub/Upful Dub Fashion/President Dub/Dub
    Skeem/Strange Dub/Bog Walk Skanking/Undercover Dub/Stop Stop Dub/Moving
    In Dub/Dub Master.
Note: Produced by Lee Perry & Bullwackie in New Jersey. Re-issued 1998 on re-
    mastered CD (RUS 8241).

MESSAGE FROM YARD – Lee 'Scratch' Perry
[Rohit (US) RRTG 7773]
Death To Anyone Who Fight/I Want A Meekie Girl/One God In Space/Rasta
    Emotions/Come By Me/The Joker/Money Me A Deal With/Message From Yard/
    Magic Dreams/Free Up The Rasta Man.
Note: Produced & mixed by Bullwackie in New Jersey. Out-takes from SATAN
    KICKED THE BUCKET.

THE DUB MESSENGER – Lee 'Scratch' Perry
[Tassa (US) 7002]
Defend Yourself/The Dubber/Miracle Dreams/ABC Dubbing/Musical Transplant/Stop
    Following Me/Come By Me/Wackie's Plan/Hard Drive/Greetings.
Note: Produced & mixed by Bullwackie in New Jersey. Out-takes from SATAN
    KICKED THE BUCKET.

PUBLIC JESTERING – Lee Perry & Friends
[Attack (UK) ATLP 108]
Public Jestering (Judge Winchester)/I'm A Dread Locks (Upsetters)/Dread Locks
    Version (Upsetters)/Stay Dread (Lee Perry)/Kingdom Of Dub (Upsetters)/Babylon
    Deh Pon Fire (Truth Fact & Correct)/Jungle Fever (Upsetters)/Hypocrites (Jimmy
    & Glen)/Nine Finger Jerry Lewis (Upsetters)/Black Candle (Leo Graham)/Bad Lamp
    (Upsetters)/Doctor Demand (Leo Graham)/Black Bat (Upsetters)/Big Tongue Buster
    (unknown deejay, miscredited to Leo Graham)/Bus-A-Dub (Upsetters)/Herb Vendor
    (Horsemouth)/Penny Reel (Prince Jazzbo).
Note: Material recorded 1973–76. Compiled & annotated by Steve Barrow.

BUILD THE ARK – Lee Perry & Friends
[Trojan (UK) PERRY 3]
My Little Sandra (Leo Graham)/Dubbing Sandra (Upsetters)/Feelings (Sharon Isaacs)/
    Version (Upsetters)/Long Long Time (Winston Heywood)/Long Time Dub
    (Upsetters)/A Wah Dat (Jr Dread)/Dub Dat (Upsetters)/White Belly Rat (Lee Perry)/
    Judas De White Belly Rat (Upsetters)/White Belly Rat (Jah Lloyd)/Freedom Street
    (Eric Donaldson)/Freedom Dub (Upsetters)/Land Of Love (Sons of Light)/Land Of
    Dub (Upsetters)/Think So (Meditations)/Dub So (Upsetters)/Cross Over (Jr
    Murvin)/Cross Over Dub (Upsetters)/At The Feast (Congos)/Travelling (Deborah
    Keese & the Black Five)/Nyambie Dub (Upsetters)/Ethiopian Land (Peter & Paul
    Lewis)/Landmark Dub (Upsetters)/Green Bay Incident (Lord Sassafrass)/Green Bay
    Version (Upsetters)/Brother Noah (Shadows)/Noah Dub (Upsetters)/Thanks &
    Praise (Jr Ainsworth)/Mr Money Man (Danny Hensworth)/Dub Money (Upsetters).
Note: Material recorded 1976–78. Compiled by Steve Barrow.

CHICKEN SCRATCH – Lee 'Scratch' Perry
[Heartbeat (US) HB 53]
Please Don't Go/Chicken Scratch/Feel Like Jumping/Solid As A Rock/By Saint Peter/
    Tackoo/Roast Duck/Man To Man/Gruma/Jane Ann & The Pumpkin/Just Keep It
    Up/Puss In Bag.
Note: Produced by Clement Dodd. Material recorded 1961–66. Compiled & annotated
    by Chris Wilson.

ALL THE HITS – Lee Perry & the Upsetters
[Rohit (US) RRTG 7758]
Run For Cover/Version/Something You Got/Version/Set Them Free/Wind Up Doll/
    Labrish/You Funny (a.k.a. You Crummy)/Version/Django Shoots First (Sir Lord
    Comic)/People (a.k.a. People Sokup Boy)/Version/Water Pump/Version/Clint
    Eastwood Rides Again/Set Me Free (Dave Barker)/Night Doctor/Rude Walking/Iron
    Claw/Newsflash (Leo Graham).
Note: Material 'licensed' from Bunny Lee, recorded 1967–73. Incorrect track listing.
    Night Doctor produced by Ansel Collins. Re-issued 1991 by Esoldun (FR) as
    NEWSFLASH.

FULL EXPERIENCE – Aura Meets Lee 'Scratch' Perry
[Blue Moon (FR) BM 116]
Young, Gifted, And Broke/Can't See You/At Midnite/Full Experience/Nar Soh, So It
    Stay.
Note: Material recorded 1977. Mini-album, plays at 45 rpm.

1991

LORD GOD MUZICK – Lee 'Scratch' Perry
[Heartbeat (US) HB 65]
Free Us/Colt The Game/Lightning And Thunder Flash/Air Manifestation/Angel
    Gabriel And The Space Boots/Lee The Upsetter/Happy Birthday Marcus/Hot Shit/
    Supersonic Man/Reggae Emperor/Collie Ruler/Lee In The Heartbeat.
Note: Produced by Lee Perry & Niney the Observer in Kingston. Re-issued by Rhino
    (UK) in 1996 as THE REGGAE EMPEROR (RN 2137) with bonus track When
    Jah Speak.

OUT OF MANY, THE UPSETTER – Lee Perry
[Trojan (UK) TRL 297]
Introducing Myself (Lee Perry)/Small Axe (Wailers)/Placed Called Africa (Jr Byles)/
    Don't Rock My Boat (Wailers)/Feeling Is Right (Susan Cadogan)/Be Thankful
    (Bunny Clarke)/Kuchy Skank (Upsetters)/Garden Of Life (Leroy Sibbles)/Kentucky
    Skank (Lee Perry)/Reaction (Wailers)/Public Jestering (Judge Winchester)/The Long
    Way (Jr Byles)/Mr Brown (Wailers)/Stick Together (U Roy)/Freak Out Skank
    (Upsetters)/Justice To The People Verse 2 (Upsetters)/Travelling (Deborah Keese &
    the Black Five).
Note: Material recorded 1970–78 and 1986.

1992

THE UPSETTER AND THE BEAT – Lee 'Scratch' Perry
[Heartbeat (US) HB 59]
Welcome Aboard/Don't Blame The Baldhead/Twiddle With Me/Coming In From The
    Cold/Big Apple Coconut/There Is A Place For Us/Love Power/Holla and Bawl/
    Musical Doctor/Happy Birthday Jamaica/Sex/Making Love.
Note: Produced by Clement Dodd in Kingston & New York. Material voiced 1988–90.

SOUNDZS FROM THE HOT LINE – Lee 'Scratch' Perry
[Heartbeat (US) HB 76]
Bionic Rat/Ashes And Dust/Righteous Oily/In This Iwa/Babylon A Fall/Rainbow Throne/
    Standing On The Hill/News Flash/When You Walk/Sweet Guava Jelly/So You Come,
    So You Go/Free Up The Prisoners/Track 13 (version of Brown Girl In The Ring).
Note: 'Licensed' from Alvin Ranglin. Material recorded 1973–79.

EXCALIBURMAN – Lee Perry
[Seven Leaves (UK) SL6]
Perry's Mood (a.k.a. Silver Locks) (Upsetters)/Hot Pipes (Jah T)/Trinity Of Life/Travelling
    (Deborah Keese)/Economic Crisis (Jackie Bernard)/Free Up The Prisoners (Lee Perry)/
    Drum Rock (Upsetters)/Dub Organizer (Upsetters)/Jungle Fever (Upsetters).
Note: Material recorded 1972–78.

1993

CONSCIOUS MAN – The Jolly Brothers
[Roots (UK) RR1]
Conscious Man/Brotherly Love/Have A Little Faith/Back Biter/Cool Down/Babylon A
    Fight Rasta/Dread Dreader/Play Play/Oppression/Colour.
Note: Material recorded 1977–78.

UPSETTING THE NATION – The Upsetters & Friends
[Trojan UK TRLS 330]
Eight For Eight/Outer Space/To Love Somebody (Busty Brown)/Soulful I/Man from
    MI5/I'll Be Waiting (Termites)/Ten To Twelve/Kiddy-O (Muskyteers)/Medical
    Operation/Night Doctor/Self Control/Crying About You (Busty Brown)/
    Thunderball/Build My Whole World Around You (Dave Barker)/One Punch/The
    Vampire/Prisoner Of Love (Dave Barker)/I Was Wrong (Dave Barker).
Note: Material recorded 1969–70. Night Doctor produced by Ansel Collins; Self
    Control produced by Martin Riley. Compiled & annotated by Chris Prete.

1994

SMOKIN' – Lee Perry
[VP (US) VPRL 1358]
Hi-Jack/Atlas Road Map/Seven/Word Sound/Cock Roach Hotel/Calamooch/
   Microtone/Ethiopian Scroll.
Note: Produced by Melvin 'Munchie' Jackson. Material recorded 1981 in New York.

PEOPLE FUNNY BOY – Various Artists
[Trojan (UK) TRL 339]
Honey Love (Burt Walters), Evol Yenoh (Burt Walters), Stranger On The Shore (Val
   Bennett), Nonesuch Busted Me Bet (Mellotones), Handy Cap (Upsetters), Blowing
   In The Wind (Burt Walters), People Funny Boy (Lee Perry), Spanish Harlem
   (Upsetters), Uncle Charlie (Mellotones), Tighten Up (Inspirations), A Place In The
   Sun (David Isaacs), What A Botheration (Mellotones), Return Of Django (Val
   Bennett & the Upsetters), Sentence (Danny & Lee), Baby Baby (Val Bennett),
   Farmers In The Den (Bleechers), Stand By Me (Inspirations), What A Botheration
   (Lee Perry), What A Situation (Slim Smith).
Note: Material recorded 1968–69. Compiled & annotated by Laurence Cane-Honeysett.

1995

SUPER APE INNA JUNGLE – Lee Perry Featuring Mad Professor, Douggie Digital, &
   Juggler
[Ariwa (UK) ARI 112]
I'm Not A Human Being/Nasty Spell/Writing On The Wall/Why Complaining?/
   Thunder And Lightning/Super Ape Inna Jungle/Jungle Roots/Black Spell/Dancing
   Boots/Sheba Dance.
Note: Produced by Mad Professor in London. Jungle & Techno-Dub remixes of out-
   takes from BLACK ARK EXPERRYMENTS.

BLACK ARK EXPERRYMENTS – Lee 'Scratch' Perry & Mad Professor
[Ariwa (UK) ARI 114]
Thank You/Super Ape In A Good Shape/Jungle Safari/From Heaven Above/Heads Of
   Government/Open Door/Black Ark Experryments/Poop Song/Come Back.
Note: Produced by Lee Perry & Mad Professor in London.

EXPERRYMENTS AT THE GRASS ROOTS OF DUB – Lee Perry
[Ariwa (UK) ARI 115]
Jungle Roots Dub/Dubbing With The Super Ape/Alien In Out A Space/Sky High Dub/
   Nucleus Dub/Dub It Wide Open/Dub Wise Experryments/Pooping Dub Song/
   Black Ark Come Again.
Note: Produced & mixed by Mad Professor in London.

LARKS FROM THE ARK – Lee Perry
[Nectar (UK) NM511]
Conscious Man (Jolly Brothers)/Nuh Fe Run Down (Lee Perry)/Freedom (Earl 16)/
   Brotherly Love (Jolly Brothers)/Groovy Situation (Keith Rowe)/Them Don't Know
   Love (Twin Roots, miscredited to Righteous Vibes)/Rastafari (Leroy Sibbles)/
   Forward With Love (Mystic Eyes, a.k.a. Mystic I)/Such Is Live (Creator)/Elaine
   (Mystic Eyes, a.k.a. Mystic I)/Don't Be Afraid (George Faith)/Cool Down (Jolly

Brothers)/School Girl Dub/I've Never Had It So Good (Jimmy Riley, miscredited to Bunny Scott)/4 & 20 Dreadlocks (Evans Jones, miscredited to Prodigal)/What's The Use (Bunny Scott)/African Freedom (Brotherhood)/Colour (Jolly Brothers).

THE QUEST – Lee Perry
[Abraham (CA)]
Militant Man/Longer Way/Kung Fu Man (Linval Thompson)/What Can I Do (Locks Lee)/Silver Locks/Episode 3/When Knotty Came (Silvertones)/Dread Locks/Johnny Reggae/Golden Locks.
Note: When Knotty Came produced by Winston Riley. Track listing partially incorrect.

THE RARITIES VOL. 1 – Bob Marley & Wailers
[Jamaica Gold (PO) JMC 200.229]
Shocks Of Mighty/Shocks Of Mighty Version/All In One/One In All/Copasetic/More Axe/Axe Man/Duppy Conqueror/Zig Zag/Run For Cover/Picture On The Wall Version 3/Picture On The Wall Version 4/Man To Man/Nicoteen/Rock My Boat/I Like It Like This.
Note: Material recorded 1970–71. Run For Cover produced by the Wailers. Compiled & annotated by Aad Ven Der Hoek (a.k.a. Dr Buster Dynamite/Dr Babylon Dread).

THE RARITIES VOL. 2 – Bob Marley & the Wailers
[Jamaica Gold (PO) JMC 200.230]
Dreamland/Dreamland Version 2/Jah Is Mighty/Turn Me Loose/Second Hand/Second Hand Part 2/Brand New Second Hand/Love Life/Keep On Moving/Keep On Skanking/Mr Brown/Mr Brown Version/Send Me That Love.
Note: Material recorded 1970–71. Compiled & annotated by Aad Ven Der Hoek (a.k.a. Dr Buster Dynamite/Dr Babylon Dread).

1996

WHO PUT THE VOODOO 'PON REGGAE – Lee 'Scratch' Perry
[Ariwa (UK) ARI 130]
I Am Happiness/Megaton Bomb/Go And Come Back/Magic Music/Don't Touch My Shadow/Mo(n)key Party/Small Morsel/Mr Arkwell Spell/Black Ark International/Messy Apartment.
Note: Produced & mixed by Mad Professor in London.

DUB TAKE THE VOODOO OUT OF REGGAE – Mad Professor & Lee Perry
[Ariwa (UK) ARI 131]
Cheerful Dub/Drummer Boy Dub/Bounce Back Dub/Dub Voodoo/Shadow Of Dub/Mystic Powers Of Dub/Mr Dubfire/Dub Connection/Messy Dub Apartment.
Note: Produced & mixed by Mad Professor in London.

WORDS OF MY MOUTH – Various Artists
[Trojan (UK) TRL 374]
Word Of My Mouth (Gatherers)/Version (Upsetters)/Kuchy Skank (Upsetters)/Rejoice Jah Jah Children (Silvertones)/Rejoicing Skank (Upsetters)/Bushweed Corntrach (Bunny & Ricky)/Callying Butt (Upsetters)/Da Ba Day (Upsetters)/Kiss Me Neck (Upsetters)/Curly Locks (Jr Byles)/Dreader Locks (Lee & Junior)/Many A Call (Unforgettables)/Too Bad Bull (Bunny & Ricky)/Too Bad Cow (Upsetters)/Fist Of Fury (Lee Perry)/Herb Vendor (Horse Mouth)/Cane River Rock (Upsetter)/

Riverside Rock (Lee Perry)/Stay Dread (Lee Perry)/Kentucky Skank (Lee Perry)/
Bathroom Skank (Lee Perry)/Spiritual Whip (Jah Lloyd).
Note: Material recorded 1973–75. Compiled & annotated by Chris Prete.

THE BLACK ARK PRESENTS RASTAFARI LIVETH ITINUALLY
[Ravensquire/Justice League (UK) JL 5001]
Ethiopian Land (Peter & Paul Lewis)/Dub Land (Upsetters)/Rise & Shine (Watty &
    Tony)/Shining Dub (Upsetters)/What A War (Watty Burnett)/What A Dub
    (Upsetters)/23rd Psalm (Juks Dread & Big Youth)/Judgement Day (Clive Hylton)/
    Well Judged Dub (Upsetters)/Forward With Jah Orthodox (Mystic I)/Orthodox
    Dub (Upsetter)/Come Along (Bluebells)/Dub Along (Upsetters)
Note: CD includes bonus tracks: 4 & 20 Dreadlocks (Evan Jones)/Dread Locks Dub
    (Upsetters)/When Jah Come (Devon Irons)/When Jah Dubs (Upsetters). Material
    recorded 1976–78. Annotated by Natty Dempster.

PEACE AND LOVE – Various Artistes
[Sprint (UK) UP 1]
Ketch Vampire (Devon Irons)/Ketch A Dub (Upsetters)/Travelling (Deborah Keese)/
    Slymbia Dub (Upsetters, a.k.a. Nyambie Dub)/Words Of My Mouth (Gatherers)/
    Version (Upsetters)/Bush Weed Corntrash (Bunny & Ricky)/Cally Butt (Upsetters)/
    Come Along (Bluebells)/Along Come A Dub (Upsetters)/This World (Milton
    Henry)/Midious Serenade (Upsetters)/Africa (Hombres)/Foundation Dub
    (Upsetters)/Peace & Love (Shuamark & Robinson)/Peace & Love Dub (Upsetters)/
    Ruffer Ruff (Horace Smart)/Ruffer Dub (Upsetters).
Note: Material recorded 1976–78. Compiled by 'Kristal Clear Water' a.k.a. Pauline
    Morrison.

VOODOOISM – Lee Perry
[Pressure Sounds (UK) PS 9]
Rise And Shine (Watty & Tony)/Wolfout Deh (Lloyd & Devon/Shepherd Rod (The
    Upsetter)/Psalms 20 (James Booms/Proverbs Of Dub (The Upsetter)/Better Future
    (Errol Walker)/Future Dub (The Upsetter)/River/Riverstone (Zap Pow)/Freedom
    (Earl 16)/Africa (Hombres)/Foundation Dub (The Upsetter)/Voodooism (Leo
    Graham)/Dubism (The Upsetter)/African Style (Black Notes).
Note: CD issue includes bonus tracks: Right Yow (Upsetters)/Mash Down (Roots)/
    African Style Version (Black Notes)/Rasta Train (Lee & Jimmy)/Yagga Yagga (Lee &
    Jimmy). Material recorded 1973–77. Tracks not produced by Lee Perry: River
    (produced by Zap Pow)/Mash Down (produced by Sean De Laire)/African Style/
    Version (produced by the Black Notes).

REBEL REVOLUTION – THE EXTENDED MIXES – Bob Marley & the Wailers
[Jamaica Gold (PO) JMC 200.277]
Small Axe/My Cup/Keep On Moving/Try Me/Don't Rock The Boat/400 Years/Put It
    On/Cornerstone/Fussing And Fighting/No Water/Duppy Conqueror/Reaction/
    Memphis/Soul Almighty/It's Alright/Riding High/Soul Rebel/Kaya/African
    Herbsman/Satisfy My Soul/Stand Alone/Rebels Hop/Sun Is Shining/Love Life/Brain
    Washing/Mr Brown/Long Long Winter.
Note: Material recorded 1970–71. All tracks except Memphis re-edited to form
    extended play with dub version. Compiled & annotated by Aad Van Der Hoek
    (a.k.a. Dr Babylon Dread).

1997

LIVE AT MARITIME HALL – Lee 'Scratch' Perry with Mad Professor
[2B1 (US) MHP 2001]
My Secret Laboratory/Introducing Myself/Jungle Safari/I Am A Madman/Roast Fish And
    Cornbread/Come Go With Lee/Heads Of Government/Bucky Skank/Open Door.
Note: Recorded April 5, 1997 in San Francisco.

TECHNOMAJIKAL – Lee 'Scratch' Perrry
[ROIR (US) RUS 8232]
Maxi Merlin/UFO Attack (ambient version)/Technologically/LSD-LSP (flute mix)/
    Unitcorn/X-Perryment/LSD-LSP (hard trance mix)/UFO Attack (instrumental)/
    Maxi Merlin (radio version)/X-Perryment (radio version)/Crazy House.
Note: Produced by X-Perrymental & Martin Kloiber. Material voiced in Zürich in 1993
    and later remixed in Zürich and Los Angeles.

ARKOLOGY – Lee Scratch Perry
[Island Jamaica (UK) CRNCD 6/524 379–2]
Dub Revolution Part 1 (Lee Perrry & Upsetters)/One Step Forward (Max Romeo)/One
    Step Dub (Upsetters)/Vampire (Devon Irons)/Vamp A Dub (Upsetters)/Sufferer's
    Time (Heptones)/Sufferer's Dub (Upsetters)/Sufferer's Heights (Jr Dread)/Don't Blame
    On I (Congos)/Much Smarter (Meditations)/Much Smarter Dub (Upsetters)/Life Is
    Not Easy (Meditations)/Life Is Not Easy Dub (Upsetters)/Tedious (Jr Murvin)/War In
    A Babylon (Max Romeo)/Revelation Dub (Upsetters)/Mr President (Heptones & Jah
    Lion)/Chase The Devil (Max Romeo)/Dreadlocks In Moonlight (Lee Perry)/Dread At
    The Controls (Mikey Dread)/In These Times (Errol Walker)/In These Times Dub
    (Upsetters)/Norman (Max Romeo & Upsetters)/Police And Thieves (Jr Murvin)/Magic
    Touch (Glen DaCosta)/Soldier And Police War (Jah Lion)/Grumblin' Dub (Upsetters)/
    Bad Weed (Jr Murvin)/John Public (Errol Walker)/John Public Version (Enos Barnes)/
    Roots Train (Jr Murvin & Dillinger)/No Peace (Meditations)/No Peace Dub
    (Upsetters)/Rasta Train (Raphael Green & Dr Alimantado)/Party Time 2 (Upsetters)/
    Vibrate On (Augustus Pablo Meets The Upsetter)/Vibrator (Upsetters)/Bird In Hand
    (Upsetters)/Congoman (Congos)/Dyon Anasawa (Upsetters featuring Full Experience)/
    Rastaman Shuffle (Upsetters & Dillinger)/Why Must I [version] (Heptones & Lee
    Perry)/Make Up Your Mind (Heptones)/Closer Together (Upsetter Revue featuring Jr
    Murvin)/Groovy Situation (Keith Rowe)/Groovy Dub (Upsetters)/To Be A Lover
    (George Faith)/Soul Fire (Lee Perry)/Curly Locks (Lee Perry)/Feast Of The Passover
    (Congos)/Roast Fish & Cornbread (Lee Perry)/Corn Fish Dub (Upsetters).
Note: Material recorded 1975–79. Life Is Not Easy produced by the Meditations.
    Compiled & annotated by David Katz, Steve Barrow, & Trevor Wyatt.

COMPLETE BOB MARLEY & THE WAILERS 1969 to 1972 PART II
[JAD/Pense À Moi (FR) 1997]
Try Me/It's Alright/No Sympathy/My Cup/Soul Almighty/Rebel's Hop/Corner Stone/
    Four Hundred Years/No Water/Reaction/My Sympathy/Soul Rebel Version/Try Me
    Version/It's Alright Version/No Sympathy Version/My Cup Version/Soul Almighty
    Version/Keep On Moving/Put It On/Fussing And Fighting/Memphis/Riding High/
    Kaya/African Herbsman/Stand Alone/Brain Washing/Keep On Moving Version/
    Don't Rock My Boat Version/Put It On Version/Fussing And Fighting Version/
    Duppy Version/Memphis Version/Riding High Version/Sun Is Shining Version/

Kaya/Love Light/Second Hand/Jah Is Mighty/Run For Cover/Man To Man/
Downpressor/Don't Rock My Boat/More Axe/Long Long Winter/All In One/Turn
Me Loose/Kaya Version 2/Battle Axe Version/Soul Rebel Version 1/Rebel's Hop
Version/Corner Stone Version/No Water Versions I & II/Reaction Version/Rebel
Version/Kaya Version/African Herbsman Version/Stand Alone Version/Brain
Washing Version/Long Long Winter Version/Second Hand Version/Dowpressor
Version/Shocks Of Might/Axe Man/Nicoteen.

Note: Material recorded 1970–71. Compiled & annotated by Bruno Blum, Roger
Steffens, & Leroy Pierson. CD issue has different track order and is missing Soul
Rebel Version 1.

1998

DUBFIRE – Lee 'Scratch' Perry
[Ariwa (UK) & RAS (US) ARI 134]
Soul Rebel/Dub Fire/Rock This Boat/Working Man/Africa Place/Doctor Dick/On The
Street Again/Why People Funny/Come Go With Lee/Keep On Learning/Covetious/I
Love You.

Note: Produced by Mad Professor in London.

FIRE IN DUB – Lee 'Scratch' Perry & Mad Professor
[Ariwa (UK) & RAS (US) ARI 135]
Working Girl/Can't Control The African/Don't Try To Capsize I (Angry Mix)/Denise
The Bitch/Fire 'Pon De Witch/Don't Try To Capsize I/Working Girl Dub/Can't
Control The African/No Stick For Denise/Dub 'Pon De Street/Witches Are Funny/
Na Go With Ravenkiller/Keep On Learning Dub/Covetious Girl/I Won't Dub You.

Note: Produced and mixed by Mad Professor in London.

UPSETTER IN DUB – Lee 'Scratch' Perry
[Heartbeat HB 77]
Noah Sugar Pan/Ketch A Dub/Version Train/Rootically Dub/Son Of The Black Ark/
Lorna Skank/If The Cap Fits/Dub A Come/Tedious Dub/Rejoice In Skank/Babylon
Thief Dub/Foundation Solid/Bagman/Better Reach/Dub In Time/Fun And Games/
Sipple Dub/Bionic Rat Dub.

Note: 'Licensed' from Alvin Ranglin. Material recorded 1972–77. Compiled &
annotated by Chris Wilson.

ARCHIVE – Lee Perry
[Rialto (UK) RM 226]
The Upsetter/You Crummy/Rub & Squeeze/Stay Dread/Justice To The People (verse
2)/Set Them Free/City Too Hot/Cow Thief Skank/Soul Man/Dr Dick/Kentucky
Skank/Shocks Of Mighty/People Funny Boy/Bionic Rats/What A Good Woodman/
Bathroom Skank/Kill Them All/What A Botheration.

Note: Material recorded 1966–1977.

DRY ACID – Various Artists
[Trojan (UK) TRL 398]
Beware Of The Vampire (a.k.a. Beware of the Pepper) (Denzil Laing)/Barbara (Val
Bennett)/Prison Sentence (Upsetters)/Not Me (Ethiopians)/Cut Down (Ethiopians)/
Uncle Desmond (Mellotones)/Down In The Park (Inspirations)/Love Oh Love

(Inspirations)/Can't Get No Peace (Eric 'Monty' Morris)/For A Few Dollars More (Upsetters)/Strange Whispering (West Indians)/Taste Of Killing (Upsetters)/Hard To Handle (Carl Dawkins)/My Mob (Upsetters)/Freedom Train (Ernest Wilson)/ Dark End Of The Street (Pat Kelly)/Since You Are Gone (Pat Kelly)/Return Of The Ugly (Upsetters)/'Til I Can't (a.k.a. Can't Take It Any More) (David Isaacs)/ Rightful Ruler (U Roy & Peter Tosh)/I Caught You (Upsetters)/Never Get Away (Eric Donaldson)/A Broken Heart (Busty Brown)/Dry Acid (Count Sticky)/Selassie (Reggae Boys)/Facts Of Life (Mellotones).

Note: Material recorded 1968–69. Compiled & annotated by Laurence Cane-Honeysett.

THE COMPLETE UK UPSETTER SINGLES COLLECTION VOL. 1
[Trojan (UK) TAL 902]

Eight for Eight (Upsetters)/You Know What I Mean (Inspirations)/Return Of Django (Upsetters)/Dollar In The Teeth (Upsetters)/Good Father (David Isaacs)/What A Situation (Slim Smith)/Ten To Twelve (Upsetters)/People Funny Fi True (Lee Perry)/What A Price (Busty Brown)/How Can I Forget (Busty Brown)/I've Got Memories (David Isaacs)/Leaving On A Jet Plane (David Isaacs)/Mini Dress (Winston Jarrett)/Mad House (Lee Perry)/Night Doctor (Upsetters)/I'll Be Waiting (Termites)/To Love Somebody (Busty Brown)/Farmer's In The Den (Bleechers)/ Kiddyo (Silvertones)/Endlessly (Silvertones)/Man From MI5 (Upsetters)/Oh Lord (West Indians)/He'll Have To Go (David Isaacs)/Since You Are Gone (David Isaacs)/Medical Operation (Upsetters)/Badam Bam (Ravers)/Live Injection (Upsetters)/Everything For Fun (Bleechers)/Come Into My Parlour (Bleechers)/Dry Up Your Tears (Mellotones)/Cold Sweat (Upsetters)/Pound Get A Blow (Bleechers)/ Hello Dolly (Pat Satchmo)/King Of The Trombone (Busty Brown)/The Vampire (Upsetters)/Check Him Out (Bleechers)/Soulful I (Upsetters)/No Bread And Butter (Milton Morris, a.k.a. Milton Henry)/Who To Tell (Bruce Bennett, a.k.a. David Isaacs)/I Can't See Myself Cry About You (Busty Brown)/Dirty Dozen (Shadows)/ Crying Too Long (Shadows)/Stranger On The Shore (Val Bennett)/Drugs And Poison (Upsetters)/Same Thing That You Gave To Daddy (Nora Dean)/A Testimony (Upsetter Pilgrims)/Same Thing (Gaylads)/I Wear My Slanders (Gaylads)/Yakety Yak (Lee Perry)/Tackro (Upsetters).

Note: Material recorded 1969–70. Night Doctor produced by Ansel Collins. Annotated by Laurence Cane-Honeysett.

WIZDOM – Lee Perry
[Ascension (AS) AN 1]

Our Man Flint (Lloyd Young & Augustus Pablo)/Pi A Ring (Groovers)/Dub The Pum Pum (Silvertones)/Kill The Music (Upsyndicates)/Ensome City Skank (Young Dillinger)/Boloman Skank (Young Dillinger)/You Can Run (Hurricanes)/Cane River Rock (Dillinger & Upsetters)/Rocky River (Upsetters)/Tighten Up Skank (Dillinger & Upsetters)/Jah Rastafari (Dennis Alcapone)/Doctor Who (I Roy)/Doctor Who Version (Upsetters)/Bhutto Girl (Inspirations)/Bhutto Version (Bunny Lee All Stars)/Ska Baby (Bobby Ellis)/Ska Version (Upsetters)/Kung Fu Part 1 (Jah Martin, a.k.a. Mandingo)/Kung Fu Part 2 (Ethnic Fight Band).

Note: Material recorded 1971–75; 'licensed' from Pauline Morrison & Omar Perry. Tracks not produced by Lee Perry: Bhutto Girl/Bhutto Version (produced by Ronnie Bop/Bunny Lee)/Kung Fu Parts 1 & 2 (produced by Larry Lawrence). Compiled & annotated by Pip Chalmers.

PRODUCED AND DIRECTED BY THE UPSETTER – Lee Perry
[Pressure Sounds (UK) PS 19]
I Man Free (King Burnett)/Free Man (Upsetters)/Zion (Flames)/Zion Version
    (Upsetters)/Bike No License (Easton Clarke)/Unlicensed Dub (Upsetters)/Crying
    Over You (Heptones)/Crying Dub (Upsetters)/Financial Crisis (Silvertones)/
    Financial Dub (Upsetters)/Back Biting (Winston Heywood & Hombres)/Chastising
    Dub (Upsetters)/House Of Parliament (Meditations)/Dub Of Parliament
    (Upsetters)/Guide Line (George Faith)/Dub Line (Upsetters)/Philistines On The
    Land (Jr Murvin)/Bingo Kid (Chinna & Upsetters)/False Teachings (Jr Murvin)/
    Teachers Dub (Upsetters).
Note: Material recorded 1976–78. 'Bike No Licence' produced by Mike Johnson.
    Annotated by Roger Eagle.

LOST TREASURES OF THE ARK – Lee Perry
[Jest Star/Orchard (UK) ORCH B2]
I Know A Place (Bob Marley)/I Know A Dub (Upsetters)/Who Colt The Game (Bob
    Marley)/Who Colt The Dub (Upsetters)/Shocks Almighty I, II & III (Bob Marley &
    Lee Perry)/More Axe (Wailers)/More More Axe (Wailers)/Stand By Me
    (Inspirations)/You Know What I Mean I & II (Inspirations)/Django Shoots First (Sir
    Lord Comic)/Dollar In The Teeth I & II (Upsetters)/Baby Baby I & II (Val
    Bennett)/Barbara (Val Bennett)/Beware Of The Pepper (Denzil Laing)/Skanky
    Chicken (Dave Barker)/Runaway Child (Dave Barker)/Glory Glory (Sister P & Full
    Experience)/Glory Glory Dub (Upsetters)/Shoulder To The Wheel (Flying
    Sensation)/Earth A Go Wheel (Upsetters)/Cost Of Living (Keithus, a.k.a. Ras
    Kiddus)/Poor Man Dub (Upsetters)/Weak Heart Feel It (Shaumark & Robinson)/
    Peace And Love (Shaumark & Robinson)/Peace And Love Dub (Upsetters)/Open
    The Gate (Watty Burnett)/Open The Gate Dub (Upsetters)/Down Here In Babylon
    (Brent Dowe)/Take Heed (Armageddeans)/Garden Of Life (Leroy Sibbles)/Garden
    Of Dub (Upsetters)/A Real Version (Upsetters)/Rainy Night In Portland (Watty
    Burnett)/Brother Noah (Shadows)/Bring It Up (Soulettes)/Connection (Dillinger).
Note: Material recorded 1968–78. 'Licensed' from Pauline Morrison & Omar Perry.
    Annotated by Peter 'Penny Reel' Siemens.

1999

THE COMPLETE UK UPSETTER SINGLES COLLECTION VOL. 2
[Trojan (UK) TAL 903]
Kill Them All (Lee Perry & Upsetters)/Soul Walk (Upsetters)/Bronco (Sir Lord Comic)/
    One Punch (Upsetters)/Do You Like It (unknown vocalist, credited to Lee Perry)/
    Touch Of Fire (Upsetters)/Consider Me (Busty Brown)/Consider Me Version
    (Upsetters)/Melting Pot (Heaters)/Kinky Mood (Upsetters)/Spinning Wheel (Melanie
    Jonas & Dave Barker)/Spinning Wheel Version (Upsetters)/Shocks Of Mighty (Dave
    Barker & Upsetters)/Set Me Free (Dave Barker & Upsetters)/Na Na Hey Hey (Kiss
    Him Goodbye) (Upsetters)/Pick Folk Kinkiest (Upsetters)/Granny Show Part 1 (Dave
    Barker & Upsetters)/Granny Show Part 2 (Dave Barker & Upsetters)/Fire Fire
    (Upsetters)/The Jumper (Upsetters)/The Pillow (Upsetters)/Grooving (Upsetters)/Self
    Control (Martin Riley & Fay Bennett)/The Pill (Martin Riley)/Let It Be (Soulettes)/
    Big Dog Bloxie (Upsetters)/Fresh Up (Upsetters)/Toothache (Upsetters)/The Thanks
    We Get (Versatiles)/Hurry Up (Versatiles)/My Cup (Bob Marley & Wailers)/Son Of

Thunder (Lee Perry & Upsetters)/Thunder Version (Upsetters)/Blood Poison (Upsetters)/Dreamland (Upsetters)/Version Of Cup (Upsetters)/Sipreano (Lee Perry & Upsetters)/Ferry Boat (Upsetters)/Some Sympathy (Dave Barker & Upsetters)/ Tender Love (Untouchables, a.k.a. Inspirations)/Same Thing All Over (Untouchables, a.k.a. Inspirations)/It's Over (Untouchables, a.k.a. Inspirations)/Bigger Joke (Upsetters)/Return Of The Vampire (Upsetters)/Sound Underground (Dave Barker & Upsetters)/Don't Let The Sun Catch You Crying (Dave Barker & Upsetters)/ Justice (Upsetters)/Duppy Conqueror (Bob Marley & Wailers)/Upsetting Station (Dave Barker & Upsetters)/Dig Your Grave (Upsetters).

Note: Self Control/The Pill produced by Martin Riley. Annotated by Laurence Cane-Honeysett.

THE UPSETTER SHOP VOLUME 2: 1969–73 – Lee Perry & the Upsetters
[Heartbeat (US/UK) 7601]

Check Him Out [take one] (Bleechers)/Uncle Charlie (Mellotones)/Uncle Charlie Version (Dillinger)/Sunshine Rock (Upsetters)/Who To Tell (David Isaacs)/Can't Take It Anymore [take four] (Pat Satchmo)/Caught You Red Handed [takes 1, 2 & 3] (Eric Donaldson & the West Indians)/In the studio listening to the Upsetter radio show on JBC (Scratch, Eric Donaldson & the Upsetters)/Water More Than Flour [take one] (Al & the Vibrators)/X-Ray Vision [take four] (Glen Adams & the Upsetters)/People Sokup Boy (Lee Perry)/Gee [take two] (Al & the Vibrators)/Some Sympathy (Dave Barker)/Tender Love (Inspirations)/Creation (Upsetters)/ Tighten Up (Inspirations)/Tighten Up Skank (Dillinger).

Note: Compiled by Chris Wilson, annotated by David Katz. CD issue has bonus tracks: Can't Take It Anymore [take four] (Pat Satchmo)/Cloud Nine [take three] (Carl Dawkins & the Wailers)/Sweets for My Sweet [rehearsal] (Silvertones).

VOCAL GUEST APPEARANCES

1988

PAY IT ALL BACK VOL. 2 – Various Artists
[On-U Sound (UK) ON-U 42]
Note: Produced by Adrian Sherwood. Includes Perry vocal Train To Doomsville (Lee 'Scratch' Perry & Dub Syndicate).

1989

MUTE BEAT DUB WISE – Mute Beat
[ROIR (US) A143]
Note: Tracks featuring Perry's voice and mixing: Thread Mill Of Life/Yackety; produced by Lee Perry & Bullwackie in New Jersey. Re-issued in Japan on Pony Canyon (685).

TRANSITION – Max Romeo
[Rohit (US) RRTG 7775]
Note: Produced by Max Romeo. Tracks featuring Perry's voice: Keep On Moving/ Maccabee Version.

1991

PEENI WAALI – Fizzè & Dizzi
[Mensch Music (SZ) AGR 4]
Note: Produced by Victor 'Fizzè' de Bros in Switzerland. Tracks featuring Perry's voice:
    Licht & Stein (and fragment of Mini Mali). Re-issued by Shanachie (US) in 1992
    (5002).

1992

QUIET REGGAE – Kazufumi Kodama
[Sony (JP) 6517]
Note: Produced by Kazufumi Kodama in Tokyo. Tracks featuring Perry's voice: Open
    The Japanese Door/Japanese Rock.

1993

ECHOMANIA – Dub Syndicate
[On-U Sound (UK)]
Note: Produced by Adrian Sherwood in London. Tracks featuring Perry's vocals:
    Dubbing Psycho Thriller/Dub Addis Ababa.

1995

STEAMING JUNGLE: THE JUNGLE DUB EXPERIENCE 2 – Rupununi Safari
    featuring Douggie Digital, Mad Professor & Juggler.
[Ariwa (UK) ARI 111]
Note: Produced by Mad Professor, Douggie Digital & Juggler in London. Track
    featuring Perry's voice: Perry In The Dub Jungle.

1997

TIBETAN FREEDOM CONCERT – Various Artists
[Grand Royal/Capitol (US) CDP 7243 8 59110 26]
Note: Recorded live at Randall's Island, New York, June 1997. Includes Perry vocal
    Heads Of Government.

1998

PEENI WAALI: THE RETURN – Fizzè
[Mensch Music (SZ) AGR 9]
Note: Produced by Victor 'Fizzè' de Bros in Switzerland. Tracks featuring Perry's voice:
    Nice Time/Nice Time (radio edit).

HELLO NASTY – The Beastie Boys
[Grand Royal (US)]
Note: Produced by the Beastie Boys in New York. Track featuring Perry's vocal: Dr Lee
    PhD.

ALBUMS CO-PRODUCED OR ENGINEERED BY LEE PERRY

1975

REVELATION TIME – Max Romeo
[Black World (JA) BWLPS 001/Tropical Sound Tracks (UK) TSL 1000]
Revelation Time/No Peace/Tacko(o)/Blood Of The Prophet (parts I & II)/Warning,
    Warning/A Quarter Pound Of I'Cense/Three Blind Mice/Open Up The Gate (parts
    I & II).
Note: Produced by Clive Hunt, except Three Blind Mice, produced by Lee Perry.
    Recorded primarily at Black Ark, except Three Blind Mice, recorded at Randy's. Re-
    issued in US by United Artists; 1999 re-issue by Blood & Fire (UK) as OPEN THE
    IRON GATE 1973–77 (BAF 27) with bonus tracks.

I'VE GOT A LOVE – The Grace Thrillers
[Showers of Blessing (JA) NW 001 LPS – DSR DT 2232]
Nothing But the Blood/I Don't Know Why (Jesus Loves Me)/Time To Go Back Home/
    Love Divine/Just About Time/Travelling On/Take Me Back/I Would Know Him/
    God's Love/I've Got A Love.
Note: Produced by Noel Willis. Several tracks recorded at Black Ark.

1976

ESCAPE FROM BABYLON – Martha Velez
[Sire (US/UK) SRK 6019]
Money Man/There You Are/Wild Bird/Disco Night/Bend Down Low/Happiness/Come
    On In/Get Up, Stand Up.
Note: Produced by Bob Marley at Harry J with Lee Perry's assistance.

REGGAE IN AMERICA – Lion Zion
[House of Natty Records (US) H of N 101]
Reggae In America/Buffalo Dub/Who Killed The Buffalo/American Revolution/
    Children, Children/Beautiful Day/3rd Century/Gas Guzzler/Arise America/Turn
    Towards The Sun.
Note: Produced by Lion Zion; recorded, engineered, & mixed by Lee Perry at Black
    Ark.

1979

PRE-MEDITATION – The Melodians
[Skynote (UK) SKY 18]
Don't Get Weary/Little Nut Tree/Swing And Dine/No Ga Long So/Love One Another/
    Better Days Are Coming/Dry Up Your Tears/I'm Gonna Fall In Love/Give Some
    Way To Love/Survival Is the Game.
Note: Produced by Sonia Pottinger. All tracks except Little Nut Tree/Swing and Dine
    recorded at Black Ark in 1974.

1979

LOVE THY NEIGHBOUR – Ras Michael & the Sons of Negus
[Jah Life (US) JL LP 5]
Don't Sell Daddy No Whiskey/Long Time Ago/Times Is Drawing Nigh/Do You
    Know/Hear River Jordan Roll/Wicked Got To Go/Little David/Jesus Christus Is
    The King.
Note: Produced by Delroy & Hyman Wright & Ras Michael. Recorded and initially
    mixed at the Black Ark by Lee Perry. First issue has incorrect track listing with three
    different songs to subsequent issues.

THE WAY IT IS – I Kong
[Top Ranking (JA) TC 82]
Life's Road/Ghetto Cry/Wolves In Sheep's Clothing/Babylon Walls/Set Black People
    Free/Sinner Man/I Wish (We'll All Be Ready)/The Way It Is.
Note: Produced by Geoffrey Chung. Certain tracks recorded at Black Ark; remainder at
    Harry J and Dynamic.

BREAKTHROUGH – The Slickers
[Tads (US) TRD 101679]
Marcus (Disco Style)/Johnny Too Bad (Disco Style)/Every Wolf (Disco Style)/Give Us
    A Break/Run Come/African Children/Black And White.
Note: Several tracks recorded at Black Ark.

1980

BLACK ARK IN DUB – Black Ark Players
[Black Ark International (UK) BALP 4000]
Jah/Cool Rockers/Lion/Rasta Man/Camp/Loving/Money/In The Valley/Dreadlocks/
    Guidance.
Note: Produced by Pauline 'Isha' Morrison; some tracks initially recorded by Lee Perry
    at Black Ark. Re-issued 1989 by Starlight (UK) and by Lagoon (FR) in 1991 (LG
    1013).

1982

LOVE THY NEIGHBOUR – Ras Michael & the Sons of Negus
[Live and Learn (US) LL LP 1]
Don't Sell Daddy No Whiskey/Times Is Drawing Nigh/Hear River Jordan Roll/Wicked
    Got To Go/Little David/Perfect Love/London Bridge Has Fallen.
Note: Produced by Delroy & Hyman Wright & Ras Michael. Recorded and initially
    mixed at the Black Ark in 1978 by Lee Perry. Alternative track listing and altered mix
    to original Jah Life pressing. Re-issued on CD in conjunction with RAS with slightly
    different mix in 1990s.

1984

BLACK ARK VOLUME 2
[Black Ark International (UK) BALP 4001]
Ethiopia (Carol Cole)/Dub (The Upsetter)/I Am I Said (Bunny Rugs)/How Deep Is
    Your Love (Inamans)/Dub (The Upsetter)/Give Praise (Silvertones)/Iry Iry

(Originals)/Dub (The Upsetter)/Let Love Touch Us Now (Bunny Rugs)/Double Wine (Upsetters)/Mumbling and Grumbling (Jr Byles, miscredited to Silvertones).

Note: Tracks produced by Pauline Morrison: Ethiopia/How Deep Is Your Love/Irie Irie (Give Praise also altered by Morrison); remainder produced by Lee Perry. Re-issued 1992 by Lagoon (FR) as STAY RED (LG 2-1034) with bonus tracks: News Splash (a.k.a. News Flash, Leo Graham)/Power To The Children (a.k.a. Justice To The People, Lee Perry)/I'll Take You Home (Silvertones)/Bless The Weed (a.k.a. Bad Lamp, Upsetters)/Thanks We Get (Upsetters).

Note: Re-issued 1998 by Orange Street (UK) as ETHIOPIA (CDUB 7) with incorrect track listing and order.

1993

PHOENIX OF PEACE – Earl Sixteen
[Seven Leaves (UK) SL8]
Apartheid System/Repatriate Your Mind/Jah Army/Set Jah Children Free/Step By Step/ Few More Miles/Freedom/Holy One/How You Been Doin'.

Note: All tracks voiced in London in 1993 over Black Ark rhythm tracks, except Freedom, voiced at Black Ark 1977.

BLACK ARK ALMIGHTY DUB VOL. 3
[Starlight (UK)]
Mandela Serenade Dub/Stone Cold Dub/Almighty Dub/Glory Glory Dub/Winnie Mandela Dub/Zion Daughters Dub/Maldonado Dub/South Africa Free Dub/Love Dub/GT 4000 Dub.

Note: Produced by Pauline Morrison. Certain tracks make use of Perry-produced rhythm tracks.

1998

WIDE PRAIRIE – Linda McCartney
[MPL/Parlophone (UK) 7243 4 979 102 2]
Note: Rhythm tracks recorded at the Black Ark, June 1977: Mister Sandman/Sugartime.

SELECTED BIBLIOGRAPHY

BOOKS

Adams, L. Emilie (1991) *Understanding Jamaican Patois*, Kingston (JA) Publishers Ltd.

Ali, Arif (ed.) (1979) *West Indians In Britain*, London: Hansib.

Alleyne, Mervyn (1989) *Roots Of Jamaican Culture*, London, Pluto Press.

Baker, Phillip (1994) *Blood Posse*, London: Picador.

Barrett, Leonard (1988) *The Rastafarians* (second edition), Boston: Beacon Press.

Barrow, Steve and Dalton, Peter (1997) *The Rough Guide To Reggae*, London: Penguin.

Beadle, Jeremy (1993) *Will Pop Eat Itself?*, London: Faber and Faber.

Bebey, Francis (1975) *African Music A People's Art*, London: Harrap & Co.

Berry, James (ed.) (1984) *News For Babylon*, London: Chatto & Windus.

Bishton, Derek (1986) *Black Heart Man*, London: Chatto & Windus.

Booker, Cedella and Winkler, Anthony (1996) *Bob Marley: An Intimate Portrait By His Mother*, London: Viking.

Brand, Dionne (1997) *In Another Place, Not Here*, London: The Woman's Press.

C., Gordon (1988) *The Reggae Files*, London: Hansib.

Campbell, Horace (1985) *Rasta And Resistance*, London: Hansib.

Cham, Mbaye (ed.) (1992) Exiles: *Essays On Caribbean Cinema*, Trenton, New Jersey: Africa World Press.

Chanan, Michael (1995) *Repeated Takes*, London: Verso.

Chang, Kevin O'Brien and Chen, Wayne (1998) *Reggae Routes*, Philadelphia: Temple University Press.

Charters, Samuel (1981) *The Roots Of The Blues*, London: Marion Boyars.

Chevannes, Barry (1994) *Rastafari Roots And Ideology*, Syracuse (NY) University Press.

Clarke, Sebastian (1980) *Jah Music*, London: Heinemann.

Cliff, Michelle (1996) *No Telephone To Heaven*, New York: Plume.

Clifford, Mike (ed.) (1982) *The Illustrated Encyclopedia Of Black Music*, New York: Harmony Books.

Condé, Maryse (1994) *Tree Of Life*, London: The Woman's Press.

Corbett, John (1994) *Extended Play*, London: Duke University Press.

Dalrymple, Henderson and Kallyndyr, Rolston (1976) *Reggae, a People's Music*, London:

Carib Arawak Publications.

Davis, Stephen (1983) *Bob Marley: Conquering Lion of Reggae*, London: Arthur Baker.

Davis, Stephen and Simon, Peter (1977) *Reggae Bloodlines*, New York: Anchor.

Davis, Stephen and Simon, Peter (eds.) (1982) *Reggae International*, New York: R&B.

Dennis, Ferdinand (1988) *Behind The Frontlines*, London: Victor Gollancz.

Fanon, Frantz (1967) *Black Skin, White Masks*, New York: Grove Press.

Faristzaddi, Millard (1987) *Itations Of Jamaica and Rastafari*, Miami: Judah Anbesa.

Fernando Jr, S. H. (1994) *The New Beats*, New York: Anchor.

Gillett, Charlie (1983) *The Sound Of The City* (Revised Edition), London: Souvenir Press.

Gilroy, Paul (1987) *There Ain't No Black In The Union Jack*, London: Hutchinson.

— (1993) *The Black Atlantic*, London: Verso.

Griffiths, Marc (1995) *Boss Sounds – Classic Skinhead Reggae*, Dunoon: ST Publishing.

Gunst, Laurie (1995) *Born Fi' Dead*, Edinburgh: Payback Press.

Hebdige, Dick (1979) *Subculture: The Meaning Of Style*, London: Methuen.

— (1987) *Cut 'n' Mix*, London: Comedia.

Henzell, Perry (1982) *Power Game*, Kingston: Ten-A Publications.

Heygood, Will (1993) *King Of The Cats*, New York: Houghton Mifflin.

Hurford, Ray (1996) *The Small Axe Reggae Album Guide*, Kuusankoski, Finland: Black Star.

Hurford, Ray (ed.) (1987) *More Axe*, Helsinki: Black Star.

— (1998) *More Axe 8*, Kuusankoski, Finland: Black Star.

Jekyll, Walter (ed.) (1966) *Jamaican Song And Story*, New York: Dover Publications.

Johnson, Buzz (1985) *I Think Of My Mother: Notes On The Life And Times Of Claudia Jones*, London: Karia Press.

Johnson, Howard and Pines, Jim (1982) *Reggae: Deep Roots Music*, London: Proteus.

Jones, Simon (1988) *Black Culture, White Youth*, London: MacMillan.

Kapuscinski, Ryszard (1984) *The Emperor: Downfall Of An Autocrat*, New York: Vintage.

Kaski, Tero and Vuorinen, Pekka (1984) *Reggae Inna Dancehall Style*, Helsinki: Black Star.

Kennaway, Guy (1997) *One People*, Edinburgh: Payback Press.

Larkin, Colin (ed.) (1998) *The Virgin Encyclopedia Of Reggae*, London: Virgin.

Lazell, Barry (1994) *Bob Marley: The Illustrated Legend*, London: Hamlyn.

Lipsitz, George (1994) *Dangerous Crossroads*, London: Verso.

Mais, Roger (1954) *Brother Man*, London: Heinemann.

Manley, Michael (1982) *Jamaica: Struggle In The Periphery*, London: Third World Media.

Marre, Jeremy (1985) *Beats Of The Heart*, London: Pluto Press.

McKenzie, Earl (1991) *A Boy Named Ossie*, Oxford: Heinemann.

Miller, Simon (ed.), *The Last Post*, Manchester University Press.

Morrish, Ivor (1982) *Obeah, Christ And Rastaman*, Cambridge: James Clarke.

Murrell, Nathaniel; Spencer, William and McFarlane, Adrian (eds.) (1998) *Chanting Down Babylon: The Rastafari Reader*, Kingston: Ian Randle.

Novi, Vitko (1991) *170 Stunden Mit Ausserirdischen*, Zürich: Lion Star.

Owens, Joseph (1976) *Dread*, Kingston: Sangster's Book Stores.

Palmer, Robert (1996) *Dancing In The Street*, London: BBC Books.

Petrie, Gavin (ed.) (1974) *Black Music*, London: Hamlyn.

Pollard, Velma (1994) *Dread Talk*, Kingston (JA): Canoe Press.

Potash, Chris (ed.) (1997) *Reggae, Rasta, Revolution*, New York: Schirmer Books.

Roberts, John Storm (1972) *Black Music Of Two Worlds*, New York: Original Music.

Roy, Namba (1989) *No Black Sparrows*, Oxford: Heinemann.

Salewicz, Chris & Adrian Boot (1995) *Songs Of Freedom*, London: Bloomsbury.

Salkey, Andrew (ed.) (1960) *West Indian Stories*, London: Faber and Faber.

Sibley, Inez Knibb (1978) *Dictionary of Place Names In Jamaica*, Kingston: Institute of Jamaica.

Siemens, Peter (a.k.a. Observer Station) (1985) *Bob Marley: The Illustrated Discography*, London: Omnibus.

Small, Geoff (1995) *Ruthless: The Global Rise Of The Yardies*, London: Warner.

Szwed, John F. (1997) *Space Is The Place*, Edinburgh: Payback Press.

Talamon, Bruce (1994) *Bob Marley: Spirit Dancer*, London: WW Norton.

Tate, Greg (1992) *Flyboy In The Buttermilk*, New York: Fireside.

Thelwell, Michael (1980) *The Harder They Come*, New York: Grove Weidenfeld.

Thomas, Michael and Boot, Adrian (1982) *Jah Revenge*, London: Eel Pie.

Thomas, Polly and Vaitilingam, Adam (1997) *The Rough Guide To Jamaica*, London: Penguin.

Toop, David (1984) *Rap Attack*, London: Pluto.

— (1991) *Rap Attack 2*, London: Serpent's Tail.

— (1996) *Oceans Of Sound*, London: Serpent's Tail.

Walker, F. Deaville (1933) *The Call Of The West Indies*, London: Cargate Press

Wallis, Roger and Malm, Krister (1984) *Big Sounds From Small Peoples*, London: Constable.

Weber, Tom and Jahn, Brian (1992) *Reggae Island*, Kingston (JA) Publishers Ltd.

White, Timothy (1991) *Catch A Fire* (Revised Edition), London: Omnibus.

Whitney, Malika Lee and Hussey, Dermott (1984) *Bob Marley: Reggae King Of The World*, Kingston (JA): Kingston Publishers Limited.

BOOKLETS, PAMPHLETS AND LINER NOTES

I have drawn from album liner notes by several authors, the largest portion of which were penned by Steve Barrow, Roger Steffens, Leroy Jodie Pierson, and Julian Jingles are also among the most noteworthy. The following items have also proved essential:

Bell-Brown, Lol and Pelling, Iain (1990) *Augustus Pablo: A Discography*, London: Boom Shacka Lacka.

Dalke, Roger (1979–95) *Record Selector/Ska To Reggae Discography Vols. 1–18*, Addlestone: TSI Publications.

— (1995) *Record Selector Master Index*, Addlestone: TSI Publications.

— (1998) *A Scorcha From Studio One (Discography) Parts 1 and 2*, Addlestone: TSI Publications.

Hurford, Ray (1989) *Rhythm Wise*, Helsinki: Black Star.

— (1992) *The Small Axe Files*, London: Muzik Tree.

Hurford, Ray (ed.) (1989) *More Axe 7*, Helsinki: Black Star.

Lesser, Beth (1989) *King Jammy's*, Helsinki: Black Star.

Morgan, Charlie (1995) *Studio One Discography*, Lakebay, Washington: Outernational.

Plum, Jeff; Rose, Jenny; Tskani, Kefentse and Anbessa-Ebanks, Kwende (1987) *Rastafari*, London: ILEA Religious Education Teachers Centre/Ethiopian World Federation.

Scrivener, Jean (1990) *Rhythm Wise Two*, Helsinki: Black Star.

— (1991) *Rhythm Wise Three*, Helsinki: Black Star.

NEWSPAPER AND MAGAZINE ARTICLES

I have found a number of publications to be consistently useful, most notably *The Daily Gleanor*, *Reggae Swing*, *Roots News*, *Reggae Times*, and *Rhythm Vibes* from Jamaica; Toronto's *Reggae Quarterly*; *The Beat*, *Dub Missive*, *Reggae Report*, *Rhythm Music*, *Dub Catcher*, *Reggae Directory*, *Cool Runnings*, and *Reggae Calendar* from the USA, Belgium's *Etna*, Germany's *Trench Town* and *Jahug*, *Reggae Trade* and *Echoes* from the UK. English fanzines *Boom Shacka Lacka*, *Distant Drums*, and *Let's Catch the Beat*, American zines *400 Years* and *Full Watts* and Malta's *Reggae World* have also been helpful. I have made specific use of the articles noted below:

Adebayo, Dotun 'Loony Tunes' in *The Voice*, January 30, 1990, page 16.

Amoruso, Carol 'A Holy Man Treads The Ism-Schisms Of Rastafari' in *Dub Missive*, Vol. 10, no. 6, pages 42–5.

Anonymous/Uncredited: 'Family Man Barrett: The Most Popular Bassman' in *Reggae Swing*, November 1976, pages 9–10.

Anonymous/Uncredited: 'Festival Song Competition Winners 1966–90' in Reggae Directory, June 1991, page 12.

— 'Lee Perry' in Reggae Directory, June 1992, page 30.

— 'Motta's 50th Anniversary Supplement' in Jamaica Daily Gleanor, March 7, 1982, pages 11–21.

— 'Lee "Scratch" Perry' in Riddim, no. 154, February 1996.

Atherton, Mike 'A Map Of The Island' in Record Collector (1996), pages 76–84.

Barnes, Winston 'Early Reggae' in Jamaica Daily Gleanor, May 23, 1982, page 4.

Bell-Brown, Lol 'Original Rocker: Augustus Pablo' in Dub Catcher, Vol. 2, no. 8, April–May 1994, pages 17–19.

Bizot, Jean-François 'Jamaïque: Reggae, Colts Et Cubans' in Actuel Almanac Des Année 1980, page 256.

Blake, Barbara 'Cimarons Take Root' in Reggae Swing, July 1976, page 17.

Blum, Bruno 'Lee Perry, Au Nom Du Père' in Best, no. 308, April 1994, pages 42–4.

— 'Out-erview De Scratch' in Best of Reggae, Hors Series no. 7 (1994), pages 40–5.

— 'Marley Rencontre Enfin Lee "Scratch" Perry, Le Producteur Dément' in Radio Nova Collector: 50 Ans de Bob Marley (1995), page 25.

Breeze, Cool 'Scratchisms', UK article published circa November 1984.

Campbell, Howard 'No One Can Like "Scratch"' in The Jamaica Sunday Observer, February 8, 1988, page 7.

Cartright, Garth 'Spear Heads Reggae Legends' in The Guardian, May 29, 1996, page 2.

Chavez, Paul 'Lee Scratch Perry & The Mad Professor Makes The Maritime Sizzle' in Reggae Calendar, Vol. 11, no. 1, pages 1 and 3.

Chirzai, Steffan 'Q & A With Lee Perry' in San Francisco Chronicle Datebook, November 9, 1997, page 48.

Clark, Carol and Liddell, Janice 'Judy Mowatt: Insights Into Reggae's Light Of The Moon' in The Beat, Vol. 3, no. 6, December 1985, pages 14–17.

Collis, Clark 'Lee "Scratch" Perry's Mysterious World' in Select, no. 60, June 1995.

Conally, Michael and Collis, Clark 'The Madness of Lee "Scratch" Perry in Yush Ponline (Internet magazine) Vol. 1, no. 12.

Davet, Stéphane 'L'Étendard de la Jamaïque Flotte Sur Bourges' in Le Monde, April 19–20, 1988, page 21.

Davis, Stephen 'Disco Nights' in The Beat, Vol. 10, no. 3, June 1991, pages 51–2.

Fadele, Dele 'Revenge Of The Totally Bananas' in NME, October 3, 1987, pages 25 and 49.

Fernando Jr, S.H. 'The Invisible Man: On-U Sound' in Dub Catcher, Vol. 2, no. 8, April–May 1994, pages 23–5.

Forman, Bill 'Dub On The Dance Floor' in Pulse!, October 1997.

Foster, Chuck 'Deepest Roots: The Meditations' in The Beat, Vol. 13, no. 5, October 1994, pages 38–41.

Foster, Chuck 'The Voodoo That You Do So Well' in The Beat, Vol. 16, no. 1, February 1997.

Frere-Jones, Sasha 'Scratching the Surface' in *Village Voice*, August 19, 1997.

Gayle, Carl 'The Upsetter (parts 1 and 2)' in *Black Music*, January 1975, pages 10–11 and February 1975, pages 42–3.

Gerlach, Russell '1997-Year of Scratch Perry In The US' in *Rhythm Vibes*, Vol 5, no. 3, (1997), page 34.

Giacomoni, Antoine 'Lee Perry' in *Rock Hebdo*, Vol. 4, no. 34, November 15, 1978.

Goldman, Vivienne 'Black Punks on Herb' in *Sounds*, October 16, 1976, pages 18–22.

— 'Black Punks On Herb Part 2' in *Sounds*, October 23, 1976, pages 18–21.

— 'Jah Punk' in *Sounds*, September 3, 1977, pages 23–7.

— 'New Musick Dub' in *Sounds*, December 3, 1977, pages 22–5.

— 'Lee Perry Has Found God, And His Name Is Pipecock Jackson' in *Melody Maker*, July 21, 1979.

— 'Bed Jamming Is A Must!' in *Melody Maker*, February 16, 1980, page 9.

Gorney, Marc 'Fire On The Wire' in *The Beat*, Vol. 17, no. 3, June 1998, pages 60–2.

Grabel, Richard 'Curse Of The Vampires' in *NME*, July 25, 1981, page 24.

Green, Joshua 'Learning From Scratch' in *SF Weekly*, November 19–25, 1997, pages 39–40.

Green, Richard 'Upsetters Boost Reggae Trend' in *NME*, October 25, 1969, page 11.

Hampton, Howard 'Seize the Daze: Lee "Scratch" Perry and the Last Crusade' in *LA Weekly*, January 26–February 1, 1990, pages 45–6.

Heath, Ashley 'Jesus Is A Soul Man' in *The Face*, April 1997, pages 127–30.

Heilig, Steve 'Scratch Attack' in *The Beat*, Vol. 9, no. 3, June 1990, pages 48–9.

— 'Scratching The Surface' in *The Beat*, Vol. 12, no. 2, April 1993, pages 28–9.

— 'Showtime With Scratch' in *The Beat*, Vol. 16, nos. 5 and 6, October–December 1997, pages 70–1 and 75.

Henderson, Richard 'A Dub Revolution' in *Soma*, Vol. 11, no. 8, October 1997, pages 64–5.

Henderson, Richard; Foster, Chuck; Heilig, Steve and Nelson, Robert 'Heart of Arkology' in *The Beat*, Vol. 15, no. 6, December 1997, pages 72–5.

Henshaw, Laurie 'The Story Behind "Django" in *Melody Maker*, December 6 1969.

Hills, Simon 'Dub Star' in *GQ*, March 1997, page 36.

Holmes, Hank 'Ras Michael: Niyabinghi Specialist' in *The Beat*, Vol. 3, no 5, October 1985, pages 15–17.

Johnson, Neville 'The Barrett Brothers' in *Cleveland Reggae Directory*, Vol. 2, no. 3, October 1990, pages 8–9.

Katz, David; Mack, Bob; Markert, Thomas and Mortensen, Shawn 'Return Of The Super Ape' in *Grand Royal*, No. 2 (1995), pages 60–86.

Kelly, Danny 'Lee Perry' in *NME*, November 17, 1984, pages 6–7 and 58.

Kessler, Ted 'Meet Lee "Scratch" Perry' in *NME*, July 26, 1997.

Kitchin, Arthur 'Legitimizing Jamaican Music' in *The Sunday Gleaner Magazine*, July 15, 1979, pages 1 and 2.

Korver, Steve 'Double Madness' in *Time Out Amsterdam*, May 1995.

Lane, Chris 'Scratch The Upsetter (part 2)' in *Blues and Soul* no.115, 3–16 August 1973, page 27.

— 'U Roy Bonanza' in *Melody Maker*, May 15, 1976, page 42.

— 'Give Us The Old Tunes Too' in *Melody Maker*, July 17, 1976, page 41.

Lee, Helene 'Reggae University' in *Best of Reggae Hors Serie*, no. 7 (1994), pages 20–1.

— 'Lee Perry, Apostrophes D'Un Dub Philosophe' in *L'Affiche*, no. 37, April 1992, page 19.

— 'Lee "Scratch" Perry, Le Reggae Aux Portes De La Folie' in *Hors Serie L'Affiche*, no. 2 (1996), pages 71–2.

Maillard, Chris 'Sparkling Perry' in *EQ*, February 1988, pages 24–8.

Martin, K. 'Echo Chamber Odysseys' in *The Wire*, May 1995, pages 29–33.

Mathieson, Kenny 'Truth Never Let Me Down' in *Cut*, November 1987, page 37.

May, Chris 'Starting From Scratch' in *Black Music*, Vol. 4, Issue 47 (October 1977), pages 13–17.

McCann, Ian 'Dub Be Good To Lee' in *NME*, April 28, 1990, page 13.

— 'Game, Upset And Scratch' in *Record Hunter*, April 1991, pages 6–7.

— 'I Am The Dub Organiser And Not The Dub Miser' in *Mixmag*, March 1997, pages 95–9.

— 'Other-Worldly' in *Q*, May 1997.

Nelson, Robert 'Special Mention: Arkology' in *Dub Missive*, pages 10, 58–9.

Novak, Hope 'Interview with Lee 'Scratch" Perry' in *Reggae Review*, Vol. 1, no. 9, November 1997, pages 4, 5 and 15.

Novick, Jeremy 'Adventures In Time And Space' in *The Observer*, 19–25 May 1996, pages 6–7.

O'Hagan, Sean 'Scratch 'n' Mix' in *The Guardian*, April 18, 1997, page 13.

Paphides, Peter 'Up To Scratch' in *Time Out*, May 22–9, 1996, page 101.

Perlich, Max 'Upfront: Clement "Sir Coxsone" Dodd' in *Grand Royal*, no. 1, 1994.

Pierson, Leroy 'Who Is Mr. Brown?' in *The Beat*, Vol. 11, no. 3, June 1992, pages 46–51.

— 'The Truth About Johnny Too Bad' in *The Beat*, Vol. 7, no. 5, October 1988, pages 16–19.

Randall, Rob 'Lee Perry: Reversing The Trernd' in *Melody Maker*, July 7, 1973, page 52.

Reckford, Verena 'Rastafarian Music' in *Jamaica Journal*, Vol. 11, Nos. 1 and 2 (1977), page 7.

Reel, Penny (a.k.a. Peter Siemens) 'Lee Perry Claims Chris Blackwell "Killed Bob Marley" ' in *NME*, March 30, 1985, page 2.

— 'Raiders Of The Lost Ark' in *Echoes*, August 9, 1997, pages 6–7.

Rodigan, David 'Echoes Uncovers The Mole In *Black Echoes*, March 1, 1980, page 5.

— 'Pressure Rock' in *Sounds*, May 19, 1979, pages 22–3.

Salewicz, Chris 'Jamaica: The Young Lion Roars' in *NME*, May 27, 1978, pages 33–9.

Salewicz, Chris 'Jamaica: The Young Lion Roars Part 2' in *NME*, June 3, 1978, pages 22–4.

Sampson, Desmond 'Yep, Beastie Boys Are Back' in *Pavement*, issue 30, August/September 1998, pages 102–5.

Sawyer, Miranda 'Song In His Heart, But What's On His Head?' in *The Observer Review*, April 20, 1997, page 11.

— 'Finish The New Album? Just Got To Finish These Trousers First . . . ' in *The Observer Review*, November 30, 1997, page 9.

Sinker, Mark 'Sore Throat Blues And Voodoo' in *NME*, June 25, 1988, page 54.

Smith, Alan 'Reggae Stops Prejudice' in *NME*, November 29, 1969, page 4.

Spellman, Robert 'King of Mess' in *Jazid*, July/August 1996, page 31.

Spencer, Neil 'Kingston Report Part 1' in *NME*, October 16, 1976, pages 29–34.

— 'Kingston Report Part 2' in *NME*, October 23, 1976, pages 30–7.

— 'Spikey Heads Meets Dreadlocks' in *NME*, October 1, 1977, pages 15–18.

— 'Lee Perry' in *NME*, May 27, 1978.

— 'Jamaican Lion Inna Concrete Jungle' in *NME*, November 10, 1979, pages 33–5, 58 and 65.

Stearns, Dave 'Lee Perry: Rapid-Fire Reggae' in *Rochester Times-Union*, July 11, 1981, page 6.

Steffens, Roger 'Scratch Greets The Beat' in *The Beat*, Vol. 10, no. 4, August 1991, pages 51–3.

— 'Jackie Mittoo' in *Dub Catcher*, Vol. 2, no. 7, December 1993/January 1994, pages 12–13.

— 'Folkes Tale' in *The Beat*, Vol. 13, no. 2, April 1994, pages 58–9.

Steinhilber, Rob '2 Records by Leo Graham' in *The Beat*, October 1984, page 25.

Stewart, Tony 'Marley's Big Toe In A Babylon' in *NME*, September 17, 1977, page 18.

Sullivan, James 'Mad Professor: The Doctor Of Dub Is In!' in *BAM*, April 4, 1997, pages 60–1.

— 'Inspector Gadget' in *Request*, July 1997, pages 48–9.

Targowski, Henry W. 'Lee Perry' in *Vinyl*, no. 6, September 1981, pages 34–5.

— 'Lee Perry: Genius, Madman, Magician' in *Vinyl*, no. 7, October 1981, pages 14–15.

Taylor, Crispin 'Return To The Ark' in *Straight No Chaser*, no. 40, Spring 1997, pages 37–47.

Terell, Tom 'Lee "Scratch" Perry' in *Seconds*, no. 44, *Fall*, 1997, pages 57–63.

Thompson, Hugh 'What Goes On: Lee Perry' in *Mojo*, no. 34, September 1996, pages 20–1.

Turner, Michael 'It Sipple Out Deh' in *The Beat*, Vol. 14, no. 1, February 1995, pages 32–4.

— 'Keep On Moving!' in *The Beat*, Vol. 15, no. 5, October 1996, pages 40–3.

— 'Get Ready, Rock Steady' in *The Beat*, Vol. 16, no. 4, August 1997, pages 58–61 and 80.

Welch, Christopher J. 'Spotlight On Reggae: The Upsetters' in *Melody Maker*, November 8, 1969, page 20.

Wendt, Doug 'Upsetter Talking' in *The Beat*, July–August 1983, pages 17–21.

— 'Blessed By A Banana Split' in *The Beat*, Vol. 6, no. 3, June 1987, pages 44, 45, 54.

— 'Satan Kicked The Bucket' in *The Beat*, Vol. 8, no. 4, August 1989, page 40.

— 'Prolific Lee "Scratch" Perry Deluges Us With Spectacular Results' in *Pulse!*, July 1990, page 93.

— 'Return of the Upsetter' in *High Times*, no. 269, January 1998, pages 64–8.

West, Bob 'The Upsetter To Return' in *Jamaica Daily News*, March 1, 1983, page 10.

Whylie, Marjorie 'Independence Is Folk Music in Jamaica' in *Jamaica Daily Gleanor*, July 27, 1979.

Wildebeest, Oscar 'Perryatrics' in *Etna*, Vol. 7, no. 2, December 1991, page 12.

Williams, John 'Ah So Me Seh' in *The Journal*, February 6–16, 1987, page 30.

SELECTED VIDEOGRAPHY

Roots Rock Reggae, BBC television broadcast, 1977; director: Jeremy Marre.

Deep Roots Music, Channel 4 television six-part series, 1982; director: Howard Johnson.

The Tube: Jools In Jamaica Special, Channel 4 television broadcast, 1982.

The Tube, Channel 4 television broadcast, 14 December, 1984 (recorded live in Newcastle).

Lee Perry: The Unlimited Destruction, Jet Star video, 1990; director: Karel Michiels.

Baadass TV, Channel 4 television broadcast, 1995.

Dancing In The Street: No Fun, BBC television broadcast, 1996; producer: Hugh Thompson.

Return Of The Super Ape, Channel 4 television broadcast, summer 1997; directors: Don Letts and Rick Elgood.

SELECTED RADIO BROADCASTS

Capital Radio, London, circa February 23, 1980; Lee Perry interviewed by David Rodigan.

BBC Radio London, *Rockers FM* show, circa November 1984; Lee Perry and Desmond Dekker interviewed by Tony Williams.

BBC Radio Lancashire, December 16, 1984; Lee Perry interviewed by Steve Barker.

BBC Radio Lancashire, 1986; telephone interview with Lee Perry conducted by Steve Barker.

BBC Radio London, 1987; Lee Perry and Winston Groovy interviewed by Tony Williams.

Radio Nova, Paris, November 18, 1987; Lee Perry interviewed by Jean-François Bizot.

Tropic FM, Paris, November 6, 1988; Lee Perry interviewed by Mary Nnankya (interview conducted in November 1987).

VPRO Radio 3, Holland, April 4, 1990; Lee Perry interviewed by Pieter Franssen.

Kiss FM, London, July 1997; Lee Perry interviewed by David Rodigan (interview conducted in April 1997).

INDEX

'A Wah Dat' 263
Ace, Richard 29
'Action Line' 63
'Action Wood' 214
'AD Vendetta' 403
Adams, Aubrey 19, 28, 46
Adams, Glen 84–5, 121, 144, 208
Adams, Lloyd ("Tin Legs") 79
'Africa' 302
African Head Charge 383
'African Head Charge In The Hackney
    Empire' 425
'African Herbman' 128, 132
African Herbman 172
'African Hitch-Hiker' 425
'African Root' 308
'African Skank' 178
'African Sound' 210
Africa's Blood 147–8, 377
Afro Jamaicans, The 202
'After The Rain' 402
Aide, Busha 2
'Ain't No Sunshine Girl' 187
'Ain't No Sunshine Rhythm' 212
Aitken, Bobby 45, 115
Aitken, Lorenzo (Laurel) 17, 140
Akabu 370, 419
Al and the Vibrators 57, 123
Alcapone, Dennis (Dennis Smith) 41,
    141–3, 161
Aldrich, Uriel 186
Alimantado, Dr (Winston Thompson)
    144, 212–13
'All Africans' 121, 123
'All Combine' 139
All For Free 214
'All For One One For All' 294
'All In One' 120

'All Over' 137
All Stars 44, 47, 69
All Stars label 19
All the Hits 421
'All Things Are Possible' 378, 381
Allah, Prince (Keith Blake) 87, 242–3
'Allergic To Lies' 385
'Alpha And Omega' 148
Alphonso, Roland 29, 45, 69, 71, 349
Alpines, The 47
Amazulu 376
'Amen' 76
'American Revolution' 253
Anderson, Alpharita 34, 38
Anderson, Gladstone 29, 44, 46–7, 55
Anderson, Lynford 58–60, 60–1, 64
Anderson, Vesta 34
Andy, Horace 52
'Angel Gabriel And The Space Boots' 431
'Angela Davis' 249
Angen label 234
'Another Chance' 77
'Apeman Skank' 178
'Appeal, The' 49
'Arab and Israelite' 209
Arawaks, The 9
'Are You Sure' 175
'Arise America' 253
Ariwa Rupununi Safari Steaming Jungle
    439
Ariwa studio 369–70, 419
'Ark Of The Covenant' 282, 284
Arkology 450
Arkwell label 392
'At Midnight' 298
'At The End' 155
'At The Feast' 333
At The Grass Roots Of Dub 197–8

Atkinson, Bryan 44
'Atlas Road Map' 352
Attack label 231
'Auntie Lulu' 166, 176
'Axe Man, The' 131, 155
Axx of Jahpostles 315

'Ba Ba' 90
'Ba Ba Boom' 49, 152
'Baby Baby' 72, 127
'Baby I Love You' 130
'Baby It's You' 243
'Baby We've Got A Date' 236
'Babylon A Fall' 211–12
'Babylon Arrest' 299
'Babylon Chapter 10' 149
'Babylon Cookie Jar A Crumble' 334,
    346, 350
'Babylon Deh Pon Fire' 241
'Babylon Falling' 319
'Babylon Feel This One' 269
'Babylon System' 290
'Babylon's Burning' 149
'Back Biting' 241
'Back Out With It' 431
'Back Weh' 234
'Backbiter' 161
'Backseat Education' 395
'Bad Case Of Loving You' 280
'Bad Food' 308
'Bad Lamp' 184
'Bad Luck' 148
'Bad Luck Natty' 251
'Bad-Minded People' 30, 32, 34
'Bad Tooth' 103
'Bad Walking' 165
'Bad Weed' 274
'Baffling Smoke Signal' 317, 334, 337,
    341
Bahama Mama 355
Bailey, Alphonso 154
Balfe, David 395
'Ball Of Fire' 54
'Bang Bang Lulu' 227
'Bangarang' 67, 85
'Bangbelly Chicken Scratch' 171
'Bank To Bank' 400
'Barbara' 72
Barker, Dave (David Crooks) 94–5,
    106–8, 109, 127, 166

Barker, Steve 375, 383, 388
Barnes, Lloyd "Bullwackie" 214, 399,
    401–2
Barnett, Dorothy 62
Barrett, Aston Francis ("Family Man")
    83–4, 110, 118–19,
    130, 395–6
Barrett, Carlton Lloyd 83–4
'Bat Bat' 400
'Bathroom Skank' 177
'Battering Down Sentence' 247
Battle Axe 154–5
'Battle Axe' 155
Battle Of Armagideon (Millionaire
    Liquidator) 378, 379, 380
Bautista, Anthony (Tony Cousins) 99,
    101
'Be Good' 52
'Be Thankful' 233
'Be With You' 52
'Beardman Feast' 276
Beastie Boys 443–4
'Beat a Way' 402
'Beat Down Babylon' 145, 146–7
Beat Down Babylon 153
'Beatitude, The' 80
Beckford, Ewart (U Roy) 91–3, 131
Beckford, Keeling 62–3, 214–15
Beckford, Neville (Jah Whoosh) 249, 382
Beckford, Theophilus 19, 28, 116
'Bed Jamming' 338, 345, 366, 395, 444
'Bed Of Roses' 140
Belgium 432, 433, 454
'Bend Down Low' 120, 236, 237
Bennett, Felix ("Deadly Headley") 29, 44,
    46, 47
Bennett, Val 9, 63, 64, 72, 97
Bernays, Lukas 435, 452
'Best Dressed Chicken In Town' 212, 213
'Best Of Both Worlds' 280
Best Of The Wailers 79
'Bet You Don't Know' 149
'Better Days' 168
'Better Future' 293
'Better Must Come' 166
'Beware' 103
'Bhutto Girl' 106
'Big Apple Coconut' 432
Big Audio Dynamite 389
'Big Boy' 258

'Big Cocky Wally' 266
'Big Gut Striker' 171
'Big May' 232
'Big Muff' 290
'Big Neck Police' 269–70, 300, 301, 312,
    337, 373
'Big Pussy Sally' 241, 266
'Big Takeover, The' 78
'Big Tongue Buster' 184
Big Youth 158
'Bigger Joke' 119
'Bike No License' 226
'Bingo Kid' 274
'Bionic Rats' 293
'Bird In Hand' 313
'Bird In The Hand' 303
Bizot, Jean-Francois 396
'Black A White' 320
Black Ark Almighty Dub Chapter Three
    441, 448
Black Ark Experryments 438–9, 440
Black Ark In Dub 345
Black Ark International label 361
Black Ark studio
    early days 180–216
    establishment 180–1
    P.'s explanation of name 182
    improved equipment 208–9, 232,
        240–1, 321
    deterioration & disintegration 329–
        30, 340
    destroyed by fire 363–5, 372
    re-building 446–7, 459–60
Black Ark Volume 2 361
Black Art label 175, 181–2
'Black Belt Jones' 198, 223
'Black Bird' 213, 214
'Black Candle' 183–4
'Black Cat' 376
'Black Cinderella' 334
'Black IPA' 169
'Black Is Our Colour' 216
'Black Lion' 251
'Black Man's Time' 169, 178
'Black Panta' 177–8
'Black People You've Got to Know
    Yourself' 345
'Black Progress' 110
Black Star Liner label 328, 331, 334, 343
'Black Vest' 255

Black Wax label 231
Blackboard Jungle Dub 277, 348, 438, 444
'Blackman Redemption' 306, 307, 322
'Blackman's Country' 52
Blackwell, Chris
    biographical 17, 18
    founds Trojan label 73–4
    and Island label 247–8, 351–2
    and 'Police And Thieves' 260
    and 'Dreadlocks In Moonlight' 270–1
    and *Heart of the Congos* 309–10
    P.'s break with Island 314
    and 'Judgement In A Babylon' 370–1
Blackwell, Joe 17–18
Blake, Keith (Prince Allah) 87, 242–3
Blake, Winston 189–92, 193
Bleechers, The 78
'Blinkers' 385, 386
'Blood Dunza' 254
'Blood of the Prophet' 229
Blood Vapour 421
Bloodvessel, Buster 376
'Blowin' In The Wind' 67, 127
Blue Bells duo 241, 256
Blue Mink 109
'Blue Moon' 155
Bluegrass Experience 230
Blues Blasters 19
Blum, Bruno 394
Blythe, Desmond 4
Blythe, Granville 3–4
Blythe, Lorna (Miss Nelle) 15
Blythe, Milton (Poppa Son) 7, 163, 347,
    363–4, 436
Blythe, Veta Aneta (Girlie) 4, 37, 102
Boboshanti 297–8, 320–1
'Bongo Man' 266
'Bongo Nyah' 122
'Bongo Red' 219
'Boogie In My Bones' 17
'Boogie Rock' 17
Booker, Cedella 307
Boothe, Ken 53
Bop, Ronnie (Lorraine Williams) 44, 47,
    63, 97, 144, 272
Bop-a Loos, The 59
Boris Gardiner Happening, The 203, 265
'Born To Love' 198
'Bosrah' 242, 243
'Boss Society' 78, 103

Boswell, George (Niney) 58, 104, 157, 169–70, 257, 430
Bovell, Dennis 222–3
Bow Tie Brothers 76
'Boy Named Tom' 126
Bradford, Bill 328, 344
Bradshaw, Carl 302
'Brain Washing' 129, 132
Braithwaite, Junior 33
'Brand New Secondhand' 129
Breakfast In Bed 193
'Breakfast In Bed' 298
Breakthrough 320
Brevett, Lloyd 28
'Broadway' 257
'Bronco' 72
Broncos, The 202
Brooks, Edmund "Mike" 235
Brooks, Hector 77
Brooks, Mike 421
Brooks, Oswald ("Baba") 29
Bros, Victor de (Fizzé) 422–5, 429, 451–2
Brother Dan All Stars 140
'Brother Noah' 315
'Brotherly Love' 337, 433
Brothers, The 219
Brown, Busty (Clive Smith) 76, 78, 94
Brown, Carlton 105
Brown, Dennis 257
Brown, Glenmore 94, 185
Brown, Lynford ("Hux") 44, 45–6, 59, 318
Bryan, Carl ("Cannonball") 29
'Bucky Skank' 169, 441
'Buffalo Dub' 253
'Buffalo Soldier' 306, 307
Bugs On The Wire 375
Bullocks, Lester ("Dillinger") 161–2, 171
'Bum Ball' 101
'Bump, The' 214
Bunny Lee & The Aggrovators Aggrovate Lee Perry & The Upsetters 438
Burke, Leslie 77
Burnett, Derrick ("Watty") 70–1, 90, 211–12, 283, 296, 309
Burnin' 236
'Burning Fire' 106
Burning Sounds label 303
'Burning Wire' 186
Burru music 9–10, 27

'Bury The Razor' 235
'Bushweed Corntrash' 231, 240
Bustamante, Alexander 20
Buster, Prince 24–7, 30, 48–50
'By Saint Peter' 35
'By The Sweat' 305
Byles, Keith ("Junior") 54, 145–6, 153, 166, 238

Cacia, Mike 354–5, 358, 360
Cactus label 166
Cadogan, Alison Anne ("Susan") 200–1, 205–7
'Calamooch' 352
Caldato, Mario 444, 455
'Call On Me' 48, 49
Caltone label 52
Cameron, Charles 29
Campbell, Al 199–200
Campbell, Cecil *see* Buster, Prince
Campbell, Lloyd F. 214
Campbell, Michael (Mikey Dread) 301
Campbell, Mireille *see* Perry, Mireille (*wife*)
Campbell, Wayne 362
Canada 455
'Cane River Rock' 212, 217, 333
'Cannot Wrong And Get Right' 32
'Can't Be Wrong' 32
'Can't Come In' 282
'Can't Conquer Natty Dreadlocks' 212
'Can't Get No Peace' 77
'Can't See You' 298
'Can't Take It Any More' 93, 103
Capo label 208
'Captive' 317, 334
'Careful How You Jump' 305
Caribbeats, The 45, 47, 80
Carlton and His Shoes 168
'Carnal Mind' 216
'Carry Go Bring Come' 44
Carter, Lynval (Prince Jazzbo) 185, 254
Carty, Sam 217
Catch A Fire 172, 236
'Catch This' 127
'Catch Vampire' 242, 266, 275
'Caught You Red–Handed' 77
Cavaliers, The 44
Caveman 105
'Caveman Shank' 165
'Caveman Skank' 178

'Chalice Ablaze' 359
Chalk Farm studio 141
Channel One studio 162
'Chant Down Babylon Kingdom' 293
'Chapter Of My Heart' 144
Charmers, Lloyd 63, 84, 85, 89
'Chase The Devil' 251–2, 255, 292, 341
'Chase Them' 316
'Chatty Chatty' 258
'Cheat Weston Head' 235
'Cheating' 303
'Check Him Out' 78, 103
'Check Your Head' 444
Checkmates, The 70
'Cheerio' 155
'Cheerio Baby' 141
'Cherry Oh Baby' 141, 142, 148, 285
'Chicken Scratch' 24–5, 32, 40
'Children Crying' 283
'Children Get Ready' 63
Chin, Albert Valentine (Tony) 114
Chin, Keith 75
Chin, Vincent 75
'Christmas' 201
Chung, Geoffrey 229
Cimarons, The 174, 243
'City Too Hot' 293
Civic label 104
'Civilization' 141
Clarendon Parish 4
Claridge, Mo 327, 332
Clarke, Danny 78, 137–8, 266, 324–5, 345
Clarke, Easton 226
Clarke, William ("Bunny") 230–1, 232, 233, 249
Clash, The 288, 357
Classics, The 141
Clemenson, Merle 60
Cliff, Jimmy 299
Clint Eastwood 89, 93
'Clint Eastwood' 93
Cloak And Dagger 164–6, 242, 333, 334
Clocktower label 209, 348
'Closer Together' 274
'Cloud Nine' 103, 126
'CN Express' 62
cocaine 352, 415
'Cockroach Motel' 352
'Cold Sweat' 90

'Cold Weather' 176
Cole, Leroy ("Cuttings") 12, 55
Cole, Wilburn Theodore ("Stranger") 21–2, 55
Coley, Keith 174
'Collie Ruler' 431
Collins, Ansel 80, 81, 166
Collins, Dave 166
Colombia Collie 250–1
'Colour' 310
'Columbia Gold Dust' 314
'Combination' 62
'Come Along' 241
'Come Da Da' 152
'Come Go With Me' 441
'Come On And Dance' 428
'Come On In' 237
'Come On Into My World' 319
'Come On Little Girl' 198
'Come On Over' 234
Comets, The 44
Comic, Sir Lord 72
'Coming In From The Cold' 432
'Complete Control' 288–9
'Concrete' 239
'Congoman' 285
Congos, The 280–3, 284, 308, 312
'Congratulations' 206
"conk" 233
Conn Rhythm Box 232
'Connection' 172
'Conquering Lion' 215
Conquering Lion of Judah label 315
Conquering Lion sound system 227
'Conqueror' 169
'Conqueror Version 3' 119
'Conscious Man' 310, 311, 433
Conscious Man 311, 433
Consciousness 311
Cook, Redvert 9
'Cookie Puss' 443
'Cool Operator' 155
Cooley, Sandra 373–4, 376–7, 387, 392, 403, 414, 416, 419–20
'Cornerstone' 126
Cosmo and Denzil 140
'Country Girl' 70
Counts, The 56
Cousins, Roy 159, 160, 283–4
Cousins, Tony (Anthony Bautista) 99,

101
"cow mooing" noise 296
'Cow Thief Skank' 169–70
Coxsone *see* Dodd, Clement Seymour
   ("Coxsone")
Crab label 74
'Crab Walking' 185
'Crab Yars' 313
'Crazy Baldhead' 238, 371, 442
'Crazy Girl' 29
'Crazy House' 453
'Creation' 165
Creation Rebel label 382
'Creeper, The' 139
Creole label 101
Crepe Souls 76
Cridland, Ansel 266, 267, 300, 347
Croaking Lizard 255
Crooks, David *see* Barker, Dave (David
   Crooks)
Crooks, Sydney Roy ("Luddy") 56, 97
'Cross My Heart Babush' 427
'Cross The Nation' 121
'Crossover' 315, 345
'Crusaders' Ball' 167
'Cry To Me' 238
Cry Tuff Dub Encounter 382
'Crying About You' 77
'Crying Over You' 272
'Crying Wolf' 306
'Curley Locks' 208–9, 223, 312, 433, 449
'Curley Dub' 256
'Cut Down (On Your Speed)' 70

D. Darling label 33
'Da Ba Da' 212
'Da Da' 151
DaCosta, Glen 294
Daddy Kool label 241
Daley, Earl (Earl Sixteen) 265
Daley, Lloyd 88, 140
Daley, Richard 115
dance
   importance for P. 4–5, 6–7
   Ettu 5
   Mash 53
'Dance All Night' 159, 281
'Dancing Mood' 262
'Daniel Saw The Stone' 361
D'Arby, Terence Trent 396

'Dark End Of The Street' 78
'Dark Moon' 155
'Darkness Falls On The City' 192
'Darling Don't Do That' 62
'Darling Here I Stand' 105
Davis, Anthony ("Sangie") 167, 168
Davis, Carlton ("Santa") 115
Davis, D. Elmyna 442
Davis, Esmee 15
Davis, Ina (*mother*) 2, 3–4, 5, 448
Davis, Pernel 4
Davis, Sangie 269
Dawkins, Carl 129–30
'Day Should Turn To Night' 400, 402
'Deacon Johnson' 35
Deans, Eric 9
'Death Trap' 216
Dekker, Desmond 99
Dekker, George 97
Delgado, Junior (Oscar Delgado Hibbert)
   210
Dells, The 73
Deltone label 62, 63
Dennis, Denzil Lynward 140–1, 194
'Dentist, The' 103
Denton, Delroy 174, 184
Derrick and Jimmy 71
Dewdroppers 19
Diamond, Mike 443–4
Diamonds, The 203, 207
'Diana' 285
'Different Experience' 223
'Dig Pit' 184
Dillinger (Lester Bullocks) 161–2, 171
Dillon, Leonard 36, 70
Dillon, Phyllis 79
Dingwalls concerts 373, 376, 388, 399
DIP label 204–5
DIP Presents The Upsetter 217
'Diplomat' 80
'Dirty Dozen' 77
Disarmament 319
'Disco Devil' 292, 341
'Disco Fits' 298
'Dispensation' 333, 345
Dixon, Phillip Texas 286
'Django Shoots First' 72, 127, 172
'Do Good' 303
'Do It Baby' 207
'Do It To Me Baby' 51, 52

'Do The Push Push' 37
'Do You Know' 319
'Do Your Thing' 147
'Doctor Demand' 184
'Doctor Dick' 40, 453
'Doctor Who' 169
Dodd, Clement Seymour ("Coxsone")
    13–14, 19–28
    P.'s early days 22–39
    P.'s disillusionment 40–3
    compared by P. with Buster 49–50
    and 'The Upsetter' 55–6
    recalled by Alcapone 143
    and 'To Be A Lover' 156
    collaboration with P. (1989) 416–17
    P. renews links 458
Dollar In The Teeth 127
dominoes 5, 6
Donaldson, Eric 77, 285
'Don't Be Afraid' 315, 332, 361
'Don't Blame The Baldhead' 432
'Don't Blame The Children' 51
'Don't Brag Don't Boast' 72
'Don't Copy' 32
'Don't Cross The Nation' 155
'Don't Get Weary' 187
'Don't Know Why' 153
'Don't Look Back' 286
'Don't Play That Song' 196
'Don't Rock My Boat' 128, 132
'Don't Run Away' 199
'Don't Sell Daddy No Whisky' 318
'Don't Speak To Me Of Love' 202
'Don't Throw Stones' 48
'Don't Touch My Shadow' 450
'Double Barrel' 127
Double Fun 279
'Double Power' 172
Double Seven 176–7, 377
'Double Six' 176
'Double Wheel' 108
Douglas, Cleon 115
Douglas, Paul 79, 233
Douglas, Val 146
Dowding, Frank (Kiddus–I) 305–6
Dowe, Brent ("Porky") 186
'Down Here In Babylon' 234
Downbeat label 23
Downey, Tyrone 130–1, 133–4
Downie, Mark 377, 412

'Downpressor' 129
'Dr Lee PhD' 455
'Dr No Go' 87, 88
Dragonaires 18
Dread, Mikey (Michael Campbell) 301
'Dread At The Control' 301
'Dread In a Jamdong' 250
'Dread In The West' 226
'Dread Lion' 256, 333
'Dread Locks Corner' 254
'Dreader Locks' 209
'Dreadlocks I' 345
'Dreadlocks In Moonlight' 269–70, 274,
    300, 312
'Dreadlocks Talking' 240
'Dreamland' 123–4, 148
'Dreamland Skank' 178
Drifter, The 196
drugs 185, 338–9, 352, 415
'Drugs And Poison' 79
drum booth 342–3
'Drum Rock' 178
'Drum Song' 379, 390
Drummond, Bill 395
Drummond, Don 29, 78, 85
'Dry Acid' 92
'Dub A Pum Pum' 212, 217
'Dub Addisababa' 437
'Dub Along' 256
Dub Blackboard Jungle 177–8
Dub Factory 377, 380
Dub Messenger, The 400
Dub Net Philosophy 448
'Dub of Justice' 262
'Dub Organiser' 171, 178, 189, 242
dub poetry 290
dub recordings 178
    first 177
Dub Syndicate 384
'Dub The Rhythm' 240
'Dub Two' 207
'Dubbing Psycho Thriller' 437
Dubfire 453–4
Duffus, Chenley 31, 149, 155–6
Duget, Nadette 308
'Duke's Cookies' 19
'Dumplings' 18
Dunbar, Charles Lowell 80–1
Dunkley, Errol 53–4
duppies 117, 120–1

'Duppy Conqueror' 117–19, 128, 139,
    386, 396, 414, 453
'Duppy Conqueror Version IV' 132
Dyce, Billy (Doraney White) 72
Dylan, Bob 67
'Dynamic Fashion Way' 92
Dynamic Sound 74, 124–5, 154
Dynamites, The 34
'Dyon Anaswa' 313, 448

Eagles, The 105
Earl, George (Earl George) 188–9, 275–6
'Early In The Morning' 174
'Earth Is The Fulness, The' 235
'Earth Is The Lord, The' 333
'Earthquake' 131, 155
'Ease Up' 78
'East Of The River Nile' 130
East Of The River Nile 314
'Eastern Standard Time' 19, 220
Eastwood Rides Again 127
'Easy Knocking' 338, 345
'Easy Snapping' 19, 155
'Easy Task' 273
Eccles, Clancy
    biographical 19–20
    work for Dodds 20
    work with P. 61–2, 69
    break with P. 71–2
    and 'A Place In The Sun' 73
    rivalry with P. 89
    Marley and P. 113
    on 'Small Axe' 125
    and 'Labrish' 170–1
    and 'Me Momma Yard' 186
    and 'Who Colt The Game' 316
    describes P.'s attack on Lee 346
Echomania 437
'Economic Crisis' 303, 427
Edwards, Max 115
Edwards, Rupie 76, 243
Edwards, Vincent ("King") 12
Edwards, Wilfred ("Jackie") 18
Edwards, Winston 195–7, 224
El Dorados 47
El Paso 142
'Elaine' 301, 303, 332
'Elephant Rock' 178, 376
Elliott, Ken 176
Ellis, Alton 19

Ellis, Bobby ("Willow") 46
Ellis, Irving 302
Emotions, The 82, 88
'End Of The World' 434
'Endlessly' 174
'Ensome City Skank' 225
'Enter The Dragon' 198, 217
Escape From Babylon 236–7
'Ethiopia' 345, 361
'Ethiopia Land' 296
'Ethiopian Lament' 230
'Ethiopian National Anthem' 92
Ethiopians, The 36, 47, 70
Ethnic Fight label 194
Ethnic label 164, 194
Ettu dancing 5
'Every Wolf' 320
'Everybody Bawling' 68
'Everybody Needs Love' 86
'Everything For Fun' 78
'Everything I Own' 217
'Evil Tongues' 312, 448
'Evol Yenoh' 64
'Ex Ray Vision' 103
'Example' 139
Excaliburman 421
'Exodus' 386, 388
Experryments At The Grassroots Of Dub
    439
'Expo '67' 47
'Extra' 103
Extra Classic 264

Fabulous Falcons 146
Faith, George 276, 285, 315, 326
Faith No More 389
Faithful Brothers 137
Falcons, The 259
'False Teaching' 273
"Family Man" see Barrett, Aston Francis
Fantails, The 320
Far I, Prince (Michael Williams) 244
'Farmer In The Den' 78
Farquarson, Joe 382
'Fashion Monkey' 159
'Fat Man' 251
Father Good 'un 80
'Fatty Fatty' 46
'Favourite Dish' 312, 453
Fay Music label 196

Fearon, Clinton Anthony 218–20, 246, 456–7
Federal records 124–5, 360
'Feel All Right' 235
'Feel It Up' 37
'Feel Like Jumping' 202
'Feel The Rhythm' 62, 68, 240, 252, 316
'Feel The Spirit' 371
'Feeling Is Right' 206
'Festival Da Da' 152
'Fever' 30, 153, 206
Fight label 194
'Financial Crisis' 234
'Finger Mash' 212
'Fire At Your Heals' 200
'Fire Fe The Vatican' 247, 255
'Fire Revelation 22' 393
'First Judgement' 392
'Fisherman' 282
'Fists Of Fury' 198
Fizzé (Victor de Bros) 422–5, 429, 451–2
'Flames Of The Dragon' 224
Flaming Phonics 265
'Flashing Whip' 187, 250
Flea, Lord 16, 33
Fletcher, Carl "Stereo" 383
'Follow Fashion' 154
Forrester, Lloyd 138
'Forward Up' 157
'Forward With Jah Orthodox' 303
'Forward With Love' 303, 332
'Four And Twenty Dreadlocks' 241, 361
'400 Years' 126, 172
Fox, Phil 349
France 396–7, 414
Francis, Jenny 388
Francis, Patrick Lloyd (Jah Lloyd) 105–6, 187–8, 249–50
Francis, Winston 54
Frantz, Chris 367
Fraser, Neil (Mad Professor) 369, 371, 375, 420, 438–9, 441, 447, 449
'Freak Out Skank' 169
'Free Angela Davis' 137
'Free Black Man' 302
Free For All 121–3, 214
'Free Reggae' 218
Free Tibet 454
'Free Up The Prisoners' 301, 315
'Free Up The Weed' 312

'Free Us' 431
'Freedom' 19, 234, 303, 310
'Freedom Blues' 313, 432
'Freedom Fighter' 231, 361
'Freedom Is Equality' 199
'Freedom Street' 285
'Freedom Train' 77, 219
'French Connection' 158, 403
'Fret Man Fret' 32, 40–1
'From Creation' 255
From The Heart Of The Congo 427
From The Secret Laboratory 425
'Frozen Sun' 402
'Fu Kung' 198
Full Experience 298–9
'Full Experience' 298
Fullwood, George 114
'Fungaa' 223
'Funky Joe' 366
'Fussing And Fighting' 128, 132

Gabbidon, Basil 19
Gale, Eric 233
Galvin, Michael 393–4
'Games People Play' 103
gangs 304–5
'Ganja Crop' 188
'Ganja Man, The' 366, 374, 380, 386
'Garden Of Life' 319
Gardiner, Boris 201–3
Garvey, Marcus 10
'Gas Guzzler' 253
Gas label 74
Gatherers, The 167–8
Gaylads 24, 37, 79
Gayle, Bunny (Devon Irons) 242
Gaylets, The 60
'Gee Baby' 382
George, Earl (George Earl) 188–9, 275–6
'Get Ready Do It Steady' 47
'Get Up, Stand Up' 237
GG's label 103
'Ghetto Sidewalk' 312
'Ghost Capturer' 119
'Ghost Dance' 49
Gibbs, Joe (Joel Gibson) 52, 53–4, 55, 57–8, 197
Gibson, Joel see Gibbs, Joe
Gifford, Marlene ("Precious") 34
'Ginalship' 138

'Girl I've Got A Date' 45
'Girl Next Door' 224
'Girl You Ruff' 78
'Girl You've Got To Run' 199
'Give It To Me' 48
'Give Love A Try' 78
'Give Me' 71
'Give Me Justice' 43
'Give Me Little Loving' 57
'Give Me Power' 138–9, 172
'Give Praises' 342
'Give Thanks' 184, 194
'Give Thanx To Jah' 346
Gladiators, The 217–20
'Go And Come Back' 450
'God Bless Pickney' 359
'Golden Locks' 209
Goldman, Vivien 264, 331
Goldmine Dub 421
'Good Nanny' 57, 85
Good, The Bad And The Upsetters, The
    101, 420
'Good Things' 185, 186
Goodall, Graeme 58–9, 99
'Goodnight My Love' 155
Gopthal, Lee 73, 74
Gordon, Ralphus ("Raleigh") 29
Gordon, Vin 143, 220–1
Grace Thrillers, The 235
Graduates, The 115
'Graduation in Zion' 305
Graham, Leo 54, 78, 171, 183, 318–19
Grant, Gilmore 179
Grant, Ricky (Errol Kong) 231
Grass Roots label 294
Gray, Owen 18
Great Lee Perry King Of Dub, The 445
'Greedy Man' 244
Green, Cherry 33
'Green Bay Incident' 300
'Green Bay Inquest' 301
Green Bay Massacre 300
Green Door Saloon 75
'Green Island' 19
'Greensleeves' 434
Gregory, Morris 114
Grennan, Winston 44–5, 79
Griffiths, Albert 217–20
Griffiths, Marcia 236
'Groove Me' 109, 155

'Grooving' 379, 400
'Groovy Situation' 277, 286, 287
'Grow Your Locks' 209
'Gruma' 34
Grumbling Dub 260
GT Moore and the Reggae Guitars 336
'Guerilla Priest' 352
'Guideline' 315
'Guilty Convict' 76
Guitar Boogie Dub 438
'Gumma' 34
'Gun Man Coming To Town' 262
'Guns Fever' 174
'Guns Of Navarone' 54
'Gypsy Woman' 274

'Hail Stone' 165
'Hail Stones' 176
'Hail To Power' 153
Haile Selassie 41, 238, 257
'Hallelujah' 30
'Hallelujah Time' 236
Hamilton, Enzo 391
'Hand To Hand, Man To Man' 35
Hanover Parish (Jamaica) 2
'Haposamane' 299
'Happiness' 237
'Happy Birthday' 378
'Happy Birthday Marcus' 431
'Hard Fighter' 122
'Hard Times' 130
Harder They Come, The (film) 162
'Hare Krishna' 442
Harriott, Derrick 46
Harris, Dennis Lascelles 204–5
'Haunted House' 108
'Have Some Fun' 217
'Have Some Mercy' 188, 189
'Hay Fever' 250
'Head Shot' 258
'Heads Of Government' 366, 439, 441,
    454
'Hear River Jordan' 318
'Heart For Sale' 199
Heart Of The Ark 361, 366, 433
Heart Of The Congos 282, 296, 308–9,
    445
'Heart Of The Dragon' 223
'Heat Proof' 77
Heavenly Singers, The 211

Heavy Metal Dub 438
'He'll Break Your Heart' 175
'He'll Have To Go' 77, 78
'Hello Carol' 218
'Hello Dolly' 78
'Hello My Love' 218
'Help The Weak' 34
Hendley, Dave 277, 327–8, 332
Henry, Aston Milton 87
Henry, Pablito (Pablo Moses) 229–30
Henry, Ras Michael 317–18
Heptones, The 46, 85, 262–3
'Herb Vendor' 184
'Here I Come' 257, 258
'Hi-Jack' 352
Hibbert, Frederick ("Toots") 29, 36–7
Hibbert, Oscar Delgado (Junior Delgado) 210
Higgs, Joe 18, 21
'High Fashion' 176
High Lite Haberdashery 31
'High Rankin Sammy' 313
Hines, Jerome ("Jah Jerry") 28
Hippy Boys 47, 81–2, 82–3, 84, 87, 88–9, 98
'Hippy John' 371
'History' 275, 277
History, Mystery, Prophecy 366–7
Hit Run 382
'Hold Down' 35
Hold Of Death 421
'Hold Them' 52, 223
'Hold You Jack' 86
'Holla And Bawl' 432
Holland 442
Holland, Jools 361
'Holly Holy' 139
Holness, Winston *see* Boswell, George (Niney)
'Home Guard' 301
Home Town Hi Fi 91
'Honey Love' 63–4
Hong Kong 445
'Hot And Cold' 153
'Hot Line' 166
'Hot Shit' 431
'Hot Tip' 168
'House Of Dread' 209
House of Natty label 253
'House Of Parliament' 299

'House Up On A Hill' 159
'How Can A Man Have One Wife' 258
'How Can You Mend A Broken Heart' 199
'How Come' 60–1
'How Deep Is Your Love' 361
'How Long Will It Take' 78
Hucknall, Mick 388
Hudson, Keith 92
Humanity 327
'Humpty Dumpty' 26
Hungry Town label 275
Hunt, Clive 192–3
'Hurt So Good' 201, 203–4, 205–6
Hurt So Good 206
'Hurting Inside' 237
'Hush Don't You Cry' 140
'Huzza A Hana' 313
'Hypocrites' 234

'I Am A Dreadlocks' 225
'I Am A Madman' 379–80, 381
'I am God' 403
'I Am I Said' 232, 361
'I Am Sorry' 242
'I Am The Government' 423
'I Am The Toughest' 38
'I Am The Upsetter' 366, 433
I Can See Clearly Now 133
'I Do Love You' 263
'I Don't Mind' 217, 254
'I Know A Place' 317, 347, 459
'I Know Something' 157
'I Live And I Love' 20
'I Love You' 23
'I Man A Grasshopper' 229
'I Man Free' 211, 217
'I Man Stand Still' 234
'I Need Money' 72
'I Need Someone' 227
'I Never Had It So Good' 332
'I Only Want To Be With You' 316
'I Remember' 85
I Roy 160, 226
'I Shall Be Released' 272
'I Shall Not Remove' 31
'I Shot the Sheriff' 451
I-Threes trio 235–6
'I Tried' 80
'I Want To Wake Up With You' 379

'I Was Appointed' 273
'I Will Keep On Loving You' 230
I-words 152
'I'd Rather Be Lonely' 73
'If I Follow My Heart' 199
'If You All Get To Heaven' 396
'If You Don't Mind' 79
'I'll Be True' 167
'I'll Be Waiting' 77, 103
'I'll Never Come Running Back To You' 57
'I'm A Believer' 140, 141
'I'm Going To Cool It' 121
'I'm In Love' 345
'I'm Yours' 155
immigration problems 397–8, 414
'Imperial Dub' 224
'In A Strange Land' 280
'In And Out The Window' 21, 55
'In The Iaah' 176
'In These Last Days' 301
'In This Whole World' 94
'Infidelity' 389
'Informer Men' 149
'Iniquity Worker' 137
Inner Circle Group 274
'Inspector Gadget' 425
Inspirations, The 72
Internet website 456
'Introducing Myself' 379
Inturns, The 234
'IPA Skank' 169
'Irie Feelings' 227
'Irie Irie' 342
'Iron Claw' 165
'Iron Fist' 223
Irons, Devon (Bunny Gayle) 242
'Iry Iry' 361
Isaac, Joe 44
Isaacs, David 73
Isaacs, Gregory 264
Ishii, Shizuo 401
Island label 247–9, 295, 314, 334, 391,
    425, 450
'Isn't It Wrong' 147
'It Hurts To Be Alone' 33, 120
'Ital Corner' 254, 348
Ital Corner 254
'Ital Drums' 209
'Ital Locks' 209
'Ital Version' 148

'It's Alright' 126, 238, 400, 442
'It's You I Love' 122
'I've Caught You' 92
I've Got A Love 235
'I've Got The Blues' 259
'I've Got The Groove' 277, 285, 425
'I've Got This Feeling' 175
'I've Got To Keep On Movin'' 28, 128
'Ivory Girl' 383

Jackson, Carlton 275
Jackson, Clifton ("Jackie") 44, 45, 59, 63,
    83, 98
Jackson, Maurice "Scorcher" 213
Jackson, Melvin "Munchie" 213, 214, 352
Jackson, Vivian "Yabby Yoo" 215–16, 219
Jackxon, Pipecock 332
'Jah Almighty' 219
'Jah Come Here' 258
'Jah Fari On A Pinnacle' 319
'Jah Is Mighty' 126
'Jah Jah Ah Natty Dread' 313
'Jah Live' 238, 239, 247
'Jah Love Is Sweeter' 333, 345
Jah Ned (Ned Willacy) 297, 321–2, 347,
    368, 416–17
'Jah Rastafari' 147
'Jah Road Block' 361
'Jah Shakin Dub' 196
'Jah Vengeance' 216, 219
Jah Warrior 378, 381
'Jailhouse' 38, 220
Jamaica
    Hanover Parish 2
    popular music 9
    racial attitudes 17
    independence 20
    social conditions 150, 415
    crime epidemic brings suppression
        192
    civil unrest (1976) 245–6
    oppression and corruption 300
    gangs 304–5
Jamaica Broadcasting Corporation 16
Jamaica Recording Studio 32
'Jamaica Theme' 217
Jammes, Patrick 394, 397
'Jammin'' 292
'Jane Ann And The Pumpkin' 35
Japan 337, 433–4, 446, 454

'Japanese Rock' 434
Jarrett, Winston 77–8, 137
'Java' 274
Java Java Dub 177
Jazzbo, Prince (Lynval Carter) 185, 254
'Jazzbo Have Fe Run' 227
'Jennifer' 258
Jennings, Paul Aston 105
'Jesse The Hammer' 334
'Jestering' 227
'Jesus Christus Is The King' 319
Jets, The 43, 44
Jews 17
'Jingling Keys' 269
Jiving Crackerballs, The 83
Jiving Juniors 19
Jobson, Wayne 280, 331
'Joe Frazer' 242
'Joe Lieges' 30
JoGib label 52
'John Public' 157, 294
'John Tom' 34
John Tom label 52
'Johnny Cool' 49
'Johnny Too Bad' 320
Johns, Vere (jnr.) 16
Johnson, Carl 43
Johnson, Cluet 19
Johnson, Earl (Earl Zero) 116
Johnson, Harry 88
Johnson, Linton Kwesi 290–1, 424
Johnson, Michael (Lord Sassafras) 300
Johnson, Roy Anthony 301–3, 308, 309
Johnson, Roydel 281–2
'Joker, The' 19, 379
'Joker In The Ring' 40
Jolly Brothers 310, 311
Jonas, Melanie 96, 108
'Joshua's Desire' 153
Judah, Pepe (Frank Warren) 333
'Judge Dread' 48
'Judge Natty' 188
'Judge Not' 33
'Judgement Day' 255
'Judgement In A Babylon' 369
'Judgement Time' 303
'Jump It' 186, 217
'Jungle' 385, 393
'Jungle Jim' 178
'Jungle Lion' 169, 176

'Jungle Skank' 178
'Just Another Girl' 432
'Just Enough' 176
'Just Keep It Up' 35
'Just Like A River' 55
'Just Once In My Life' 77
Justice League label 139
'Justice To The People' 171, 176

Kapetanovich, Vlado (Vitko Novi, Vitko) 432
'Kasha Macka' 178
Kawongolo, Kalo 427
'Kaya' 128, 132
'Kaya Skank' 178
Keary, Vic 141
'Keep On Moving' 128, 132, 157, 178, 227, 290, 293, 361, 392, 399, 412, 414, 448
'Keep On Skanking' 184, 453
Keese, Debra 301
Kelly, Pat 78
Kelso, Beverley 33
Ken and Glen 85
Kendal (birthplace) 1
Kenner, Chris 50, 95
'Kentucky Skank' 177
Kes Chin and The Souvenirs 201–2
Khouri, Ken 16
Kiddus-I (Frank Dowding) 305–6
'Kiddyo' 174
Kilik label 231
'Kimble' 57
Kimwangala, "Kalo" Kawongolo ("Buffalo") 308
King, Whoppi 12
'King Alpha' 148
King Iwah 139
'King Of Babylon' 149, 150, 151
King Of Dub 438
'King Of Kings' 106
'King Of The Punks' 390
'King Of The Trombone' 78, 103
'King Pharaoh' 227
King Tubby Meets The Upsetter At The Grass Roots of Dub 197–8
King Tubby's Hometown Hi-Fi 142, 158–9
'Kingston Rock' 294
'Kinky Fly' 232
'Kinky Mood' 109

'Kiss Me In The Rain' 230
'Kiss Me Neck' 212
'Kiss The Champion' 385
Knibb, Lloyd 28, 44
Knight, Kenneth 82
'Knock On Wood' 127
'Knock Three Times' 139, 155
'Know Love' 283
Kodama, Kazufumi "Echo" 400–1, 434
'Kojak' 239
Kong, Errol (Ricky Grant) 231
Kraut, Jim 357
'Kuchy Skank' 172
Kulu Hatha Mamnua 423
'Kung Fu' 194
'Kung Fu Man' 198, 217, 223
Kung Fu Meets The Dragon 223–4
Kuypers, Robert 427

'La La Bam Bam' 282, 283
'Labor Wrong' 138
'Labrish' 170–1
Lacey, Brynn 349
Lack, Ken 52
'Lady Lady' 192, 193, 427
'Lady Lovelight' 94
Laing, Denzil ("Pops") 44
'Lama, The' 187, 188, 250
'Lama Lava' 274, 428
Lambert, Barrington 59
'Land Of Kinks' 108, 109
'Land Of Love' 315
Lane, Chris 182–5, 276–7
Lasher, Count 16
Lass, David 349
'Last Dance Is Over, The' 199
'Late September and May' 280
Lawrence, Clifton ("Larry") 99, 100, 164,
    175, 194–5, 204
Lawson, Beryl 60
Leaders, The 87, 242
Lee, Byron 18–19, 154
Lee, Edward ("Bunny", "Striker")
    biographical 51
    joins WIRL 53
    and Max Romeo 82, 86
    works with Adams 85
    and The Hippy Boys 89
    and 'Let The Power Fall' 150–1
    meets Lane 183

    and 'White Belly Rat' 265
    and 'Who Colt The Game' 431
'Lee in the Heartbeat' 431
Lee Perry & The Upsetter(s) Meet Scientist
    At Black Ark Studio 448
Lee Perry Meets King Tubby In Dub
    Confrontation 422
Lee Perry Meets Mafia And Fluxy In
    Jamaica 438
Lee Perry Meets Scientists At The Blackheart
    Studio 445
Lee Perry Meets The Mad Professor In Dub
    421
Lee Perry Presents Gregory Isaacs 438
Lee Perry The Upsetter Presenting Dub 438
Lee Scratch Perry And The Upsetters Meet
    At King Tubby's 438
'Lee The Upsetter' 431
'Leggo' 247, 333
'Leggo Skanga' 227
Lenks, Jah 167, 168
'Let George Do It' 26
'Let Him Go' 38
'Let It Be' 123
'Let Love Touch Us Now' 361
'Let The Power Fall' 150
'Leticia' 32
'Let's All Unite' 275, 333
'Let's Move' 298
Lewis, Alva (Reggie) 85–6, 110, 118, 158,
    318
Lewis, Aura (Aurelia Msimang) 289–90,
    298, 299
Lewis, Hopeton 44
Lewis, Jerry 186, 200
Licensed To Ill 443
'Licht & Stein' 424
'Lick Samba' 133
'Lick The Pipe Peter' 153
'Life Is A Flower' 217, 254
'Life Is Gonna Easy' 254
'Life Is Not Easy' 300
'Lightning And Thunderflash' 431
'Lightning Strikes Twice' 376
Limit, The 428, 435
Lindo, Blanche 17
Lindo, Earl ("Wire") 115, 395
Linkers, The 266
Lion, Jah 250, 251
'Lion, The' 313

'Lion A De Winner' 345
'Lion of Judah' 149
'Lion Rock' 333
'Liquid Serenade' 165
'Liquidator, The' 89, 165
'Little David' 318
'Little Honey' 26
Little Ian Rock 123
Little London 8
'Little Nut Tree' 186
Little Roy (Earl Lowe) 121–3, 213, 214
'Little Sally Dater' 251
'Little Sheila' 17
'Little Suzy' 90
Live ! 237
'Live As One' 54, 145
Live At Maritime Hall 451
'Live Good Today' 254
Live In Montreux 422
'Live Injection, A' 81, 100
'Live It Up' 276
'Live Wire' 218
'Lively Up Yourself' 172
'Living My Life' 277, 287
Livingston, Neville 33
Livingstone, Bunny 34
Lloyd, Cecil 29
Lloyd, Jah (Patrick Lloyd Francis) 105–6, 187–8, 249–50
Lloyd's Stereophonic Hi-Fi 140
'Lockjaw' 107–8
Locks label 231
'Lolita' 32
London, Jimmy (Ransford White) 72
London
    Notting Hill Carnival 260–2, 392
    P.'s years in England 369–414
    Thames excursion 384–5
'London Bridge Has Fallen Down' 318
London Underground (group) 383, 403
'Long Long Time' 241, 259
'Long Sentence' 148
'Long Time Ago' 319
'Long Way, The' 209, 240, 454
'Look Around' 294
'Look Who A Bust Style' 106
Lord, Derrick 36
Lord God Muzick 430
'Lorna Banana' 224
Lost Treasures Of The Ark 459

'Love And Affection' 120
'Love And Unity' 227
'Love Can Run Faster' 279
'Love Fire' 389
'Love Is Better Now' 352
'Love Is For Fools' 140
'Love Is Not A Gamble' 400
'Love (of) My Life' 200
Love On A Shelf 287
'Love Power' 432
Love Thy Neighbour 318
Lover, Johnny 209
'Lover's Skank' 178
'Loving Is Good' 205
'Loving Skank' 188
'Low Lights' 103
Lowe, Earl (Little Roy) 121–3, 213, 214
Lowe, Winston 84
LSD 338–9
'Lucifer' 273
'Lucky Boy' 94
'Lying Lips' 210

Ma-Ashanti 297
'Maccabee The Third' 144
'Maccabee Version' 139, 399
McCartney, Paul 278, 337
McCook, Tommy 43
Machuki, Count 20
McIntosh, Peter 33
Mack, Bob 444
McKenzie, Candy 298
MacLean, Bertram ("Ranchie") 80
McLeod, Enos 227
'Mad Head' 32
'Mad House' 93
Mad Professor see Fraser, Nell
Madden, David 294–5
'Maggie Breast' 257
'Magic Touch' 262
Magnet label 205, 206
Magnetic Mirror Master Mix 421
Mahfood, Margarita 85
Majestics, The 355, 356–7, 358, 360
'Malaika' 299
Malcolm, Carlos 202
Malcolm, Hugh 44, 45, 53
'Mama Look Deh' 90
'Man And Wife' 32
'Man From Carolina' 103

'Man From MI 5 '81
'Man In Your Life' 138
'Man Of Destiny' 227
'Man To Man' 120, 238
Mango label 231, 350
Manley, Michael 38, 191–2, 245–6, 251
'Manny Oh' 18
Manoeuvres d 'automne 423
Mantronick 388
'Many A(re) Call(ed)' 234
Many Moods Of The Upsetters 102–3
'Marcus' 320
'Margaret' 196
marijuana 185
Marijuana World Tour 382
'Marjie' 19
Marley, Rita 123, 368
Marley, Robert Nesta
    and the Wailers 33, 109, 110–13,
        119–12
    and the Soulettes 34
    marries Rita Anderson 38
    at the Carib Theatre 94
    in Sweden 129
    in London 132–3
    relationship with P. 134–5, 145
    Escape From Babylon 236–7
    Rastafarian faith 239
    and 'Smile Jamaica' 268–9
    attacked and shot 270
    toe operation 292
    One Love Peace Concert 305, 306–7
    'Who Colt The Game' 316
    'I Know A Place' 317
    refuses loan to P. 346–7
    collapses 348
    death 355
Maroon label 131
Marshall, Bucky (Aston Thompson) 304
Marshall, Steve 376, 402–3
Martin, Alan 140
Martin, "Honey Boy" 44
Martin, Jah (Martin Williams) 194
Martyn, John 263–4, 290, 367
Marx, Rema 349
Mascoll, Jennifer (Romeo) 378–9
Mascoll, Rudy 378, 397, 399, 412
Mash (dance) 53
'Mash Down' 294
Mason, Lloyd 28

Massop, Claudie ("Jack") 304
'Master Key' 151
'Masters of the Universe' 403
Matthews, Brenton 93
Matthias, Nathaniel ("Jerry") 29
Matumbi 173
'Maxi Merlin' 453
'May Sound Funny' 380
Maytals 29–30
'Me Breda You A Go Feel It' 275
Me Momma Yard' 186
Meads, Patrick 378, 387
'Mean And Dangerous' 103
'Mean The World To Me' 249
'Meaning Of Life' 235
'Medical Operation' 81, 103
Meditations, The 138, 266–7, 299
Meditators, The 45, 105
medleys 120
'Meekly Wait And Murmur Not' 84
'Meet Mr Nobody' 280
'Megaton Bomb' 450
Megaton Dub 366, 433
Meggy 114
Meier, Dieter 435–6, 439–40, 453
Mellotones, The 54, 65, 70, 71
Mellow Larks 19
Melodians, The 46
Melody Enchanters, The 167
'Melting Pot' 109
'Memories' 274
'Memories Of Flora' 202
'Memphis' 128, 132
Mento music 15–16, 16
'Merry Christmas, Happy New Year' 378,
    381
Message, The 177
Message From The King 382
Message From The Meditations 266
'Message From The Top' 224
Message From Yard 400
'Messy Apartment' 450
Micron Dub 247
Micron label 224, 226
'Midnight Hour' 174, 285
'Mighty Chin' 412
'Mighty Clouds of Joy' 151
'Mighty King Reveal Yourself' 417
Mighty Merritone sound system 190
Mighty Mystics 146

'Mighty Quinn' 412
Mighty Virtues 146
Miles, Desmond 46
'Militant Rock' 209
Miller, Jacob 199
'Million Dollar Baby' 31
Mindwarp, Zodiac 395
'Mini Dress' 77–8
'Minstrel And Queen' 37, 274
'Miss Cushy' 258
'Mistry Babylon' 277
Mittoo, Jackie 29, 44, 72, 121–2
Monama 308, 310
'Money Man' 237
'Money Me A Deal With' 400
'Monkey Fashion' 159
'Monkey Man' 319
"mooing cow" noise 296
'Moonlight Lover' 79
Moonwalk 427
Moore, Gerald Thomas 336, 339–42
Moore, Joe 193
Moore, Johnny ("Dizzy") 29, 44
Moore, Stainton ("Archie") 7, 15, 64,
    104–5
'Mooving Version' 157
'More Axe' 131
'More Power' 139
'More Proof' 20
Morgan, Earl 247, 262, 263, 270
Morris, Eric ("Monty") 21, 55, 62, 77
Morris, Sylvain 237
Morrison, Aston 36
Morrison, Pauline
    birth of Michelle 36–7
    meets P. 36–7
    birth of Marvin 58
    birth of Omar 74
    attacks P. with knife 96
    birth of Marsha 102
    affair with Clarke 323–5
    own productions 333, 345, 361, 441
    with P. in New York 352
    returns to Jamaica 437
Moses, Pablo (Pablito Henry) 229–30
Mosukola, "Seke" Molenga 308
'Mother In Law' 34
'Mother Long Tongue' 227
'Mother's Choice' 76
Motta, Stanley Beresford 16

'Mount Zion' 137
'Move Me' 148
'Move Out Of My Way' 233, 239
'Moving Skank' 178
Mowatt, Judy 60, 61, 96, 268
'Mr Baldwin' 219
'Mr Biah' 249
'Mr Brown' 120–1, 139
'Mr Cop' 264
'Mr DJ Man' 312, 393
'Mr Dobberman' 428
'Mr Fire Coal Man' 432
'Mr Money Man' 315
'Mr Music' 373, 374
'Mr Phong, Mr Wong, Mr Chin' 226
'Mr President' 272
'Mr T' 213
Msimang, Aurelia (Aura Lewis) 289–90,
    298, 299
'Much Smarter' 299
'Mule Train' 103
'Mumbling and Grumbling' 192, 194,
    361
Mundell, Hugh 274–5
'Muriel' 19
Murvin, Junior (Murvin Smith Junior)
    258–60, 273–4, 315
'Music' 390, 391, 392
'Music and Science Lovers' 385
'Music Breeze' 359
'Music Field' 51, 52
Music Mountain studio 365
'Music Well' 392
Musical Bones 220, 221
'Musical College' 49
'Musical Transplant' 165
Muskyteers, The 77
Mute Beat 400, 401–2
Mute Beat Dubwise 434
'Mutiny' 445
Mutron phaser 241
'My Baby' 23
'My Boy Lollipop' 414
'My Conversation' 227
'My Cup' 113, 126, 127
'My Girl' 140, 148, 165
'My Heart Is Gone' 117
'My Jamaican Girl' 106
'My Little Sandra' 318, 333
'My Sympathy' 126

'My Way' 140
Mysterious 303
'Mystery Babylon' 319
Mystic I 301, 302–3
Mystic Miracle Star 359
'Mystic Mood' 294
Mystic Warrior 371, 420
Myton, Cedric 281, 309

'Na Na Hey Hey (Kiss Him Goodbye)' 109, 319
'Nanny Goat' 68, 202
Nash, Johnny 110, 129
Natty Dread 235–6
Natty Locks Dub 196
'Natty Natty' 158
Natty Passing Thru 254, 348
'Natty Plant It' 243
'Natty Roots' 198
'Natural Mystic' 268, 371
'Nature Man' 217
Nature Survival (film) 335
Nazarines, The 242
'Nebuchadneezer' 151
'Necoteen' 120
Negril 233–4
Nelson, Vicky 344–5, 362, 365, 368, 398, 415–16, 430
'Never Before' 165
'Never Get Away' 77
'Never Get Weary' 32
'Never Had A Dream' 139
New Age Steppers 383
New York 164, 348–58, 399–400, 454
'News Flash' 171
News Flash 421
Next Move, The 98
'Nice And Easy' 207
'Nice Time' 120, 361, 373, 393, 451
'Nicodeemus' 284
'Night Doctor' 80, 81, 100
Night Food 263
'Night Shift' 238
Niney (George Boswell) 58, 104, 157, 169–70, 257
Niyabinghi Slaughters The Dragon 320
Niyabinghi Theocracy 297–8, 304, 306, 320–2
'No Bread And Butter' 87
'No More Heartaches' 88

'No Need To Buy Newspaper Any More' 210
'No No No' 68, 202
'No Peace' 229, 299
'No Stocky Shop' 430
'No Sympathy' 126
'No Time To Lose' 236
'No Water' 126
'Nonesuch' 64
'Norman' 252, 273
'Norman the Gambler' 334
'Norwegian Wood' 379
'Not For Me' 70
'Not Guilty' 148
Notting Hill Carnival 260–2, 392
Novi, Vitko (Vlado Kapetanovich) 432
'Now Generation' 146–7, 272
NuBeat label 74

Obeah 64, 181–2
'Observe Life' 223
Observer label 104
'Oh Carolina' 27, 103
'Oh Lord' 77
'Oh Me Oh My' 264
'Oil Crisis' 212
'OK Corral' 93, 313
'Old For New' 32
Olive Blossom label 27, 49
On The Rock 243
On Top label 234
On-U Sound 382, 383–4
'Once A Man' 137
'One Cup Of Coffee' 33
'One Drop' 370, 373, 374, 388, 442
'One Horse Race' 400
One Hundred Drums (play) 321
'100 Pounds Of Clay' 160
'One I Love, The' 52
'One Love' 120, 290
One Love Peace Concert 304, 307
'One Step Beyond' 72
'One Step Forward' 251, 254
'Only You' 24
'Ooh La La' 400
'Open Door' 439, 441
'Open The Gate' 283, 345
'Open The Iron Gate' 229
'Open Up (Cook Book)' 35
'Open Up The Gate' 282

'Open Up The Japanese Door' 434
'Operation' 172
'Opportunity '286
Orchid label 208
Original Blackboard Jungle 445
Original Super Ape 459
Osbourne, Brad 353
Ossie, Count 27, 90
Ossie and The Upsetters 69
Ostrowe, David ("Dro") 349, 350, 351, 353
'Out Of Many, We Are One' 287
'Outer Space' 103
'Outformer Version' 149
Overheat records 401
Overtakers, The 54, 78
Owens, Tony 100, 289, 311, 337, 361, 365
'Own Man' 240

P-Son *see* Blythe, Milton (Poppa Son!
Pa Ashanti 297
Pablo, Augustus (Horace Swaby) 130–1, 153, 189, 274–5
'Pablo Satta' 251
Palmer, Harry 63, 74, 89
Palmer, Robert 278–80
Pama label 74, 76, 194
'Pampas Judas' 184, 194
Paris 396–7, 414
Parks, Arkland 28
Parks, Lloyd 77, 80, 127, 151
'Party, The' 423
'Party Time' 202, 319, 334
Party Time 272
'Patience' 256
Patterson, Alvin ("Seeco") 33
'Paul Bogle' 244
Pauline (Morrison) *see* Morrison, Pauline
Paul's Boutique 443
Pay It All Back 402
'Peek A Boo' 265
Peeni Waali 423, 429
'Penny Reel' 185, 186
'People Funny Boy' 66–7, 290–1
'People Funny Fi True' 72
'People Grudgeful' 67
'People Sokup Boy' 161
'People's Court, The' 49
'Perfect Love' 318

'Perilous Time' 303
Perkins, Eddy 19
Perries label 204
Perry, Beryl (Dulcie) (*sister*) 2
Perry, Cleopatra (*daughter*) 392
Perry, Delano (*son*) 96
Perry, Gabriel Merlin Zay (*son*) 434
Perry, Henry (*father*) 2
Perry, Icelyn (Sitta) (*sister*) 2
Perry, Ina (mother) 2, 3–4, 5, 448
Perry, Lesbert (Sonny) (*brother*) 2, 4, 7
Perry, Mark Anthony ("Omar") (*son*) 74, 207, 416, 437, 446, 448
Perry, Marsha Rachel (*daughter*) 102, 208, 364, 398, 416, 426–7, 436, 458
Perry, Marvin Hugh ("Sean") (son) 58, 315, 363, 416, 436–7, 449, 458
Perry, Michelle ("Yawnie") (*daughter*) 36–7, 362–3, 398, 416, 436, 458
Perry, Milton (*brother*) 128
Perry, Mireille (*wife*) 447
    biographical 413–14
    and Switzerland 417–20
    marries P. 433
    makes demands 438
    injured by P. 440–1
    reconciliation 442
    files for divorce 445
Perry, Rainford Hugh Lee ("Scratch")
    birth & origins 1
    name 1
    childhood 3
    dancing 4–5, 6–7, 22
    education 4
    dominoes 5, 6
    spirit world 5–6, 433
    work 6
    construction industry 7–8
    marries Ruby 8, 25
    early days in Kingston 21–39
    origin of "Scratch" 24
    relationship with Pauline 36–7, 96, 323–5
    disillusionment with Studio One 40–3
    treatment by Buster 49–50
    birth of Marvin 58
    church going 66, 225
    moves house 69
    perfectionist 69
    birth of Omar 74

divorce from Ruby 74
trip to London (1969) 76
on The Upsetters 87–8, 98
and Rastafarianism 90, 152–3, 325
birth of Delano 96
knife wound 96
relationship with Junie 96
relationship with Lou 95–6
relationship with Melanie 96
sex life 95–6
car accident 96–7
UK tour (1969) 98–100
adopts Renal (Enoch) 102
birth of Marsha 102
sponsors radio show 102
relationship with Bunny Wailer 124
relationship with Marley 134–5,
    135–6, 145
violence by Wailers 135
recalled (at Dodd's) by Alcapone 143
further car accident 151
at Dynamic Sound 154
declines film appearance 162
builds own studio 163
in New York 164
involvement with Obeah 181–2
and marijuana 185
records children 207–8
drastic behaviour 252–3
and studio murals 256–7
further odd behaviour 277, 319
London visit (1977) 287–8
paints Xs 319
family problems, stress and
breakdown 322–6
P.'s betrayal & departure 323–5
disintegration and alienation 329–31
in Amsterdam 335–9
denies taking hard drugs 338–9, 352
attacks Lee and Tubby 346
in New York (1981) 348–58
enacts rituals 362
Black Ark studio fire 363–5
5 years in England 369–414
drinks petrol 380
birth of Cleopatra 392
immigration problems 397–8, 414
dictates proclamations for this
    book   404–12
in Switzerland 418–61

birth of Shiva 426
marries Mireille 433
birth of Gabriel 434
Perry, Shiva Elaine Sharon (*daughter*) 426
'Pharaoh Hiding' 149, 150
'Philistines On The Land' 274
Phillips, Delroy ("Jubie") 75
Phillips, George *see* Pratt, Phil
Phoenix Of Peace 437
'Pick Up The Pieces' 160
'Pickpocket Skank' 166
'Picture On The Wall' 130, 155
'Piece Of My Heart' 139
Pinkney, Dwight 38, 294
Pioneer label 16
Pioneers, The 56–7, 85, 98
'Pipecock Jackson' 341, 350
'Pipecock Jackstone' 373
Pipecock Jackxon 332, 380
'Pitta Patta' 165
'Place Called Africa' 147, 155, 178, 453
'Place Called Africa Version 3' 148
'Place In The Sun, A' 73, 74
'Play On Mr Music' 284
Playboys, The 46
'Please Don't Go' 35
'Please Stay' 62
'Please Stop Your Lying' 54
Pocomania 65–6
'Police And Thieves' 259–60, 262, 274
Police And Thieves 273
Polly Wog Stew 443
'Poor Chubby' 148, 153
'Poor People Rights' 390
'Pop A Pop' 155
'Pop A Top' 59, 60, 139
'Popcorn' 127
popular music
    Jamaica 9
'Positive Vibration' 430
Pottinger, Sonia 61, 186
'Pound Get A Blow' 71
'Power Cut' 90
'Power Pack' 127
Pratt, Phil (George Phillips) 24, 52,
    199–200, 421–2
Pre-Meditation 186
'Preacher Man' 157
'President Mash Up The Resident, The'
    227

Prince, Winston 144, 212–13
'Prince And Duke' 32
'Prince In The Back' 32
'Prisoner Of Love' 93, 94
Prisoner Of Love 127
Produced And Directed By The Upsetter 447
'Professor Ironside' 151, 165
Progressions, The 87
'Prophecy' 213, 249
'Prophet Live' 254
Prophets, The 215–16
'Prove It' 103
'Psalm 53' 244
Psalms For 1 244, 382
'Psyche and Trim' 313
'Public Enemy Number One' 156, 157
'Public Jestering' 191
Pukumina 65–6,
Punch label 74
punk rock 288
'Punky Reggae Party' 289, 291–2
'Puss See Hole' 160
'Pussy Galore' 38, 40, 195
'Pussy I Cocky I Water' 359
'Put It On' 38, 120, 128, 132, 371

'Quarter Pound of I'Cense' 228
'Queen Can't Shit, The' 390
'Queen Majesty' 274
Quiet Reggae 434

Rabbit and the Jungles 129
racial attitudes
    Jamaica 17
'Radication Squad' 359
Radio Jamaica Rediffusion 16
Rae, Clifford 50
'Rain Drops' 240
'Rainbow' 82
'Rainbow Country' 267, 268, 361
'Rainy Night In Georgia' 283
'Rainy Night In Portland' 283
'Ram Goat Dub' 207
'Ram Goat Liver' 207
'Ram You Hard' 78
Randy's label 75
Ranglin, Alvin 103
Ranglin, Ernest 16, 28, 62
'Rape Bait' 35

Ras Michael (Henry) 317–18
'Rasta Band Wagon' 156–7
'Rasta Dreadlocks' 211
'Rasta Dub' 157
'Rasta No Born Ya' 257
'Rasta No Pickpocket' 166
'Rasta Train' 212, 275, 299
'Rastafari' 361
Rastafarianism 10–11, 41, 90–1, 92
    use of I–words 152
    and non–Africans 156
    and church going 225
'Rastaman Live Up' 306, 322
'Rastaman Prayer' 267
'Rastaman Shuffle' 276
Rastaman Vibration 238
'Rat Race' 238
'Reach Out' 52
'Reaction' 126, 210
'Real Rock' 220
'Real True Dub' 220
'Rebel's Hop' 126
Reconstruction 309
'Red Hot' 127
Redwood, Ruddy 91
Reggae Best: Heavy Manners 421
Reggae Blue 336
Reggae Boys 90
'Reggae Emperor' 431
Reggae Emperor, The 431
'Reggae Got Soul' 122
Reggae In America 253
reggae music 67–8, 73–4
'Reggae Music' 275
'Reggae Rock' 187
Reggae To UK With Love 87
Reid, Arthur (Duke) 12, 14, 19
    P.'s early days 21
    anti-Rasta 41
    'Lockjaw' session 107–8
'Rejoice' 361
'Rejoice Jah Jah Children' 175
'Rejoicing Skank' 175, 250
Reminah Dub 247
'Rescue Jah Children' 273
'Result, The' 103
'Retail Love' 165, 186
'Return Of Django' 95, 378
Return Of Peeni Waali, The 451
Return Of Pipecock Jackxon 345

Return Of The Super Ape 313, 333, 459
'Return Of The Ugly' 103
Return Of Wax 223
'Revelation Time' 224, 228
Revelation Time 228
'Revolution' 214
'Revolution – Boo Tax Boo VAT' 442
Revolution, The 428
Revolution Dub 239–40, 337
'Revolution Is For The Chinaman' 224
Reynolds, Monty 16
RHT Invincibles 80
Rhythm Aces, The 201
'Rhythm Land' 131
Rhythm Raiders 114–15
Rhythm Shower 172, 377
Richards, Winston 45
'Ride On' 212
'Riding High' 128, 132
'Right Now' 167
'Right To Live' 227
'Right Yow' 310
Righteous Flames, The 77–8
Righteous Souls 137
Rightful Brothers 219, 282
'Rightful Ruler' 91, 92
Riley, Jimmy 234
Riley, Martin James Norman (Jimmy)
     104–5, 106, 113
'Ring Of Fire' 148
'Rinky Dink' 35
Rio label 140
'Ripe Cherry' 142
'Rise And Fall' 243
'Rise And Shine' 283
'River' 294, 295, 447
'River Jordan' 20
'River To Cross' 234
'Road Of Life' 272
'Roast Duck' 34
'Roast Fish And Cornbread' 241, 350,
     393, 442, 451
Roast Fish Collyweed And Cornbread
     311–12, 333
'Rob Oil' 138
Robinson, Jackie 57, 98
Robinson, "Prince" Tony 209
Robinson, Sandra 378
Robotics, The 441, 442
'Rock Me in Your Soul' 174

'Rockaman Soul' 219
'Rockstone' 280
Rodigan, David 327
Rodriguez, Emmanuel 29
Roland Space Echo 241
'Roll On' 71
'Rolling Poland' 402
Romeo, Jennifer (Mascoll) 378–9
Romeo, Max (Maxie Smith)
     biographical 82
     on Family Man 83–4
     on Bunny Lee 86
     on 'Ginalship' 138
     and 'Let The Power Fall' 150
     and 'Rasta Band Wagon' 156
     and 'Sipple Out Deh' 246, 247
     and 'Chase The Devil' 252
     on P.'s odd behaviour 325, 348–9
     visits P. in London 389–90
     with P. in New York 399–400
'Roots Natty' 219
Roots Radics 384
'Roots Rock Reggae' 267, 361
Roots Rock Reggae (film) 284–5
Roots, The 294
'Roots Train' 273, 276
'Rough and Smooth' 155
'Rough And Tough' 21–2
'Round And Round' 158
Rowe, Keith 286–7
Royals, The 160
'Royalty' 32
'Rub And Squeeze' 38, 40
'Rub Up 71' 146
Ruddock, Osbourne ("Tubby") 91
'Rude Boy Get Bail' 38
'Rude Boy Gone A Jail' 38, 46
'Rude Boy Ska' 38
'Rude Boys Rule' 48
Rude Flower 401
'Rude Walking' 165
'Rudie' 220
'Rudie Barn Barn' 38
rudies 37–8, 48
Ruegg, Mireille *see* Perry, Mireille (*wife*)
'Rumplesteelkin' 172
'Run Baldhead' 211
'Run Come Feel' 200
'Run Come Rally' 216
'Run For Cover' 50, 119

'Run Rudies Run' 37, 38
'Run To The Rock' 186
'Run Up Your Mouth' 139, 148
'Runaway Child' 127
'Running From Jamaica' 267

'Safe Travel' 52
'Same Thing All Over' 101
'Samfy Girl' 214
San Francisco 451, 457
'Sandman' 278
Sang Hugh 257
Sassafras, Lord (Michael Johnson) 300
Satan Kicked the Bucket 399
Satan's Dub 400
Satchmo, Pat 78
'Satisfy My Soul' 453
'Sat (t) a' 251, 254
'Saving My Love For You' 199
'Saw Dust' 148
'Say A Little Prayer' 285
'Say A Prayer' 244
'Say Say' 266
'Say What You're Saying' 62, 68
'Scandal Corner' 294
'School Girls' 301, 332
Schwarz, Jim 360
Scientist Upset The Upsetter 445
Scorchers, The 88
'Scorching Iron' 223
Scott, Bunny 232
Scott Brothers 45
Scratch (punk group) 316
Scratch And Company Chapter I 353
Scratch On The Wire 334
'Scratch On The Wire' 375
Scratch The Super Ape 255
Scratch The Upsetter Again 103
'Screwdriver' 121, 155
'SDI' 385
Sea Bat Cloud 9 (film) 335
Seaga, Edward 18, 20, 37
Seaton, Harris Lloyd ("Bibi") 24, 79, 82
'Second Avenue' 232
'Second Judgement' 393
'Security In The Streets' 305
'See Me' 188
'Seeing Is Knowing' 5, 57
Seke Molenga And Kalo Kawongolo 310
'Selassie' 90, 103

'Self Control' 104–5
'Semi-Nyah' 184
Sensations, The 50, 104
Sensi Dub 1 and 2 421
Serious Dub, A 422
'Serious Time' 272
'Set Back' 264
'Set Me Free' 127
'Set Them Free' 50
'Seven' 352
'7 and 3/4 Skank' 170
Seven Leaves label 311, 337
'Sex Education' 141
Sex Pistols, The 288
'Sex Vibration' 427
'Sexy Boss' 427
'Sexy Lady' 379, 381
'Sexy Natty' 273, 334
'Shake It Up' 85
Shakespeare, Lloyd 82
'Shame' 230
Shanackie's Megawatt Dub 453
'Shanty Town' 48
'Sharp Razor' 165
Shaw, Donald "Tabby" 203
Shaw, Trevor 72
'She Is Gone Again' 103
'She Used to Call Me Daddy' 269
'She Wreng Ep' 212
Sheiks, The 44
'Shenk I Sheck' 44
Shepherd label 305
Sheridons, The 159
Sherwood, Adrian Maxwell
    biographical 381–2
    On-U Sound label 383
    recalls P.'s behaviour 384–5
    radio broadcast 388
    P. criticises 392, 394–5
    Pay It All Back 402
    From The Secret Laboratory 425
    recalls Belgian performance 432
    at wedding of P. and Mireille 433
    Echomania 437
    P.'s behaviour unacceptable 446
    praise for P. 447
'Shirley' 52
Shirley, Roy 52–3, 133
'Shocks Almighty' 106–7, 126
'Shocks Of Mighty' 106–7, 126, 127

'Shocks 71' 131
Shorty the President 227–8
'Show Me That River' 379
Showers of Blessing label 235
'Shufflin' Jug' 23
'Si Senor' 70
Sibbles, Leroy 262
'Sick And Tired' 86, 95, 169
'Side Gate' 165
'Sign Of The Times' 103
'Sign Your Name' 396
Sihillig, Rich 440
'Silent Satta' 251
Silver Bullets 175–6
'Silver Locks' 209
Silvertones, The 77, 174–5
'Simmer Down' 38, 120
Simonon, Paul 288
Simpson, Fitzroy "Bunny" 203
Sims, Danny 110, 119, 358
'Since You Are Gone' 77, 78
'Sincerely' 155
Sinclair, David ("Tappa Zukie") 242, 243
Singers and Players 383
'Sinner Man' 129
'Sipple Out Deh' 245–7, 252
'Sitting By The Seaside' 386
'Sitting On The Sidewalk' 266
'Six And Seven Books Of Moses' 30
Sixteen, Earl (Earl Daley) 265, 322
ska 28–9
Ska Beat label 43
'Ska-ing West' 72
'Skango' 223
"skanking" 169
'Skanking' 172
Skatalites 15, 29
'Ski Wa Wa' 167
Sky Rocket sound system 189
'Skylarking' 165, 192
slavery influence 5
Sleeper, Mick 456
'Slip Away' 94
'Slipping' 258
'Small Axe' 125, 131, 172, 221, 394, 419
'Smile Jamaica' 268–9
'Smile out of Style' 252
Smith, Clive (Busty Brown) 76, 78, 94
Smith, Dennis (Dennis Alcapone) 41,
    141–3, 161

Smith, Earl ("Chinna") 116–17, 238,
    275, 316
Smith, Marvin (Junior Soul) 71
Smith, Maxie see Romeo, Max (Maxie
    Smith)
Smith, Murvin Junior (Junior Murvin)
    258–60, 273–4, 315
Smith, Slim 71, 80, 84, 104
Smithsonian Folkways label 18
'Smokey Room' 252
Smokin' 352, 437
'So Many Times' 342
'Sodom And Gomorrow' 282
'Soldier And Police War' 262
'Soldier Round The Corner' 188
'Solid Foundation' 282, 284
'Solomon' 139, 258, 273
'Some Have Fe Halla' 346
Some Of The Best 377
'Someone To Love' 63
'Something About My Man' 60
'Something You Got' 50
'Sons Of Negus' 212
Sons of Negus 317–18
'Sons Of Slaves' 275, 333
'Sons Of Thunder' 122, 165
Soul, Junior (Marvin Smith) 71
'Soul Almighty' 126, 441
'Soul Fire' 312, 337, 350, 373
'Soul Man' 176
'Soul Rebel' 119, 125, 453
Soul Rebels 125–7
Soul Revolution 127–8, 131
Soul Revolution II 131–2
Soul Shack 133
'Soul Sister' 175
'Soul Stew' 103
Soul Syndicate 114, 115–16, 117, 118–19
'Soul Too' 314
Soul Twins 71
Soulettes, The 34, 38, 39, 123
'Soulful I' 77
sound systems 11–12, 190
Sound Tracks label 228, 230
Soundcraft mixer 208–9
Soundzs From The Hotline 431
'South Parkway Mambo' 59
Southern Studio 390
'Souvenir Of Mexico' 175
Souvenirs, The 201–2

Space Echo 241
Spanglers, The 38, 304, 322–3
'Spanish Harlem' 74
Sparrow, Jack 36
Spectaculars, The 56
Spence, Lloyd 44
Spencer, Tim 387, 390, 398–9
Spinning Wheel label 108
spirit world 5–6, 433
'Spiritual Healing' 427
Spiritual Healing 449
'Spit In The Sky' 31
spliff 338, 352
Stackman, Ron 357, 359
'Stagger '189
'Stand Alone' 128, 132, 237
'Stand And Look' 320
'Stand By Me' 103, 170, 214
'Stand Up' 285
'Standing On The Hill' 281
Starship Africa 382
'Start Over' 168
'Station Underground News' 171
'Stay Dread' 212, 234
'Stealin'' 252
Steck, Jeannot 435
'Step On The Dragon' 257
Sterling, Keith 116
Sterling, Lester 29, 85–6
Stewart, Roman 200
Stewart, Web 82
'Stick Together' 176
Stingers, The 138
'Stop That Train' 286
'Stop the War In A Babylon' 247, 255
'Storm Clouds' 272
'Story Come To Bump' 254
'Straight To I Roy's Head' 227
'Strange Country' 70
'Strange Whispering' 77
'Stranger On The Shore' 64, 162
Strictly Roots 228
'Strictly Roots' 298, 299
Strong Like Sampson label 303
Stud, Johnny 138
Studio One 15–39
    P.'s disillusionment 40–3
    power and influence 124–5
Studio One label 33
Studio Six 377

'Such A Good Woodman' 43
'Such Is Life' 337
Sufferer sound system 222–3
'Sufferer's Heights' 263, 266
Sufferer's Heights label 327
'Sufferer's Time' 263, 272
'Sugar Bag' 37
'Sugar Sugar' 175
'Sugartime' 278
'Summertime' 294
'Sun Is Shining' 114, 117, 129, 132, 139
Sunpower label 299
'Sunshine Rock' 165
Super Ape 254–5
'Super Ape In A Good Shape' 439
Super Ape Inna Jungle 439
Super Eight 286
'Supersonic Man' 431
Supersonics, The 45
'Sure Shot' 443
Survival 290
'Survival Is The Game' 186, 187
'Suspicious Minds' 139
Swaby, Horace (Augustus Pablo) 130–1,
    153, 189, 274–5
'Sweat Suit' 301
'Sweet and Loving Baby' 174
'Sweet Caroline' 232
'Sweet Dreams' 400
'Sweet Soul Music' 218
'Swing and Dine' 186
Switzerland 418–61

'Tables Turning' 192
'Tacko(o)' 229
'Tackro, The' 93
Tafari label 213
Taitt, Nerlyn 43, 46, 63
'Take It Easy' 44
'Take One' 103
'Take Your Belongings' 140
'Talk About It' 207
'Talking Blues' 38, 243
Talking Heads 367
'Tan and See' 252
Tanamo, Lord 16, 36–7
'Tang Tang Festival' 258
Targowski, Henry W. 328–31, 332–3,
    334–5, 339
Tartans, The 159

'Taste of Killing' 103
Taylor, Stephen 36, 70
'Tea Pot' 224
Teardrop Explodes, The 395
'Teardrops Falling' 63
Techniques, The 104
Technomajikal 435, 452–3
'Teddy Bear' 403
'Tedious' 273, 274
Teem label 187
Teenagers, The 33
'Telephone Line' 100
'Tell Me Something Good' 313
Tempests, The 159
Termites, The 77
Terrel, Lloyd 63
Terrorists, The 349–50, 351–2, 353–4
Thames excursion 384–5
Thameside studio 378
'Thank You Baby' 56
'Thanks We Get, The' 207, 208
'That Wonderful Sound' 106
'That's the Way' 348
'That's The Way You Like It' 78
'That's When It Hurts' 175
'Theme From Hong Kong' 223
'There Is A Place For Us' 432
'There Must Be A First Time' 267
'There You Are' 237
'There's A Train' 188, 286
Thing, The (label) 214
'Things A Come Up To Bump' 432
'Think So' 299
Third World 249
'This Girl Is Mine' 380
'This Heart Of Mine' 80
'This Is Reggae Music' 294
'This World' 153
Thompson, Aston (Bucky Marshall) 304
Thompson, Derrick 227–8
Thompson, Errol ("ET") 86, 114, 181
Thompson, Linval 198
Thompson, Uziah ("Sticky") 54, 62, 113
Thompson, Winston (Dr Alimantado)
　　144, 212–13
Thoroughbreds, The 127
'Thousand Teardrops' 201
'Thread Mill Of Life' 402
'Three Blind Mice' 184, 224, 225–6
'Three Little Birds' 247

'Three 'Pon One A Murder' 243
'Three Times Three' 226
Thrillers, The 199
'Throw Some Water In' 312
'Thunderball' 81
'Tidal Wave' 77
'Tight Spot' 127
Tighten Up 74, 162
'Tighten Up' 72, 74
Tilley, Jerry 378, 386
Tilley, John 386, 387, 389
'Time' 217, 219, 220, 234
Time Boom – De Devil Dead 384, 385–6,
　　389, 392, 394
'Time Conquer' 385
'Time Has Come, The' 55
'Time Is Drawing Nigh' 318
'Time Marches On' 379, 402
'Time to Pray' 19
Time Unlimited 210–11
T'ings And Time 424
'Tip Of My Tongue' 139, 144
'Tipper Special' 172
Tippertone 144
'To Be A Lover' 155–6, 172, 178, 187,
　　188, 189, 194, 251, 276
To Be A Lover 286
'To Love Somebody' 77
To Love Somebody 232–3
Tom the Great Sebastian 13
'Tonight' 286
'Too Bad Bull' 231
'Too Fat' 306
'Too Hot To Handle' 77
Tortchaninoff, Marc "Nof-Nof" 422
Tosh, Peter 34, 90–1, 124, 126, 129, 393
Tots, The 235
'Tougher Than Tough' 38
'Train Is Coming Back' 218
'Train Is Coming, The' 212
'Train To Doomsville' 402, 403
'Train To Skaville' 54, 218
'Train To Soulsville' 54
Tramp label 84
'Travelling' 301
Treasure Isle label 19
'Trench Town Rock' 134, 172
'Trial And Crosses' 34
'Tribal War' 213–14
Tribal War 14

Trojan label 73–4, 101, 127, 194, 377–8, 391
'True Confession' 174
'True Love' 69, 130
'Try A Thing' 249
'Try Me' 125–6
'Trying Faith' 234
'Trying To Conquer Me' 212
Tuff Gong label 119
Turn And Fire 421
'Turn Back The Hands Of Time' 286
'Turn Me Loose' 184
'Turn Me On' 69
Turntable label 192
Twelve Tribes of Israel 156, 167, 305
'25 Years Ago' 371–2
'Twiddle with Me' 432
Twinkle Brothers 117
'Two Of A Kind' 62
'Two Roads Before You' 84
Two Tones, The 93
Ty and the Titans 45

U Roy (Ewart Beckford) 90–3, 131
'UFO Attack' 453
'Uglyman' 88
'Uncle Charley' 70, 172
'Uncle Desmond' 70
'Underground Root' 255
Underground Roots 449
Unforgettables, The 234
'Ungrateful Skank' 208
Uniques, The 84, 104
Unity label 74
Unlimited Destruction, The (video) 429
'Unos Dos Tres' 85
'Untitled Rhythm' 396
'Untrue Girl' 219, 220
'Upfull Living' 314
Upset label 60, 64
Upset The Upsetter 420
Upsetter, The 76–7
'Upsetter, The' 56, 76
Upsetter All Stars, The 69
Upsetter And The Beat, The 431–2
Upsetter Collection 377
Upsetter label 70, 108
Upsetter Meets The Upsetress In Dub Around The World 448
Upsetter Record Shop 75–6

Upsetter sound system 102
'Upsetter The Righteous Organiser' 189
Upsetters, The 69, 88, 98, 144, 380
Upsetters Disco Bum 292
Upsetters 14 Dub Blackboard Jungle 177–8
Upsetters Junior 430
'Upsetting Station' 119
'Uptown Babies' 251
'Uptown Top Ranking' 301
'Use Me' 232

'Van Cleef' 89
Vandells, The 243
'Vendetta' 428
'Vengeance' 89
Versatiles, The 54, 63
'Version Ironside' 165
'Version Panta Rock' 178
Version To Version 151
versions 149
'Vibrate On(n)' 274, 275, 293, 299, 425
Viceroys, The 234
Vikings, The 46, 94
Vin, Duke 11–12
Voice of the People label 27
Voice Of Thunder 382
Voiceroys, The 234
'Voodoo Economic' 442
'Voodooism' 184, 446

'Waap You Waa' 176
Wackies studio 399, 401–2
Wailer, Bunny 34, 121, 124, 360
Wailers, The 33, 38–9, 102–36, 172–3, 236–7, 268, 316
Wail'n Soul'm label 109
'Waiting For My Rude Girl' 380
'Wakey Wakey' 165
Walker, Constantine ("Vision") 34
Walker, Earl George ("Bagga") 115, 167, 168, 293
Walks, Dennis 196
Wallace, Leroy ("Horsemouth") 115, 138, 157
Walters, Burt 63
'Wam Pam Pa Do' 168
'Want A Wine' 176
'Want To Be Loved' 160
'War In A Babylon' 245, 246, 251–2, 255, 403

War inna Babylon 309
'Warning To The Nation' 220
'Warning Warning' 229
Warren, Frank (Pepe Judah) 333
'Warrior No Tarry Ya' 210
'Wash Wash' 379
'Watch This Sound' 84, 110
'Water Genesis' 393
'Water More Than Flour' 123
'Water Pump' 160, 178
'Water The Garden' 78
Waterman, Pete 205, 206
Watson, Winston 266
Way It Is, The 319
'We Are In The Mood' 159
'We Are Neighbours' 176
We Care A Lot 389
'We Have Got A Date' 186
'We Love Jamaica' 434
'We Want Some Money' 430
website 456
'Weeping And Wailing' 254
'Welcome Aboard' 431
'Well Charge' 196
'Well Dread' 143
'Well Dread Version 3' 148
West Indians, The 77
West Indies Records Limited 18, 58–9, 74
Weston, Pete 224
'Wet Dream' 86
'Wet Up Your Pant Foot' 196
Weymouth, Tina 367
'What A Botheration' 71
'What A Confusion' 121, 209
'What A Disaster' 31
'What A Situation' 71, 294
'What A War' 283
'What Am I To Do' 89
'What An Agony' 105
'What Can I Do' 251
'What Is This' 90
'What Makes Honey' 19
'What The World Is Coming To' 54, 145
'What Will Your Mama Say' 62
'What's The Use' 232, 332, 361
'When Jah Come' 242, 255, 392
'When Jah Speak' 157
'When The Grass Is Green' 199
'When Will Better Come' 166
'Where Were You' 199

'Whiplash' 158
White, Bruce 98, 101, 166
White, Doraney (Billy Dyce) 72
White, Joy 192
White, Ransford (Jimmy London) 72
White, Thomas 383
'White Belly Rat' 265, 333, 43
'Who Colt The Game' 316–17, 347, 431, 459
'Who Killed The Buffalo' 253
'Who Killed The Chicken' 346
Who Put The Voodoo *'Pon* Reggae 449
'Who The Cap Fits' 120, 238
Whoosh, Jah (Neville Beckford) 249, 382
'Whup Whup Man' 50
'Why Did She Cry' 210
'Why Did You Leave Me To Cry' 432
'Why Do Black Man Fuss And Fight' 275
'Why Must I' 272
'Why Should You' 200
'Wicked Got To Go' 318
Wide Prairie 278
Wiggle Spoon label 52
Wild Bells label 27
'Wild Bird' 237
'Will You Still Love Me' 103
Willacy, Ned (Jah Ned) 297, 321–2, 347, 368, 416–17
Williams, Lorraine ("Ronnie Bop") 44, 47, 63, 97, 144, 272
Williams, Luther 9
Williams, Martin (Jah Martin) 194
Williams, Michael (Prince Far I) 244
Williams, Michael L. 294, 295
Williams, Oswald *see* Ossie, Count
Williams, Ruby ("Tootsie") ('wife') 8, 25, 74
Wilson, Chris 355–6
Wilson, Delroy 30
Wilson, Ernest 77
Wilson, Ron 44
Wilson, Roy 18
'Wind Up Doll' 50
'Winner, The' 53
WIRL (West Indies Records Limited) 18, 58–9, 74
'Wisdom' 250
'Wishes Of The Wicked' 34
Wizzdom label 139
'Wolf And Leopards' 257

'Wolf Out Deh' 293
Wolfe, Sidney 319
'Woman A Come' 85
'Woman And Money' 194
'Woman Is Like A Shadow' 266
'Woman's Gotta Have It' 234, 239
'Wonder Thirst' 84
Wong, Tom 11
'Woodman, The' 43
'Word Sound And Power' 359
'Words' 275
'Words Of My Mouth' 167–8, 172, 250
Working On The Guideline 315
'Working Time' 138
'World and Me, The' 277
World Disc label 19
World Service 376
Wright, Winston ("Brubeck") 44, 47, 81
'Wrong Thing, The' 282

X Perrymental 435, 438–9

'Yackety' 402
'Yagga Yagga' 212
'Yakkety Yak' 93
'Yama Khy' 207
Yank, The (dance step) 7
Yardbrooms, The 81
Yardies 374
Yashiki, Gota 401
Yello 435, 452
Yesehaq, Abuna 225

'You Are A Fool' 234
'You Are The Girl' 218
'You Can Run' 137, 138, 178
'You Can Wake Up With Me' 379
'You Can't Stop Me' 87
'You Crummy' 71
'You Don't Care' 202
'You Gonna Miss Me' 141
'You Know What I Mean' 72
'You Thought I Was Dead' 425
'You Were Meant For Me' 62
'You'll Be Sorry' 139
Young Experience 259
'Young, Gifted And Black' 202, 298
'Young, Gifted And Broke' 298
'You're Gonna Feel It' 78
'You're Gonna Need Me' 53
Youth Professionals 130
'Yu Squeeze Me Panhandle' 312
'Yucky Skank' 169
'Yuppy Conqueror' 396

Zap Pow 203, 294–5, 305
Zero, Earl (Earl Johnson) 116
'Zig Zag' 119
Zion, Lion 253
'Zion I Love You' 78
'Zion Rock' 187, 188
'Zion's Blood' 255
Zodiac Mindwarp 395
Zukie, Tappa (David Sinclair) 242, 243
Zurich 418–61

ACKNOWLEDGMENTS

I am indebted to a great number of people, each of whom has helped shape a particular aspect of this biography. Without the help of such dedicated and committed individuals, the book would clearly never have existed, and I take great pleasure in thanking each of them below.

Lee Perry's family has been especially helpful, and I would like to thank each member for bravely confronting the turmoil of the past in response to my intrusive questions. His mother, Ina Blythe, even insisted that I occupy her bedroom during my few days in Hanover, while she shared the spare room with other relatives. Siblings who spoke of early days in Hanover included Beryl ('Dulcie'), Lesbert ('Sonny'), and Icelyn ('Sitta') Perry, plus Desmond ('Lloyd'), Veta ('Girlie'), and Lorna ('Miss Nell') Blythe. Half-brother Milton 'P-Son' Blythe deserves special mention for locating a number of musicians and other family members, including Stainton 'Archie' Moore of Caveman sound system, as well as accompanying me around the northwest of Jamaica, and being a fountain of reliable information about the Black Ark. Though Perry's adopted daughter Michelle and son Mark ('Omar') gave me only reluctant snippets of information, his son Marvin ('Sean') spoke at length about his relationship with his father, as did his daughter Marsha, who deserves extra special thanks for finding a space for me to occupy during one of my trips to Jamaica, and for making me feel a part of the family through home cooking, shared spliffs, and domino games. Their mother, Pauline 'Isha' Morrison, was also reluctant to provide much information, but clarified certain specifics over time, and introduced me to the delights of the Blue Mountains. Present wife Mireille Perry provided much frank information and allowed me to retain a strong link with Scratch after he moved to Switzerland, while former girlfriends Vicky Nelson and Sandra Cooley also provided useful information, as did daughter Cleopatra.

The many musicians, singers, producers, executive producers, and engineers who worked with Scratch or his material provided the bulk of information presented in this text, several graciously answering my questions on more than one occasion. Extra-special thanks are due to my former neighbour, Winston 'Dr Alimantado' Thompson, for friendship and three trips to Belgium with his band; to Rudy Mascoll and Jennifer Romeo, for making me feel I had family outside the USA and for always including me; and to Maxwell Livingston Smith (a.k.a. Max Romeo) for driving me all over Jamaica, locating numerous musicians, and for making sure I always had the best spliff. I would like to thank each of those other individuals who worked directly with Scratch with whom I conducted formal interviews in alphabetical order by surname: Glen 'Capo' Adams, the late, great Roland Alphonso, Gladstone 'Gladdy' Anderson, Lynford 'Andy Capp' Anderson, Aston 'Family Man' Barrett, Ewart 'U Roy' Beckford, Keeling Beckford, Neville 'Jah Whoosh' Beckford, Lukas Bernays, Chris Blackwell, Keith 'Prince Allah' Blake, Winston Blake OD,

Cedella Booker, George 'Niney the Observer' Boswell (a.k.a. Winston Holness), Dennis Bovell, Lloyd Brevett, Tony Brevett, Edmund 'Mike' Brooks, Clinton 'Tennessee' Brown, Lynford 'Hux' Brown, Radcliffe 'Douggie' Bryan, Lester 'Dillinger' Bullocks, Derrick 'Watty' Burnett, Mike Cacia, Alison 'Susan' Cadogan, Mario Caldato Jr, Al Campbell, Cecil 'Prince Buster' Campbell, Errol 'Flabba Holt' Carter, Linval 'Prince Jazzbo' Carter, Albert 'Tony' Chin, Danforth 'Danny' Clarke, William 'Bunny Ruggs' Clarke, Wilburn 'Stranger' Cole, Keith Coley, Ansel Collins, Bernard 'Satta' Collins, Roy Cousins, Mike Craig, Ansel Cridland, Dave 'Barker' Crooks, Glen DaCosta, Earl 'Sixteen' Daley, Anthony 'Sangie' Davis, Carlton 'Santa' Davis, 'Bongo' Herman Davis, Carl Dawkins, Victor 'Fizzè' de Bros, Denzil Dennis, Mike Diamond, Leonard 'Sparrow' Dillon, Clement 'Sir Coxsone' Dodd, Paul Douglas, Val Douglas, Frank 'Kiddus-I' Dowding, Brent 'Porky' Dowe, Tyrone Downey, Mark Downie, Chenley Duffus, Lowell 'Sly' Dunbar, Errol Dunkley, Clancy Eccles, Rupie Edwards, Winston Edwards, Ken Elliot, Clinton Fearon, the Mighty Fatman, Carl 'Stereo' Fletcher, the late Patrick 'Jah Lloyd' Francis (a.k.a. Jah Lion), Neil 'Mad Professor' Fraser, George 'Fully' Fullwood, Boris Gardiner, Earl 'George Faith' George, Vin Gordon, Leo Graham, Gilmore Grant, Winston Grennan, Albert Griffiths, Marcia Griffiths, Aston Milton Henry, 'Ras' Michael Henry, Pablito 'Pablo Moses' Henry, Frederick 'Toots' Hibbert, Oscar 'Junior Delgado' Hibbert, Clive Hunt, David Isaacs, Carlton Jackson, Clifton 'Jackie' Jackson, Vivian 'Yabby You' Jackson, Lloyd 'Prince Jammy' James, Winston 'T-Man' Jarrett, Wayne Jobson, Roy Anthony Johnson, Linton Kwesi Johnson, Roydel 'Congo Ashanti Roy' Johnson, Euton Jones, Vic Keary, Martin Kloiber, Kazufumi Kodama, Lloyd Knibb, Robert Kuypers, Clifton 'Larry' Lawrence, Byron Lee, Edward 'Bunny' Lee, Alva 'Reggie' Lewis, Aurelia Msimang Lewis-Berton, Earl 'Little Roy' Lowe, David Madden, Rita Marley, John Martyn, Skip McDougal, Dieter Meier, Gerald T. Moore, Earl Morgan, Sylvain Morris, Judy Mowatt, Cedric Myton, David 'DRO' Ostrowe, Tony George Owens (a.k.a. Tony J), Marcus Owens, Lloyd Parks, George 'Phil Pratt' Phillips, Dwight Pinkney, Ernest Ranglin, Ras Kidus, Winston 'Reedy' Reid, Michael 'Mikey Boo' Richards, Martin 'Jimmy' Riley, Emmanuel 'Rico' Rodriguez, Keith Rowe, Trevor 'Jimmy London' Shaw, Trevor Starr, Jim Schwartz, Harris 'Bibi' Seaton, Robbie Shakespeare, Donald 'Tabby' Shaw, Adrian Sherwood, Roy Shirley, Zoot 'Scully' Sims, David 'Tappa Zukie' Sinclair, Dennis 'Alcapone' Smith, Earl 'Chinna' Smith, Murvin Smith Jr (a.k.a. Junior Murvin), Ron Stackman, Lester Sterling, the late Horace 'Augustus Pablo' Swaby, Nerlynn Taitt, Henry W. Targowski, Derrick 'Shorty the President' Thompson, Linval Thompson, Uziah 'Sticky' Thompson, Winston 'Groovy' Tucker, Earl 'Bagga' Walker, 'Jah Ned' Willacy, Lorraine 'Ronnie Bop' Williams, Michael 'Reverend Mikey Zappow' Williams, Winston Watson, Sidney Wolfe, and Gota Yashiki. Further relevant information came from informal discussions with musicians and engineers including Renford Bailey, Sonny Binns, Glenmore Brown, Syd Bucknor, Benjamin Del Sesso, Franklyn Dunn, Alton Ellis OD, Vyries Edghill, the late Alric Forbes, Locksley Gichi, Lascelles James, Harry Johnson, Donald Marvin Kerr Jr (a.k.a. Junior Marvin), Andy Montgomery, Carlton 'Bubblers' Ogilvie, Reuben, Everton Samuels, Berry 'Prince Hammer' Simpson, Valerie Skeete, Black Steel, Tawanda, Lloyd 'Charmers' Terrell, Joe Whyte, and Martin 'Mandingo' Williams (a.k.a. Jah Martin). Other music-industry contacts also provided useful information about their work with Scratch, including documentary-film assistant Frank 'Pepe Judah' Warren, former lawyer Tim Spencer, Caroline Robertson of the esteemed Westbury Music, and promoter Marc 'Nof Nof' Tourtchaninoff. Journalists Chris Lane and Vivienne Goldman, photographer Dave Hendley and film-makers Don Letts and Rick Elgood also shared tales of their experiences with the man, while further background information arose from formal interviews with producers Bertram Brown and Enos McLeod, singers Joshua Bailey, Edi Fitzroy, Olive 'Senya' Grant, Joseph Hill, and Lindburgh 'Preps' Lewis, sound system operator Duke Vin, poet Mutabaruka, toaster Anthony 'Lone Ranger' Waldron, and herbalist Owen S. 'Dr Bagga' Forrester.

Interview co-ordination was provided by a range of individuals, including in the UK: Maxine B of Genesis FM, James Dutton and Mike Coe of the estimable Motion Records, Nikki Eder of Culture Promotions, Dean Ellis of Alltone records, Michael McGeachy of Rockers International, Joe 'The Nose' Hennessy of Independent Music, Gerry Lyesight of Palm Pictures, Gaylene Martin of the Coalition, Clive Plummer, Tricia Renee, Andy Richie, Yoshi Terashima of Respect Productions, Delroy Washington, and Anita and Liam of Zest Agency; in Jamaica: Tricia Archibald of Moses, A. Doeman of I & I studio, Marcia Elliott of Judy M Music, Derrick Harriott, Rudy Isaacs, Miss James at Talent Corporation, Andrea Corinne Lewis, Cathy Snipper, Simon Stewart of Coyaba River Garden, Chester Synmoie, Julia Vaz of Tuff Gong International, and Bunny the juice man on Marcus Garvey Drive; in the USA: Marc Gorney, Barbara Kennedy, Nancy Lewis of Entertainment Works, Gina Rankin of Grand Royal, Prince Philip Smart of H, C & F studio and Derrick Williams of Dangerous One Productions in the East Bay; in France, Philippe Maurizi of Bernard Mokett Agency; in Switzerland, journalist Reto Baumann of *Loop* magazine; in Japan, Rika Kuji of Soytzer Music and the woman known as Highbridge; in Canada, Dave Kingston. Affordable accommodation was provided in Kingston by actress and night-life specialist Dionne Silvera.

Individuals who conducted joint interviews with me also deserve my gratitude, including Lol Bell-Brown of the sorely missed *Boom Shacka Lacka*, loyal friend Ray Hurford of the inspiring *Small Axe*, Patricia Meschino of *Rhythm*, Adrian Christani of Greensleeves mail-order department and Dave Hallworth, who also has my thanks for providing translations of French and German items. I also thank photographer Adrian Thomas for his fine work in what were often very trying circumstances.

Several key people have allowed access to their record collections or provided me with tapes, news clippings, and other items. Foremost among them is pioneering radio disc jockey Doug Wendt, whose *Midnight Dread* radio programme on KTIM San Rafael was where I first heard Perry's music in my youth. Professor Steve Barrow of Blood and Fire Records must have one of the most complete collections of Jamaican music outside Jamaica – indeed, the only person I have met with a bigger stash was Winston Blake of Merritone sound system – and he has shared much of his knowledge with me; I also thank him for ensuring my involvement in Island's *Arkology* retrospective, while his partner, Sue Green, deserves thanks for providing the antidote of non-reggae discussions and fine meals at Avenue Road. Jeremy Collingwood of *Distant Drums* magazine/*Yalp* extended much time and energy to make the discography more accurate and complete, while Jean Scrivener sent me several tapes and news items (in combination with Kevin Eden and Jake Frost); others were gleaned from Roger Steffens, founder of *The Beat* magazine, John Mason of Trybute Records and Colin Moore of Fencebeater Records, from Marley enthusiasts Olivier Albot, Laurent Campos, and Dave Millar and Congos specialist Micke Tsiparis, from cordial collectors Ron de Groot and Jos and Tom Klijn, from sound engineer Joel Dos Santos, fanzine editor Steve Milne, and from poet and sleeve-note scribe Geoff Parker. Endless tapes were also traded with graphic artist Ian 'Mystic' Martindale, always in inventive re-cycled packaging. Gary Simons has provided numerous helpful clippings and a couple of crucial tapes, while other music and news items have come from road manager Bernard Warin, KUSF deejay Andrew Rush, drummer Mike Bordin,

Jonathan Hess, Nuff Sed records founder Brandan Kearney, and James Dillon of Green Apple records and books – one of my oldest and closest friends. Further discography information came most extensively from Roger Dalke of TSI publications, Laurence Cane-Honeysett of Trojan Records (who also provided key news items), Maggie Agard of Island records, Chris Prete of TOTAS, David Sedlock of niyabinghi.com and Rangan Momen. Crucially, Trevor Wyatt, former A & R at Island Records and presently with Palm Pictures, opened Island's vaults to allow my perusal of Perry product, including archive film material from Jeremy Marre and Gary Weiss. The availability of Adrian Boot's excellent photographic material was co-ordinated by Mary Belle of Palm Pictures, while additional video footage was obtained from Pierre Aragon of Le Speaker Masqué in Toulouse and from Brian 'Planet' Jackson, premier sound system operator on the Lancashire/Yorkshire border. John Sergent assisted with video transfers, and made many helpful comments on the initial draft of the first completed chapter of the book. Bethlehem Tekle and Tekle Alemu helped make sense of Amharic adaptations.

Further thanks are due to the many record vendors who have supplied and traded Lee Perry material with me, including Charlie Morgan of Outernational Records in Washington, Markus Vogel and Lucien Solloway of Mill International in Switzerland, Michael de Koningh of the UK's Reggae Reggae Reggae, Joe Saroce in Connecticut, Andreas Forker in Hamburg (associate of Selekta Sound record shop), Bob Brooks of London's Reggae Revive, Greg Lawson in Toronto, Matt Downs of Brixton's Lion Vibes, Paul at Flash Forward in Camden, Pete Trodahl of Arlequin Records in Brussels, Major P of Genesis FM/Maestro Records in Peckham, and especially the consistently courteous Darren from Nation's Vibration sound system in New Cross.

Other disc jockeys who have helped educate me include Hank Holmes of KCRW's syndicated *Beat* programme, the Ion Lion at KPOO San Francisco, Drepenba of KPFA Berkeley, David Rodigan of Capitol and Kiss FM London, Nick Raphael and the Manasseh crew and Joey Jay, formerly of Kiss FM, Lepke of pioneering London pirate station Dread Broadcasting Corporation, the Ranking Miss P of Greater London Radio, Daddy Ernie of South London's Choice FM, Bounty Hunter of Harlesden's People's FM and Challenger of Willesden's JBC. Extra special mention must be made of the late Jack Ruby, who introduced me to the mind-boggling reality of the sound system experience by bringing his entire hand crafted 50,000-watt set on a coast-to-coast tour of America in 1982.

I have used several pertinent quotations from fellow journalists in this book. Many of the strongest came from interviews conducted by Bruno Blum, former staff writer for *Best*; the permission he granted for use of the material is readily acknowledged. Other crucial quotations were culled from the work of Carl Gayle and Chris May in *Black Music*, Danny Kelly in *NME*, and from interviews conducted by Karel Michiels. This book has also been informed by the work of writers such as Michael Turner, Richard Henderson, and Leroy Pierson in the *Beat*, Peter 'Penny Reel' Siemens, John Masouri, and John Williams in *Echoes*, and Beth Kingston in the greatly-missed *Reggae Quarterly*. Though a full list of books appears in the bibliography, I acknowledge a particular debt to the work of Stephen Davis, Sebastian Clarke and Timothy White. I have also enjoyed tapping into Mick Sleeper's Lee Perry website on the Internet.

I must also thank the many editors who have published my work on Scratch and others over the years, including Eric 'Black Dog Bone' Cope of *Murder Dog*, who published my first article on Lee Perry in a 1986 edition of *Wiring Department*; Marc Hutsebaut at the sadly defunct *Etna*; CC Smith at the *Beat*, who consented to publishing the second edition of the *Upsetter* magazine; Gibson Keddie, who has always made space for reggae music in *Bassist*; Larry Birnbaum of the adventurous *Rhythm* (formerly *Rhythm Music*), and Tero Kaski of Black Star press in Finland; Bob Mack, disgraced former editor of *Grand Royal* also deserves a salutation, though certain of his editorial decisions at that magazine almost resulted in the abandonment of this book. I also express gratitude to regular London stockists of the *Upsetter* and *Musical Root* magazines, particularly Noel Hawks at Dub Vendor, Mike Williams at Fat Shadow, Chris Rentham at Compendium, Chris Sedgwick, Chris Cracknell, Chris O'Brien, Ian Taylor and all at Greensleeves, and especially Judith Crighton at Rough Trade, whose words of encouragement came at precisely the right moment, while Jeff Pretes of Naked Eye News and Video in San Francisco and Pierre-Alexandre Mestcherimoff of Patate Records in Paris receive my additional appreciation, as does Ira Heaps of New York's Jammyland, who has also been kind enough to relay crucial fax and email data.

Jamie Byng, Colin McLear, Peter Collingridge, Mark 'Stan' Stanton, and all at Payback Press deserve applause for realising the worth of this biography, and for providing the necessary support to ensure its completion. Other less tangible support has been provided by those closest to me, including my father, Dr Lawrence Katz, who gave much encouragement and occasional financial cushioning; his partner, Edith Freeman, who brought the Asmat fishing song to my attention; my sister Deborah Katz, who gave much positive feedback and sent relevant news clippings; my sister Sharon Katz, who provided encouragement by email; my mother, Shirley Katz, who endowed me with an inquisitive mind and a respect for other cultures; my Aunt Ethel and Uncle Harold Grill, who gave further encouragement and provided accommodation in New York; Heather and Derrick Bernard, Monica and Selwyn Walton, and the rest of the family for accepting me as one of their own; and most of all, my long-term partner, Claudia Bernard, whose love, patience, and understanding has allowed for notable transgressions connected with this book.

My final word of thanks must be to none other than Lee 'Scratch' Perry, the mighty Upsetter, who is easily the most original man I have ever had the pleasure to meet. I feel the greatest debt connected with this book is owed to Scratch himself, not only as he realised my potential for penning this text long before I was willing to accept it, but more importantly for providing the world with such truly exceptional music. The publication of this book makes years of struggle in an alien land seem finally worthwhile to me; I hope its realisation has also given something back to the man whose life it investigates.